D0207897

RELIGIOUS PERIODICALS OF THE UNITED STATES

RECENT TITLES OF HISTORICAL GUIDES TO THE WORLD'S PERIODICALS AND NEWSPAPERS

This series provides historically focused narrative and analytical profiles of periodicals and newspapers with accompanying bibliographical data.

Black Journals of the United States
Walter C. Daniel

Mystery, Detective, and Espionage Magazines
Michael L. Cook

American Indian and Alaska Native Newspapers and Periodicals, 1826–1924
Daniel F. Littlefield, Jr., and James W. Parins

British Literary Magazines: The Augustan Age and the Age of Johnson, 1698–1788
Alvin Sullivan, editor

British Literary Magazines: The Romantic Age, 1789–1836
Alvin Sullivan, editor

British Literary Magazines: The Victorian and Edwardian Age, 1837–1913
Alvin Sullivan, editor

Children's Periodicals of the United States
R. Gordon Kelly, editor

International Film, Radio, and Television Journals
Anthony Slide, editor

Science Fiction, Fantasy, and Weird Fiction Magazines
Marshall B. Tymn and Mike Ashley, editors

American Indian and Alaska Native Newspapers and Periodicals, 1925–1970
Daniel F. Littlefield, Jr., and James W. Parins, editors

Magazines of the American South
Sam G. Riley

RELIGIOUS PERIODICALS OF THE UNITED STATES

Academic and Scholarly Journals

Edited by

Charles H. Lippy

Historical Guides to the World's Periodicals and Newspapers

Greenwood Press
New York • Westport, Connecticut • London

Library of Congress Cataloging in Publication Data

Lippy, Charles H.
  Religious periodicals of the United States.

  (Historical guides to the world's periodicals and
newspapers, ISSN 0742–5538)
  Includes index.
  1. Religious newspapers and periodicals—United States.
2. Scholarly periodicals—United States.   I. Title.
II. Series.
PN4888.R4L5   1986   016.2′005   85–9861
ISBN 0–313–23420–5 (lib. bdg. : alk. paper)

Library of Congress Catalog Card Number: 85–9861
ISBN: 0–313–23420–5
ISSN: 0742–5538

First published in 1986

Greenwood Press, Inc.
88 Post Road West, Westport, Connecticut 06881

Printed in the United States of America

The paper used in this book complies with the
Permanent Paper Standard issued by the National
Information Standards Organization (Z39.48–1984).

10 9 8 7 6 5 4 3 2 1

Contents

Preface

Students of religion undertaking research on virtually any topic in the discipline are immediately confronted with a dazzling array of periodicals that may contain information of value in determining work already done on a topic, the state of knowledge in a particular subfield, or ideas that have helped shape later reflection on a given subject. Having a sense of what focus or orientation particular journals have makes preliminary research easier and more efficient. This book represents an effort to survey more than 100 periodicals and journals in the field of religion to provide students and scholars with an introduction to the kinds of periodical literature available and the types of concerns manifested in their pages. Taken together, the profiles also provide a history of religious periodical publishing in the United States and the ways in which periodicals mirror not only the changes in religious scholarship over the years but also the impact of other social and cultural forces on the character of academic work in religious studies.

With more than 2500 religious periodicals in print in the United States in 1985, profiling selected representative journals in a single book would be virtually impossible. Hence this book concentrates on a sampling of those that focus on academic and scholarly concerns. Even this limitation poses some difficulties, for the types of periodicals that might be included in this category are numerous. They include those currently in print whose articles are written by scholars in the many areas that constitute the academic discipline of religion, as well as those that seek to distill scholarly research and work to an educated lay audience. Even so, identification of a periodical as academic and scholarly is complicated by the fact that several publications contain a variety of materials, mixing together items of general interest with matters of scholarly interest. In addition, there are hundreds of religious periodicals that were once influential but are no longer in print. But it is more difficult to categorize periodicals formerly in print into general interest and academic and scholarly groupings, for prior to the twentieth century publishers of religious periodicals could assume that even a general readership had a lively interest in the technical matters of religion. Hence their offerings frequently dealt with religious or doctrinal controversies, provided rather sophisticated analyses of the intricacies of particular religious viewpoints, or promoted a rigid denominational perspective, as well as giving news of important events, material designed to foster religious nurture and growth, and a variety of poetry, moralistic stories, and inspirational items. Indeed some of the periodicals that once were vehicles to promote the beliefs and practices of a particular sect or group and were intended to bolster the commitment of the faithful are now primarily of interest to academicians and scholars for historical or sociological reasons.

The profiles that follow were selected with all of these concerns in mind. There has been an effort to include periodicals that reflect:

1. The publications of a representative grouping of academic, scholarly, and professional societies in the disciplines that constitute the field of religion.
2. The range of religious groups—Protestant, Catholic, Jewish, humanist, sectarian—that publish journals.
3. The variety of institutions, such as theological seminaries and universities, that sponsor periodicals.
4. A concern to draw on current research in religion in materials geared to a lay audience.
5. A mixture of popular and academic fare in their articles.
6. Types of journals no longer in print but that disseminated scholarly work in the past.
7. Matters that are currently of interest primarily to scholars but were not necessarily so when they were being published.

Incidental factors, such as availability of and access to a complete run of a journal, also played into the selection process. Even with these guidelines in mind, however, an element of subjectivity enters, for scholars will always disagree over what titles are the most representative of their genre. Hence the editor must bear responsibility for the final determination of the periodicals profiled in this volume, aware that many deserving titles have been omitted.

Each profile seeks to provide a capsule history of the periodical under scrutiny, noting the factors that gave it birth and the rationale offered by founders for the particular focus the journal would take. The profiles also discusss some of the materials that have appeared in the periodicals surveyed, paying special attention to seminal articles. The respective profile authors have attempted to assess the contribution an individual periodical has made within its own field, as well as within the discipline of religion. Material at the end of each profile includes suggestions for further reading and identifies index sources for the periodicals under review, whether reprint or microform editions are available, and selected libraries that contain the periodical in their collection. Finally, the profiles offer an appended summary publication history, noting title changes that may have occurred over the years, volume and issue data, a listing of publishers and places of publication, a listing of editors and their years of service if available, and estimated circulation figures. The profiles reflect the work of the individual contributors; consequently each emphasizes those dimensions of a periodical's story that the scholars writing the profiles thought best provided an understanding of the nature and significance of each journal.

Generally periodicals profiled are listed under the title in use currently, if the periodical is still being published, or the final title, if the journal is no longer published. Occasionally, however, when a final title of a defunct periodical is less familiar than a title used over several years, the more familiar designation has been used. In every case, though, the various titles used by an individual journal are given in the appropriate place alphabetically, with a note identifying the title that readers should consult for the complete profile.

Asterisks in the text following mention of a particular journal indicate that this journal is also profiled. Readers can use this cross-reference system to gain a more complete understanding of the relationships among periodicals.

Appendix A provides a chronological listing of the periodicals by date of founding in a format that relates the emergence of particular periodicals to movements within U.S. religious history as a whole. Appendix B identifies the periodicals profiled by sponsoring society or agency and by religious tradition, if a profile's orientation is linked to a particular religious heritage.

In preparing this book, I have benefited from the assistance and counsel of many individuals. I am most grateful to the individuals who consented to write the profiles. More than 50 scholars from around the nation shared in the creation of this book. In addition, I particularly appreciate the advice of Robert T. Handy (Union Theological Seminary, New York), E. Brooks Holifield (Emory University), Martin E. Marty (University of Chicago), Russell E. Richey (Drew University), John F. Wilson (Princeton University), and many others in suggesting possible contributors. A sabbatical leave from Clemson University in the spring semester of 1984 and designation as a visiting scholar in the Department of History at the University of North Carolina-Chapel Hill that term provided an opportunity to do the bulk of the editorial work. It was a pleasure to have the resources of the Davis Library at UNC-Chapel Hill at my disposal, along with those of Duke University, North Carolina State University, and Clemson University. Marian Withington of the Clemson University Library deserves special thanks for her help in tracking down many technical details. I also appreciate the guidance provided by Cynthia Harris at Greenwood Press.

Introduction

From the eighteenth century to the present, religious periodicals have accounted for a significant proportion of all journals published in the United States. Indeed, one religious periodical, *Christian History*, which was published briefly in Boston beginning in 1743, ranks among the earliest of the periodicals and magazines published in the English colonies that later became the United States. Now nearly two and one-half centuries later, current religious periodical titles number in excess of 2500. The development of religious journals in the United States is itself a microcosm of the story of periodical publication in general, for the titles that have appeared reflect the cultural changes and diversity of American life.

Prior to the Civil War, most religious periodicals consisted of reprints of sermons and articles, which argued various positions in the many theological controversies of the day. In a secular age, it is difficult to recall that printed sermons once represented some of the most popular leisure reading in literate circles and that minor points of theology once generated as heated debates as do topics such as the nuclear arms race and civil rights in the later twentieth century. The *Arminian Magazine*, published in Philadelphia in 1789–90, offered readers ongoing discussion of the doctrine of the freedom of the will, a hotly contested notion in a day when many thought that espousal of freedom of the will denied belief in the absolute sovereignty of God.

In addition to sermons and theological debates, antebellum religious periodicals also regularly provided short biographical essays, usually of clergy; religious poetry that rarely had literary significance; narratives of conversions, which often emphasized the dramatic nature of religious experience; and other pieces intended for the edification and spiritual nurture of readers. Indeed, magazine journalism in general during this period did not seek so much to entertain or to advance knowledge in a specialized field as to provide a means for moral improvement. Religious periodicals were not necessarily pitched to a particular constituency, although many were published under the aegis of the emerging denominations, but to a public living in a culture where an evangelical Protestant tone permeated the whole. There were exceptions, to be sure, and some of these will be noted here, but for the most part, antebellum religious periodicals sought to explain doctrine, lift up examples of pious living, and offer clues for spiritual growth and development.

The *Theological Magazine* (1795–99), for example, reported on numerous conversion experiences and carried many rather dry doctrinal pieces, while the *Connecticut Evangelical Magazine* (1800–15) regularly featured accounts of revivals, as well as missionary news, articles of biblical exposition, and occasional pieces explaining the differences among various Protestant denominations. A few journals were oriented to groups that were then religious minorities. In the second quarter of the nineteenth century, the Unitarians were especially prolific in producing periodical literature. The *Christian Examiner*, which began publication in 1824 and continued for nearly a half-century while undergoing many title changes, was one of the most important Unitarian publications, counting many Harvard University faculty and alumni as contributors. In Roman Catholic circles, one of the earliest periodicals to appear was the *U.S. Catholic Miscellany*, published in Charleston, South Carolina, from June 1822 through December 1832. While containing much general news, the *Miscellany* owed its existence to the conviction that the Catholic minority not only needed a magazine that would bolster commitment to the faith in a highly Protestant environment but had a duty to explain the contours of Catholic belief and practice to a hostile majority. American Judaism also spawned a few periodicals near midcentury. The most significant, largely because of its association with Isaac M. Wise, was the *American Israelite*, which first appeared in 1854.

In addition, there were some antebellum periodicals of a more academic cast, though the division of religious periodical literature into readily definable categories such as academic and scholarly, general interest, and denominational did not reach fruition until the later nineteenth century. The *Biblical Repertory*, later known as the *Princeton Review* and an antecedent of the *Princeton Theological Review*, was among the first periodicals geared to a professional readership, the Presbyterian clergy. Edited by the venerable Charles Hodge for nearly half a century after its founding in 1825, the journal was a mainstay of the Old School (antirevival) movement, a vehicle for the exposition of what became known as the Princeton Theology, and a bulwark of defense for Calvinist beliefs in original sin and the impropriety of church structure centered around bishops. Another journal that generally reflected an orthodox Calvinist perspective is *Bibliotheca Sacra*, founded in 1843 and still published today. In 1871 dubbed the "prince of theological quarterlies" by a writer in the *Lutheran Review*, *Bibliotheca Sacra* is a prism through which are refracted all the major religious issues, controversies, and debates that cascaded across the American Protestant landscape in the second half of the nineteenth century.

By midcentury, however, currents of social reform, most conspicuously seen in the abolitionist movement, were sweeping across American society. They too left their mark on religious periodicals. Although publication of religious journals at midcentury was dominated by the Baptists, Congregationalists, Methodists, and Presbyterians, few escaped the impact of social reform regardless of sponsorship. *The Independent*, for example, which was founded in 1848 as a periodical oriented to a Congregationalist audience outside Congregationalist New England and continued until well into the twentieth century after merging in 1870 with *Outlook*, had a distinctive social reform focus and printed the text of Harriet Beecher Stowe's *Uncle Tom's Cabin* in the 1850s, when abolitionist sentiment was feverish.

By midcentury, too, however, several journals were taking on a more obvious intellectual and scholarly cast, devoting their pages to rather heady theological discussions. The *Mercersburg Review*, edited at different times by John Williamson Nevin and Philip Schaff, became a major voice for the liturgical, historical, and christological theology associated with the Reformed tradition at midcentury, while the *American Theological Review* (later the *American Presbyterian Review*), strongly influenced by the faculty of New York's Union Theological Seminary, devoted itself almost exclusively to articles on doctrine and belief, often moving beyond points of interest primarily or exclusively to Presbyterians. The scholarly journals of a later generation have their roots in periodicals such as these, which were clearly not intended for a lay readership but for a clerical and academic audience possessed of theological sophistication.

The first two decades after the Civil War saw many changes in the nature and number of religious periodicals in the United States. On the one hand, as American higher education began to assume a different cast, largely influenced by developments in Germany, with the emergence of distinctive academic disciplines and specializations and the organization of academic and professional societies, a new kind of religious periodical began to appear: that geared to a specialized scholarly audience. The rise of the secular press, particularly in terms of daily newspapers, meant that religious periodicals that had been concerned with general news as well as religious matters could now devote their pages exclusively to religious topics for a general or perhaps denominational readership. This period, for example, witnessed the rapid rise of periodicals designed to promote denominational programs and viewpoints as much as to offer broadly based religious edification for readers. The dramatic increase in immigration, which witnessed the arrival of millions of Roman Catholics and Jews, also brought an increase in the number of periodicals designed to perpetuate and enhance allegiance to those traditions and, to a lesser extent, combat criticism from the Protestant majority. Within American Protestantism, the burgeoning Sunday School movement generated a need for a new kind of periodical literature focused primarily on children and youth and intended as a medium of instruction. Frank Luther Mott, in his classic study of the history of American magazines, noted that while some 350 religious periodicals were published in the United States in 1865, that number had increased to more than 650 by 1885 and that Sunday School periodicals easily accounted for more than half the circulation in 1885. Although the profiles in this book will deal primarily with periodicals of the first sort—the academic and scholarly—their appearance and place in the overall story of religious journals must be understood in the context of these other changes, which altered the character of religious journalism drastically.

Many of the more academic journals were outlets for scholars identified with particular religious groups, often seminary professors or teachers in church-related colleges, and their contents often reflected the growing interest in historical studies. Representative examples include the *Quarterly Review of the Evangelical Lutheran Church* (1878), the *U.S. Catholic Magazine* (1887), the reorganized *Methodist Review* (1885), the *American Catholic Quarterly Review* (1876), and the influential *Journal of Biblical Literature* (1882). Some scholarly societies regularly published papers presented at meetings until a permanent journal was established (for example, the American Society of Church History's *Church History*, published quarterly since 1932, replaced periodic publication of papers begun in 1888). There was as well a concern to disseminate scholarly knowledge among an educated readership. In this area, the faculty of the University of Chicago's Divinity School led the way with the founding of the *Hebrew Student*, later known as the *Biblical World*, in 1882. The intent of this journal was to provide articles that reflected the latest work in biblical scholarship, a field that had witnessed great transformation with the rise and acceptance of biblical criticism, in language and form comprehensible to nonspecialists. To balance this approach, the Divinity School faculty in 1897 established another periodical, the *American Journal of Theology*, which concentrated on more technical matters. The two were merged into the *Journal of Religion* in 1921.

Another genre of sophisticated religious periodicals sought to argue for particular viewpoints, often promoting perspectives that gained currency in intellectual circles with the growing interest in scientific method and the desire to reconcile religious affirmation of some sort with scientific knowledge. Although they are ultimately different in focus and tone, in their genesis the *Journal of Christian Science* (1883), the predecessor of the *Christian Science Monitor*, *The Index: A Weekly Paper Devoted to Free Religion* (1870), and the *Radical* (1865) belong in this category. Others became popularly identified with identifiable schools of thought, even if they were not intentionally designed to promote a specific position. The *Andover Review* (1884–93), for example, was intended to replace *Bibliotheca Sacra* as a forum for that seminary's faculty when the latter journal's editorship shifted to Oberlin College in Ohio, but it quickly became linked to the liberal Social Gospel movement, which captured the attention of many Protestant denominational leaders in the late nineteenth century. Some journals continued to promote the earlier interest in social reform. The *Arena* (1889–1909), for instance, in its early years maintained a clear focus on religiously based social reform, counting many clergy among its contributors, but in time its social interests superseded its religious foundation, and the periodical became primarily a journal crusading for social change.

So diverse and expansive had religious periodical publication become by the close of the nineteenth century that Frank Luther Mott identified at least thirteen different types of religious journals in print, noting that the heterogeneous nature of the religious press made simple definition and easy categorization difficult:

1. Periodicals that commented on national and international affairs and literary developments from a religious perspective (*Independent, Outlook*).
2. Journals with a liberal slant but published by denominational presses (*Churchman, Christian Register*).
3. Denominational periodicals, frequently well edited, that were geared to a lay constituency and contained a mix of articles, some promoting denominational programs, some designed for religious nurture, and some of a sophisticated nature (*Christian Advocate, Congregationalist*).
4. Hundreds of regional and diocesan denominational journals.
5. Nondenominational or interdenominational periodicals that offered a combination of inspirational material and serious doctrinal or theological pieces (*Christian Herald*).
6. Magazines that advanced the programs of religious action groups (the Salvation Army's *War Cry*).
7. Journals of various missionary societies that reported, generally in a pietistic vein, on activities of missionaries in both the United States and overseas.
8. Quarterly or monthly theological reviews sponsored by denominations.
9. More strictly scholarly periodicals published by academic societies, colleges and universities, or nondenominational groups (*American Journal of Semitic Languages and Literature*).
10. Journals and magazines prepared by Roman Catholic organizations, which would include examples in many of the previous categories and some written in languages other than English.
11. Journals and magazines published by various Jewish agencies and groups, including examples drawn from many of the previous categories but, as with Catholic parallels, with some written in foreign languages.
12. Other religious periodicals written in foreign languages (*Lehre und Wehre*).
13. Peripheral journals that promoted the special interests of small groups and with a very limited circulation.

In the twentieth century, all of these categories, with the exception of the foreign language religious periodicals, have continued to grow in number and volume. The expansion of the discipline of religious studies has accounted for much of the increase in the number of academic periodicals for two reasons. First, the study of religion is no longer the exclusive bailiwick of theological seminaries and church-related colleges and universities. The twentieth century has witnessed the establishment of numerous religion departments and ancillary programs at unaffiliated and state schools and universities, resulting in a proliferation of methodological approaches to religious questions, as well as in a dramatic shift in the presuppositions undergirding the study of religion. Simply put, analysis has replaced apologia. Second, the academic discipline of religion, like other areas of scholarly concern, has become increasingly specialized. The rise of new areas of specialization has led in many cases to the formation of additional professional societies, many of which have established their own journals to disseminate the latest work in their respective subfields. In addition, as the U.S. population continues to achieve a higher educational level, there has been a demand for religious periodicals designed for nonspecialists but nevertheless manifesting considerable intellectual sophistication in content and approach.

One could point to countless examples of this proliferation in periodical publication, but a few will suffice. The interdisciplinary character of much academic work in religious studies may readily be seen in the contents of the *Journal of the American Academy of Religion* (1965), first established as the *Journal of the National Association of Biblical Instructors* in 1933, and in *Soundings* (1968), formerly known as *Christian Scholar* (1953) and as *Christian Education* (1917). The interest in application of social scientific methodologies to religious material led to the formation of the Society for the Scientific Study of Religion, which in turn established the *Journal for the Scientific Study of Religion* in 1961. That same year, advocates of the comparative study of religion pioneered in the publication of the now highly respected quarterly *History of Religions*. The expansion of archaeological work in the Near East spurred the establishment of *Biblical Archaeologist* (1938) and the more popular *Biblical Archaeology Review* (1975). Other journals established in recent years reflecting the range of specializations that have developed within religious studies include the *Thomist* (1939), the *Journal of Church and State* (1959), and the *Journal of Religious Ethics* (1973).

The concern to explore in a scholarly fashion the interaction of religion and science led to the founding of *Zygon* in 1966, and the need to advance a solid academic foundation for resurgent Protestant evangelicalism resulted in the publication of the first issue in 1958 of the *Bulletin* (now *Journal*) *of the Evangelical Theological Society*. The desire to place Catholic scholarship on a firm foundation generated such journals as the *Catholic Historical Review* (1915) and the *Catholic Biblical Quarterly* (1939), both regarded as in the front ranks of periodicals in their respective fields. The pages of the *Jewish Quarterly Review*, the *Journal of Reform Judaism, Conservative Judaism*, and *Judaism* reflect the coming of age of the American Jewish community. Some newer religious groups that have come to maturity in the twentieth century have also sponsored scholarly periodicals and in some cases witnessed minority movements establish their own journals to provide an alternative to official viewpoints. *Dialogue: A Journal of*

Mormon Thought first appeared as a quasi-official publication of the Latter-day Saints in 1966; less than a decade later (1975) the first issue of a dissident journal, *Sunstone*, came off the presses.

Periodicals that offer commentary on current events, book reviews, and carefully written scholarly essays but geared to an educated religious readership continue to flourish. *Christian Century*, for example, first appeared in 1884 under the auspices of the Disciples of Christ but within half a century had become an interdenominational biweekly with a moderate liberal focus. More liberal yet is *Christianity and Crisis*, founded by Reinhold Niebuhr of New York's Union Theological Seminary in 1941. A conservative Protestant analogue is *Christianity Today* (1956); *Commonweal* (1924) is the Roman Catholic parallel and *Commentary* (1945) the Jewish one. All continue the tradition of cognate periodicals of the nineteenth century in seeking to relate religious beliefs to the events and currents of the times.

Thus the publication of religious periodicals oriented to academic and scholarly concerns continues to be a vital dimension of American journalism.

Bibliography

Albaugh, Gaylord P. "American Presbyterian Periodicals and Newspapers, 1752–1830, with Library Locations." *Journal of Presbyterian History* 41 (1963): 165–87, 243–62; 42 (1964): 54–67, 124–44.

Allen, Frederick L., et al. *American Magazines, 1741–1941*. New York: New York Public Library, 1941.

Barrett, John P. *The Centennial of Religious Journalism*. 2d ed. Dayton: Christian Publishing Association, 1908.

Baumgartner, Apollinaris W. *Catholic Journalism: A Study of Its Development in the United States, 1789–1930*. New York: Columbia University Press, 1931.

Berger, Tom. *Baptist Journalism in Nineteenth-Century Texas*. Austin: University of Texas Press, n.d.

Bisbee, Robert E. "The Religious Press and Social Reform." *Arena* 20 (August 1898): 210–15.

Brigham, Clarence S. *History and Bibliography of American Newspapers, 1690–1820*. 2 vols. Worcester: American Antiquarian Society, 1947.

"Centennial of Religious Journalism," *Independent* 65 (1 October 1908): 800–801.

Dobbins, Gaines S. "Southern Baptist Journalism." Th.D. dissertation, Southern Baptist Theological Seminary, 1914.

Dunn, James J. "Journalism of the Catholic Church in the United States." *Chautauquan* 20 (March 1895).

Edgar, Neal L. *A History and Bibliography of American Magazines, 1810–1820*. Metuchen, N.J.: Scarecrow Press, 1975.

Elsbree, Oliver W. "The Rise of the Missionary Spirit in New England, 1790–1815." *New England Quarterly* 1 (1928): 295–322.

English, Carl D. "The Ethical Emphases of the Editors of Baptist Journals Published in the Southeastern Region of the United States, 1865–1915." Th. D. dissertation, Southern Baptist Theological Seminary, 1948.

Foik, Paul J. *Pioneer Catholic Journalism*. New York: U.S. Catholic Historical Society, 1930.

Ford, Edwin H. *History of Journalism in the United States: A Bibliography of Books and Annotated Articles*. Minneapolis: Burgess Publishing Co., 1938.

Gohdes, Clarence L. F. *Periodicals of American Transcendentalism*. Durham: Duke University Press, 1931.

Gotwald, Frederick G. "Pioneer American Lutheran Journalism." *Lutheran Quarterly* 42 (April 1912): 161–98. Also published separately.

Index to Early American Periodical Literature, 1728–1870, Part I: The List of Periodicals Indexed. New York: Pamphlet Distributing Co., 1941.

Jensen, Howard Eikenberry. "The Rise of Religious Journalism in the United States." Ph.D. dissertation, University of Chicago, 1920.

Lewis, Benjamin. "A History and Bibliography of American Magazines, 1800–1810." Ph.D. dissertation, University of Michigan, 1955.

Lucey, William L., S.J. "Catholic Magazines, 1865–1880." American Catholic Historical Society of Philadelphia *Records* 63 (March 1952): 21–36; 63 (June 1952): 85–109; 63 (September 1952): 133–56; 63 (December 1952): 197–223.

McDonald, Erwin L. *Across the Editor's Desk: The Story of the State Baptist Papers*. Nashville: Broadman Press, 1966.

Martin, David, C.S.C. "A History of Catholic Periodical Production." Master's thesis, University of Chicago, 1955.

Marty, Martin E., et al. *The Religious Press in America*. New York: Holt, Rhinehart, and Winston, 1963.

Meehan, Thomas F. "First Catholic Monthly Magazines." Catholic Historical Society *Records and Studies* 31 (1940): 137–44.

Middleton, Thomas C. "Catholic Periodicals Published in the United States from the Earliest in 1809 to the Close of the Year 1892." American Catholic Historical Society of Philadelphia *Records* 19 (1908): 18–41.

———. "A List of Catholic and Semi-Catholic Periodicals Published in the United States from the Earliest Date down to the Close of the Year 1892." American Catholic Historical Society of Philadelphia *Records* 4 (1893): 213–42.

Morehouse, Clifford P. "Origins of the Episcopal Church Press from Colonial Days to 1840." *Historical Magazine of the Protestant Episcopal Church* 11 (1942): 199–318.

Morrison, Alfred J. "Presbyterian Periodicals of Richmond, 1815–1860." *Tyler's Quarterly Historical and Genealogical Magazine* 1 (1920): 174–76.

———. "The Virginia Literary and Evangelical Magazine, Richmond, 1818–1828." *William and Mary Quarterly*, 1st ser. 19 (1911): 266–72.

Mott, Frank L. "The Christian Disciple and the Christian Examiner." *New England Quarterly* 1 (1928): 197–207.

———. *A History of American Magazines, 1741–1930*. 5 vols. Cambridge: Belknap Press of Harvard University Press, 1957.

Newman, A. H. *A Century of Baptist Achievement*. Philadelphia: American Baptist Publication Society, 1901.

Norton, Wesley. *Religious Newspapers in the Old Northwest to 1861: A History, Bibliography, and Record of Opinion*. Athens: Ohio University Press, 1977.

Osmer, Harold H. *U.S. Religious Journalism and the Korean War*. Washington, D.C.: University Press of America, 1980.

Peterson, Theodore. *Magazines in the Twentieth Century*. Urbana: University of Illinois
   Press, 1964.
Postal, Bernard. "The Early American Jewish Press." *Reflex* 2 (1928).
Regazzi, John J., and Theodore C. Hines. *A Guide to Indexed Periodicals in Religion*.
   Metuchen: Scarecrow Press, 1975.
Reilly, C. *Catholic Journalism: A Study of Its Development in the United States, 1789–
   1930*. New York: Columbia University Press, 1931.
Reilly, Louis W. "The Weak Points in the Catholic Press." *American Ecclesiastical
   Review* (1894).
Reilly, Sister Mary Lonan. *The Catholic Press Association*. Metuchen: Scarecrow Press,
   1971.
Sheerin, John B. "The Development of the Catholic Magazine in the History of American
   Journalism." U. S. Catholic Historical Society *Historical Records and Studies*
   41 (1953): 5–13.
Smith, Walter W. "Periodical Literature of the Latter-day Saints." *Journal of History*
   14 (July 1921).
Spence, Thomas H. "Southern Presbyterian Reviews." *Union Seminary Review* 56 (1945):
   93–109.
Stevens, Daniel G. *The First Hundred Years of the American Baptist Publishing Society*.
   Philadelphia: American Baptist Publishing Co., 1925.
Stroupe, Henry. *The Religious Press in the South Atlantic States, 1802–1865: An An-
   notated Bibliography with Historical Introduction and Notes*. Durham: Duke Uni-
   versity Press, 1956.
Thaman, Mary Patricia. *Manners and Morals of the 1920's: A Survey of the Religious
   Press*. New York: Bookman Associates, 1954.
Wakefield, Dan. "Slick-Paper Christianity." *Nation* 184 (19 November 1957): 56–59.
Walsh, Michael J. *Religious Bibliographies in Serial Literature: A Guide*. Westport,
   Conn.: Greenwood Press, 1981.
White, R. C. "Writings Pertaining to Religion in Eighteenth-Century American Maga-
   zines." Ph.D. dissertation, Harvard University, 1945.
Willging, Eugene P., and Herta Hatzfeld. "Catholic Serials in the Nineteenth Century
   in the United States: A Bibliographical Survey and a Union List." American
   Catholic Historical Society of Philadelphia *Records* 65 (1954): 158–75; 66 (1955):
   156–73, 222–38.
———. *Catholic Serials of the Nineteenth Century in the United States*. Washington,
   D.C.: Catholic University of America Press, 1962.
Wolseley, Roland E. *Careers in Religious Journalism*. Rev. ed. Scottdale, Pa.: Herald
   Press, 1966.
———. *Interpreting the Church through Press and Radio*. Philadelphia: Muhlenberg
   Press, 1951.
———. "The Influence of the Religious Press." *Religion in Life* 26 (Winter 1956–57):
   75–87.
———. *Writing for the Religious Market*. New York: Association Press, 1956.
Woods, James E., Jr. "Baptist Historical and Theological Journals." *Baptist History
   and Heritage* 1 (October 1966): 47–58.

PROFILES OF RELIGIOUS PERIODICALS OF THE UNITED STATES: ACADEMIC AND SCHOLARLY

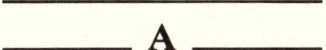

ACADEMY

The Lutheran Academy for Scholarship has published a modestly sized quarterly since 1943 to communicate with members and to feature their reflections on the liberal arts, the professions, and Lutheran theology. First entitled the *Lutheran Scholar*, the journal was renamed in 1974 *Academy: Lutherans in Profession*. Until 1967 academy membership was limited to Lutherans holding graduate degrees who were also members of the Synodical Conference, a federation of strictly orthodox Lutheran bodies dominated by the Missouri Synod.[1] Membership was opened to all Lutherans in 1967, the same year that the Lutheran Church–Missouri Synod, the American Lutheran Church, and the Lutheran Church in America founded the Lutheran Council in the U.S.A. to further the cause of inter-Lutheran cooperation.

Although the *Scholar* has never exceeded a circulation of 700, it merits historical attention because it logs the efforts of restive intellectual leaders within the Missouri Synod to raise standards of scholarship for synodical schools and clergy, to nurture Lutheran sensibilities among an increasingly educated laity, and to explore the relationship between their church and American culture. The foundations for this movement were laid by the academy and other organizations financially independent of the Synod, such as Valparaiso University and the Lutheran Education Association, during the 1940s and 1950s. By the mid–1960s efforts to usher the Missouri Synod with its distinctive educational and theological heritage into dialogue with America's religious and intellectual mainstream appeared destined for success. Yet the movement had attracted opponents who scored political victory in 1969 with the election of J. A. O. Preus as Synod president. By the mid–1970s strife between the factions yielded a breakaway seminary, Concordia Seminary in Exile, and church body, the Association of Evangelical Lutheran Churches. The ''Seminex'' faculty now dominated the academy and its mouthpiece. During the ensuing decade, the academy struggled to build a new constituency and to stabilize its leadership. This drama unfolds in the pages of the *Scholar* and *Academy*.

During the 1940s and 1950s the customary 32-page issues of the *Scholar* carried news on the scholarly and career achievements of members, including women, reports on academy projects, and two or three brief articles by members. The academy was especially proud of its role in prompting the Synod to contract with the University of Chicago for a translation and adaptation of the fourth edition of Walter Bauer's *Greek-German Lexicon of the New Testament*. The project, begun in 1949, was completed in 1957 by William F. Arndt and F. Wilbur Gingerich as *A Greek-English Lexicon of the New Testament*.[2] The academy also pressed for inclusion of new fields in theological education, particularly the social sciences.[3] Beginning in 1951 with the Institute on Church and Modern Culture, the academy began to cosponsor a series of conferences designed to explore the relationship between Lutheran theology and contemporary trends. The journal, which advertised and reported on these events, also published manuscripts of speeches. University staff assemblies for academicians and for campus pastors and conferences on law, medicine, social welfare, and public policy followed.

In its years as the *Lutheran Scholar*, the tone of the journal was set not by the editor, who served more as a host than a critical commentator, but by the academy president, who articulated standards of scholarship, reported on the progress of academy and synodical research projects, and expressed the intellectual mission of Lutheranism (particularly Missouri Lutheranism) in the United States. The president became a public conscience for the Synod's intellectual life. In 1943 Einar Anderson, the first president, sounded the mission call in the opening issue of the *Scholar*:

> The greatest need in our world today is for a leavening influence of sound scholarship and orthodox theology, a synthesis of the practical and the ideal, the pessimistic and the optimistic, in other words, of the influences of the Reformation and the Renaissance.[4]

In its second president, Martin H. Scharlemann, the academy gained a public presence that would dominate the journal from 1946 to 1970. Scharlemann's powerful voice derived from his own experience as a broker for contemporary New Testament scholarship in the Missouri Synod and as a chaplain facing the challenges of relating faith to members of the U.S. Air Force from the time of World War II. He viewed the Synod's position in American Protestantism as an unequaled opportunity for mission.[5] Yet not until the early 1960s would he become candid about the pressures applied to those who shared his convictions in the Synod.

During the 1950s, the academy and its journal came under the wing of the Synod's establishment. In 1952 Lorenz Blankenbuehler, editor of the *Scholar* from 1943 to 1954, was called to the seminary faculty at Concordia, St. Louis, to edit the Synod's popular magazine, the *Lutheran Witness*. Scharlemann, who had joined the faculty the same year, became director of its graduate school in 1954. Andrew J. Buehner, *Scholar* editor from 1956, continued that responsibility once he joined the editorial department of the Synod's Concordia Publishing House in 1964, from then on printer and distributor of the journal. In 1959 the academy acquired nonprofit status under Missouri law and began receiving annual grants from the favored fraternal insurance company of Missouri Lutherans, the Aid Association for Lutherans.

By the early 1960s the *Scholar* documented the emerging confidence within the academy that the case for contemporary scholarship had been accepted. Scharlemann's regular column, "Gnomon" ("interpreter"), claimed that changes in Missouri under its new president Oliver Harms paralleled changes in Catholicism under Pope John XXIII:

> Men can be themselves. There was a time when they were afraid, fearful of what someone might report to higher echelons. In fact we remember when men dreaded to present exegetical papers. . . . A kind of theological renaissance is quietly going on also among us.[6]

Now Scharlemann openly challenged biblical positions that had not taken into account current scholarship. For example, Bernard Keiser's article, "Can the Scientist Today Believe in Genesis 1?" (October 1962), was criticized for its fundamentalist orientation by both Martin Scharlemann and his brother Robert.[7] Keiser's later rebuttal cited such standard Missouri authorities as C. F. W. Walther, Franz Pieper, and the Brief Statement of 1932. Scharlemann expressly denounced this form of argumentation by quoting a more recent Missouri savant, Theodore Craebner, on Missouri's "burden of infallibility."[8]

In a further expression of this confidence, Scharlemann stated that the academy had reached that moment in its organizational life "when it must act boldly or perish."[9] Included in the "five-year plan" was the proposal to invite scholars of other Lutheran bodies to join. As part of the academy's self-study, the journal was reevaluated prior to its publication at Concordia Publishing House, and a features editor was appointed to provide more thematic coherence. Symposia on contemporary social and/or peculiarly Lutheran concerns became a frequent format.[10]

The theme of lay competence again soon came to the fore. Academy member Arthur Carl Piepkorn argued against the "scandalizing" of the erudite when the church exalts "a human opinion to the status of dogma without a clear word of God to support it." He held the church and its theologians accountable for so instructing "the educated man that he takes to his daily tasks the best insight into the divine revelation that under God we can communicate to him."[11] Scharlemann, who stated that the academy ought "to articulate the Lutheran ethic for various disciplines and professions," engaged in such teaching in a four-part series of articles, "Biblical Interpretation Today," in which he rejected "liberal" and "fundamentalist" approaches for the scholarship developing in post–Vatican II Catholicism.[12]

By the time a retrospective on the academy's first 25 years appeared in the *Scholar* in 1969, the era of good feelings was closing in Missouri.[13] Members of the Academy became polarized as Missourians took sides on both biblical and cultural interpretation. By the time Scharlemann's presidency ended in 1970, the 1960s had taken their toll. Scharlemann had broken with Missouri scholars who shared his understanding of contemporary biblical scholarship but not his social views in an age of "revolution" and anti-American sentiment. Scharlemann viewed the social order as "an undeserved blessing" and South Vietnam as a "crucible of freedom."[14] When Robert H. Smith, also a New Testament scholar at Concordia and one who, unlike Scharlemann, would join the Seminex faculty, became academy president, the tenor of the *Scholar* shifted. While continuing to press traditional aims of the academy, Smith expressed more of the values of the political Left, as embodied in Common Cause.[15]

Beginning in 1974 when Buehner retired from the editorship of the *Scholar* and when the split between one faction in Concordia Seminary and the Missouri Synod was institutionalized, leadership in the academy grew increasingly provisional. During the following decade, the academy had four presidents and six different arrangements of editors, joint and single. All the men holding these posts had been ordained in and were formerly connected with the Synod. Under Richard Jeske, editor since 1980 and faculty member at the Lutheran Theological Seminary in Philadelphia, the journal moved from St. Louis and showed signs of becoming more explicitly inter-Lutheran. Jeske, for example, published the papers of the Lutheran Campus Ministries Staff Conference and the annual meeting of the Association of Lutheran College Faculties in 1981.[16]

Editors and presidents voiced the academy's traditional cause of maintaining contact and the flow of ideas among Lutheran academicians. Nevertheless, their task had become more difficult now that members came from diverse Lutheran backgrounds and were largely strangers to each other. Both journal and academy compete for the loyalty of a clientele with stronger loyalties to more regional manifestations of the church and to their academic guilds. That editors and presidents find it difficult to make the enterprise a priority is evidence of a problem facing the entire membership in the mid–1980s.

Notes

1. At the time of the academy's founding, the Synodical Conference was made up of the Evangelical Lutheran Synod of Missouri, Ohio, and Other States, the Wisconsin Evangelical Lutheran Synod, and the Slovak Evangelical Lutheran Church. Missouri members provided the impetus and leadership. Because of Missouri's national network of junior colleges (inclusive of high schools and modeled on the German *Gymnasium*) all feeding into Concordia Theological Seminary in St. Louis and the strength of kinship ties, academy members, heavily clerical in number, were well known to each other.

2. William F. Arndt and F. Wilbur Gingerich, *A Greek–English Lexicon of the New Testament* (Chicago: University of Chicago Press, 1957).

3. See the *Lutheran Scholar* (July 1948) (hereafter cited as TLS), and Roger Beese, "The First Quarter Century," *TLS* 26 (January 1969): 28–32.

4. *TLS* 1 (March 1943).

5. See his account of the Institute on Church and Modern Culture in "The Lutheran Church and Its American Environment," *Concordia Theological Monthly* 26 (August 1955): 597–602.

6. *TLS* 21 (July 1964): 84.

7. At the time, Keiser, a Missouri layman, was a senior staff member in communications systems at the RCA laboratories, Princeton, N.J. See *TLS* 19 (October 1962): 84–91, and 20 (October 1963): 99–101. For M. Scharlemann's views, see 20 (January 1963): 18, and 22 (July 1965): 19–20; for R. Scharlemann's, "The Scientist and Genesis 1: A Reply," 20 (April 1963): 36–39.

8. *TLS* 22 (April 1965): 45.

9. "Gnomon," *TLS* 20 (July 1963): 74.

10. See "A Symposium on Ethics and the Public Service," *TLS* 25 (July 1968); "Symposium: Changing Conceptions of Vocation," *TLS* 26 (January 1969); "Symposium: Violence in Contemporary Political Life," *TLS* 27 (October 1970).

11. "The Educated Man and the Church," *TLS* 20 (July 1963): 68, 70.

12. *TLS* 21 (October 1964): 91–92; 24 (January, April 1967): 9–23, 35–48; 25 (April, July 1968): 54–61, 80–83.

13. Beese, pp. 28–32, 45–61.

14. See "The Credibility Gap in Theology," *TLS* 28 (January 1971): 26. His views on Vietnam were articulated as early as 1963.

15. See "Asterisk . . . An Occasional Comment," *TLS* 28 (July 1971): 95–96.

16. *Academy* 37 (1980–81).

Information Sources

BIBLIOGRAPHY:

Adams, James E. *Preus of Missouri and the Great Lutheran Civil War*. New York: Harper & Row, 1977.

Danker, Frederick W. *No Room in the Brotherhood: The Preus-Otten Purge of Missouri*. St. Louis: Clayton Publishing House, 1977.

Leuker, Erwin L., ed. *Lutheran Cyclopedia*. St. Louis: Concordia Publishing House, 1975.

Meyer, Carl S. *Log Cabin to Luther Tower*. St. Louis: Concordia Publishing House, 1965.

Nelson, E. Clifford, ed. *The Lutherans in North America*. Philadelphia: Fortress Press, 1975.

INDEX SOURCES: *Religion Index One*.

REPRINT EDITIONS: University Microfilms International.

LOCATION SOURCES: University of Illinois (Urbana), Andover-Harvard Theological Library, Princeton Theological Seminary, Catholic Central Verein of America, and others.

Publication History

MAGAZINE TITLE AND TITLE CHANGES: *Lutheran Scholar* (1943–74), *Academy: Lutherans in Profession* (1974–).

VOLUME AND ISSUE DATA: *Lutheran Scholar* 1 (Winter 1943)–31 (Winter 1974); *Academy* 31 (Spring 1974–); 32 (January 1975) is a newsletter only, 33 (Autumn 1976) is a roster of academy members, 37 (nos. 1–2, nos. 3–4) covers 1980–81.

PUBLISHER AND PLACE OF PUBLICATION: Lutheran Academy for Scholarship, St. Louis (1943–49), Lake City, Minn. (1949–64); St. Louis (1964–79); Philadelphia (1980–).

EDITORS: Lorenz Blankenbuehler (1943–55), Andrew J. Buehner (1956–73), Duane Mehl (1974–76), Earl Gaulke (1974), Richard LaBore (1975–79), Kurt K. Hendel (1976), Richard Jeske (1980–).

CIRCULATION: 500 (1983).

Christa R. Klein

THE A.M.E. CHURCH REVIEW

Since its initial appearance in 1884, the *A.M.E.* (African Methodist Episcopal) *Church Review* has appeared continuously on a quarterly basis, making it the longest surviving journal published by blacks in the United States. Although the *Review* has explicitly been an organ of a denomination, it has also served as a forum for the advancement of black learning and culture. While emphases have shifted over the century of its existence, the *Review*, particularly before the 1930s, constitutes an important chronicle for developments in black Christianity and culture from the post-Reconstruction period on.

The first editor of the *Review*, Benjamin T. Tanner (1835–1923), proffered this rationale at the end of the first volume in 1885:

> The object aimed at in the publication of the . . . Review is to give an outlet to negro scholarship a) of the A.M.E. Church, b) and of the world. At present, this scholarship is practically hedged in. White Magazines and Reviews stand in no need of it. . . . Nothing remains but for the negro to open a channel for himself. The men of this organization are prepared to lead in the work of cutting the ditch. They only ask that the negro scholars of the country, of the West Indies, of Africa, and of the world come to their help.[1]

Reflecting these encompassing purposes to promote black scholarship and the A.M.E. Church, Tanner published articles on a variety of subjects, including anatomy, literature, politics, and education, as well as higher criticism of the Bible, theology, and the ordination of women.

Tanner, who had edited the *Christian Recorder*, the A.M.E. weekly newspaper, before taking responsibility for the *Review*, was elected bishop in 1888.

At that time Levi Jennings Coppin (1848–1924) was named editor, a post he held until he was elected a bishop in 1896. The character of the *Review* changed little under Coppin's leadership; he worked within the framework established by Tanner. Coppin attempted to increase the readership of the journal, adding, among other things, a feature dedicated to short stories and fiction.[2]

After Coppin's election to the episcopacy, the *Review* was edited by Hightower T. Kealing (1859–1932), a layperson and educator who held important administrative positions in several A.M.E. colleges. Kealing's special interests, while working within the young tradition he inherited from Tanner and Coppin, were reflected in his concern to use the journal as a vehicle for the continuing education of black clergy.[3]

In 1912 when Kealing gave up the editorship to take a college presidency, Reverdy C. Ransom (1861–1959) was elected to succeed him. Ransom charted a new course for the *Review*, expressing a desire for continuity as well as the necessity for more sustained attention to social and political issues. In one of his first editorials Ransom wrote:

> Our purpose is, by God's help, to endeavor to maintain the high literary character which the Review has held for more than a quarter of a century, but while doing this we shall deal chiefly with *potential literature*. . . . We shall concern ourself not less about Israel or Egypt, but more about the Negro in America.[4]

A regular feature during the early years of Ransom's leadership, which extended until 1924, was the Department of Social Service, edited by George Edmund Haynes (1880–1960), the first director of the Urban League and later secretary for race relations of the Federal Council of Churches. Ransom's practical concerns were also evident in his concentration on U.S. foreign policy during the Wilson administration and on the contributions of Negro soldiers to the war effort. On the domestic front, Ransom published articles about lynching, the Ku Klux Klan, and voting rights for Negroes. Articles also appeared during this period about the work of the A.M.E. Church in South Africa, which former editor L. J. Coppin had been assigned to serve after his election as bishop. In a fortieth anniversary number, an editorial reflected that "the *Review* had always looked upon itself less as the organ of a denomination and more as the mouthpiece of a race."[5]

Upon Ransom's election as a bishop in 1924, the editorship passed to J. G. Robinson (1866–1947) who, during the 16 years of his leadership of the *Review*, shifted the focus of the journal more decisively in the direction of the A.M.E. Church and its associated institutions than had any previous editor. Robinson used the *Review* as a vehicle for promoting his commitments to evangelism and revival, as well as for occasional critical probes at Franklin Roosevelt and the New Deal. In part, Robinson's disappointment in Roosevelt was caused by the repeal of the Eighteenth Amendment ending prohibition. Robinson changed the character of the *Review* substantially, moving toward a more magazine-like format and giving greater attention to current events in the denomination.

Robinson was succeeded by three editors during the 1940s: H. D. Gregg, M. W. Thornton, and J. S. Brookens. In 1951 George A. Singleton was elected editor of the *Review*, which continued to focus principally on the denomination and the work of its bishops past and present. Singleton's abiding concern was to chronicle the history of the A.M.E. Church, devoting attention to such subjects as Richard Allen, the first bishop of the A.M.E. Church; Daniel Alexander Payne, a leading bishop of the late nineteenth century; and Wilberforce University, the oldest educational institution of the denomination. From the period beginning with the 1954 Supreme Court decision, *Brown v. Board of Education of Topeka*, declaring school segregation unconstitutional, he also gave regular notice to the civil rights movement and to the work of Martin Luther King, Jr.

By the 1970s, the *Review* began to evince a shift away from scholarship and anlaysis, its pages increasingly focusing on denominational concerns. Reports of denominational meetings and the work of church agencies replaced articles appraising various dimensions of black religious history, life, and culture. Today the *Review* generally features only one major article per issue of interest to persons not A.M.E. adherents. By and large it has ceased to be a significant organ.

Notes

1. *A.M.E. Church Review* 1 (1884): 412.
2. Penelope Bullock, *The Afro-American Press, 1838–1909* (Baton Rouge: Louisiana State University Press, 1981), p. 94.
3. Ibid., p. 95.
4. *A.M.E. Church Review* 29 (1913): 80–81.
5. Ibid., 40 (1924): 41.

Information Sources

BIBLIOGRAPHY:
Bullock, Penelope L. *The Afro-American Press, 1838–1909*. Baton Rouge: Louisiana State University Press, 1981.
Cunningham, Dorothy Homes. "An Analysis of the A.M.E. Church Review, 1884–1900." *A.M.E. Church Review* 68 (1952): 12–18; 69 (1953): 21–29.
Singleton, George A. *The Romance of African Methodism: A Study of the African Methodist Episcopal Church*. New York: Exposition Press, 1952.
Wright, Richard R., ed. *The Encyclopedia of the African Methodist Episcopal Church*. 2d ed. Philadelphia: n.p., 1947.
INDEX SOURCES: None.
REPRINT EDITIONS: University Microfilms International.
LOCATION SOURCES: Complete or virtually complete holdings at Wilberforce University, Howard University, Schomberg Center for Research in Black Culture of the New York Public Library, Robert W. Woodruff Library of the Atlanta University Center; partial holdings widely available.

Publication History

MAGAZINE TITLE AND CHANGES: *The A.M.E. Church Review* (1884–).
VOLUME AND ISSUE DATA: 1:1 (1884–); appears quarterly.
PUBLISHER AND PLACE OF PUBLICATION: A.M.E. Sunday School Union, Nashville, Tenn.
EDITORS: Benjamin T. Tanner (1884–88), Levi J. Coppin (1888–96), Hightower T. Kealing (1896–1912), Reverdy C. Ransom (1912–24), J. G. Robinson (1925–40), H. D. Gregg (1940–43), M. W. Thornton (1943–44), J. S. Brookens (1944–51), George A. Singleton (1951–66), B. Hill (1966–70), W. D. Johnson (1970–84), Jayne Williams (1984–).
CIRCULATION: 3000 (1984).

Eugene Y. Lowe

AMERICA

America, together with its lay-edited counterpart *Commonweal*,* has served since the first decade of the century as one of the two leading Catholic journals of opinion in the United States. It began publication on 17 April 1909 under the editorship of John J. Wynne, S.J., who was also a major force in the preparation of the first edition of the *Catholic Encyclopedia*, and is staffed by members of the Jesuit order.[1] Its purpose originally was to provide a more sophisticated alternative to diocesan and popular Catholic newspapers in order to address the social, political, and cultural issues of the day for an increasingly literate Catholic readership, as well as to undertake the apologetic task of expounding Catholic teaching and counteracting erroneous information about Catholicism in the secular and Protestant press.[2] It was established with an *Ordinatio*, or constitution, provided by the general of the Jesuits, and its editors have been appointed by and responsible to the heads of the Jesuits' provinces in the United States (and, later, Canada); however, with some significant exceptions, its staff has been largely self-supervising, and the journal has always been careful not to present itself as an official vehicle for the Jesuit order.[3] Its most direct model was the *Tablet* of London, a sophisticated English Catholic journal, and its enunciated goal in its first issue was "to meet the needs of the time" and to provide "a review and conscientious criticism of the life and literature of the day."[4]

The concerns and topics dealt with in *America* have been similar to those of cognate religious opinion journals such as *Commonweal* and the *Christian Century** and, to an extent, such secular counterparts as the *New Republic*. The first pages generally have dealt with contemporary political and social issues (including specifically, for some years, regular sections on "Education" and "Sociology"), while the latter part of the magazine has featured columns on literature and the arts. Articles on specifically theological topics have appeared with some frequency but do not generally dominate the contents.

Political opinion, though always avowedly nonpartisan, has ranged from moderately liberal to fairly conservative over the years, depending on the particular editors and the degree to which specifically Catholic interests have been involved (such as in the case of the role of the Catholic Church in Mexico and Spain during periods of civil war). The informing philosophy, however, at least since the 1920s, has been the application of Catholic teachings as enunciated by contemporary popes, such as the social encyclicals of Leo XIII and Pius XI, to the issues of the day, especially where matters of general moral interest or specifically Catholic concerns have been involved.

In looking back on the first decade or so of *America* from the vantage point of 50 years of publication, later editors have characterized the journal's early stance as negatively preoccupied with the threat of socialism in the political realm and given in uncritical terms to the promotion of the Catholic writing of the day as superior to its secular counterparts. *America* achieved a greater measure of sophistication during the 1920s and began to take a moderate to liberal stance on contemporary affairs, reflecting the impact of the Catholic Bishops' Program of Social Reconstruction of 1919.[5] Although its editorials were generally supportive of President Franklin Roosevelt and the New Deal during the early 1930s, a more conservative tone began to emerge during the later part of that decade, with the Spanish Civil War's drawing an increasing amount of attention as the editors took a position of solidarity with the vast majority of the Catholic press in uncritical support for Franco.[6] A preoccupation with communism became increasingly apparent during these years as well, and editorials praised the work of the Dies committee in its investigations of alleged internal subversion.[7]

One of the most controversial periods for the journal took place during the early 1950s as Americans, including Catholics, were becoming increasingly divided over the tactics of Senator Joseph McCarthy. Beginning with McCarthy's attack on George Marshall in 1951, *America* became increasingly critical of McCarthy's method of innuendo and undocumented attack and began to receive hostile correspondence on the matter from the Wisconsin senator himself, as well as from many of his followers, together with open criticism by fellow Jesuits in the secular as well as the religious press. In May 1954 the superiors of the editors imposed a ban on any further discussion of the issue, which was subsequently modified upon appeal by editor in chief Robert C. Hartnett. This compromise was again reversed by the father-general of the order in Rome, who cited a prohibition against intra-Catholic controversy in the journal's pages as his rationale. Hartnett retired the following year, and McCarthyism was not again discussed for a long period.[8]

Opposition to Senator McCarthy, however, was a much more controversial stance than that usually taken on such issues by *America*'s editors. Perhaps the topics that elicited a consistently liberal position were those involving the rights of labor and social welfare. Questions of civil liberties drew forth variable positions, with editorial outrage expended on such questions as Bertrand Russell's employment at New York's City College or "Can We Get Rid of Red Teachers?"

(The answer: yes.)[9] Such positions varied with the times and the editorial staff, however, so it is difficult to generalize for the whole span of the journal's life. On the question of race relations, *America* has generally taken an advanced position, especially under the distinguished editorship of John LaFarge, who was extremely active in the cause of interracial understanding and harmony.[10] Attitudes on women's issues have varied from opposition to the early version of the equal rights amendment introduced in 1924 to a cautious openness to a wide range of such concerns from the 1970s on.[11] Even on the delicate issue of the ordination of women to the priesthood, recent editorials have called for a careful evaluation of the situation and have tacitly refused to advocate a definitive position.[12] On abortion, editorials in recent years have been pro-life, while not attempting to polemicize or oversimplify the complex issues involved, and have even openly advocated improved nonabortive birth control as an alternative.[13]

Education has been an area of concern that has consistently received attention in *America*. During the 1920s and 1930s, considerable attention was given to the question of the alleged secularism of the National Education Association and the public school system it attempted to control. The editors of *America* simultaneously promoted the classical virtues of Catholic education while consistently opposing the use of federal funds to benefit public schools to the detriment of Catholics, both financially and philosophically. The issue of federal support came to a head during the late 1940s especially, and America Press published several pamphlets by the journal's editor, Robert Hartnett, advocating a distinctive Catholic educational policy.[14] Beginning with the late 1950s, hostility to the secular realm in education began to erode, and even John Dewey, the previously reviled philosopher of progressive education, began to be presented more kindly. The issue of governmental support, however, has never entirely disappeared as a concern.

In addition to controversial issues in the public sector, *America*, like other journals of opinion, has dedicated a considerable amount of attention to the arts in general and to literature in particular. The early years featured the "leisurely literary essay," the subject of which was, as often as not, the writing of the past rather than that of the present.[15] The 1920s through the 1950s might be described as the heyday of an aggressive campaign for a distinctively Catholic culture in which the Jesuit literary editors of *America* played a significant role. Francis X. Talbot, Leonard Feeney (later excommunicated for an unacceptably strict interpretation of the relationship between Catholic Church membership and the possibility of salvation), and Harold C. Gardiner oversaw the journal's literary dimensions during these decades, and widely known Catholic authors, both American and European, contributed essays, including G. K. Chesterton, Hilaire Belloc, Flannery O'Connor, and Daniel Berrigan.[16] In more recent years, the notion of a specifically American Catholic culture has receded as a self-conscious guiding principle, but discussions of Catholic writers such as Mary Gordon are often part of *America*'s literary dimension.[17]

In addition to *America* itself, a number of auxiliary enterprises have arisen from America Press. These include a variety of books and pamphlets on a wide range of Catholic subjects, such as positions on church-state issues (especially education) and papal teachings on various current topics; anthologies of verse originally published in *America*;[18] and the *Catholic Mind*, an anthology of Catholic writings from various sources whose editorship has been closely associated with that of *America*.[19] The Catholic Book Club was another related enterprise founded by Francis X. Talbot in 1928 as part of that generation's campaign to promote actively a culture significantly distinct from that of the secular Book of the Month Club.[20]

In general, *America* has in many ways proved to be a good indicator of American Catholic thought and culture at various stages in its growth during the twentieth century. Its editorship has been generally sophisticated without being avant-garde; liberal but cautious, especially where specifically Catholic interests have been thought to have been at stake; involving the laity widely as contributors but retaining control in the hands of the Jesuit editors, who have ultimately been accountable to their superiors. As such, it has been a more accurate barometer of Catholic opinion than its lay-edited counterpart *Commonweal*, which from time to time has taken stands (for example, on the Spanish Civil War) too far to the left of official Catholic positions and perhaps somewhat less cautious on issues involving moral and cultural concerns. On the whole, however, its contents have been thoughtful and literate, and *America* can take considerable credit as one of the major vehicles through which Catholic opinion in the United States has gradually come to prove itself both sophisticated and influential.

Notes

1. Thurston N. Davis, "What Is 'America'?" *America* 101 (11 April 1959): 92. (This issue contains a number of valuable articles by several of *America*'s editors, which provide information on the journal's history since it is the fiftieth anniversary issue. "Week after Week since 1909," also by Davis, appears in the seventieth anniversary issue, 140 [12 April 1979]: 326–29.) *America* superseded an earlier Jesuit publication, variously titled the *Messenger of the Sacred Heart*, the *Messenger of the Sacred Heart of Jesus*, and simply the *Messenger*, which was published by Fordham University in New York from April 1866 until March 1909.

2. Davis, "What Is 'America'?" p. 92. See also the "Editorial Announcement" of the first issue, *America*, 1 (17 April 1909): 5, reprinted in the fiftieth anniversary issue, p. 95.

3. Davis, "What Is 'America'?" p. 100; John LaFarge, S.J., *The Manner Is Ordinary* (Garden City, N.Y.: Doubleday Image, 1957), p. 254. Chapter 18 of that autobiography, "Hoisting a Visible Sign," deals with LaFarge's career as editor of *America* toward the end of World War II. (I have omitted use of "S.J." following the names of editors, as is *America*'s usual practice, and have included them only when they appear in book citations.)

4. Davis, "What Is 'America'?" p. 92.

5. Benjamin L. Masse, "A Half-Century of Social Action," *America* 101 (11 April 1959), pp. 138–39, 142. Masse was one of *America*'s most vigorous editors in promoting progressive social policies.

6. Ibid., p. 142; John David Valaik, "American Catholics and the Spanish Civil War, 1931–1939" (Ph.D. dissertation, University of Rochester, 1964), p. 53. *Commonweal* and the *Catholic Worker* were vitually the only Catholic publications even to advocate a policy of U.S. neutrality in the Spanish struggle. See also Valaik, "American Catholic Dissenters and the Spanish Civil War," *Catholic Historical Review* 58 (1968): 537–55.

7. *America* 56 (15 October 1936): 27.

8. Donald F. Crosby, S.J., *God, Church, and Flag: Senator Joseph McCarthy and the Catholic Church, 1950–1957* (Chapel Hill: University of North Carolina Press, 1978), pp. 81–83, 101, 178–85. See also Rodger Van Allen, *The Commonweal and American Catholicism* (Philadelphia: Fortress Press, 1974), pp. 107–16.

9. *America*, 62 (23 March 1940), pp. 646–47; 63 (6 April 1940), pp. 208–9; and 82 (25 March 1950) p. 715.

10. In addition to La Farge, *Manner*, see his "Views of a Country Pastor," *America* 101 (11 April 1959), pp. 124–25, 127–28.

11. On the first proposed amendment, see *America*, 31 (1 May 1924), p. 289. See also "Split Ticket on the E.R.A.," *America*, 133 (22 November 1975), p. 343.

12. "On Ordaining Women," *America*, 133 (1 November 1975), p. 269; "The Ordination of Women," *America*, 139 (25 November 1978), pp. 374–75.

13. "Abortion Statistics," *America*, 143 (12 July 1980), p. 2. An editorial in *America*, 143 (26 July 1980) p. 24, endorsed the Hyde amendment.

14. For example, *Federal Aid to Education* (New York: America Press, 1950).

15. Harold C. Gardiner, "Literature and Arts in 'America,' " *America*, 101 (11 April 1959), p. 181.

16. Ibid, pp. 181, 184. On Gardiner himself and other of *America*'s literary editors, see William M. Halsey, *The Survival of American Innocence: Catholicism in an Era of Dissillusionment, 1920–1940* (Notre Dame: University of Notre Dame Press, 1980), pp. 64–65, 108, 112.

17. Madonna Kolbenschlag et al, "Man, Woman, Catholic," *America*, 126 (4–11 July 1981) pp. 4–11, a three-part symposium on Mary Gordon's *The Company of Women*.

18. Francis X. Talbot, ed., *The America Book of Verse* (New York: America Press, 1928); *The Second America Book of Verse, 1930–1955* (New York: America Press, 1955).

19. Benjamin L. Masse, "The *Catholic Mind*," *America*, 101 (11 April 1959), pp. 192–93.

20. Harold C. Gardiner, "The Catholic Book Club," *America*, 101 (11 April 1959), pp. 190–92.

Information Sources

BIBLIOGRAPHY:

Crosby, Donald F., S.J. *God, Church, and Flag: Senator Joseph R. McCarthy and the Catholic Church, 1950–1957*. Chapel Hill: University of North Carolina Press, 1978.

Davis, Thurston N. "What Is 'America'?" *America*, (11 April 1959), pp. 92–103.

———. "Week after Week since 1909." *America*, (21 April 1979) pp. 326–29.

Deedy, John G., Jr. "The Catholic Press: The Why and Wherefore." In Martin E. Marty et al, eds. *The Religious Press in America*. New York: Holt, Rinehart and Winston, 1963.

Duff, Edward. "Wilfrid Parsons: An Appreciation." *Social Order* 8 (March 1955): 104–16.

Halsey, William M. *The Survival of American Innocence: Catholicism in an Age of Disillusionment, 1920–1940.* Notre Dame: University of Notre Dame Press, 1980.

LaFarge, John, S.J. *The Manner Is Ordinary.* New York: Harcourt Brace, 1954.

Talbot, Francis X. *Richard Henry Tierney.* New York: America Press, 1930.

Valaik, John David. "American Catholics and the Spanish Civil War, 1931–1939." Ph.D. dissertation, University of Rochester, 1964.

Van Allen, Rodger. *The Commonweal and American Catholicism.* Philadelphia: Fortress Press, 1964.

INDEX SOURCES: *Book Review Digest, Book Review Index, Catholic Periodical Index, Reader's Guide to Periodical Literature.*

REPRINT EDITIONS: Bell and Howell Micro Photo Division, University Microfilms International, Microforms International Marketing Company.

LOCATION SOURCES: Catholic University of America, Union Theological Seminary (New York), Princeton University, Boston College, Library of Congress, and others.

Publication History

MAGAZINE TITLE AND TITLE CHANGES: *America: A Catholic Review of the Week* (17 April 1909–21 January 1950), *America: A National Catholic Weekly Review* (28 January 1950–26 June 1965), *America* (3 July 1965–   ).

VOLUME AND ISSUE DATA: Volumes span six months, with the exception of 107 (October-December 1962), beginning with 17 April 1909. In 1964 came the change to a January-June and July-December volume division.

PUBLISHER AND PLACE OF PUBLICATION: America Press, New York.

EDITORS: John J. Wynne (1909–10), Thomas C. Campbell (1910–14), Richard H. Tierney (1914–25), Wilfrid Parsons (1925–36), Francis X. Talbot (1936–44), John LaFarge (1944–48), Robert C. Hartnett (1948–55), Thurston N. Davis (1955–68), Donald R. Campion (1968–75), Joseph A. O'Hare (1975–   ). All editors have been Jesuits.

CIRCULATION: 5400 (1909), 50,000 (1959), 35,000 (1982).

Peter W. Williams

AMERICAN BAPTIST QUARTERLY

Foundations: A Baptist Journal of History and Theology was first published in 1958 by the American Baptist Historical Society, Rochester, New York. It was successor to the *Chronicle*, founded in 1938; became a journal subtitled *History, Theology, and Ministry* in 1978; and was succeeded in 1982 by the *American Baptist Quarterly*. Attention to nomenclature of both journal and society is necessary for their own descriptive purposes, as well as to distinguish them from the *Baptist History and Heritage: A Southern Baptist Journal**, published quarterly by the Southern Baptist Convention and the Southern Baptist Historical Society, and the *Quarterly Review*, published by the Sunday School Board of the Southern Baptist Convention, Nashville, Tennessee.

Foundations had five editors in its 25 years. The first and longest in tenure,

George D. Younger (1958–68), set the editorial policy of the journal in its first issue: "To search to discover those foundations on which we Baptists have built"; hence, it was to be a journal of history. And since history must interpret as well as chronicle, "pointing beyond the past to the life of the present and the way of the future," there was required the "assistance of Biblical study and theology"; hence, it was also to be a journal of history and theology.[1] To these ends the first issue offered a piece on the early seventeenth century by Edwin S. Gaustad, "Roger Williams and the Principle of Separation," and another on the later twentieth century by Lynn Leavenworth, "American Baptists Face Theological Issues."[2] Such interplay between matters historical and theological was to be a characteristic and a strength of the journal under Younger.

In its third year, 1960, *Foundations* focused on a prominent concern (some might argue *the* concern) for Baptists: baptism itself. Not without humor Younger anticipated two possible reactions among readers of the journal: "At long last, an issue on baptism!" and "Why do they have to be so Baptist?" To the second of these he responded by restating the intent of the journal, noting that while "there are any number of good journals and quarterlies . . . that seek to represent an interdenominational [Christian] perspective and claim as broad an audience," *Foundations* sought to "help Baptists learn more of their own history and discuss with ever-increasing precision and depth their theological reasons for existence as Christians and Baptists."[3]

To his Baptist enthusiasts Younger cautioned against reduction and closure. He was not "willing to assume that our Baptist position is so well defined and understood that all we have to do is spin out exposition of statements drawn from our history." In fact, he continued, "as Baptists we have done so little creative reflection on our practice of believers' baptism that it is difficult to say what we need to be discussing among ourselves, let alone what we should be bearing witness to among our fellow Christians in ecumenical discussion."[4] Thus the journal offered several pieces on baptism, as well as a major review by Norman H. Maring of Markus Barth, *Die Taufe—Ein Sakrament?*[5]

Foundations did not focus on concerns germane only to Baptists. In 1962, the journal committed an issue to the examination of one biblical passage, the story of the confession of Peter at Caesarea Philippi, Matthew 16:13–20. Included were a summary by Lyle O. Bristol of recent New Testament scholarship, a survey by Bernard L. Ramm of patristic and Reformation treatment, and examples by David H. Wallace and Leander E. Keck of contemporary American exegetical scholarship.[6] In 1968, the journal devoted an issue to the study of Christology, with articles by Oscar Cullmann, Robert F. Meye, George Eldon Ladd, and others.[7] Other issues were committed to biographical histories and to preaching.[8] In short, *Foundations* during the Younger years was an active, informative, proud, but not parochial, journal of broadly based Baptist concerns and interests.

Under its second editor, John E. Skoglund (1969–74), *Foundations* continued the pattern of concentration on a given topic with an issue devoted to "rethinking'' worship and preaching and another to ''rethinking'' ordination.[9] Of special merit in this latter matter was the inclusion of ''Recommended Procedures'' for ordination adopted in 1969 by the American Baptist Ministers Council and the Commission on the Ministry.[10] Such procedures articulated the responsibilities of all parties in establishing and maintaining a professional clergy. There was also a series of conversations, edited by James B. Ashbrook, with Paul Tillich and the faculty of Denison University.[11]

In the midst of this continuity with the past, there appeared, though at first muted, definite change in policy and practice. With respect to books reviewed, Robert P. Meye recalled in 1971 that it had been ''customary'' for the journal to give ''preference to works about Baptists . . . or concerned with Baptist life and thought'' and ''some preference to books *by* Baptists.'' Now, ''longer reviews, particularly on works bearing more directly upon Baptist life and thought,'' would remain, while ''for the rest,'' Meye would ''regularly survey in capsule form recent religious publications received for review.'' The result would be ''a much wider reach of literature under review.''[12] Left unsaid was that the new practice would be more scholarly and less Baptist than before.

Another change under Skoglund concerned the subject matter of the journal. In 1970 he asked, ''Why are there not more women working as professionals in theology and the related disciplines?'' He offered no answer but remarked that ''*Foundations*, for its part, will welcome articles by women: biblical studies, historical studies, and theological essays. And not only articles by women but *about* women and the church.''[13] The same issue offered pieces on black religion, slavery, lay views of the church (Baptist and Roman Catholic), and counterculture students in theological seminaries.[14] Later would come articles on revolution in Latin America and on human rights violations and one issue devoted to ''War and Peace.''[15] In sum, under Skoglund *Foundations* not only reached its highest scholarship, but did so while opening its institutional eye to crucial, even explosive, concerns of contemporary culture.

Under its third editor, Eldon G. Ernst (1975–77), *Foundations* moved to its third stage. It was now ''one kind of literary instrument facilitating Christian life and thought with a Baptist flavor.'' It also represented ''an American Baptist involvement in world Christianity'': perhaps the latter, clearly the former.[16] A high level of scholarship was maintained, and there was another attempt to treat the matter of women in American religion.[17] There was also a provocative issue, with sequel, to mark the U.S. bicentennial. One issue focused on sexual orientation and Christianity.[18] These three issues were the journal's finest under Ernst.

Ernst was succeeded as editor by Joseph R. Sweeny (1978–81), who placed the emphasis of the journal on ''a creative tension between the scholarly and professional arenas.'' There was also a very real concern to maintain the journal in the face of deficit expenditures and diminishing subscriptions.[19] One change was the addition of the word *ministry* in the subtitle of the journal to demonstrate a move ''consciously in the direction of providing current thinking on critical issues vital to the life and ministry of the church."[20] There were two issues of special focus: one on Baptists in Canada, 1760–1980 and another on Winthrop S. Hudson, Baptist historian. There was also a briefly renewed interest in critical book reviews.[21]

The years 1980–81 meant continued financial and subscription difficulty for *Foundations*. William H. Brackney (1981–82) succeeded Sweeny for a time, to be followed himself by guest editors. Then in the first issue of 1982 an unsigned "Editorial Report: The Past and the Future" anticipated with "enthusiasm" the creation of a new journal, the *American Baptist Quarterly*, under the editorship of William R. Miller. This *Quarterly* promised high scholarship in such considerations as "history, theology, polity, missions, biblical studies, professional ministry, and reviews of contemporary literature."[22]

Notes

1. *Foundations* 1 (January 1958): 3.
2. Ibid. (January 1958): 55–64; 38–45.
3. Ibid. 3 (January 1960): 3.
4. Ibid., pp. 3, 4.
5. Ibid. 3 (January 1960): 74–83.
6. Ibid. 5 (July 1962).
7. Ibid. 11 (January 1968).
8. Ibid. 5 (January 1962), 6 (January 1963).
9. Ibid. 12 (January 1969), (April 1969).
10. Ibid. (April 1969): 172–82.
11. Ibid. 14 (January 1971), (April 1971), (July 1971).
12. Ibid. (January 1971): 89–90.
13. Ibid. 13 (October 1970): 293–94.
14. Ibid. (October 1970).
15. Orlando Costas, "Latin American Revolutions and the Church," *Foundations* 14 (April 1971): 116–27; Thomas B. McDormand, "Contemporary Threats to Human Rights," ibid., 128–35; *Foundations* 15 (October 1972).
16. Ibid. 18 (January 1975): 4.
17. Ibid. 19 (January 1976).
18. Ibid. 19 (April 1976), (July 1976), 20 (April 1977).
19. Ibid. 21 (January 1978): 4.
20. Ibid. 22 (October 1979): 291.
21. Ibid. 23 (January 1980), (April 1980), (July 1980).
22. Ibid. 25 (January 1982): 3–4.

Information Sources

INDEX SOURCES: *Religion Index One, Historical Abstracts, America: History and Life, Religious and Theological Abstracts*.

REPRINT EDITIONS: University Microfilms International.

LOCATION SOURCES: American Baptist Historical Society, Yale University, Emory University, Union Theological Seminary (New York), Southern Methodist University, University of Chicago, and others.

Publication History

MAGAZINE TITLE AND TITLE CHANGES: *The Chronicle* (1938–57), *Foundations: A Baptist Journal of History and Theology* (1958–78), *Foundations: A Baptist Journal of History, Theology, and Ministry* (1978–82), *American Baptist Quarterly* (1982–   ).

VOLUME AND ISSUE DATA: *Chronicle*, vols. 1–20 (1938–57); *Foundations*, vols. 1–25 (January 1958-January 1982); *American Baptist Quarterly*, vols. 1– (1982-   ).

PUBLISHER AND PLACE OF PUBLICATION: (*Foundations*): American Baptist Historical Society, Rochester, N.Y.

EDITORS: (*Foundations*): George D. Younger (1958–68), John E. Skoglund (1969–74), Eldon D. Ernst (1975–77), Joseph R. Sweeny (1978–81), William H. Brackney (1981–82).

CIRCULATION: (*Foundations*): 1500 (1960), 1100 (1979), 630 (1982).

Stephen H. Snyder

THE AMERICAN BIBLICAL REPOSITORY. *See* THE BIBLICAL REPOSITORY AND CLASSICAL REVIEW

AMERICAN CATHOLIC QUARTERLY REVIEW

American Catholic apologetics was a recent development in periodicals and journals of the day when Charles A. Hardy and D. H. Mahony of Philadelphia set out in 1876 to add a new publication to the growing list. The *U.S. Catholic Miscellany*,* founded in 1822, had long attempted, with varying success, to do literary battle with the secular (Protestant) press, and the *Boston Quarterly Review* (1838), later *Brownson's Quarterly Review*,* had mirrored the zeal of its founder, editor and publisher, Orestes Brownson, in appraising the relationship between Catholic religious belief and social issues such as the labor problem and states' rights.[1] These two journals, one in Massachusetts and the other in the Carolinas, inspired Hardy and Mahony to provide a similar service to the public in Philadelphia and its neighboring communities. It was not surprising, therefore, when the publishers hired the Reverend James Andrew Corcoran, formerly of the *Miscellany*, as editor and asked Brownson to contribute one of the first articles to their new journal, the *American Catholic Quarterly Review*.[2]

That the quarterly intended to take up where the *Miscellany* left off was evident from the first issues edited by Corcoran:

Its aim therefore will be to explain and defend the Catholic theory of revealed Truth moral and dogmatic as it really is, as it has been left to us by the Apostles and defined by the Church, and to let men see how different is the base counterfeit of the same, wickedly forged to our discredit by some and received in good faith as our doctrine by many others outside our communion.[3]

But the quarterly would depart significantly from the pioneering social and political commentary of Brownson. While attempting to demonstrate "the practical development and working of the Catholic principle in the history of the world" with articles on philosophy, religion, and science, the *American Catholic Quarterly Review* would have nothing to do with politics, under the premise that "it little concerns us who sits in the Presidential chair once hallowed by George Washington."[4]

This aloof stance was calculated to ward off criticism of church meddling in affairs of state, but it did not inhibit Corcoran and his small staff from approaching the topic of government from an analytical and historical perspective, if not a purely political one. Indeed, the review proclaimed, it was not only a Catholic publication but an American one as well; as such, it was within the purview of the journal to chronicle and illustrate the progress of the church in its American incarnation and to lift up and praise that which was worthy of preservation in the New World. Thus the review carried numerous articles on U.S. history and government, many written by the noted Catholic historian John Gilmary Shea, and a series written by Edward McGlynn, outlining the advantages to the church of the U.S. democratic system.

In general articles varied in tone from the didactic to the polemical, from topics such as "The Philosophy of the Supernatural" to "Anti-Catholic Prejudice," but the journal lacked the spark and controversy of Brownson's review. Nonetheless, many of the pieces were aimed at non-Catholics who, "though misdirected by unhappy training," were still possessed of an "inherent love of justice, truth and the spirit of religion." The articles attempted to redress the fact that "they dislike and condemn us [Catholics] because they know us only, not as we are, but as we have been falsely presented to their view."[5] During Corcoran's tenure as editor (1876 to his death in 1890), the *American Catholic Quarterly Review* was perhaps the most informative of all Catholic periodicals in matters of Catholic thought and scholarship. There were included in the review during these years installments explaining the Catholic theory of biblical inspiration, Catholic teaching regarding social reform, and papal instruction in the encyclical *Sapientiae Christianae*. Charles Mercier contributed an article on the interconnection between education and democracy, scientist John Zahm of Notre Dame pointed to the proper distinction between scientific dogmatism and true Catholic dogma, and Herman Heuser of the *American Ecclesiastical Review** researched the thought of Cardinal Newman for the pages of Corcoran's quarterly.

To broaden its appeal to the general public, the quarterly included works that were only indirectly related to Catholicism, or to religion at all for that matter. Interspersed among treatment of dogmatic and ethical matters were travel pieces, art criticism, and short biographies of famous non-Catholics such as Brigham Young.[6]

When Corcoran died in 1890, the *American Catholic Quarterly Review* lost a vital force, a man with "an unsurpassed catholicity of knowledge."[7] His successor, Archbishop Patrick John Ryan, pledged to continue the *Review* on the lines set out by that "great pioneer" in his mission to "the higher intellects, Catholics and non-Catholics alike" and to explain to those readers "the philosophy, theology, and sociology of the old Church."[8]

Under Ryan's leadership, the review became bolder in its approach to politics. Whereas elections and endorsements were still avoided, the ethical concerns behind political decisions were seen as open for analysis by Catholic journalism. Because all truth is harmonious and the church is entrusted with the Ultimate Truth about reality, it might well comment with a watchful eye on the advances of science and the programs of government, declared Ryan.[9] Furthermore, the American milieu was particularly suited to the ways of Catholicism, for there existed in the pluralism of programs, beliefs, and heritages in the United States a diversity resembling that of the Catholic Church. From diversity came an overarching unity in the church; so should it be in American society, to which Catholics belonged in equal degree with Protestants. Thus in Ryan's solicitations for the *Review* and in his own writing, there was a heightened awareness of questions of political philosophy and church-state relations. The approach to these issues, however, was theoretical rather than topical, dealing with ideas rather than contemporary events. The implication was obvious: the Catholic belongs in the United States, is at home here, is not a threat to democracy or to freedom of religion.[10]

Ryan served as editor until 1912, at which point the journal began a slow decline, ending in its termination in 1924. Its era of inventiveness under Corcoran and Ryan was spent, and it lost subscribers even as it returned to a less controversial format, with features covering such esoterica as medieval Latin poetry. It went the way of its counterparts, *Brownson's Quarterly Review* and the *U.S. Catholic Miscellany*, an apologetic exercise that had outlived its appropriate setting.

Notes

1. Clarence L. F. Gohdes, *The Periodicals of American Transcendentalism* (Durham: Duke University Press, 1931), p. 47.

2. Paul J. Foik, C.S.C., *Pioneer Catholic Journalism* (New York: U.S. Catholic Historical Society, 1930), p. 77.

3. "Introduction," *American Catholic Quarterly Review* 1 (1876): 1.

4. Ibid., p. 2.

5. Rev. James O'Connor, "Anti-Catholic Prejudice," *American Catholic Quarterly Review* 1 (1876): 5–21; "Salutatory," ibid., p. 4.

6. See, for example, *American Catholic Quarterly Review* 48 (April 1929).

7. Patrick John Ryan, "Salutatory," *American Catholic Quarterly Review* 15 (1890): 385.

8. Ibid., pp. 385–386.

9. Ibid., pp. 386–87.

10. This theme was generally espoused by other American Catholic periodicals of the nineteenth century. See Sister Mary Lonan Reilly, *The Catholic Press Association* (Metuchen, N.J.: Scarecrow Press, 1971).

Information Sources

BIBLIOGRAPHY:

Gohdes, Clarence L. F. *The Periodicals of American Transcendentalism*. Durham: Duke University Press, 1931.

Henesey, James, S.J. *American Catholics*. New York: Oxford University Press, 1981.

Marty, Martin E., John G. Deedy, David Wolf Silverman, and Robert Lekachman, *The Religious Press in America*. New York: Holt, Rinehart and Winston, 1963.

New Catholic Encyclopedia. New York: McGraw-Hill, 1967. Vol. 3.

Reilly, Sister Mary Lonan. *The Catholic Press Association*. Metuchen, N.J.: Scarecrow Press, 1971.

INDEX SOURCES: *Religious Periodicals in the United States, Catholic Periodical Index*.

REPRINT EDITIONS: University Microfilms International (American Periodicals Series).

LOCATION SOURCES: Stanford University, Yale University, Union Theological Seminary (New York), University of Chicago, Harvard University, and others.

Publication History

MAGAZINE TITLE AND TITLE CHANGES: *American Catholic Quarterly Review* (1876–1924).

VOLUME AND ISSUE DATA: 1 (1876)–48 (1924). Issued quarterly.

PUBLISHER AND PLACE OF PUBLICATION: Hardy and Mahony, Philadelphia.

EDITORS: Rev. James Andrew Corcoran (1876–90), Archbishop Patrick John Ryan (1890–1912), Rev. Edmund F. Prendergast (1912–24).

CIRCULATION: 7500 (1910), less than 1500 (1923).

R. Scott Appleby

AMERICAN ECCLESIASTICAL REVIEW

In January 1889 the Reverend Herman J. Heuser, a 37-year-old German-born priest of the archdiocese of Philadelphia and professor of sacred Scripture at Overbrook Seminary, published the first issue of the *American Ecclesiastical Review*. In taking up the challenge of the Third Plenary Council of Baltimore to foster solid and reputable Catholic journalism, Heuser addressed himself to a need he perceived among the clergy and their coworkers:

Our monthly will address itself not only to the clergy, but to those, also, who more or less directly aid them in their sacred tasks, teachers and assistant laborers in the vineyard of Christ, whether they work in Church, or school, or in the world.[1]

Heuser targeted an audience somewhat broader in scope than that of the Reverend W. J. Wiseman, whose *Pastor* was also a journal published for priests in the United States. Whereas the *Pastor* saw itself as a conduit of information from Rome, "to keep working priests posted as to all decrees and decisions emanating from the Holy See,"[1] the *American Ecclesiastical Review* sought to meet specific pastoral needs unique to American clergy and their associates. Heuser's theological journal would counsel and educate American priests in order to

> be a help in carrying out the legislation of our Holy Church, and in particular, the decrees of the Councils of Baltimore. Our next object will be to strive for the promotion of what has been called the higher education of the clergy. By calling attention to whatever may touch the special interests of the latter body, in the domains of ecclesiastical letters, or art, or science, it hopes to serve the increase of knowledge unto sanctification.[3]

In this instruction of the clergy, the journal would be directly dependent on the magisterium (teaching authority) of the church. The symbol chosen to represent the *Review*, the dolphin and anchor, was thus exceedingly appropriate, for, as Heuser explained in an article published in February 1890, the dolphin was the earliest Christian symbol for Christ and the anchor represented the solidarity of belief, confidence, and hope of the church. The first motto of the journal, taken from 1 Corinthians 14:5—"that the Church may receive edification"—further asserted a reliance on orthodox teaching. Heuser insisted, "Truth and the glory of God, loyalty to legitimate authority . . . are our passwords."[4] He did not seem to mind early criticism that his publication was seen as a mouthpiece for the magisterium; indeed, he seemed to relish it: "If our authority offends, it may be that truth offends and that those who demur have simply judged themselves."[5]

Sooner than he anticipated, Heuser had the chance to champion orthodoxy. In 1891, the journal began a series of articles written by Monsignor Schroeder, professor of dogmatic theology at Catholic University, on the subject of European modernism. Schroeder sought to engage modernist Salvatore di Bartolo in debate regarding the scope and extension of the infallibility of the church and the pope, a teaching that the latter interpreted in a highly critical manner. The debate was to enliven the pages of the *American Ecclesiastical Review*. But in May 1891, when di Bartolo's book was placed on the Index, Heuser terminated the series of articles on the grounds that the *Review* must not contain, even indirectly, any ideas or teachings that could "offend, even by implication, against the respect due to the Vicar of Christ, or the sacred deposit of the Catholic faith."[6] The liberty granted to theological discussion, Heuser explained, did not extend past a boundary "unmistakably defined in matters of Catholic faith."[7] Any doctrines that deviated from that boundary must be eliminated from thoughtful discussion.

This incident set the tone for Heuser's 30-year tenure as editor of and chief contributor to the *Review*. He wrote numerous articles and over 2000 book reviews and solicited contributions from theologians who would join him in the endeavor to protect and nourish the Catholic Deposit of Faith. Pragmatic to a fault, Heuser often preferred European authors for his journal, deigning to wait until American priests "form the literary habit and certain traditional disciplines of mind fit for instructing others."[8] But in fact the number of American authors appearing in the pages of the *Review* increased steadily under Heuser, writing on such topics as proper pastoral care of the sick and dying, instruction in homiletics, and surveys of the latest encyclicals from Rome.

Father Heuser served as editor (excepting a five-year hiatus from 1914 to 1919) until 1927, when Monsignor William J. Kerby, professor of sociology at Catholic University, succeeded him in that post. Kerby moved the editorial offices from Philadelphia to Washington, D.C., but in all other respects continued the work of his illustrious predecessor. In editing the *Review* he, like Heuser before him, avoided potentially controversial subject matter, focusing his efforts instead on traditional approaches to traditional subjects, mostly pastoral in nature. Articles broached subject areas such as the "social mission of charity", the "young priest and his elders," and the "virtue of hope."[9]

At the death of Kerby on 27 July 1936, the helm of the *Review* was passed to Joseph LaRue, who steered the journal through the war years. As procurator of Catholic University, LaRue was able to apply the considerable business expertise he acquired in that post to the financial problems facing the journal because of a wartime shortage of materials and ongoing problems with workers. After the war, the business office of the *Review* joined the editorial offices in Washington, D.C., and the journal began a transfer of ownership to Catholic University. After 1944 the journal was published by Catholic University Press. The first and most important editor of this era was Monsignor Joseph Clifford Fenton, an instructor in dogmatic theology who had first appeared in the pages of the *Review* in 1936 with an essay on apologetics as art and science. During his tenure as editor, which spanned two decades, Fenton contributed articles on ecclesiology and prayer and solicited articles from such noted Catholic University professors as Patrick Granfield, O.S.B., Eugene Burke, C.S.P., and Edmond Benard, who wrote on sacred theology, the concept of the diocesan priesthood, and other related topics.

But it was the Reverend Francis J. Connell who came to embody the new era inaugurated by Fenton. A Redemptionist labeled a reactionary by his opponents, Connell had been the first president of the Catholic Theological Society of America. Together he and Fenton entered into strenuous debate with the editor of *Theological Studies*,* John Courtney Murray, S.J. They opposed Murray on behalf of what they considered to be perennial and unchangeable Catholic doctrine. In articles spanning the years 1945–55, Fenton and Connell expressed the ideal that there should be only one religion in American society, the Catholic faith, and that it should work in concert with the state, one tending to temporal needs and the other to spiritual matters. In short, Catholicism should be professed by the state.[10] To the editor and main contributor of the *American Ecclesiastical Review*, Murray's seeming embrace of religious pluralism and freedom of choice in the United States was wrong and bordered on heresy. They pointed to the papal condemnations of the Americanist heresy in the previous century to invoke precedent for their attack on Murray.

At the same time, Fenton in his later years as editor sought to prepare the American clergy for the changes that were to take place during the Second Vatican Council. He was an original member of the Preparatory Theological Commission and *peritus* of the council.

These proclivities were evident as early as 1949 when Fenton modified the motto of his journal to: "That you are steadfast in one spirit with one mind striving together for the faith of the gospel."[11] Fenton felt that this explained and expanded on the old motto by noting how the "edification of the Church" might be achieved in the conciliar age: "through work for the unity of the Church and of the Faith."[12] In a sense, Fenton and his associates at the *Review* wanted to co-opt the movement of change sweeping the church and in no small measure control it or at least illustrate the continuity between old ways and new. This principle lay behind articles dealing with the development of theology, canon law, and liturgy. In these years of Vatican II, the *American Ecclesiastical Review* reflected as well cultural change in the United States and its pertinence to Catholic teaching and thus attempted to aid American priests in effecting the radical changes and innovations promulgated by the council.

The pages of the *Review* since the close of the council continued to emphasize its pastoral purpose. Patrick Granfield (editor, 1963–71) and James P. Clifton are but two of the several writers who have taken a hand in editing the *Review* in the years following the long reign of Fenton. They opened up the *Review* to dialogue with the church in the modern world in ways that would have been impossible before the council. A survey of the themes of the articles in the decade after Vatican II helps to underscore that point: there were treatments of current issues in moral theology (John Giles Milhaven), analyses of the "uncertain priests of the '60's" (John Tracy Ellis), and articles on divorce and remarriage in the church and on the expanding role of the diaconate. Thus the *American Ecclesiastical Review* continued its stated purpose of edifying the American clergy until it ceased publication in 1975.

Notes

1. *American Ecclesiastical Review* 1 (1889): 4.

2. Patrick Granfield, "Seventy-five Years of the *AER*," *American Ecclesiastical Review* 150 (1964): 21.

3. Herman J. Heuser, "Literature and the Clergy," *American Ecclesiastical Review* 1 (1889): 15.

4. Frontispiece, *American Ecclesiastical Review* 1 (1889).

5. Herman J. Heuser, "The 'Ecclesiastical Review' and Theological Discussions," *American Ecclesiastical Review* 3 (1891): 48.

6. See the articles in *American Ecclesiastical Review* 3 (1891) by Monsignor Schroeder, "Theological Minimizing and Its Latest Defender," for an accounting of the initial attack on di Bartolo.

7. Heuser, "Ecclesiastical Review," p. 51.

8. Granfield, p. 23.

9. For an example of editorial concerns of the *Review* as they appeared in the writings of one editor, see William J. Kerby, *The Social Mission of Charity* (New York: Macmillan, 1921).

10. James Hennesey, S.J., *American Catholics* (New York: Oxford University Press, 1981), p. 302.

11. Joseph Clifford Fenton, "Editor's Note," *American Ecclesiastical Review* 121 (October 1949): 339–40.

12. Ibid., p. 340.

Information Sources

BIBLIOGRAPHY:

Hennesey, James, S.J. *American Catholics*. New York: Oxford University Press, 1981.

Heuser, Herman J. *The Harmony of the Religious Life*. New York: Benziger Brothers, 1902.

———. *The Parish Priest on Duty*. New York: Benziger, 1904.

Kerby, William J. *The Social Mission of Charity*. New York: Macmillan, 1921.

Martin, David, C.S.C. "A History of Catholic Periodical Production." Master's thesis, University of Chicago, 1955.

INDEX SOURCES: *Catholic Magazine Index, Catholic Periodical Index, Guide to Social Science and Religion in Periodical Literature*.

REPRINT EDITIONS: University Microfilms International.

LOCATION SOURCES: Catholic University of America, Union Theological Seminary (New York), University of Chicago, University of Texas-Austin, New York Public Library, and others.

Publication History

MAGAZINE TITLE AND TITLE CHANGES: *American Ecclesiastical Review* (1889–1901), *Ecclesiastical Review* (1901–43), *American Ecclesiastical Review* (1944–75).

VOLUME AND ISSUE DATA: *American Ecclesiastical Review* (January 1889-October 1901), *Ecclesiastical Review* (December 1901-December 1943), *American Ecclesiastical Review* (January 1944–75).

PUBLISHER AND PLACE OF PUBLICATION: Dolphin Press, Philadelphia (1889–1944); Catholic University of America Press, Washington, D.C. (1944–75).

EDITORS: Herman J. Heuser (1889–1927), William J. Turner (interim editor, 1914–19), Monsignor William J. Kerby (1927–36), Joseph LaRue (1936–44), Joseph Clifford Fenton (1944–63), Patrick Granfield (1963–71), James P. Clifton (1971–75).

CIRCULATION: Slightly over 10,000 (1960s).

R. Scott Appleby

AMERICAN JOURNAL OF THEOLOGY

In 1897, writing in the inaugural issue of the *American Journal of Theology*, Alexander B. Bruce remarked:

> Particular systems of theology may have outlived their day, but zest for theological inquiry has not died out. Let a man only think vigorously, and above all sincerely, on dogmatic problems. . . . What honest men object to is not conservatism but zeal for orthodoxy having another source than intelligent, pure love of truth.[1]

This passion for truth, unrestrained by the bounds of traditional theological method, was to characterize the *Journal*'s 23-year history. Edited by the divinity faculty of the University of Chicago, the publication became a forum for scholarly reflection within several spheres of the academic study of Christianity. With few exceptions each issue carried at least one article on church history, contemporary theology, and biblical exegesis. In addition, many issues carried a reflective essay on the nature of theological education and its impact on American culture. In retrospect, this last category proves to be particularly interesting, for it provides a fascinating account of the shifting attitudes of American theologians in the epoch framed by the advent of the Social Gospel and World War I. Articles carrying titles such as "The Scope of Theology and Its Place in the University," "The Proper Use of Science in the Pulpit," and "What Does Modern Psychology Permit Us to Believe in Respect to Regeneration," are fascinating in this regard.[2] Clearly, these were attempts by progressive theologians to address their rapidly changing cultural milieu. Apart from these scholarly essays, each issue of the *Journal* contained other information useful to academicians. Brief critical notes on issues of concern were regularly included, as were notices of recent theological and periodical literature.[3]

Some of America's greatest scholars regularly contributed to the enterprise. Articles by Frank Hugh Foster, Arthur Cushman McGiffert, Augustus H. Strong, and Henry Preserved Smith appeared often. Other notable contributors included B. B. Warfield, Charles A. Briggs, and Williston Walker.

Beginning in 1907 the *Journal* gave increasing prominence to the scholarship of the prolific Shirley Jackson Case, sometime president of the American Society of Church History and the Society of Biblical Literature. Case, a guiding force in the American Association of Theological Schools, became one of the *Journal*'s managing editors in 1916 and helped engineer the merger of the *Journal* with *Biblical World** into the *Journal of Religion** in 1921. This merger itself culminated a process that the *American Journal of Theology* had undergone. Begun as a progressive forum for the study of Christianity, it had naturally evolved into a journal committed to the study of the generic topic of religion.

Notes

1. Alexander B. Bruce, "Theological Agnosticism," *American Journal of Theology* 1 (January 1897): 14–15.

2. Charles A. Briggs, "The Scope of Theology and Its Place in the Pulpit," *American Journal of Theology* 1:i (January 1897): 38–70. John Merle Coulter, "The Proper Use of Science in the Pulpit," *American Journal of Theology* 3:iv (October 1899): 641–53. George Albert Coe, "What Does Modern Psychology Permit Us to Believe in Respect to Regeneration," *American Journal of Theology* 12: iii (July 1909): 353–68.

3. These notes varied in subject matter and length. See, for instance, Samuel MacComb, "Do We Need Dogma?" *American Journal of Theology* 6: iv (October 1902): 753–57, and, Edgar J. Goodspeed, "The Syntax of I Cor. 7:18, 27," *American Journal of Theology* 12: iii (April 1908): 249–50.

Information Sources

INDEX SOURCES: *American Journal of Theology* 24 (October 1924): 529–629 contains a general index; also in *Poole's Index, Reader's Guide to Periodical Literature, Writings in American History*.
REPRINT EDITIONS: American Theological Library Association Microtext.
LOCATION SOURCES: Andover-Harvard Theological Library, Yale University, Princeton Theological Seminary, Catholic University of America, Library of Congress, University of Chicago, Los Angeles Public Library, Union Theological Seminary (New York), and others.

Publication History

MAGAZINE TITLE AND TITLE CHANGES: *American Journal of Theology* (1897–1920).
VOLUME AND ISSUE DATA: 1:1 (January 1897)–24:4 (October 1920). Appeared quarterly in January, April, July, and October.
PUBLISHER AND PLACE OF PUBLICATION: University of Chicago Press, Chicago.
EDITORS: Not listed (1897–1915), Shirley Jackson Case and Gerald B. Smith (managing editors, 1916–1920).
CIRCULATION: Unknown.

John R. Fitzmier

THE AMERICAN ORTHODOX MESSENGER. *See* THE RUSSIAN AMERICAN ORTHODOX MESSENGER

AMERICAN PRESBYTERIAN AND THEOLOGICAL REVIEW

The *American Presbyterian and Theological Review* was first published in 1859 as the *American Theological Review* under the editorship of the liberal Presbyterian theologian, Henry Boynton Smith. In 1862, Smith merged the quarterly with the *Presbyterian Review*, edited by James Manning Sherwood, because Smith's increasing involvement with the General Assembly of the New School wing of the Presbyterian Church and other denominational activities left less time for his editorial work. The journal then became the *American Presbyterian and Theological Review*, with both Smith and Sherwood as editors. Smith retired to Europe in 1871, and the *Review* continued under Sherwood's direction. Another merger followed shortly after, and the quarterly became part of *Biblical Repertory*, which itself evolved into the *Presbyterian Quarterly and Princeton Review* until in 1877 it finally became the well-known *Princeton Review.**

From 1859 through 1871, the *Review* served as a chronicle for some of the most important religious issues and controversies of the nineteenth century. Smith's elegantly written essays covered politics, the arts, current literature (including favorable reviews of the work of Charles Dickens), as well as religious topics that promoted the perspective of liberal Presbyterianism. The statement of purpose in the first volume of the *Review* made clear that the basic aim of the quarterly was to make the tenets of Calvinism plainly understood and accepted by a religious public that had been too influenced by either excessive religious enthusiasm or by the transcendentalist movement. Smith believed that the old truths would provide the best understanding of religion if one relied on the Scriptures alone as the basic authority. In this approach, Smith's intent was not far different from that of many other religious writers of the time. He differed from the majority, however, in insisting that his objective should be achieved while keeping "an amenity of spirit and courtesy of manner."[1] The search for religious truth could continue among those holding opposing views if the consequences of human depravity, especially hostility and animosity toward those of contrary opinion, were kept in check. In all of his writings, Smith kept to his conviction that opponents could differ yet still act as gentlemen. This high tone marked the *Review* for its entire existence.

The most famous essay to appear in the *American Theological Review* or its immediate successor was Smith's "British Sympathy with America," published in July 1862. In it Smith questioned not only the British government's position of offering tacit support to the Confederacy during the Civil War but also the support given to the South by former British allies of the northern churches. Smith clearly elucidated the differing viewpoints. He noted, for example, that the United States saw Confederates as rebellious traitors who had attacked federal government property and "annulled the laws of the land; they attempted to overrun states that had never seceded; they threatened to take and destroy the national capitol."[2] These were the legal grounds, he argued, that the United States government had for the war. Smith acknowledged that 40 years of political strife concerning the question of slavery provided the moral basis for action, but he also carefully asserted that the legitimacy of his argument rested on the legality of northern actions. The essay pointed out as well that British support for the South might well result in great commercial gains for Britain, for the British could supply the South with the manufactured goods previously obtained from the North. But what troubled Smith more was the notion that the various churches of England and Scotland could support a governmental policy that was not only based on financial gain but in his mind contrary to biblical teaching. Smith closed by expressing the hope that the future would bring reconciliation between the warring states, as well as between the divided churchmen. In spite of his deep personal disappointment with his British fellow clergy, Smith maintained a directness of style and reasonable expression that make the essay a model for moderately displayed righteous indignation.

The *Review* proved to be one of the most consistent quarterlies of its time, never failing to deal with the contemporary subjects of the age. An essay by Francis A. March in the January 1869 issue, for example, tackled the thorny issue of the proper role of the Christian scholar in an age when Darwinism, fascination with scientific method, and the rise of biblical criticism had made the intellectual life suspect in many Christian circles. Operating from a liberal Christian perspective, March carefully correlated Calvinist doctrines with new scientific discoveries, noting that some discoveries might result in error. The constant emphasis was on hope for the future but a hope that recognized human propensity for error because of human imperfection. March resolved the contradiction that others found impossible to reconcile by proclaiming, ''The scholar, as he labors for the progress of the race, will seek to use the expulsive power of new truth. . . . Such is the method which Lord Bacon inculcates. Such is the method of Christian progress.''[3]

The *Review*, under the guidance of Smith and with the help of Sherwood, was an important vehicle for the cause of common sense and good faith in religious writing. Without Smith's enlightened views of reasonable exchange, the controversial political, social, and religious debates of the age would have been more vitriolic than they were. Smith's insistence on tolerance of opposing views and his spirit of seeking reconciliation helped set the tone for much of the Presbyterian Church in later years.

Notes

1. *American Theological Review* 1 (1859): 14.
2. Ibid. 4 (1862): 488.
3. Ibid. n.s. 1 (1869): 86.

Information Sources

INDEX SOURCES: *Poole's Index*.
REPRINT EDITIONS: American Periodicals Series, University Microfilms International.
LOCATION SOURCES: Yale University, Union Theological Seminary (New York), University of Chicago, Princeton Theological Seminary, Duke University, Andover-Harvard Theological Library, Library of Congress, and others.

Publication History

MAGAZINE TITLE AND TITLE CHANGES: *American Theological Review* (1859–62), *American Presbyterian and Theological Review* (1863–71); became part of *Biblical Repertory and Princeton Review*.

VOLUME AND ISSUE DATA: *American Theological Review* 1–4 (January 1859-October 1862); *American Presbyterian and Theological Review*, n.s. 1–6 (January 1863-October 1868); *American Presbyterian and Theological Review*, n.s. (3d ser.) 1–3 (January 1869–71). Appeared quarterly.
PUBLISHER AND PLACE OF PUBLICATION: Charles Scribner, New York.
EDITORS: Henry Boynton Smith (1859–71), James Manning Sherwood (1862–71).
CIRCULATION: Under 1500 (est.).

Linda K. Varkonda

AMERICAN THEOLOGICAL REVIEW. *See* AMERICAN PRESBYTERIAN AND THEOLOGICAL REVIEW

THE AMERICAN WESLEYAN. *See* THE WESLEYAN ADVOCATE

AMERIKANSKII PRAVOSLAVNYI VIESTNIK. *See* THE RUSSIAN AMERICAN ORTHODOX MESSENGER

ANDOVER REVIEW

The maxim of the *Andover Review*, announced in the opening editorial of the first issue published in January 1884, was "let us learn to *think* according to Christianity." In language fashionable among serious-minded Christians who attempted to respond to the advances occurring in science and scientific thinking, the editors proclaimed that "whatever is truly rational is in harmony with Christianity and allied to it. All thinking not in harmony with Christianity is irrational." If Christianity was true, the editors reasoned, then it could not be "discordant with any other truth." Secure in this belief, they sought to develop a Christian theology free of anachronism and consistent with the intellectual advances that were sweeping the lives and minds of Christians everywhere. The truth of the new theology they were proclaiming was revealed and self-authenticating:

That for which we contend is that Christianity is a revelation, the crowning revelation of God to men; that it is [of] a given historical and spiritual magnitude; that it brings into evidence its own truth, its own laws, and is to be understood in its own clear light. Attested by its own evidences, announcing and substantiating its own origin and purpose, master in its own sphere, it demands of right a scientific construction of its doctrines harmonious with its own genius and ruled by its own central and supremely authoritative principle.

The editors urged that a scientific construction of Christian doctrine should cause no alarm among less self-assured Christians. To fashion such a construction was "to *think* according to Christianity."[1]

This approach to the theological task became known as progressive orthodoxy. Two series of articles outlining the new theology appeared in the *Review* in 1885 and 1892 and subsequently separately as books. One book, *Progressive Orthodoxy*, set out to represent "the modern attempt to Christianize theology." The other, *The Divinity of Jesus Christ*, presented what the editors called "the realities of Incarnation and Redemption, as they are understood in the light of the most recent Biblical and historical scholarship and of the Divine revelation in nature, in humanity, and in the eternal son."[2]

A cursory glance at the contents of these books and of the *Andover Review* in which they first appeared shows that progressive orthodoxy was less a fully developed systematic theology and more an approach to Christian truth that tried to take serious account of current scientific thought. It was marked by a spirit of free inquiry, polite discourse, and, most of all, a supreme confidence that everything would come out right. Progressive orthodoxy moved confidently into social ethics, education, and evangelization. With tolerance toward others and other points of view, progressive orthodoxy appropriated truth where it found truth and prepared the ground for the ultimate triumph of the truth that only Christianity possessed.

The founders and principal editors of the *Review*, all professors at Andover Theological Seminary, were Egbert C. Smyth, William J. Tucker, J. W. Churchill, George Harris, and Edward Y. Hincks. Seldom does the reader encounter these persons as individual writers in the *Review*. Although they occasionally signed editorials individually, nearly all editorials appeared unsigned and so with the sanction of the whole body. Progressive orthodoxy was therefore more than the creation of one inspired or strong-willed individual. It was a viewpoint that drew its energy from several like-minded apologists. In fact, all of the important writings of these men during the years between 1884 and 1893 appear in the *Review*.[3]

Two major controversies embroiled the editors of the *Review* soon after the enterprise was underway. One grew out of the problem of the relationship of Christianity to other faiths. The world missionary enterprise of American Christianity had grown in size and importance throughout the 1800s, and the issue of relating Christianity to the religions encountered on the mission field became more acute as the century drew to a close. The Andover School became embroiled in a phase of doctrinal discussion that centered on one question: "What shall Christians think about the fate of those who die without saving repentance? Are they condemned to everlasting punishment?" The Andover answer was that although knowledge of the gospel was necessary to saving repentance, those who did not hear the gospel in this life might still have the opportunity to hear it and repent in the life after death. That doctrine, called future probation, was propounded in the *Review* and *Progressive Orthodoxy*. The controversy over this notion raged for many years and involved the seminary, the Congregational Church, and the American Board of Commissioners for Foreign Missions who refused to send out as missionaries Andover graduates who subscribed to this view.

The second controversy involved the editors more directly. Andover Theological Seminary had been established in 1808 as a center of New England orthodoxy and a counter to Unitarian tendencies at Harvard. To ensure the steadfastness of its faculty, a creed had been developed to which faculty gave allegiance. Outwardly allegiance to the creed was maintained until 1880 when William J. Tucker joined the faculty, though the seeds of change had been sown as early as 1863 when Egbert Smyth had become professor of ecclesiastical history. Tucker prefaced his oath of allegiance with this often-quoted remark: "The creed I am about to read and to which I subscribe, I fully accept as setting forth the truth against the errors which it was designed to meet. No confession so elaborate and with such intent may assume to be the final expression of the truth or an expression equally fitted in language or tone to all times."[4]

The storm now began to break upon the seminary. After Edwards A. Park, a champion of New England orthodoxy and long-time Andover faculty member, retired in 1881 and was replaced by George Harris in 1883, Park wrote a pamphlet denouncing the apostasy of the new faculty—the same faculty who were about to found the *Andover Review*. In 1886 the board of visitors of the seminary brought charges against the editors, and an attempt was made to remove Smyth from his faculty post. Litigation lasted five years until the judicial court of Massachusetts decided in Smyth's favor. In 1892 the visitors dismissed the charges against Smyth.

The *Review* appeared monthly every year from 1884 through 1892. In 1893 the *Review* appeared bimonthly, and then publication ceased. The editors announced its closing with these words: "For the last two years the increasing demands of work in the Seminary, incident to the enlargement of the course of studies under the elective system," made it difficult to give proper attention to the *Review* and meet the demands of its high editorial standards.[5] Furthermore, one of the editors, William Tucker, had left to become president of Dartmouth. During the course of its 10-year history, some of the leading writers of the day appeared in its pages. In some respects, the controversies that embroiled the editors and seminary overshadowed the broad range of issues addressed in the *Review*. All in all, the publication remains an important historical document of one serious effort to meet the difficult intellectual challenges that confronted American Christianity on the eve of the twentieth century.

Notes

1. *Andover Review* 1 (1884): 1–13. The author of the editorial was Egbert C. Smyth.
2. Ibid. 19 (1893): 714.
3. Daniel Day Williams, *The Andover Liberals: A Study in American Theology* (New York: King's Crown Press, 1941), p. 31.
4. Quoted in ibid., p. 31.
5. *Andover Review* 19 (1893): 713.

Information Sources

BIBLIOGRAPHY:

Andover Review. *The Divinity of Jesus Christ. An Exposition of the Origin and Reasonableness of the Belief of the Christian Church*. Boston: Houghton Mifflin, 1893.

————. *Progressive Orthodoxy. A Contribution to the Christian Interpretation of Christian Doctrine*. Boston: Houghton Mifflin, 1886.

Williams, Daniel Day. *The Andover Liberals: A Study in American Theology*. New York: King's Crown Press, 1941.

INDEX SOURCES: *Andover Review* (1888), for vols. 1–10; *Poole's Index*.

REPRINT EDITIONS: American Theological Library Association; American Periodicals Series, University Microfilms International.

LOCATION SOURCES: Princeton Theological Seminary, University of Chicago, Library of Congress, University of Southern California, Union Theological Seminary (New York), Duke University, University of Texas-Austin, and others.

Publication History

MAGAZINE TITLE AND TITLE CHANGES: *Andover Review: A Religious and Theological Monthly*.

VOLUME AND ISSUE DATA: 1–18 (January 1884-December 1892), appeared monthly; 19–20 (January-November 1893), appeared bimonthly.

PUBLISHER AND PLACE OF PUBLICATION: Houghton Mifflin, Boston and New York.

EDITORS: Egbert C. Smyth, William J. Tucker, J. W. Churchill, George Harris, Edward Y. Hincks.

CIRCULATION: Unknown.

Kent Druyvesteyn

ANGLICAN THEOLOGICAL REVIEW

The *Anglican Theological Review* emerged from the intellectual and publishing chaos of World War I as a project sponsored by a group of professors at Western (now Seabury-Western) Theological Seminary in Chicago. These men thought that two problems made theologizing difficult within the Episcopal Church: the lack of any scholarly theological journal in that denomination and the exigencies of war, which had cut Americans off from regular access to European theological journals. The new journal was intended to remedy those two problems.

More significant, the journal was intended to be more than an in-house publication for the Protestant Episcopal Church in the United States of America (the denomination's official title in 1918). The founders self-consciously chose the name *Anglican* to reflect their desire to be supranational. They proposed to appeal "to all serious students of theology in the Anglican Communion, and to those in other communions who wish to know the Anglican point of view."[1]

This magisterial task—to speak authoritatively for the Anglican tradition—was accomplished in an unofficial manner. Although the journal's editorial offices have been at Seabury-Western Theological Seminary for most of the *Review*'s life and although the denomination's seminaries support and lend their names to the *Review*, the journal has no official denominational ties. Not until 1930 was the Corporation of the Anglican Theological Review, "a not-for-profit corporation registered in the State of Illinois," organized to provide continuity and financial support. Thus, although the corporation that publishes the *Review* is controlled by Episcopalians (along with representatives from two seminaries of the Anglican Church of Canada), the Episcopal Church as an institution does not control the corporation or fund its work.

During the first six years of the *Review* (1918–24), six coeditors supervised it. From 1924, however, until his retirement in 1955, Frederick C. Grant dominated the journal. Grant was assisted by Burton Scott Easton, a professor at General Theological Seminary, who was coeditor, 1921–50. Grant taught at several Episcopal seminaries east of the Mississippi and ended his academic career at Union Theological Seminary.

Under Grant's editorship, the *Review* published articles by some of the giants of Anglican scholarship between the wars: Angus Dunn, Joseph F. Fletcher, DuBose Murphy, Percy V. Norwood, Edgar Legare Pennington, W. Norman Pittenger, Vida Dutton Scudder, Massey H. Shepherd, Jr., Evelyn Underhill, and Alexander C. Zabriskie. A few non-Anglicans appeared, most notably Henry Sloane Coffin and Andreas Rinkel (the Old Catholic Archbishop of Utrecht). The articles tended to be historical in the classic Anglican style; either they were historical studies or they approached theological issues with a historical bent. Historical-theological studies of the early church fathers and of the Caroline Divines were common in this period of the *Review*'s life.

After World War II, the journal's direction began to change, as it became concerned with more contemporary issues. Rose Phelps's article, "The Place of Women in the Anglican Tradition" (vol. 28, 1946), raised the question of admitting women to the priesthood for perhaps the first time in a major Anglican theological journal. Other articles analyzed the theology of Rudolf Bultmann, Reinhold Niebuhr, and Paul Tillich and examined the theological implications of extrasensory perception. This trend continued during the editorship of John S. Marshall (1959–65), professor of philosophy at the University of the South. Marshall devoted whole numbers of the *Review* to symposia on "Justice," "God, Time, and History," and the theology of Paul Tillich.

John Coolidge Hurd, Jr., professor of New Testament at the Episcopal Theological Seminary of the Southwest (Austin, Texas), became editor in 1966 and resigned in 1968. Under his direction the *Review* formalized what had become an unstated editorial policy. The *Review* declared itself to be interested in "major issues both historical and contemporary" and was "especially receptive to articles touching upon Anglicanism, but only to the end that we may make such contribution as we may to the ecumenical discussion."[2] The turmoil of the late 1960s was reflected in the journal, however, as finances declined, publication of numbers fell behind schedule, and a backlog of articles grew.

After Hurd's resignation, Robert M. Grant, professor of New Testament and early Christianity at the University of Chicago Divinity School, served as interim editor until 1970, paving the way for Jules Laurence Moreau, professor of ecclesiastical history at Seabury-Western, whose tenure was intended to be long term, but Moreau died suddenly in 1971. During this period, the *Review* devoted whole numbers to papers arising from special topic seminars. For instance, an issue on "Christian Missions in a Secular Society" included a paper by Saul Alinsky, the famous neighborhood organizer; "A Seminar on the Development of Catholic Christianity" included a contribution by Georges Florovksy; "Religion and Literature" was devoted to an analysis of the poetry of Denise Levertov; and "Theology and Culture" was a series of articles on radical theology.

A permanent editor appeared when W. Taylor Stevenson (of Marquette University, later of Seabury-Western) was appointed. He became editor in chief in 1976 when Robert M. Cooper (of Nashotah House; later of the Episcopal Theological Seminary of the Southwest) was appointed editor. Under these men's direction, the *Review* went further along the editorial path that it had taken since the mid–1950s. Their editorial policy was clear: "An Anglican theological journal as such is an anachronism. There is no need for a journal written entirely or largely by Anglicans on distinctively Anglican subjects for an Anglican audience." Rather, the *Review*'s role, in their view, was to bring "a distinctively Anglican style" to "the new theology and the larger Church."[3]

In keeping with this editorial line, the *Review* has published articles by Wolfhart Pannenberg and Paul Ricoeur (the latter's papers being reprints of previously published works) and about process theology, phenomenology, Bernard Lonergan, Edward Schillebeeckx, Jungian psychology, and other current trends in theological thinking. Poetry appears in almost every number. Ten recent numbers of the *Review* (January 1979 to January 1981) contain 50 lengthy articles; only 14 have to do with concerns primarily Anglican (such as clergy oversupply, Anglican ethics, Prayer Book revision); the rest are of general interest or application. So the *Review* is not concerned primarily with "distinctively Anglican subjects." On the other hand, the journal continues to be "written . . . largely by Anglicans." Of the 79 contributors of articles or comments in those recent numbers, at least 45 can be identified as Anglican.

In addition to its quarterly numbers, the *Review* has published eight supplements since 1973. Some of these supplements emerge from symposia (which the *Review* likes to call "consultations") on areas of topical concern (such as "Theology of Mission," 1974; "Prayer, Ritual, and Spiritual Life," 1975; "Evangelism," 1979); others are festschriften (for Sherman E. Johnson, 1974; John B. Coburn, 1976; Albert T. Mollegen and Clifford L. Stanley, 1976).

In sum, the *Anglican Theological Review* in its first 65 years of publication has evolved from a self-consciously Anglican journal engaged in the exposition of that tradition's magisterium to one that transmits to that tradition the latest theologizing of liberal Roman Catholicism and churchly Protestantism.

Notes

1. *Anglican Theological Review* 1 (1918–19): 3.
2. Ibid. 47 (1965): 347.
3. Ibid. 54 (1972): 67.

Information Sources

INDEX SOURCES: *Bulletin Signaletique, Index to Religious Periodical Literature (Religion Index One), Internationale Bibliographie der Zeitschriften Literatur, New Testament Abstracts, Religious and Theological Abstracts.*
REPRINT EDITIONS: University Microfilms International.
LOCATION SOURCES: Yale University, Catholic University of America, Union Theological Seminary (New York), Emory University, University of Chicago, Southern Methodist University, and others.

Publication History

MAGAZINE TITLE AND TITLE CHANGES: *Anglican Theological Review* (1918–   ).
VOLUME AND ISSUE DATA: Vol. 1 (1918–19) through 12 (1929–30) begin in October; volume 12 contains six numbers to reconcile publication with the calendar year. From vol. 13 (1931) on, each volume covers the calendar year.
PUBLISHER AND PLACE OF PUBLICATION: Columbia University Press, New York (1918–24); Kenyon College, Gambier, Ohio (1924–25); Bexley Hall, Rochester, N.Y. (1925–26); Berkeley Divinity School, Middletown, Conn. (1926–27); Western Theological Seminary, Chicago (1927–29); Anglican Theological Review, Inc., Evanston, Ill. (1930–   ).
EDITORS: Samuel A. B. Mercer (1918–24), Leicester C. Lewis (1918–20), Arthur Haire Forster (1920–23), Frank H. Hallock (1921–24), Frederick C. Grant (1921–55), Burton Scott Easton (1923–50), Sherman E. Johnson (1955–59), Alden D. Kelley (1955–56), John S. Marshall (1959–65), John C. Hurd, Jr. (1966–68), Robert M. Grant (1968–70), Jules Laurence Moreau (1970–71), W. Taylor Stevenson (1972–   ), Robert M. Cooper (1976–   ).
CIRCULATION: 2400.

Denis G. Paz

ASSOCIATION FOR JEWISH STUDIES REVIEW

The *Association for Jewish Studies Review* (*AJSreview*) is a publication of the Association for Jewish Studies, an organization composed of those involved in Jewish studies in North America and elsewhere. The association also publishes a *Newsletter*.

The first volume of *AJSreview* appeared in 1976 under the editorship of Frank Talmage (University of Toronto), who remained in this position through 1983. Robert Chazan (Queens College, City University of New York) succeeded Talmage as editor.

Volumes 1–8 appeared once a year (volume 7–8 is a double volume) in a hardcover format. In addition to the editor, associate editor, consulting editors, and managing editor, an editorial advisory board, whose members have "significant evidence of publications as well as a willingness to assist the Editor in reading manuscripts and in offering comments in a prompt and complete manner," has played a major role in the production of *AJSreview*.[1] Each volume, consisting of more than 200 pages, contains articles in English and Hebrew. Articles vary in length from a few to over 40 pages and cover a wide variety of topics ranging from the Hebrew Bible to developments in the twentieth century. Among articles printed are "Maimonides and Thomas Aquinas: Natural or Divine Prophecy?" "The Hebrew First Crusade Chronicles: Further Reflections," and "A Sociological Portrait of German Jewish Immigrants in Boston." Prior to acceptance for publication, all material is subjected to an anonymous appraisal by a body of international scholars.[2]

Beginning in 1984 the journal shifted its format to softcover and increased its frequency of publication to twice a year. Along with these changes came the decision to include lengthy review-essays and to change the makeup of the group responsible for producing *AJSreview*. This responsibility passed to an editorial board consisting of the editor, six associate editors, and one corresponding editor in Israel.[3] Overseeing all of the publications of the association is a publications committee, chaired by the association's vice-president for publications. The editor of *AJSreview* serves as an ex officio member of this committee and the association's board of directors.

Arnold J. Band, editor of the *Newsletter*, has commented as follows on the quality and significance of *AJSreview*: "When I receive a new volume of our *Review*, I am both delighted and awed by the editorial standards it maintains. Few of our members can imagine the talent and energy invested in the editing of our *Review*—or the loneliness, the sense every editor harbors that no one out there knows what goes into each page.... The *Review* is, after all, the most important permanent contribution of the Association to the history of Jewish studies."[4] As stated in *AJSreview*, the publication of this journal is made possible by a grant from the National Foundation for Jewish Culture.

Notes

1. *AJS Newsletter* 28 (March 1981): 4. For further details of organization, see ibid. 31 (March 1982): 2.
2. As indicated in the "Notes for Contributors" at the beginning of each volume.
3. Robert Chazan, personal correspondence (January 1983); also *AJS Newsletter* 33 (Winter 1983): 2.
4. *AJS Newsletter* 31 (March 1982): 1.

Information Sources

BIBLIOGRAPHY:
Association of Jewish Studies Newsletter 28, 31, 33.
AJSreview, "Notes for Contributors."
INDEX SOURCES: None.

LOCATION SOURCES: University of Arizona; University of California, Santa Barbara; Cornell University; Duke University; Emory University; Harvard University; and others.

Publication History

MAGAZINE TITLE AND TITLE CHANGES: *Association for Jewish Studies Review* (1976–   ).
VOLUME AND ISSUE DATA: Volume 1 (1976–   ).
PUBLISHER AND PLACE OF PUBLICATION: Association for Jewish Studies, Cambridge, Mass.
EDITORS: Frank Talmage (1976–83), Robert Chazan (1983–   ).
CIRCULATION: 1500 (1982).

Leonard J. Greenspoon

THE AUGUSTANA QUARTERLY. *See* THE LUTHERAN QUARTERLY

AVE MARIA

Ave Maria magazine, which ceased publication in 1969, was one of the oldest and longest running of American Catholic periodicals. It was founded in 1865 by Father Edward Sorin as a devotional family magazine, devoted to the Blessed Virgin:

The Ave Maria is, in the true and widest sense of the word, a *Family Newspaper*, in which we intend to speak exclusively of our own family affairs. It is published to meet the wants and interest the heart of every Catholic, from the grey-haired grandsire who tells his beads at eventide, to the prattling child who kisses his medal as he falls asleep in his downy cradle, with rosy dreams in which the loved images of his mother on earth and his Mother in Heaven are sweetly blended.[1]

Having founded the University of Notre Dame in 1842, Sorin was continuing his efforts to bring the benefits of civilization (Christian) to the Midwest. As the university was to honor the Blessed Virgin, so was the new magazine.[2]

Mother Angela, a Civil War nurse and the second founder of St. Mary's, Notre Dame, and her brother, Father Neal Gillespie, assisted Father Sorin. The two were involved in the editing, in obtaining literary contributions from prominent Catholics, and in preparing translations of essays in foreign languages. Alfred Talley was in charge of the Ave Maria Press, although, because of technical difficulties, the first two issues were printed in Chicago.

In 1866, Father Gillespie took over many of the editorial duties and in 1868 became editor. Though editor for seven years, his name did not appear in the magazine during this period.

Many of the articles in these first years were devoted to Mary ("How to Say the Hail Mary," "Luther's Tribute to the Blessed Virgin") as well as to fiction ("Legends of the Blessed Virgin") and poetry ("Hymn to Our Blessed Lady," by Edgar Allan Poe and "Rose Plant of Jericho," by Henry Wadsworth Longfellow).[3] Also included were pious and devotional articles on such subjects as altar boys and the apostleship of prayer. The pastoral letters of the bishop of Fort Wayne were reprinted along with the sermons and pastorals of other members of the American Catholic hierarchy and papal encyclicals. Notable contributors in these first years included Orestes Brownson, Bishop John Timon of Buffalo, Archbishop Martin John Spalding of Baltimore, Father John Lancaster Spalding, and Catholic writers such as Lady Georgiana Fullerton, Francis Howe, Eliza Ellen Starr, Maurice Francis Egan, and Andrew Arnold Lambing. After the first several issues, a children's section was included.

In the first years, the editor of *Ave Maria* (along with the editors of many other Catholic publications) printed long selections from the letters and speeches of Pius IX, who was often referred to in the Catholic press as the "prisoner of the Vatican." (From the time of the unification of Italy into a single national state until the concordant with Mussolini in 1929, popes refused to leave the Vatican as a protest against their loss of political control of the former Papal States, now incorporated into the new Italian state.) These were the years when American Catholics vigorously protested their loyalty to the Roman pontiff. *Ave Maria* collected money to send to Rome to be used for the pope's defense.

The early volumes reflected something of the antiworldly posture of mid-nineteenth-century Catholicism and also the Protestant-Catholic antagonisms of the period. The former was seen, for example, in a two world mentality that gave to the priestly and religious calling higher status and sacredness. The treatment of topics and figures from Scripture exhibited confidence in the ability to fill in gaps in the scriptural stories.

There were articles encouraging a pious and wholesome life, such as on temperance, family prayer, and courage in everyday life. There were also articles on current events, such as "The Fire in Chicago" and "Celebration of the Twenty-Fifth Anniversary of the Holy Father's Election."[4] There were others of a more controversial nature dealing with the public school system, such as "Defective Education" and "Compulsory Education."[5]

Father Daniel Hudson took over the editorship in 1875 and continued in this position until 1928. His editorial policy remained what it had been under Father Gillespie. In a short time, there were over ten thousand subscribers. The first issue of 1876 announced a reduction (from $3.00 to $2.50) in the annual subscription rate, a response to the financial hardships following the panic of 1873.[6] In 1879, four additional pages were added, bringing the number of pages up to 20.

Father Hudson was a true intellectual. During the early years of his editorship,

Ave Maria reflected the richness of Catholic literary achievements. The number of regular contributors grew, and there was a broadening of subject matter. Contributors included some who had written under Father Gillespie and new ones: Maurice Francis Egan, Francis Marion Crawford, Andrew A. Lambing, Bishop John Lancaster Spalding of Peoria, Eleanore C. Donnelly, Anna T. Sadlier, and Austin O'Malley. In 1872, Orestes Brownson contributed a 10-part series "Religious Orders."[7] Charles Warren Stoddard wrote of the South Seas, shrines on the West Coast, and his conversion. He contributed a series of articles, "The Martyrs of Molokai," which was later published as *The Lepers of Molokai.*[8] Father Hudson corresponded with missionaries in China, Southwest Asia, India, and the Pacific Islands. The pages of *Ave Maria* were used to collect money and aid for these missionaries.

In the 1880s, a series of brief biographical sketches of distinguished Catholics appeared. There were also articles on political figures (such as Otto von Bismarck) and the conversion stories of Chopin, a "Protestant doctor," and "Robespierre's valet."[9] There was a European correspondent who submitted letters, several of a political and secular nature.

Editorials after the turn of the century touched on religious, political, and social issues. They were somewhat biased against Theodore Roosevelt. Dissatisfied with the schools chosen for young Filipinos brought to the United States for an education, Father Hudson gained the sympathy of William Howard Taft, who came to Notre Dame to speak. He was a favorite of the editor in the elections of 1908 and 1912.

After 1900, Hudson became more political. He voiced objections to both Woodrow Wilson and the League of Nations. In his later years, the general quality of the magazine and its editorial policy declined. One editorial called attention to the plight of the Negro in the South, who was becoming more and more educated but who was perhaps also being "inoculated" with the "Bolshevik microbe."[10] Another editorial drew attention to "the present agitation among our Anglican friends in regard to women preachers. Some of the disputants hold that no good reason exists why women should not preach, others quite as stoutly maintain that there is no good reason why they should."[11]

In the Americanist controversy, Father Hudson appeared to be sympathetic with the Americanists, especially with Bishop John Keane of Richmond and Archbishop John Ireland of St. Paul. But he was also sympathetic to several conservative editors and with Bishop Bernard McQuaid of Rochester. With the Americanists, he supported the founding of the Catholic University. With the conservatives, he continued in his support of Catholic schools. Hudson criticized any sign of friendship on the part of the U.S. government toward the British. His sympathies were with the Irish, not with their "oppressors." Yet English contributors to the *Ave Maria* were not turned away nor were English subscribers.

New contributors were added in the years before World War I. Subscriptions rose to 25,000. In 1914, subscriptions had risen to 26,000, and by the time of

Hudson's resignation in 1928, they had risen to 35,000. After 1910, the intellectual level of American Catholic writing went down, affecting the *Ave Maria*.

In the 1920s, articles appeared dealing with different lands ("Europe and the Church," "Christianity and the Japanese"); there were also several on the church: "The Mission of the Church," "The Church and the Ministry of Women," "The Dignity of the Priesthood."[12] Articles of a pious and hortatory nature continued—"The Bread of Mystery," "Great Deeds vs. Common Duty," "Our Materialism"—along with many articles on Mary and the saints.[13] The *Ave Maria* continued to be rather defensive and triumphalist in its attitude toward other religions.

After Father Hudson's resignation in 1928, Father Eugene Burke took over the editorship but only until 1934. Father Burke and his young assistants, hoping to bring a Catholic perspective to the new humanism of the day, were perhaps burdened by the long tradition of Father Hudson's editorship.

Misunderstanding among editors, contributors of long standing, and readers was bound to occur. Just as this began to lift, Father Patrick Carroll was appointed to replace Father Burke. Father Carroll was strongly Catholic and conservative in his views, representative of his fellow Catholics of European origin who identified things American with things secular and past traditions as having a greater value than the modern. Rejection of new methods in both education and government bore witness to this attitude.

During World War II, attention was given to the war effort at home and abroad in news columns and in articles. There were even articles dealing with women in the war effort, among them "The Strength of Catholic Women" and "War-weary Women."[14] The conservatism of *Ave Maria* in the war years and those following the war was seen especially in the strong opposition to communism, with which no compromise was to be tolerated. Many articles appeared dealing with the U.S. political system and the American way of life, including "An Essential of Democracy," "Democracy and Law," "The Church and Politics," and "The Catholic Church and Politics."[15] Espousal of Marxist ideals was seen as a rejection of things Catholic.

Father Carroll was succeeded by Father Felix Duffy, who served as editor from 1952 until 1954. During his brief editorship, color and photography were added to the *Ave Maria*.

In 1954, Father John Reedy took over as editor. Father Reedy moved the *Ave Maria* from the conservatism of the earlier decades into the Catholicism of Vatican II. In these years, the *Ave Maria* reflected the broad range of issues discussed by American Catholics and the many positions held. Differences of opinion were often expressed in the letters to the editor. The new theology and new liturgy were made available to many Catholics through the *Ave Maria*. A new format was introduced under Father Reedy and a new professionalism in the use of paper and photography. During the years of his editorship, subscriptions were up to 50,000 and 60,000.

Articles of a high caliber devoted to political and social issues appeared in the last decade of *Ave Maria*'s publication; examples are "Laos, Issues and Questions," "Negroes and Property Values," and "South Africa, 1961."[16] "Khrushchev and the Labor Leaders" was among some of these.[17] Striking covers introduced such articles as "Who's Helping Miami's Cuban Refugees,"[18]"The Italy Nobody Knows," and "TV—The Electronic Classroom."[19] Editorials dealt with race problems ("Race—An Integrated Problem"), famine in the People's Republic of China, and church-state problems in Sweden.[20]

Essays and reports dealing with family life were much more open and realistic than those of earlier decades. They faced problems that the church as an institution would face in the 1970s and 1980s: problems of the aging, the widowed, the retarded. As in the rest of Catholicism generally, the laity became visible and active; "The Layman in the City" and "The Laity and Christian Unity" reflected these views.[21]

Leading Catholic clergy and laypersons of a variety of perspectives contributed to the *Ave Maria*. Rev. Virgil C. Blum, Dorothy Dohen, Rev. Leo Trese, George N. Shuster, Rev. Carroll Stuhlmueller, and Donald Thorman were among the many who wrote for the magazine.

In the last years, the *Ave Maria* faced severe financial problems and was losing money. The subscribers were generally family oriented and middle-brow. The confusion in the church after Vatican II affected the subscribers and thereby *Ave Maria*'s circulation. Since the nineteenth century, many of the subscribers were drawn through door to door sales. This method of promotion was discontinued after Vatican II. According to Father Reedy, after the council, Catholic families seemed to lose their loyalty to things Catholic. Circulation dropped to under 30,000, and in 1969, the decision was made to cease publication.

The *Ave Maria* was published weekly for 104 years. Its more than 5000 issues reflected Catholic family life, Catholic piety and beliefs, and Catholic attitudes toward the sacred and the secular. The many authors who contributed serve as a good index of the variegated quality of American Catholic literary achievements, especially on the popular level. The volumes of the *Ave Maria* provide a rich source for the history of Catholic lay folk.

Notes

1. *Ave Maria* 1 (May 1, 1865).
2. Thomas T. McAvoy, C.S.C., American Catholic historian and archivist at the University of Notre Dame, who died in 1969, wrote two histories of the *Ave Maria*: "The *Ave Maria* after 100 Years," *Ave Maria* 101 (May 1, 1965): 6–9, 21; "The First 100 Years of a Great Catholic Magazine" pt. 1, *Notre Dame* (Spring 1965): 16–19; pt. 2, *Notre Dame* (Summer, 1965): 14–17. These articles provided the major source for this history. All references to individual articles are taken directly from the volumes of *Ave Maria*.
3. *Ave Maria* 1 (1865): 214, 443, 10, 38, 91.
4. Ibid. 7 (1871): 697, 449, 499.
5. Ibid. (1871): 610, 611.
6. Ibid. 12 (1876): 12.

7. Ibid. 7 (1871): 65, 81, 114, 233, 425, 473, 505, 521, 553, 585.
8. Ibid. 29 (1889): 49.
9. Ibid. 22 (1886): 229, 437, 492, 466.
10. Ibid., n.s. 13 (January-June 1921): 55.
11. Ibid. (January-June 1921): 57.
12. Ibid. (January-June 1921): 566, 232, 822, 737, 533.
13. Ibid. (January-June 1921): 532, 595, 372.
14. Ibid., n.s. 53 (January-June 1941): 624, 116.
15. Ibid. (January-June 1941): 199, 85, 583, 135.
16. Ibid., n.s. 93 (January-June 1961) 20, 5.
17. Ibid., n.s. 91 (January-June 1960): 20.
18. Ibid., n.s. 93 (January-June 1961): 3.
19. Ibid., n.s. 91 (January-June 1960); 5, 20.
20. Ibid., n.s. 93 (January-June 1961): 16, 17.
21. Ibid., pp. 24, 9.

Information Sources

BIBLIOGRAPHY:
Hope, Arthur J., C.S.C. *Notre Dame: One Hundred Years*. Notre Dame: University of Notre Dame Press, 1943.
McAvoy, Thomas T., C.S.C. "The Ave Maria after 100 Years." *Ave Maria* 101 (May 1965): 6–9, 21.
———. "The First 100 Years of a Great Catholic Magazine." *Notre Dame* (Spring 1965): 16–19; (Summer 1965): 14–17.
Unger, Henry F. *Writers in Roman Collars*. Fresno: Academy Guild Press, 1959.
Willging, Eugene P., and Herta Hatsfeld. *Catholic Serials of the Nineteenth Century in the United States*. 2d ser., 4. Washington: Catholic University of America Press, 1962.
INDEX SOURCES: *Catholic Periodical Index* (since 1930).
REPRINT EDITIONS: Microfilm, University Libraries, University of Notre Dame.
LOCATION SOURCES: Catholic University, University of Notre Dame, St. Meinrad's Abbey, Creighton University, St. Louis University, Boston College, and others.

Publication History

MAGAZINE TITLE AND TITLE CHANGES: *Ave Maria* (1865–1969).
VOLUME AND ISSUE DATA: 1–78 (1865–1914), n.s. 1–111 (1915–69).
PUBLISHER AND PLACE OF PUBLICATION: Ave Maria Press, Notre Dame, Ind.
EDITORS: Edward Sorin, C.S.S. (1865–68), Neal Gillespie, C.S.C. (1868–75), Daniel Hudson, C.S.C. (1875–1928), Eugene Burke, C.S.C. (1928–34), Patrick Carroll, C.S.C. (1934–52), Felix Duffy, C.S.C. (1952–54), John Reedy, C.S.C. (1954–69).
CIRCULATION: 6000 (1867), 10,000 (1878), 19,000 (1886), 22,500 (1900), 33,600 (1928), 58,200 (1948), 59,500 (1961), under 30,000 (1965–69).

Judith Wimmer

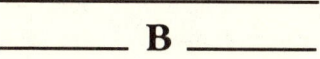

B

THE BAPTIST. *See* THE CHRISTIAN CENTURY

BAPTIST HISTORY AND HERITAGE

The first issue of *Baptist History and Heritage* appeared in July 1965. Published under the joint auspices of the Historical Commission of the Southern Baptist Convention and the Southern Baptist Historical Society, the journal, in the words of the editorial committee on the inside front cover of the inaugural issue, was "dedicated to the pursuit of historical information that will enable Baptists to understand themselves, to appreciate their past, and to discover historical perspective for the future." It was no accident that the periodical emerged during the decade in which the Southern Baptist Convention became the largest Protestant denomination in the United States. Keenly aware that the denomination's evangelical heritage had fostered the impression that Southern Baptists were nonintellectual, if not anti-intellectual, and that the Baptist polity that granted considerable autonomy to local congregations all too often meant that Southern Baptists themselves had little sense of the larger church and their own history as a denomination, the first editorial committee sought to provide a forum for scholarly inquiry into the Baptist past, as well as to prod Baptists to become more historically conscious.

The journal was warmly received. After publishing three issues in the first volume, the editorial committee announced that beginning in 1967, the journal would appear each January and July. Beginning with volume 5 (1970), *Baptist History and Heritage* became a quarterly.

From the start, the journal has devoted considerable attention to articles profiling notable Baptist leaders from the past, many of whose work has given shape to the Southern Baptist denomination. Pieces about Joseph Martin Dawson, John

Leadly Dagg, William O. Carver, Benjamin Franklin Riley, Basil Manly, Jr., and Hight C. Moore have appeared. Figures drawn from the larger Baptist heritage have not been neglected. Anabaptist leader George Blaurock and eighteenth-century New England Baptist spokesman Isaac Backus, for instance, have both been subjects of articles. In addition, early issues contained brief book reviews and notes about the activities of the various state Baptist historical societies in the denomination.

When *Baptist History and Heritage* became a quarterly, its focus expanded. Two issues each year have been printed from camera-ready copy, and two have been typeset. The second issue annually is now devoted to reports from the annual meeting of the Southern Baptist Convention, which sets guidelines for denominational policy and positions on current issues. Since the mid–1970s one or two issues each year have been devoted to a single theme, often drawing articles from papers presented at annual conferences sponsored by the Southern Baptist Historical Commission and the Southern Baptist Historical Society. Although official policy is still to consider unsolicited as well as invited scholarly articles and to include material not necessarily restricted to Southern Baptist topics, most articles are in-house essays on matters germane to the denomination and its history.

Theme issues have been devoted to standard topics such as the national bicentennial (11:3, 1976), Baptist theology (13:3, 1978), Baptist missions (14:1, 1979), Baptist polity (14:3, 1979), and Baptist Sunday Schools (18:1, 1983). But there has also been a conscious attempt to explore generally neglected themes and those that are related to currents of interest in the culture at large. Theme issues of this nature include those focusing on women in the Baptist heritage (12:1, 1977), blacks in Southern Baptist history (16:3, 1981), and ethnic minorities and the Southern Baptist tradition (18:3, 1983). In addition, issues have been devoted to efforts to increase historical awareness on a local level. For example, one issue was devoted to oral history techniques and how they can be used to write local histories (10:3, 1975), and another was devoted to resources for congregational and community histories (12:3, 1977).

Over the years, major Baptist and non-Baptist scholars have contributed articles. Penrose St. Amant, Robert Baker, Robert T. Handy, C. C. Goen, Kenneth C. Bailey, J. Wayne Flynt, Leon McBeth, and W. Harrison Daniel have all authored pieces for inclusion in the journal. In addition, since 1968 *Baptist History and Heritage* has provided an annual bibliography of works published during the previous year that treat topics relevant to the denomination.

Although the periodical has never gained a large circulation, it has offered Southern Baptists important glimpses into their complex past, prompted readers to explore historical resources often neglected, and reminded non-Baptists that the Southern Baptist Convention is far from a monolithic denomination. In so doing, it has provided a valuable service for scholars and laypersons, Baptists and non-Baptists.

Information Sources

INDEX SOURCES: *Religion Index One*, *Southern Baptist Periodical Index*, *America: History and Life*.

LOCATION SOURCES: Union Theological Seminary (New York), Princeton Theological Seminary, Duke University, Library of Congress, Indiana University-Bloomington, and others.

Publication History

MAGAZINE TITLE AND TITLE CHANGES: *Baptist History and Heritage* (1965–   ).

VOLUME AND ISSUE DATA: 1:1 (August 1965–   ); three issues in vol. 1 (1965–66). Semiannually (January and July), vols. 2–4 (1967–70); quarterly (January, April, July, October), vol. 5 (1971–   ).

PUBLISHER AND PLACE OF PUBLICATION: Historical Commission, Southern Baptist Convention, and the Southern Baptist Historical Society, Nashville, Tenn.

EDITORS: Editorial Committee (1965); Davis C. Woolley (1966–71); Lynn E. May, Jr. (1971–   ).

CIRCULATION: 2250 (1982).

Charles H. Lippy

BIBLICAL ARCHAEOLOGIST

Biblical Archaeologist, a publication of the American Schools of Oriental Research, was founded by G. Ernest Wright, who served as editor for 14 years and then as coeditor for another 11. He stated in the first issue, published in February 1938, that the purpose of the new journal was to meet the need of a "readable, non-technical, yet thoroughly reliable account of archaeological discoveries as they are related to the Bible."[1] He identified his audience as "the hundreds of ministers and Bible teachers who are not specialists in the field."[2] Underlying this statement of purpose and intended audience was Wright's conviction that, in the words of W. G. Dever, "philosophically the enterprises of biblical theology and biblical archaeology belonged together."[3]

As both editor and frequent contributor—36 articles, numerous book reviews, and more or less regular columns on archaeological news—Wright gave the journal its distinctive character as a publishing outlet for the discipline of biblical archeology as he understood it. In 1947 he wrote:

To me, at least, biblical archeology is a special "armchair" variety of general archeology, which studies the discoveries of the excavators and gleans from them every fact that throws a direct, indirect, or even diffused light upon the Bible. It must be intelligently concerned with stratigraphy and typology, upon which the methodology of modern archeology rests; but its chief concern is not with strata or pots or methodology. Its central and absorbing interest is the understanding and exposition of the Scriptures.[4]

Expressing dissatisfaction with journals and books that serve as "repositories of odds and ends of pedantic research," Wright insisted that

> because the Bible is the type of literature that it is and because its intensive study today is largely carried on by those interested in prospering the life of church and synagogue, biblical archeology cannot remain content with the mere pedantics of scholarship. It must insist on knowing to what end the matters of technique and detail lead; and it is even more interested in the conceptual life of Israel's neighbors than it is in their pottery and grammar, when the latter are conceived as ends in themselves.[5]

Although Wright never took the position that "archaeology proves the Bible," over the years he became increasingly aware of the limitations of archeology for understanding and exposition of the Scriptures. He later penned these words for an article published in a 1971 issue of the journal:

> With regard to biblical events, however, it cannot be overstressed that archaeological data are mute. . . . Yet the mute nature of the remains does not mean that archaeology is useless. . . . What archaeology can do for Biblical study is to provide a physical context in time and place which was the environment of the people who produced the Bible or are mentioned in it.[6]

The early issues of *Biblical Archaeologist* were received enthusiastically by a small but steadily growing audience. The journal quickly grew from a four-page pamphlet to quarterly issues of eight, 12, 16, 20, and then 24 pages. In the first progress report to his readers, included in the May 1945 issue, Wright noted that the paid circulation of the journal had reached 2027 and then observed: "There is a certain degree of pride in the fact that already our journal has a larger circulation than any other dealing specifically with Biblical, archeological, or oriental subjects."[7] Although Wright had overlooked the larger circulation of the Dutch journal *Jaarbericht Ex Oriente Lux* (as its editor promptly called to Wright's attention), *Biblical Archaeologist* had quickly established itself as the leading English-language journal of its kind.[8] Only five years later Wright announced that 5000 copies of each issue were being printed, nearly 600 of them going to foreign countries.[9]

The early popularity of the journal was helped by the excitement over the discovery of the Dead Sea scrolls. The May 1948 issue announced the discovery of the scrolls ("the most important discovery ever made in Old Testament manuscripts"), and the following issue was devoted entirely to the new finds. Over the years, *Biblical Archaeologist* published numerous articles on the Dead Sea scrolls.

Although the early period of the journal was one of remarkable growth and widespread popularity, the next 25 years (1950–75) witnessed no significant growth in terms of production and circulation. During this time the journal's articles became increasingly technical in an attempt to keep abreast of the rapid pace of archeological discovery and scholarly reports. The journal was guided during these years by Wright and coeditors F. M. Cross, Jr. (1952–58) and E. F. Campbell, Jr. (1959–62). After Wright's retirement from the journal in 1962, Campbell served as editor from 1963 to 1971 and then as coeditor with H. D. Lance from 1972 to 1975. Under the capable editorial hands of these men, the journal gained an international reputation for its scholarly excellence. With only a little exaggeration, it can be said that the journal had gained a scholarly audience while losing many of the nonspecialists for whom it was originally intended.

When the journal was placed in the editorial hands of D. N. Freedman in 1976, the new editor announced a return to the original policy of the journal: "an interpretation of the meaning of new archeological discoveries for the biblical heritage which Jews and Christians share."[10] Acknowledging that "the extraordinary pace of archeological discovery during the past generation—the generation of the Dead Sea Scrolls—led to a kind of scholarly inflation at *Biblical Archeologist*,"[11] Freedman stated his intention to make the journal more appealing to nonprofessionals without losing the core audience, who "will continue to be the scholars of the American Schools of Oriental Research and their colleagues around the world."[12] A new format and background articles to help nonprofessional readers understand the more technical reports on archeological discoveries were instituted. By 1981 the journal could report a total paid circulation of nearly 8500, approximately double the figure before Freedman's "new" *Biblical Archeologist* was introduced.

During Freedman's term as editor, the journal carried a number of articles on the discoveries of ancient Ebla in northern Syria and several others that debated the appropriateness of the term *biblical archeology* and the discipline it denotes. Some scholars dislike the term *biblical archeology*, contending that it is too closely tied to Wright's and others' attempts to use archeology to illuminate biblical matters. William G. Dever, for example, prefers the term *Syro-Palestinian archeology* because, in his view, archeology should operate with an autonomy and integrity of its own. He maintains that "from an archaeological perspective, 'biblical archaeology' has no *independent* rationale, methodology, objectives, status, or support."[13] The view expressed by H. Darrell Lance, however, will likely govern the editorial policy of the journal in the future:

> So long as the flood of new material keeps pouring from the tells and sites of the biblical world, the biblical exegete has only two options: either to ignore the flood or to take it into account when interpreting the Bible. Ultimately, only the second option is viable: therefore, biblical archeology's past is only a swelling prologue to a long and productive future.[14]

When Eric M. Meyers became editor of the journal in 1983, it was clear that the original objective of the journal would be upheld. Meyers instituted several new departments to preserve the generalist orientation of the journal, including regular articles on "enigmatic Bible passages" illuminated by archaeology, "portraits" of archeologists of major significance to biblical archeology, and the "Museum Trail," which features articles on museums that house collections of Near Eastern artifacts. Acknowledging that he intended to work in continuity with the "past stewardship of this magazine," he observed that "after nearly a half-century of publication . . . the forces which led Ernest Wright to found *BA* are still very much a part of the study of the Bible and the ancient Near East today."[15]

Notes

1. *Biblical Archaeologist* 1 (1938): 4.
2. Ibid.
3. William G. Dever, "Biblical Theology and Biblical Archaeology: An Appreciation of G. Ernest Wright," *Harvard Theological Review* 73 (1980): 1.
4. G. Ernest Wright, "The Present State of Biblical Archaeology," in *The Study of the Bible Today and Tomorrow*, ed. Harold R. Willoughby (Chicago: University of Chicago Press, 1947), p. 74; also in *Biblical Archaeologist* 10 (1947): 7.
5. Wright, p. 74; also in *Biblical Archaeologist* 10 (1947): 8–9.
6. *Biblical Archaeologist* 34 (1971): 73.
7. Ibid. 8 (1945): 59.
8. Acknowledged by Wright in ibid. 10 (1947): 85.
9. Ibid. 13 (1950): 100.
10. Ibid. 39 (1976): 2.
11. Ibid.
12. Ibid., p. 3.
13. Ibid. 45 (1982): 103.
14. Ibid., p. 101.
15. Ibid. 46 (1983): 3.

Information Sources

BIBLIOGRAPHY:
Campbell, Edward F., Jr., and David Noel Freedman, eds. *The Biblical Archaeologist Reader*, Vol. 3. Garden City, N.Y.: Doubleday, 1970.
Dever, William G. "Biblical Theology and Biblical Archaeology: An Appreciation of G. Ernest Wright." *Harvard Theological Review* 73 (1980): 1–15.
Freedman, David N., and Edward F. Campbell, Jr., eds. *The Biblical Archaeologist Reader*. Vol. 2. Garden City: Doubleday, 1964.
———, eds. *The Biblical Archaeologist Reader*. Vol. 4. Sheffield, Eng.: Almond Press, 1983.
King, Philip J. *American Archaeology in the Mideast: A History of the American Schools of Oriental Research*. Winona Lake, Ind.: Eisenbrauns, 1983.
Wright, G. Ernest. "The Present State of Biblical Archeology." In Harold R. Willoughby, ed., *The Study of the Bible Today and Tomorrow*. Chicago: University of Chicago Press, 1947.
Wright, G. Ernest, and David N. Freedman, eds. *The Biblical Archaeologist Reader*. Garden City: Doubleday, 1961.
INDEX SOURCES: *Art Index, Religion Index One, Christian Periodical Index, Elenchus*

Bibliographicus Biblicus, Internationale Zeitschriftenschau für Bibelwissenschaft und Grenzgebiete, Religious and Theological Abstracts, Catholic Periodical and Literature Index, Chemical Abstracts, Old Testament Abstracts.

REPRINT EDITIONS: University Microfilms International.

LOCATION SOURCES: Yale University, Library of Congress, Catholic University of America, Andover-Harvard Theological Library, New York Public Library, Duke University, and others.

Publication History

MAGAZINE TITLE AND TITLE CHANGES: *Biblical Archaeologist* (1938–75), *Biblical Archeologist* (1976–82), *Biblical Archaeologist* (1983–).

VOLUME AND ISSUE DATA: *Biblical Archaeologist* 1:1 (February 1938)–38:4 (September-December 1975), *Biblical Archaeologist* 39:1 (March 1976)–45:4 (Fall 1982), *Biblical Archaeologist* 46:1 (Winter 1983–).

PUBLISHER AND PLACE OF PUBLICATION: American Schools of Oriental Research, New Haven, Conn. (1938–65); Cambridge, Mass. (1965–75); Missoula, Mont. (1976–77), in cooperation with Scholars Press); Cambridge, Mass. (1978–82); Philadelphia Pa. (1982–).

EDITORS: G. Ernest Wright (1938–51); G. Ernest Wright and Frank M. Cross, Jr. (1952–58); Edward F. Campbell, Jr., and G. Ernest Wright (1959–62); Edward F. Campbell, Jr. (1963–71); Edward F. Campbell, Jr., and H. Darrell Lance (1972–75); David Noel Freedman (1976–82); Eric M. Meyers (1983–).

CIRCULATION: 8500 (1982).

Carl D. Evans

BIBLICAL ARCHAEOLOGY REVIEW

The first issue of the *Biblical Archaeology Review* was published in March 1975 by the Biblical Archaeology Society, Washington, D.C. The society is a nonprofit organization based on the premise that archaeological scholarship should be understood and enjoyed by the lay public as well as by the professional. Hershel Shanks, an attorney in Washington, has been the president of the society since 1974 and editor of the *Review* since its founding.[1]

The *Biblical Archaeology Review* lists reports from digs, scholarly examinations of origins of legends, analysis of artworks and artifacts of the cultures relating to the Bible, and even essays on the wildlife of the Middle Eastern region among its articles. Many contributors examine biblical accounts to see if modern scientific information can substantiate them as fact. The aim is "to make available in understandable language the current insights of professional archaeology as they relate to the Bible."[2] Aiming for the middle ground between the scholar and the reader who is completely untutored in archaeological terminology, the journal necessarily uses language that gives basic technical data and definitions in a direct and precise manner. It is this characteristic that makes it a helpful general reference for information on scientific progress in the study of the history of the Middle

East. Although the focus is on Christianity and Judaism, any other aspect of Middle Eastern culture that pertains to the Bible is included.

The *Biblical Archaeology Review* started as a small publication, with most of its articles being written by the staff. By March 1976, it had started to include four pages of high-quality color photographs with longer articles and comments from professional archaeologists and religious commentators. The March 1980 issue was further enlarged with more articles, bolder type, and a glossy format. These changes added clarity and detail to the articles without sacrificing article length or quality.

The *Review* has reported and commented on several major archaeological issues and philosophic debates during its short life. The ongoing debate between the literal interpretations of the Bible and use of scientific data is reflected in reader reaction to articles such as "A Futile Quest: The Search for Noah's Ark" by William H. Steibing, Jr.,[3] and "How It Came About: From Saturday to Sunday" by Samuele Bacchiocchi.[4] The readers' reactions come despite the editor's stated intent that

> our commitment is to scientific truth, not to sacred truth. . . . Neither do we believe one's faith will be destroyed by a study of Biblical archeology— regardless of the archeologists' findings. . . . In short, our view of the parameters of faith is that they do not infringe upon, nor are they thwarted by, a search for scientific truth.[5]

Shanks has carefully guided the editorials through this area of controversy without losing sight of the journal's aims. Articles are balanced to preserve scientific theory while allowing room for individual authors to make statements of faith.

Because of its enthusiastic commitment to scientific truth, the *Review* has raised some startling questions. One of these was posed by editor Shanks in "Kathleen Kenyon's Anti-Zionist Politics—Does It Affect Her Work?"[6] Here he postulates that Dame Kathleen, one of the most prestigious British archaeologists, was not scientifically objective in her professional writings because she had a pro-Arab bias. Shanks charged her with refusing to recognize Jerusalem as a legitimate part of the state of Israel and with constantly challenging the methods of Israeli archaeologists. Kenyon replied, defending her position and making clear that the editor had violated the aim of his own magazine with his admitted pro-Zionist view of her work.[7] The debate was never fully settled in print when she died in 1978.

Several other interesting articles have enlivened the *Review* and helped explain the magazine's interest to laity. A cover photo in 1980 of the comet Kohoutek led to an article written by astronomer Carl Sagan, "A Scientist Looks at Velikovsky's 'Worlds in Collision.' "[8] He discussed Immanuel Velikovsky's old but popular theory that near-fatal cosmic collisions caused the plagues, pillars of fire, and sea partings in the Exodus story. Although the scientific community never upheld this theory, it had popular appeal. Sagan summarized the problem:

The attempt to rescue old-time religion, in an age which seems desperately to be seeking some religious roots, some cosmic significance for mankind, may or may not be creditable. I think there is much good and much evil in the old time religions. But I do not understand the need for half-measures. If we are forced to choose between them—and we *decidedly* are not—is the evidence not better for the God of Moses, Jesus and Muhammed than for the comet of Velikovksy?[9]

Although many of the questions raised in the journal would seem to lack depth in the scientific community, the *Review* does expose these issues in a serious, sincere manner; however, serious international issues of scholarship and censorship have also been raised.

The Ebla question centered around the deciphering of approximately 17 thousand clay tablets found at Tell Mardikh in northern Syria. They date from c. 2400–2250 B.C. and were reported to have been found at the site of the ancient city of Ebla. Syrian government officials were outraged at the publicity surrounding the find and at the biblical interpretations given to the contents of the tablets. The Syrians claimed that the pro-Zionist scholars were weighting the evidence of the tablets away from pro-Arab interpretations. The *Review* pointed out that the Syrian government was playing politics with scientific information and forcing scholars to publish findings favorable to the Syrian viewpoint in order to continue to work on the project.[10] The Ebla question is still being discussed in the journal, and it has raised many thoughtful points about accepted scientific practices in the archaeological field.

The *Biblical Archaeology Review* stands alone as a general reference magazine for readers interested in the subject. The articles are stimulating for readers who care to use them as a starting point for further research while still containing enough information, often augmented by well-chosen color photographs, to satisfy basic curiosity on biblical archaeological subjects.

As the journal has grown, so have the services offered to readers. A book review section was added to the existing format, along with a short description of the authors. The *Review* encourages readers to participate in lectures and tours of the Middle Eastern region, and by 1980 it organized and sponsored its own tours, with noted scholars and interested laypeople as guides. Trips to Jerusalem and surrounding areas became so popular that it went on to sponsor summer programs in the United States. The most notable are vacation seminars at Chautauqua, New York.

Notes

1. *Who's Who in America, 1982–83*, 42d ed. (Chicago: Marquis–Who's Who, 1982), p. 3026.

2. *Biblical Archaeology Review* 1:1 (1975): 2, 16.

3. Ibid. 2:2 (1976): 1.

4. Ibid. 4:3 (1978): 32.

5. Ibid. 1:1 (1975): 1, 16.
6. Ibid. 1:3 (1975): 3.
7. Ibid. 2:1 (1976): 12.
8. Ibid. 6:1 (1980): 41.
9. Ibid. 6:1 (1980): 51.
10. Ibid. 6:3 (1980): 49.

Information Sources

INDEX SOURCES: *Guide to Social Science and Religion in Periodical Literature*, *Old Testament Abstracts*, *Religious and Theological Abstracts*.
LOCATION SOURCES: Library of Congress, Columbia University, New York Public Library, Brown University, University of Texas (Austin), University of Washington, and others.

Publication History

MAGAZINE TITLE AND TITLE CHANGES: *Biblical Archaeology Review* (1975–).
VOLUME AND ISSUE DATA: Vol. 1 (March 1975–).
PUBLISHER AND PLACE OF PUBLICATION: Biblical Archaeology Society, Washington, D.C.
EDITORS: Hershel Shanks (1975–).
CIRCULATION: 65,000 (1981).

Linda K. Varkonda

BIBLICAL ARCHEOLOGIST. *See* BIBLICAL ARCHAEOLOGIST

BIBLICAL REPERTORY. *See* THE PRINCETON REVIEW

BIBLICAL REPERTORY AND PRINCETON REVIEW. *See* THE PRINCETON REVIEW

BIBLICAL REPERTORY AND THEOLOGICAL REVIEW. *See* THE PRINCETON REVIEW

THE BIBLICAL REPOSITORY. *See* THE BIBLICAL REPOSITORY AND CLASSICAL REVIEW

THE BIBLICAL REPOSITORY AND CLASSICAL REVIEW

The *Biblical Repository* was founded in 1831 to "promote a spirit of ardent and judicious inquiry in the wide field of Biblical literature."[1] To accomplish this goal, founder and editor Edward Robinson (1794–1863) chose what seemed a rather narrow focus. Indeed, during the first year of publication, the *Repository* depended on the labor of only two men. As "Professor Extraordinary in the Theological Seminary at Andover," Robinson was able to draw on the considerable talents of senior colleague Moses Stuart. In return, the journal served as something of a showcase for Stuart. He was the most prolific contributor, publishing one or two articles in each number of the first year alone. His contributions ranged from the exegetical to the philological and the theological.

In contrast, the second laborer, Robinson himself, contributed primarily the fruits of a peripatetic nature. In a feat rare for American theologians of the time, he had traveled to Germany in 1826, remaining four years to study at Göttingen, Halle, and Berlin. He gained the acquaintance of such scholars as Wilhelm Gesenius, E. Rödiger, Friedrich Tholuck, Joachim Neander, and Karl Ritter. He acquired some insight into the contemporary German theological scene, particularly that of scholars he admired. He married Therese Albertine Louise, "the brilliant daughter of Ludwig Heinrich von Jakob, professor of philosophy at Halle," who as Mrs. Robinson earned her own place in American biography.[2]

Yet for all of the potential of this background, Robinson's contributions to the *Repository* were largely derivative. With slight exception, he appeared content to use his fluent command of German to render translations of his Continental mentors. Thus, his own labors served to highlight further the reputation of Moses Stuart, setting the latter's original work in juxtaposition with translations of contemporary German scholars. Robinson's talents, at least as revealed in the *Repository*, were those of organizer, collaborator, and observer. The "ardent and judicious inquiry" was supplied by Stuart of Andover and scholars of Göttingen, Halle, and Berlin.

The *Biblical Repository* marked a unique contribution in a crowded marketplace. The second quarter of the nineteenth century witnessed numerous enterprises in religious journalism. Most were oriented toward domestic doctrinal concerns and British theological, biblical, and philosophical influences. German scholarship was treated less thoroughly and with more suspicion, particularly in response to the growing romantic movement. The *Repository* set out to familiarize an American audience with the work of German scholarship, not by secondhand evaluation but by translation of the originals. Moreover, since this audience radiated outward from a center of rigorous, revivalistic orthodoxy—rather than learned Unitarianism or an ethnic denominational base—this contribution was doubly unique, serving to broaden the field of inquiry and to legitimate the scholarship of the orthodox coalition behind Andover Seminary. Ironically then, the scholarship that would impel the Mercersburg movement and the work of

Philip Schaff and John Williamson Nevin touched shore earlier in the stronghold of the very revivalist Calvinism that Nevin would oppose.

The *Repository*'s first series was interrupted in 1834 by the resignation of the editor. Robinson was replaced by another Andover graduate, Bela Bates Edwards (1802–52). In a manner typical of the journalistic individualism of the day, Edwards brought his own creation, the *American Quarterly Observer* (1833), to the new post, thus expanding his charge to the *Biblical Repository and Quarterly Observer*. Since the emphasis of the latter journal corresponded more closely to that of other American religious periodicals—"the discussion of those principles of literature, politics, morals and religion, which are of general interest and are recognized as such by the mass of Christians"—the combined publication entered a transitional stage.[3] Edwards continued to publish translations of German scholars, including Friedrich Schleiermacher, but he also published more articles of general interest to an American audience, such as Lyman Beecher's "A Plea for the West."[4] This expansion was intended to attract more subscribers to the Andover-based journal, and it apparently succeeded. Robinson's parting complaint, that the *Repository* could not sustain its editor financially, was replaced by the estimation of Edward's successor, in 1840, that the journal was a moderately successful and prestigious publication worthy of expansion.[5] Unfortunately, this success was purchased at the cost of the *Repository*'s original forte. By 1840, translations of German scholarship were rare, replaced by critical reviews of that scholarship by Americans.

The second series commenced in 1839 after the *Repository* had been acquired by its third editor, Absalom Peters (1793–1869), merged with another general publication, the *Quarterly Christian Spectator*, and moved from Andover to New York. A New School Presbyterian, Peters maintained the tradition of a Calvinism of "the more liberal, or New England, type" but with a fondness for New School politicking.[6] A professional editor with an eye on the market and a taste for including in the format all that that market would demand—a potpourri approach illustrated in Peters's other endeavor, the *American Eclectic* (1841)—Peters committed the journal to a comprehensive statement of purpose reflected even in its title, the *American Biblical Repository. Devoted to Biblical and General Literature, Theological Discussion, the History of Theological Opinions, etc*. The transformation of Robinson's original design was complete. And though the *Repository* would have four more editors, one additional change of title, and a third series before merging with *Bibliotheca Sacra** in 1850, its course as a journal of general religious knowledge—initiated by Edwards and established by Peters—would persist.

Five editors followed Edwards. They shared important qualities, some of which marked their profession, some the bond they shared with their clientele. All were pastors turned professional journalists who came to the job with previous editorial experience, often among the number of similar, New York-based religious periodicals. Three of the five also edited Peters's more secular *Eclectic*. All earned their living by seeking to provide a segment of American Protestantism with a journal that met as many needs as possible between two covers. By doctrine and party they embodied the "Presbygationalism" of those who adhered to the Plan of Union of 1801, which linked Presbyterian and Congregationalist expansion efforts. Both New School Presbyterians and New England Congregationalists served as editors. Thus, fine points of disagreement with Old School opponents were argued by such lights as Moses Stuart, Albert Barnes, Lyman Beecher, and Edwards A. Park.[7] On the other hand, ambivalence regarding the excesses of revivalism prompted opposition to Finneyite perfectionism and the Campbellites.[8] Concern for an educated ministry found expression in book reviews, articles on literary subjects, doctrinal exposition, and detailed exegesis.[9] The frontier mission of the Plan of Union opened the pages of the *Repository* to regular contributions by such westerners as Julian Sturtevant of Illinois College.[10] Interdenominational cooperation through voluntary associations for missions, tracts, and Sunday Schools was regularly advocated, as were such benevolences and reforms as temperance, poor relief, and antislavery.[11]All of the points of interest shared by the editors and their public found a place in the *Biblical Repository*. Unfortunately, the end product then had little to distinguish it from several other periodicals aimed at the same public. By becoming more American, the editors of the *Repository* hastened the day of its eventual merger and demise.

Notes

1. Edward Robinson, "Theological Education in Germany," *Biblical Repository* 1:1 (1831): 1.

2. Dumas Malone, ed., *Dictionary of American Biography* (New York: Charles Scribner's Sons, 1963), 8: 39–40, 55.

3. Absalom Peters, "Introductory Observations," *American Biblical Repository*, 2d ser. 1:1 (1839): 3.

4. Friederich Schleiermacher, "On the Discrepancy between the Sabellian and Athanasian Method of Representing the Doctrine of the Trinity," trans. Moses Stuart, *Biblical Repository and Quarterly Observer* 6:19 (1835): 1–116; Lyman Beecher, "A Plea for the West," *Biblical Repository and Quarterly Observer* 6:20 (1835): 437–50.

5. Peters, p. 3.

6. See, for instance, Erastus C. Benedict, "The Presbyterian Controversy: Its Occasions and Present State," *American Biblical Repository*, 2d ser. 1:2 (1839): 472–500.

7. See Asa D. Smith, "Extremes in Theology," *American Biblical Repository*, 3d ser. 6:21 (1850): 39–53.

8. Enoch Pond, "Christian Perfection," *American Biblical Repository*, 2d ser. 6:1 (1839): 44–57, and R. W. Landis, "Campbellism," ibid., pp. 94–129.

9. So marked was this facet of the publication that the final title chosen for the periodical was *The Biblical Repository and Classical Review*. See Peters, pp. 7–11.

10. J. M. Sturtevant, "The Levitical Law of Incest," *American Biblical Repository*, 2d ser. 8:16 (1842), 423–43; Don Harrison Doyle, *The Social Order of a Frontier Community: Jacksonville, Illinois, 1825–70* (Urbana: University of Illinois Press, 1978), pp. 39–61.

11. Although the editors strongly favored voluntary associations and benevolent en-

terprise (see Peters, pp. 18–24, and Bela B. Edwards, "Introductory Observations," *American Biblical Repository* 9:25 [1837]: 14–21), the latter was rarely treated in detail. Only temperance called forth extensive articles. See William G. Schauffler, "What Drink Did Our Lord Jesus Christ Use at the Institution of the Eucharist?" *Biblical Repository and Quarterly Observer* 8:24 (1836): 285–308.

Information Sources

BIBLIOGRAPHY:
Marsden, George W. *The Evangelical Mind and the New School Presbyterian Experience.* New Haven: Yale University Press, 1970.
Woods, Leonard. *History of the Andover Theological Seminary.* Boston: James R. Osgood and Co., 1885.
INDEX SOURCES: *Poole's Index.*
REPRINT EDITIONS: American Periodicals Series, University Microfilms International.
LOCATION SOURCES: Colorado College, Andover-Harvard Theological Library, University of Chicago, Yale University, Duke University, Princeton University, and others.

Publication History

MAGAZINE TITLE AND TITLE CHANGES: *The Biblical Repository* (1831–34), *The Biblical Repository and Quarterly Observer* (1835–36), *The American Biblical Repository* (1837–38), *The American Biblical Repository: Devoted to Biblical and General Literature, Theological Discussion, the History of Theological Opinions, etc.* (1839–44), *The Biblical Repository and Classical Review* (1845–50).
VOLUME AND ISSUE DATA: 1:1–12:32 (January 1831-October 1838); 2d ser. 1:1–12:24 (January 1839-October 1844), also known as 13:33–24:56; 3d ser. 1:1–6:24 (January 1845-October 1850), also known as 25:57–30:80.
PUBLISHER AND PLACE OF PUBLICATION: Flagg, Gould and Newman, Andover, Mass. (1831–38); Leavitt, Lord and Co., New York (1834); Perkins and Marvin, Boston (1835–38); Wm. B. Peters and Platt & Peters, New York (1839); Seth Bliss, Boston (1839); Whipple and Damrell, Boston (1840–41); Saxton & Pierce, Boston (1842–47); Wiley and Putnam, London (1839–47); Leavitt, Trow and Co., New York (1845–47); J. M. Sherwood, New York (1848–50); G. L. Weed, Cincinnati, Ohio (1848–50); John Snow, London (1848–50).
EDITORS: Edward Robinson (1831–34), Bela Bates Edwards (1835–37), Absalom Peters (1838–42), Selah B. Treat (1840–41), John Holmes Agnew (1842–46), Walter Hilliard Bidwell (1846–47), James Manning Sherwood (1848–50).
CIRCULATION: Unknown.

Daniel L. Swinson

THE BIBLICAL REPOSITORY AND QUARTERLY OBSERVER. *See* THE BIBLICAL REPOSITORY AND CLASSICAL REVIEW

THE BIBLICAL WORLD

The origins of the *Biblical World* are rooted in the efforts of William Rainey Harper to bring modern scientific knowledge and educational theory to bear upon the use of the Bible for preaching and teaching in U.S. churches. Although the title of the journal changed several times before becoming the *Biblical World*, the changes indicated a broadening of subject matter, which Harper believed would improve the religious instruction offered by ministers and church workers in local congregations.

Harper's interest in the reform of religious education predated his ascendancy as the first president of the University of Chicago. In December 1880, soon after becoming professor of Hebrew at Baptist Union Theological Seminary in Morgan Park near Chicago, Harper launched a campaign to extend the emerging fruits of modern scholarship to ministers and church workers.[1] Under the aegis of what later became the American Institute of Sacred Literature, he developed a multifaceted extension program, which included various levels of correspondence courses in Hebrew and summer schools and winter institutes conducted mostly in churches around the country.

To tie these endeavors together and to disseminate information on the activities of the institute, he started a monthly "Bulletin" in August 1881. By the next February, Harper's desire to include scholarly articles as well resulted in a full-fledged journal, the *Hebrew Student*.[2] His decision to include material on archaeology, higher criticism, comparative religions, and other emerging approaches to the Bible and religion was the outgrowth of his conviction that pastors in the United States should emulate their counterparts in Germany by combining scholarly pursuit with pastoral duties. Never the cynic or pessimist, he cajoled, challenged, and entreated his readers to learn Hebrew and to enter into the current critical debates about the Bible in order to be more adequately prepared for their work.

Although he officially declared the journal's stance toward higher criticism to be "conservative," his openness—even eagerness—to hear out even the most radical approaches then being advanced in Germany revealed a young man with an insatiable curiosity and a maturing intellectual position.[3] To him "conservative" meant not a literalistic or Princetonian view of Scripture but a cautious, dispassionate attitude that balanced his willingness to entertain any critical approach. Many churchmen frowned on such a policy as being too liberal and harmful to faith in the Bible as the word of God. But Harper tactfully maneuvered through this barrage of criticism time after time without yielding his position and continued to reprint articles by German scholars and published others by Charles A. Briggs, Henry Preserved Smith, and Francis Brown, as well as contributions by several Jewish scholars.

At the end of the first year, circulation approached 1000 mainly because students in the correspondence courses were automatically given a subscription. However, Harper began to sense that because the scholarly articles often were too technical or contained lengthy passages in Hebrew, the journal was over the heads of most of his readers and was failing in its reform purpose. To correct this problem, he started a quarterly, *Hebraica*, in 1884 to carry articles by and for Hebrew specialists and changed the name of the original journal to the *Old Testament Student* to signal his shift toward a more popular orientation.

This move was followed by the inclusion of a broader range of concerns about the Bible while Harper was teaching at Yale in the late 1880s. In editorials and articles he began to press for the establishment of English-language Bible courses on the collegiate level. But closer to his heart was the Sunday School. Harper's distate for the uniform approach that made no age differentiation in the learning levels of students and used the Bible uncritically led him to develop his own graded, inductive Sunday School lessons and to crusade for improved pedagogical techniques, an effort that led to his involvement in the founding of the Religious Education Association in 1903. Harper's circle of interests widened also to include the New Testament. A ''New Testament Supplement'' in each issue appeared in 1888, and a year later the name of the journal was changed to the *Old and New Testament Student*.

Harper's move back to Chicago meant no major shift in editorial policy, but it did mean a new and final name for the journal, *Biblical World*. Because of the university's demands on Harper's time and energy, he delegated the bulk of the work on the journal to the Bible faculty of the Divinity School, which he had formed by transferring the old Baptist seminary from Morgan Park to the new university. While he leaned heavily on George S. Goodspeed in the early years and later Clyde W. Votaw and Shailer Mathews to tend to the details of each issue, he nonetheless retained final control and oversaw general policy as editor.[4] It was always understood by associates and readers alike that the *Biblical World* was the expression of Harper's personal interests and concerns.

By the mid-1890s Harper again sensed that the journal was losing its appeal to its readership, especially pastors. What it needed, he wrote to Ernest DeWitt Burton, a close associate in the Divinity School, was ''more of a magazine element'' with more ''literary and historical'' features and less ''critical and theological'' elements.[5] The result was a new look that included colorful covers, occasional poetry, photographs, and special numbers devoted to a single topic. Harper remained dissatisfied, however, and the result of his discontent was another spinoff journal for scholars, the *American Journal of Theology*,* which first appeared in 1897 and which Harper insisted be explicitly connected with the Divinity School as an institutional effort rather than be associated with himself as a personal endeavor.[6]

Harper built *Biblical World* into a modestly successful journal with a circulation of between 2000 and 3000. In the early 1900s, his steadying hand calmed occasionally turbulent relations among his associates at the Divinity School, especially between Mathews and Votaw. However, in 1906 cancer struck him down, and the direction of the journal fell to Burton, who continued Harper's policy of promoting and improving the study of the Bible and avoiding becoming a forum for technical biblical research. Rarely did he deviate from the policies set down by the journal's guiding light.

In 1912 Burton was tapped as the university's third president, and the editorship was filled by Shailer Mathews, a member of the New Testament faculty. More than Burton, Mathews altered the direction established by Harper. While continuing to promote responsible Bible study and the reform of the Sunday School, Mathews added his own causes of ecumenism, modernism, and the Social Gospel. These interests flowed from his position as president of the fledgling Federal Council of Churches and his leadership at the Divinity School, which was emerging as a center of the modernist movement. More theologically combative than his predecessors, Mathews did not hesitate to use the journal to battle the fundamentalist movement by defending evolution and criticizing premillennialism. World War I prompted Mathews at first to stress the peacemaking impulse of Christianity, but when the United States entered the conflict, he worked hard to show modernism's support of American democracy and values and to put some distance between liberal Christian causes and the "taint" of German scholarship.

By this time *Biblical World* was a bimonthly and had moved away from Harper's passion to keep it a scholarly journal of popular biblical interest and religious educational reform. The Divinity School wanted to shift the emphasis of the *American Journal of Theology* away from theology proper to a broader view of religion as a dynamic force in human life. Consequently the two journals were reunited in late 1920 under the editorship of Gerald Birney Smith as the *Journal of Religion.**

Notes

1. Francis W. Shepardson, "Biographical Sketch," *Biblical World* 27 (March 1906): 162–66.
2. Richard A. Myers, "The American Institute of Sacred Literature," typescript, 26 March 1943, American Institute of Sacred Literature Papers, Department of Special Collections, University of Chicago Library.
3. *Hebrew Student* 1 (April 1882): 10.
4. Shailer Mathews, "As an Editor," *Biblical World* 27 (March 1906): 205–07.
5. Harper to Burton, 19 August 1895, William Rainey Harper Papers, Department of Special Collections, University of Chicago library.
6. Harper to C. R. Brown, 10 March 1896, Harper Papers.

Information Sources

BIBLIOGRAPHY:
Biblical World 27 (March 1906). The entire number is dedicated to William Rainey Harper.
Goodspeed, Thomas Wakefield. *Ernest DeWitt Burton: A Biographical Sketch*. Chicago: University of Chicago Press, 1926.
———. *William Rainey Harper: First President of the University of Chicago*. Chicago: University of Chicago Press, 1928.
Mathews, Shailer. *New Faith for Old: An Autobiography*. New York: Macmillan, 1936.

Mayer, Milton S. *Young Man in a Hurry: The Story of William Rainey Harper, First President of the University of Chicago.* Chicago: University of Chicago Alumni Association, 1957. First printed in 1941 as a supplement to the *University of Chicago Magazine.*

Presidents' Papers, 1889–1925. University of Chicago Library. Department of Special Collections.

William Rainey Harper Papers, 1889–1925. University of Chicago Library. Department of Special Collections.

INDEX SOURCES: *Poole's Index* (1893–1906).

REPRINT EDITIONS: American Periodicals Series, University Microfilms International.

LOCATION SOURCES: University of Chicago, Purdue University, and others.

Publication History

MAGAZINE TITLE AND TITLE CHANGES: *The Hebrew Student* (1882–83), *The Old Testament Student* (1883–89), *The Old and New Testament Student* (1889–92), *The Biblical World* (1893–1920).

VOLUME AND ISSUE DATA: *The Hebrew Student* 1–2 (April 1882-June 1883); *The Old Testament Student* 3–8 (September 1883-June 1889); *The Old and New Testament Student* 9–15 (July 1889-December 1892); *The Biblical World*, n.s. 1–54 (January 1893-November 1920).

PUBLISHER AND PLACE OF PUBLICATION: American Publication Society of Hebrew, Chicago (1883–89); Student Publishing Company, Hartford, Conn. (1889–92), University of Chicago Press, Chicago (1893–1920).

EDITORS: William Rainey Harper (1882–1906), Ernest DeWitt Burton (1906–12), Shailer Mathews (1912–20).

CIRCULATION: 3000 (peak).

L. David Lewis

BIBLIOTHECA SACRA

Bibliotheca Sacra (*BS*), which means "sacred library," holds the distinction of being the oldest continuing religious journal in the United States. Its founding dates to 1843 when Edward Robinson, a biblical philologist and topographer who taught at Union Theological Seminary, New York, determined that his new journal would contain articles that would give such a "full and thorough discussion" of biblical and theological topics as to make it of "permanent value as a work of reference" for the religiously literate.[1]

Permanence under Robinson was not to be. After only three numbers that first year, his academic work load forced him to turn it over to Bela Bates Edwards, his trusted friend and former colleague at Andover Theological Seminary. Under Edwards and his coeditor, Edwards Amasa Park, and with assistance from the faculty, *BS* became a primary literary vehicle for upholding the modified Calvinism of the New England theology. The editors not only included articles of interest to ministers, missionaries, and serious Bible students, but also covered a wide range of literary and philosophical subjects from Greco-Roman classicism to appeal to those in undergraduate education. Jerusalem and Athens, it seems, were well balanced.

The continuing goal to make *BS* something of lasting value was translated editorially to mean only minimal consideration for current issues such as slavery and the Civil War and a preponderance of lengthy, often pedantic, articles on exegetical and archaeological subjects of interest to a small circle of scholars. German scholarship was duly honored by frequent reprints of articles translated from the original publications. The editors granted considerable latitude to contributing authors to express their own opinions on controversial subjects while continuing their own support for the New England theology.

In 1851 a merger with the *Biblical Repository and Classical Review*,* whose roots also went back to Robinson and the Andover faculty and whose editorial policy and content were similar to that of *BS*, added valuable subscribers and contributors. With Edwards's death the next year, Park assumed the editorship, a position he was to occupy for 32 years. He maintained its broadly evangelical spirit, although a disproportionate number of articles continued to be authored by Congregational and Baptist ministers in New England, the latter partly as a result of the takeover in 1863 of a Baptist quarterly, the *Christian Review*. A third merger occurred in 1871 when the *Theological Eclectic*, which specialized in translating and reprinting European articles, was absorbed, reinforcing *BS*'s ties with European scholarship.[2]

The latter years of Park's tenure were marked by a dramatic shift at Andover toward modern theological liberalism. The thought that the liberal faculty might try to take over *BS* and promote such doctrines as the future probation of the heathen so disturbed Park, who himself retired from the faculty in 1881 as the last of the orthodox Hopkinsians, that he cast about for a successor to himself who would move the journal away from Andover to some other center of Congregationalism where the publication's theological tradition might be safeguarded. His search ended with George Frederick Wright, a professor of New Testament at Oberlin in Northern Ohio. Wright had previously written articles for the periodical while holding two pastorates in New England, one of them at Andover where he and Park became fast friends. In 1884 Wright became editor, a title he would hold until his death 38 years later in 1921. Thus a key to *BS*'s continuity has been the stability of its editors, with Park and Wright's tenures together totalling a remarkable 78 years.

Wright sympathized with Park's concern over encroaching theological liberalism, but his special interest in geology led him to take a moderating position on the burning issue of the day, evolution and the broader relationship between science and religion. Park had reacted negatively to the developmentalism of Darwin and his predecessors that necessitated a reinterpretation of the Genesis account of creation. Wright, however, a published author and recognized authority on glacial geology and an advocate of human antiquity, was close friends with Asa Gray, the Harvard botanist and proponent of Charles Darwin's theory. Thus Wright advocated a reconciliation between science and religion, a Christian or theistic evolution that defined evolution as God's method of creation. Indeed from 1892 until his retirement in 1907, he occupied a faculty position at Oberlin especially designed for him and named the Chair of the Harmony of Science and Revelation.

This mediating position was reflected in the journal's stance toward the social turmoil of the 1890s and early 1900s. He rejected the growing demand of Social Gospelers that government take action to solve social problems, asserting that "the hope of the nation" lay not "in the paternal hands of centralized authority, but in allowing the utmost freedom to her well-meaning citizens."[3] He even wrote an article defending trusts and monopolies as efficient and criticizing the muckrakers.

On the other hand, he recognized the winds of change blowing at Oberlin and within Congregationalism and thus printed articles by Washington Gladden and enlisted for his staff such progressives as Z. Swift Holbrook and Frank Hugh Foster. Indeed, there was a conscious effort in 1888 to enliven the pages of BS with "current topics of practical interest," a departure from past policy.[4] A special department, "Sociological Notes," informed readers of pressing social concerns for the Christian and a subtitle for the journal was added in 1895, "A Religious and Sociological Quarterly," a designation that remained into the 1930s.

But Wright himself remained basically conservative and by the turn of the century was showing signs of alarm at the growing trend to accommodate traditional theology to modern thought, despite his own willingness to do so on the issue of human origins. He began printing more articles by conservatives such as B. B. Warfield and William Green of Princeton, James M. Gray of Moody Bible Institute, and Abraham Kuyper. Wright came to view science as less an equal partner with religion in revealing the full scope of God's activity and more a handmaid to be used to demonstrate the scientific credibility and historical accuracy of the Bible. He contributed three articles to the *Fundamentals*,* a multivolume anthology by 65 conservative authors, and he carried on a five-year feud with Foster, the most liberal member on his staff, over Foster's dismissal of New England theology as a thing of the past, a dispute that culminated in the latter's resignation in 1912.

With his retirement from teaching and Oberlin's own shift toward a more liberal stance, Wright leaned less on his former Oberlin associates for articles and more on his old New England friends and missionaries, less on critical German writers and more on conservative British spokesmen.

Wright's death in 1921 created a crisis for the journal since the Oberlin faculty had their own publication, the *Oberlin Review*.* It was finally sold to Xenia Theological Seminary, St. Louis, whose president, Melvin G. Kyle, an associate editor under Wright, now assumed the editorship. A Presbyterian minister and biblical archaeologist, Kyle even more than Wright moved BS toward a fundamentalist stance, declaring in the first number he edited that he and his staff were "those who believe in the eternal verities that do not need to adapt themselves to the shifty precociousness of the twentieth century, but need only to be sought and found."[5] However, he was not especially combative, as evidenced by his pastoral and anecdotal comments and in a new editorial section he added. The range of subject matter for articles focused more narrowly on biblical, theological, and homiletical subjects, and a new section on critical and exegetical notes often became as long as the major articles themselves.

Xenia's decreasing enrollment and financial difficulties forced it to merge in late 1930 with Pittsburgh Theological Seminary, and the combined institution continued publishing *BS* under Kyle's leadership. The deaths of both Kyle and his trusted associate, John H. Webster, in May 1933 removed the two major forces keeping the journal alive at Pittsburgh-Xenia. The seminary offered it to other institutions before a young fundamentalist seminary in Texas, Evangelical Theological College (now Dallas Theological Seminary), seized the opportunity to realize a dream of several years to publish its own theological review.

The move was not a drastic step. Two members of the new editorial board and many early contributors had studied under Wright at Oberlin. Kyle himself was on the regular lecture staff of the institution and had come to know many of the school's professors through his participation in summer Bible conferences and as archaeology editor of the fundamentalist *Sunday School Times*.

But the move did change some long-standing policies. The new editor, Rollin Thomas Chafer, made the major articles the responsibility of the faculties of the various departments of the school. The departmental plan more closely aligned the journal with the school and its views in an official way than had ever been the case before. Also, the long-standing policy of providing for the expression of divergent views on theological and biblical subjects gave way to one that saw the journal's purpose as that of defending the doctrinal distinctives of the institution. This doubtless reflected the battle scars and continuing tensions from the fundamentalist-modernist controversy earlier in the century. Chafer also tried to broaden the appeal of the journal by publishing worthy articles by graduate students and by absorbing a lively fundamentalist quarterly, *Christian Faith and Life*, in 1939.[6]

Upon his death the same year, his brother, theologian Lewis Sperry Chafer, became editor. Even more than his brother, Lewis made *BS* a defense of the fundamentalist position. As such he toned down its popular appeal and concentrated on making it a means of systematically instructing its readers. He was replaced at his death in 1952 by John F. Walvoord, who for over 30 years has maintained the strict doctrinal approach but has shifted the format to literature by dropping the departmental plan and the editorial sections while increasing the book reviews and starting an unusual section of reviews of articles in current periodicals.

BS has become an established mouthpiece for the conservative premillennial wing of the broader evangelical movement in the post–World War II period. A list of its contributors reads like a who's who in American Protestant fundamentalism: Charles C. Ryrie, J. Dwight Pentecost, Kenneth S. Kantzer, Everett

F. Harrison, Merrill C. Tenney, Earle E. Cairns, and George W. Dollar. Dallas Seminary professors continue to write regularly, but other institutions and individual conservatives are well represented. *BS* generally eschews articles on contemporary social and political issues, choosing instead to focus on biblical and theological matters. As such it appears to be trying to fulfill the original vision of Robinson in 1843 that *BS* be of "permanent value."

Notes

1. Edward Robinson, "Advertisement," *Bibliotheca Sacra* 1 (February 1843): iii.
2. An excellent genealogical chart is included in Arnold D. Ehlert, "Genealogical History of Bibliotheca Sacra," *Bibliotheca Sacra* 100 (January-March 1943): 40–41.
3. Quoted in William James Morrison, "George Frederick Wright: In Defense of Darwinism and Fundamentalism, 1838–1921" (Ph.D. dissertation, Vanderbilt University, 1971), p. 374.
4. "Prospectus," *Bibliotheca Sacra* 44 (1888): 1.
5. "Editorial," *Bibliotheca Sacra* 79 (January 1922): 3.
6. "Brief Statement by the New Owners of Bibliotheca Sacra," *Bibliotheca Sacra* 91 (January 1934): n.p.

Information Sources

BIBLIOGRAPHY:
Bennetch, John Henry. "The Biography of Bibliotheca Sacra." *Bibliotheca Sacra* 100 (January-March 1943): 8–30.
Ehlert, Arnold D. "Genealogical History of Bibliotheca Sacra (with Genealogical Chart)." *Bibliotheca Sacra* 100 (January-March 1943): 31–52.
Hannah, John D. "*Bibliotheca Sacra* and Darwinism: An Analysis of the Nineteenth-Century Conflict between Science and Theology." *Grace Theological Journal* 4 (Spring 1983): 37–58.
Houghton, George C. "Bibliotheca Sacra: Its Beginning in 1843." *Bibliotheca Sacra* 126 (July-September 1969): 214–23.
Morrison, William James. "George Frederick Wright: In Defense of Darwinism and Fundamentalism, 1838–1921." Ph.D. dissertation, Vanderbilt University, 1971.
Mott, Frank Luther. "The Bibliotheca Sacra." *A History of American Magazines*. Cambridge: Harvard University Press, 1930; repr. 1968.
Wright, George Frederick. *Story of My Life and Work*. Oberlin: Bibliotheca Sacra Co., 1916.
INDEX SOURCES: W. F. Draper, *Index to the Bibliotheca Sacra and American Biblical Repository, Second Series, Volumes I to XIII* (Andover: W. F. Draper, 1857), and *Index to the Bibliotheca Sacra, Volumes I to XXX (1844–1873)* (Andover: W. F. Draper, 1874); Wayne D. Knife and Eduard M. van der Maas, "Subject Index to Bibliotheca Sacra: 1933 through 1966" (mimeographed); also in *Internationale Zeitschriftenschau für Bibelwissenschaft und Grenzgebiete, Religion Index One, Christian Periodicals Index, Poole's Index, Religious and Theological Abstracts, New Testament Abstracts*.
REPRINT EDITIONS: University Microfilms International.

LOCATION SOURCES: Andover-Harvard Theological Library, Library of Congress, Union Theological Seminary (New York) have complete runs; partial collections widely available.

Publication History

MAGAZINE TITLE AND TITLE CHANGES: *Bibliotheca Sacra, Tracts and Essays on Topics Connected with Biblical Literature and Theology* (1843), *Bibliotheca Sacra and Theological Review* (1844–50), *Bibliotheca Sacra and Biblical Repository* (1851–70), *Bibliotheca Sacra and Theological Eclectic* (1871–75), *Bibliotheca Sacra: A Religious and Sociological Quarterly* (1895–1933), *Bibliotheca Sacra* (1876–94, 1934–   ).

VOLUME AND ISSUE DATA: 1:1–3 (February, May, December 1843); n.s. 1 (1844–   ).

PUBLISHER AND PLACE OF PUBLICATION: Wiley and Putnam, New York (1843); Allen, Merrill and Wardwell, Andover, Mass. (1844–49); W. F. Draper, Andover, Mass. (1850–83); E. J. Goodrich, Oberlin, Ohio (1884–94); Bibliotheca Sacra Co., Oberlin, Ohio (1895–1921), St. Louis (1922–31), Pittsburgh (1932–33); Dallas Theological Seminary, Dallas (1934–   ).

EDITORS: Edward Robinson (1843); Bela B. Edwards and Edwards A. Park (1844–52); Edwards A. Park and Samuel Harvey Taylor (1852–71); Edwards A. Park and George E. Day (1871–83); George Frederick Wright (1884–1921) with Judson Smith (1884), Frank H. Foster (1885–92), W. G. Ballantine (1884–91), and Z. Swift Holbrook (1894–99); Melvin G. Kyle (1922–33); Rollin T. Chafer (1934–39); Lewis S. Chafer (1940–52); John F. Walvoord (1952–   ).

CIRCULATION: 9515 (1982).

L. David Lewis

BIBLIOTHECA SACRA AND BIBLICAL REPOSITORY.
See BIBLIOTHECA SACRA

BIBLIOTHECA SACRA AND THEOLOGICAL ECLECTIC. *See* BIBLIOTHECA SACRA

BIBLIOTHECA SACRA AND THEOLOGICAL REVIEW.
See BIBLIOTHECA SACRA

BIBLIOTHECA SACRA, TRACTS AND ESSAYS ON TOPICS CONNECTED WITH BIBLICAL LITERATURE AND THEOLOGY. *See* BIBLIOTHECA SACRA

BOSTON QUARTERLY REVIEW. *See* BROWNSON'S QUARTERLY REVIEW

BOSTON RECORDER. *See* CONGREGATIONALIST AND
HERALD OF GOSPEL LIBERTY

BOSTON RECORDER AND RELIGIOUS TELEGRAPH.
See CONGREGATIONALIST AND HERALD OF GOSPEL
LIBERTY

BOSTON WATCHMAN AND REFLECTOR. *See* THE
INDEX

BROWNSON'S QUARTERLY REVIEW

In January 1838, Orestes A. Brownson (1803–76), published the first issue
of the *Boston Quarterly Review*. Brownson, a religious seeker who had formerly
been both a Presbyterian and a Universalist, was then steward of the U.S. Marine
Hospital in Chelsea, Massachusetts, and a Unitarian clergyman, although his
pursuit of religious truth was already leading him to Roman Catholicism. The
Boston Quarterly Review, he thought, would be a public forum in which to
explore religious and philosophical questions and to appraise the relationship
between religious belief and social issues. Indeed, determining the proper connection between religion and society was a task that dominated Brownson's adult
life. In the inaugural issue he wrote, "I am not wise enough to say dogmatically
what is or is not for the public good; but I know what I think, what comes to
me as truth; and as a watchman, I would tell what I see, or seem to see, and
let them of the city treat it as they will."[1]

For five years, Brownson singlehandedly ran the journal, authoring most of
its essays. The *Review* was essentially a "private journal."[2] Others did contribute, but since articles usually appeared unsigned, it is difficult to determine
authorship of particular pieces. Henry Brownson, in his biography of his editor-
father, claimed that Bronson Alcott, George Bancroft, B. H. Brewster, A. H.
Everett, Margaret Fuller, Anne Charlotte Lynch, Theodore Parker, H. S. Patterson, Elizabeth Peabody, George Ripley, Miss R. A. Taylor, and Sarah H.
Whitman all wrote for the *Review*.[3] Clarence Gohdes has identified Albert Bris-
bane, William Ellery Channing, J. S. Dwight, S. D. Robbins, and John F.
Tuckerman as additional authors.[4] But the focus and content clearly reflected
Brownson's own passion for religion and politics.

This passion brought controversy when Brownson addressed two vital issues
of the day—the labor problem and states' rights—in *Review* articles. In two
essays on "The Laboring Classes," Brownson argued that since Christianity's
organized clergy was concerned only with the salvation of individual souls,
Christianity could never improve the social condition of the laboring masses,

but the "Christianity of Christ" was oriented to social reform and improving the lot of the poor. By chaining workers to selfish employers, the wage system of northern industrial capitalism was, to Brownson, more reprehensible morally than southern slavery. At least the slave did not face potential unemployment! An authentic Christianity, Brownson claimed, would seek emancipation for both the workingman and the slave. More important was Brownson's insistence that love mark all human relationships. This principle, he argued in the opening essay in the first issue, represented the stance encapsuled in the actions of Jesus.[5] Brownson's assault on the churches and capitalism and his seeming acceptance of slavery brought many attacks, but as Arthur M. Schlesinger, Jr., has noted, "No other American of his day and few Europeans inquired so deeply into the weaknesses and contradictions of industrial society."[6]

The national turmoil over slavery and abolition provided the occasion for Brownson to support states' rights theory, regarded as dogma by southern politicians, such as John C. Calhoun, whom he admired. In the first volume of the *Boston Quarterly Review*, he wrote two articles in which he claimed that although slavery was bad in itself, slaveholders personally could render slavery tolerable if they were Christians. He went on to argue that the states rather than the federal goverment should determine the outcome of the slavery issue because, as he propounded more forcefully in a later article, the states alone could protect minority rights effectively.[7] Indeed, he followed Calhoun in endorsing the position that states should have veto power over congressional legislation for this very reason.

Philosophically Brownson drew heavily on the "eclectic philosophy" advanced by Victor Cousin, the French thinker, in his early articles. For a time, he was also attracted to transcendentalism, which he later denounced, although he spent time at the transcendentalist commune, Brook Farm, in 1841. Despite the controversy it engendered, his journal never gained wide circulation, with circulation never attaining 1000 subscribers. Hence in 1843, Brownson suspended publication and merged his efforts with the more politically oriented *Democratic Review*, to which he had already contributed several pieces. When the *Boston Quarterly Review* ceased publication, William Henry Channing was moved to write: "Take it all in all, it was the best journal this country has ever produced, at once the most American, practical, and awakening; the more so because its editor was a learner and shared his studies with his readers."[8]

Personal shifts in Brownson's religious quest were soon to leave him discontent without a mouthpiece for his own views. By 1844, the pursuit of religious truth was leading Brownson to Roman Catholicism. Although he denied early that year that he was contemplating conversion, in October he was received into the Roman communion.[9] The transition completed Brownson's spiritual journey for despite his later conflict with the church hierarchy, he remained a devout Catholic until his death and believed his writings articulated a stance that combined a democratic, American perspective with a genuine Roman Catholic viewpoint.

Even before his conversion, Brownson severed his ties with the *Democratic*

Review. Since his agreement with that periodical's editor, John O'Sullivan, precluded his using the *Boston Quarterly Review* name for a new publication, Brownson betrayed the intensely idiosyncratic nature of his publications when, in 1844, he dubbed his new journal *Brownson's Quarterly Review.* At first, the new quarterly seemed based on the same premises as the old one, but after its founder committed himself to Roman Catholicism, the journal became a vehicle for his efforts to apply his understanding of Catholic belief to the social problems and political system of the United States. Encouraged initially by Boston's Archbishop Fitzpatrick, who also guided him in reading Catholic theology, Brownson quickly found his position again the center of controversy. And again, circulation remained so low that at one point Brownson nearly went bankrupt.[10]

In 1853, Brownson launched a series dealing with the relationship between temporal and spiritual power from what he thought to be the Catholic stance.[11] He claimed that spiritual power was supreme over temporal power in all areas of life because Christ had made the Roman Catholic Church the only valid guardian of God's law on earth. To resist spiritual authority, symbolized by the papacy, was sin in Brownson's mind. Also, because of the supremacy of the spiritual, obedience to the temporal was mandated only when the demands of the state were in harmony with the will of God as discerned by the church. In an evangelical Protestant America, this position fueled nativist fires that assumed Catholic immigrants could never be committed citizens since their primary loyalty was to a "foreign prince," the pope, who was indeed the political ruler of the Papal States in Italy. Even Brownson's Catholic readership balked, for they realized that Brownson had, perhaps unwittingly, provided ammunition for the increasing anti-Catholic sentiment in the United States. In addition, Brownson's apparent ultramontanism angered Irish immigrants, then the base of American Catholicism, for the Irish church had long resented papal supremacy within the church.

Brownson sought to remedy this problem in 1854–55 in five articles on the Know-Nothing party, the political arm of nativism. But here too his views pleased neither his ideological foes nor the church hierarchy.[12] While Brownson did condemn the bigotry of the Know-Nothing position, he also expressed understanding of the forces that propelled nativist sentiment. It was only logical, he claimed, for persons to love their own country and seek to protect it, and he called on American Catholics to demonstrate their patriotism by rapid acculturation to American ways. Specifically he insisted that Catholic immigrants abandon the traditions and mores of their former homelands but without forsaking their religion. One way to do so was to give up the expanding parochial school network. Brownson admitted that the public schools were not only Protestant in temper but also anti-Catholic. Yet he claimed that parochial education was not only inferior in quality to public education but also a factor that delayed cultural accommodation.[13] Protestant critics remained suspicious since Brownson was a Catholic, and church leaders feared that rapid acculturation and abandonment of old traditions would ultimately mean an erosion of commitment to the Catholic

Church. Catholic critics also rejected Brownson's seeming acceptance of nativism in his appreciation of the patriotism that undergirded it.

Consequently, Archbishop Fitzpatrick hedged in his support of Brownson's endeavors, and Brownson sought a more favorable religious climate in which to carry on his journal. In 1855, he moved his base of operations to New York City, where he hoped to receive greater encouragement from Archbishop John Hughes. Whatever reassurances Brownson anticipated from Hughes vanished both because of Hughes's doubting the wisdom of the Americanization of the Catholic faithful that Brownson demanded and because of the furor that ensued after the appearance of "The Church and the Republic" in the July 1856 issue of *Brownson's Quarterly Review*.

In this article, Brownson offered Roman Catholic Christianity as the only agency that could balance an anarchic individualism that, he believed, Protestantism fostered with the potentially despotic power of the state.[14] American Catholics did not seek to overthrow or control the U.S. government, he asserted, but expected only guarantees of freedom of conscience and freedom to fulfill the church's mission. Catholic and Protestant alike took this to be an insistence that the Roman Catholic Church was the only genuinely Christian body. Indeed, after his conversion, Brownson consistently argued that the Catholic Church was not only the sole source of salvation but also the only means by which the supernatural could penetrate society. The *Universalist Quarterly and General Review*,* for one, attacked Brownson in print,[15] while sensitive Catholics such as Archbishop Hughes realized that the position Brownson espoused was implausible in the religiously pluralistic culture that had emerged in the United States.

One response Brownson made was to move in 1857 to Elizabeth, New Jersey, where he was in a different diocese, although he continued to publish the *Review* in New York. But opposition continued. In 1862, Philadelphia's Bishop Wood excoriated Brownson, saying that the *Quarterly Review* should not be considered a Roman Catholic publication or a legitimate expositor of Roman Catholic principles.[16] Ultimately Brownson was even denounced to the prefect of the Congregation for the Propagation of the Faith in Rome, although his writings were not formally condemned.[17] Circulation, never high, continued on a downward trend. Finally, Brownson could not endure the criticism. In 1864, he suspended publication of the *Review*. For nearly nine years, Brownson devoted his attention to writing articles for *Ave Maria*,* a magazine established by University of Notre Dame founder, the Very Reverend Edward Sorin; *Catholic World* (later *New Catholic World**), edited by Isaac Hecker; and the *New York Tablet*. He also published his most sophisticated statement of political philosophy in the *American Republic*.[18]

Much of the material in the *American Republic* had appeared earlier in the *Boston Quarterly Review* and *Brownson's Quarterly Review*. For example, Brownson again asserted his views that government itself was divine in origin and that religion stands above the state. But there were important shifts, which brought fresh charges that Brownson was inconsistent in his thinking. Gone were two claims advanced in previous essays: the supremacy of spiritual power over temporal and the sovereignty of the states (states' rights). The abandonment of the latter came most forcefully in his castigation of southern secession in the Civil War. Where his earlier positions, depending on the issue in question, had seemed sometimes liberal and sometimes conservative—hence the basis for the charge of inconsistency—Brownson's stance now seemed to defy categorization.

Perhaps to counter his critics or perhaps to articulate his evolving views more publicly, Brownson revived *Quarterly Review* in 1873. In the opening issue, he freely admitted that some of his earlier positions had been in error and acknowledged that his own social thought was becoming more conservative.[19] But in this last series of *Brownson's Quarterly Review*, the uneasy balance between a moderate conservatism and a moderate liberalism, exemplified in the essay "The Democratic Principle," is apparent.[20] Consequently Brownson continued to reap criticism for being inconsistent. Yet as Americo Lapati has noted, it was Brownson's ongoing quest for the truth, especially religious truth, that brought his seemingly too frequent changes in viewpoint; as his concept of the truth shifted, so too did its application to social and political issues.[21]

In addition to the discussion of religious and political questions, Brownson devoted considerable space in most issues to literary reviews. Over the years, more than five hundred review essays appeared, most—if not all—written by Brownson. The subjects ranged from poetry to fiction to Roman Catholic religious thought, although there was a tendency to discuss works by American authors. The same convictions that propelled Brownson's political and theological writing also guided his rather romantic analysis of literature: since literature by his definition instructs readers, it should be subservient to Christian (Catholic) doctrine and ethical teaching. Hence, for example, although he generally admired Nathaniel Hawthorne, he sharply criticized *The Scarlet Letter* since neither of its main characters ultimately repented of sin.[22] Brownson was concerned too about the apparent dearth of a distinctively American literature in general and of an American Roman Catholic literature in particular. Although he knew that a body of American Catholic literature would develop only gradually because of the Protestant hostility to Roman Catholics and the meager educational achievement of the mass of Catholic immigrant laborers, he nevertheless saw a special need for it. American Catholic literature, based on religious truth that only Roman Catholicism possessed, could "cultivate, refine, and humanize barbarous nature." It should not focus on theology but on those practical matters that would allow Christian morals to penetrate society. "The office of popular literature," Brownson claimed, "is not precisely to spiritualize, but to civilize a people."[23]

When Brownson resumed his *Quarterly Review* in 1873, he was in his seventieth year, and age was beginning to take its toll. Failing eyesight required that he dictate several of his final articles, and declining health finally forced him to stop publication with the October 1875 issue. He died some six months later, without ever having enjoyed a steady following. From the first issue of the *Boston Quarterly Review* to the final one of *Brownson's Quarterly Review*, Orestes Brownson was controversial, although he retained his commitment to harmonizing American democratic principles with religious truth as he saw it. As Schlesinger noted, "The lonely pursuit of truth, with its worship of unflinching honesty and rigorous logic, was the secret of his failure. While the quest for goodness might have united him to his fellows and given him power to move them, the quest for truth only led to bleak isolation."[24] Ironically, however, in time Roman Catholicism in the United States did take on a distinctively American character, though not necessarily along the same lines as Brownson envisioned. In time, too, the bigotry of anti-Catholicism was recognized. And in the late nineteenth-century labor movement, the Social Gospel, and Progressive politics, many of the features of industrial capitalism that had aroused Brownson's ire were acknowledged and partially corrected. If Brownson as a journalist and editor was a failure, he was also a prophet.

Notes

1. *Boston Quarterly Review* 1 (1838): 4. Also see Thomas R. Ryan, *Orestes A. Brownson: A Definitive Biography* (Huntington, Ind.: Our Sunday Visitor, 1976), pp. 124–40.

2. "End of the Volume," *Boston Quarterly Review* 5 (1842): 513.

3. Henry F. Brownson, *Orestes A. Brownson's Early Life: From 1803 to 1844* (Detroit: H. F. Brownson, 1898), pp. 214, 215, 220, 224, 227, 228, 231, 235.

4. Clarence L. F. Gohdes, *The Periodicals of American Transcendentalism* (Durham: Duke University Press, 1931), p. 48.

5. "The Laboring Classes," *Boston Quarterly Review* 3 (1840): 358–95, 420–512; "Christianity Not an Original Revelation with Jesus," *Boston Quarterly Review* 1 (1838): 8–21. Also see Ryan, pp. 164–90.

6. Arthur M. Schlesinger, Jr., *Orestes Brownson: A Pilgrim's Progress* (Boston: Little, Brown, 1939), p. 99.

7. "Slavery," *Boston Quarterly Review* 1 (1838): 238–60; "American Liberties and American Slavery," ibid. 1 (1838): 473–500; "Speech of Mr. Calhoun, of South Carolina, on the Distribution Bill," ibid. 5 (1842): 84–119.

8. William Henry Channing, "The Democratic Review and O. A. Brownson," *The Present* 1 (1843): 72.

9. "Introduction," *Brownson's Quarterly Review* 1 (1844): 15.

10. Schlesinger noted, p. 195n, that even by 1850, the year after financial ruin seemed imminent, circulation was just 1400. For a time, though, *Brownson's Quarterly Review* attracted an English readership, and briefly in the 1850s an English edition was published. See ibid., pp. 198, 209; Henry F. Brownson, *Orestes A. Brownson's Middle Life: From 1844 to 1855* (Detroit: H. F. Brownson, 1899), pp. 47–53; and Ryan, pp. 226–29.

11. "The Two Orders, Spiritual and Temporal," *Brownson's Quarterly Review* 3d ser. 1 (1853): 22–62; "The Spiritual Not for the Temporal," ibid. 1 (1853): 137–65; "The Spiritual Order Supreme," ibid. 1 (1853): 281–315. Also see Ryan, pp. 560–70.

12. "Native Americanism," *Brownson's Quarterly Review*, 3d ser. 2 (1854): 328–54; "The Know-Nothings," ibid. 2 (1854): 447–87; "The Know-Nothings," ibid. 3

(1855): 114–35; "A Know-Nothing Legislature," ibid. 3 (1855): 393–411; "The Know-Nothing Platform," ibid. 3 (1855): 473–98. Also see Ryan, pp. 468–86.

13. This point is developed forcefully in "Public and Parochial Schools," *Brownson's Quarterly Review*, New York ser. 4 (1859): 324–42. Also see Ryan, pp. 548–59.

14. "The Church and the Republic," *Brownson's Quarterly Review*, New York ser. 1 (1856): 273–307.

15. "A Response to O. A. Brownson,' *Universalist Quarterly and General Review* 14 (1857): 155–66; "Christianity as an Organization," ibid. 14 (1857): 353–73.

16. Henry F. Brownson, *Orestes A. Brownson's Later Life: From 1855 to 1876* (Detroit: H. F. Brownson, 1900), pp. 287–91.

17. Ibid., pp. 254–58.

18. Orestes A. Brownson, *The American Republic: Its Constitution, Tendencies, and Destiny* (New York: P. O'Shea, 1866). Also see Ryan, pp. 644–61.

19. "Introduction to the Last Series," *Brownson's Quarterly Review*, last ser. 1 (1873): 1–8. Also see Ryan, pp. 676–94.

20. "The Democratic Principle," *Brownson's Quarterly Review*, last ser. 1 (1873): 253–59.

21. Americo D. Lapati, *Orestes A. Brownson*, Twayne's United States Authors Series (New York: Twayne Publishers, 1965), pp. 126–32.

22. "Literary Notices and Criticisms," *Brownson's Quarterly Review*, n.s. 4 (1850): 528–31.

23. "Catholicity and Literature," *Brownson's Quarterly Review*, New York ser. 1 (1856): 70. Also see Ryan, pp. 347–65.

24. Schlesinger, p. 292.

Information Sources

BIBLIOGRAPHY:

Brownson, Henry F. *Orestes A. Brownson's Early Life: From 1803 to 1844*. Detroit: H. F. Brownson, 1898.

———. *Orestes A. Brownson's Later Life: From 1855 to 1876*. Detroit: H. F. Brownson, 1900.

———. *Orestes A. Brownson's Middle Life: From 1844 to 1855*. Detroit: H. F. Brownson, 1899.

Gohdes, Clarence L. F. *The Periodicals of American Transcendentalism*. Durham: Duke University Press, 1931.

Lapati, Americo D. *Orestes A. Brownson*. Twayne's United States Authors Series. New York: Twayne Publishers, 1965.

Marshall, Hugh. *Orestes Brownson and the American Republic: An Historical Perspective*. Washington, D.C.: Catholic University of America Press, 1971.

Ryan, Thomas R. *Orestes A. Brownson: A Definitive Biography*. Huntington, Ind.: Our Sunday Visitor, 1976.

Schlesinger, Arthur M., Jr. *Orestes A. Brownson: A Pilgrim's Progress*. Boston: Little, Brown, 1939.

Sveino, Per. *Orestes A. Brownson's Road to Catholicism*. New York: Humanities Press, 1970.

INDEX SOURCES: *Poole's Index to Periodical Literature*.

REPRINT EDITIONS: AMS Press (New York, 1965); American Periodicals Series, University Microfilms International.

LOCATION SOURCES: Yale University, Los Angeles Public Library, Boston Public Library, Harvard University, University of North Carolina-Chapel Hill, University of Illinois-Urbana, and others.

Publication History

MAGAZINE TITLE AND TITLE CHANGES: *Boston Quarterly Review* (1838–42), *Brownson's Quarterly Review* (1844–64, 1873–75).

VOLUME AND ISSUE DATA: *Boston Quarterly Review* 1–5 (January 1838-October 1842); *Brownson's Quarterly Review* 1–3 (January 1844-October 1846), n.s. 1–6 (January 1847-October 1852), 3d ser. 1–3 (January 1853-October 1855), New York ser. 1–4 (January 1856-October 1859), 2d and 3d New York ser. 1–4 (January 1860-October 1863), national ser. 1 (January-October 1864), last ser. 1–3 (January 1873-October 1875).

PUBLISHER AND PLACE OF PUBLICATION: B. H. Greene, Boston (*Boston Quarterly Review*, 1838–42; *Brownson's Quarterly Review*, 1844–55); E. Dunigan & Bro., New York (*Brownson's Quarterly Review*, 1856–64, 1873–75).

EDITOR: Orestes A. Brownson.

CIRCULATION: Less than 1500 (est.).

Charles H. Lippy

BULLETIN OF FRIENDS' (FRIENDS) HISTORICAL ASSOCIATION. *See* QUAKER HISTORY

BULLETIN OF FRIENDS' HISTORICAL SOCIETY OF PHILADELPHIA. *See* QUAKER HISTORY

BULLETIN OF THE EVANGELICAL THEOLOGICAL SOCIETY. *See* JOURNAL OF THE EVANGELICAL THEOLOGICAL SOCIETY

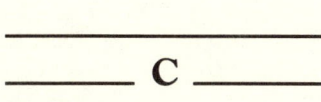

C

CTM. *See* CONCORDIA THEOLOGICAL MONTHLY

CALVIN THEOLOGICAL JOURNAL

First appearing in 1966, the *Calvin Theological Journal* is published biannually by the faculty of Calvin Theological Seminary, the denominational seminary of the Christian Reformed Church. To a degree, the content and thrust of the *Journal* are reflected in the "Calvin Bibliography," published first in the November 1971 issue (6:2) and continuing yearly to the present. This preoccupation with things Calvin indicates not only the *Journal*'s conscious ties to the past but the denomination's as well. While Scripture remains the touchstone of Reformed life, practice, and thought, the sixteenth-century reformer's understanding of its content (though mediated and refined by the historic confessions of the Dutch Reformed faith) continues to form the basis of this tradition.

During the rather chaotic theological situation of the 1960s, the *Calvin Theological Journal* emerged out of "the urge to speak to the world on the issues of the day."[1] Robert Handy has noted that theological trends during this decade "were varied and complex; secular and radical positions sparred for a hearing with new movements of liberal and natural theologies and fresh articulations of confessional and evangelical options."[2] The *Journal*, then, sought to give a fresh articulation to the Christian Reformed faith. As John H. Kromminga stated in his *apologia* for the new publication, "It is our conviction that Reformed theology must remain abreast of changes for its own sake and for the sake of its constituency. It must do this, not in denial of the Reformation heritage, but in obedience to the mandate which the church has from Scripture, past tradition, and the present challenge."[3]

The objectives of the *Journal* were twofold: "to serve the community of

Reformed theological scholarship, and through it, the ministers and members of the Reformed churches'' and to ''provide the conservative Reformed community with a window on the complex world of theology.'' According to Kromminga, there is ''much in contemporary theology to be criticized and rejected. . . . Theology's platform appears to be one of quicksand,'' where none of the ''institutions, formulas, standards, traditions . . . it would appear, ought to be defended or used.'' The *Journal* based its theology on the historical doctrine of divine revelation, contending that if this doctrine were denied, there would be ''no profit whatsoever in going on with theology.'' Contrary to what a handful of radical theologians were saying in the 1960s, Kromminga asserted: ''God is not dead, but speaking and acting in our day; and that his will has had an inspired, authoritative and perpetually relevant expression in the Sacred Scriptures.'' Still, the *Journal* recognized the ''profitable new insights'' in present-day theology and hence the need to balance rejection of some contemporary theological trends with the acceptance of others. ''We hope,'' concluded Kromminga, ''that the distinctive note of our journal will include affirmation as well as negation.''[4]

The *Journal*'s editors originally divided its space into three sections: articles, book reviews, and ''Scholia,'' subtitled ''Notes and Comments for the Minister.'' Contributors to the first issue were drawn exclusively from faculty at Calvin College and Seminary, as well as from the Christian Reformed sister colleges of Trinity Christian (Palos Heights, Illinois) and Dort (Sioux Center, Iowa). Subsequently the range of contributors has expanded to include pastors and other academics within the Christian Reformed Church, those from a Reformed background other than the Christian Reformed, and still others without formal ties to the Reformed faith.

During the first decade of publication, articles in the *Calvin Theological Journal* were generally supplied by the seminary faculty, but since then the majority of article contributors have come from outside the faculty. Topics receiving the most space relate to the life and thought of John Calvin,[5] Reformed confessions of faith,[6] and ecumenism.[7] Also included are a broad range of theological and biblical studies and the valuable compilation of Calvin studies (''Calvin Bibliography'') by Peter DeKlerk, the theological librarian at Calvin Seminary. Running anywhere from 15 to 40 pages, this extensive bibliography includes the previous year's published material dealing with some aspect of the life and thought of Calvin. A special issue (7:2, 1972) was devoted to missions from a Reformed perspective. Ties to the Dutch Reformed heritage are evident in the contributors to articles, the contents of articles, and in the books reviewed.[8]

The last two sections of the *Journal* may be briefly summarized. Nearly one-half of the *Journal* is devoted to book reviews. This section mirrors the original objectives of the editors: to inform the Reformed community of current scholarship and to offer ''constructive criticisms of that community on such thought.''[9] Many of the books reviewed are published by such Reformed-connected companies as Eerdmans, Zondervan, and Westminster. A ''Book Notices'' section was added in April 1976. The final section, called ''Scholia'' in reference to the marginal notes in medieval manuscripts, was intended "to pass along to pastors such observations, flashes of insight, and tidbits of information" that might assist them in their work.[10] For no reason offered by the journal, this section was dropped after April 1974 (9:1).

In its brief history, the *Calvin Theological Journal* has undergone few changes in format, tone, or substance. The scholarship, consistently high in quality, continues to reflect the ongoing dialogue of Reformed thought with contemporary theology. The editorship is carried on by three Calvin Seminary faculty members on an unevenly rotating basis.

Notes

1. John H. Kromminga, "Editorial: Why We Speak," *Calvin Theological Journal* 1 (April 1966): 5 (hereafter cited as *CTJ*).

2. Robert T. Handy, *A Christian America: Protestant Hopes and Historical Realities*, 2d ed. (New York: Oxford University Press, 1984), p. 200.

3. Kromminga, p. 7.

4. Ibid., pp. 6–8.

5. Examples include Anthony A. Hoekema, "The Covenant of Grace in Calvin's Teaching," *CTJ* 2 (November 1967): 133–61; Pieter A. Verhoef, "Luther's and Calvin's Exegetical Library," *CTJ* 3 (April 1968): 5–20; and the articles by Joseph Tylanda in *CTJ* 8 (April 1973), 8 (November 1973), 9 (November 1974), and 10 (April 1975).

6. For examples, see Anthony A. Hoekema, "Needed: A New Translation of the Canons of Dort" (Scholia), *CTJ* 3 (April 1968): 41–47; "A New Translation of the Canons of Dort," *CTJ* 3 (November 1968): 133–61; Fred H. Klooster, "Recent Studies on the Heidelberg Catechism" (Scholia), 1 (April 1966): 73–78; "The Heidelberg Catechism and Comparative Symbolics" (Scholia), *CTJ* 1 (November 1966): 205–12; and John H. Kromminga, "The Shape of a New Confession," *CTJ* 7 (November 1972): 146–57.

7. Examples include Fred H. Klooster, "Uppsala on 'The Holy Spirit and the Catholicity of the Church,' " *CTJ* 4 (April 1969): 51–98; John H. Kromminga, "Evangelical Influence on the Ecumenical Movement," *CTJ* 11 (November 1976): 149–80; Paul G. Schrotenboer, "Current Trends in the Ecumenical Movement," *CTJ* 10 (April 1975): 28–45; "The Bible in the World Council of Churches," *CTJ* 12 (November 1977): 144–63; and Klaas Runia, "The World Council of Churches and Interreligious Dialogue," *CTJ* 15 (April 1980): 27–46.

8. For example, N. J. Hommes ("Let Women Be Silent in Church," *CTJ* 4 [April 1969]: 5–22) was a minister of the Gereformeerde Kerken in the Netherlands; Henry Zwaanstra considered Abraham Kuyper, the Dutch Reformed thinker and leader from the Netherlands in "Abraham Kuyper's Conception of the Church," *CTJ* 9 (November 1974): 149–81; and there appeared a review of Johannes Verkuy's *Breek de muren af! (Break Down the Walls!)* in *CTJ* 5 (November 1970): 227–30.

9. Kromminga, p. 10.

10. Ibid.

Information Sources

INDEX SOURCES: *Christian Periodical Index, Religious and Theological Abstracts, Religion Index One, Old Testament Abstracts, New Testament Abstracts, Internationale Zeitschriftenschau für Bibelwissenschaft und Grenzgebiete.*

REPRINT EDITIONS: University Microfilms International.
LOCATION SOURCES: Calvin College and Seminary Library, Yale University, Union Theological Seminary (New York), Princeton Theological Seminary, Duke University, and others.

Publication History

MAGAZINE TITLE AND TITLE CHANGES: *Calvin Theological Journal* (1966–   ).
VOLUME AND ISSUE DATA: 1:1 (April 1966–   ). Published biannually in April and November.
PUBLISHER AND PLACE OF PUBLICATION: Calvin Theological Seminary, Grand Rapids, Mich.
EDITORS: Andrew J. Bandstra, Fred H. Klooster, Carl G. Kromminga (1966–68); Andrew J. Bandstra (1968–69); Anthony A. Hoekema and Carl G. Kromminga (1969); Anthony A. Hoekema, Fred H. Klooster, Robert Recker (1970); Anthony A. Hoekema, Marten H. Woudstra, Robert Recker (1970–71); Marten H. Woudstra, Robert Recker, Henry Zwaanstra (1971–72); Marten H. Woudstra, Henry Zwaanstra, Henry Strob (1972–73); Marten H. Woudstra, John H. Kromminga, Henry Strob (1973–74); John H. Kromminga, Henry Strob, John H. Stek (1974–75); John H. Stek, John H. Kromminga, Bastiaan Van Elderen (1976); John H. Stek, Bastiaan Van Elderen, Anthony A. Hoekema (1977); John H. Stek, Richard R. DeRidder, Anthony A. Hoekema (1977–78); John H. Stek, Richard R. De Ridder, Harold Dekker (1978–79); John H. Stek, Harold Dekker, Theodore Minnema (1979–80); John H. Stek, Theodore Minnema, J. Marion Snapper (1981); John H. Stek, Cornelius Plantinga, J. Marion Snapper (1981–82); John H. Stek, Cornelius Plantinga, Andrew J. Bandstra (1982–   ).
CIRCULATION: 2400 (1982).

David Kling

CATHOLIC ACTION

Although non-Catholic Americans in the early twentieth century believed the American Catholic Church to be a monolithic body, in reality the American church at that time was almost hopelessly fragmented. As Charles H. Shanabruch notes, "Catholics did not have a sense of unity common to most Americans. They did not see themselves as American Catholics, but continued to see themselves as Irish Catholics, German Catholics, Bohemian Catholics, and the like."[1] Residual ethnic loyalties were joined by distrust between liberal and conservative members of the hierarchy as a result of the unfortunate Americanist controversy of the closing years of the nineteenth century. Individual bishops from both camps resisted any movement toward interdiocesan unity and cooperation. Moreover, many American Catholic leaders, lay and clerical, feared that any attempt to form a truly unified American Catholic body would inevitably lead to the creation of an American equivalent of the Centre party of Germany and inflame nativist feelings.

The entrance of the United States into World War I, however, afforded the church an opportunity to overcome its internal divisions and to contribute in a positive way to U.S. political life. The government depended on voluntary associations to tackle the almost innumerable problems of gearing up for war.[2] The Knights of Columbus spearheaded the Catholic response to the nation's call but were unable to handle all the problems posed by mobilization. Moreover, the absence of a hierarchically controlled and coordinated war effort led to needless duplication of activities in Catholic war work. In the summer of 1917, John J. Burke persuaded the hierarchy and then the American Federation of Catholic Societies and the Catholic Press Association to form a supradiocesan agency that could coordinate and direct the wartime activities of all American Catholics.[3] By the end of 1917, the National Catholic War Council had been formed, led by the American hierarchy.

After the war, when the church faced the question of whether to continue the existence of the council, its champions argued that the council could serve the church in a vital way: it could be a national voice capable of asserting and protecting Catholic interests in public life.[4] In short, the partisans of the War Council wished to create a national Catholic lobby that could represent the church in the national capital. It would also signal the development of a self-conscious national Catholic identity.

In order to further its multifaceted plans, the council founded the *National Catholic War Council Bulletin* in June 1919. In its 35-year history, the *Bulletin* underwent four changes of name, altered its format with some regularity, and displayed an often chaotic editorial policy. These shifts were the result of the *Bulletin*'s being the house organ of an ambitious, sometimes beleaguered and disparate organization that pursued multiple goals, had to fight for its life in its early years, and emphasized different aspects of its mission at different times in its history.

The early history of the *Bulletin* was dominated by the War Council's desire to demonstrate the congruence between Catholicism and American democratic principles. In the inaugural issue, Peter J. Muldoon, bishop of Rockford, Illinois, and the chairman of the Executive Committee of the War Council, announced that the purpose of the *Bulletin* was the creation of positive public opinion with regard to the American church:

But the creation and sustaining of enlightened and favorable public opinion, which is the proper function of publicity when applied to the furtherance of any worthy purpose, is now a most essential part of the work of the Council. Our best energies may well be employed in disseminating among the citizens of our country a wide and continuing knowledge of the nature, the extent and the importance of the work being done by the Catholic Church in America through the agency of the National Catholic War Council.[5]

In order to fulfill this mandate, the *Bulletin* emphasized the contributions that American Catholics had made to the war effort and published glowing tributes by non-Catholics concerning such work. Even when the move toward the creation of a permanent peacetime agency, the National Catholic Welfare Council (NCWC), brought about the *Bulletin*'s first name change (to the *National Catholic Welfare Council Bulletin*), this desire to educate the American public remained the primary task of the *Bulletin*. In the first issue published under the new masthead, the editors announced:

> The Bulletin will continue to report the actions and pronouncements of the
> Hierarchy and the various departments of the Welfare Council acting under
> its authority, and to chronicle the national accomplishments of our patriotic
> Catholic men and women in their efforts to uphold American traditions,
> to promote our national ideals and to work for the restoration of the
> Kingdom of Christ on earth.[6]

But the *Bulletin* also began to shift its attention toward the peacetime undertakings of the council. Slowly but surely the *Bulletin* devoted itself more and more to an internally directed mission, the creation of a national Catholic self-consciousness. This goal was to be accomplished by the publication of articles of common interest to all American Catholics and of news of activities of local groups affiliated with the council.[7] During this period, Charles A. McMahon was named editor, and some degree of order began to replace the randomness of earlier issues.

Following a 1922 crisis brought about by a nearly successful attempt by some of the hierarchy to have the NCWC suppressed,[8] the journal settled down under McMahon's leadership. As a result of a Roman decree changing the name of the Welfare Council, the *Bulletin* underwent its third change of name and became the *National Catholic Welfare Conference Bulletin*. Although it continued to report on the meetings and pronouncements of the hierarchy and activities of groups such as the National Councils of Catholic Men and Women, the most energetic departments of the NCWC began to contribute a disproportionately large number of articles. The legal, social action, immigration, and media departments of the conference began to dominate the *Bulletin*'s pages. William Montavon, head of the legal department, sought to alert Catholics to legislation affecting their interests and principles. In the 1920s and into the 1930s, his staff directed attention to discussions of the proposals that surfaced periodically to inaugurate a federal department of education. Montavon endeavored to expose the dangers that would thus be posed to Catholic families.[9]

John A. Ryan, director of the social action department, and two of his staff, Raymond A. McGowen and Lenna Bresette, covered questions of industrial rights, social legislation, and immigration. In addition, they covered meetings of the NCWC-sponsored Catholic Conferences on Industrial Problems and undertook to explain and defend the Bishops' Program of Social Reconstruction of 1919. For its part, the media department followed a two-part strategy in its articles: it sought to educate the laity to support a strong Catholic press, and it adopted the issue of censoring sexually suggestive motion pictures as an issue of particular importance for maintaining morality and family life.[10]

But the *Bulletin* began slowly to change its emphasis and to discover both its true mission and its true audience. It began to conceive of its task in terms of intramural education. In line with Pope Pius XI's enunciation of the concept of Catholic Action as a "true apostolate in which Catholics of every social class participate," the editors began to devote more of their energies to educating American Catholics in the meaning of Catholic social principles.[11] In December 1931, they announced their intent to change the name of the journal to *Catholic Action* (it had become the *NCWC Review* just the previous year):

> This change of title was deemed appropriate in view of the fact that the NCWC is the expression of that informed faith and devoted service to the Living Church which our Holy Father has included in the term "Catholic Action." . . . The change of name will serve to inform the clergy and laity of the country that the Conference magazine is a source of information with regard to programs, methods and results of Catholic action. . . . The magazine should prove invaluable to all Catholic societies and their members in planning and carrying on their local activities.[12]

With the adoption of the new title, the journal assumed a more aggressive air. An editorial section, "Our Catholic Interests," was inaugurated, and the magazine began to publish this statement of purpose in every issue: "It aims to defend and to advance the welfare both of the Catholic Church and of our beloved country. It seeks to inform the life of America of right fundamental principles of religion and morality." In line with their determination to teach America "right fundamental principles," the editors and contributors did not hesitate to lecture America on those national faults that stemmed from a failure to follow Catholic principles. Thus in the course of the 1930s, John A. Ryan and his colleagues in the social action department excoriated the laissez-faire economic philosophy on which the United States had built the false prosperity of the 1920s. They contributed articles calling for a reconstruction of the social and economic orders along the lines suggested by Pius XI in *Quadragesimo Anno*[13] and later praised the New Deal because it seemed to do so.[14] This willingness to lecture America showed up in *Catholic Action*'s strong protest against U.S. support for the Republican forces in the Spanish Civil War.[15] In short, in the 1930s, *Catholic Action* displayed a robust self-assurance rather than a servile patriotism.

This work did not exhaust the educational endeavors of the journal. In 1929 the old *NCWC Review* launched a feature called "Our Common Catholic Work," a symposium devoted to some topic of Catholic interest. In 1932, this feature became "Study Topics"; in the late 1930s, "Study Club Discussions"; and finally in 1942, "Forum." It consistently presented a topic of current interest, the Catholic viewpoint on the topic, and a series of questions to stimulate small group discussion.[16] As Henry P. Lefebure makes clear, the rationale was both educational and apostolic:

> Each year's series, which consists of eight articles, is designed as minimum material to inform lay organization leaders of Catholic teaching in fields of common social and religious interest, and to suggest opportunities and means by which these Catholic societies may spread this teaching and put it into effect for the betterment not only of the community, but through sensitive effort, of the country itself.[17]

During 1942, the journal suffered the death of its first editor, Charles A. McMahon. He was replaced by the Rev. Paul F. Tanner, the journal's final editor. Tanner's tenure saw some minor changes in format, such as the introduction of a bookshelf section, the publication of papal and episcopal documents in their entirety, and the inauguration of a devotional column by the Reverend Charles A. Hart. All reflected a growing awareness that the magazine's audience needed more specialized grounding in Catholic principles of social responsibility if the American church was to become that leaven in public life that Pius XI believed it should. In December 1953, the editorial board announced that since the American Catholic community was ably served by a wide range of publications, the Welfare Conference decided to discontinue publication. But in the course of its history, *Catholic Action* and its predecessors had helped unify the church and educate generations of Catholic leaders.

Notes

1. Charles G. Shanabruch, "The Catholic Church's Role in the Americanization of Chicago's Immigrants, 1833–1928" (Ph.D. dissertation, University of Chicago, 1975), 1: 203.

2. Robert D. Cuff, "The Ideology of Voluntarism and the War Organization during the Great War," in *Herbert Hoover: The Great War and Its Aftermath, 1914–1933*, ed. Lawrence E. Gelfland (Iowa City: University of Iowa Press, 1979), p. 147.

3. See Michael Williams, *American Catholics in the War: National Catholic War Council, 1917–1921* (New York: Macmillan, 1921), p. 113.

4. Elizabeth McKeown, "War and Welfare: A Study of American Catholic Leadership" (Ph.D. dissertation, University of Chicago, 1972), p. 120.

5. Peter J. Muldoon, "Announcement," *National Catholic War Council Bulletin* 1 (June 1919): 1.

6. Editorial, *National Catholic Welfare Council Bulletin* 2 (November 1920): 24.

7. Editorial, *National Catholic Welfare Council Bulletin* 3 (January 1922): 12.

8. See John B. Sheerin, *Never Look Back: The Career and Concerns of John J. Burke* (New York: Paulist Press, 1975), pp. 83ff.

9. See, for instance, Charles N. Lisschka, "The Case against a Federal Department of Education," *National Catholic Welfare Conference Review* 12 (February 1930): 9–10.

10. See, for instance, Frederic Siedenburg, "Motion Picture Censorship," *National Catholic Welfare Council Bulletin* 3 (February 1921): 18, and "Movie Industry on Trial," *National Catholic Welfare Council Bulletin* 3 (May 1921): 13.

11. Cited by *National Catholic Welfare Conference Bulletin* 10 (March 1929): 9.

12. Editorial, *National Catholic Welfare Conference Review* 13 (December 1931): 16.

13. Since 1936 marked the fifth anniversary of the publication of *Quadragesimo Anno*, *Catholic Action* devoted a great deal of attention to discussions of the social principles contained in the encyclical. See the April, May, and June 1936 issues.

14. See Raymond A. McGowan, "Testing the NRA by Catholic Teaching," *Catholic Action* 15 (October 1933): 10.

15. See, for instance, "Keep the Spanish Embargo Aim of Catholic Group," *Catholic Action* 21 (January 1939): 3.

16. The journal was aiming specifically at the formation of the consciences of Catholic lay leaders in the hope that they would act as a leaven in the Catholic community. See "Crucial Questions of the Day," *Catholic Action* 29 (August 1947): 8.

17. Henry P. Lefebure, "Conquering a World at Home," *Catholic Action* 27 (August 1945): 5.

Information Sources

BIBLIOGRAPHY:

Ebersole, Luke E. *Church Lobbying in the Nation's Capital.* New York: Macmillan, 1951.

Halsey, William M. *The Survival of American Innocence: Catholicism in an Era of Disillusionment, 1920–1940.* Notre Dame: University of Notre Dame Press, 1980.

Hawley, Ellis W. *The Great War and the Search for a Modern Order: A History of the American People and Their Institutions, 1917–1933.* New York: St. Martin's Press, 1979.

McKeown, Elizabeth. "War and Welfare: A Study of American Catholic Leadership." Ph.D. dissertation, University of Chicago, 1972.

Sheerin, John B. *Never Look Back: The Career and Concerns of John J. Burke.* New York: Paulist Press, 1975.

Williams, Michael. *American Catholics and the War: National Catholic War Council, 1917–1921.* New York: Macmillan, 1921.

INDEX SOURCES: *Catholic Periodical Index*, the Catholic Magazine index of the *Catholic Bookman*.

REPRINT EDITIONS: University Microfilms International.

LOCATION SOURCES: Catholic University of America, Library of Congress, St. John's (Collegeville), New York Public Library, St. Meinrad's Archabbey, and others.

Publication History

MAGAZINE TITLE AND TITLE CHANGES: *National Catholic War Council Bulletin* (1919–20), *National Catholic Welfare Council Bulletin* (1920–21), *National Catholic Welfare Conference Bulletin* (1922–29), *NCWC Review* (1930–31), *Catholic Action* (1932–53).

VOLUME AND ISSUE DATA: *National Catholic War Council Bulletin* 1:1–2:1 (June 1919-October 1920), *National Catholic Welfare Council Bulletin* 2:2–4:5 (November 1920-October 1922), *National Catholic Welfare Conference Bulletin* 4:6–

11:7 (November 1922-December 1929), *NCWC Review* 12:1–13:12 (January 1930-December 1931), *Catholic Action* 14:1–35:12 (January 1932-December 1953).
PUBLISHER AND PLACE OF PUBLICATION: National Catholic War/Welfare Council/Conference, Washington, D.C.
EDITORS: Charles A. McMahon (1920–42), Paul F. Tanner (1942–53).
CIRCULATION: 31,500 (1919), 15,500 (1930s), 12,000 (1953).

Joseph M. McShane, S.J.

THE CATHOLIC BIBLICAL QUARTERLY

The first issue of the *Catholic Biblical Quarterly* appeared in January 1939, just three years after a group of Catholic Scripture scholars had met at the Sulpician Seminary, Washington, D.C., to plan the preparation of a revised edition of the Challoner-Rheims version of the New Testament. In the context of this meeting, Romain Butin, S.M., proposed the formation of an association of Catholic Scripture scholars. His proposal was unanimously received, and plans were made for the organization of the new association under the patronage of the Confraternity of Christian Doctrine.[1] At the first general meeting of the newly created Catholic Biblical Association of America in St. Louis, 9–10 October 1937, the question of the publication of a quarterly was raised, and after discussion the projected publication was approved by a vote of 26 to five.[2] A questionnaire presented to the members of the association had identified the creation of a biblical periodical as a major activity that the association should undertake.

Wendell S. Reilly, S.S., the first chief editor of the *Catholic Biblical Quarterly*, discussed the question, "Why a biblical quarterly?" in the first issue of the new journal. His answer to this question was direct: "First of all because the Catholic Biblical Association of America needs an organ."[3] Thus, the *Quarterly* from its inception was envisioned as a vehicle for communication among members of the Catholic Biblical Association and a forum for the publication of papers presented at their meetings. In addition, the *Quarterly* would aim to make itself useful "not only by encouraging our biblical scholars to write and discuss subjects which are of interest to themselves, but to make them useful to those students of the Bible who are not enclosed by the walls of seminaries and scholasticates."[4] It would be "the only Catholic review devoted exclusively to the Bible in the English-speaking world."[5] The intention from the outset was that the new journal would be both scholarly and popular. The Most Reverend Edwin V. O'Hara, who because of his patronage and support of the Biblical Association in its formative years came to be regarded as the father and founder of the association,[6] expressed the hope that the work of the association would "put the Bible in its exalted place in the teaching of Religion."[7] Throughout the editorial tenure of Father Reilly (1939–41) and his successor, Michael J. Gruenthaner, S.J. (1941–51), the *Quarterly* was characterized by this dual concern for scholarly and popular communication in the service of spiritual development.

The initial focus of the association, revising the Challoner-Rheims version of the New Testament and subsequently the Challoner-Douay Old Testament, is reflected in the papers on translation and textual criticism read at the early meetings of the association and published in its *Proceedings* and the *Quarterly*.[8] A variety of other scholarly and confessional concerns are also given expression in the pages of the *Quarterly* in its early years. Juxtaposed in the first issue were articles on "The Synoptic Problem" and "The Essence of the Sacrifice of the Mass and Scripture." As part of a continuing feature on "Obscurities in the Latin Psalter," there was an exegetical note, "Homiletical Notes on the Magi: Gospels for the Feast of the Epiphany." In addition, there were several features in the first issue that have characterized the *Quarterly* throughout most of its history, although some have undergone evolution and modification. Among these were the report on the general meeting of the Catholic Biblical Association, "Biblical News," notes on the death of members of the association, book reviews, and an archaeological note, "The Archaeological Corner," contributed by E. A. Cerny. Cerny identified the attraction of archaeology to be, in part, its confirmatory results against the radical skeptical treatment of scripture.[9]

During these early years, the members of the association and the contributors to the *Quarterly*, all devout Catholics,[10] received encouragement and direction from the encyclical of Pius XII, *Divino Afflante Spiritu*, issued on 30 September 1943.[11] This encyclical, with its emphasis on the importance of biblical and related languages and textual and literary criticism for biblical study, was regarded as a Magna Carta for scientific biblical work.[12] Despite this encouragement from the Vatican, the biblical movement in Catholicism experienced sharp criticism from conservative ranks within the church. This criticism reached its peak just before Vatican II, when attacks on the Pontifical Institute in Rome expanded to include American biblical scholarship. The third and fourth editors of the *Quarterly*, Edward F. Siegman C.PP.S. (1951–58) and Roland Murphy, O.Carm. (1958–65), guided the *Quarterly* through this difficult period. However, the pages of the *Quarterly* provide only the briefest glimpses of this controversy. In a memorial note for Father Siegman, Roland Murphy credited Siegman with making the *Quarterly* what it is today and alluded to the personal difficulties Siegman had experienced in this difficult period.[13] A brief note in volume 23 (1961), presumably by editor Roland Murphy, notes the difficulty "that many people have had in accepting the principles laid down in the *Divino Afflante Spiritu*."[14]

An indication of the emphasis on scholarly communication under the editorship of Father Siegman was the continuing expansion of the book review section and the "Survey of Periodicals," which had been initiated in volume 3. By 1955, the number of books reviewed annually exceeded one hundred. The evolution of the *Quarterly* into a mature scholarly journal was essentially completed under the editorial direction of Roland Murphy. The appearance of a new periodical, the *Bible Today* (1962), which was intended for a general audience, obviated the need for the popular and confessional dimension of the *Quarterly* although, as Rossiter observed, the tension between the popular and the scientific concerns had usually been resolved in favor of the scholarly.[15] Among his other contributions, Father Murphy added a section, "Miscellanea Biblica," to take the place of the "Survey of Periodicals," which had been dropped in 1958 because of the number of periodical indexes that by then had appeared.[16] Father Murphy hoped that the new section "would attract surveys of literature of a chiefly critical, as opposed to expository, type."[17] In his report to the association in 1960, Editor Murphy could announce that 2100 copies of the journal were being printed.

During Murphy's tenure also, the *Quarterly* celebrated its silver anniversary with two special issues, one for the Old Testament (25:1, January 1963) and one for the New Testament (25:3, July 1963), and in a foreword to volume 25:1 (1963) he paid tribute to the work of the members of the Catholic Biblical Association, indicating that most of the articles over the 25-year history of the *Quarterly* had been contributed by members of the association.[18] The twenty-fifth year of the *Quarterly* was also the twentieth anniversary of the encyclical, *Divino Afflante Spiritu*. A letter of congratulation to the association from Cardinal Meyer noted this fact and observed that "the success of CBQ has been due in no small way to its fidelity to the principles of this important and forward-looking document."[19]

The *Quarterly* was steadily becoming more ecumenical and international. In the silver anniversary volume, in addition to articles by Ephraim Speiser, W. F. Albright, and Robert M. Grant, there were articles in German by Georg Fohrer and Oswald Loretz; three articles in French, two by Pierre Benoit, O.P., and the other by Joseph Coppens; and an article in Italian by Giovanni Rinaldi, C.R.S.

At the end of 1965, Father Murphy resigned, and Bruce Vawter, C.M., was named editor. Vawter promptly dropped the title, "Miscellanea Biblica" in favor of "Shorter Communications." In 1968 the association voted to undertake a monograph series "to facilitate the publication of books of scholarly nature in the biblical field that would otherwise find publication difficult to secure."[20] The series was to be named the Catholic Biblical Quarterly Monograph Series, the first volume of which was a collection of studies by Patrick Skehan, *Studies in Israelite Poetry and Wisdom* (1971). Father Vawter was succeeded by Monsignor Francis S. Rossiter (1968–1972), who also served for some 25 years as the publishing editor, and George T. Montague, S.M. (1972–75). During the editorship of Father Montague, Roland Murphy was called upon to serve as a special editor for a festschrift issue of the *Quarterly* to honor Patrick W. Skehan on his sixty-fifth birthday and on the occasion of his achieving the rank of professor emeritus. This issue (October 1974) contained contributions from a distinguished array of scholars, Catholic and non-Catholic, reflecting the increasing use of articles by scholars who were not members of the Catholic Biblical Association that had developed during the editorial tenures of Vawter, Rossiter, and Montague. Perhaps nothing else is as symbolic of the full maturity of the *Catholic Biblical Quarterly* as this festschrift for Skehan, characterized as it was by a scholarship that clearly transcended confessional and national boundaries.

In 1976, Richard Clifford, S.J, became editor. Under the editorship of Rossiter, the book review section had grown to the extent that Neil J. McEleney, the book review editor, reported to the thirty-fourth general meeting of the Catholic Biblical Association that over the past year the *Quarterly* had carried approximately two hundred book reviews, the majority by members of the association.[21] Under Clifford, the continuing emphasis on book reviews led to the appointment of two book review editors, one responsible for reviews relating to the Old Testament and Qumran and the other responsible for those relating to the New Testament as well as intertestamental and rabbinic materials. During the period of Clifford's editorship, the *Quarterly* underwent a redesign of its format, with a new cover and a compatibility of the typefaces. Joseph A. Fitzmyer, S.J., assumed editorial responsibilities in 1980, the year in which the association agreed to help the *Journal of Biblical Literature** celebrate its centennial by jointly sponsoring a panel on the topic "Should Biblical Scholarship Have an Impact on the Churches?"

The *Catholic Biblical Quarterly* for some 44 years has served as a vehicle for the Catholic Biblical Association and has mirrored the growth and developments of that association. The evolution of the *Quarterly* has contributed to and reflected the changing view of biblical scholarship within Catholicism under the encouragement of *Divino Afflante Spiritu* and Vatican II. It has taken its place alongside the *Journal of Biblical Literature* as a leading vehicle for the communication of the best biblical scholarship. While the majority of the membership of the Catholic Biblical Association continue to be Catholics and while the editors and most of the contributors have been members of that association, it has nevertheless become a journal characterized by scholarship that transcends religious and national boundaries.

Notes

1. *Proceedings of the Catholic Biblical Association of America* (First General Meeting: St. Louis, Missouri, 9–10 October 1937), p. 133. Francis S. Rossiter's brief presidential address, read at the meeting of the Catholic Biblical Association on 18 August 1975, provides an insightful sketch of the history of the association and the *Quarterly*. The address, "Forty Years Less One," was published in *Supplement to the Catholic Biblical Quarterly* 39 (1977): 1–14. Brief historical notes are also to be found in the later *Supplements* to the *Catholic Biblical Quarterly* (1939–1940, January 1954, January 1960, April 1964).

2. Reverend John F. Rowan, "The Hartford Meeting," *Catholic Biblical Quarterly* 1 (1939): 77.

3. Wendell S. Reilly, "Editorial Notes," *Catholic Biblical Quarterly* 1 (1939): 5.

4. Ibid.

5. Ibid., p. 6.

6. Stephen J. Hartdegen, O.F.M., "Sinite Parvulos Venire," *Catholic Biblical Quarterly* 17 (1955): 1 (121). The April number of volume 17 was a festschrift honoring O'Hara for his patronage of the association.

7. "Report of the General Secretary," *Proceedings of the Catholic Biblical Association of America*, p. 136.

8. The revision of the Challoner-Rheims version of the New Testament appeared in 1941. The revision of the Challoner-Douay version of the Old Testament was scheduled for completion on 1 June 1944. The encyclical, *Divino Afflante Spiritu*, emphasized the importance of the original languages, and as a result, the revision of the Challoner-Douay Old Testament, although nearly complete, was abandoned in favor of a new translation from the original languages. This translation, the *New American Bible*, appeared in 1970.

9. E. A. Cerny, "The Archaeological Corner," *Catholic Biblical Quarterly* 1 (1939): 83.

10. The constitution adopted at the St. Louis meeting in 1937 specified that active members of the association must be Catholic. The most recent language on membership in the constitution and bylaws of the association is less specific, and active membership in the association now includes Protestant and Jewish biblical scholars. However, from its earliest days there was an ecumenical thrust to the Catholic Biblical Association. This is reflected, for example, in the invitation to Protestant biblical scholar William F. Albright to address the 1944 meeting of the association and granting him honorary life membership in the association. His address was subsequently published in the *Quarterly* 3 (1945).

11. An English translation of the encyclical is published in *Rome and the Study of Scripture*, 7th ed., rev. and enlarged (St. Meinrad, Ind.: Grail Publications, 1962), pp. 80–107.

12. This is the language used in the letter sent to all the Catholic bishops of the United States on 14 September 1973 containing a resolution of the association in support of fellow biblical scholars under attack for attempting to follow the direction for biblical research laid down in *Divino Afflante Spiritu*. The letter was published in the *Catholic Biblical Quarterly* 35 (1973): 502–7.

13. Roland Murphy, "In Memoriam," *Catholic Biblical Quarterly* 29 (1967): 96. Among other achievements with which Murphy credits Siegman are the primary responsibility for the O'Hara festschrift (April 1955) and the issues on messianism. See also the praise of Father Siegman by Francis Rossiter in "Forty Years Less One," p. 5.

14. "The Close of a Controversy," *Catholic Biblical Quarterly* 23 (1961): 269. In addition to this brief note, see the letter addressed to the Catholic bishops of the United States cited in n. 12; Edward Siegman, "The Decrees of the Pontifical Biblical Commission: A Recent Clarification," *Catholic Biblical Quarterly* 18 (1956): 23–29; and Joseph A. Fitzmyer, S.J., "A Recent Roman Scriptural Controversy," *Theological Studies* 22 (1961): 426–44. The pertinent documents are published in translation in *Rome and the Study of Scripture*: "A Response of the Biblical Commission to the Most Eminent Father, Archbishop Emmanuel, Celestine Suhard, Cardinal," 16 January 1948, (pp. 150–53); "An Instruction of the Biblical Commission," 13 May 1950, (pp. 154–57); "An Instruction of the Biblical Commission," 15 December 1955 (pp. 168–72); and the "Monitum of Holy Office to Biblical Scholars," 20 June 1961, (p. 174). For a brief nontechnical discussion of the conflict, see Robert Blair Kaiser, *Pope, Council and World: The Story of Vatican II* (New York: Macmillan, 1963), pp. 154–64.

15. Rossiter, "Forty Years Plus One," p. 7.

16. Among the surveys particularly cited were the *Internationale Zeitschriftenschau für die Bibelwissenschaft und Grenzegebiete* (1951); *New Testament Abstracts* (1956);

La Bibliographie Biblique (Montreal, 1958); *Religious and Theological Abstracts* (1958); and "the practically exhaustive" *Index Bibliographicus* of *Biblica* (*Catholic Biblical Quarterly* 21 [1959]: 59).

17. Ibid.
18. *Catholic Biblical Quarterly* 25:1 (January 1963), "Foreword."
19. Ibid., 25:3 (July, 1963), n.p.
20. Ibid. 31 (1969): 533.
21. Ibid. 33 (1971): 539.

Information Sources

BIBLIOGRAPHY:

Proceedings of the Catholic Biblical Association of America: First General Meeting, St. Louis, Missouri, October 9 and 10, 1937. St. Meinrad, Indiana: Abbey Press, 1938.

Rome and the Study of Scripture: A Collection of Papal Enactments on the Study of Holy Scripture Together with the Decisions of the Biblical Commission. 7th ed. rev. and enlarged. St. Meinrad, Ind.: Grail Publications, 1962.

Rossiter, Francis S. "Forty Years Less One: An Historical Sketch of the C.B.A. (1936–1975). " Supplement to the *Catholic Biblical Quarterly* 38 (July 1977): 1–14.

INDEX SOURCES: Decennial indexes to the *Catholic Biblical Quarterly*: vols. 1–10 (1939–48), vols. 11–20 (1949–58), vols. 21–30 (1959–68). Also in *Religious and Theological Abstracts, Catholic Periodical and Literature Index, Religion Index One (Index to Religious Periodical Literature), Current Contents, New Testament Abstracts, Old Testament Abstracts.*

REPRINT EDITIONS: University Microfilms International.

LOCATION SOURCES: Catholic Biblical Association of America, Yale University, Catholic University of America, University of Chicago, Union Theological Seminary (New York), and others.

Publication History

MAGAZINE TITLE AND TITLE CHANGES: *Catholic Biblical Quarterly* (January 1939–   ).

VOLUME AND ISSUE DATA: 1:1 (January 1939–   ); appears quarterly.

PUBLISHER AND PLACE OF PUBLICATION: Catholic Biblical Association of America, Catholic University of America, Washington, D.C.

EDITORS: Wendell S. Reilly, S.S. (1939–41), Michael J. Gruenthaner, S.J. (1941–51), Edward F. Siegman, C.PP.S. (1951–58), Roland E. Murphy, O.Carm. (1958–65), F. Bruce Vawter, C.M. (1965–68), Msgr. Francis S. Rossiter (1968–72), George T. Montague, S.M. (1972–75), Richard J. Clifford, S.J. (1976–79), Joseph A. Fitzmyer, S.J. (1980–   ).

CIRCULATION: 3640 (paid, 1982); 3913 (total, 1982).

Harold O. Forshey

CATHOLIC CHARITIES REVIEW

In 1833, Frederic Ozanam, a young French Catholic studying at the Sorbonne in Paris, gathered a group of his fellow students together to found the Saint Vincent de Paul Society. Named after a seventeenth-century French priest who had founded religious communities to evangelize the urban poor and the rural areas of France, Ozanam's society stressed poor relief, but it also offered assistance to other charities such as industrial and vocational schools and homes for working boys.[1] Organized in conferences at the parish level, the St. Vincent de Paul Society spread rapidly. The first conference in the United States was organized in St. Louis in 1845. Organizational unity was achieved through an international directorate headquartered in Paris and the bulletin, which the directors published. In 1856, the Superior Council of the Society in Ireland began the publication of an English edition of the bulletin, which over the years gave some coverage to the activities of the society in the United States.[2]

When the fifth national convention of the St. Vincent de Paul Society in the United States met in New York City in September 1895, it adopted the proposal of a special bulletin committee to publish a journal for the society in North America.[3] The first issue appeared in November 1895, and an editorial in the opening pages stated the publication's objectives: "This is not a literary periodical or social magazine. It is intended simply to voice the sentiments of the Society, a chronicle of its doings and a mirror of its conduct." The new publication, entitled *St. Vincent de Paul Quarterly*, would offer "American news of the Society" to educate its readers: "We hope to demonstrate to the Catholics of America that our organization is something more than a mere relief agency, and that our aims extend far beyond the mere food and clothing we give."[4] Over the next 21 years the *St. Vincent de Paul Quarterly* carried news of the society, editorials on the Catholic Church and national issues, articles on the means to alleviate distress among the population, and essays reflecting on the theology of charitable works, such as "A Responsibility of Wealth" by John M. Farley, later the cardinal archbishop of New York, which appeared in the February 1897 issue. One historian has remarked that "the most valuable literature of Catholic charity in existence was in the *St. Vincent de Paul Quarterly*."[5]

Although it held national conventions at frequent intervals, the society in the United States did not achieve national unity until 1915 when the Superior Council of the United States was organized under the leadership of Thomas Mulry.[6] From its inception the journal had been published under the auspices of the Superior Council of New York, and repeated efforts to transform it from a quarterly into a monthly publication had failed. With the organization of the National Conference of Catholic Charities in 1910, the *St. Vincent de Paul Quarterly* in effect had been turned over to the new organization whose secretary, Rev. William J. Kerby, served as editor from 1911 until the publication ceased in 1916.[7]

The first National Conference of Catholic Charities convened at the Catholic University of America in Washington, D.C., in September 1910. It was attended by 17 laymen, Thomas Mulry among them, all of whom were members of the St. Vincent de Paul Society, and nine clergymen who were active in charitable work. The purpose of the new organization was to integrate and coordinate Catholic charitable organizations in the United States.[8]

At the fourth National Conference of Catholic Charities in 1916, a proposal to launch a publication was approved. The new journal, *Catholic Charities Review*, made its appearance in January 1917. One section was regularly devoted to news of the St. Vincent de Paul Society, and a notice in the first issue cited arrangements whereby the new review was the successor to the *St. Vincent de Paul Quarterly* and would reserve a portion of each issue for the service of the society. *Catholic Charities Review* thus became the official organ of the society.[9]

Over the next 58 years, *Catholic Charities Review* dealt with the practical problems in Catholic benevolent work in the United States. There was a recurring emphasis in its pages that not only must distress among the poor be alleviated but that the causes of poverty and destitution had to be removed. It supported most of the federal social legislation of the 1930s. While it took the position that government programs should support rather than supplant private agencies, it backed housing programs for low-income families on the grounds that slums strained the resources of charitable agencies. Although in its early years it encouraged the professionalization of social work, by the 1940s and 1950s the *Review* was asking whether professionalization had brought a loss of the "spiritual component" of Catholic charitable work.

Rev. John A. Ryan served as editor for the first 15 years of the *Review*'s existence. In its first four years, he wrote all the editorials, and his legacy to the journal was a strong doctrinal thrust based on a definite philosophy of life that characterized it down to its last issue. Poverty, for example, was not to be reduced by artificial and immoral devices of birth prevention and mothers' pensions did not derive from childbearing as a hired and delegated function of the state.[10]

When it ceased publication with the issue of October 1974, an editorial advised readers that *Catholic Charities Review* would be continued as a quarterly journal cosponsored by the National Conference of Catholic Charities and the National Catholic School of Social Service at the Catholic University of America.[11] The first issue of the new publication, *Social Thought*, appeared in the spring of 1975.

Notes

1. F. MacMillan, "Ozanam, Antoine Frederic," *New Catholic Encyclopedia* (New York: McGraw-Hill, 1967), 10: 847–58.

2. D. T. McColgan, *A Century of Charity* (Milwaukee: Bruce Publishing Co., 1951), 2:315–17.

3. Ibid., p. 318.

4. "Greeting," *St. Vincent de Paul Quarterly* 1:1 (November 1895): 3–4.

5. D. P. Gavin, *National Conference of Catholic Charities, 1910–1960* (Milwaukee: Bruce Press, 1962), p. 46.

6. D. Baker, "Mulry, Thomas Maurice," *New Catholic Encyclopedia*, 10:68.

7. McColgan, pp. 319–20.

8. D. P. Gavin, "National Conference of Catholic Charities," *New Catholic Encyclopedia*, 10:229–30.

9. "Editorials," *Catholic Charities Review* 1:1 (January 1917): 1–6.
10. "Editor's Notes," *Catholic Charities Review* 58:7 (October 1974): 3.
11. Ibid., pp. 1–3.

Information Sources

INDEX SOURCES: *St. Vincent de Paul Quarterly*: none; *Catholic Charities Review*: self-indexed in the last issue of each volume, also in *Catholic Periodical Index* (1930–74).
REPRINT EDITIONS: *Catholic Charities Review*: University Microfilms International.
LOCATION SOURCES: Catholic University of America, University of Illinois, Boston Public Library, University of Missouri, University of Notre Dame, and others.

Publication History

MAGAZINE TITLE AND TITLE CHANGES: *St. Vincent de Paul Quarterly* (1895–1916), *Catholic Charities Review* (1917–74); superseded by *Social Thought*.
VOLUME AND ISSUE DATA: *St. Vincent de Paul Quarterly* 1:1 (November 1895)–21:4 (November 1916), five issues in vol. 1 and four thereafter; *Catholic Charities Review* 1:1 (January 1917)–58:7 (October 1974). Monthly except for July and August.
PUBLISHER AND PLACE OF PUBLICATION: *St. Vincent de Paul Quarterly*: Superior Council of New York, Society of St. Vincent de Paul, New York; *Catholic Charities Review*: National Conference of Catholic Charities, Washington, D.C.
EDITORS: *St. Vincent de Paul Quarterly*: none listed (1895–1910), Rev. William J. Kerby (1911–16); *Catholic Charities Review*: Rev. John A. Ryan (1917–31), Rev. John J. O'Grady (1931–61), Rev. Raymond J. Gallaher (1961–65), Rev. Lawrence J. Corcoran (1965–74).
CIRCULATION: 6000 (*St. Vincent de Paul Quarterly*, 1916), 7000 (*Catholic Charities Review*, 1973).

James T. Connelly, C.S.C.

THE CATHOLIC HISTORICAL REVIEW

The first issue of the *Catholic Historical Review*, a scholarly quarterly devoted to the history of the Catholic Church and Catholicism, appeared in April 1915. Bishop Thomas J. Shahan, professor of church history and rector of the Catholic University of America, served as editor in chief of the journal from its inception until 1929. However, the principal force behind both the *Review* and the American Catholic Historical Association (ACHA), which was founded in Cleveland four years later, was Monsignor Peter Guilday, also professor of church history at the Catholic University. Guilday himself became chief editor after Shahan and held the title until his death in 1947.[1] From the beginning, the Catholic University has both published the *Review* and hosted its offices, which since 1963 have been under the supervision of the managing editor, Robert Trisco.

Since the late 1960s, the membership of the ACHA has hovered at the 1100 mark, a drop from its peak of 1333 in 1961, but still a sizable increase from the 730 who belonged at its twenty-fifth year. The *Review* enjoys a circulation of approximately twice the number of the current ACHA roster.[2] Membership has been open to all who are professionally interested in the history of Catholicism, including historians of the Catholic Church, historians of American Catholicism, those interested in Catholic spiritual values, and Catholic historians generally. A recruitment drive is currently underway to attract non-Catholic members and subscribers.[3]

From 1915 until 1921, the *Review* was devoted exclusively to the history of the American church but was thereafter expanded to embrace the history of Catholicism in Europe and elsewhere. Although the majority of the journal's articles have attended to the church and its leaders, pieces on Catholic organizations and missions, especially social bodies, have not been uncommon. Studies treating the political relationships of Catholic institutions have been frequent. As is true for the historical profession as a whole, a growing sensitivity to social history—in the *Review*'s case, "the sociography" of ordinary Catholics—has been evident.[4]

The principal motivation for the founding of both the *Review* and the ACHA was to affirm the contributions of the Catholic Church to American life. At a time when Catholic loyalties were questioned by periodic outbursts of anti-Catholic feeling, a national publication "devoted to the discussion of Catholic history on a scale corresponding to the importance which Catholicity has assumed in the life of the nation" was deemed crucial "to rescue from oblivion the names and deeds of those who from the days of Columbus have planted the faith in the new world, and who have striven to realize in new and frequently hostile surroundings the precepts of the Master."[5] Similarly, at the first annual meeting of the ACHA in Washington, D.C., the president, Lawrence F. Flick, remarked: "What the Catholic Church has done for our country and what Catholics as individuals and as a body have contributed to the development of our free institutions and the formation of the character of our people has never been woven into our history or our literature. To have done this likewise is one of the functions of this organization."[6]

Peter Guilday, who had adopted American Catholicism as his chief intellectual interest, was especially concerned to revive among Catholics a sense of their own history, one that had waned since John Gilmary Shea completed his four-volume work, *The History of the Catholic Church in the United States*, in 1892.[7] Further, Guilday hoped that both the journal and the association, in conformity with the rapid professionalization of history as a discipline, would strengthen the intellectual reputation of American Catholics, a predominantly lower-class immigrant constituency just beginning to produce trained scholars.[8]

Since its inception, however, the *Catholic Historical Review* has consistently committed itself to the nurture of uniquely Catholic views of historical processes and actors. The presidential addresses of the ACHA have returned often to discussions of Catholicism's place in history, the role of the Catholic historian, and the nature of the Catholic view of history.[9] Theological and ecclesiological purposes were particularly noticeable in the years before the Second Vatican

Council dramatically altered the posture of the church toward modern social movements and thought, toward other Christian bodies and religious traditions, and even toward its own laity.[10]

The *Review*'s contributors warily attended to, and at times even rejected, modern historical methods from the vantage of historical theologizing. "An interest in historical studies and the fashion of viewing actions and events in their historical relations are the natural inheritance of Catholics," Bishop Shahan reflected in the first issue. He commented on the increasing secularization of the discipline as the result of its adaptation of methods used in the physical sciences. Now the plane of historical investigation had shifted from a concern for "nature and essence" to "origins and development." Even religious beliefs were being "traced to causes which lie far outside the object of religious inspiration." In response, the Catholic historian had to assert "the principle that God rules over the affairs of mankind and disposes all things according to His own purposes. The urgency of the call for the theologian, who is at the same time a trained historian, is manifest from the fact that historical science of the present demands of its votaries hermeneutical powers rather than the mere capacity for research."[11] Over twenty years later, a contributor firmly recommended that history be de-secularized, that is, divorced "from the entanglements of philanthropy, social service, psychology and economics" and transformed instead into a record of man's actions in society as they "advance toward God or turn away from Him."[12]

The authority of the church and its teachings evoked appropriate judgments from the *Review*'s writers and reviewers. A London cleric confidently denied any discrepancy between Catholic truth and historical truth. "Whatever record leaps to light," he asserted, the church "never shall be harmed. It is her place to live in the light, while those who assail her shall perish in the darkness." Yet he supported the occasional "suppression and withholding of facts" out of "reverence for those in authority."[13] Authors of books on Protestantism saw their errors exposed. A biographer of Luther was criticized for having misinterpreted Paul's justification by faith "as successfully as did Luther himself."[14] The writer of *The World's Debt to Protestantism*, according to the reviewer, illustrated "how much of its muddled thinking and distorted perspectives the world owes to Protestantism."[15]

The decline in such obvious theological and ecclesiological judgments, as one ACHA presidential address of the mid–1970s pointed out, attested not only to the Vatican Council's encouragement of ecumenism but also to the inappropriateness of those perceptions according to the canons of the historical profession. The "aims and methods" of Catholic historiography generally were unacceptable to other schools "be they Marxist, neo-positivist, *Annales*, or just plain American social sciences-oriented history."[16] The use of such radically opposed categories as good and evil to describe historical phenomena and the labored ascriptions of historical change, whether good or bad, to single individuals, violated standard understandings of historical causation. The vision of church doctrine as immutable, which underlay much Catholic historical investigation, not only ran up against the comprehension of history as developmental but even lost favor among Catholic theologians sensitive to the historical contexts of church teachings.[17]

Yet as the same presidential address concluded, a distinctly Catholic perspective on history could be affirmed that was simultaneously loyal to prevailing historical methodologies and to tradition. The Catholic historian could be set apart by his appreciation for "the historical importance of theological questions," his nonreductive treatment of religious motivations, and the possibility that individuals "no matter how hemmed in they may be by economic curves and social structures, can be active agents in the historical process." Moreover, the Catholic historian recognized the sanctity of his vocation and his obligation to achieve the broadest possible audience for historical knowledge. A "new" Catholic history was arising—one "constantly in dialogue with the latest currents of non-Catholic historiographies, yet one still faithful to the lasting values of its own 2,000-year-old tradition."[18]

That alteration of the criteria for Catholic historiography spoke at least as much for the changing status of American Catholics as it did for the effects of Vatican II or for the inevitable triumph of social scientific history. As the priest and sociologist, Andrew Greeley, has documented, the certainties of the immigrant garrison church raised against an often unfriendly environment disintegrated with the achievement by Catholics of educational and economic parity with, even superiority over, traditionally dominant national and ethnic groups. Yet consistent with his rejection of melting pot models of assimilation, Greeley asserted that a Catholic collectivity has continued to thrive—only now independent of the teaching authority of the church leadership—which has retained its loyalty to the Catholic heritage and its values.[19]

Throughout its history, the ACHA has preserved its uniqueness and defended its special purposes in its relationships with other historical organizations. Its founding occurred simultaneously with the annual convention of the American Historical Association (AHA), and to the present, the ACHA still holds its annual meeting in conjunction with that of the larger body. Yet the minutes of the first ACHA convention articulated the new group's different obligations. As the AHA provided guidance in the historical sciences to public schools and nonsectarian colleges, so the ACHA needed to provide the same for Catholic institutions. Moreover, the minutes expressed that the AHA's dependence on government support and its relationship to the Smithsonian Institution would inevitably mean its deemphasis of religious history. Finally, the report implied that the predominantly Protestant American Society of Church History (ASCH), founded by Philip Schaff in 1888, provided an inadequate forum for Catholic history, despite the presence of a few Catholic members and the periodic appearance of papers by Catholic authors in the society's journal, *Church History*.* A distinctly Catholic organization was necessary "if the Church is to be recognized in her true position as the sacred and perpetual mother of all that is best and holiest in modern civilization."[20]

Nevertheless, the ACHA, especially in recent years, has encouraged exchanges with other historical groups. Joint sessions with the AHA and the ASCH for the presentation of papers are common at annual conventions, and the *Review* reports fully on the activities of related associations in its quarterly issues. Book reviews in the journal are comprehensive. They cover works dealing with every major period in the history of Christianity, all exponents of the tradition whether institutional or popular, Catholic or non-Catholic, and provide assessments of works of general historical importance. Reviewers are selected for their scholarly competence.

Stronger ties have emerged between the ACHA and the ASCH. Although the Catholic association rejected the ASCH's proposal of a merger in 1969 for fear that the obligation to the history of Catholicism would be lost in a union with a substantially larger organization, both the editorial boards and governing bodies of the two have seen exchanges of prominent figures between the two groups. Perhaps the best-known American Catholic historian, John Tracy Ellis, who served as managing editor of the *Review* from 1947 until 1963, was president of the ASCH. Methodist scholar Albert Outler and Lutheran historian Martin Marty have both been presidents of the ACHA.[21]

While membership reports at annual meetings have often stressed the difficulty in retaining new members in the ACHA, both the association and the *Review* are well established.[22] The *Review*'s continued vitality attests not only to its application of professional historical methodologies to Catholic history but also because it has affirmed and revitalized a unique historical vision.

Notes

1. John Tracy Ellis, "Peter Guilday 1884–1947," *Catholic Historical Review* 23 (1947): 257–68 (hereinafter cited as *CHR*).

2. *CHR* 55 (1970): 108; ibid. 68 (1982): 275–78.

3. Ibid. 68 (1982): 278.

4. See the presidential address of John Lukas, "The Historiographical Problem of Belief and Believers: Religious History in the Democratic Age," *CHR* 63 (1978): 153–67.

5. Rt. Rev. Thomas J. Shahan, "Introductory: The Spirit of the Catholic Historical Review," *CHR* 1 (1915): 12. The most recent general history of Catholicism in the United States is that of James Hennesey, S.J., *American Catholics: A History of the Roman Catholic Community in the United States* (New York: Oxford University Press, 1981). See especially pp. 221–79, which cover the period from the outbreak of World War I to the election of Franklin Roosevelt.

6. *CHR*, n.s. 1 (1921): 16.

7. John Gilmary Shea, *The History of the Catholic Church in the United States* (New York: J. G. Shea, 1886–92).

8. See Ellis on Guilday, and Carl Wittke, "The Catholic Historical Review—Forty Years," *CHR* 42 (1956): 3–4.

9. William J. McGill, "Something of Worth from Boetia: The Presidential Addresses of the American Catholic Historical Association, 1920–68," *CHR* 55 (1970): 26.

10. The Vatican Council is the focal point of the last volume of the monumental series edited by Hubert Jedin, *History of the Church*, vol. 10: *The Church in the Modern Age*, trans. Anselm Biggs (New York: Seabury Press, 1981), esp. chap. 4.

11. Shahan, "Introductory," pp. 5, 6, 8.

12. *CHR* 22 (1937): 426–32.

13. W. H. Kent, "Catholic Truth and Historical Truth," *CHR* 6 (1920): 275–93.

14. Ibid. 21 (1935): 214.

15. Ibid. 20 (1934): 64.

16. Eric Cochrane, "What Is Catholic Historiography?" *CHR* 61 (1975): 176.

17. Ibid., esp. pp. 176–81.

18. Ibid., pp. 183–90.

19. *The American Catholic: A Social Portrait* (New York: Basic Books, 1977), pp. 270–74.

20. Peter Guilday, "The American Catholic Historical Association," *CHR* 6 (1920): 3–14.

21. Hennesey, p. 325.

22. Most recently in the last secretary's report, *CHR* 68 (1982): 275–76.

Information Sources

BIBLIOGRAPHY:

Cochrane, Eric. "What is Catholic Historiography?" *Catholic Historical Review* 61 (1975): 169–90.

Greeley, Andrew. *The American Catholic: A Social Portrait*. New York: Basic Books, 1977.

Hennesey, James, S.J. *American Catholics: A History of the Roman Catholic Community in the United States*. New York: Oxford University Press, 1981.

McGill, William J. "Something of Worth from Boetia: The Presidential Addresses of the American Catholic Historical Association, 1920–1968." *Catholic Historical Review* 55 (1970): 25–41.

Wittke, Carl. "The Catholic Historical Review—Forty Years." *Catholic Historical Review* 62 (1956): 1–14.

INDEX SOURCES: *Guide to Social Science and Religion in Periodical Literature*, *Catholic Periodical and Literature Index*, *Humanities Index*, *Index to Religious Periodicals* (*Religion Index One*), *Current Contents*.

REPRINT EDITIONS: University Microfilms International.

LOCATION SOURCES: Catholic University of America, Yale University, University of Chicago, Union Theological Seminary (New York), and others.

Publication History

MAGAZINE TITLE AND TITLE CHANGES: *The Catholic Historical Review* (1915–).

VOLUME AND ISSUE DATA: 1–6 (1915–20) old series. 1– (April 1921–), new series. Issues released quarterly (January, April, July, October).

PUBLISHER AND PLACE OF PUBLICATION: Catholic University of America, Washington, D.C.

EDITORS: Thomas J. Shahan (1915–29), Peter Guilday (1929–47), John Tracy Ellis (1947–63), Robert Trisco (1963–).

CIRCULATION: 2100 (approx.).

Shelley Baranowski

CATHOLIC UNIVERSITY BULLETIN

When John Lancaster Spalding, bishop of Peoria, called for the establishment of a national Catholic university during an impassioned speech at the Third Plenary Council of Baltimore in 1884, the congregated bishops of the Catholic Church in the United States were forced to confront an issue as costly as it was controversial. A number of the assembled prelates, concerned to repudiate any potential challenge to their own prized diocesan seminaries, opposed the notion outright on financial and ideological grounds. However, with the backing of James Cardinal Gibbons, archbishop of Baltimore, and the material support of a providential pledge of $300,000 from a young heiress, the idea came to fruition in 1889 when the Catholic University of America opened its doors as a graduate school of theology for priests. In 1895, studies in the social sciences and philosophy began, and lay undergraduates were admitted beginning in 1905. The early history of the university reflects the lack of unanimity and focus that plagued its founding: the institution endured a series of financial and ideological crises and never quite attained the lofty goals set for it by Gibbons, Spalding, and others.[1]

Part of the problem concerned the identity of the university as a center for American Catholic scholarship. Could top-notch scholarship and critical inquiry into all subjects be reconciled with the particular claims of a religious tradition? Which methods of instruction might best facilitate the goals of the university? What would be the scope and extent of faculty research interests? In order to provide substantive answers to these and similar pressing questions, the priests charged with administering the university issued in 1895 the first number of a publication by the faculty designed to inform the general public as to the character and scope of their labors, the *Catholic University Bulletin*.

Published quarterly, the journal was perceived by its editors as a vital tool in the process of explaining and publicizing the "object and nature of our new university," a topic "easily misunderstood," as well as the range of its studies and the gravity of its work, lest they be "less highly esteemed than is proper."[2] The founders of the journal recognized its potential for generating goodwill toward the university and attracting financial support in the early days of the growth of the university when "the need of sympathy and cooperation is more vividly felt than at a later time when a multitude of honored graduates, accumulated wealth, and great services rendered, forbid any apathy or opposition."[3]

Like the university it sought to promote, the bulletin's reach exceeded its grasp. Planned on a grand scheme as "a hyphen between the academic corps on one hand and the world of American thought and action on the other," it targeted a nationwide audience of "the great Catholic body and the scientific world in general" presumably interested in "the aim, plans, and methods . . . the spirit of the University."[4] In addition to publicizing the administrative endeavors, material progress, and endowment of the growing university, it was to focus on educational matters—the system of instruction at Catholic University and its results, the history of pedagogies, and the growth of culture. At the same time, it was not to be strictly a pedagogical journal but a publication on the cutting edge of the latest researches and discoveries in the various sciences taught at the university.

In achieving these goals, the actual publication met with only partial success. Intended as a competitor to the popular *American Catholic Quarterly Review** and the *Catholic World*,* the *Catholic University Bulletin* never reached its general audience, becoming instead a review by and for university professors whose articles reflected the views and trends of American Catholic intellectual circles at the time.[5] However, under the leadership of Rev. Thomas J. Shahan, who edited and contributed articles to the *Bulletin* throughout its history, it prospered as a journal of scientific scholarship, exploring and reporting on new, and often controversial, advances in the sciences.

As a student of church history at the University of Berlin and the Catholic Institute in Paris, Shahan had worked with Adolf von Harnack and Louis Duchesne, two historians whose names were closely identified with the modernist crisis that ravaged European Protestantism and Roman Catholicism at the turn of the century. To his post as editor of the *Bulletin* he brought an informed curiosity about modern science and a propensity for careful scrutiny of issues facing the churches in the modern age. Thus, in the pages of the journal alongside scholarly reviews of the latest theories of education there appeared frequent articles investigating the new philosophies and theologies gaining currency in Europe.

To set this enterprise in its proper orthodox context, Shahan opened the first issue with a clear statement from James Cardinal Gibbons on the church and the sciences. Echoing the words of Pope Leo XIII encouraging Catholics to make the best use of their freedom to further the interests of science, Gibbons contended that the church makes allowance for the "real progress" of science. If not a thorough endorsement of every aspect of modern science, this statement by the archbishop served nonetheless as a keynote for the subsequent reportage of the *Catholic University Bulletin*. In the years that followed, a small but erudite group of faculty members submitted articles on the International Scientific Congress of Catholics at Brussels; on new theories of biblical inspiration, exegesis, and hermeneutics; and on topics such as "the evolution theory of morality" and "the human element in Scripture." In an article by John Zahm, C.S.C., of Notre Dame, later suspected of modernist tendencies, Leo XIII was characterized as seeing in science not an enemy of faith but an invaluable auxiliary to religion.[6]

But hint of Roman reaction against the new sciences was in the air as early as 1896, the year in which the first rector of Catholic University of America, Bishop John J. Keane, was removed from his position by Rome, putatively for his progressive views. The *Bulletin* lamented the move.[7] And the editorial policy of the journal was affected significantly by the formal condemnation of modernism by Pius X in 1907: authors that had once reported noncommittally or favorably on the new hermeneutics and theology were now invited to criticize and condemn them. Shahan affirmed that "the Apostolic See has spoken with all the dignity becoming the supreme tribunal'' and promised that the *Bulletin* would ''treat in greater detail some of the more pervasive and perilous errors condemned by these solemn pontifical utterances'' and begin regular publication of pontifical documents to assure to the subscribers ''the guidance of the Apostolic See in the various modern lines of thought and action.''[8]

For seven years the *Bulletin* continued to publish scholarly articles from all fields of study, its vigor diminished somewhat by the condemnations. In 1915 it changed format abruptly, abandoning its role as an organ for the dissemination of the teaching and research of the university faculty and adopting the style of an alumni newsletter. The editors dropped the $3 subscription fee and sent the newsletter free to all former subscribers. It published the texts of public discourses, listed gifts, described social and athletic events, and reported on alumni interests until it too ceased publication in 1928. As for the old bulletin, it had run its course, destined to be replaced later by more specialized journals such as the *Catholic Historical Review*.*[9]

Notes

1. James Hennesey, S.J., *American Catholics: A History of the Roman Catholic Community in the United States* (New York: Oxford University Press, 1981), p. 187.

2. ''Prospectus'', *Catholic University Bulletin* 1 (1895): 1.

3. Ibid., p. 1.

4. Ibid., p. 2.

5. ''Catholic Press,'' *New Catholic Encyclopedia* (New York: McGraw-Hill, 1967), 3: 319.

6. John Zahm, C.S.C., ''Leo XIII and Science,'' *Catholic University Bulletin* 2 (January 1896): 37. On Shahan, cf. ''Thomas Joseph Shahan,'' *New Catholic Encyclopedia* (New York: McGraw-Hill, 1967), 13: 157.

7. ''John J. Keane,'' *Catholic University Bulletin* 2 (October 1896): 219.

8. ''Editor's Note,'' *Catholic University Bulletin* 13 (January 1907): 1.

9. ''A Special Announcement,'' *Catholic University Bulletin* 21 (January 1915): 1.

Information Sources

BIBLIOGRAPHY:

Ellis, John Tracy. *The Formative Years of the Catholic University of America*. Washington, D.C.: Catholic University of America Press, 1946.

Hennesey, James, S.J. *American Catholics: A History of the Roman Catholic Community in the United States*. New York: Oxford University Press, 1981.

McCluskey, Neil P. *A Modern Appraisal of the Catholic University*. Notre Dame: University of Notre Dame Press, 1970.

INDEX SOURCES: *Catholic Periodicals in the United States, Poole's Index*.

REPRINT EDITIONS: University Microfilms International.

LOCATION SOURCES: Catholic University of America, Marygrove College, St. Louis University, University of Michigan, and others.

Publication History

MAGAZINE TITLE AND TITLE CHANGES: *Catholic University Bulletin* (1895–1928) (not to be confused with the Catholic University's *Bulletin*).

VOLUME AND ISSUE DATA: 1–34 (January 1895-April 1928). Published quarterly, 1895–1907, 1926–28; published eight or nine times a year, 1908–25; new series, without break in volume numbering, began in 1915.

PUBLISHER AND PLACE OF PUBLICATION: Catholic University of America, Washington, D.C.

EDITORS: Thomas J. Shahan (1895–1909), William Turner (1909–14), Thomas J. Shahan and Patrick J. Healy (editor in chief and editorial board chairman, respectively, 1914–28).

CIRCULATION: 2500–3000 (est.).

R. Scott Appleby

CATHOLIC WORLD. *See* NEW CATHOLIC WORLD

CENTRAL BLATT. *See* CENTRAL BLATT AND SOCIAL JUSTICE and SOCIAL JUSTICE REVIEW

CENTRAL BLATT AND SOCIAL JUSTICE

Central Blatt and Social Justice (known as *Social Justice Review** since April 1940) was the product of a rejuvenation movement of Der Deutsch Römisch-Katholische Central Verein von Nord-Amerika (Central Verein), a national federation of German American Catholic parish benevolent societies founded in 1855.[1] At the turn of the century the leaders of the Central Verein realized that the organization, then in decline, needed refocusing around some new mission. Prompted by the drop in German immigration, the challenge of the newly formed American Federation of Catholic Societies, and the great upsurge of socialist activity in the Progressive period, the Central Verein at its 1909 annual convention decided on social reform as its new mission.

Undoubtedly the social writings and activities of the German bishop Wilhelm Emmanuel von Ketteler and reports of the German Catholic congresses of the late nineteenth century influenced the leaders of the Verein to promote the social question. Within the context of events in the American Catholic community of the day, the establishment of this social mission is seen as part of the reaction of the conservative German American party to the liberal Catholic faction and its seemingly unquestioning acceptance of America.[2] A critique of the social problems of America became the central theme of the *Central Blatt and Social Justice*.

In February 1909, Frederick P. Kenkel was appointed the director of the

Central Bureau, the agency charged with supervising the social reform activities of the Central Verein. One of his main tasks was to establish a journal devoted to the examination of the social question in the light of Catholic principles. This he did by expanding *Central Blatt*, an already existing journal sponsored by the Central Verein and edited by its financial secretary, Rudolph Krueger. The newly christened *Central Blatt and Social Justice* first appeared as a bilingual monthly in March 1909 with Kenkel editing the German section and the Rev. Peter Dietz the English section.[3] In 1910 Kenkel became the sole editor and remained such until his death in 1952.

Kenkel gave significant shape to the social message of the periodical for the most vigorous years of its existence. Frederick Kenkel was born in 1863 in Chicago to well-off German immigrants of Protestant ancestry.[4] Although he studied for a time at German universities, his immense knowledge and interest in the medieval social order was achieved by personal study. Kenkel became a Catholic in 1892. After a brief but disappointing career in business, he became a journalist and a successful editor of several German Catholic newspapers. In 1905 he moved to St. Louis to become editor of *Die Amerika*, a position he maintained until 1920. Kenkel's romantic vision of the reconstruction of modern society modeled after the Catholic society of the Middle Ages permeated *Central Blatt and Social Justice* until his death. He propagated solidarism, the social philosophy best exemplified by the twentieth-century German Jesuit, Heinrich Pesch.[5] This view of society envisioned a corporate state built on Catholic principles. The motto of the periodical incorporates this theme: *Pax Christi in regno Christi* ("the peace of Christ in the rule of Christ"). It stood as a cricitism of both modern liberal capitalist states and the modern totalitarian socialist states. Within the perspective of solidarism, the significant social questions of the day were addressed by *Central Blatt and Social Justice*: labor, unions, family wage, totalitarian states, welfare state, lay apostolate, Catholic Action, farmers' co-operatives, and the like. It was within the context of the solidarism that the great social encyclicals of Pope Leo XIII and Pope Pius XI were received with approbation by the periodical's writers and editor.

Under the leadership of Kenkel, *Central Blatt and Social Justice* changed format several times. The most significant change was the gradual expansion of the English-language section from 10 percent in 1909 to 75 percent in 1930 and 100 percent in 1940 when the name was changed to *Social Justice Review*. The periodical certainly suffered from anti-German sentiment before and during both world wars. It usually contained several brief yet serious articles in German and English, as well as extensive items of information about activities of the Central Verein and the Central Bureau on the local and international levels. For the first three decades, most issues contained a section dedicated to the women's apostolate in the church. In 1917 Kenkel introduced as a regular monthly feature a section devoted to the history of German Catholics in America. These essays, especially those of the Reverend John Lenhart, O.F.M. Cap., were well-researched contributions to the history of American Catholicism.

Among the major contributors to the periodical during the Kenkel years were Kenkel himself as editor, Rev. Charles Bruehl, Rev. William J. Engelen, S.J., Rev. Alfred Muntsch, S.J., Rev. (later Cardinal) Aloisius Muench, Rev. Adolph Frenay, O.P., L. S. Herron, Franz Mueller, Rev. J. Elliott Ross, C.S.P., and Liam Brophy. Several significant series of articles appeared during the Kenkel years. Three by Father Engelen ("Social Reflections" in volumes 12, 13, and 14; "Social Observations" in volumes 14, 16, and 17; and "Social Reconstruction" in volumes 17, 18, and 19) gave a systematic presentation of the social ethics of solidarism.[6] Kenkel's negative critique of the New Deal policies of Franklin D. Roosevelt is contained in a long series, "New Deals, Past and Present," in volumes 26–30.

The periodical's vigorous approach to social issues diminished in the later years of Kenkel's editorship. Pessimism about modern society came to dominate his writings. However, the vigor of his ethical vision remained evident in his essays against the use of atom bombs in the post–World War II years. These were among the earliest ethical evaluations of nuclear warfare.

In the post-Kenkel years, *Social Justice Review* turned its back on the themes of solidarism and corporate order in society and emphasized issues such as the dangers of communism and secularism, the error of abortion, the dangers of some post–Vatican II movements in religious education, sex education, and the general cultural crisis of the times. The essayists and editors in general carried forward the traditional approach of Kenkel to the topics addressed. However, some writers such as James Likoudis, the administrative assistant to the president of Catholics United for the Faith, represented a more reactionary stance.

The primary import of *Central Blatt and Social Justice* lies in the fact that it was the first Catholic journal in the United States devoted primarily to the discussion of social problems. The solutions it proposed were based on a social philosophy, medieval solidarism, that proved too utopian and too unrealistic for twentieth-century America. The periodical has consistently advocated an approach to social ethics that is tradition oriented. In its earlier years, *Central Blatt and Social Justice* was concerned with social issues of interest to the wider American society such as the labor movement, the problems of farmers, credit unions, and the like. In later years the traditional approach of the periodical has perdured and even become somewhat reactionary. But the social issues now addressed arise from the interests of a limited segment of American society.

Central Blatt and Social Justice remains an important source for understanding the development of the issues of social justice among American Catholics. It highlights a major contribution of German Catholics—mostly laymen—to American Catholic history and destroys the myth that social justice issues are the domain of liberals.

Notes

1. For information about the history of the Central Verein, see Philip Gleason, *The Conservative Reformers: German-American Catholics and the Social Order* (Notre Dame: University of Notre Dame Press, 1968).

2. Ibid., p. 78. For a discussion of the struggle between conservative and liberal American Catholic leaders in the late nineteenth century, see James Hennesey, S.J., *American Catholics* (New York: Oxford University Press, 1981), chap. 15, and Thomas T. McAvoy, C.S.C., *The Great Crisis in American Catholic History* (Chicago: Regnery, 1957).

3. Ibid., pp. 109ff. See Mary Harrita Fox, B.V.M., *Peter E. Dietz, Labor Priest* (Notre Dame: University of Notre Dame Press, 1953).

4. Ibid., pp. 91ff., and memorial tributes to Kenkel in *Social Justice Review* 45 (1952): 23f., 44f.; 46 (1953): 34f., 71f., 107f.

5. See Richard E. Mulcahy, *The Economics of Heinrich Pesch* (New York: Henry Holt, 1952), and William Engelen's essays on Pesch in *Central Blatt and Social Justice* 9 (1916): 7f., 41f.; 19 (926): 77ff., 111f. Also see Ruper Ederer's essay on Pesch in *Social Justice Review* 61 (1968): 372f.

6. See Charles E. Curran, *American Catholic Social Ethics: Twentieth Century Approaches* (Notre Dame: University of Notre Dame Press, 1982), pp. 92–129. This chapter of Curran's book presents an analysis of the social ethics of William J. Engelen.

Information Sources

BIBLIOGRAPHY:

Curran, Charles E. *American Catholic Social Ethics: Twentieth Century Approaches.* Notre Dame: University of Notre Dame Press, 1982.

Dye, Mary E. *By Their Fruits: A Social Biography of Frederick Kenkel, Catholic Social Pioneer.* New York: Greenwich Book Publishers, 1960.

Fox, Mary Harrita. *Peter E. Dietz, Labor Priest.* Notre Dame: University of Notre Dame Press, 1953.

Gleason, Philip. *The Conservative Reformers: German-American Catholics and the Social Order.* Notre Dame: University of Notre Dame Press, 1968.

———. "The Early Years of Frederick P. Kenkel: The Background of an American Catholic Social Reformer." *Records of the American Catholic Historical Society of Philadelphia* 74 (December 1963): 195–212.

Hennesey, James. *American Catholics.* New York: Oxford University Press, 1981.

Kenkel, Frederick P. Papers. University of Notre Dame.

McAvoy, Thomas T. *The Great Crisis in American Catholic History.* Chicago: Regnery, 1957.

Mulcahy, Richard E. *The Economics of Heinrich Pesch.* New York: Henry Holt, 1952.

INDEX SOURCES: *Guide to Catholic Literature, Catholic Periodical and Literature Index (Catholic Periodical Index).*

LOCATION SOURCES: Catholic Central Union of America (St. Louis), New York Public Library, St. John's University (Collegeville), Catholic University of America, and others.

Publication History

MAGAZINE TITLE AND TITLE CHANGES: *Central Blatt* (1908–9), *Central Blatt and Social Justice* (1909–40), *Social Justice Review* (1940–   ).

VOLUME AND ISSUE DATA: *Central Blatt* 1 (April 1908-March 1909), *Central Blatt and Social Justice* 2–32 (April 1909-March 1940), *Social Justice Review* 33–   (April 1940–   ).

PUBLISHER AND PLACE OF PUBLICATION: Central Bureau of the Central Verein, St. Louis, Missouri.
EDITORS: Rudolph Krueger (1908–09), Frederick P. Kenkel (1909–52), Rev. Victor T. Suren (1952–61), Don A. Livingston (1961–62), Harvey J. Johnson (1962–   ).
CIRCULATION: 13,000 (1913), 1740 (1974).

Bernard Noone

CHICAGO STUDIES

In 1962, the year in which the Second Vatican Council was convened, the priests of the Roman Catholic Archdiocese of Chicago joined the faculty of the major seminary of that archdiocese, St. Mary of the Lake Seminary, in founding a journal "for the continuing theological development of priests and other religious educators."[1]

The fruit of this effort, *Chicago Studies: An Archdiocesan Review*, grew within a few years from a semiannual to a triannual publication. Under the editorship of Father George Dyer since its founding, it has been shaped essentially to meet the needs of the Catholic clergy on two levels. First, it translates recent contributions to Roman Catholic theology into language accessible to nonspecialists and offers suggestions as to the usefulness of such scholarship to pastoral work. This purpose is served typically by articles such as "The Historical Meaning of the *Humanae Vitae* Controversy," "Pluralism in Roman Catholic Theology," and "Why Confess to a Priest?"[2] This role of the journal is stated explicitly in the introduction to an issue devoted entirely to canon law:

> Much fine canonical research reaches the light of day only in scholarly journals. It does not reach the pastoral life of the Church. The same is true of post-conciliar canonical documents and the canonical implications of other ecclesiastical statements. Because of this, there is a need for translation of this rich data into ecclesial practice. The research of scholars and the documents of the church must both inform and enter into dialogue with the living church.[3]

Second, the journal publishes articles bearing on the problems and challenges encountered in ministry. Articles representative of this type include "Stress, Sexuality, and Ministry," "Alcoholism: A Response to Stress in Ministry," "Ministering to Marriage," and "Communicating Moral Values."[4]

In addition to discussions of Roman Catholic theology and articles on pastoral work, *Chicago Studies* publishes writings that draw insights from disciplines such as sociology and psychology to help organize and interpret church doctrines.[5] The historical context of American Catholicism is also considered in a variety of ways. In essays on American civil religion, the arms race, and public policy, social, economic, and political circumstances of life in the United States are concretely related to church teachings.[6] More recently, *Chicago Studies* has begun to publish the work of women theologians such as Anne Carr and Agnes Cunningham.[7]

Chicago Studies is not a scholarly journal in the traditional sense; notes are rare, bibliographies are absent, and most of the articles are summaries of larger, more complex theological writings. The popularity of the journal is to be located in its ability to bridge the academy and the parish, to bring the ideas of Catholic theological scholars together with the interests and concerns of the parish clergy. *Chicago Studies* has received three first-place awards from the Catholic Press Association. The Catholic Theological Society of America has presented the journal with the John Courtney Murray Award for Distinguished Achievement in Theology. Several of the thematic issues of *Chicago Studies* have been translated into German, Spanish, and Italian and distributed abroad.

Notes

1. *Chicago Studies* 1 (Spring 1962): 2.
2. Norbert Rigali, S.J., "The Historical Meaning of the *Humanae Vitae* Controversy," *Chicago Studies* 15 (Summer 1976): 127–38; Charles E. Curran, "Pluralism in Roman Catholic Theology," *Chicago Studies* 14 (Fall 1975): 310–34; Kenan B. Osborn, "Why Confess to a Priest," *Chicago Studies* 14 (Fall 1975): 260–78.
3. *Chicago Studies* 15 (Fall 1976): 235.
4. James J. Gill, S.J., M.D., "Stress, Sexuality and Ministry," *Chicago Studies* 18 (Spring 1979): 45–68; Andrew J. McDonagh and Vincent D. Pisani, "Alcoholism: A Response to Stress in Ministry," *Chicago Studies* 18 (Spring 1979): 69–86. "Ministering to Marriage" and "Communicating Moral Values" are the titles of theme issues of *Chicago Studies* 18 (Fall, 1979) and *Chicago Studies* 19 (Fall 1980), respectively.
5. Andrew D. Thompson, "Toward a Social-Psychology of Religious Valuing," *Chicago Studies* 19 (Fall 1980): 271–88; James J. Gill, S.J., "Psychiatry, Psychology, and Spirituality Today," *Chicago Studies* 15 (Spring 1976): 27–38.
6. George S. Weigel, Jr., "The Common Covenant: Catholic Theology and American Civil Religion," *Chicago Studies* 15 (Summer 1976): 211–31; George S. Weigel, Jr., "The Catholics and the Arms Race: A Primer for the Perplexed," *Chicago Studies* 18 (Summer 1979): 169–96.
7. See "The Voices of Women," a theme issue, *Chicago Studies* 19 (Summer 1980).

Information Sources

INDEX SOURCES: *Catholic Periodical and Literature Index, New Testament Abstracts, Religious and Theological Abstracts.*
REPRINT EDITIONS: University Microfilms International.
LOCATION SOURCES: Yale University, Catholic University of America, Fordham University, University of Chicago, Loyola University (New Orleans), University of Portland, St. Benedict's College (Atchison, Kans.), and others.

Publication History

MAGAZINE TITLE AND TITLE CHANGES: *Chicago Studies: An Archdiocesan Review* (1922–   ).
VOLUME AND ISSUE DATA: 1:1 (Spring 1962–   ). Now appears three times each year.
PUBLISHER AND PLACE OF PUBLICATION: St. Mary of the Lake Seminary, Mundelein, Ill.
EDITOR: George Dyer (1962–   ).
CIRCULATION: 10,000 (1983).

John Corrigan

CHRISTENDOM. *See* THE ECUMENICAL REVIEW

CHRISTIAN BAPTIST. *See* MILLENNIAL HARBINGER

THE CHRISTIAN CENTURY

The most influential individual in the history of the *Christian Century* is undoubtedly Charles Clayton Morrison. The point where his ministry converges with the work of the journal provides a natural starting point for attempting to understand the historical development of the periodical itself. This convergence occurred in 1908. At that time, Morrison was a rather disillusioned pastor in Chicago. The neighborhood surrounding his church was increasingly attracting immigrants with little or no interest in Protestantism. The frustrations Morrison experienced in this setting caused him to become aware of new opportunities for ministry.

During the summer of 1908, Morrison discovered that the local Disciples of Christ publication was about to expire because of financial difficulties. Putting together $1500, much of it borrowed from a life insurance policy, he bought the magazine. With only 600 subscribers (each subscription costing $2), the periodical faced obvious difficulty. Morrison's organizational abilities, coupled with his diehard tenacity, brought a sorely needed measure of stability to the enterprise.

October 1983 marked the seventy-fifth anniversary of the date that Morrison purchased the *Century*. That transaction actually constituted a refounding of the journal. Prior to Morrison's intervention, the periodical was a small, respectable religious voice for the Disciples of Christ in Chicago and was not well known outside its denominational readership. Originally named the *Christian Oracle*, the journal's first issue was printed in the summer of 1884. At the turn of the twentieth century, the magazine's editor, George A. Campbell, Jr., changed the masthead of the periodical to read the *Christian Century*. In an editorial published in the last issue bearing the old name, Campbell wrote, "We believe that the coming century is to witness greater triumphs in Christianity than any previous century has ever witnessed, and that it is to be more truly Christian than any of its predecessors."[1] Obviously Campbell felt that the new name would better reflect liberal Protestantism's optimistic faith.

When Morrison assumed control of the periodical, he was completely comfortable with carrying on in the tradition of his predecessors. Both the name and the focus of the periodical seemed appropriate to him. In 1916, however, Morrison discovered something that caused him to begin to change the focus of the *Christian Century*. According to his own recollection, sometime during that year Morrison realized that the *Century*'s subscription list included numerous non-Disciples. Based on this revelation, he decided to broaden the *Century*'s agenda to include nondenominational concerns.

Soon after Morrison's decision to turn the periodical into a nondenominational publication, the *Century*'s readership began to grow considerably. Eventually, mostly attributable to Morrison's long and skillful leadership, the journal established a reputation as one of the premier liberal Protestant publications in the country. As one observer has noted, Morrison was extremely "bold and he counted courage a higher virtue than caution."[2] Martin E. Marty, a long-time staff member of the periodical, has written that "Morrison had a genius for locating the magazine at those junctures and sore points in social life where it could participate in freedom."[3] Throughout his tenure as editor, Morrison subjected most dimensions of American life to thorough and critical examination.

Within two months of the time that he took over as the journal's editor, Morrison was defending Social Gospel concerns. In an editorial entitled "Labor and the Federal Council of Churches," he emphasized the church's responsibility for "the gospel of social righteousness and industrial justice."[4] Throughout the early twentieth century, the periodical's coverage of labor concerns was substantial and entirely sympathetic. Condemnation of child labor appeared early and often within its pages. Further, when the organized labor movement began, the *Century* consistently praised it and urged it on to greater successes. Largely as a result of Morrison's early leadership in this area, the *Century* has always been "a great and true champion of the workingman."[5] In 1936, for example, it was the only mainline church paper to support the reelection of Franklin Delano Roosevelt. The reasons given for the endorsement rested on Roosevelt's New Deal reforms. And this was at a time when 70 percent of the clergy in the United States disapproved of New Deal policies.[6]

Somehow the *Christian Century* avoided many of the pitfalls that befell American Protestantism during the prosperous 1920s. When American churches were adopting the success-oriented practices and materialistic standards of contemporary businessmen, the *Century* resoundingly and repeatedly criticized the "gospel of wealth" sell-out of prophetic religious expression. The *Century*'s editorials (along with those of a few other liberal Protestant periodicals) exemplified an enlightened and critical perspective in an otherwise sympathetic and culture-affirming Protestant community.

Another area in which the *Century* was outspoken during the years of Morrison's editorship involved the issue of war. Perhaps feeling guilty for its wartime advocacy of a tough peace, the *Christian Century* criticized the 1919 Treaty of Versailles, calling it "punitive, vindictive, terrorizing . . . not Christian."[7] From that time on Morrison continually emphasized his belief that war should be outlawed. He was instrumental in engineering the Kellogg-Briand Pact of 1928 and was present at its signing.

The *Century*'s attitude toward war eventually led to a significant rift in liberal Protestant journalism. As a result of its noninterventionist stance with regard to World War II, the *Century* lost the services of one of its most renowned contributing editors. In 1940, Reinhold Niebuhr, who as a Detroit pastor had been brought to the attention of the religious reading public through the efforts of Morrison, resigned his position with the *Century*. Shortly after, Niebuhr had a hand in forming the more interventionist liberal Protestant journal, *Christianity and Crisis*.*

Perhaps one of the most stirring editorials Morrison ever wrote was occasioned by the bombing of Pearl Harbor and the resultant U.S. declaration of war, a declaration Morrison had fought for several years. Dated 17 December 1941, the editorial was entitled "An Unnecessary Necessity." Though he stated his support for the U.S. war effort, he made it clear that he felt that U.S. involvement in the war had resulted from an American "course of action which was neither necessary or just." Execution of the war, he went on, would involve "unimaginable cost and doubtful morality." Nevertheless, he felt that support for the war effort, once the declaration was made, was a necessity, though he considered it a tragic and "unnecessary necessity." In closing his editorial he wrote:

> We make no claim that we know the will of God or the mind of Christ. But with heart bowed in grief that even such a choice had to be made, we shall keep an open mind and a listening ear for the truth and the right and the faith in which on some better day our conscience may find peace.[8]

As such words would indicate, Morrison retained his right to criticize what he viewed as immoral in the U.S. prosecution of the war. The *Century* was the first national magazine to condemn the internment of Japanese Americans.[9]

Morrison should also be remembered for inaugurating the *Century*'s well-known "Mind Change" series. The first series appeared in 1939 as several prominent theologians reflected on how developments of the previous decade had affected their life and work. Every 10 years, the *Century* has continued the series by asking important religious thinkers to write on the subject of "How My Mind Has Changed." The first series is particularly notable in that it brought Karl Barth to the attention of the periodical's readership.

Although he was progressive in his social and political views, Morrison nevertheless reflected the Protestant provincialism of his day. That is, perhaps, most apparent in the anti-Catholicism found in *Century* pages during the Al Smith candidacy of 1928. With Morrison and his successor, Paul Hutchinson, the periodical was devoted to Protestant concerns, speaking, as Marty has noted, "chiefly to Protestantism on 'closed-circle' terms."[10]

Harold E. Fey, the *Century*'s third editor, moved the periodical "from the Protestant cultural setting into pluralism."[11] Fey began his work at the *Century* in 1940. His appointment to the editorship came in 1956, the year after his extremely significant series on American Indians had appeared in the journal. Fey's series of five articles, ultimately published under one cover as *Indian Rights and American Justice*, is credited with being one of the contributing factors toward the halting of a governmental attempt to terminate all contractual responsibilities regarding Indian welfare.

Fey also brought the *Century* into the middle of the fight for civil rights. Even in its early years, the periodical had "displayed a sensitivity toward the Negro probably unmatched in any papers in the country, religious or secular."[12] Early in the emerging civil rights battle, the *Century* began publishing articles written by Martin Luther King, Jr. In its fiftieth anniversary issue in October 1958, the *Century* announced that King had accepted the invitation to become an editor at large. Further, in 1963, the periodical provided Americans with the first national publication of King's "Letter from Birmingham Jail." When Fey retired, he was replaced by Kyle Haselden. Haselden had recently written a book, *The Racial Problem in Christian Perspective*, and possessed strong credentials in the area of civil rights. Thus his leadership provided the *Century* with an educated and consistent position on this critical problem.

The combined leadership of Fey, Haselden, and Alan Geyer, Haselden's successor, moved the *Christian Century* toward a more sophisticated theological concern in ecumenical affairs. James Wall, the current *Century* editor, has continued this emphasis while stressing the periodical's status as a forum for open discussion of religious issues from various theological perspectives. Wall's direction has provided other than mainline voices—those from evangelicalism, for example—with an opportunity for expression. This shift away from the seemingly ideological posture of earlier years has helped to make the periodical truly ecumenical in the range of theological dialogue it addresses.

As an independent weekly possessed of a long and clearly distinguished tradition of religious journalism, the *Christian Century* is unsurpassed in its position as one of the most quoted Protestant periodicals. Its circulation, since the 1920s, has remained at between 35,000 and 40,000. Yet because of the large numbers of libraries that subscribe to the journal, the *Century* enjoys a much higher actual readership. Individual subscribers are generally religious professionals, either teachers in colleges and seminaries, or ordained and lay workers in the parish setting.

The *Christian Century* has long possessed one of the most perceptive and literate voices among Protestant publications. Always open and plain spoken, the periodical has consistently provided its readership with conscientious discussion of controversial issues. Further, its nondenominational status, its ecumenical concern, and its international focus have most certainly been factors in its ability to maintain the loyalty of its readers.

Notes

1. George A. Campbell, Jr., *Christian Oracle* 26 (23 November 1899): 4.
2. Robert Moats Miller, *American Protestantism and Social Issues, 1919–1939* (Chapel Hill: University of North Carolina Press, 1958), p. 59.
3. Martin E. Marty, "The Protestant Press: Limitations and Possibilities," in *The Religious Press in America*, ed. Martin E. Marty, John G. Deedy, Jr., David Wolf Silverman, and Robert Lekachman (New York: Holt, Rinehart and Winston, 1963), p. 59.
4. Charles Clayton Morrison, "Labor and the Federal Council of Churches" (26 December 1908), reprinted in *The Christian Century Reader*, ed. Harold E. Fey and Margaret Frakes (New York: Association Press, 1962), p. 273.
5. Miller, p. 247.
6. Ibid., p. 122.
7. Quoted in ibid, p. 122.
8. Morrison, "An Unnecessary Necessity" (17 December 1941), reprinted in *Christian Century Reader*, pp. 245–51.
9. See "Citizens or Subjects?" (29 April 1942), reprinted in *Christian Century Reader*, pp. 251–55.
10. Marty, p. 59.
11. Ibid., p. 60.
12. Miller, p. 312.

Information Sources

BIBLIOGRAPHY:
Delloff, Linda-Marie. "C. C. Morrison: Shaping a Journal's Identity." *Christian Century* 101 (18 January 1984): 43–57.
———. "The Century in Transition: 1916–1922." *Christian Century* 101 (7 March 1984): 243–46.
Fey, Harold E., and Margaret Frakes, eds. *The Christian Century Reader*. New York: Association Press, 1962.
———. *How I Read the Riddle: An Autobiography*. St. Louis: Bethany Press, 1982.
"Fiftieth Anniversary Issue." *Christian Century* 75 (8 October 1958).
Hefley, John Theodore. "The *Christian Century* in American Culture, 1920–1941." Ph.D. dissertation, University of Minnesota, 1953.
Marty, Martin E., et al. *The Religious Press in America*. New York: Holt, Rinehart and Winston, 1963.
Miller, Robert M. *American Protestantism and Social Issues, 1919–1939*. Chapel Hill: University of North Carolina Press, 1958.
"A Special Anniversary Issue." *Christian Century* 101 (12 October 1983).
Other selected issues in 101 (1984) contain articles dealing with the history of the *Christian Century*; each 1984 issue bears the subtitle, "Celebrating Our Centennial: 1884–1984." Archival materials for the *Christian Century* are housed in Special Collections, Morris Library, Southern Illinois University.

INDEX SOURCES: Self-indexed in the last issue of June and December annually; also in *Reader's Guide to Periodical Literature, Religion Index One, Religious and Theological Abstracts*; book reviews in *Book Review Digest* and *Book Review Index*; media reviews in *Media Review Digest*; poetry in *Index of American Periodical Verse*.

REPRINT EDITIONS: University Microfilms International, Bell and Howell Micro Photo Division.

LOCATION SOURCES: Partial collections widely available; *Union List of Serials* lists complete collections only at Andover-Harvard Theological Library and University of Vermont.

Publication History

MAGAZINE TITLE AND TITLE CHANGES: *Christian Oracle* (1884–99), *The Christian Century of the Disciples of Christ* (1899–1901), *The Christian Century* (1902–   ); absorbed *Christian Tribune* (1900), *Christian Work* (1926), *The Baptist* (1933), and *World Tomorrow* (1934).

VOLUME AND ISSUE DATA: *Christian Oracle* 1:1 (July 1884)–26:47 (November 1899), *The Christian Century of the Disciples of Christ* 26:48 (December 1899)–28:52 (December 1901), *The Christian Century* 29:1 (January 1902–   ). Appears weekly, except for the first two weeks of January and February, the last two weeks of March, the months of June, July, and August, the first three weeks of September, and the last two weeks of December when biweekly issues appear.

PUBLISHER AND PLACE OF PUBLICATION: Christian Century Foundation, Chicago.

EDITORS: Prior to 1908, editor information did not appear; Charles Clayton Morrison and Herbert L. Willett (1908–13), Charles Clayton Morrison (1913–47), Paul Hutchinson (1947–56), Harold E. Fey (1956–64), Kyle Haselden (1964–68), Kyle Haselden and Alan Geyer (1968), Alan Geyer (1968–72), Dean Peerman (1972), James M. Wall (1972–   ).

CIRCULATION: 40,000 (1984).

Mark G. Toulouse

THE CHRISTIAN CENTURY OF THE DISCIPLES OF CHRIST. *See* THE CHRISTIAN CENTURY

THE CHRISTIAN CENTURY PULPIT. *See* THE CHRISTIAN MINISTRY

CHRISTIAN EDUCATION. *See* SOUNDINGS

THE CHRISTIAN FRONT. *See* CHRISTIAN SOCIAL ACTION

THE CHRISTIAN MINISTRY

The milieu of 1969 is not what it was in 1929. The church is not what it was. The clergy are not what they were. The mission of the church requires a new style with new skills for its fulfillment. . . . We wonder about these things and the cluster of issues they portend. But wondering is not enough. We must assume risks, make decisions, render judgements, undertake commitments. . . . We believe that progress is made not by monological pronouncements but by dialogical sharing. We think the time has come for clergymen to reassess themselves—to determine who they are and what their roles are in a new day. Who can do that better than one clergyman in dialogue with another?[1]

With these words, printed in September 1969, Robert Graham Kemper simultaneously announced the "literary death" of the *Pulpit* and its resurrection ("that which was continues to be") in the form of the *Christian Ministry*. The *Pulpit*, founded in 1929 by Charles Clayton Morrison as the *Christian Century Pulpit* (the name was shortened in the spring of 1942), consistently devoted itself to bringing "inspiration to ministers" and to raising "the standard of preaching by presenting the best sermonic utterances of the contemporary pulpit."[2] Through its interdenominational approach to preaching, the *Pulpit* served its readership well.

Despite Morrison's pledge to "to keep the new periodical free from the illusion of great names" and his determination that the "periodical shall be a *finder* of great preachers," its pages were constantly graced with sermons of the great preachers of the period: Harry Emerson Fosdick, Ralph Sockman, Henry Sloane Coffin, George A. Buttrick, Clovis G. Chappell, John Haynes Holmes, Paul Scherer, Leslie Weatherhead, and Rufus Jones, to name just a few.[3] Thus, past issues of the *Pulpit* provide the researcher with a cornucopia of pulpit masters. Doubtless, many preachers were able to nourish themselves and their congregations as a result of this sermonic horn of plenty.

Ironically, if one applies the traditional standard of success (retention of readership mixed with a gradual increase of subscriptions), the *Pulpit* was a journalistic failure. Further, if one accepts the criteria established by Morrison in his opening editorial as a standard, the journal not only failed, it failed abysmally. According to Morrison, "We shall not be satisfied until the new periodical is found on the study table of at least 75,000 of the 100,000 ministers in American and Canadian Protestantism."[4] Even allowing for editorial hyperbole, Morrison's hopes remained unfulfilled.

Because of its sibling relationship with the *Christian Century*,* the inaugural issue was mailed to 20,000 charter subscribers. Readership leveled off rather quickly to a little over half that figure; however, once the leveling process was completed, the journal maintained a respectable readership numbering over 12,000 for 40 years.

Given the faithful audience enjoyed by the *Pulpit*, the move to a new format represented a risky venture. As Robert G. Middleton, editor of the *Pulpit*, expressed it, "Always there will be those who prefer to have things kept the way they are. In our case we are sure that there will be some who will regret and oppose the change we are going to make."[5] This prediction proved to be true. By 1971, one-third of the *Pulpit's* subscribers allowed their subscriptions to lapse. The *Christian Ministry* has yet to regain the readership held by the *Pulpit* at the time the transition was made.

Alan Geyer, president of the Christian Century Foundation from 1968 to 1972, was the prime mover behind the decision to introduce the *Christian Ministry*. He wanted to produce a magazine concerned with the whole of pastoral ministry. Throughout the 1960s American society went through a period of social upheaval, which left its mark on the parish ministry. The tendency toward activism that emerged as a result of issues like the Vietnam war and civil rights cut ministers loose from the conventional moorings of ministry inside the church. Middleton, looking forward to the advent of *Ministry*, commented:

The old image of the pastor as a kindly and benevolent person, deeply interested in good causes, but somewhat isolated from contact with life's grubby realities is giving way. He is now the activist, and there is little reason to believe this is going to change in the foreseeable future.[6]

Preaching was no longer viewed as the single vital function of the contemporary minister. The *Pulpit*, reasoned Geyer, needed to be replaced by a professional magazine that would address the changed nature of the ministerial vocation. What better way to begin than to use the subscriber list of the *Pulpit*?

Geyer hoped to involve other organizations committed to ministry in the project. A meeting was called to discuss the possibilities. The New York office of Jack Biersdorf of the National Council of Church's Department of Ministry provided the setting. Besides Geyer and Biersdorf, Reuel Howe of the Institute for Advanced Pastoral Studies, Connolly Gamble of the Society for the Advancement of Continuing Education for Ministry (SACEM), Edgar "Ted" Mills (editor of the National Council of Churches' quarterly entitled *Ministry Studies*), and Robert G. Kemper (pastor in Montclair, New Jersey) attended. Kemper emerged as leader of the project.

Bob Kemper found his heart "strangely warmed" by Geyer's proposal. As with John Wesley, the sensation led to commitment. He became the magazine's first editor. Kemper knew from experience that support systems for activist ministers were virtually nonexistent.[7] *Life* magazine picked up on this problem in an article entitled "Crunch in the Churches," which noted that congregations were splitting over the new style of ministry.[8] Disillusioned and cynical ministers were leaving the church altogether. From Kemper's vantage point, something had to be done.

After the initial meeting, Kemper spent hours attempting to work through the problem of how a new journal might best address the crisis facing the ministerial profession.[9] His conclusions were published in his first editorial:

> We intend to be an advocate of ministry. We want to amplify the call to do it. We want to broadcast to an entire profession the risks and the progress of our common venture. Presuming to know the angel's side, we want to celebrate what is good and deplore what is not. But most of all, we want to minister to ministers. We want to instruct, exhort, provoke, criticize, heal, expose, console, and surprise our readers. Whatever we do, our intention is to advance the practice of ministry.[10]

Not all who attended the initial meeting shared Kemper's enthusiasm. Geyer's hope was to involve all the institutions represented in financial support of the project. None was forthcoming. As a result, the *Christian Ministry* has never attained the stature its founders intended. When Jim Wall became editor in 1973, the ship was sinking. As Kemper has pointed our, "During its first four years, *Ministry* was a drain on the foundations's resources."[11] Both the *Century* and *Ministry* were in danger of going under. As if things were not bleak enough, Kemper contracted an eye disease, which left him legally blind.

Wall assumed control of both publications. Essentially he saved the *Century* by making *Ministry* a self-supporting magazine. The staff was cut back. No articles were solicited, and many articles intended for the *Century* began to appear in *Ministry*. Naturally, these changes affected the quality of *Ministry*. No one single person was giving the magazine undivided attention. However, readership remained constant, and *Ministry* stopped losing money.

Although the *Christian Ministry* never developed into the forceful influence coveted by its originators, it has served as a valuable resource for those in the ministerial vocation. The closing paragraph of Kemper's initial editorial captures the philosophy of *Ministry* throughout its existence: "Our reach may extend our grasp, but we would rather endure muscle strain than suffer atrophy. The faith and the profession deserve at least that."[12]

Notes

1. Robert G. Kemper, "Ministry Begins at 40," *Pulpit* 40 (September 1969): 3.

2. Charles Clayton Morrison, "Event of the Month," *Christian Century Pulpit* 1 (October 1929): 23.

3. Ibid.

4. Ibid.

5. Robert G. Middleton, *Pulpit* 40 (July–August 1969): 3.

6. Ibid. (April 1969): 3.

7. Robert G. Kemper, "Reflections on a Decade," *Christian Ministry* 10 (November 1979): 5–8.

8. "Crunch in the Churches," *Life*, 4 October 1968, pp. 79–84.

9. Kemper, "Reflections," p. 7.

10. Robert G. Kemper, "What Are We For," *Christian Ministry* 1 (November 1969): 5.
11. Kemper, "Reflections," p. 7.
12. Kemper, "What Are We For," p. 5.

Information Sources

BIBLIOGRAPHY:
Christian Century Foundation Collection, Morris Library, Special Collections, Southern Illinois University, Carbondale, Ill.
Kemper, Robert G. *An Elephant's Ballet*. New York: Seabury Press, 1977.
———. "Reflections on a Decade." *Christian Ministry* 10 (November 1979): 5–8.
Morrison, Charles Clayton, ed. *The American Pulpit*. New York: Macmillan, 1925.
INDEX SOURCES: *Religion Index One, Guide to Social Science and Religion in Periodical Literature*.
REPRINT EDITIONS: University Microfilms International.
LOCATION SOURCES: Brigham Young University, Hartford Seminary Foundation, Library of Congress, University of Chicago, and others.

Publication History

MAGAZINE TITLE AND TITLE CHANGES: *Christian Century Pulpit* (1929–42), *The Pulpit* (1942–69), *The Christian Ministry* (1969–   ).
VOLUME AND ISSUE DATA: *Christian Century Pulpit* 1:1–13:3 (October 1929-April 1942), *The Pulpit* 13:4–40:8 (May 1942-October 1969), *The Christian Ministry* 40:9 (November 1969–   ). Bimonthly.
PUBLISHER AND PLACE OF PUBLICATION: Christian Century Foundation, Chicago.
EDITORS: Charles Clayton Morrison (1929–55), Theodore A. Gill (1956–60), Kyle Haselden (1960–68), Robert G. Middleton (1968–69), Robert G. Kemper (1969–73), James M. Wall (1973–   ).
CIRCULATION: 10,000 (1982).

Mark G. Toulouse

CHRISTIAN ORACLE. *See* THE CHRISTIAN CENTURY

THE CHRISTIAN REGISTER. *See* THE INDEX

CHRISTIAN SCHOLAR. *See* SOUNDINGS

CHRISTIAN SCHOLAR'S REVIEW

In February 1955, the *Gordon Review* was launched by the faculties of Gordon College and Seminary (Wenham, Massachusetts). The *Review*, disclaiming any official connection with these institutions, was, however, "an independent effort spontaneously undertaken'' by its faculties.[1] The goal of the *Review*, as stated by Lloyd F. Dean in his inaugural editorial, was to ''bring together the various disciplines that they may be seen as only individual aspects of the one truth.''[2] As an evangelical publication, the *Review* intended to examine the liberal arts and sciences from the perspective that all truth is God's truth. ''Knowledge is one,'' wrote Dean. ''There is no field of investigation which can be successfully and ultimately isolated from the other disciplines which go to make up the totality of man's knowledge-experience.''[3] Recognizing the isolation of the various disciplines, the new editor hoped the *Review* would become part of ''a new period of vigor of thought and expression which will challenge the mind of the world to consider seriously and prayerfully the claim of Christ in every aspect of life and culture.''[4]

Although the goals of the *Gordon Review* were broadly conceived, the intended audience was the past and present Gordon community. Dean expressed hope that the *Review* would attract readers in New England and the nation at large, but clearly the primary audience was the Gordon constituency. The *Review* would be a means of maintaining ties with Gordon students and graduates: ''Our students will have the opportunity to acquaint themselves with scholarly material in the various fields . . . written by men with whom they are, in many cases, already acquainted.''[5]

However inauspicious its beginnings, the *Gordon Review* signaled the maturing of the evangelical community. Just as the nation in general experienced a boom in higher education in the 1950s, so did the Christian liberal arts colleges, many of which had their origins as Bible schools during the fundamentalist-modernist controversy of the 1920s. Until the *Gordon Review*, there was no vehicle for scholarly evangelical expression, theological journals excepted. ''This is a scholarly review,'' contended Dean, *''from the perspective of the historic Christian faith,''* in which theology would have a place ''as one discipline among others.''[6]

Response to the first issue of the *Review* was so favorable that the editor asked readers to return back issues for recirculation. Contributors to the first few numbers of this quarterly journal were almost entirely Gordon faculty members, but within the first year a spate of articles appeared written by academics from other evangelical institutions. An article by Richard K. Curtis from Bethel College (St. Paul, Minnesota) entitled ''Language and Theology: Some Basic Considerations'' (1:3), touched off an extended controversy when Roger Nicole (Gordon Seminary) and Gordon H. Clark (Butler University) took issue with Curtis's statement regarding the reliability of Scripture. Curtis contended that ''to label the Scriptures *as we have them* as the *Absolute* word of God is to hold a position completely untenable in view of but a cursory examination of the evidence.''[7] Charges and countercharges were parried back and forth until the controversy was finally dropped.

More in keeping with the masthead that appeared a decade later—''A Christian Quarterly of the Arts and Sciences''—were articles on such topics as ''Characteristics of a Christian College'' by Hudson T. Armerding (later of Wheaton

College, Illinois), "The Place of Drama in a Christian College" by Miriam Rose Bonner, "The Christian in the World" by historian W. Stanford Reid of McGill University, "Anthropology in the Christian College" by James O. Buswell III, and "Aesthetics and Church Music" by frequent contributor Arthur Holmes. These kinds of articles dealt with integrating a particular academic discipline with evangelical Christianity. In the years following, many of the early contributors to the *Gordon Review* became leading spokespersons within the evangelical academic community.

Several issues have been thematic, such as the Calvin commemorative in 1959, an issue on African nationalism and missions, and a special feature on missionary outreach.[8] Most of the *Review* issues, however, contained four or five unrelated articles. A book review and books received section appended the main body of articles.

In the fall of 1970, the *Christian Scholar's Review* succeeded the *Gordon Review*. At this time Gordon College and Seminary were in the midst of severing their ties with each other, and in order to avoid legal entanglements, *Gordon* was dropped. Additionally, the name change conveyed a less parochial image, though the *Christian Scholar's Review* remained true to the philosophy of its predecessor. Fifteen Christian liberal arts colleges sponsored the fledgling journal, a move that broadened the financial basis of support.[9]

Coinciding with the separation of the Gordon schools was the acceptance by George K. Brushaber, a former editor of the *Gordon Review*, of an academic post at Westmont College (California). Largely because of his initiative, the *Christian Scholar's Review* was launched. In becoming the new journal's first editor, Brushaber moved the publication to the West Coast.

A statement of purpose on the inside cover of the new quarterly summarized the intention of its sponsors:

> The Christian scholar, experiencing the redemptive love of God and welcoming the enriching perspective of divine revelation, accepts as part of his vocation the obligation not only to pursue his academic discipline but also to contribute toward a broader and more unified understanding of life and the world. His vocation therefore includes the obligation to communicate his understanding to the Christian community and to the entire world of learning.
>
> The *Christian Scholar's Review* is intended as a medium through which Christian scholars may cooperate in pursuing these facets of their tasks. Specifically, this publication has as its primary objective the integration of Christian faith and learning on both the intra- and inter-disciplinary levels. As a secondary purpose, this journal seeks to provide a forum for the discussion of the theoretical issues of Christian higher education. The *Review* is intended to encourage communication and understanding both among Christian scholars, and between them and others.[10]

During Brushaber's eight-year tenure as editor and publisher, the journal assumed a format different from that of the *Gordon Review*. Roughly half of the *Review* included articles, discussion, and on occasion, symposia, while the remainder consisted of an expanded book review section. In addition, the content of the articles in the *Christian Scholar's Review* was more scholarly than those in the *Gordon Review*. Most were written by scholars in the fields of philosophy, theology, history, science, and literature.

A double issue considered the tensions between psychology and Christianity, and the integration of sociology and Christianity was the featured theme in another issue.[11] Theoretical issues of Christian higher education received continuing attention.[12] The symposia section considered contemporary issues from several scholars' viewpoints. A recent issue featured a position paper on nuclear arms policy with two respondents.[13] On occasion, book review articles of three to four pages preceded the book review section. Of particular interest was the decade-long dialogue between Ernest Sandeen and George Marsden over defining fundamentalism and tracing its history. Marsden began the exchange by reviewing Sandeen's *The Roots of Fundamentalism* (1970), and Sandeen concluded it with his review of Marsden's *Fundamentalism and American Culture* (1980).[14]

Contributors to the *Christian Scholar's Review* are not exclusively conservative Protestants, nor are its present sponsoring institutions exclusively conservative Protestant ones. Still, most articles are written by those representing the evangelical strain. Since 1978, Clifton Orlebeke of Calvin College has served as editor. Few substantive changes have taken place under his guidance.

Notes

1. Lloyd F. Dean, "Editorial: A New Journal," *Gordon Review* 1, reprinted in *Gordon Review* 8:3–4 (Winter 1964–65): 59.

2. Ibid., p. 62.

3. Ibid., p. 61.

4. Ibid., p. 60.

5. Ibid.

6. Ibid.

7. On this controversy, see *Gordon Review* 1:4 (December 1955); 2:1 (February 1956); 2:4 (December 1956); 3:1 (February 1957); 3:2 (May 1957); 3:4 (December 1957).

8. Ibid. 5:4 (Winter 1959); 7:1 (Fall 1963); 9:1 (Fall 1965).

9. The *Christian Scholar's Review*'s first sponsors were Anderson College, Barrington College, Bethel College (Minnesota), Calvin College, Geneva College, Gordon College, Houghton College, Northwestern College (Iowa), Nyack College, Spring Arbor College, Taylor University, Trinity Christian College, Trinity College (Illinois), Westmont College, and Wheaton College (Illinois).

10. The statement of purpose appears on the inside cover of each issue.

11. *Christian Scholar's Review* 8:1–2 (Fall-Winter 1977); 10:3 (Spring 1979).

12. For examples, see Edmund Clowney, "The Christian College and the Transformation of Culture," *Christian Scholar's Review* 1:1 (Fall 1970): 5–18; Nicholar Wolterstorff, "Academic Freedom in the Christian College," *Christian Scholar's Review* 1:2

(Winter 1970): 99–108; William Hasker, "Academic Freedom: Secular and/or Christian," *Christian Scholar's Review* 2:2 (Winter 1971): 127–31; James Steven Counelis, "The American Christian University: A Position Paper," *Christian Scholar's Review* 2:3 (Spring 1972): 236–41; Walter C. Hobbs, "On the Necessity and Feasibility of Conflict among Christian Faculty," *Christian Scholar's Review* 4:2 (Winter 1973): 134–39; James W. Skillen, "Theology, Philosophy, and the Christian Liberal Arts College," *Christian Scholar's Review* 5:3 (Spring 1975): 241–51; Mark A. Noll, "Christian Thinking and the Rise of the American University," *Christian Scholar's Review* 9 (Fall 1978): 3–16.

  13. *Christian Scholar's Review* 12:3 (1982).

  14. See George M. Marsden, "Defining Fundamentalism," *Christian Scholar's Review* 1:1 (Fall 1970): 141–51; Ernest Sandeen, "Defining Fundamentalism: A Reply to Prof. Marsden," *Christian Scholar's Review* 1:3 (Spring 1971): 227–33; and Sandeen's review of Marsden's *Fundamentalism and American Culture, Christian Scholar's Review* 10:3 (Spring 1980): 255–58.

Information Sources

INDEX SOURCES: *Gordon Review*: *Christian Periodical Index, Abstracts of English Studies, New Testament Abstracts, Religious and Theological Abstracts. Christian Scholar's Review*: *American Literature Abstracts, Bibliography of English Language and Literature, Journal of Ecumenical Studies, New Testament Abstracts, Religious and Theological Abstracts, PMLA* (bibliography).

LOCATION SOURCES: *Gordon Review*: Library of Congress, University of Chicago, New York Public Library, Gordon College, Pacific School of Religion, McCormick Theological Seminary, Goshen College Biblical Seminary, Concordia Theological Seminary, Union Theological Seminary (Virginia). *Christian Scholar's Review*: Gordon College, Union Theological Seminary (New York City), Yale University, University of Massachusetts, George Washington University, Auburn University, University of Oklahoma, and others.

Publication History

MAGAZINE TITLE AND TITLE CHANGES: *Gordon Review* (1955–70), *Christian Scholar's Review* (1970–   ).

VOLUME AND ISSUE DATA: *The Gordon Review* 1–3:1–4 (February, May, September, December 1955–57), 4–5:1–4 (Spring, Summer, Fall, Winter 1957–59), 6:1 ("1st issue 1960–61"), 6:2–3 (Winter 1961); 4 (Winter 1962–63), 7:1 (Fall 1963), 7:2–3 (double issue, Winter 1963–64), 7:4 (Summer 1964), 8:1 (Fall 1964), 8:2–3 (double issue, Winter 1964–65), 8:4 (Spring 1965), 9:1 (Fall 1965), 9:2–3 (Winter 1966), 9:4 (Spring 1966), 10:1 (Fall 1966), 10:2 (Winter 1967), 10:3 (Summer 1967), 10:4 (Fall 1967), 11:1 (Winter 1968), 11:2 (Spring 1968), 11:3 (Fall 1968), 11:4 (Summer 1969), 11:5 (Spring 1970); *Christian Scholar's Review* 1:1 (Fall 1970–   ). Published quarterly.

PUBLISHER AND PLACE OF PUBLICATION: Gordon College and Divinity School Faculties, Wenham, Mass. (*Gordon Review*); George K. Brushaber, Westmont College, Calif. (*Christian Scholar's Review*, 1970–76), J. Edward Hakes, Trinity College, Ill. (*Christian Scholar's Review*, 1977), Edward H. Pauley (*Christian Scholar's Review*, 1978–80), Thomas A. Askew, Jr., Gordon College, Wenham, Mass. (1980–   ).

EDITORS: Lloyd F. Dean (*Gordon Review*, 1955–56), Charles A. Huttar (*Gordon Review*, 1957), Lloyd F. Dean (*Gordon Review*, 1958), Charles A. Huttar (*Gordon Review*, 1959), Board of Editors (*Gordon Review*, 1960–70), George K. Brushaber (*Christian Scholar's Review*, 1970–78), Clifton Orlebeke (*Christian Scholar's Review*, 1978–).
CIRCULATION: 4000 (1983).

David Kling

THE CHRISTIAN SCIENCE JOURNAL. *See* THE CHRISTIAN SCIENCE MONITOR

THE CHRISTIAN SCIENCE MONITOR

A new religion was born in Lynn, Massachusetts, in 1866, when Mary Baker Eddy attributed her sudden recovery from a back injury to be confirmation of a scientific principle of healing that she had detected in the Bible. A former patient of New England mesmerist-healer Phineas Parkhurst Quimby and a convert to his theory that disease is essentially a trick upon the mind, Eddy spent the next 10 years refining her ideas. In 1875 she published *Science and Health*, in which she claimed that matter was unreal (the body, disease, and death were illusions) and that all phenomena harmonized in "Mind." In that same year, she organized public religious services in Massachusetts, and the new religion, Christian Science, began to attract followers. The movement was widely criticized, and in 1878, Eddy determined that a public defense of Christian Science was necessary:

> We have not a newspaper at our command through which to right the wrongs and answer the untruths, we have not a pulpit from which to explain how Christian Science heals the sick, but if we had either of these, the slanderer and the physician would have less to do, and we should have more.[1]

Eddy's concern was not limited to a defensive campaign. When she launched the *Journal of Christian Science* five years later, she stressed as well the active, constructive role the publication would play:

> After looking over the newspapers of the day, very naturally comes the reflection that it is dangerous to live, so loaded seems the very air with disease. These descriptions carry fears to many minds, to be depicted in some future time upon the body. This error we shall in great measure be able to counteract.[2]

Under Eddy's editorship, the monthly *Christian Science Journal* (as it was called beginning in April 1885) printed testimonials, poems, and articles that explained Christian Science doctrine and met the charges of critics. A column entitled "Animal Magnetism" was introduced in 1886 and advised readers on another sort of defense. According to Eddy, malicious animal magnetism (or MAM) was an invisible force that stole into the human body, especially during sleep or at other times when a person's guard was down, and caused physical illness. Moreover, MAM could lead to errors in thought; inability to see that matter was an illusion was often attributed to its influence. The monthly "Animal Magnetism" columns explained how to identify and defend against this danger.

After James Henry Wiggins, an ex-Unitarian minister and nonbeliever, was hired as editor in 1886, the *Journal* began to take on a more sophisticated look. In the 1890s and early 1900s, under the editorships of Septimius J. Hanna and Archibald McClellan, the upgrading was continued. In addition to testimonials to the curative powers of Christian Science and comments on MAM, the *Journal* published a body of articles on two issues: the "labor-capital conflict" and the scientific character of Christian Science. Commentary on the former issue took a point of view reflective of the values of the church's middle-class membership.[3] Conspicuous in the articles on labor and capital was a vision of the middle class under attack from below and above. The social body, like the physical body, could be threatened by powerful disruptive forces. The *Journal* lamented the error of mind that "leads the mortal who has too much to accumulate more, and causes the mortal who has too little to try to plunder his neighbor."[4] On the one hand, the seeming impatience in the demands of organized labor was a threat to the social order. Because "secure progress cannot be assured through rapid and unordered chance," Christian Science "will steady the revolutionary purpose, and take from the vengeful hand of the 'white slaves' the weapon of retaliation, that the fair morning of labor's long delayed millennium may not be sullied by blood."[5] On the other hand, it was pointed out that "no successful business is carried on without a certain amount of systematic conformity to the rules of order," and a "desire to monopolize from business transactions" was surely a breach of those rules, an attempt to undermine opportunity for others to advance.[6]

Other *Journal* articles drew religious lessons from scientific discoveries. New theories in atomic physics were interpreted as scientific support for certain Christian Science beliefs. Einstein's theory of the equatability of mass with energy was particularly compatible with Eddy's own claim that matter was only a misapprehension of mind. Articles such as "Methods of Reasoning Used in Christian Science" served to inform *Journal* readers of advances in physics and mathematics and to argue such theses as the following: "Like pure mathematics, Christian Science is a system of deductive reasoning."[7]

Eventually it became apparent to Eddy that the *Journal* was not reaching a large enough audience. Her thinking on the matter crystalized when John L.

Wright, a Christian Scientist and Chicago newspaperman, wrote to Eddy in 1908 suggesting that the church publish a daily newspaper in Boston. Eddy responded with the following message:

> I have had this newspaper scheme in my thought for quite a while and herein send my name for our daily newspaper
> *The Christian Science Monitor*
> This title only classifies the paper and it should have departments for what else is requisite.[8]

Eddy soon after set the wheels in motion for the publication of the *Monitor*; the first issue appeared on 25 November 1908. Eddy had intended that the *Monitor* evince high journalistic standards, that it be moderate and constructive rather than sensationalist, and that religious articles be regularly included but limited in number. The *Monitor* was to report news of uplifting events from around the world, to analyze ideas and culture critically, and, most important, "to spread undivided the Science that operates unspent."[9] While similar in purpose to the *Journal*, the *Monitor* thus differed in strategy. Publication of positive news, rather than personal testimonials, was to be the primary means by which it impressed on its readers the harmony of reality. Indeed, editor McClellan was successful from the beginning in achieving the requisite soothing tone for the paper, as the *New York Herald* observed: "Readers afflicted with heart trouble may open up the newspaper with absolute safety."[10]

In its first few months, the *Monitor* included on its editorial page essays with explicitly religious themes; however, after 23 April 1909, all references to Christian Science were confined to a section entitled "The Home Forum." Generally a full page in length, "The Home Forum" included poems, essays, and reproductions of art exemplifying or illuminating Christian Science doctrines. The Christian Science point of view continued to shape other stories in the paper. For example, weather reports could not be found in the paper in 1909–10. Weather, as an aspect of matter, was an illusion, and it was therefore unscientific to draw attention to it. On Eddy's instructions, a section entitled "Weather Predictions" was later added. It was apparently felt that this nomenclature was less offensive to church doctrine.

The stance the *Monitor* took on certain political issues, and on the matter of prohibition in particular, is also demonstrative of its Christian Science viewpoint. Christian Scientists believe that alcohol, as well as tobacco and drugs, are not only harmful to the body but are injurious to a person's spiritual welfare as well. In the 1920s, when the repeal of national prohibition was a constant issue, the *Monitor* consistently beseeched voters to elect candidates who supported prohibition. Such encouragement took the form of editorial comment, as well as articles refuting claims made by pollsters that opposition to repeal was waning.[11]

Mary Baker Eddy claimed to be little interested in politics: "I have none, in reality, other than to support a righteous government, to love God supremely, and my neighbor as myself.''[12] The *Monitor*, with some exceptions, has been nonpartisan. With regard to international politics, it has been guided from its beginning by a concern for world unity. The first issue of the *Monitor*, 18 pages available for two cents at the newsstand, contained articles on the Philippines, China, Canada, the Balkans, Russian language courses at the University of Michigan, and the popularity of baseball in the Orient.[13] Occasionally, however, application of the Christian Science doctrine of harmony to an understanding of international affairs has led to a naive position. For example, on 7 June 1941, while the world witnessed the escalation of warfare in Europe and the Pacific, the *Monitor* ran the following headlines: ''Americans Set for Gala Vacation Year—Travel Links Unity of Western Hemisphere.''

Other *Monitor* articles have been more thoughtful. In the aftermath of World War I, the *Monitor* published an editorial proposing that world peace might best be ensured by the passage of a constitutional amendment through which ''all possibility of wartime profit would be eliminated'' from wartime economy.[14]

After Mary Baker Eddy died in 1910, the trustees of the Publishing Society, the corporation responsible for publishing the *Monitor*, claimed independence from the editorial supervision of the board of directors of the Mother Church. Sensing disloyalty on the part of the trustees, church members withdrew advertising and cancelled subscriptions; between 1919 and 1922, circulation dropped from 123,000 to 20,000. The courts eventually ruled that the Publishing Society was legally bound to conform to the wishes of the board of directors, and the paper recovered.[15]

Since World War II the *Montior*, which bears the subtitle *An International Daily Newspaper*, has acquired a reputation for high journalistic and artistic standards and has received numerous awards, including the Pulitzer Prize and the N. W. Ayer Cup. In addition to its coverage of world events, the *Monitor* includes sections on business, sports, real estate, the arts, and a foreign language translation of a religious article in ''The Home Forum.'' The ''Opinion and Commentary'' section often includes columns by university professors and government experts. In general, the *Monitor* has become a more lively paper than it was under McClellan but is still moderate in its presentation of the news, still faithful to Eddy's vision.

Although the *Monitor* has replaced the *Journal* as the chief voice of Christian Science, the latter publication still fulfills an important in-house function. In addition to several short devotional articles, each issue contains the names of all Christian Science practitioners.

Notes

1. Mary Baker Eddy, *Science and Health with Key to the Scriptures*, 2d ed. (Lynn, Mass.: A. G. Eddy, 1878), p. 166.

2. *Christian Science Journal* 1 (April 1883): 3.

3. Stephen Gottschalk, *The Emergence of Christian Science in American Life* (Berkeley: University of California Press, 1973), p. 256; Harold W. Pfautz, ''Christian Science:

The Sociology of a 'Social Movement and Religious Group' '' (Ph.D. dissertation, University of Chicago, 1954).

4. *Christian Science Journal* 20 (November 1902): 465.

5. Ibid. 26 (September 1908): 342–43.

6. Ibid. 25 (February 1908): 643, 12 (February 1895): 479.

7. Clarence A. Buskirk, ''Methods of Reasoning Used in Christian Science'' *Christian Science Journal* 21 (October 1904): 404–5.

8. Quoted in Robert Peel, *Mary Baker Eddy: The Years of Authority* (New York: Holt, Rinehart, and Winston, 1977), p. 309.

9. Mary Baker Eddy, *The First Church of Christ Scientist and Miscellany* (Boston: Published by the Trustees under will of Mary Baker Eddy, 1913), p. 353.

10. Quoted in Erwin Canham, *Commitment to Freedom: The Story of the Christian Science Monitor* (Boston: Houghton/Mifflin, 1958), p. 84.

11. *Christian Science Monitor*, 7 October 1924, editorial page; *Christian Science Monitor*, 4 October 1924, editorial page.

12. *Miscellany*, p. 276.

13. *Christian Science Monitor*, 25 November 1908.

14. Ibid., 15 November 1923: 18.

15. Canham, *Commitment*, p. 397; Charles S. Braden, *Christian Science Today* (Dallas: Southern Methodist University Press, 1958), pp. 61–95.

Information Sources

BIBLIOGRAPHY:

Braden, Charles. *Christian Science Today*. Dallas: Southern Methodist University Press, 1958.

Canham, Erwin. *Commitment to Freedom: The Story of the Christian Science Monitor*. Boston: Houghton/Mifflin, 1958.

Gottschalk, Stephen. *The Emergence of Christian Science in American Life*. Berkeley: University of California Press, 1973.

Peel, Robert. *Mary Baker Eddy: The Years of Discovery*. New York: Holt, Rinehart, and Winston, 1956.

———. *Mary Baker Eddy: The Years of Trial*. New York: Holt, Rinehart, and Winston, 1971.

———. *Mary Baker Eddy: The Years of Authority*. New York: Holt, Rinehart, and Winston, 1977.

INDEX SOURCES: DeWitt Talmage Finley, *Practitioners and Students Index of a Selection of Articles Which Have Been Published in the Christian Science Journal and the Christian Science Sentinel* (Tulsa: Index Publishing Co., 1932); Helen M. Cropsey, ed., *The Christian Science Monitor Indexes* (Corvallis, Oregon: H. M. Cropsey, 1960–   ).

LOCATION SOURCES: *Christian Science Journal*: New York Public Library, Library of Congress, Union Theological Seminary (New York), Wisconsin State Historical Society (Madison). *Christian Science Monitor*: Los Angeles Public Library, Rosenberg Library (Galveston, Texas), Boston Public Library, State Library of Massachusetts (Boston), Cornell University, New York Public Library, Wisconsin State Historical Society (Madison).

Publication History

MAGAZINE TITLE AND TITLE CHANGES: *The Journal of Christian Science* (1883–85), *The Christian Science Journal* (1885–   ), *The Christian Science Monitor* (1908–   ).

VOLUME AND ISSUE DATA: *Journal of Christian Science* 1–3 (April 1883-March 1885), *Christian Science Journal* 3- (March 1885–   ), *Christian Science Monitor* 1- (November 1908–   ).

PUBLISHER AND PLACE OF PUBLICATION: Christian Science Publishing Society, Boston (*Journal of Christian Science*, *Christian Science Journal*, and *Christian Science Monitor*).

EDITORS: *Christian Science Journal*: Mary Baker Eddy (1883–84), Emma Hopkins (1884–86), James Gill (1886), James Henry Wiggin (1886–89), Joshua P. Bailey (1889–92), Julia Field-King (1892), Septimius J. Hanna (1892–1902), Archibald McClellan (1902–8). *Christian Science Monitor*: Archibald McClellan (1908–14), Frederick Dixon (1914–22), Willis J. Abbott (1922–27), Frank Perrin (1927–34), Rose Drummond (1934–40), Erwin Canham (1940–64), John Dewitt (1964–70), John Hughes (1971–79), Earl Foell (1979–83), Kay Fanning (1983–   ).

CIRCULATION: *Christian Science Monitor*: 149,913 (1983).

John Corrigan

CHRISTIAN SOCIAL ACTION

The publication of the *Christian Front* (the name was later changed to *Christian Social Action*) in January 1936 represented an effort on the part of Richard Deverall (1911–80), who was to become the guiding spirit of the magazine, and two associates to establish "a lay Catholic magazine for intellectuals" which could provide "a framework for social Catholicism."[1] Influenced by Dorothy Day (1899–1980) and the Catholic Worker movement, Thomistic social ethics, and a desire to live out the social implications of the Mass, the magazine sought to interpret a social gospel for American Roman Catholicism.

The *Christian Front* appeared monthly at a time when many of the barriers constraining Roman Catholic participation in American life were eroding. It sought simultaneously to identify with the awakened social conscience of the secular-based New Deal and to assert a theistic and Catholic grounding for federal policies directed toward alleviating the economic distress of the Great Depression. It was especially supportive of the labor union movement and the Congress of Industrial Organizations. Thus it sought to convey substantive continuities with the direction of public policy, as well as to vindicate a distinctive Roman Catholic tradition that asserted social solidarity over and against laissez-faire individualism.

In many respects, Deverall presupposed the foundation laid by the work of the Reverend John A. Ryan (1869–1945), professor of political economy and moral theology at the Catholic University of America, who had been the author of the (Roman Catholic) Bishops' Program of Social Reconstruction (1919) and the director of the National Catholic Welfare Conference. Ryan had been the most influential interpreter of the papal social encyclicals, *Rerum Novarum* (1891) and *Quadragesimo Anno* (1931), both of which addressed the relation of Roman Catholic thought to the conflicts of modern industrial development. Deverall himself attributed a more direct stimulus to the work of the "radio priest," the Reverend Charles Coughlin (1891–1979) of Royal Oak, Michigan, whose weekly broadcasts protesting the "unchristian character of the nation's economic and political life" reached millions during the early 1930s.[2]

The *Christian Front*, while sympathetic with the reformist ethos of the New Deal on domestic issues, became more critical of what it discerned as increasing tendencies toward militarism and interventionism in the late 1930s. In so doing it lost support from Ryan, among others.

The magazine, which never had more than a few hundred subscribers, reached many in leadership positions in the Roman Catholic Church, as well as in secular and religious print media. Initially published at Villanova, Pennsylvania, it moved its offices in September 1939 to Detroit under the aegis of Archbishop (later Cardinal) Edward Mooney (1882–1958). At the same time the name of the magazine was changed in response to the use of the name "Christian Front" by another group influenced by Coughlin, which had begun to disseminate harshly anti-Semitic views. Confusing the two groups, many of Deverall's supporters had withdrawn support and cancelled subscriptions.

In Detroit Deverall became involved in the publication of the *Michigan Labor Leader* (later the *Wage Earner*) and also served as executive secretary to the Association of Christian Trade Unionists. Consequently there was less time for *Christian Social Action*. Six months after the Japanese attack on Pearl Harbor in December 1941, Deverall, who amended his conscientious objection application to include the qualification that he would not take up arms "unless my country is attacked by an external foe," prepared to enter military service, and the magazine ceased independent publication.

From the beginning Deverall had been motivated by a longing to rediscover and communicate a Roman Catholic social ethic applicable to the situation obtaining in the United States during the 1930s. His use of the encyclicals was an important foundation for establishing the relevance of Roman Catholicism to modern economic life. Reflecting the influence of the liturgist Dom Virgil Michel (1890–1938) of St. John's Abbey, Collegeville, Minnesota, Deverall framed the conjunction of liturgy and ethics as "prayer, action and sacrifice"—the essence of Catholic action—anticipating important developments in subsequent American Roman Catholic history.[3]

Notes

1. Richard L.-G. Deverall, "The Way It Was," *Social Order* 11:7 (1961): 302.
2. Deverall, *Social Order*, 11:4 (1961): 199; and David J. O'Brien, *American Catholics and Social Reform* (New York: Oxford University Press, 1968) p. 152.
3. Deverall, *Social Order* 12:4 (1962): 183.

Information Sources

BIBLIOGRAPHY:
Abell, Aaron, I. *American Catholicism: A Search for Social Justice*. Garden City: Doubleday, 1960.
Flynn, George Q. *American Catholics and the Roosevelt Presidency: The New Deal Years*. Lexington: University of Kentucky Press, 1968.
O'Brien, David J. *American Catholics and Social Reform, 1932–1936*. New York: Oxford University Press, 1968.
INDEX SOURCES: None.
LOCATION SOURCES: Catholic University of America, Fordham University, Library of Congress, St. John's University (Collegeville), St. Louis University, University of Detroit, and others.

Publication History

MAGAZINE TITLE AND TITLE CHANGES: *The Christian Front* (1936–39), *Christian Social Action* (1939–42).
VOLUME AND ISSUE DATA: *Christian Front* 1:1–4:6 (January 1936-August 1939); *Christian Social Action* 4:7–7:6 (September 1939-June 1942).
PUBLISHER AND PLACE OF PUBLICATION: *Christian Front*, Villanova, Penn. (1936–39); *Christian Social Action*, Detroit (1939–42).
EDITOR: Richard L.-G. Deverall (1936–42).
CIRCULATION: Less than 1000 (est.).

Eugene Y. Lowe

THE CHRISTIAN TRIBUNE. *See* THE CHRISTIAN CENTURY

THE CHRISTIAN UNION. *See* THE OUTLOOK

CHRISTIAN UNION QUARTERLY. *See* THE ECUMENICAL REVIEW

CHRISTIAN WORK. *See* THE CHRISTIAN CENTURY

THE CHRISTIAN WORKER'S MAGAZINE. *See* THE MOODY MONTHLY

CHRISTIANITY AND CRISIS

From its beginnings in 1941, *Christianity and Crisis* has asked readers to exercise "discriminate judgment" as part of a responsible Christian witness. The journal was born in a time of crisis. Reinhold Niebuhr and a small group of colleagues at Union Theological Seminary considered the Christian pacifism of prewar America dangerously blind to the real threat of the Axis powers. Niebuhr had previously launched the quarterly *Radical Religion* but found it unable to combat effectively the vocal pacifism of popular and influential journals such as the *Christian Century*.* Hence, Niebuhr introduced a biweekly, *Christianity and Crisis*. His first signed editorial set the tone for the journal during the war years: "As Protestant Christians we stand confronted with the ultimate crisis of the whole civilization of which we are a part and whose existence has made possible the survival of our type of faith and our type of church."[1] The journal consistently pointed out the real moral issues involved in the war yet criticized as either unnecessary or immoral the relocation of Japanese-Americans, Allied obliteration bombing, and the call for unconditional surrender. During the later years of the war, the journal supported the creation of the United Nations and called attention to the importance of worldwide social and economic reconstruction. "Our job," Niebuhr said, is to "establish a tolerable community within the limits set by man's recalcitrance." Other articles also called attention to crises that would occupy many pages of future issues: racial injustice in the United States and the tensions between Jews and Palestinians in the Middle East.[2]

Crises did not cease with the end of hostilities. In the first of many retrospective glances, Niebuhr and his colleagues on the editorial board decided that postwar crises justified continued publication. The journal examined the growing tensions between the Soviet Union and the West, warned readers about the perils of the atomic age, and began to probe the troublesome legacies of colonialism in underdeveloped nations.

Two major crises occupied much of the journal's attention in the early 1950s: McCarthyism and the Cold War. Liston Pope's essay, "The Great Lie," condemned Senator Joseph McCarthy's tactics and message. Pope accused the senator of "incredible human irresponsibility [that] threatens the foundations of politics as well as morality."[3] John Bennett's editorials continued to attack McCarthy throughout this period of national hysteria. Niebuhr consistently warned readers about the danger of communism, more serious than national socialism, he thought, for it was "more plausible in its appeal and more terrible in turning dreams of justice into nightmares of cruelty."[4] Yet even as he uttered such warnings, he never failed to urge the United States to be on guard against national self-righteousness, against misuse of power. John Bennett also warned against totalitarian danger (arguing, for example, that U.S. military intervention in Korea was justified) but also pointed out that communism was not monolithic and that too many Americans were convinced that there was "no difference between Polish or Yugoslav Communism or Russian Communism."[5]

In 1947, Niebuhr wrote that "acrimonious relations between Catholics and Protestants in this country are scandalous."[6] *Christianity and Crisis* was an early leader of the ecumenical movement that gained importance in the next decade. The journal allowed its readers to share the thought of Catholic scholars such as Jacques Maritain, Gustave Weigel, and John Courtney Murray. Bennett, carefully acknowledging Protestant concerns, wrote that "the vision of many Protestants of a monolithic Catholic Church . . . is very wide of the mark. Historically, it has proved itself capable of adjustment to the greatest variety of cultural conditions instead of being one kind of religious ethos exported from Rome."[7] In early 1960, editorials took aim at the so-called Catholic issue in the presidential campaign and helped in its elimination. Other editorials broached the subject of the merits of federal aid to parochial schools, taking to task extremist Protestant groups whose arguments sounded like "a broken record stuck in the 18th century."[8] The journal's ecumenical stance did not please everyone, especially the critic who labeled it the *"L'Osservatore Romano* of Morningside Heights."[9]

The late 1950s and early 1960s were a time of growth and expansion. Wayne Cowan, who joined the staff in 1954, became managing editor in 1956. The format and content of the journal changed because there was a growing conviction that "God has a concern for all of life and that we must be prepared to discern His hand at work in the most unlikely places."[10] Reviews of movies, television, and books and the satire of St. Hereticus appeared regularly, complementing discussion of various political and economic crises. In 1960, an editorial stated that it was time to "illumine the problems faced by the rising nations of Asia and Africa."[11] The continuing struggle for human rights around the world thus led to one of the enduring concerns of *Christianity and Crisis*. Articles such as "Torture and Mind-Breaking in South Africa," "The Price of Progress in Brazil," and "Torture in Democracy's Homeland" were harbingers of the journal's ongoing outcry against the "panoply of witnesses against inhuman oppression, and American complicity therein, in Greece, Brazil, Uruguay, Korea, and elsewhere."[12]

The journal celebrated its twenty-fifth anniversary amid the trauma of Vietnam. When Vice-President Hubert H. Humphrey joined others in honoring Reinhold Niebuhr, John Bennett read him and the assembled audience words from a forthcoming editorial attacking the nation's policy in Vietnam. The journal often served as a gadfly on the body politic, reminding its readers that its voice must risk "displeasure of the powers that be in order to challenge dogmatisms that imperil ourselves and the world."[13] The thirtieth anniversary year, 1971, brought the death of Reinhold Niebuhr and the retirement of John Bennett, but *Christianity and Crisis* has continued to point out social and economic injustice at home and abroad. The journal has responded to these kinds of crises by letting victims speak in its pages. Readers have been introduced to various theologies of liberation through the writings of James Cone, José Miguez-Bonino, Rosemary Ruether, and others. Articles also struggled to liberate readers from oppressive stereotypes, arguing, for example, that there is no longer "a tenable case for excluding homosexuals from full participation in the life of the church."[14] Listening to victims has also brought controversy. Attacked by some for being too sympathetic to Palestinians, Niebuhr's wife and son requested in 1972 that his name be removed from the masthead because the journal "consistently publishes articles with anti-Israeli animus."[15]

Recent issues of the journal have introduced readers to a wide variety of crises that call for sober analysis and reasoned response. Bioethical issues, U.S. policy in Central and Latin America, world hunger, "Thinking about the Bomb," and resurgent militarism in the United States illustrate that the editors have remained faithful to the initial mission of the journal: to work for the "establishment of justice, instead of priding ourselves incessantly upon the unique resources of Christian grace."[16]

Criticized occasionally for paying more attention to crises than to Christianity, the journal continues to alert readers to significant human crises and challenge them to translate Christian ethical insights into humane and practical social responses.

Notes

1. "The Crisis," *Christianity and Crisis* (10 February 1941): 1.

2. "World Community and World Government," in Wayne H. Cowan, ed., *Witness to a Generation* (Indianapolis: Bobbs-Merrill, 1966), p. 30. For early statements on racial justice and the Jewish-Palestinian question, see the following articles in *Christianity and Crisis*: "Balance Sheet of the Negro in America" (20 March 1944); "The Church and Race Segregation" (1 April 1946); "Can We Abolish Jim Crow in the Armed Forces?" (18 October 1948); "The Jewish Problem Is a Christian Problem" (28 June 1943); and "The Voice of the Arabs" (10 January 1944).

3. Liston Pope, "The Great Lie," in Cowan, p. 35.

4. "Ten Fateful Years," *Christianity and Crisis* (5 February 1951): 1.

5. *Christianity and Crisis* (24 June 1947): 81. See also "The Communist Threat: Past and Present," *Christianity and Crisis* (8 December 1952).

6. "Our Relation to Catholicism," *Christianity and Crisis* (15 September 1947): 5.

7. "A Protestant Looks at American Catholicism," in Cowan, p. 52.

8. "Federal Aid to Education: A Call to Action," *Christianity and Crisis* (28 October 1963): 170.

9. Related by editor Wayne Cowan to the writer.

10. Quoted in Robert T. Handy, "Continuity and Change through Twenty Years," *Christianity and Crisis* (6 February 1961): 11.

11. "Why Christianity and Crisis?" (Editorial), *Christianity and Crisis* (8 February 1960): 1.

12. *Christianity and Crisis* (20 January 1975): 314.

13. "We Protest the National Policy in Vietnam," in Cowan, p. 77.

14. See the special issue on homosexuality in *Christianity and Crisis* (30 May, 13 June 1977). This statement is on p. 114.

15. *Christianity and Crisis* (29 May 1972): 129.

16. "The Christian Perspective on the World Crisis," *Christianity and Crisis* (1 May 1944): 3.

Information Sources

BIBLIOGRAPHY:

Cowan, Wayne H., ed. *Witness to a Generation: Significant Writings from Christianity and Crisis (1941–1966).* Indianapolis: Bobbs-Merrill, 1966.

Kegley, C. W., and R. W. Bretall, eds. *Reinhold Niebuhr: His Religious, Social, and Political Thought.* New York: Macmillan, 1956.

Marty, Martin, et al. *The Religious Press in America.* New York: Holt, Rinehart, and Winston, 1963.

Merkley, Paul. *Reinhold Niebuhr: A Political Account.* Montreal: McGill-Queen's University Press, 1975.

INDEX SOURCES: *Humanities Index, Public Affairs Information Service, Religion Index One (Index to Religious Periodicals), Guide to Social Science and Religion in Periodical Literature.*

REPRINT EDITIONS: Johnson Reprints, University Microfilms International, Bell and Howell Micro Photo Division.

LOCATION SOURCES: University of Chicago, Union Theological Seminary (New York), Andover-Harvard Theological Library, Duke University, Princeton University, University of Pennsylvania, and others.

Publication History

MAGAZINE TITLE AND TITLE CHANGES: *Christianity and Crisis: A Journal of Christian Opinion* (1941–57), *Christianity and Crisis: A Christian Journal of Opinion* (1957–   ).

VOLUME AND ISSUE DATA: 1:1 (10 February 1941–   ). Published 24 times a year, 1941–75; published 22 times a year, 1975–   .

PUBLISHER AND PLACE OF PUBLICATION: Christianity and Crisis, New York.

EDITORS: Reinhold Niebuhr was chairman of the editorial board, 1941–53. Niebuhr and John C. Bennett served as co-chairmen, 1953–66. In 1966, Niebuhr retired and became special contributing editor until named founding editor in 1969. Bennett was chairman, 1966–68, when he retired and became senior contributing editor. Wayne Cowan served as managing editor, 1956–68, and editor, 1968–82. In 1982, Cowan became editor-in-chief, and Robert Hoyt became editor.

CIRCULATION: 19,000–20,000 (1982).

Edward Tabor Linenthal

CHRISTIANITY TODAY

Christianity Today, a fortnightly "magazine of evangelical conviction," debuted 15 October 1956, the fruition of a vision of L. Nelson Bell, a layman involved in conservative activities in the Presbyterian Church in the United States; his son-in-law, evangelist Billy Graham; and Wilbur M. Smith, evangelical scholar associated with Fuller Theological Seminary.[1]

While a medical missionary in China, Bell was impressed by the Philadelphia-based *Christianity Today* published during the 1930s by conservatives in the largely northern Presbyterian Church in the U.S.A. The name remained with him, even though the magazine soon ceased publication.[2] After he returned to the United States in 1941, Bell promoted founding a journal representing evangelical concerns within his largely southern denomination. The result was the monthly *Southern Presbyterian Journal* (1942), which in 1959 became the *Presbyterian Journal*. Bell gradually became convinced of a need for a more broadly based magazine, national rather than denominational, that would be an alternative to the dominant theological liberalism and its interdenominational *Christian Century*.* He fastened on *Christianity Today* as a title for it.

Similar concerns moved Billy Graham, as he revealed on the twenty-fifth anniversary of *Christianity Today*: "Late in . . . 1953, I was awakened at about 2 A.M. I went to my desk and wrote out ideas about a magazine similar to the *Christian Century*, one that would give theological respectability to evangelicals. I even named it *Christianity Today*."[3] John C. Pollock notes that "Billy Graham found that his father-in-law's dream magazine not only had the same aim and scope as his own dream, but the very same name, though Billy had never heard of the earlier, defunct *Christianity Today*. . . . They acquired the copyright to the name."[4]

Graham began to develop a financial base for the magazine that involved the rather heavy commitment of oil magnate J. Howard Pew and to search for an editor. He approached Wilbur M. Smith, who initially declined the offer to be editor. Graham renewed the invitation about a year later. Smith recalled: "Our discussion of the journal revealed at once a most interesting fact. I had prepared a four-page, tentative outline of what such a journal ought to contain, and gave a copy to Dr. Graham for his further study. In the meantime, not knowing that I had done this, he had made some notes regarding the very same subject. In not less than eight different points he expressed to me, almost word for word, what I had already recorded in this typewritten syllabus, which he had never before seen."[5] Smith had also developed more detailed proposals for similar ventures discussed in 1926 with Lewis Sperry Chafer, founding president of Dallas Theological Seminary, and in 1945 with Will H. Houghton, president of the Moody Bible Institute. In 1946 Professor Carl F. H. Henry of Northern Baptist Seminary, who eventually became founding editor of *Christianity Today*, expressed similar concerns to Smith.

After Smith declined the editorship, Fuller Seminary professor Harold Lindsell proposed Henry's name to Graham.[6] Graham's response was favorable but mixed. He thought the journal should avoid the extreme fundamentalism associated with Henry, and he wondered whether Henry could develop a popular rather than strictly academic style. He also doubted whether Henry would assume the position fulltime and move to Washington where the journal's headquarters would be. Finally, he pondered how Henry would react to sharp criticism from thoroughgoing fundamentalists. Graham felt the journal had to promote a middle-of-the-road evangelical position positively rather than simply condemn liberalism negatively.[7] Lindsell's reply noted that while Henry wished Graham to initiate any further discussions of the editorship, Henry was committed to a conservative but irenic evangelical theology.[8] Sensitivity to all these matter provides the framework for an assessment of *Christianity Today*.

Appointed editor in 1955, Henry sought contributors for a journal pitched to neoevangelical teachers and clergy. In a letter to potential contributors, he indicated the thrust of *Christianity Today*: "There is a movement on foot to establish a Christian magazine, along the lines of the *Christian Century*, but from the evangelical standpoint. Its purpose is to reach ministers whose theological training has been inadequate, weak, and erroneous. Especially is there a desire to restore their confidence in the Scriptures as the very Word of God. It is intended to send the magazine to all Protestant ministers in the United States and Canada. This provides a wonderful opportunity to present Christian truth and action in the spirit of Christian love, scholarship and ethics. . . . It is our *purpose* to win over those of liberal leaning and training. Therefore an attempt should be made not to antagonize."[9] A news release announcing the journal's founding gave as its objectives:

1. The articulation of "the central doctrinal distinctives of historic Christianity."
2. The pursuit of a biblical ecumenicity grounded in a biblically valid Christology and expressed in a biblically shaped ecclesiology.
3. The advocacy of a biblical theology of creation that makes it possible to integrate "true science and revealed religion."
4. The formulation of a biblical ethic and attention to its application to the personal, social, political, and economic dimensions of life.
5. The incitement of the church to the fulfillment of its missionary, evangelistic, and educational mandate in the world.
6. The uncovering of theological and philosophical aberrations that are inimical to the Christian faith.[10]

Editorials in the inaugural issue made it clear that the evangelical view of Scripture and the evangelical understanding of evangelism are the twin foci that *Christianity Today* seeks to underscore and that link its articles together.

Reactions and assessments of the new fortnightly were varied in the media, both secular and religious. Kenneth Dole in the *Washington Post and Times Herald* for 5 May 1956 stated that the announcement of *Christianity Today*'s publication was "what may turn out to [be] a historic" event, that the intended magazine is a "high brow" one "aimed at evangelical Christians" and as such it would "be to conservative, Fundamentalist, orthodox Protestants what the *Christian Century* is to more liberal believers."[11] In the *Post* for 13 November 1956 Dole mistakenly commented: "As may be surmised, the magazine reflects the fundamentalist position of the American evangelist."[12] Carl McIntyre's

Christian Beacon, because of its separatist stance, criticized *Christianity Today*'s irenic approach, while *Eternity* questioned its lack of explicit millennial commitment.[13] Liberal religious journalism was somewhat slower to refer to or speak about *Christianity Today*. It took nearly two years for the journal to be mentioned in *Christian Century* or for articles to discuss it to appear in *Christianity and Crisis*.*[14]

After 12 years as editor, Henry resigned in order "to give the next years to theological research and writing."[15] For the next 10 years, the editor's chair was filled by Harold Lindsell who had originally proposed Henry as editor. Lindsell retired in 1978, succeeded by Kenneth Kantzer, dean of Trinity Evangelical Divinity School. Kantzer served until October 1982 when V. Gilbert Beers, who holds doctorates in both theology and communications, took over. Kantzer still serves as advisory editor and writes many editorials.

A survey of the content and emphases of *Christianity Today* since the Henry years reveals the following:

1. Fidelity to the original theological commitments of the magazine, particularly regarding the focus on Scripture as plenarily inspired and authoritatively infallible. Under Lindsell, the emphasis on Scripture as inerrant and not simply infallible may have received increased attention, causing the irenic posture to diminish as controversy arose within evangelical circles over what some would consider Lindsell's rigid insistence on Scripture as inerrant in every respect. Lindsell's position is more evident, however, in his books on the subject (such as *The Battle for the Bible*) than in the journal.[16]

2. A subtle shift in the audience of the magazine from intellectually sophisticated pastors and professors to a mass readership. The shift comes to view as one notices the language and vocabulary of articles becoming ever more simple. The pool of authors has also changed. In 1959–60, for example, academics wrote 58 percent of the articles; in 1982–83, they accounted for just 36 percent of the material. Thus the conceptual focus of *Christianity Today* since Henry's departure as editor has moved from a scholarly to a more popular one, pitched more to the layperson than the clergy or professor. In contrast, *Christian Century*, still the major liberal competitor, while written in a popular style, has retained its scholarly focus.

These shifts may also reflect the differing theological reputations of the editors. Although all four hold earned doctorates in theological and/or philosophical disciplines, with the first and fourth having earned two each, only Henry has occupied a place of centrality in the evangelical theological world and also been widely recognized in nonevangelical circles. In contrast, the present editor, although he has written valuable evangelical theological literature, is better known for his children's books.

What may be said about the achievements, impact, and significance of the magazine? Martin E. Marty, associate editor of *Christian Century*, addressed these issues in the silver anniversary issue of *Christianity Today*:

> Modern evangelicalism under some name or other would have existed without *Christianity Today*, but not likely in anything of the shape it has assumed. . . . Without this magazine, the movement would likely have been more cramped and mean, less full of vision and venture. On these pages, at least, there have been calls for civility and culture to match the passion and firmness of faith—and this is the blend needed at this moment when an epochal shift in the Christian consciousness is called for. . . .
>
> . . . *Christianity Today* has often come up with the right blend. The editors spoke not in the name of a God as predator but God as persuader. . . . The stakes are too high for people to be other than deep and serious about contention. But to the degree that *Christianity Today* has resolved to state and has learned to state its case with some respect for those who do not share its every detail, the magazine has brought a gift to go with its evangelical claims.
>
> I know that the magazine has only won a subculture, not *the* culture. It has shaped an evangelical world, not *the* world. But, one must ask in a consoling spirit, where does it say that the Lord asked the steward to be successful? Not successful. Only faithful.[17]

Notes

1. For an overview, see Daryl Alan Porter, "*Christianity Today*: Its History and Development" (Th.M. thesis, Dallas Theological Seminary, 1978).

2. On Bell, see John C. Pollock, *A Foreign Devil in China: The Story of Dr. L. Nelson Bell, an American Surgeon in China* (Minneapolis: Published for the Billy Graham Evangelistic Association by World Wide Publications, [1971]).

3. "In the Beginning . . . Billy Graham Recounts the Origins of *Christianity Today*," *Christianity Today*, 17 July 1981, p. 26.

4. Pollock, p. 239.

5. Wilbur M. Smith, *Lest I Forget* (Chicago: Moody Press, 1971), p. 178.

6. "In the Beginning," p. 27.

7. Billy Graham to Harold Lindsell, 25 January 1955, Archives of the Billy Graham Center, Wheaton College, collection 192, box 6, folder 2.

8. Harold Lindsell to Billy Graham, 31 January 1955, Archives, Collection 192, box 6, folder 2.

9. Carl F. H. Henry to potential contributors, memorandum, n.d., Archives, collection 8, box 15, folder 11.

10. News release, 3 May 1956, Archives, collection 8, box 14, scrapbook, October 1956-May 1857.

11. Kenneth Dole, "News of the Churches," *Washington Post and Times Herald* (5 May 1956).

12. Kenneth Dole, "News of the Churches," *Washington Post and Times Herald* (13 November 1956).

13. "Christianity in Eclipse," *Christian Beacon* (25 October 1956); "Journalism," *Eclipse* (October 1956).

14. *Christian Century* 30 April 1958; John C. Bennett, "The Depth of Difference," *Christianity and Crisis* 27 October 1958.

15. Carl F. H. Henry, "Editor's Note," *Christianity Today*, 5 January 1968, p. 2.

16. Harold Lindsell, *The Battle for the Bible* (Grand Rapids: Zondervan Publishing House, 1976).

17. Martin E. Marty, "The Marks and Misses of a Magazine," *Christianity Today*, 17 July 1981, pp. 51, 58.

Information Sources

BIBLIOGRAPHY:

Archives of the Billy Graham Center, Wheaton College, Wheaton, Illinois, collection 8, boxes 1, 3, 14, 15; collection 192, box 6.

"Declaration of Principles." *Christianity Today*, 14 October 1957, p. 20.

"In the Beginning . . . Billy Graham Recounts the Origins of *Christianity Today*." *Christianity Today*, 17 July 1981, pp. 26–27.

Marty, Martin E. "The Marks and Misses of a Magazine." *ChristianityToday*, 17 July 1981, pp. 51, 58.

Pollock, John C. *A Foreign Devil in China: The Story of Dr. L. Nelson Bell, an American Surgeon in China*. Minneapolis: Published for the Billy Graham Evangelistic Association by World Wide Publications, [1971].

Porter, Daryl Alan. "*Christianity Today*: Its History and Development." Th. M. thesis, Dallas Theological Seminary, 1978.

"Reflections: Five Years of Change." *Christianity Today*, 26 November 1982, p. 19.

Smith, Wilbur M. *Lest I Forget*. Chicago: Moody Press, 1971.

"Why 'Christianity Today'?" *Christianity Today*, 5 October 1956, p. 22.

INDEX SOURCES: *Reader's Guide to Periodical Literature, Christian Periodical Index, Religion Index One, Religious and Theological Abstracts, Old Testament Abstracts, Guide to Social Science and Religion in Periodical Literature.*

REPRINT EDITIONS: University Microfilms International.

LOCATION SOURCES: Library of Congress, Yale University, University of Chicago, Southern Methodist University, Union Theological Seminary (New York), Princeton Theological Seminary, Duke University, Andover-Harvard Theological Library, and many others.

Publication History

MAGAZINE TITLE AND TITLE CHANGES: *Christianity Today* (1956–   ).

VOLUME AND ISSUE DATA: 1:1 (15 October 1956–   ). Appears fortnightly.

PUBLISHER AND PLACE OF PUBLICATION: Today's Publications, Washington, D.C. (1956–57); Christianity Today, Washington, D.C. (1957–77); Christianity Today, Carol Stream, Ill. (1977–   ).

EDITORS: Carl F. H. Henry (1956–68), Harold Lindsell (1968–78), Kenneth Kantzer
    (1978–82), V. Gilbert Beers (1982–   ).
CIRCULATION: Nearly 182,000 (1984).

John G. Merritt

THE CHRONICLE. *See* AMERICAN BAPTIST QUARTERLY

CHURCH AND STATE

In September 1946, a number of concerned religious and political leaders met in Washington, D.C., to discuss the problem of the relationship between church and state. This meeting led to a series of similar ones that culminated in the creation of Protestants and Other Americans United for Separation of Church and State (POAU) on 20 November 1947. Officers of the group included "president, Edwin McNeill Poteat, president of Colgate-Rochester Divinity School; first vice president, Charles Clayton Morrison, editor of the *Christian Century**; second vice president, John A. MacKay, president of Princeton Theological Seminary and former moderator of the Presbyterian Church, U.S.A.," and other prominent Protestant leaders.[1] The group drew up a manifesto, hired Glenn L. Archer as executive director, and mandated publication of a newsletter that was to become *Church and State* magazine.

The series of meetings and the group that arose from them were a response to Roman Catholicism in the United States. The founders of POAU feared that Catholic efforts to win funding for parochial schools and the appointment of Myron C. Taylor as Franklin D. Roosevelt's personal representative to the Vatican threatened the First Amendment separation of church and state.[2] Although the founders insisted that theirs was not to be an anti-Catholic organization, one of them later conceded that "the practical effect of the Manifesto was to pit the organization directly against the United States hierarchy of the Roman Church."[3] The manifesto accused that church of trying "to secure total support of its extensive system of parochial schools from the public treasury." It also decried the church's "ominous progress in its strategy of winning for itself a position of special privilege in relation to the state" as represented in the U.S. diplomatic mission to the Vatican.[4] Over the next three decades POAU (later renamed Americans United) crusaded against any entanglement of church and state. This crusade involved it in countless legal disputes and pamphlet wars with Roman Catholics and other religious groups.

One of the chief weapons of POAU was its magazine. *Church and State Newsletter* began on 15 May 1948 as a mimeographed report of issues and activities of the organization. It was published in that form approximately every other month until July 1949, when the first four-page typeset edition was issued.

The new format appeared monthly until the journal was redesigned and renamed in September 1952. Now known as *Church and State: A Monthly Review*, it expanded to eight pages. In June 1961 it shortened its name to *Church and State* and doubled in length again to 16 pages. In 1970 the journal expanded to 24 pages and currently fluctuates between 16 and 24 pages. Although most editions deal with a variety of short features, there have been occasional issues devoted to special subjects, including population problems (April 1967), church wealth and church tax exemption status (July 1967), and anniversary editions (December 1967 and February 1973).[5]

Throughout its history *Church and State* has crusaded against the entanglement of church and state. Initially the magazine struggled against Roman Catholic advances in federal and state aid to parochial schools and political recognition of the Vatican as a secular state. One of the leaders of POAU, Paul Blanshard, became nationally prominent for his attacks on the Roman Catholic Church.[6] Since the 1950s the journal has polled political candidates on their attitudes about the relationship between religion and politics. It was particularly vocal during the 1960 presidential campaign of John F. Kennedy, ultimately supporting this Catholic candidate because of his statements opposing aid for parochial schools. More recently *Church and State* has opposed tuition tax credits to assist private schools and the political involvement of the Moral Majority and religious Right.

Notes

1. C. Stanley Lowell, *Embattled Wall* (Washington, D.C.: Protestants and Other Americans United for Separation of Church and State, 1966), pp. 28–29.

2. Ibid., pp. 6–7.

3. Ibid., p. 38.

4. Protestants and Other Americans United for Separation of Church and State, *Basic Documents Relating to the Religious Clauses of the First Amendment* (Washington, D.C.: Protestants and Other Americans United for Separation of Church and State, 1965).

5. Albert J. Menendez, ed. *The Best of Church and State: 1948–1975* (Washington, D.C.: Americans United, 1975), pp. ix-x.

6. Blanshard's work included publication of many controversial treatments of Roman Catholicism. These included Paul Blanshard, *American Freedom and Catholic Power* (Boston: Beacon Press, 1949), *God and Man in Washington* (Boston: Beacon Press, 1960), and *Religion and the Schools* (Boston: Beacon Press, 1963). He was also a prominent speaker at mass rallies sponsored by Americans United.

Information Sources

BIBLIOGRAPHY:

Blanshard, Paul. *American Freedom and Catholic Power*. Boston: Beacon Press, 1949.
———. *God and Man in Washington*. Boston: Beacon Press, 1960.
———. *Religion and the Schools*. Boston: Beacon Press, 1963.
Lowell, C. Stanley. *Embattled Wall*. Washington: Protestants and Other Americans United for Separation of Church and State, 1966.
Menendez, Albert J. *The Best of Church and State: 1948–1975*. Washington, D.C.: Americans United, 1975.

Protestants and Other Americans United for Separation of Church and State. *Basic Documents Relating to the Religious Clauses of the First Amendment.* Washington, D.C.: Protestants and Other Americans United for Separation of Church and State, 1965.
INDEX SOURCES: Self-indexed annually; also in *Religion Index One (Index to Religious Periodical Literature).*
REPRINT EDITIONS: University Microfilms International.
LOCATION SOURCES: Back issues available from Americans United. Also at Union Theological Seminary (New York), Emory University, Cornell University, Colgate-Rochester Divinity School, and others.

Publication History

MAGAZINE TITLE AND TITLE CHANGES: *Church and State Newsletter* (15 May 1948-August 1952), *Church and State: A Monthly Review* (September 1952-May 1961), *Church and State* (June 1961–   ).
VOLUME AND ISSUE DATA: *Church and State Newsletter* 1:1–5:7 (1948–52), *Church and State: A Monthly Review* 5:8–14:5 (1952–61), *Church and State* 14:6- (1961–   ).
PUBLISHER AND PLACE OF PUBLICATION: Protestants and Other Americans United for Separation of Church and State (later called Americans United), Washington, D.C.
EDITORS: Glenn L. Archer (July 1948-February 1964), C. Stanley Lowell (February 1964-May 1976), Ed Doerr (May 1976-February 1982), Joseph L. Conn (February 1982–   ).
CIRCULATION: 50,000.

Michael R. McCoy

CHURCH HISTORY

The year 1888 was a banner year for those in the United States interested in religious history, for in that year Philip Schaff founded the American Society of Church History (ASCH). Americans had finally come to the point when they valued the contemplation of history. Thus far they had been busy with the making of their short history. Only four years earlier the American Historical Association (AHA) had been founded. The latter organization reflected new ideas about "doing history" in a scientific age, while the former reflected the ideas of the founder concerning the unique features of religious history. Whereas the AHA was larger and the presidency changed each year, the ASCH was smaller, composed mainly of historians of the Christian religion, and had the same president for the first six years of its existence, Philip Schaff. For this reason the importance of the ideas of the founder and first president of the ASCH on this organization's later history cannot be emphasized too much. The driving force in Schaff's life at this time was to nurture in every way possible ecumenical activity that might lead in the direction of the reunion of Christendom. Without question this was the major reason for his giving American church historiography an outlet by means of the ASCH.

Swiss-born Philip Schaff had come to the United States in 1844 to assume a teaching position at the small German Reformed Seminary in Mercersburg, Pennsylvania. He and John W. Nevin developed what became known as the Mercersburg theology, a theological position keenly aware of history, the creeds, and the broader denominational spectrum.[1] While there Schaff experienced two heresy trials[2] and produced several major theological volumes, including *The Principle of Protestantism* (1845), *What Is Church History?* (1846), and *America* (1854).[3] The last work has been judged by Perry Miller as one of the finest tributes to the United States ever paid by an immigrant.[4] Outgrowing little Mercersburg, Schaff moved to New York City in 1864 and in 1870 joined the faculty of Union Theological Seminary, where he remained until his death in 1893.[5] During this period he made a positive international name for himself through his scholarly writings, travels, and major connections with the Evangelical Alliance (he was the driving force behind the 1873 international meeting of the alliance in New York City), the Bible translation project of 1870–85, and the founding of the ASCH. Appropriately, the last scholarly activity of his life was the presentation of the visionary paper, "The Reunion of Christendom," at the Parliament of Religions meetings in Chicago in 1893.[6]

From the commencement of his career, Scahff was committed to the principle of "evangelical catholicism."[7] This principle anticipated and yearned for a future age of some kind of higher unity of Protestantism and Catholicism that would combine in a creative way the best of the two traditions.[8] Part of the pilgrimage in this direction would involve leaving biased sectarianism behind and moving forward toward the expression of healthy denominationalism in which each group values its own history while remaining open to points of contact with other traditions.[9] Nurturing this goal was the major commitment of Schaff's life. Teaching church history by whatever means would only support this goal, he believed. One could not come away from a full study of church history and remain provincial in outlook.

The union Schaff sought, then, was one in which scholars of varying denominational backgrounds could stand and view religious history free from a sectarian bias. Thus, on 23 March 1888, he founded the American Society of Church History in New York City and remained its president until his death. To those scholars invited to his home with such an organization in mind, he delivered a founder's day address. The theme was the need for and aims of such a society:

> Dr. Schaff spoke upon the desirability and prospective usefulness of an American Society of Church History on a catholic and irenical basis in the development of a taste and talent for historical theology by special researches, and by bringing into personal contact the workers in this department, and thus indirectly aiding the cause of Christian union.[10]

At the first meeting of the society on 28 December 1888, he set forth the scope of the group: "It was formed for the purpose of cultivating church history as a science, in an unsectarian, catholic spirit, and for facilitating personal intercourse among students of history as a means of mutual encouragement."[11] The founding was noted quite favorably in Germany by Adolf von Harnack:

> It . . . was a great pleasure to hear that a Society of Church History had been formed in the United States. I greet it as the beginning out of which we may hope a fine spirit will develop. America has put us in Europe to shame by this association and I can only hope that in the interests of our science at home it may still more decidedly put us to shame.[12]

During his presidency Schaff was present at every session of the society, and the program of each meeting was largely of his own suggestion. The proceedings, as well as papers read at each session, were printed in *Papers of the American Society of Church History* and circulated yearly to the subscribing members. The programs and papers were varied in topic and personnel and presented a cross-section of the church universal. No particular age in the history of the church was overemphasized nor was any historical period or subject intentionally neglected.[13] The society, under Schaff's direction, was also concerned with keeping its members informed of the most recent materials available in the field of church history through its papers and bibliographies. From its inception the society published extensive bibliographical notations for the use of its members.[14]

Perhaps the most important early literary achievement of the society from the standpoint of ecumenics was the American Church History Series, a series of 13 volumes, 11 of them histories of major American denominations. Schaff instructed that the volumes were "to present a clear view of its [the denomination's] present condition and relation to other Christian Churches. The style should be scholarly, yet popular and interesting, so as to attract intelligent readers of all classes and creeds."[15] Schaff further expressed a major ecumenical hope: "The study of history—'with malice toward none, but with charity for all'—will bring the denominations closer together in an humble recognition of their defects and a grateful praise for the good which the same spirit has wrought in them and through them."[16]

After Schaff's death in 1893, the presidency of the society passed to men with similar ideas but not with the amazing energies and driving force of this doyen. By 1896 the society came under the control of those who believed that "Church History is only a part of general history, its students should ally themselves with the students of the general subject."[17] Because of this greater interest in scientific methodology rather than ecumenicism or theological matters, the ASCH terminated its separate existence in 1896 and became a permanent Section of Church History in the American Historical Association.

For 10 years this relationship continued. On 27 December 1906, several members of the Church History Section reconstituted the American Society of

Church History as a separate and independent organization from the AHA. The membership included scholars of a wide variety of church and professional commitments, and a diversity of opinions was present from the start. Some clung to Schaffian ideas about ecumenicity, and others were more interested in scientific methodology. One pragmatic, yet important, reason for this reconstitution must be mentioned. Because of editorial policies in relation to the publishing of the *American Historical Review* and some connection with governmental agencies not wishing to offend the principle of the separation of church and state, the papers from the Church History Section had been turned down regularly and were not being published in the association's literary outlet. As much as anything else, the reconstitution was done in order to provide more opportunities for the publication of scholarly and other worthy articles in the field of religious history.[18] The *Papers, Second Series*, were circulated among members and carried the transactions of the society, scholarly papers, source translations, and bibliographical aids. The last volume of this series was published in 1934, for the role played by these volumes had been assumed by the quarterly publication of *Church History*, which had commenced in 1932.

From 1932 until the present, *Church History* has been the scholarly organ of the ASCH. Circulated among the members, libraries, and interested lay and clerical subscribers, it contains the proceedings of the society, news items, erudite book reviews, and cogent articles on various phases of church history, including quite often bibliographical essay articles. *Church History* continues to reflect to the present day a variety of ideas about church history. The ecumenical hopes, goals, and commitments of Philip Schaff are reflected alongside more scientific methodological interests. The two viewpoints are definitely not opposed to one another; it is perhaps best to say that they reflect the two ends of a spectrum that meet in the minds of most members of the society somewhere around midpoint. Many of the members of the ASCH are also members of the AHA and the cross-fertilization of ideas is perhaps best reflected in the fact that both national meetings are held every year at the same time and the same place and that there are always joint sessions. Members of the AHA and the ASCH often cross lines in their attendance at sessions, reading papers, chairing sections, and publishing articles. In other words, religious historians and secular historians get along much better than they did in 1906. Perhaps Henry W. Bowden has said it best about the society and its literary organ, *Church History*:

No single conception has ever dominated all thinkers since the turn of the century, and that open-ended search for truth has produced a great deal of fruitful debate and a beneficial exchange of ideas. The continued vitality of the ASCH during this later era can be taken as evidence of man's interest in religion and his persistence in trying to understand its past.[19]

Notes

1. For the best interpretation of this theological school, see James H. Nichols, *Romanticism in American Theology* (Chicago: University of Chicago Press, 1961), passim.

2. See George H. Shriver, *American Religious Heretics* (Nashville: Abingdon Press, 1966), chap. 1.

3. The *Principle* has been reprinted in the *Lancaster Series on the Mercersburg Theology*, vol. 1 (Philadelphia: United Church Press, 1964) and *America* was redone by the Belknap Press of Harvard University Press (Cambridge, 1961).

4. *America*, p. xxxv.

5. For a biographical account, see David S. Schaff, *The Life of Philip Schaff* (New York: Charles Scribner's Sons, 1897).

6. See *Reunion of Christendom* (New York: Evangelical Alliance Office, 1893).

7. See Klaus Penzel, "Church History and the Ecumenical Quest: A Study of the German Background and Thought of Philip Schaff" (Th. D. dissertation, Union Theological Seminary, New York, 1962), and George H. Shriver, "Philip Schaff's Concept of Organic Historiography" (Ph.D. dissertation, Duke University, 1961).

8. See James H. Smylie, "Philip Schaff, Ecumenist: The Reunion of Protestantism and Roman Catholicism," *Encounter* 28 (1967).

9. See Schaff, *History of the Christian Church* (Grand Rapids: Eerdmans, 1950), 7:43.

10. *Papers of the American Society of Church History, First Series* (New York: Putnam's 1889), 1:vi–vii. Also see P. Schaff, "Autobiographical Scrapbook", Schaff Papers, Union Theological Seminary, 2:124–26. The formation of the society was noted in *New York Evening Express*, 24 March 1888, and *New York Daily Tribune*, 26 March 1888.

11. Ibid., p. xv.

12. *Autobiographical Scrapbook*, 2:159.

13. See *Papers of the American Society of Church History, First Series* (New York: Putnam's 1889) vol. 1 passim. The papers in this first volume are exemplary of the ecumenical character of the society: Philip Schaff, "The Progress of Religious Freedom as Shown in the History of Toleration Acts," H. C. Lea, "Indulgences in Spain," J. C. Moffat, "A Crisis in the Middle Ages," F. H. Foster, "Melanchthon's Synergism," H. M. Scott, "Some Notes on Syncretism in the Christian Theology of the Second and Third Centuries," E. C. Richardson, "The Influence of the Golden Legend on Pre-Reformation Culture History," A. C. McGiffert, "Notes on the New Testament Canon of Eusebius," and S. M. Jackson, "A Note on the Need of a Complete Missionary History in English."

14. This desire to be aware of the most recent research finds expression in volume 4 (1892) of the *Papers* in a review article by A. H. Newman entitled "Recent Researches Concerning Medieval Sects." This volume also commences a series that list in alphabetical order all the works of interest to students of church history that have appeared during the preceding year. This bibliographical series carries valuable information regarding primary source materials, as well as scholarly secondary works.

15. *Papers, First Series* (New York: Putnam's 1892) 4:xix.

16. See P. Schaff, *Reunion of Christendom*, p. 35.

17. *Papers, First Series* (New York: Putnam's 1897) 8:xxviii–xxix.

18. See Henry W. Bowden, *Church History in the Age of Science* (Chapel Hill: University of North Carolina Press, 1971), pp. 239ff. This excellent book poses the issues carefully and perceptively.

19. Ibid., p. 245.

Information Sources

BIBLIOGRAPHY:

Bowden, Henry W. *Church History in the Age of Science*. Chapel Hill: University of North Carolina Press 1971.

Nichols, James H., ed. *The Mercersburg Theology*. New York: Oxford University Press, 1966.

————. *Romanticism in American Theology*. Chicago: University of Chicago Press, 1961.

Schaff, Philip. *America*. Reprinted, Cambridge: Belknap Press of Harvard University Press, 1961.

————. *The Principle of Protestantism*. Reprinted, Philadelphia: United Church Press, 1964.

————. *The Reunion of Christendom*. New York: Evangelical Alliance Office, 1893.

————. *What is Church History?* Philadelphia: J. P. Lippincott and Co., 1846.

Shriver, George H. *American Religious Heretics*, Nashville: Abingdon Press, 1966.

INDEX SOURCES: Indexes for both series of *Papers* and for *Church History* are available from the treasurer of the ASCH: William B. Miller, 305 East Country Club Lane, Wallingford, Pa. 19086. Also *Religion Index One, Guide to Social Science and Religion in Periodical Literature, Christian Periodical Index, Humanities Index, Religious and Theological Abstracts, Old Testament Abstracts, Current Contents*.

REPRINT EDITIONS: Microfilm reproductions of both series of *Papers* and *Church History*, vols. 1–17 (1932–48) are available from the ATLA Board of Microtext. Inquiries should be sent to Charles Willard, Princeton Theological Seminary, Speer Library, Box 111, Princeton, N.J. 08540. Microfilm reproductions of *Church History*, vols. 18-, are available from University Microfilms International.

LOCATION SOURCES: Union Theological Seminary (New York), Library of Congress, University of Chicago, University of California-Los Angeles, and others.

Publication History

MAGAZINE TITLE AND TITLE CHANGES: *Papers of the American Society of Church History*, 1st ser. (1888–97); *Papers of the American Society of Church History*, 2d ser. (1908–34); *Church History* (1932–   ).

VOLUME AND ISSUE DATA: *Papers*, 1st ser., vols. 1–8 (1888–97); *Papers*, 2d ser., vols. 1–9 (1908–34); *Church History*, vols. 1- (1932–   ). Published quarterly.

PUBLISHER AND PLACE OF PUBLICATION: Putnam's, New York (*Papers*, 1st and 2d ser.); Science Press, Ephrata, Pa. (*Church History*).

EDITORS: S. M. Jackson (*Papers*, 1st ser., vols. 1–8; 2d ser., vols. 1–2); W. W. Rockwell (vols. 3–5); F. W. Loetscher (vols. 6–9); Matthew Spinka, et al. (*Church History*, vols. 1–19); J. H. Nichols, Wilhelm Pauck, et al. (vols. 20–22); J. H.

Nichols, L. J. Trinterud, et al. (vols. 23–24); J. H. Nichols, F. A. Norwood, et al. (vols. 25–30); J. C. Brauer, R. M. Grant, and M. E. Marty (vols. 31-). CIRCULATION: 3400 (approx.).

George H. Shriver

CHURCH RECORD. *See* EPISCOPAL RECORDER

CHURCH UNION. *See* THE OUTLOOK

COMMENTARY

In November 1945, the American Jewish Committee began publication of *Commentary*, the most ambitious literary project ever attempted by the American Jewish community. Created to present thought and opinion on Jewish affairs, *Commentary* was the first Jewish journal to include articles targeted for a non-Jewish audience. Thus *Commentary* became the first periodical that intentionally sought to be both Jewish and nonparochial. Its aim was to "be hospitable to diverse points of view and belief," to provide a forum for both Jewish and non-Jewish writers, and to be a serious intellectual and objective publication in an effort to avoid the provincialism characteristic of previous Jewish publications.[1] Although editorially independent from its publisher, *Commentary* has consistently reflected the general aims and purposes of the American Jewish Committee as part of the committee's "general program to enlighten and clarify public opinion on problems of Jewish concern, to fight bigotry and protect human rights, and to promote Jewish cultural interests and creative achievement in America."[2]

The creation of *Commentary* was the American Jewish Committee's affirmation of the faith that it held for the possibilities of Jews in the United States and for their influence throughout the world after the Holocaust. The founding members of the committee (including Jacob H. Schiff, Louis Marshall, Oscar S. Straus, Mayer Sulzberger, Julius Rosenwald, Cyrus Adler, Cyrus L. Sulzberger, Judah L. Nagnes, Julian W. Mack, and Adolf Lewisohn) believed that American democracy offered Jews a unique opportunity to develop a life-style in accordance with the highest values of Jewish religion and tradition. The committee vigorously asserted that "Judaism and Americanism were more than compatible, they were complementary." For this reason the committee was hostile to the Zionist movement, opposing any ideology that considered the United States as exile.[3] The committee adhered to the conviction that Jews were at home in the United States and sponsored *Commentary* to affirm and promote that conviction. The members of the American Jewish Committee seemed to have known intuitively what Arthur A. Cohen argued in his study of the American

Jewish community half a century later: the most thoroughly assimilated American Jews were among the most devoted supporters of Jewish religious institutions.[4]

The oldest Jewish defense organization in the United States, the American Jewish Committee was founded in 1906 to safeguard the civil and religious rights of the Jewish people and protect their well-being. Most of its work has been designed to prevent and counteract anti-Jewish sentiments and activities in the United States, although efforts also have been made abroad. The committee has actively encouraged legislative, judicial, and social reform to eliminate discrimination and prejudice against Jews and other minorities in general. In its early years the committee fought for a liberal immigration policy because of the plight of Russian Jewry before World War I. Its lobbying contributed to the 1907 and 1913 defeats of an immigrant literacy requirement that would tend to disqualify the poor and the minorities.[5] In 1911, the committee successfully campaigned for the abrogation of the Russian-American treaty of 1832 because the Russians refused to allow American Jews into Russia for visitation purposes, although all other American groups were allowed.[6]

Following World War I, the committee supported the inclusion of provisions guaranteeing the rights of minorities in the peace treaties. It also actively sought to counter the violent anti-Semitism erupting in Poland and Rumania. With the rise of fascism in Germany, the committee became a major source for informing the world of the plight of German Jews and exposed the Nazi plan to annihilate them, as evidenced in the committee's booklet, *The Jews in Nazi Germany: The Factual Record of Their Persecution by the National Socialists.*[7] The committee was also remarkably effective in combating domestic anti-Semitism and discrimination in the early twentieth century. For example, it succeeded in securing the passage by the New York legislature in 1913 of an amendment to the state's civil rights law explicitly forbidding advertisements that Jews were unacceptable as guests at hotels or resorts.[8] The committee often used personal persuasion to approach influential people to abate discrimination against Jews, as when committee members persuaded Henry Ford to apologize for and publicly retract the anti-Semitic propaganda he had published in the *Dearborn Independent.*

With the increase of organized anti-Semitism in the United States during the 1930s, the committee began a long-range educational campaign "to create a wholesome understanding between Jews and non-Jews in America," discarding the apologetic reaction to anti-Semitism and arguing that persecution undermined the foundations of democratic society. Following World War II the committee further demonstrated its strong support for a pluralistic democratic society by aggressively participating in the black struggle for equal opportunities in housing, education, employment, and public accommodations. Eventually blacks and Jews marched together and died together for civil rights progress.[9]

Among the efforts of the American Jewish Committee to educate the Jewish people themselves was the launching of *Contemporary Jewish Record: A Review of Events and a Digest of Opinion* in September 1938. The primary goal of *Contemporary Jewish Record* was to keep American Jews informed about the events and opinions that affected Jews worldwide and their repercussions on American Jewry. With the rise of Adolf Hitler and the spread of European totalitarianism, events of special interest to Jews had increased drastically. For seven years *Contemporary Jewish Record* provided authoritative and responsible coverage and analysis of the most turbulant and traumatic period in the history of modern Jewry. Although somewhat provincial in scope since the magazine was written primarily for American Jews, the publication gained a reputation for "fairness, high standards, and an unfailing sense of responsibility."[10]

With the prospects of a new era of peace following the war, the publishers of the *Contemporary Jewish Record* felt the time ripe for a new publication, one broader in scope, less provincial, focusing more on American Jewry, and exploring the basic issues of peace, freedom, and human destiny that challenged all humanity. Out of the ashes of war and with this challenge ahead, *Commentary* was born, incorporating as one of its dominant concerns the ongoing analysis of and search for the meaning of the Holocaust. Over the past four decades *Commentary* has been committed to keeping a vigil with history, for its editors and publishers realize that the mentality that set loose the nightmare of the Holocaust remains dormant within civilization. *Commentary* has sought to identify and resist this mentality in both individuals and governments, as well as reaffirm and restore a sense of the sanctity of human life and of basic inalienable human rights.[11]

Following the war it was "natural for non-Jews everywhere to believe, as Jews now had more reasons than ever to believe, that Jewish survival and Jewish self-determination related to everything in the world. The particular distinction of *Commentary* among Jewish periodicals," according to Alfred Kazin, "has been to articulate and to support this many-sided relatedness."[12] The multitude of articles in *Commentary* over the last 40 years treating the Holocuast and its meaning demonstrate how this event bound Jews worldwide to every fundamental question of human nature as Jewish sociologists, economists, political scientists, art critics, and others have repeatedly related the Holocaust to their disciplines and areas in contemporary culture. The present editor of *Commentary*, Norman Podhoretz, has recently reiterated the centrality of the Holocuast to contemporary Jewry: "World Jewry . . . has served notice that it will not be bullied or cajoled into forgetting that in our generation Jews are above all else forbidden to give posthumous victories to Hitler."[13]

One service of *Contemporary Jewish Record* that *Commentary* has continued to provide is authentic information on world events undistorted by propaganda or factionalism. Special attention has been given to the role of the United States in international affairs and to the meaning of world events to American Jewry. Beginning with an article in the first issue by George Orwell on the British general elections, *Commentary* has closely monitored and boldly interpreted political, social, and economic events in Europe, especially in Germany, Britain, and France. For example, when pressures arose within European Jewry for a new exodus after the war, *Commentary* warned that "if Jews cannot hope to live in dignity and security in Europe, then the cause of democracy itself, not only that of the Jews, has suffered a terrible defeat in this war."[14]

Another specific area of world events that *Commentary* has monitored concerns the Soviet Union and its allies. *Commentary* has had a threefold interest in this sphere: the spread of communism, the persecution of Jews in the Soviet Union, and the development of East-West relationships. Its focus has been on the history and practice of anti-Semitism in the Soviet Union. A third important area of concern has been the Middle East, especially Israel. From its earliest years, *Commentary* has kept readers abreast of developments relating to the creation and survival of the state of Israel, emphasizing the importance of American political and financial support for the state and even encouraging American Jewry to make investments there. In 1983 the editor declared, "Thanks to Israel, world Jewry is still a reality."[15] Even with its strong support for Israel, *Commentary*'s writers have pleaded with Israeli officials to allow religious freedom in the state and to take the initiative to establish friendly relations with Arabs inside and outside Israel.

Another subject that *Commentary* has examined is Jewish culture. Over the years *Commentary* has offered wide-ranging discussion of the Jewish heritage, Jewish beliefs and philosophies, and Jewish literary efforts. It has reached into the wealth of the past but also explored the riches of contemporary American Jewish life. *Commentary* has appraised not only the elusive nature of Jewishness (Jewish identity understood historically and sociologically) but also the current diversified condition of Judaism (the Jewish system of beliefs and practices). It has dealt with such difficult questions as: does the Jew exist? who is a Jew? what is basic Judaism? what is the task of being an American Jew? Moreover, *Commentary* has examined such contemporary cultural issues as ethnicity in the United States, civil rights progress, problems in education, the character of the American middle class, the menace of nuclear war, and world survival out of a concern to make sense of the contemporary world.[16] The editors have intentionally tried to reach the general public through articles by such outstanding non-Jewish writers as John Dewey, Paul Tillich, and Reinhold Niebuhr.

To achieve the aims and goals for which *Commentary* was created, founding editor Elliot Cohen divided the publication into six sections: featured articles, "The Month in History," "Cedars of Lebanon," "From the American Scene", "Study of Man," and "Books in Review". "The Month in History" chronicled major developments in world events as they affected Jewish people. "Cedars of Lebanon" presented classic essays on the fundamental ideals underlying Jewish life and thought. "From the American Scene" was devoted to people, institutions, places, and events in the United States. "The Study of Man" noted research in anthropology, sociology, ethics, social psychology, philosophy, education, economics, and political science. Except for two changes in format, the periodical remained consistent until 1960. The two features added later included one for letters from readers (1946) and another entitled "On the Horizon," a review primarily of plays, films, music, and art.

During its first 15 years of existence, *Commentary* clearly reflected the personality of Cohen. When Norman Podhoretz became editor in 1960 upon the death of Cohen, the publication underwent several changes. *Commentary*'s format now emphasized letters from readers, with as many as 10 to 30 pages devoted to them. World events were still covered in a section entitled "Observations," and the arts were treated in sections entitled "Fiction," "Movies," and "Music." "Books in Review" remained a vital part of the periodical, but the other regular features were dropped. These changes reflected the fact that Podhoretz was less concerned with the sociology of the American Jewish community, with the social sciences in general, and with the character of the American middle class. *Commentary*, however, has remained faithful to its original goals, purposes, and philosophies. This periodical has not only made a significant contribution to the American Jewish community but has also influenced the more intellectual American general public.

Notes

1. *Commentary* 1 (November 1945): iii.

2. Ibid., "On the Fiftieth Anniversary of the American Jewish Committee," *Commentary* 24 (January 1957): iv.

3. Oscar Handlin, "The American Jewish Committee: A Half-Century View," *Commentary* 24 (January 1957): 3.

4. Arthur A. Cohen, *The Natural and the Supernatural Jew: An Historical and Theological Introduction* (New York: McGraw-Hill, 1962), pp. 193–94.

5. "American Jewish Committee," *Encyclopedia of Zionism and Israel* (New York: Herzl Press/McGraw-Hill, 1971), 1:30.

6. "American Jewish Committee," *Encyclopedia Judaica* (New York: Macmillan, 1971), 2:823.

7. American Jewish Committee, *The Jews in Nazi Germany: The Factual Record of the Persecution by the National Socialists* (New York: American Jewish Committee, 1933).

8. "American Jewish Committee," *Universal Jewish Encyclopedia* (New York: KTAV Publishing House, 1939), 1:243.

9. Ibid.; "American Jewish Committee," *Encyclopedia Judaica*, 2:824.

10. Elliot E. Cohen, "An Act of Affirmation," *Commentary* 1 (November 1945): 2–3.

11. Ibid., p. 2.

12. Alfred Kazin, "Introduction," in *The Commentary Reader: Two Decades of Articles and Stories*, ed. Norman Podhoretz (New York: Atheneum, 1966), p. xxii.

13. Norman Podhoretz, "The State of World Jewry," *Commentary* 76 (December 1983): 45.

14. Zachariah Shuster, "Are Jews Finished in Europe?" *Commentary* 1 (November 1945): iv.

15. Podhoretz, "State of World Jewry," p. 39.

16. Podhorett, *Commentary Reader*, p. ix.

Information Sources

BIBLIOGRAPHY:

Cohen, Elliot E., ed. *Commentary on the American Scene: Portraits of Jewish Life in America.* New York: Knopf, 1953.

Hammelfarb, Milton, ed. *The Condition of Jewish Belief: A Symposium Compiled by the Editors of Commentary Magazine.* New York: Macmillan, 1966.

Podhoretz, Norman, ed. *The Commentary Reader: Two Decades of Articles and Stories.* New York: Atheneum, 1966.

Schachner, Nathan. *The Price of Liberty: A History of the American Jewish Committee.* New York: American Jewish Committee, 1948.

INDEX SOURCES: *Readers' Guide to Periodical Literature, Book Review Digest, Public Affairs Information Service, Index to Jewish Periodicals, ABC Political Science, Historical Abstracts, America: History and Life, Humanities Index, International Index to Periodicals, Index to Labor Articles, Magazine Subject Index.*

REPRINT EDITIONS: University Microfilms International, Bell and Howell Micro Photo Division, International Mkt. Co.

LOCATION SOURCES: Union Theological Seminary (New York), Library of Congress, Yale University, University of Chicago, University of Texas-Austin, University of California-Los Angeles, Princeton University, Duke University, and others.

Publication History

MAGAZINE TITLE AND TITLE CHANGES: *Contemporary Jewish Record: Review of Events and Digest of Opinion* (1938–42), *Contemporary Jewish Record* (1943–45), *Commentary: Incorporating Contemorary Jewish Record* (1945–60), *Commentary* (1960–   ).

VOLUME AND ISSUE DATA: *Contemporary Jewish Record: Review of Events and Digest of Opinion* 1–5 (September 1938-December 1942), *Contemporary Jewish Record* 6–8 (January 1943-June 1945), *Commentary: Incorporating Contemporary Jewish Record* 1–29 (November 1945-January 1960), *Commentary* 29 (February 1960–   ).

PUBLISHER AND PLACE OF PUBLICATON: American Jewish Committee, New York.

EDITORS: Morris David Waldman (1938–45), Harry Schneiderman (1938–45), Sidney Wallach (1938–42), John Slawson (1943–45), Adolph S. Oko (1942–44), Elliot Ettleson Cohen (1945–59), Norman Podhoretz (1960–   ).

CIRCULATION: 45,000 (1983).

Paul G. Chappell

THE COMMONWEAL

The *Commonweal*, a Catholic periodical devoted to "public affairs, literature and the arts," was founded in 1924 by the lay journalist, Michael Williams. From its inception, the magazine has taken unmistakably liberal positions in secular political matters, both domestic and international. On ecclesiastical issues, it has consistently advocated ecumenism among Catholics, Protestants, and Jews. Especially since the Second Vatican Council, it has grown increasingly forthright in theological affairs, maintaining that such questions concern "the entire Christian community" and are "too important to be left solely to 'official' spokesmen." Thus, although the *Commonweal* has often supported papal pronouncements, particularly those related to social concerns, and has championed efforts on behalf of peace and social justice by the American hierarchy, it has not hesitated to question theological conservatism and unresponsive ecclesiastical hierarchicalism.[1]

At its founding, the *Commonweal* illustrated the desire of its predominantly well-assimilated Anglo-Catholic supporters to present a Catholic outlook, one that stood firmly on Catholic moral principles while affirming American democracy and pluralism. The noted historian, Carlton J. H. Hayes, produced three articles during the first year of publication that set forth the magazine's view of the obligations and contributions of its coreligionists. Catholics, Hayes argued, should dispense with their deep-seated inferiority complex, break away from their clannishness, and actively participate in American political life. They should especially support responsible social activism following the norms implicit in Pope Leo XIII's encyclical, *Rerum Novarum*. Although they should willingly serve in the armed forces, they should oppose war and strident, jingoistic nationalism.[2]

The *Commonweal* meant to elucidate "orthodox religious principles and their application to subjects that fall within its purview" and reflect the "continuous unbroken tradition and teachings of the historic mother church." Yet the editors of the new magazine were to be laymen, even if clerical contributions would be sought. The *Commonweal*'s editorial positions, furthermore, would stand independent of those of the church. Its contributors would be drawn even among those "holding different forms of Christian belief and in some cases to authors who do not profess any form of Christian faith."[3] Consequently the periodical's writers have been both diverse and distinguished: G. K. Chesterton, Hilaire Belloc, Jacques Maritain, Karl Rahner, Hans Küng, Edward Schillebeeckx, John Tracy Ellis, Will Herberg, Garry Wills, Michael Harrington, Walter Lippmann, Daniel Berrigan, Daniel Callahan, Robert McAfee Brown, and Harvey Cox are but a few of the prominent figures who have appeared in the *Commonweal*'s pages.

The magazine has retained its distinct perspective, one that incorporates approval of specific social and economic remedies as consistent with Catholic understandings of the gospel but rejects the espousal of any comprehensive secular ideology as normative.[4] The magazine's commitment to peace and social justice has implicitly or explicitly urged the avoidance of what it sees as the sterile alternatives of pure capitalism and Marxist collectivism. Both are viewed as destructive of the human person. Thus, the present executive editor, Peter Steinfels, applauds the U.S. hierarchy's moral sensitivity to the international arms race but criticizes the bishops for having failed to acknowledge sufficiently the evils of the Soviet system: "As a totalitarian society, it has been matched only by Hitler's Germany in this century as a source of human degradation."[5] The visit of Pope John Paul II to Central America in the winter of 1983, heavily criticized because of the pope's seemingly inconsistent stances on behalf of social justice and against clerical political involvement, is seen as having provided some open space in the midst of the political violence in that region. John Paul's position, the editorial continues, prevents the church from either accommodating oligarchies or being "co-opted" by Marxist-Leninists.[6] The Jesuit superior general, Father Pedro Arrupe, is praised for his intelligent assessment of Marxism, one that recognizes the value of Marxian social analysis while urging a critical distance from both dogmatic Marxism and individualistic capitalism.[7]

The *Commonweal*'s devotion to social action was, according to one of its earliest supporters and its long-time managing editor, George Shuster, a dominant concern from the beginning. The magazine presented as a model for implementation the Bishops' Statement on Social Reconstruction of 1919. Radical for its time, the message called for better housing, social insurance, minimum wage laws, the curtailment and even abolition of monopolies, and worker participation in industrial management. As a result, the magazine has generally supported the rights of labor and spoken against unrestrained capitalism. It supported the New Deal, although not without criticism, and the Great Society of President Lyndon Johnson. It was an early advocate of racial integration.[8]

Johnson's election in 1964 prompted the *Commonweal*'s reaffirmation of its mission: the common good. "Thus we have rejected those economic theories which hold that unfettered competition, based on personal self-interest, will insure a decent living standard for all." Thus too, the magazine opposed a self-centered American nationalism that did not consider the legitimate interests of other nations and the claims of states' rights that prevented minority groups from achieving equal participation in American society. Barry Goldwater's defeat for the presidency in 1964 was to be welcomed because he "represented the spirit of the rampantly acquisitive society, a society of atomized individuals each seeking his own good."[9]

On only two occasions, however, has the *Commonweal* endorsed presidential candidates. Both were liberals: Adlai Stevenson in 1952 and George McGovern 20 years later. In the latter case, argued the editorial, "the overriding issues" were "moral ones." In contrast to Richard Nixon, whom the magazine found guilty of having abused the power of the presidency, McGovern better represented the ecumenical view that "God has given man freedom and responsibility to work for a just society on earth." The Democratic candidate would support the equitable distribution of wealth; the integration of minorities; the right to organize, work, and bargain collectively; the accessibility of decent housing and health care; and finally, the negotiated settlement of the war in Vietnam.[10]

Despite its consistent antipathy toward Soviet communism, the *Commonweal* has created its greatest controversies by its equally persistent warnings about the dangers of militant anticommunism. While it generally backed U.S. support of South Vietnam in the 1950s and early 1960s, it grew increasingly critical of the ideological rigidity and conduct of U.S. policy after the Gulf of Tonkin resolution in 1964.[11] Yet even before the 1960s, the magazine's critical distance from anticommunism placed it in opposition to accepted church policy.

The Spanish Civil War, during which Catholic sympathies leaned heavily and uncritically toward the Falangists, prompted the managing editor, George Shuster, to take a more searching view. While disliking Moscow's involvement on the side of the Spanish Republic and the violent anticlericalism of republican supporters, he found Franco an unattractive alternative. Franco's dependence on Hitler and the reactionary, militaristic character of the Falangist movement were anything but worthy of the praise the church was currently offering. The "evident perils" of fascism, noted Shuster, could not be ignored because it was "preferable to communism." Shuster's comments not only brought denunciations and subscription cancellations from without but produced conflict within the *Commonweal*'s editorial board itself. The magazine's acute financial position at the time, partially the consequence of Shuster's criticism of European fascism, led the *Commonweal*'s founder, Michael Williams, to endorse openly the opposite position. In the end, the turmoil forced both Shuster and Williams to resign.[12]

In the 1950s, the *Commonweal*'s attitude toward McCarthyism provoked responses nearly as hostile as those that greeted the periodical's view of the Spanish Civil War. Although it was not immune itself to suggestions of communist infiltration in government during that period, it condemned what it termed the Wisconsin senator's irresponsible and reckless demagoguery that threatened the reputations of even innocent liberals. The *Commonweal* stood virtually alone among Catholic national and diocesan newspapers in its opposition to McCarthy's anticommunist zeal.[13]

Consistent with its purpose as an organ of lay Catholic expression, the *Commonweal* since its inception has advocated a revitalization of the church through increased lay participation. It has periodically evinced impatience with the commonly held understanding of laypersons as mere vessels for clerical and episcopal dicta. The magazine's communal ecclesiological vision has incorporated respect for both the authority of the church and its officers and the initiatives of creative, responsible laypersons. Even before Vatican II, editorials argued "that the Church had much to learn from democratic society, that concepts like due process of law would improve ecclesiastical life, that democratic society came closer to the Gospel than any authoritarian regime."[14]

Yet it was not until the Second Vatican Council, which the *Commonweal* covered exhaustively, that the magazine became deeply concerned with internal church affairs and theological controversies. The unprecedented renaissance in Catholic theology after well over a century of stasis obviously encouraged the new editorial commitment. The *Commonweal* took note of the seismic shift in ecclesiology in its fiftieth anniversary issue in 1974: "The static concept of the Church is now dead; it was dying before Vatican II, and the Council Fathers laid it to rest once and for all. Today the predominant concept . . . is that of the pilgrim Church, the Church on the move, seeking the right path, not supplying easy answers but perhaps asking the right questions—a Church perpetually in need of self-examination and self-renewal."[15]

Articles presenting a diversity of theological opinion on issues ranging from abortion to birth control appear frequently. Characteristically they include Protestant contributions as well.[16] Yet the theme of active lay participation remains constant in the *Commonweal*. Regardless of its position on specific issues, the periodical urges repeatedly that clerical authorities respect the integrity of lay consciences. An editorial that underscores the magazine's opposition to the 1972 U.S. Supreme Court decision on abortion nonetheless criticizes the hierarchy's rigidity on that issue, birth control, and divorce: "The hierarchical church, we suggest, has lost its members by refusing to listen to them, by refusing to respect the integrity of their consciences, by failing to see the degree to which the consensus of good and sincere people is itself a guide to the moral law, by refusing to listen to the Spirit when the Spirit is not saying what the curia and the chancery usually like to hear."[17]

The Vatican as well has heard dissent. Pope Paul VI's genuine concern for social justice, the *Commonweal* claimed, was "rendered limp by an out-dated ecclesiology, an inappropriate life-style, and an understanding of his own historical role that rob his sincerest and noblest moments of compassion and just outrage of their proper force."[18] The controversial theologian Hans Küng's declaration against papal infallibility was perceived as having formidable critics even outside Rome. Yet the Vatican's defensive theology, its "feudal judicial procedures" that undermine the authority of Küng and others to speak as expositors of the faith, and its denigration of the teaching function of theologians were seen as a futile repression of legitimate and needed debate.[19] The same editorial that praised John Paul II for his peacemaking efforts in Central America still criticized the style of that pope's frequent travels as characteristically "Vatican"—from the top down.[20]

After nearly 60 years of publication, the *Commonweal* continues to provide its perceptions of church, politics, and society not only for the benefit of its Catholic readers but also for a broad ecumenical audience concerned with similar issues.[21]

Notes

1. See Rodger Van Allen, *The Commonweal and American Catholicism: The Magazine, the Movement, the Meaning* (Philadelphia: Fortress Press, 1974), pp. 1–14. The quotations are drawn from *Commonweal* 101 (15 November 1974): 126 (hereinafter cited as *Com.*).

2. Van Allen, pp. 12–14.

3. *Com.* 1 (12 November 1924): 5.

4. Ibid. 91 (20 November 1964): 269.

5. Ibid. 108 (18 December 1981): 708.

6. Ibid. 110 (25 March 1983): 163–64.

7. Ibid. 108 (22 May 1981): 294.

8. Ibid. 91 (20 November 1964): 262. See also James Hennesey, S.J., *American*

Catholics: A History of the Roman Catholic Community in the United States (New York: Oxford University Press, 1981), pp. 228–29, and Van Allen, pp. 41–50, 80–84.

9. *Com.* 91 (20 November 1964): 257.

10. Ibid. 99 (13 October): 27–28.

11. Van Allen, pp. 152–60.

12. *Com.* 14 (23 April 1937): 716–17; Van Allen, pp. 60–74.

13. Van Allen, pp. 107–16.

14. *Com.* 101 (15 November 1974): 125; Van Allen, pp. 56–60.

15. *Com.* 101 (15 November 1974): 126.

16. See, for example, "What Is Shaping My Theology," *Com.* 108 (30 January 1981): 41–54, an article that calls attention to the theological diversity that has arisen since Vatican II.

17. *Com.* 103 (2 January 1976): 3–4.

18. Ibid. 102 (3 January 1975): 284.

19. Ibid. 107 (1 February 1980): 37–38.

20. Ibid. 110 (25 March 1983): 163.

21. See, for example, Peter Steinfels' recent contribution, "Neoconservative Theology," to the new American leftist journal, *Democracy* 2 (April 1982): 18–27.

Information Sources

BIBLIOGRAPHY:

"Commonweal's 50th Anniversary." *Commonweal* 101 (15 November 1974): 125–26.

"A Symposium of Commonweal Editors." *Commonweal* 91 (20 November 1964): 261–80.

Van Allen, Rodger. *The Commonweal and American Catholicism: The Magazine, the Movement, the Meaning.* Philadelphia: Fortress Press, 1974.

INDEX SOURCES: *Readers' Guide to Periodical Literature, Humanities Index, Religion Index One, Guide to Social Science and Religion in Periodical Literature, Catholic Periodical and Literature Index, Book Review Digest.*

REPRINT EDITIONS: University Microfilms International, Bell and Howell Micro Photo Division, Microforms International Marketing Co.

LOCATION SOURCES: Catholic University of America, University of California-Berkeley, New York Public Library, Yale University, University of Chicago, and others.

Publication History

MAGAZINE TITLE AND TITLE CHANGES: *The Commonweal* 1 (1924–   ).

VOLUME AND ISSUE DATA: Vol. 1 (1924–   ). Published weekly until 6 December 1974 when it became biweekly.

PUBLISHER AND PLACE OF PUBLICATION: Commonweal Publishing Co., New York.

EDITORS: Michael Williams (1924–38), Philip Burnham (1938–47), Edward Skillin (1938–67), James O'Hara (1967–   ).

CIRCULATION: Peak of 46,000 (1962–66, the years of Vatican II); 30,000 (est. 1983).

Shelley Baranowski

THE CONCORDIA JOURNAL. *See* CONCORDIA THEOLOGICAL MONTHLY

CONCORDIA THEOLOGICAL MONTHLY

In June 1929 the thirty-fourth convention of the Evangelical Lutheran Synod of Missouri, Ohio, and Other States (hereafter LCMS, Lutheran Church Missouri Synod) met in River Forest, Illinois. The delegates decided to merge several journals into one monthly, referring the matter to Concordia Publishing House and the faculty of Concordia Seminary, St. Louis.[1] The *Concordia Theological Monthly* resulted from this decision. Its first number was published in January 1930, and it continued until January 1974. With but two exceptions, it consistently appeared as a monthly of about 80 pages per issue. From 1964 summer issues were combined, and in 1973 the journal changed to five issues per year. The new journal did not break with the policies of the journals it replaced. On the contrary, it consciously sought to continue them and to pursue a conservative confessional Lutheran point of view in "full allegiance to all the Confessions of the Lutheran Church as collected in the Book of Concord of 1850."[2] Though the name and format were new, the journal's priorities were and remained those of *Lehre und Wehre** and the *Magazin,* two of its predecessors.[3]

Throughout its history, the *Concordia Theological Monthly* was edited by the faculty of Concordia Seminary with a managing editor chosen from among them. The faculty or a representative faculty committee approved articles for publication until mid–1964 when Herbert T. Mayer became managing editor. Then the faculty took on functions more related to planning and clarity rather than approval.

Until 1941 the magazine was bilingual. German and English began on an approximately equal basis until German gradually disappeared. Conceived largely for pastors, articles catered to their interests and needs. They included sermons, along with studies of biblical materials, theology, history, liturgy, education, church music, hymnody, and similar topics. A column, "Theological Observer," reacted to current events related to the church. There was also a book review section.

At first, William Frederick Arndt (1880–1957) and Paul Edward Kretzmann (1883–1965) coedited the journal.[4] Arndt had taught New Testament at Concordia Seminary since 1921. He was an irenic, scholarly sort with a firm commitment to the doctrine of verbal inspiration of Scripture.[5] Arndt opposed liberalism and modernism in the LCMS, but he also opposed separatism and isolationism. He argued that the proper course was to follow the LCMS founders and steer between those extremes.[6] Kretzmann was more prolific and less irenic. Editor and production manager of Concordia Publishing House, he joined the Concordia Seminary faculty in 1923. His articles fill the early volumes of *Concordia Theological Monthly.* He argued that Lutherans in the United States could get together, but his requirements were narrowly defined: they included "a common and solid confessional basis" with "the Word of God, inerrant and infallible in its entirety and in all its parts . . . as the *norma normans,* the one and only source of doctrine and norm of life";[7] "creation *ex nihilo,* which certainly excludes both an atheistic and theistic evolution";[8] and opposition to church "unionism" and "lodgery."[9]

Eventually Kretzmann regarded even the LCMS as too liberal. In 1946 he left Concordia Seminary, helped form the Orthodox Lutheran Church, and became president of the Orthodox Lutheran Seminary in Minneapolis.[10]

Generally the journal tried to steer a course between the extremes Arndt had noted, but it often reflected the LCMS by turning in a conservative direction. A change evidenced itself in 1950 when Frederick Emmanuel Mayer (1892–1954) became managing editor. He had worked as an assistant editor since 1940, having joined the faculty of his seminary alma mater in 1937. Mayer also opposed "unionism" but was interested in defining the beliefs of differing religious groups. His "Foreword" at midcentury took a long view. Tracing the journal back to *Lehre und Wehre*, he called the church to a traditional Lutheran vision of law and gospel (rather than liberalism and separatism).[11] The form of the journal remained much what it had been, but a more attractive typeface was adopted and the content of articles gently broadened. Verbal inspiration and narrow LCMS themes received less emphasis, while traditional theological, historical, liturgical, and similar topics were now treated in a broader context, always with high scholarly standards.

Frederick Mayer's tenure as editor was brief. He died in July 1954. Walter R. Roehrs (b. 1901) succeeded him. Roehrs, another Concordia Seminary graduate, was first listed as managing editor in November 1954. He did not write a foreword or advance an editorial position when he took over. He did not even write many articles.[12] He served for 10 years as a competent caretaker who continued the journal on a path set by its history and the faculty. From 1954 to 1964 the journal was not conceived as a place for lively dialogue and debate.

Nevertheless over the years to this point, the *Concordia Theological Monthly* had yielded a rich harvest of learning, which earned it a place of honor among American religious periodicals. The contributions of John Theodore Mueller, Carl Stamm Meyer, Arthur Carl Piepkorn, Herbert J. A. Bouman, Martin E. Marty, and Jaroslav Pelikan, to name a few, bear witness to the quality of scholarship that could develop within a seemingly narrow tradition. The journal's commitment to the needs of the parish clergy and to the importance of the Missouri Synod's growing involvement in world missions remained strong, offering as much in the way of preaching helps as its predecessors.

The last editor, Herbert T. Mayer (b. 1922), considerably changed the journal's tone. He assumed managing editorial responsibilities in July 1964, having come to Concordia Seminary in 1959. Like his father, Frederick, he began with an editorial placing things in perspective. Articles would "continue to reaffirm traditional positions," but they would "not hesitate to reexamine them to reorient them;"[13] they would also keep readers up to date on theological developments in the LCMS and world Christianity, which meant exploring "new and promising fields of study even though the final answers may not be at all apparent."[14] Two years later the staff of the journal expanded Mayer's comments and indicated they would follow the instructions of the Synod of 1963 by examining "major theological issues confronting the church throughout the world" and by discussing "the pros and cons of major trends in Biblical studies."[15]

The journal, as in the past, reflected the issues and struggles of the LCMS itself. It now presented a variety of writers and perspectives on Scripture; on ecumenism; on sex, marriage, and divorce; on the gospel; on choices the Synod had to face—"legalistic, immigrant sect" versus "ecumenical, evangelical" church, as one writer expressed it;[16] along with numerous other topics and the usual book reviews and sermonic materials.

The ferment in the LCMS became more evident in September 1969 when Herbert Mayer wrote an editorial delineating three key issues that troubled the denomination: "the doctrine of the Word, the nature of the mission of the people of God, and the quest for fellowship."[17] In November John Tietjen (b. 1928) became president of Concordia Seminary and defined the seminary's "chief objective" as "bringing God's life to the world."[18] This ruled out other alternatives such as size and pride and narrow Lutheran commitments, focus on the church's internal life, or focus on church politics either of Left or Right.[19] That same year Jacob A. O. Preus was also elected president of the LCMS. He immediately began to move the denomination strongly to the right, and eventually the seminary faculty found itself under investigation as heretics. The opening editorial of 1971 noted the investigation and then printed its own confession of faith, accepting "without reservation the Scriptures of the Old and New Testaments as the written Word of God and the only rule and norm of faith and of practice and all the Symbolical books of the Evangelical Lutheran Church as a true and unadulterated statement and exposition of the World of God."[20]

In the next several years, the journal continued its course with high-quality articles on a variety of subjects and with relatively little space devoted to conflicts in the LCMS. In view of the strictures against the faculty and the dismissal of like-minded church officials throughout the denomination, this was somewhat remarkable.[21] But the business-as-usual calm could not continue in this atmosphere of civil war. In 1973 the journal was cut to five publications per year, and the initials *CTM* replaced *Concordia Theological Monthly*. The seminary faculty persisted in publishing what it considered important without regard to official synodical opinion. The first article in 1973, for instance, concerned the ordination of women, an impossible thought for the Preus forces.[22]

By September the breach was irreconcilable. The seminary faculty protested what it considered unconstitutional and coercive acts by the Synod, and it again confessed its orthodox Lutheran posture.[23] An issue of *CTM* followed in November and one again in January 1974, this the last. After that the seminary faculty founded Concordia Seminary in Exile or "Seminex" (which became Christ Seminary), and it with its supporters eventually formed the Association of Evangelical Lutheran Churches (AELC). Appropriately the last issue of *CTM* was a tribute to John Tietjen for his presidency and leadership throughout this troubled, adversarial period.

The Seminex faculty, with support from Evangelical Lutherans in Mission who became the AELC, kept Herbert Mayer as managing editor and began another journal, *Currents in Theology and Mission*, in August 1974. Published initially by ELIM (Evangelical Lutherans in Mission, an organization of Missouri Synod moderates), *Currents* was placed under the supervision of an editorial review staff consisting of Seminex faculty, pastors, and laypeople. The decision was made to return to something like the division of labor that obtained between *Lehre und Wehre* and the *Magazin*: articles of topical interest reserved for *Currents* and homiletical material provided in a separate periodical, *Preaching Helps*. The intention was to broaden the appeal of *Currents* to the laity. Contributors have included prominent writers throughout American and world Lutheranism, as well as persons involved in parish ministry or missions. *Currents* has avoided numbers devoted to a single topic and esoteric scholarly apparatus. Seminex Old Testament professor Ralph Klein has served as managing editor of both *Currents* and *Preaching Helps* since 1975. In 1977 ELIM transferred publication of *Currents* to Seminex. *Preaching Helps* is published jointly by Seminex, the Lutheran School of Theology at Chicago, Pacific Lutheran Theological Seminary, and Wartburg Theological Seminary. Both periodicals are issued bimonthly.[24]

Meanwhile the LCMS formed another faculty on the old Concordia Seminary campus. In 1975 they began another periodical, *Concordia Journal*, edited by H. Richard Klann. Its editorial policy has remained consistent with a statement of purpose proposed by Martin Scharlemann, then acting president of Concordia Seminary: (1) a theological orientation consistent with the Missouri Synod's historic position; (2) an accurate reflection of the Concordia faculty's theology; (3) exegetical studies in keeping with the directives of the Synod's Commission on Theology and Church Relations; (4) vigilance "against all manner of contemporary doctrinal aberrations," particularly with reference to Holy Communion; (5) writing with "perceptive laypersons" in mind; (6) emphasis of peculiarly Missourian accents as part of the journal's ecumenical responsibility; (7) printing important denominational documents; (8) providing "sound homiletical materials in the solid tradition of the old *Homiletisches Magazin*"; and (9) maintaining a critical Lutheran stance vis-à-vis "what might generically be called conservative Protestantism."[25] Circulation greatly increased in 1979 when the Missouri Synod decided to provide free copies to all of its more than 8000 clergy. Major contributors continue to be members of the Concordia Seminary faculty, though others may submit manuscripts.[26]

The firm bonds that obtain between periodical and church in *Currents in Theology and Mission*, *Preaching Helps*, and *Concordia Journal* bespeak a commitment on the part of all three descendants of *Concordia Theological Monthly* to serve the church in a Lutheran context. Failure to agree on what constitutes such service made the demise of the parent journal and the separate publication of its descendants necessary.

Notes

1. The resolutions are detailed in the first editorial of *ConcordiaTheological Monthly* 1 (January 1930): 1. Four magazines were involved: *Lehre und Wehre* (75 vols., 1855–1929), *Theological Quarterly* (1897–1920), and *Theological Monthly* (1920–29; combined

total of 33 vols.), and *Magazin für Ev.-Lutherisches Homiletik* (53 vols., 1877–1929). See F. E. Mayer, "Foreword," *Concordia Theological Monthly* 21 (January 1950): 7n.

2. "By Way of Introduction," *Concordia Theological Monthly* 1 (January 1930): 1.

3. Ibid.

4. The Concordia Historical Institute, Concordia Seminary, St. Louis, has some biographical material on Arndt. To honor his retirement in 1951, the faculty dedicated the December issue that year to Arndt. Also see Paul M. Bretscher, "William Frederick Arndt," *Concordia Theological Monthly* 28 (June 1957): 401–8.

5. For example, see W. Arndt, "Foreword," *Concordia Theological Monthly* 12 (January 1941): 406, and the series of articles on this subject in 1941 and 1942.

6. See W. Arndt, "Foreword," *Concordia Theological Monthly* 11 (January 1940): 1–11.

7. P. E. Kretzmann, "Foreword," *Concordia Theological Monthly* 4 (January 1933): 1–2.

8. Ibid., p. 4.

9. Ibid., pp. 9–10.

10. Typescripts opposing the LCMS and other materials by and about Kretzmann are in the Concordia Historical Institute.

11. See F. E. Mayer, "Foreword," *Concordia Theological Monthly* 21 (January 1950): 1–7.

12. A list of 19 articles between 1946 and 1958, largely Old Testament and sermon studies, is in Theodore E. Allwart, comp., *Index to Concordia Theological Monthly, Volumes I-XXX, 1930–1959* (St. Louis: Concordia Publishing House, 1963), p. 134.

13. See H. T. M[ayer], "Editorial," *Concordia Theological Monthly* 35 (July-August 1964): 389.

14. Ibid., p. 391.

15. Staff, "A Statement of Editorial Policy," *Concordia Theological Monthly* 37 (January 1966): 3.

16. John George Huber, "Theses on Ecumenical Truth and Heresy," *Concordia Theological Monthly* 40 (May 1969): 299.

17. Herbert T. Mayer, "The Task Ahead," *Concordia Theological Monthly* 40 (September 1969): 527.

18. John H. Tietjen, "In God for the Word," *Concordia Theological Monthly* 41 (January 1970): 3.

19. Ibid., pp. 3–4.

20. "Statements Adopted by the Faculty of Concordia Seminary, St. Louis, Mo.," ibid., pp. 46–47.

21. See, for instance, "Structure and Mission," *Concordia Theological Monthly* 43 (November 1972): 643–44, where the dismissal of Dr. Martin Luther Kretzmann from his 30-year tenure as missionary in India is noted.

22. John Reumann, "What in Scripture Speaks to the Ordination of Women," *CTM* 44 (January 1973): 5–30.

23. See "Editorial," *CTM* 44 (September 1973): 243–44.

24. Guy C. Carter, interview with Ralph Klein, 26 September 1983.

25. Martin Scharlemann, "Born of Anguish and Travail," *Concordia Journal* 1 (Jan., 1979): 6, 7.

26. Robert G. Hoerber, "Concordia Journal Expands," *Concordia Journal* 5 (Jan. 1979): 1.

Information Sources

BIBLIOGRAPHY:
Concordia Historical Institute (St. Louis) has limited biographical information on *Concordia Theological Monthly*'s editors, but the Institute, Concordia Seminary, and Concordia Publishing House do not know where galley proofs, drafts, or related data may be found.
Baepler, Walter A. *A Century of Grace: A History of the Missouri Synod, 1847–1947.* St. Louis: Concordia, 1947.
INDEX SOURCES: Allwardt, Theodore E. *Index to Concordia Theological Monthly, Volumes I-XXX, 1930–1959.* St. Louis: Concordia Publishing House, 1963; "Author and Subject Index of Main Articles, 1960–1964," *Concordia Theological Monthly* 36 (January 1965): 43–55. Also *Religion Index One* and its predecessor, *Index to Religious Periodicals* indexed/indexes *CTM, Currents in Theology and Mission,* and *Concordia Journal.*
REPRINT EDITIONS: University Microfilms International (*Concordia Theological Monthly*).
LOCATION SOURCES: *Concordia Theological Monthly* and *CTM*: Library of Congress, University of Chicago, Augustana College, University of Illinois-Urbana, Los Angeles Public Library. *Currents in Theology and Mission*: Yale University, Princeton Theological Seminary, University of Illinois-Urbana, Drew University, Southern Methodist University, Union Theological Seminary (Virginia), St. Mary of the Lake Seminary. *Preaching Helps*: Andover-Harvard Theological Library, Union Theological Seminary (Virginia). *Concordia Journal*: Louisiana State University, University of Santa Clara.

Publication History

MAGAZINE TITLE AND TITLE CHANGES: *Concordia Theological Monthly* (1930–1972), *CTM* (1973–74). Succeeded variously by *Currents in Theology and Mission* (1974–   ), *Preaching Helps* (1974–   ), and *Concordia Journal* (1975–   ).
VOLUME AND ISSUE DATA: *Concordia Theological Monthly* 1–43 (January 1930-December 1972), *CTM* 44–45 (January 1973-January 1974), *Currents in Theology and Mission 1 (1974–   ), Preaching Helps* 1 (1974–   ), *Concordia Journal* 1 (1975–   ).
PUBLISHER AND PLACE OF PUBLICATION: Concordia Publishing House, St. Louis, Mo. (*Concordia Theological Monthly, CTM, Concordia Journal*); Evangelical Lutherans in Mission (*Currents in Theology and Mission, Preaching Helps,* 1974–76); Christ Seminary-Seminex, St. Louis (*Currents in Theology and Mission, Preaching Helps,* 1977–83); Christ Seminary-Seminex, Chicago (*Currents in Theology and Mission, Preaching Helps,* 1983–   ).
EDITORS: *Concordia Theological Monthly (CTM)*: Faculty of Concordia Seminary, St. Louis, with the following managing editors: William Frederick Arndt and Paul Edward Kretzmann (1930–37), William Frederick Arndt (1938–49), Frederick Emmanuel Mayer (1950–54), Walter R. Roehrs (1954–64), Herbert T. Mayer (1964–74). *Currents in Theology and Mission*: Herbert T. Mayer (1974), Ralph Klein (1974–   ). *Preaching Helps*: Ralph Klein (1974–   ). *Concordia Journal*: H. Richard Klann (1975–76), Robert Hoerber (1976–82), Quentin Wesselschmidt (1982–   ).

CIRCULATION: *Concordia Theological Monthly*: 2100 (1944), 2800 (1950), 4300 (1955), 9235 (1966), 3465 (1970). *Currents in Theology and Mission*: 3800 (1982). *Preaching Helps*: 2700 (1982); *Concordia Journal*: 8600 (1982).

Guy C. Carter and Paul Westermeyer

CONGREGATIONAL QUARTERLY

The *Congregational Quarterly* was first published in January 1859, partly under the auspices of the Congregational Library Association. This body was represented by its secretary, Joseph S. Clark, who joined with two other giants of Congregationalism, Henry Martyn Dexter and Alonzo Quint, to prepare a publication with broad appeal to educated Congregationalists. They intended their effort to complement the *Congregationalist*, a successful magazine for the laity of the denomination. Dexter was invited into the venture because of his leading role on the editorial board of that magazine.[1] Four months later the American Congregational Union of New York joined in the plans and designated its secretary, Isaac P. Langworthy, to sit on the editorial board. Thus, with its editorial board composed of representatives of key Congregational bodies, the *Congregational Quarterly* became a semiofficial organ of American Congregationalism.

From the beginning, the *Congregational Quarterly* was devoted to matters concerning Congregationalism and its leaders. It included biographical sketches of famous figures in the denomination, histories of the various regional associations, and articles about Congregational philosophy and theology. Other regular features of the magazine included "Congregational Necrology" and reviews of a wide variety of books ranging from denominational publications to works of German theology. Perhaps the most significant regular feature of the *Congregational Quarterly* was the publication of denominational statistics. The *Quarterly* took this task from the American Congregational Union, which had previously published statistics in its *Congregational Year Book*. In 1859, shortly after its founding, the *Congregational Quarterly* pledged to present comprehensive statistics on a regular basis. The American Congregational Union suspended publication of its yearbook immediately, leaving the *Quarterly* to present the official denominational statistical record.

Within its departments, the *Congregational Quarterly* offered its readers a striking variety of information and opinion. While much of its space was given to matters of purely denominational interest, virtually every issue devoted some of its pages to articles of broader concern. Congregational theologians analyzed currents of European philosophy and theology in serial articles that ran through several issues. Historical articles extolled the virtues of Congregational luminaries but also examined key figures and events from Reformation and pre-Reformation periods. The editors of the *Congregational Quarterly* conceived of their publication as a scholarly journal for the educated clergy and laity.

The quasi-official standing of the *Quarterly* remained unchallenged as long as the publication remained in the hands of representatives of Congregational bodies and other leaders of the denomination. These men were old, however, and death soon began to thin their ranks. The first decade of publication was marked by a nearly complete turnover of members of the editorial board. In 1867, Christopher Cushing purchased one-quarter of the publication from Isaac Langworthy. Cushing, well known in Congregational circles, was interested in the publication as a commercial venture as much as an ecclesiastical one. He continued to buy shares of the *Quarterly* until, in 1874, he became sole proprietor. The *Quarterly* no longer bore the imprimatur of either the Congregational Library Association or the American Congregational Union.

Cushing made relatively few changes in the form or content of the *Congregational Quarterly*. He preserved the original departments in the *Quarterly* but increased the space given to philosophy and theology. Cushing continued to solicit articles from leading Congregationalists, restricting his own pronounced theological views to the editorial table and an occasional article about theology or church practice. He never ceased to call for a return to the forms of Congregationalism that had prevailed a century before.

While the *Congregational Quarterly* never won a broad following outside its own denomination, it continued, under Cushing, to exercise substantial influence in Congregational circles. It served as a vehicle for contemporary Congregational opinion and in some cases managed to influence that opinion. In at least one case the *Quarterly* influenced the course of the denomination. Hastings Ross's 1874 article, "An Ecumenical Council of Congregational Churches," appears to have been the initial stimulus that led to the creation of the International Congregational Council in 1889.[2] Ross's plea for ties with British Congregationalism, repeated by Christopher Cushing, aroused such interest that the national councils of Congregationalism finally responded with a series of initiatives that culminated in a formal relationship.

Despite Cushing's insistence that he had labored hard for the *Quarterly*, that he had "not spared labor or expense to raise its character and extend its influence," circulation of the magazine did not grow.[3] Most of his subscribers were the ministers and leading laity of Congregationalism. They were primarily interested in the quarterly statistics of the denomination, which could be found only in the *Congregational Quarterly*. In 1879, disaster overtook Cushing's publication. Following an annual meeting in Detroit, the National Council of the Congregational Churches in the United States announced its intention to publish a yearbook that would, "principally, officially contain those statistics of the churches," which had "been long annually printed by private enterprise."[4] Cushing's protests could not dissuade the council. Not only did the council propose to publish the same statistics that were the mainstay of the *Congregational Quarterly*, but it proposed to distribute them, free of charge, to every church and every minister in American Congregationalism. Cushing appealed to national and state councils, arguing that such a duplication of his material "sweeps the whole field of the *Quarterly*, that the Year Book is designed to be a condensation of the material of the *Quarterly* into an annual.''[5] The council responded by offering to share the plates of its statistical tables with Cushing, but it refused any further compromise. At the same time, the publication committee of the council sought advertising from the same sources that had supported the *Congregational Quarterly*. Without this last source of funds, the *Quarterly* was mortally wounded. Unable to find a buyer for the magazine, Cushing could do nothing but appeal for payment of delinquent subscriptions and cease publication. The *Congregational Quarterly* offered its final edition in October 1878.

Notes

1. Allen Johnson and Dumas Malone, eds., *Dictionary of American Biography* (New York: Charles Scribner's Sons, 1930), 5:279–280.
2. Manfred W. Kohl, *Congregationalism in America* (Oak Creek, Wis.: Congregational Press, 1977), p. 59.
3. Christopher Cushing, ed., *Congregational Quarterly* 20 (October 1878): 639.
4. Cushing quotes a circular issued by the National Council. The circular is reproduced in the *Congregational Quarterly* 20 (October, 1878): 640–41.
5. *Congregational Quarterly* 20 (October 1878): 641.

Information Sources

BIBLIOGRAPHY:
Hoornstra, Jean and Heath, Trudy, eds. *American Periodicals 1741–1900: An Index to the Microfilm Collections.* Ann Arbor, Mich.: University Microfilms, 1979.
Johnson, Allen, and Malone, Dumas, eds. *Dictionary of American Biography.* 22 vols. New York: Charles Scribner's Sons, 1928–40.
Kohl, Manfred W. *Congregationalism in America.* Oak Creek, Wis.: Congregational Press, 1977.
INDEX SOURCES: The *Congregational Quarterly* contains its own indexes; volume 10 contains the index for the first 10 volumes, volume 20 the index for volumes 11 to 20. Also in *Poole's Index.*
REPRINT EDITIONS: University Microfilms International.
LOCATION SOURCES: University of California-Berkeley, Union Theological Seminary (New York), Yale University, University of Chicago, University of Texas-Austin, and others.

Publication History

MAGAZINE TITLE AND TITLE CHANGES: *Congregational Quarterly* (1859–78).
VOLUME AND ISSUE DATA: Vols. 1–10 (January 1859-October 1868); vols. 11–20, also listed as n.s., vols. 1–10 (January 1869-October 1878).
PUBLISHER AND PLACE OF PUBLICATION: Congregational Publishing House, Boston (1859–74); Christopher Cushing, Boston (1874–78).
EDITORS: Joseph S. Clark (1859–61), Henry Martyn Dexter (1859–65), Alonzo H. Quint (1859–75), Isaac P. Langworthy (1859–72), Christopher Cushing (1868–78), Samuel Burnham (1869–73). Until 1874, editorial control was vested in an

editorial board with as many as four members; in 1874, Christopher Cushing assumed editorial control, assisted for a time by Alonzo H. Quint.

CIRCULATION: Unknown.

Michael R. McCoy

CONGREGATIONALIST. *See* CONGREGATIONALIST AND HERALD OF GOSPEL LIBERTY

CONGREGATIONALIST AND CHRISTIAN WORLD. *See* CONGREGATIONALIST AND HERALD OF GOSPEL LIBERTY

CONGREGATIONALIST AND HERALD OF GOSPEL LIBERTY

The *Boston Recorder* was "the prototype of that numerous class of periodicals called 'religious newspapers.' "[1] It began in 1816 as one of the first efforts to combine journalism and religion. As such, it modeled itself more on the newspapers of the day than on the theological reviews and journals that had begun to appear a few years earlier. In addition to religious news, it contained many other staples of nineteenth-century religious periodicals, including poetry, missionary reports, anecdotes, and articles about pressing social issues.

In the middle of the nineteenth century there was a debate about whose claim to be the founder of the *Boston Recorder* was just. The sons of both Nathaniel Willis and Sidney Edwards Morse claimed for their fathers the honor of devising "the plan of connecting religion and journalism as embraced in the *Boston Recorder*."[2] The claim for Willis rested on his position as the first printer of the newspaper. In that role he also controlled the business arrangements at the outset. He remained a guiding figure for 28 years.

Morse's claim seems somewhat stronger. As a young law student, he was approached by his father, Jedidiah Morse, and Jeremiah Evarts, editor of the *Panoplist*, who proposed that he establish a religious newspaper.[3] Despite his broad experience in writing for newspapers, Morse was reluctant to accept because of his inexperience as an editor and because of the financial risks. Both concerns were assuaged when Evarts agreed to train Morse and supervise the work, and Nathaniel Willis agreed to print the paper at his own risk. Morse "wrote and issued the prospectus of the *Recorder*, a weekly newspaper, on an original plan" in October 1815.[4] As the first issue approached, however, Evarts withdrew from the enterprise. Willis, who lost money because the prospectus had attracted only about five hundred subscribers, also withdrew after the fourth week of publication. Encouraged and supported by his father, Morse secured another printer and continued to publish. Within a few months another six hundred subscribers were added, and the paper began to show a small profit. Willis asked to be restored as printer and was accepted. Thus, although Willis was the initial printer, Morse was the original editor and proprietor.

Morse's claim to be the founder of *Recorder* must not be taken to indicate that his influence over the publication was greater than Willis's. Morse left the *Recorder* "after about a year to enter Andover Theological Seminary."[5] Willis took the lead and guided the newspaper for nearly three decades. He was assisted by a series of editors who included important journalists and leaders of New England Congregationalism. Among those who assisted him were Gerard Hallock, later renowned for his work as a New York journalist. Hallock edited the *Recorder* in 1825, immediately before moving to New York. Calvin Ellis Stowe, later married to Harriet Beecher Stowe, edited the paper in 1830.[6]

Sidney Morse's official connection with the *Recorder* ended when he left for seminary. There remained an unofficial connection, however. In 1823 Sidney Morse and his younger brother, Richard Cary Morse, moved to New York and founded the *New York Observer*, a religious newspaper designed on the same plan as the *Recorder*. The *New York Observer* continued to be a house organ for orthodox Congregationalism for many years. During its early years the *Observer* drew many of its assistant editors, and later its senior editors, from the *Boston Recorder*. Gerard Hallock, Nathaniel Willis's partner in the *Recorder*, sold his half of that paper in 1826 in order to join the Morse brothers "as joint owner and editor of the *New York Observer*."[7] Joseph Tracy joined the *Observer* in 1835 after a year as editor of the *Recorder*. Tracy continued as publisher of the *Recorder* with Nathaniel Willis until 1837.

From its beginning, the *Recorder* was very much a newspaper. Although it combined the features of weekly newspapers and religious journals of the day, both its founders and its readers understood it to be a newspaper. It provided a mixture of religious and secular news in a four-page, five-column format, which resembled most of the weekly papers of the time. Secular news included local reports about Boston, broader information about national affairs, reports of Congress, marriages and deaths, and advertisements.[8]

This strong identification with the newspaper format continued until 1825 when the *Recorder* merged with the *Boston Telegraph* to form the *Recorder and Telegraph*. Under the combined leadership of Nathaniel Willis and Gerard Hallock, who had owned the *Telegraph*, the focus of the new publication changed. There was less emphasis on secular news and more stress on religious matters. Although the paper still came out on a weekly basis, there was less effort to offer a compromise between secular newspapers and religious journals. Secure in its identity and with a steadily increasing list of subscribers, the *Recorder and Telegraph* became an outspoken voice of Congregational orthodoxy, a role it maintained throughout its existence.

Religious material covered by the *Recorder* and its successors varied according to the important issues of the day. Many editions reported on foreign missions and the progress of Congregationalism in other parts of the world. Early issues (up to the mid–1820s) and editions in the 1840s and 1850s reported the revivals that continued to excite the churches of New England. Samuel Ware's account of the revival in Ware, Massachusetts, in 1819 is of particular interest.[9] In other editions there were discussions of Sabbath Schools, religious societies (including the American Bible Society, the Boston Society for the Religious and Moral Instruction of the Poor, and many others), and other important concerns of the day. The uniting feature in all of these reports and discussions was a clear sense of denominational identity. The editors summarized their position in 1850: "Our aim is rather to hold fast what we have—to illustrate, enforce and defend the doctrines of our Puritan fathers, and of the leading divines of New England from that day to this. This we desire to do, as little as possible, in the language of controversy."[10]

Although the editorial stance of the *Recorder* and its successors is fairly clear, the history of the publication itself is a confusion of mergers and name changes. Initially known as the *Recorder*, the title was changed to *Boston Recorder* not long after the departure of Sidney Morse. In 1825 it became the *Recorder and Telegraph* (or sometimes the *Telegraph and Recorder*) when Gerard Hallock entered partnership with Nathaniel Willis and merged his *Boston Telegraph* with the *Boston Recorder*. The name of the publication was lengthened and clarified in 1826 to *Boston Recorder and Religious Telegraph*, but four years later, after the departure of Hallock, it became simply the *Boston Recorder* again. Another merger, this time with the *New England Puritan* in 1849, led to the *Puritan Recorder*. After 10 years the name was restored to *Boston Recorder* and was not changed again until 1867 when the *Boston Recorder* joined with the *Congregationalist* to form the *Congregationalist and Recorder*. This name was maintained until the end of 1869 when it became simply the *Congregationalist*. Another merger in 1901 led to the *Congregationalist and Christian World*, which was again shortened to the *Congregationalist*, after 20 years, in 1921. Another merger in 1930 formed the *Congregationalist and Herald of Gospel Liberty*, the usual listing for the complex. This publication continued until 1934, when it was superseded by the *Advance*.

Notes

1. Frederick Hudson, *Journalism in the U.S. from 1690 to 1872* (New York: Harper and Bros., 1873), p. 294.

2. Ibid., p. 294.

3. Allen Johnson and Dumas Malone, eds., *Dictionary of American Biography* (New York: Charles Scribner's Sons, 1930), 13:251.

4. Hudson, p. 294.

5. Johnson and Malone, 13:251.

6. Ibid., vols. 8, 18.

7. Ibid., 8:157.

8. Neal L. Edgar, *A History and Bibliography of American Magazines, 1810–1820* (Metuchen, N.J.: Scarecrow Press, 1975), p. 135.

9. *Boston Recorder* 5 (1 January 1820): 1.

10. *Puritan Recorder* 35 (1850): 178.

Information Sources

BIBLIOGRAPHY:

Edgar, Neal L. *A History and Bibliography of American Magazines, 1810–1820.* Metuchen, N.J.: Scarecrow Press, 1975.

Hoornstra, Jean, and Trudy Heath, eds. *American Periodicals 1741–1900: An Index to the Microfilm Collections.* Ann Arbor, Mich.: University Microfilms, 1979.

Hudson, Frederick. *Journalism in the U.S. from 1690 to 1872.* New York: Harper and Bros., 1873.

Johnson, Allen, and Dumas Malone, eds. *Dictionary of American Biography.* 22 vols. New York: Charles Scribner's Sons, 1928–40.

INDEX SOURCES: Most volumes of the *Boston Recorder* contain annual indexes at the close of the volume. There are no cumulative indexes or external index sources.

REPRINT EDITIONS: University Microfilms International (under the various titles; some editions not preserved).

LOCATION SOURCES: Boston Public Library and the Congregational Library (Boston) have the only known complete sets.

Publication History

MAGAZINE TITLE AND TITLE CHANGES: *Recorder* (1816), *Boston Recorder* (1817–24, 1830–49, 1858–67), *Recorder and Telegraph* (1825), *Boston Recorder and Religious Telegraph* (1826–30), *Puritan Recorder* (1849–58), *Congregationalist and Recorder* (1867–69), *Congregationalist* (1870–1901, 1921–30), *Congregationalist and Christian World* (1901–21), *Congregationalist and Herald of Gospel Liberty* (1930–34).

VOLUME AND ISSUE DATA: Numbering confused by the many mergers and title changes; most contemporary citations follow Hoornstra and Heath (see Bibliography) in numbering volumes consecutively from the first volume (1) of *Recorder* (1816) to the last (119) of *Congregationalist and Herald of Gospel Liberty* (1934), but this scheme omits volumes of merged publications printed prior to the mergers.

PUBLISHER AND PLACE OF PUBLICATION: Complete list of publishers unknown, but all were in Boston.

EDITORS: Complete list unknown; where known, individuals are noted in the text.

CIRCULATION: Ranged from 500 to 5000.

Michael R. McCoy

CONGREGATIONALIST AND RECORDER. *See* CONGREGATIONALIST AND HERALD OF GOSPEL LIBERTY

CONSERVATIVE JUDAISM

Conservative Judaism is a publication of the Rabbinical Assembly and the Jewish Theological Seminary of America. While topics of interest to Conservative rabbis and laypersons are the special concern of this journal, *"Conservative Judaism* is [also] of great interest to those not affiliated with the Conservative movement, insofar as its perspective is worldwide, extending beyond denominational lines."[1]

With the exception of volume 34, which was published as a bimonthly, *Conservative Judaism* has appeared as a quarterly since its inception in 1945. In keeping with the Jewish calendar, in which the new year begins in the autumn, the fall issue is the first number of each volume, followed by issues in the winter, spring, and summer. (Thus 33:1 carries a fall 1979 date, with winter 1980, spring 1980, and summer 1980 completing the volume.)

The editors of *Conservative Judaism* (there have been nine) are Conservative rabbis. They have usually been assisted in their task by an editorial board, a managing editor, an associate editor, and various department editors. These groups have devised several formats in which to present the journal's material. A typical issue of the journal in the early 1980s contained between four and eight articles, a few review essays, approximately a half-dozen book reviews, and several communications. In addition, each issue generally included one or more of the following sections: "State of the Field," "Open Forum," "Beineinu," and "Letter from Jerusalem." The average number of pages for these issues is between 80 and 100.

The following describes the breadth of coverage provided by this journal:

> *Conservative Judaism* is concerned with Jewish life in all of its variety, as reflected in articles about Jews in the French Foreign Legion, in Latin America, in Sweden, and in the Havurah movement in the United States. Life in Israel has been discussed . . . and examined. . . . Special issues have focused on the lives and teachings of Abraham Joshua Heschel and of Mordecai M. Kaplan. . . . Topics of current interest are related to Jewish sources and placed into perspective. Thus the journal has dealt with various issues of the changing role of women in the Jewish community, and with issues encompassing medical ethics.[2]

Three cumulative indexes of *Conservative Judaism* have been published: volumes 1–17, volumes 18–30 (printed in the summer 1977 issue), and volumes 31–33 (printed in the summer 1980 issue). The 1977 and 1980 listings are divided into an author index, a subject index, and a book review index.

Notes

1. Notice of *Conservative Judaism* in *Religion and Related Areas* catalog of Human Sciences Press (New York: Human Sciences Press, n.d.), page 1.
2. Notice of *Conservative Judaism*.

Information Sources

INDEX SOURCES: *Index to Jewish Periodicals, Religious and Theological Abstracts*.
LOCATION SOURCES: Boston University, Jewish Theological Seminary, New York
Public Library, Yale University and others.

Publication History

MAGAZINE TITLE AND TITLE CHANGES: *Conservative Judaism* (1945–).
VOLUME AND ISSUE DATA: 1:1 (1945–). Appears quarterly in fall, winter, spring,
and summer; vol. 34 only was bimonthly.
PUBLISHER AND PLACE OF PUBLICATION: Rabbinical Assembly and the Jewish
Theological Seminary of America, New York.
EDITORS: Leon S. Lang (1945–52), Samuel H. Dresner (1952–64), Jack Riemer (1964–
65), S. Gershon Levi (1965–69), Mordecai Waxman (1969–74), Stephen C. Lerner
(1974–77), Myron Fenster (1977–79), Arthur A. Chiel (1979–80), Harold S.
Kushner (1980–).
CIRCULATION: 2000 (1982).

Leonard J. Greenspoon

CONTEMPORARY JEWISH RECORD. *See*
COMMENTARY

CROSS CURRENTS

In 1976 *Cross Currents* celebrated its twenty-fifth anniversary with a glance
at its beginnings in December 1950. "From our first article," the editors declared,
"we have been forced to recognize the failures of Christendom, seeing its com-
promises with war, capitalism, colonialism, racism, and sexism as our own
betrayal writ large."[1]

The journal was born out of the trauma of World War II, reacting in large
part to the failure of culture-Christianity. Its editors were young Catholic laypeople (teachers and students), many of them graduates of Catholic colleges.
The first issue pointed out the need for both humility and critical thinking if
Christians were to address the modern world meaningfully and "reintroduce
Christianity to Christendom." The primary function of the journal was to reprint
the outstanding articles from European sources that would "indicate the relevance
of religion to the intellectual life."[2] Early contributors included Emil Brunner,
Henri de Lubac, Karl Barth, Karl Rahner, Simone Weil, Karl Jaspers, and Jean
Daniélou.

Emmanuel Mounier's "Christian Faith and Civilization" illustrated the journal's attention to the relationship of Christianity and culture. Mounier stated that
"Christianity commands man to take an active place in the temporal world" but
also demands that one give up the "horrible illusion" that Christianity can be

identified with the cultural forms it takes.[3] Early issues of *Cross Currents* are filled with articles on the meaning of history, the Christian-Marxist dialogue, the issue of religious freedom, and the relationship of Christianity to the secular state. In the winter 1951 issue, for example, Karl Barth's significant article on the East-West struggle suggested to readers that "[we] must be all the more on our guard against regarding our Western judgment as the right and Christian judgment."[4]

Articles by Carl Rogers, Martin Buber, C. G. Jung, and others introduced readers to the relationship between religion and psychiatry. In 1964 a number of *Cross Currents* articles by Roman Catholics on this subject were included in the book *Cross Currents of Psychiatry and Religion*, which attempted to ease the then "inflammable relationship between religion, psychiatry, and psychoanalysis."[5]

Cross Currents turned more and more to American resources and issues in the turbulent 1960s. Bemoaning the quality of the debate surrounding the impact of John Kennedy's Catholicism on his presidential candidacy, the editors suggested that "the sense of God, the idea of the holy, cannot make their impact on men busy with the clatter of heated argument over irrelevancies," and time would be better spent attending to the crucial national and international issues of the times.[6]

The Second Vatican Council was a highly significant event for the journal. The spring 1962 issue, "Looking toward the Council," had contributions from Roman Catholic scholars from Europe, Asia, and Africa, as well as contributions from Orthodox and Protestant spokesmen. The issue was published in book form by Herder and Herder in 1962. The journal also published a lengthy commentary on the council and considered Vatican II "a public vindication of many European Catholic theologians published earlier in *Cross Currents* when they were under varying degrees of fire from Vatican authorities."[7]

As the radical upheavals of the decade continued, a variety of issues attracted the journal's attention. Bernard Gilligan introduced an issue concerned with sexuality, declaring it was important to discuss "the personal and changing problems associated with human sexuality."[8] Louis Dupré criticized the Catholic position on birth control, stating that the choices available to Catholics (abstinence or the rhythm method) "would seem to require more solid justification than reference to the intrinsic finality of man's biological nature."[9]

The journal's editors asked its readers to abandon faulty mythologies of all kinds. They castigated the church for its ambivalence on the race question, asking if the church had the moral power to confront this evil. Hervé Chaigne continued the journal's attention to socialism by illustrating the church's movement from total rejection to "implicit acceptance of a large part of the positive program of socialism."[10] Jean Lecourtre introduced readers to the complex political situation in Vietnam, and W. Richard Comstock examined the death of God movement, suggesting that man's new secular maturity might be preparatory for a "new religious adulthood whose final shape we now can only dimly see."[11]

Part of this religious adulthood was evident in the growing sense of advocacy as an integral part of Christian witness. "Abundant evidence," the editors declared, "indicates that . . . we know too little about how to live and how to exchange the gift of life with others."[12] More than ever before, *Cross Currents* looked to others to help define ideological and cultural ghettoes that impeded understanding of subcultures in the United States and non-Christian cultures around the world. The editors hoped that these unheard minority voices might sensitize readers to the "interlocking forms of injustice from which all these groups suffer" and might help prevent a "new glorification of nationalism" in the United States.[13] Hence, *Cross Currents* expanded its interest in material from feminist theologians, black theologians, and numerous voices from Third World churches.

Although *Cross Currents* was immersed in the public issues of the day, the editors never lost sight of the importance of the cultivation of the inner life. One of the journal's distinctive contributions has been its issues on spirituality: "A Symposium of World Spiritualities," with contributions from David Steindl-Rast, Thomas Berry, Kallistos Ware, Joshu Sasaki Roshi, and Inayat Khan; "The Good Red Road: Native American Spirituality"; and "Spirituality in Secularized Society: The Maritain-Merton Symposium." Jacques Maritain and Thomas Merton represented the values *Cross Currents* most desired to foster: Maritain's "true humanism" and Merton's combination of a "deep interior life and profound compassion for the oppressed."[14]

The rich variety of viewpoints expressed in these issues suggests that *Cross Currents* had moved beyond the ecumenical interests of its early days—when articles about non-Christian religions tended toward paternalism—to a genuine desire for interreligious dialogue.[15] The efforts of Raimundo Pannikar were significant in this respect, and a special issue in his honor examined his efforts to help create the "new modes of consciousness required by a global environment."[16]

In addition to offering articles on the cutting edge of so many controversial issues, since 1957 *Cross Currents* has provided its readers James Collins's "Annual Review of Philosophy" and has consistently published substantive book reviews.

Cross Currents, while remaining true to its original purpose, has expanded its interests. Impressed in its early years with the personalist philosophy of Mounier, *Cross Currents* asked its readers to consider responsible action as well as interior development. To their credit, the editors understood that to consider this diligently, inquiry could not be limited by parochial constraints or comfortable illusions. The journal asks its readers to abandon these illusions and develop "more of a readiness for the supreme risk of the total abandonment of ourselves to God."[17]

Notes

1. Joseph E. Cunneen, "After 25 Years: An Introduction to Our 100th Issue," *Cross Currents* 25 (Winter 1976): 355.

2. Both quotes from the first issue's editorial, *Cross Currents* 1 (Fall 1950): 1.

3. Emmanuel Mounier, "Christian Faith and Civilization," *Cross Currents* 1 (Fall 1950): 9.

4. Karl Barth, "The Church between East and West," *Cross Currents* 1 (Winter 1951): 69.

5. William Birmingham and Joseph E. Cunneen, eds., *Cross Currents of Psychiatry and Catholic Morality* (Cleveland: World Publishing Co., 1966), p. v.

6. Joseph E. Cunneen, "The 'Religious Issue' and the Limits of National Purpose," *Cross Currents* 10 (Fall 1960): 313.

7. Correspondence from Joseph E. Cunneen, editor of *Cross Currents*.

8. Bernard Gilligan, "Sexuality and the Modern World: An Introduction,"*Cross Currents* 14 (Spring 1964): 129.

9. Louis Dupré, "Toward a Re-Examination of the Catholic Position on Birth Control," *Cross Currents* 15 (Winter 1964): 69.

10. Hervé Chaigne, "The Catholic Church and Socialism," *Cross Currents* 15 (Spring 1965): 163.

11. W. Richard Comstock, "Theology after the 'Death of God,' " *Cross Currents* 16 (Summer 1966): 301. The journal offered its readers substantive discussion regarding various trends in contemporary theology. For example, the summer 1968 issue was devoted to "A Symposium on Hope," edited by Walter H. Capps. Contributors included Ernest Bloch, Wolfhart Pannenberg, Johannes B. Metz, and Jurgen Moltmann.

12. "For White America: Perspectives on Development and Social Change," *Cross Currents* 18 (Fall 1968): 385.

13. Both quotes from Cunneen, "After 25 Years," p. 354.

14. See "A Symposium on World Spiritualities," *Cross Currents* 24 (Summer and Fall 1974); "The Good Red Road: Native American Spirituality," *Cross Currents* 26 (Summer 1976). The comment about Thomas Merton is from "Spirituality in a Secularized Society: The Maritain-Merton Symposium," *Cross Currents* 31 (Fall 1981): 258.

15. For example, see J. M. Abd-el-Jalil, "Islam, the Koran, and History," *Cross Currents* 3 (Fall 1952), and Emile Gauthier, "Hinduism and Christian Thought," *Cross Currents* 3 (Winter 1953).

16. "Symposium in Honor of Raimundo Pannikar," *Cross Currents* 29 (Summer 1979): 131.

17. Joseph E. Cunneen, "We—and They," *Cross Currents* 14 (Spring 1964): 292.

Information Sources

BIBLIOGRAPHY:

Cassidy, Sally Whelan. "Catholic Revival." *Catholic World* 171 (September 1950): 460–61.

Cogley, John. "Cross Currents." *Commonweal* 53 (30 March 1951): 608.

Wolf, D. "Emmanuel Mounier: A Catholic of the Left." *Review of Politics* 22 (1960): 324–44.

INDEX SOURCES: *Catholic Periodical and Literature Index, Humanities Index, Old*

Testament Abstracts, Guide to Social Science and Religion in Periodical Literature, Religious and Theological Abstracts.
REPRINT EDITIONS: University Microfilms International.
LOCATION SOURCES: Los Angeles Public Library, University of Southern California, Boston Public Library, Yale University, University of Chicago, Princeton University, and others.

Publication History

MAGAZINE TITLE AND TITLE CHANGES: *Cross Currents* (1950–   ).
VOLUME AND ISSUE DATA: *Cross Currents* 1:1 (Fall 1950–   ).
PUBLISHER AND PLACE OF PUBLICATION: *Cross Currents*, Mercy College, Dobbs Ferry, N.Y.
EDITOR: Joseph E. Cunneen (1950–   ).
CIRCULATION: 7000 (1982).

Edward Tabor Linenthal

THE CUMBERLAND PRESBYTERIAN REVIEW

In February 1810, three disgruntled Presbyterians ended a long-standing ecclesiastical dispute. Samuel McAdow, Finis Ewing, and Samuel King withdrew from the Presbyterian Church in which they had been ordained:

> Having waited in vain more than four years [we] . . . do hereby agree, and determine, to constitute into a presbytery. On the following conditions (to wit) all candidates for the ministry, who may hereafter be licensed by this presbytery . . . shall be required . . . to receive, and adopt, the confession of the Presbyterian Church, except the idea of fatality, that seems to be taught under the mysterious doctrine of predestination.[1]

So began the Cumberland Presbyterian Church, an ecclesiastical body conceived in revivalism, born of theological controversy, and nurtured on America's western frontier. The Cumberland patriarchs' scruples against traditional Presbyterian schemes of predestation were more than short-lived squabbles, however. A self-conscious position midway between Calvinism and Arminianism was to become the lasting theological hallmark of the new denomination. The editor of one of the *Cumberland Presbyterian Review*'s antecedents urged seekers to "take passage in the safe care of the Bible, and you will soon arrive at Cumberlandtown, situated on the highway of truth between Calvinburg and Arminianville."[2]

The Cumberland Church was indeed a nineteenth-century American ecclesiastical hybrid. Theologically it stood between the classic doctrinal poles of Arminianism and Calvinism. But the denominations's ecclesiology was also a blend of distinct traditions. Although some Cumberland ministers served settled congregations, the church's early history was marked by the presence of itinerant clergy as well. The staunchly traditional *Biblical Repository and Princeton Review** suspected that the Cumberlanders had "a presbyterian warp, but a Methodist filling," an assessment with which many Cumberland ministers were happy to agree. As one church leader claimed, strictly Presbyterian polity and Methodist zeal combined to make the Cumberlanders "the most orthodox Presbyterians on the American Continent."[3]

In many respects the *Cumberland Presbyterian Review* and its antecedents reflected the changes and shifting emphases of the denomination itself. Begun in 1845 as the *Theological Medium*, the publication sought to define—in terms intelligible to the popular mind—the uniqueness of the denomination. Milton Bird, the journal's founding editor and publisher, included items of polemic theological character, such as attacks on the Calvinist notion of the divine decrees, as well as more filiopietistic essays by denominational clergy. Subsequent editors, T. C. Blake and M. B. DeWitt, continued this editorial stance, adding book reviews and later advertisements aimed at Cumberland laypeople.

In 1880 the *Theological Medium* changed hands and was published under the name *Cumberland Presbyterian Quarterly*. The editorial task fell to the theological faculty of the denomination's university. This development was accompanied by an editorial shift in a scholarly direction. Essays on "Augustine and Augustinianism" and "Hebrew Poetry" appeared in the first issue and were typical of the new approach. Despite the academic emphasis, however, the editors had the everyday faith of Cumberlanders in mind. The *Quarterly* addressed several issues of the day. Articles on tobacco, suicide, and temperance—the last examined under the question of the propriety of using alcohol in the Lord's Supper—offered scholarly analyses of traditional frontier-revival concerns.

In 1881 the *Quarterly* took another title, *Cumberland Presbyterian Review*, and began to include the work of authors whose opinions were not wholly acceptable to the Cumberland University faculty. The last page of one issue included the disclaimer, "The Editors of the *Review* do not hold themselves responsible for all the views of their correspondents."[4]

Appeals for increased reader support were scattered throughout nearly all the issues of the *Review*. In 1884 W. C. Logan attempted to revitalize the periodical, but financial constraints made the publication of further issues impossible. Five years later, the denomination itself made an attempt to resurrect the enterprise under the title *Cumberland Presbyterian Review: A Quarterly Magazine* but was able to publish only four volumes. When the circulation dropped to approximately 300 in 1892, the periodical was discontinued.[5] A last attempt to revive it a decade later was also unsuccessful.

Notes

1. *A Circular Letter Addressed to the Societies and Brethren of the Late Cumberland Presbytery* (Russellville, Ky.: Printed by Matthew Duncan at the Office of the Farmer's Friend, 1810).

2. Editor's comment, *Theological Medium: A Monthly Journal* 4:7 (May 1849): 193.

3. Ibid. 2:7 (May 1847): 453–54.

4. *Cumberland Presbyterian Review* 19:4 (October 1883): back leaf.

5. Ben Barrus et al., *A People Called Cumberland Presbyterians* (Memphis: Frontier Press, 1971), p. 249.

Information Sources

BIBLIOGRAPHY:

Barrus, Ben, et al. *A People Called Cumberland Presbyterians*. Memphis: Frontier Press, 1971.

Foster, Robert V. *A Sketch of the History of the Cumberland Presbyterian Church*. American Church History Series, vol. 11. New York: Christian Literature Co., 1894.

INDEX SOURCES: None.

REPRINT EDITIONS: American Periodicals Series, University Microfilms International (missing vols. 1, 3, 5–6, 8, 10, 14 [o.s.] and 1–4 [final ser.]).

LOCATION SOURCES: Historical Library of the Cumberland Presbyterian Church, Memphis Theological Seminary; most complete partial collections at Library of Congress, Yale University, and Historical Foundation of the Presbyterian and Reformed Churches.

Publication History

MAGAZINE TITLE AND TITLE CHANGES: *The Theological Medium: A Monthly Journal* (1845–50), *The Theological Medium: A Cumberland Presbyterian Quarterly* (1853, 1871–79), *The Cumberland Presbyterian Review* (1880–84), *The Cumberland Presbyterian Review: A Quarterly Magazine* (1889–92).

VOLUME AND ISSUE DATA: *The Theological Medium: A Monthly Journal* 1–5 (November 1845-October 1850); *Theological Medium: A Cumberland Presbyterian Quarterly* 6–15 [also n.s. 1–10] (January-October 1853, January 1871-October 1879); *Cumberland Presbyterian Review* 16–20 (January 1880-October 1884); *Cumberland Presbyterian Review: A Quarterly Magazine* 1–4 (January 1889-October 1892).

PUBLISHERS AND PLACES OF PUBLICATION: Milton Bird, Uniontown, Pa. (1845–47), Louisville, Ky. (1848–49); Cumberland Presbyterian Board of Publication, Nashville, Tenn. (1853, 1871–79); J. D. Kirkpatrick, Lebanon, Tenn. (1880–83); W. C. Logan, St. Louis, Mo. (1884); Board of Publication of the Cumberland Presbyterian Church, Nashville, Tenn. (1889–92).

EDITORS: Milton Bird (1845–49), T. C. Blake (1853, 1871–79), M. B. DeWitt (1873–79), Theological Faculty of Cumberland University (1880–84), Board of Publication of the Cumberland Presbyterian Church (1889–92).

CIRCULATION: 300 (1892).

John R. Fitzmier

CURRENTS IN THEOLOGY AND MISSION. *See* CONCORDIA THEOLOGICAL MONTHLY

DIAKONIA

The era of Vatican II prompted an increased ecumenical awareness in Roman Catholic circles and a desire to inaugurate dialogue with other branches of Christianity or to enhance dialogue already underway. Among some Catholics, dialogue with Eastern Orthodox Christianity seemed paramount, for there were within Roman Catholicism several subgroups that retained the Eastern rite in liturgy or had roots in areas where Eastern Christianity remained dominant. To promote this association with Eastern Orthodox Christianity, Fordham University's John XXIII Center for Eastern Christian Studies in 1966 launched the journal *Diakonia*. Its initial subtitle evidenced its aim: *A Quarterly Devoted to Advancing Orthodox-Catholic Dialogue*.

From its inception, *Diakonia* has organized material into four departments: articles, comment, documentation (minutes of dialogue consultations and the like), and a list of books received (not book reviews). The articles have tended to concentrate more on various aspects of Eastern Orthodox history, theology, and liturgy, as well as on practical matters (such as positions on divorce) than on comparative Roman Catholic–Eastern Orthodox studies. Authors have been drawn from within and outside the ranks of both religious bodies. Well-known figures who have contributed to *Diakonia* have included Cardinal Bea, Georges Florovsky, Franklin Clark Fry, John Meyendorff, and Louis Bouyer.

Frequent discussion has been directed to various theological topics in the thought of the early church fathers common to both traditions but now more directly associated with Eastern Christianity: Irenaeus, Gregory of Nyssa, Origen, John Chrysostom, Gregory Nazianzus, and others. Contemporary Orthodox thinking, however, has not been neglected. For instance, in 1975, *Diakonia* carried a lengthy, two-part appraisal, "The Holy Spirit's Role in the Deification of Man According to Contemporary Orthodox Theology (1925–1972)" by Sister

Marta Ryk, O.S.U. In addition, Eastern liturgy and devotional life, as well as its relationship to Western practices, has been a frequent subject of analysis. Louis Bouyer, for example, addressed the theme, "Western Catholics and the Byzantine Liturgy" (7:2, 1972), and Catherine Aslanoff discussed "Veneration of Icons" (6:4, 1971). Occasionally specifically historical topics come under scrutiny, as in "Public Opinion, the Schism, and the Fourth Crusade," by Raymond H. Schmandt (3:3, 1968). Issues that have been bones of contention between Eastern and Western Christians have also been appraised, as in the three-part series (4, 1969) by Bernard Schultze of the Pontifical Institute on the primacy of the bishop of Rome (the pope) and the numerous articles dealing with the controversial filioque clause in the Nicene Creed, which have appeared over the years. Finally, some issues have concentrated on single themes such as unitism (2:2, 1967) and ecclesiology (2:3, 1967).

Although from its beginning *Diakonia* has counted Eastern Orthodox adherents as associate editors, much of the character of the journal has revolved around the editor, who regularly has contributed not only an editorial in each issue but often articles as well. For many years, the driving force behind *Diakonia* was George Maloney, coeditor in the first year of publication and then editor until 1982. Maloney did not hesitate to take a firm position on matters of concern in Eastern-Western Christian dialogue, even at the risk of rebuke. In 15:2 (1980), Maloney editorially criticized papal actions with regard to Ukrainian Orthodox Christians. The issue contained a special disclaimer indicating that Maloney's views did not represent those of the sponsoring agency. Maloney was replaced as editor just over one year later by John F. Long, S.J., the more conservative director of the John XXIII Center.

In 1975, as ecumenical advocates recognized that dialogue was a long-term process and the enthusiasm for ecumenical ventures begun by Vatican II waned, *Diakonia* adopted a new subtitle, which also reflected Maloney's personal agenda: *Devoted to Promoting Eastern Christianity in the West.* The transfer of editorial leadership to Long witnessed another change in subtitle to *Devoted to Promoting a Knowledge and Understanding of Eastern Christianity.* The subtle shift in emphasis was indicative of a desire to stem the advocacy role that *Diakonia* had assumed and bring its orientation more in keeping with official church policy.

Information Sources

INDEX SOURCES: In 1975, *Diakonia* published an index to vols. 1–10.
REPRINT EDITIONS: University Microfilms International.
LOCATION SOURCES: Yale University, Catholic University of America, Library of Congress, Union Theological Seminary (New York), Princeton Theological Seminary, Duke University, University of Chicago, Harvard University, and others.

Publication History

MAGAZINE TITLE AND TITLE CHANGES: *Diakonia: Devoted to Advancing Orthodox-Catholic Dialogue* (1966–74), *Diakonia: Devoted to Promoting Eastern Christianity in the West* (1975–82), *Diakonia: Devoted to Promoting a Knowledge and Understanding of Eastern Christianity* (1982–   ).

VOLUME AND ISSUE DATA: 1:1–9:3 (1966–74), three issues per year; 10:1 (1975–), quarterly.
PUBLISHER AND PLACE OF PUBLICATION: John XXIII Center for Eastern Christian Studies, Fordham University, Bronx, N.Y.
EDITORS: Thomas Bird and George A. Maloney (1966–67), George A. Maloney (1967–81), John F. Long, S.J. (1982–).
CIRCULATION: 1500 (1982).

Charles H. Lippy

THE DIAL

A major force in shaping American religious thought in its liberal expression was the transcendentalist movement, and the major literary expression of this movement was the *Dial*. Transcendentalism has been defined rather loosely at times. Terms such as *faith, temper, mood, attitude, mystical spirit, enthusiasm, wave of sentiment,* and *intuitive* have been used.[1] In 1842, C. M. Ellis, in his "Essay on Transcendentalism," defined it as follows: "That belief we term transcendentalism which maintains that man has ideas, that come not through the five senses, or the powers of reasoning; but are either the result of direct revelation from God, his immediate inspiration, or his immanent presence in the spiritual world."[2] The referent of transcendentalism was definitely that order of reality that transcends the experience of the senses. The transcendentalists held to the immediacy of reality through their intuitional theory of knowledge. They subscribed to an order of truths that transcends the sphere of external fact.[3] It is next to impossible to trace all the roots of the movement, for at times it seems to draw upon the entire intellectual history of humanity. Within it one sees Platonism and neo-Platonism, Cambridge Platonism, philosophical idealism, the British moral sense tradition, Scottish realism, and French eclecticism. Further, it was inscribed in the much larger romantic movement of the nineteenth century.[4]

Perry Miller described the historical emergence of the movement: "The Transcendentalists were a number of young Americans, most of them born into the Unitarianism of New England in the early nineteenth century, who in the 1830s became excited, or rather intoxicated, by the new literature of England and of the Continent (and also by a cursory introduction to that of the Orient), and who thereupon revolted against the rationalism of their fathers."[5] Many of these "young Americans" were clergymen liberated by Unitarianism from orthodox Calvinism but moving a giant step forward even from Unitarianism. They were now impatiently objecting to the religion of rationalism just as they had earlier objected to Calvinistic orthodoxy. They rejected the lingering authoritarianism and biblicism in the enlightenment themes.[6] Indeed, "a few bold American spirits made a gallant effort to introduce this mercantile and pragmatic nation to some of the deeper currents in the intellectual life of the West—and of the East."[7]

It was out of the Transcendental Club that the *Dial* had its birth. On 8 September 1836, F. H. Hedge, George Putnam, George Ripley, and Ralph Waldo Emerson met at Willard's Hotel in Cambridge, Massachusetts, to form an informal symposium. Such discussion clubs were common at this time. Ripley volunteered his home for the second meeting, and all agreed that more persons would be invited. New participants were Bronson Alcott, Orestes Brownson, James Clarke, and Convers Francis. This lively group, reveling in dissent, adopted only one rule: "no man should be admitted whose presence excluded any one topic." Soon other important figures were invited to the meetings, including William Ellery Channing, Margaret Fuller, and Theodore Parker.[8]

At the meeting of 18 September 1839, the subject of the publication of a journal was first discussed, and Alcott proposed a title, the *Dial*. The club was now preparing to give its members a public voice. There had been informal talk of such before, but this was the first formal discussion. The transcendentalists had generally found all avenues for expressing themselves and their ideas cut off. They believed that they needed a magazine that would be religious and give some space to literary and philosophical material. Early on, there were two models for such a venture: the English journal, the *Monthly Magazine*, and the *Western Messenger*. Both journals had taken a friendly attitude toward the transcendentalists, and both were successful. After this initial interest from the club, the driving forces to establish the journal were Fuller, Emerson, and Ripley and their closest friends.[9]

Emerson soon announced that Fuller would edit the journal and that Ripley would be involved in the business side of it. Fuller's enthusiasm was catching, and Emerson got caught up in it, even receiving the first literary contribution for the *Dial*, an "Elegy" from Henry David Thoreau. The Boston house of Weeks, Jordan and Co. agreed to publish the *Dial*. By April 1840, Fuller was planning the contents of the first number. In May a "Prospectus" of the journal was sent out with its final statement: "The *Dial*, as its title indicates, will endeavor to occupy a station on which the light may fall; which is open to the rising sun; and from which it may correctly report the progress of the hour and the day." Volume 1, number 1 appeared in July 1840. The *Dial*'s brief history was underway.[10]

Although there were some appreciative responses, in the main the *Dial* was greeted with ridicule or simply ignored. One reviewer reported that after reading the *Dial*, he had been left "perfectly in the dark." The *Boston Times* called it "one of the most . . . ridiculous productions of the age." The few words of praise were only whispers amid the critical chatter. Transcendentalism itself continued to be discredited as almost "sheer midsummer madness," and since the *Dial* was linked so closely to this movement, its future was bleak indeed.[11]

The second number in October 1840 appeared amid better reviews, but actually less attention was given to it. Surprisingly, one of the best reviews came from the *Knickerbocker*, a source of heavy criticism of the first number. Fuller and Emerson were encouraged by the better reception and the increased interest.

After two more issues (one year of publication), however, the outlook was rather dim. Only local papers and friends paid attention to the *Dial*, the publishers were in financial straits, and the editor was in poor health. In the second year the *Dial* was damned by unattention far more than by negative attention. Established journals simply did not mention the *Dial*. Publishers were changed several times, and Fuller's state of mind was "deeply grave, deeply lonely." Other strains were made even more intense by financial matters; a salary promised the editor had not been paid.[12]

In March 1842, Fuller wrote Emerson of her firm decision to resign as editor because of financial matters and severe health problems. Within a few days Emerson agreed to take over the journal "for a time." Wishing Fuller better health, he requested information and details about running the *Dial*. Emerson was mainly faced with the mammoth problem of reviving interest in a journal that was hardly receiving notice except among its closest friends.[13]

Ralph Waldo Emerson was urged from the start by Fuller to be his own editor and form the *Dial* according to his own interests. Theodore Parker suggested that he ensure its success by writing a great deal for it himself. The first number with Emerson as editor appeared in July 1842, published by E. P. Peabody of London. Nearly all the reviews were favorable. It was obvious from the start, however, that the heavy editorial duties were a real trial for Emerson, and just how long he would last was highly debatable. Encouragingly, though, reviews continued to be positive, especially of the October 1842 number. James Russell Lowell referred to it as "the most popular one ever published." Meanwhile Emerson was busy with lecture tours. By March 1843, he was expressing strong uncertainties about the *Dial*'s future; it was making no profit, and the public was not urging its continuation. The last year was continued for certain friends only.[14]

Nothing in the situation changed to dissuade Emerson. Lack of sales and public attention continued. Furthermore, many friends of the *Dial* had either moved or were traveling, and Emerson hardly had enough worthy material to print. By now the *Dial* was even costing Emerson money, and he began to plan that volume 4 would be his last as editor. April 1844 was the final number of the four-year-old *Dial*. Emerson himself evaluated:

> I have just done with the *Dial*. Its last number is printed; and having lived four years, which is a Presidential term in America, it may respectably end. I have continued it for some time against my own judgment to please other people, and though it has now some standing and increasing favour in England, it makes a very slow gain at home, and it is for home that it is designed. It is time that each of the principal contributors to it, should write in their own names, and go to their proper readers. In New England its whole quadrenium [*sic*] will be a pretty historiette in literary annals. I have been impatient to dismiss it as I am a very unable editor, and only lose good time in my choosing and refusing and patching, that I want for more grateful work.[15]

And so, after four years, the trancendentalists lost their major literary voice, not because of qualitative matters but quantitative ones. In retrospect, however, this journal of such brief duration played a major role in shaping liberal American religious thought.[16]

Notes

1. H. S. Smith, R. T. Handy, and L. A. Loetscher, eds., *American Christianity* (New York: Charles Scribner's Sons, 1963), 2:119ff.

2. Perry Miller, ed., *The American Transcendentalists* (Garden City: Doubleday, 1957), p. 23.

3. Smith, Handy, and Loetscher, pp. 122ff.

4. Ibid.

5. Miller, p. ix.

6. Ibid.

7. Ibid., p. xi. Also see Catherine L. Albanese, *Corresponding Motion* (Philadelphia: Temple University Press, 1977). She presents an excellent interpretive statement on and description of transcendentalism. Also, always helpful is O. B. Frothingham, *Transcendentalism in New England* (1876; reprinted New York: Harper, 1959).

8. Joel Myerson, *The New England Transcendentalists and the Dial* (Rutherford, N.J.: Fairleigh Dickinson University Press, 1980), p. 20.

9. Ibid., p. 35ff.

10. Ibid., p. 37ff.

11. Ibid., p. 51ff.

12. Ibid., p. 54ff.

13. Ibid., p. 74ff.

14. Ibid., p. 77ff.

15. Cited in Ibid., p. 98.

16. For the legacy of the movement, see M. Simon and T. H. Parsons, eds., *Transcendentalism and Its Legacy* (Ann Arbor: University of Michigan Press, 1966).

Information Sources

BIBLIOGRAPHY:

Albanese, Catherine L. *Corresponding Motion: Transcendental Religion and the New America*. Philadelphia: Temple University Press, 1977.

Frothingham, O. B. *Transcendentalism in New England*. 1876. New York: Harper, 1959.

Gohdes, Clarence L. F. *The Periodicals of American Transcendentalism*. Durham, N.C.: Duke University Press, 1931.

Miller, Perry, ed. *The American Transcendentalists*. Garden City: Doubleday, 1957.

Myerson, Joel. *The New England Transcendentalists and the Dial*. Rutherford, N.J.: Fairleigh Dickinson University Press, 1980.

Simon, M., and Parsons, T. H., eds. *Transcendentalism and Its Legacy*. Ann Arbor: University of Michigan Press, 1966.

Smith, H. Shelton; Handy, R. T.; and Loetscher, L. A., eds. *American Christianity*. Vol. 2. New York: Charles Scribner's Sons, 1963.

INDEX SOURCES: Joel Myerson, *The New England Transcendentalists and the Dial*, provides a list of the contents for each number of the *Dial*. A complete report on the *Dial*'s contents is found in Joel Myerson, ''An Annotated List of Contributors to the Boston *Dial*," *Studies in Bibliography* 26 (1973): 133–66. Also in *Poole's Index*.

REPRINT EDITIONS: In 1902, the Rowfant Club, a book fancier's club in Cleveland, reprinted the complete *Dial*. In 1961, Russell and Russell of New York City did an offset reprint of the entire *Dial*, using the Rowfant Club edition. Also in the American Periodicals Series, University Microfilms International.

LOCATION SOURCES: Harvard University, University of California-Berkeley, Boston Public Library, New York Public Library, University of Texas-Austin, University of Michigan, and others.

Publication History

MAGAZINE TITLE AND TITLE CHANGES: *The Dial: A Magazine for Literature, Philosophy, and Religion* (1840–44).

VOLUME AND ISSUE DATA: 1:1 (July 1840)–4:4 (April 1844).

PUBLISHER AND PLACE OF PUBLICATION: Weeks, Jordan and Co., Boston (1:1–2:1); Jordan and Co., Boston (Vol. 2:2–2:4); E. P. Peabody, London (3:1–4:4).

EDITORS: Margaret Fuller (vols. 1–2), Ralph Waldo Emerson (vols. 3–4).

CIRCULATION: Never more than 300.

George H. Shriver

DIALOG

Dialog: A Journal of Theology, is a theological quarterly published since 1962. While not affiliated with any American Lutheran church body or agency, it is oriented to a Lutheran readership, particularly nonprofessional theologians. Offering attractive graphics and articles that rarely exceed thirty-five hundred words, each issue centers on a single theme—societal, cultural, ecclesial, biblical, dogmatic, or liturgical—chosen by the editorial board.[1]

Dialog grew out of the experience of a cadre of midwestern Lutheran theologians who came to maturity after World War II, the first generation of American Lutherans whose graduate work was shaped by the theological explosion of the mid-twentieth century. All left the Lutheran heartland to study in the Northeast, in Germany, or in both. Interest in the kerygmatic function of theology incited them to reexamine Lutheran theology and to promote theological ferment within their own denominations.[2] Since no existing journal was devoted to that cause or sufficiently open to it, they launched their own.[3]

A disproportionate number of the founders belonged to an even tighter circle. They shared ethnic and educational backgrounds within the old (Norwegian) Evangelical Lutheran Church (ELC). Many cut their teeth, theologically speaking, on Søren Kierkegaard at the denomination's colleges. Most took their first theological degree from Luther Seminary in St. Paul, Minnesota, where theological controversy among the diverse Norwegian-Lutheran traditions making up the ELC remained a lively pastime.

Non-Norwegians who joined the effort in the founding years usually had experienced European study, a midwestern German or Swedish background, and the same concern to reexamine Lutheran theology. Most of the first members of the self-chosen Editorial Council (Editorial Board since 1980) of some three dozen were in the initial stages of academic careers, usually in Lutheran institutions. Within 10 years, many would hold major theological professorships in the seminaries and colleges of the Lutheran Church in America and the American Lutheran Church. Members with backgrounds in the Lutheran Church-Missouri Synod, such as Robert Sharlemann and Robert Wilken, were by then teaching in non-Lutheran university settings.

The inter-Lutheran character of the journal was also a mark of the era of founding. By the 1960s ethnicity no longer separated Lutherans from each other or isolated them from general cultural trends. Merger had created the American Lutheran Church in 1960, supplanting the old ELC and three other denominations of Norwegian, German, and Danish extract. In 1962 the Lutheran Church in America joined together Swedish, Finnish, and Danish-American denominations with the older and originally Eastern German–American United Lutheran Church in America. In 1967 even the largely German-American Missouri Synod, which had never participated in a merger, was cooperating with the two new bodies in the Lutheran Council in the United States of America. *Dialog* editors welcomed the new age, hoping it would prompt greater theological sophistication and commitment.

The aims of *Dialog* were specified in the initial winter 1962 issue. The editors claimed that "the presuppositions of DIALOG coincide with the theological principles which faithfully interpret that original primary dialogue" between Creator and creature that reached its "supreme and final focus" in the historical biblical Christ and is known concretely in the church. The vertical dialogue initiates a horizontal one. Hence "the journal DIALOG seeks to be a rendezvous where the mind of the church and the cultural consciousness of our age encounter each other in mutual ferment, exposure, criticism and questioning."[4]

Noting that the "profound paradoxes and polar principles" of Luther's thought antedated the dialectical visions of Jakob Böhme, Georg Hegel, and Karl Barth, the editors agreed "that the data of revelation compel the interpreter to correlate concepts which seem to move in opposite directions" and asked rhetorically why theology should "be any less tense than life itself." They intended that the journal work in the gaps between church and world, between theology and "the plethora of relatively autonomous areas of research and knowledge," and between European and American theological movements.[5]

At the start, each issue contained editorials, a half-dozen articles on a particular theme, and three other forms of commentary. In "Views and Counterviews" readers were encouraged to comment on *Dialog* articles or other theological matters. "Ecumenical Perspectives" provided information and analysis of Lutheran and other developments in this arena. "Criticism of Current Literature" supplied thorough reviews of books.

The Editorial Council chose themes that addressed social and political concerns of the 1960s, such as civil rights, cities, war, and the women's movement and also the interpretive problems for Lutheran theology raised by contemporary biblical scholarship and ecumenical and Reformation research. Often a plurality of views were represented; at other times council members wrote lead articles with a more particular viewpoint. Among the regular council authors were Carl Braaten, Robert W. Jenson, James Burtness, Roy Harrisville, Franklin Sherman, and Arthur Olsen. They also solicited the work of Edmund Schlink, Hans Küng, Paul Tillich, Gabriel Vahanian, Helmut Thielicke, Anders Nygren, Regin Prenter, Paul Ramsey, Peter Brunner, Wolfhart Pannenberg, Jurgen Moltmann, and Rosemary Radford Ruether.

In time editorial consensus proved less attainable. By 1969 unsigned editorials had been replaced by initialed ones. As the *Dialog* generation aged and the young turks became the Lutheran theological establishment, they disagreed over the nature of theology's role in the church. Robert Jenson of the LCA's Gettysburg Seminary hoped that *Dialog* would become "more unfair, annoying, and inventive than it has been." He saw *Dialog* as an "upsetter of the church" lest the church be too satisfied with the status quo to upset the world.[6] James Burtness of the ALC's Luther Seminary, on the other hand, argued "that theology will best serve the church in the present time which is more concerned about the essence of the Gospel than about its relevance, which seeks to embrace the many members rather than to sever them, which speaks softly and clearly rather than arrogantly and rudely."[7]

The council did agree that whatever the position, *Dialog* ought to do less reporting of theology and more constructing of it. In its second decade, European contributions virtually ceased.[8] Editor Braaten summarized a developing perspective when he criticized theology as "essentially dialogue" for being "overly reductive and restrictive," since "what the world wants to talk about is not necessarily its greatest need." Braaten called for *Dialog* to become more theological, even at the risk of appearing "monological," by going into something more than ethics, ecumenics and communications, that is to go back into history, to invent new doctrine, to soar into speculation, to challenge basic horizons, to explore the limits of heresy, to provoke the church establishment, to encourage subversive beliefs, etc."[9]

Martin Marty's critique of the first decade hit a nerve. Marty noted that Lutheranism, freshly emergent from its ethnic cocoon, had not made a "substantive witness" on the American scene and that the *Dialog* generation were neither adept as church politicians nor had sufficient "clarity of purpose" to "try to see and press for a specific shape of church-in-culture" as others had done. He argued that for Lutherans "the time had come . . . to see whether in a late secular and enduringly pluralistic environment [the church] can emit signals or images and shapes which should threaten or attract men."[10]

Robert Jenson mentioned Marty's challenge when, beginning his editorship in 1975, he called for *Dialog* to be "a force" for the gospel, for reason, and for the recovery of national hope. According to him, such forcefulness would come from stoking the fires of Lutheranism: "Perhaps DIALOG can yet help give Lutheranism its American chance—not, probably, by promoting it among Catholics and Protestants, but by promoting it among Lutherans."[11] Under Jenson's leadership, analysis of contemporary Lutheranism has been a continuous theme, especially with the prospect of a new Lutheran denomination made up of the ALC, the LCA, and the Association of Evangelical Lutheran Churches, a breakaway body from the Missouri Synod.[12] A new column, "Merger Watch," was added in 1983 to evaluate developments and propose alternatives. *Dialog* staff and council have been active in forums discussing the new church but are notably missing from the body elected to design it. There has been more attention to worship since Jenson's editorship began, and the column "Viva Vox" featuring sermons was added in 1977.[13] Also new are departments for other articles "Near the Theme" or "Outside the Theme."

Cultural discussion has also taken new directions. The state of American education and Christian nurture are recurrent subjects.[14] American culture and religion have come under greater scrutiny.[15] Moreover, in his editorials, Jenson has pushed Lutheran sacramental and incarnational theology in ethical directions challenging to traditional Lutheran ethics.

Beginning its third decade, *Dialog* continues a commitment to the reconstruction of theology. Staff and authors are ready to criticize and to propose alternatives. The *Dialog* inner circle has, however, remained white and overwhelmingly male, though articles manifest broader representation. *Dialog* has never included high-ranking members of either the Missouri Synod or the breakaway moderates, although the latter have joined its circle through ALC or LCA connections. With circulation just above 2000, *Dialog* continues primarily as a journal directed to the conscience of Lutheran pastors and lay leaders who either enjoy its provocation in range and substance or, if they are in positions of denominational power, want to know what the opposition thinks.

Notes

1. A kindred journal is Princeton Theological Seminary's older *Theology Today**. *Lutheran Forum*, another independent journal, is generally less technical. *Dialog*'s art and layout have been handled by professors and students of Augsburg College, Minneapolis.

2. Roy Harrisville, "A Theology of Rediscovery," *Dialog* 2 (Summer 1963): 188–90.

3. The widely read Lutheran journals of the day included *Concordia Theological Monthly** and the *Lutheran Quarterly**.

4. "Dialog: a Journal of Theology," *Dialog* 1 (Winter 1962): 5–6.

5. Ibid., pp. 5–8.

6. "About Dialog, and the Church, and Some Bits of the Theological Biography of Robert W. Jenson," *Dialog* 11 (Winter 1972): 42.

7. "Who Cares about Theology Now?" *Dialog* 11 (Winter 1972): 24.

8. Prominent American and European churchmen and theologians were listed as contributing editors until 1972 and as "Dialog Associates" from then until 1979 when the category was dropped.

9. "The Colliding of Eschatology and Establishment," *Dialog* 11 (Winter 1972): 21–22.

10. "After Ten Years—Observations, Reflections," *Dialog* 11 (Winter 1972): 43–45.

11. "A Jeremiad from the New Editor," *Dialog* 14 (Winter 1975): 4–6.

12. Relevant issues include "Lutheran Identity" (Fall 1977), "Lutheran Merger" (Spring 1981), and "Mission and Merger" (Spring 1983).

13. Relevant theme issues include "Worship" (Spring 1975), "Liturgy" (Spring 1979), "Easter" (Winter 1980), and "Christmas" (Fall 1982).

14. Issues include "Religion and Schooling" (Winter 1979), "The Liberal Arts" (Spring 1980), and "Christian Nurture" (Winter 1982).

15. See, for example, "American Theology" (Fall 1975), "Religion and the Dilemmas of Nationhood" (Winter 1976), and "Once More for the Bicentennial" (Winter 1976).

Information Sources

BIBLIOGRAPHY:

Jensen, John M., Gerald Giving, and Carl E. Linder, comps. *A Biographical Directory of Pastors of the American Lutheran Church*. Minneapolis: Augsburg Publishing House, 1962.

Nelson, E. Clifford, ed. *The Lutherans in North America*. Philadelphia: Fortress Press, 1975.

Thomas, Shirley L. "American Epistemology and the Role of the Specialist in Society as Revealed in the Work of the American Lutheran Theologians Who Have Edited *Dialog*." Ph.D. dissertation, Washington State University, 1978.

INDEX SOURCES: *Dialog*'s winter issue contains an annual index; also in *Old Testament Abstracts*, *New Testament Abstracts*, *Religion Index One*, *Religious and Theological Abstracts*.

REPRINT EDITIONS: University Microfilms International.

LOCATION SOURCES: Yale University, Library of Congress, University of Chicago, Princeton University, Duke University, University of Texas-Austin, and others.

Publication History

MAGAZINE TITLE AND TITLE CHANGES: *Dialog: A Journal of Theology* (1962–).

VOLUME AND ISSUE DATA: 1:1 (Winter 1962–). Winter, spring, summer, and fall quarterly issues.

PUBLISHER AND PLACE OF PUBLICATION: Sacred Design Associates, Minneapolis (1962); *Dialog*, St. Paul (1963–).

EDITORS: Carl E. Braaten (1962–65, 1972–74), Kent S. Knutson (1966–68), James H. Burtness (1969–71), Robert W. Jenson (1975–).

CIRCULATION: 4450 (1964), 1910 (1979), 2050 (1983).

Christa R. Klein

DIALOGUE

Dialogue: A Journal of Mormon Thought, an independent voice of avowedly faithful but somewhat troubled divergency within the Mormon Church, offers a forum where Mormons and non-Mormons can exchange opinions on matters

Mormon in an informed and scholarly way. The editors have uniformly insisted that their purpose was not dissent or even advocacy but providing a place to trade ideas and information.[1]

Initiated in the mid–1960s by Mormon graduate students and professors at Stanford University, *Dialogue* was the work of a "generation of young Mormons who came of age in the 50's and 60's, whose faith was tested in the colleges and universities, and in a world of dramatic social change."[2] One of these students, George Eugene England, a Ph.D. candidate in English and first editor, believed that the church needed a journal broader than prevailing church-sponsored periodicals. Stung by Wallace Stegner's lament that Mormonism had created its share of bigots, England said in the first issue in 1966 that "the freedom that exists in our religion and in our culture is determined essentially by how willing we are to create it." England said he sought a rational faith, informed and responsive to the intellectual and social issues of the day. He expressed concern about the lack of sensitivity to literature in the church and the seeming diminishing quality of Mormon thought, particularly in Mormon history: "there is something terribly dangerous about the implication that the less we know about our past the more apt we are to have faith in it."[3]

From the first the editors of *Dialogue* were open to a broad spectrum of issues and individual viewpoints. They found that most contributors were professionals concerned about church traditions in the face of modern social and intellectual trends.[4] The first issue contained historian Leonard Arrington's discussion of the limitations of secular doctoral dissertations on Mormonism and his lament that "there is . . . not even a satisfactory general history of the Mormons." Arrington urged the "promotion of research and writing that will give the Mormon heritage a fuller and more sympathetic hearing."[5]

In the same issue, Francis Lee Menlove, a psychologist, said that there is a growing passion for honesty among Roman Catholic and Protestant communities, and Mormons need to respond in kind. How free is a Mormon to admit doubts to self or community? "The tendency seems to be to conform silently or leave the Church." Said Menlove: "there should not be two churches, one as it actually is and another that is offered to the public."[6]

Topics that received attention in succeeding issues were diverse, including "Reappraisals of Mormon History," which offered new interpretations from several well-known historians of Mormonism;[7] a roundtable on the conflicting values of the marketplace versus religion and art;[8] a discussion by an actor of the conflict between his professional and religious values in considering a role in a Eugene O'Neill play;[9] and a roundtable on the modern Mormon family from the viewpoint of several academic disciplines.[10]

During these first few years, there was heavy emphasis on Mormon history as many in the church looked for new answers to vexing questions created by the discovery of numerous new historical sources. Typical were two articles in 1968 on the discovery of the Joseph Smith papyri from which, according to tradition, Joseph Smith translated the Book of Abraham, one of the standard works of Scripture in the Utah church.[11]

In autumn 1969, an issue was devoted to literary concerns. Karl Keller, associate professor of literature at San Diego State College, commented that "for all the Church's emphasis on the spiritual worth of intelligence and knowledge . . . there is no literary tradition in the Church, no serious use of literature . . . and barely a sign of interest." Keller said that "our puritanic-paranoic-apocalyptic fundamentalism is at fault" and that good literature "cannot be written in the service of religion."[12]

In summer 1971, Claudia Bushman and Laurel Ulrich, two Mormon women living in the Boston area, edited an issue devoted to women in the church. Bushman indicated that their small group was made up of single and married women in their thirties, college educated, city bred, wives of professional men. They were concerned about the rigidity of the roles for women traditionally prescribed in the church: "We argue for acceptance of diversity that already exists in the lifestyles of Mormon women."[13]

That winter there appeared selections of Utah-born Bernard DeVoto, with a few of DeVoto's personal letters, edited by Wallace Stegner, which affirmed the tensions experienced by a Utah Catholic at odds with the prevailing Mormon culture in the 1930s and 1940s. DeVoto explained his scathing critique of the Mormon Church in a 1930 issue of *American Mercury* as the work of a "young buck intoxicated with the newly achieved privilege of publication." But DeVoto said that even after rendering a very favorable treatment of the Mormons in his *Year of Decision* (1946), he received vilification from some Utahans because the "orthodox Mormon mind cannot tolerate any objective treatment of Mormon history whatever."[14]

Despite success in attracting important scholars and presenting diverse views, not always liberal, *Dialogue* experienced financial difficulties between 1970 and 1975. Rising publication costs and diminishing subscriptions placed the continuance of the journal in jeopardy. Pleas by editor Robert Rees brought sufficient donations to enable continuation, although with thinner and more infrequent issues. A factor in decreasing community support was a popular image of the journal and its editors as liberals or even apostates.[15] A statement in a "Priesthood Bulletin," sent from church headquarters in 1967, which declared that articles in *Dialogue* were "never submitted to Church Authorities for approval," probably made many conservatives wary.

Still the publication continued, with quality remaining high. In 1972, for example, sociologist Armand Mauss argued from a study of Mormons in Salt Lake City and urban areas in California that these Latter-day Saints (LDS) were not particularly conservative on political or social issues, that 57 percent in Salt Lake City were Democrats or moderate Republicans, and that in California 65 percent were such.[16]

Lester E. Bush, Jr., contributed in the spring of 1973 a potent historical essay, "Mormonism's Negro Doctrine," then a critical issue in Mormon circles. He demonstrated that in the earliest years there was no proscription on blacks holding the priesthood, that the gospel was preached to every nation and people, and that at least one black was ordained an elder. Bush said, "There is no contemporary evidence that the Prophet [Joseph Smith] limited Priesthood eligibility because of race or biblical lineage." Brigham Young, however, was far more reactionary on this question, and church policy against blacks hardened during his administration. Not until the presidency of David O. McKay in the 1960s were there changes that moved the church away from its hard-line policies.[17]

An article in the summer 1973 issue by John Sorenson spoke for conservatives in the church generally when he argued that despite social changes in the nineteenth century, the church and its people had retained their worldview: faith in progress, the idea of salvation on merit, belief in the millennium, authority, and Scripture were still intact. In the same issue, Michael D. Coe, professor of Mesoamerican archaeology at Yale University, pointed out that Mormon defense of the Book of Mormon through archaeology was bankrupt but noted the church's contribution to understanding ancient culture in Central America through support of the New World Archeological Society.[18]

An entire issue in 1974 was devoted to the subject of science and religion. Richard F. Hogland, Jr., maintained that science, like religion, is based on opinions and human values and that they should develop mutually supportive attitudes based on their common interest in preserving moral and intellectual freedom and science's need for fresh categories and concepts. Duane Jeffrey wrote that "the question of whether species evolve is no longer open; it has long since been resolved affirmatively." Jeffrey said the "gap theory," where God is seen as a cause in those areas we do not yet understand, is self-destructive of religious faith as knowledge expands. Jeffrey contended that Mormon views of the origin of humanity and the age of the earth are not so conservative as some suppose.[19]

Robert Rees surrendered the editorship in 1976 to Mary Lythgoe Bradford and Lester E. Bush, Jr., who worked out of Arlington, Virginia. At the time the journal was some $10,000 in debt. The editorial change took *Dialogue* away from the liberal California academic environment, yet the new editors still sought to provide breadth and depth of commentary on the Mormon scene, continuing to speak as "outlanders," beyond the overriding influence of church authorities in Salt Lake City.

An issue in 1978 gave considerable space to Leonard J. Arrington and developments in Mormon history. David J. Whittaker wrote of Arrington's major contribution to Mormon studies through his own numerous publications and his role as church historian, where he encouraged professional standards at the church archives. Whittaker added a bibliography of Arrington's works, which listed over 150 books and published articles on the West and the Mormons.[20]

A year later came an issue commemorating the revelation in 1978 by church president Spencer W. Kimball granting priesthood to all worthy blacks. At the time, said Lester Bush, church liberals heralded the day as "not to be forgotten, like the bombing of Pearl Harbor, or the assassination of President Kennedy." Yet in the year that had followed there were few changes in the church, no large exoduses of white members or large influx of black converts, suggesting that social changes would come slowly despite the new doctrine.[21]

An issue in the spring of 1980 heralded church growth in Latin America and in parts of Asia, noting that there were at that time 600,000 members in Latin America alone. Lamont Tullis, a Brigham Young University professor of political science, pondered whether Mormon commitment to Americanism and the American "civil religion" might hinder growth and development among a people unconvinced of the merits of the mission of the United States.[22]

A year later *Dialogue* published a rather sympathetic "Odyssey of Sonia Johnson" and "Oral History Interview with Fawn Brodie," two ex-Mormons whose names were anathema to many of the conservative Saints. "Odyssey," written by Mary L. Bradford, traced ERA champion Johnson's early life in the church in Logan, Utah, her subsequent education, marriage, quarrel with the church, excommunication, and divorce. The Brodie interview traced the noted biographer's initial disenchantment with Mormonism as she took classes at the University of Utah. While attending the University of Chicago, she began studying the life of Joseph Smith and concluded in her biography that the leader was a fraud. Brodie said frankly, "I was a heretic—and especially for writing the book."[23] Subsequent issues carried letters from readers that both praised and condemned *Dialogue* for carrying these pieces.

As *Dialogue* was midway through its second decade of publication, new editors Jack and Linda Newell voiced their faith in the freedom that had inspired *Dialogue* in the past. Their prospects seemed bright as the journal was now out of debt. Yet a move to Salt Lake City placed *Dialogue* in the Mormon heartland where the editors risked greater pressures from conservative LDS and even church leaders. With a few liberals in Mormondom already lamenting that *Dialogue* had been "baptized" and had become another *B.Y.U. Studies*, the Newells faced a challenge to prevent too great a narrowing of the perspective.[24] The appearance of a new liberal journal in Utah, *Sunstone*,* persuaded them that the future for *Dialogue* rested toward the center.

Notes

1. See Eugene England, "The Possibility of Dialogue," *Dialogue* 1 (Spring 1966): 9. Also see the statement of purpose on page 1 of each issue, and Eugene England, *Dialogue: The Idea and the Journal* (Salt Lake City: L.D.S. Institute of Religion, 1967), pp. 7, 11; Robert A. Rees, "A Continuing Dialogue," *Dialogue* 6 (Spring 1971): 4–5; Mary L. Bradford, "Famous Last Words, or Through the Correspondence Files," *Dialogue* 15 (Summer 1982): 11; and L. Jackson Newell and Linda King Newell, "Ongoing Dialogue," *Dialogue* 15 (Autumn 1982): 11.

2. Rees, p. 4.

3. England, "Possibility," p. 8, and England, *Dialogue*, pp. 2, 3, 6, 7.

4. Don Holsinger, "An Interview with Eugene England," *Carpenter* (Winter 1969–70): 13–14.

5. Leonard J. Arrington, "Scholarly Studies of Mormonism in the 20th Century," *Dialogue* 1 (Spring 1966): 15–29.

6. Francis Lee Menlove, "The Challenge to Honesty," *Dialogue* 1 (Spring 1966): 44–53.

7. *Dialogue* 1 (Autumn 1966): 23–140. Some of the authors included Richard Bushman, Robert Flanders, Klaus Hanson, and P. A. M. Taylor.

8. "Art, Religion and the Market Place," *Dialogue* 1 (Winter 1966): 73–99.

9. Ronald Wilcox, "Morality or Empathy," *Dialogue* 2 (Spring 1967): 15–28.

10. "The Mormon Family in the Modern World," *Dialogue* 2 (Autumn 1967): 41–108.

11. John A. Wilson, "Summary Report," and Hugh Nibley, "Phase I," *Dialogue* 3 (Summer 1968): 67–92, 99–105.

12. Karl Keller, "On Words and the Word of God: The Delusions of a Mormon Literature," *Dialogue* 4 (Autumn 1969): 13–20.

13. Claudia L. Bushman, "Woman in Dialogue: An Introduction," *Dialogue* 6 (Summer 1971 : 5–8.

14. Leland Fetzer, "Bernard DeVoto and the Mormon Tradition," and Wallace Stegner, "Bernard DeVoto and the Mormons: Three Letters," *Dialogue* 6 (Autumn-Winter 1971): 23–47.

15. From conversations with Mary L. Bradford and Linda K. Newell, but also see Edward Geary, "Is Dialogue Worth Saving?," a circular letter dated 1972, *Dialogue* files, Salt Lake City.

16. Armand L. Mauss, "Moderation in All Things: Political and Social Outlooks of Modern, Urban Mormons," 27 January 1976, journal files.

17. Lester E. Bush, Jr., "Mormonism's Negro Doctrine: An Historical Overview," *Dialogue* 8 (Spring 1973): 11–66.

18. John Sorenson, "Mormon World View and American Culture," and Michael Coe, "Mormons and Archeology: An Outside View," *Dialogue* 8 (Summer 1973): 17–29, 40–48.

19. Richard F. Haglund, Jr., "Religion and Science: A Symbiosis," and Duane Jeffrey, "Seers, Savants and Evolution: The Uncomfortable Interface," *Dialogue* 8 (Autumn-Winter 1974): 23–40, 41–75.

20. David J. Whittaker, "Leonard James Arrington: His Life and Work," *Dialogue* 11 (Winter 1978): 23–47.

21. Lester E. Bush, Jr., "Introduction," *Dialogue* 12 (Summer 1979): 9–12.

22. Lamont Tullis, "The Church Moves outside the United States," *Dialogue* 13 (Spring 1980): 63–73.

23. Mary L. Bradford, "The Odyssey of Sonia Johnson," and Shirley E. Stephenson, "Fawn McKay Brodie: An Oral Interview," *Dialogue* 14 (Summer 1981): 14–26, 99–116.

24. Samuel W. Taylor to the Editors, *Dialogue* 15 (Autumn 1982): 7.

Information Sources

BIBLIOGRAPHY:

There is no volume that would consider the full implications of *Dialogue* in the contours of Mormon thought in the twentieth-century, nor is there any study of the journal's origins. A few recent general histories of Mormonism provide some background against which to assess the publication.

Allen, James B., and Glen M. Leonard. *The Story of the Latter-day Saints*. Salt Lake City: Deseret Book Co., 1976.

Arrington, Leonard J., and Davis Bitton. *The Mormon Experience*. New York: Knopf, 1979.

Hansen, Klaus J. *Mormonism and the American Experience*. Chicago: University of Chicago Press, 1981.

INDEX SOURCES: *Dialogue: A Journal of Mormon Thought: A Ten Year Index* (Arlington: Dialogue Foundation, 1976).

REPRINT EDITIONS: Individual reprints may be purchased through the Dialogue Foundatigon, Salt Lake City; also University Microfilms International.

LOCATION SOURCECS: University of California-Berkeley, Library of Congress, Yale University, Harvard University, University of Chicago, University of Utah, and others.

Publication History

MAGAZINE TITLE AND TITLE CHANGES: *Dialogue: A Journal of Mormon Thought* (1966–   ).

VOLUME AND ISSUE DATA: *Dialogue* 1 (Spring 1966–   ).

PUBLISHER AND PLACE OF PUBLICATION: Dialogue Foundation, Stanford, Calif. (1966–76); Arlington, Va. (1977-Summer 1982); Salt Lake City (Autumn 1982–   ).

EDITORS: George Eugene England (Spring 1966-Winter 1971), Robert A. Rees (Spring 1971-Winter 1976), Mary L. Bradford (Spring 1977-Summer 1982), Linda K. Newell and L. Jackson Newell (Autumn 1982–   ).

CIRCULATION: 2500 (1982).

Marvin S. Hill

THE DREW GATEWAY

Like many other journals, the *Drew Gateway* has evolved considerably over the years. Begun in 1930 "in the interest of the alumni of Drew Theological Seminary," in its early years the *Gateway* (named after a landmark on Drew's Madison, New Jersey, campus) featured notes on alumni and news of the Methodist seminary. Book reviews, reports from missionaries, and theological discussions gradually crept into its pages, and by its third volume the *Gateway* published a symposium, "The Selection and Training of the Methodist Ministry." From 1931 to the early 1940s, alumni news and campus building plans competed for editorial space with articles like "Mental Hygiene and the Minister" and "Training Rural Pastors for the Orient."

Accepting the editorial reins in 1943, Stanley R. Hopper, professor of Christian ethics and later the first dean of Drew's graduate school, warned that the " 'interests of the alumni' could easily circumscribe the *Gateway's* usefulness by narrowing it to a sort of parochial preclusiveness."[1] This Hopper wanted to avoid, seeking instead to balance "news items of former classmates" with more serious and scholarly matters.[2]

With Hopper at the masthead, the *Gateway* veered steadily toward more cerebral concerns, and the editor himself contributed a regular column on some issue of theological moment. In 1950, after a year's lapse, the *Gateway* resumed publication, this time with two changes: it adopted the subtitle *A Quarterly Journal of Comment and Criticism* and the smaller, journal-sized format that it retains to the present. The abandonment of alumni news in 1963 completed the *Gateway*'s transition to a scholarly publication.[3]

Drew Gateway has consistently resisted becoming a journal of strictly esoteric concerns. Darrell J. Doughty outlined its purposes most recently in 1977, when he took over as editor. "It is not our intention that the *Gateway* should be a depository of academic scholarship comprehensible only to specialists," he wrote. "Neither do we conceive our task as merely the mediation of esoteric wisdom to a mundane world through interpretation of latest theological trends."[4] Doughty sought instead to provide a forum "in which issues of church and ministry can be addressed in a serious and scholarly way."[5]

Because of its in-house orientation, the *Gateway* through the years has reflected the interests and concerns of the Drew faculty. Articles such as John Dillenberger's "Introduction to Tillich's Theology," "Theological Presuppositions of Social Philosophy" by Will Herberg, and Russell Richey's "Liberalism, Theological Education and the Churches" mirror that diversity of interests. The *Gateway* occasionally has opened its pages to a festschrift for one of Drew's faculty or to a symposium on a particular figure or topic. Examples of the latter include neo-orthodoxy, John Wesley, Rudolf Bultmann, and Friedrich Gogarten.

Notes

1. "Editorial Notes," *Drew Gateway* 14 (Summer-Autumn 1943): 8.
2. Ibid.
3. For a brief outline of the *Gateway*'s earlier history, including comments on the elimination of alumni news, see David J. Bort, "The Drew Gateway: A Brief History," *Drew Gateway* 41 (Fall 1970): 13–16.
4. "The New Drew Gateway," *Drew Gateway* 48 (Fall 1977): 2.
5. Ibid.

Information Sources

INDEX SOURCES: *The Drew Gateway: An Index, Volumes 13–39* (issued as *Drew Gateway* 38:3 [1967]). Also in *Religion Index One* (*Index to Religious Periodicals*).
REPRINT EDITIONS: University Microfilms International.
LOCATION SOURCES: Drew University, Duke University, and others.

Publication History

MAGAZINE TITLE AND TITLE CHANGES: *Drew Gateway* (1930–49), *The Drew Gateway: A Journal of Comment and Criticism* (1950–77), *The Drew Gateway* (1977–   ).
VOLUME AND ISSUE DATA: First issue dated 19 April 1930 (originally printed as 18:3). Appeared quarterly beginning with vol. 2 (1930–31); appeared three times a year starting with vol. 28 (1957–58); publication suspended 1949–50.

PUBLISHER AND PLACE OF PUBLICATION: Published by Drew Theological Seminary.
EDITORS: Harry J. Smith (1930); F. Taylor Jones and William P. Tolley (1930–31); F.
Taylor Jones (1931–41); Stanley R. Hopper and Harry M. Taylor (1942–43);
Stanley R. Hopper (1943–57); Nelle K. Morton (acting editor, 1957–58); Gordon
Harland (1958–64), Lawrence O. Kline (1964–67); Charles Courtney (1967–77);
Darrell J. Doughty (1977–83); Edward L. Long, Jr. (1983–   ).
CIRCULATION: 4000 (1977); 1000 (1982).

Randall H. Balmer

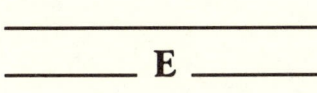

E

ECCLESIASTICAL REVIEW. *See* AMERICAN
ECCLESIASTICAL REVIEW

THE ECUMENICAL REVIEW

The *Ecumenical Review* has been the official journal and house organ of the World Council of Churches since its inception in 1948 at the First Assembly in Amsterdam. W. A. Visser 't Hooft, the first general secretary, was its founding editor; the succeeding general secretaries, Eugene Carson Blake (1967–73) and Philip A. Potter (1973–   ), later served as the journal's editors. The journal was preceded by *Christendom*, published from 1935 to 1948, and that journal's immediate predecessor, the *Christian Union Quarterly*. While the *Ecumenical Review* is published quarterly from the headquarters of the World Council of Churches in Geneva, Switzerland, its immediate predecessor, *Christendom*, was published in New York, and the World Council of Churches maintains an editorial office in that city. It is published only in English.

The purpose of the *Review* is to enhance communication between the World Council of Churches and its supporters, as well as to report on ecumenical developments around the world. Bishop Yngve Brilioth, chairman of the editorial board in 1948, outlined the journal's purpose in its first issue:

It will be the task of this review to be the continuous record of the World Council's history. On these pages its decisions are to be registered, the events in its evolution are to be reported and commented on. Here also the ecumenical discussion is to be carried on.[1]

In its years of publication, the *Ecumenical Review* has faithfully fulfilled its purpose as further articulated in an editorial in the initial issue:

> This Review is not an end in itself. Its one and only purpose is to help in the creation of true fellowship between the Churches. It is an instrument to be used by the Churches in order to give substance and reality to the new relationships between them which are implied in their participation in the World Council of Churches.[2]

It would intentionally reflect the weaknesses of the ecumenical movement and thereby lack a "clearly defined theology." But it would also reflect the strengths of the movement by its openness to the new directions of God's leading.

Most issues have followed the same format. In addition to several scholarly articles on topics in ecumenism, each issue included an Ecumenical Chronicle, which published significant ecumenical documents and reports; an Ecumenical Diary, which summarized significant events; book reviews; a listing of the contents of other important ecumenical journals; and bibliographies of books received at the World Council of Churches. It recorded all major happenings in the growing fellowship among the churches around the world.

A number of important periodicals had been published furthering the cause of Christian unity prior to the establishment of the *Ecumenical Review*. In the United States, Peter Ainslie had edited the *Christian Union Quarterly* from 1918 until his death in 1934. He was succeeded by Charles Clayton Morrison; the magazine ceased publication in 1935 and was immediately replaced by *Christendom*. Morrison continued as editor until succeeded by Harlan Paul Douglass in 1938. During the formative years of the World Council of Churches, *Christendom* was published in New York by the American Committee for the World Council of Churches. Its valedictory came in the autumn 1948 issue with an editorial farewell:

> With this issue, which completes its thirteenth year, *Christendom* ceases to be a separate publication and is incorporated in *The Ecumenical Review*. . . . After the provisional setting up of the World Council of Churches in 1938, *Christendom* was very generously presented by the publishers to The American Section of the World Conference on Faith and Order and The Universal Christian Council for Life and Work—later the American Committee for the World Council.[3]

At the same time that *Christendom* was being published in the United States, the Provisional Committee of the World Council of Churches was planning for the publication of a journal for the ecumenical movement. Differences within the committee in 1946 centered on the intended readership, but the opposition of Visser 't Hooft to a popular magazine won the day. In 1947 the Provisional Committee began negotiations for a cooperative publishing venture with *Chris-*

tendom, which finally resulted in the termination of that journal. At the same time, the proposed title *Koinonia* was found unsuitable.[4] The preliminary issue of the *Ecumenical Review* was circulated at the First Assembly of the World Council of Churches at Amsterdam, with the first number of the new journal being published in autumn 1948 from Geneva.

The contribution of the journal has been in publishing addresses, reports, and essays that reflect the progress of the ecumenical movement on numerous fronts, including theology, church union, and biblical studies, as well as international affairs. The topics themselves give a clearer indication of the progress of the ecumenical movement than any one particular essay. Every seven years, the World Council of Churches meets in assembly, its most important gathering, for it is the only meeting when all member churches are represented. Each of the six assemblies held thus far has dominated the pages of the *Ecumenical Review*. During the year or two preceding an assembly, the *Review* includes essays on the theme of the upcoming assembly and reports on all preparations for the event. Following each assembly, impressions, reactions, and assessments from varying ecclesiological perspectives fill its pages. The volumes of 1948, 1954, 1961, 1968, 1975, and 1983 are thereby critical for assessing the progress of the World Council of Churches.

Two other major events in the ecumenical story received extensive treatment. Although the Roman Catholic Church is not a full member of the World Council, there has been a growing sense of cooperation and participation by Rome in various programs of the council. The publications of the World Council gave full coverage of the Second Vatican Council. The April 1962 issue (14:3) contained an important essay by Lukas Vischer, "The World Council of Churches and The Vatican Council," and other articles on the growing comprehensiveness of the ecumenical movement. Ongoing dialogue with the Roman Catholic Church has often reappeared in the *Review*, notably in the July 1964 issue. The other event of special note was the integration of the World Council of Churches and the International Missionary Council, completing the merger of most major ecumenical bodies. Articles on the proposed merger began appearing in July 1957 and continued through actual integration at the Third Assembly in New Delhi in 1961. Since the merger, the *International Review of Missions*, the journal of the International Missionary Council, has continued publication.

Regularly included in the *Ecumenical Review* are the annual reports of the moderator of the Central Committee and the general secretary. Major world conferences sponsored by units of the World Council were reported in full. For example, the regular meetings of the Faith and Order Commission published most of their presentations in the *Review*; the World Conference on "Faith, Science and the Future" held at the Massachusetts Institute of Technology in 1979 was featured in the October 1979 issue and the Sheffield Conference on the Community of Women and Men in the Church in October 1981 and April 1982. The issue of July 1956 was devoted to topics of international affairs honoring the Commission of the Churches on International Affairs; that of April

1958 examined the place of the laity in the churches; and the October 1975 issue focused in its entirety on women's issues. A transition in emphasis can be detected from a focus on the history and progress of the ecumenical movement in the early years of publication to giving more attention on issues of international problems, such as the efforts of the churches to combat racism, sexism, poverty, and economic and political injustice. Yet at no time have the core questions of church unity such as those involving the sacraments, the nature of ministry, church order, theology, and dialogue with peoples of other faiths and ideologies been neglected. Key contributors have been the general secretaries: Visser 't Hooft, Blake, and Potter, along with other senior staff of the council and elected leaders.

The *Ecumenical Review* has continued to be a journal of high quality in its editing and writing. It has fulfilled its mandate that was stated as early as 1939 in a meeting of the Provisional Committee of the World Council to "serve as a means for furthering discussion on a fully ecumenical and international scale."[5]

Notes

1. *Ecumenical Review* 1 (Autumn 1948): 4.
2. Ibid., pp. 1–2.
3. *Christendom*, 13 (Autumn 1948): xiv–xv.
4. *The World Council of Churches, Its Process of Formation* (Geneva: World Council of Churches, 1946), p. 45.
5. Ibid., p. 131.

Information Sources

BIBLIOGRAPHY:

Gaines, David P. *The World Council of Churches: A Study of Its Background and History*. Peterborough, N.H.: Richard R. Smith, Noone House, 1966.

World Council of Churches. *The World Council of Churches, Its Process of Formation*. Geneva: World Council of Churches, 1946.

————. *Minutes and Reports of the Meeting of the Provisional Committee, Buck Hill Falls, Penn., April 1947*. Geneva: World Council of Churches, 1947.

————. *Evanston to New Delhi, 1954–1961. Report of the Central Committee to the Third Assembly of the World Council of Churches. Geneva: World Council of Churches, 1961*.

————. *New Delhi to Uppsala, 1961–1968*. Report of the Central Committee to the Fourth Assembly of the World Council of Churches. Geneva: World Council of Churches, 1968.

INDEX SOURCES: *Guide to Social Science and Religion in Periodical Literature, Humanities Index, Current Contents, Old Testament Abstracts, Religion Index One*.

REPRINT EDITIONS: University Microfilms International.

LOCATION SOURCES: Union Theological Seminary (New York), University of Texas-Austin, University of Chicago, Catholic University of America, Yale University, Andover-Harvard Theological Library, Stanford University, and others.

Publication History

MAGAZINE TITLE AND TITLE CHANGES: *Christian Union Quarterly* (1918–34), *Christendom* (1935–48), *The Ecumenical Review* (1948–   ).

VOLUME AND ISSUE DATA: *Ecumenical Review* 1:1 (Autumn 1948–   ).

PUBLISHER AND PLACE OF PUBLICATION: World Council of Churches, Geneva, Switzerland, and New York.

EDITORS: Peter Ainslie (1918–34), Charles Clayton Morrison (1934–38), Harlan Paul Douglass (1938–48), W. A. Visser 't Hooft (1948–66), Eugene Carson Blake (1966–73), Philip A. Potter (1973–   ).

CIRCULATION: 4000 (1982).

Robert J. Williams

EPISCOPAL RECORDER

Founded on 5 April 1823, on the eve of the great missionary expansion of the Protestant Episcopal Church, the *Philadelphia Recorder* (which in April 1831 became the *Episcopal Recorder*) declared its "one great object" to be cultivation of "an intense interest" in missions, dissemination of "information" essential to the "welfare and prosperity" of the church, and "general advancement of that 'knowledge' which one day is to 'cover the earth as the waters cover the sea.' "[1] Successor to the *Church Record*, the paper heralded a new day:

> We are aware that our church has not hitherto taken that stand among Christian denominations to which she is entitled; and while we rejoice in God that better things are in prospect, we would lend our exertions to hasten the period when all reproach shall be taken off her shoulders. It was with this object, that some few of the clergy of the Episcopal Church, residing in this city, undertook the editing of a little weekly paper entitled the *Church Record*. This, however, is found to have been conducted on too small a scale to give that general satisfaction which was desirable, but the success of which has emboldened the present editors to undertake a much larger work, suitable to the exigencies of the times.[2]

Born in the cradle of the denomination and its evangelical stronghold, the paper included among its original sponsors a core of the church's vanguard: William White (1748–1836), presiding bishop and a principal architect of the liturgy and government of the church; Jackson Kemper (1789–1870) and William H. De Lancey (1797–1865), future bishops in the upper Midwest and western New York; and Gregory Townsend Bedell (1793–1834), a gifted preacher for whom St. Andrew's Church in Philadelphia was under construction as an inducement for his becoming rector.

The new paper took up the unexpired subscriptions to the *Church Record* and retained as publisher Seldon Potter, printer of the superseded journal. On 20 January 1823, Potter had lost most of his property in a fire: "It is hoped that the profits of the paper may give him something by which his losses may in some measure be repaired."[3] In April 1824, however, he was replaced by Stavely and Bringhurst. Initially the Protestant Episcopal clergy of the city collectively assumed editorial responsibility. They were succeeded by Edward R. Lippitt in 1824, Bedell later that year, Benjamin Bosworth Smith (1794–1884), future bishop of Kentucky, in 1829, and George A. Smith two years later, a founding cadre of great future significance.[4]

The long-term emphases of the journal were evident in its earliest years. The paper, though free of a denominational bridle, tied its interests to those of the church. Its strongly Protestant, evangelical, missionary, and cooperative stance closely resembled that of the institutions for which it unofficially spoke. Reports of transdenominational Bible, tract, Sunday School, and colonization societies, and of national meetings and missionary agencies of sister denominations appeared side by side with quasi-official accounts of Protestant Episcopal diocesan and general church meetings and agencies. Coverage was both comprehensive and ecumenical.

The *Episcopal Recorder* was decidedly evangelical (even evangelistic) and nonritualist from the start. In the face of the spread of Puseyism after 1833, the paper stood fast in defense of low church positions. The moderate and strongly pro-tractarian stands of Bishops Kemper and De Lancey, now long removed from the evangelically charged atmosphere of Philadelphia, counted for little. Instead midcentury editors favored stands taken by the dioceses of Virginia and Ohio under the leadership of Bishops William Meade (1789–1862), Charles Pettit McIlvaine (1799–1873), and Gregory Thurston Bedell (1817–92), son of one of the journal's founders. In these years in which missionary expansion and the slavery controversy shared the platform with tractarianism, doctrinal and liturgical controversy smoldered while social and sectional conflicts that led to Civil War burst into flame.

With civil peace came a renewal of churchly conflict. In 1868 Stephen H. Tyng (1839–98), rector of the Church of the Holy Trinity, New York, and son of a former editor of the *Recorder*, was brought to trial and "admonished" for having preached in a Methodist church in New Jersey.[5] The anonymous publication that year of Franklin Samuel Rising's 43-page tract, *Are There Romanizing Germs in the Prayer-Book?* raised the specter of liturgical sanction for regarding baptism as a converting ordinance, with the result that 11 evangelical bishops petitioned the 1869 General Convention to approve either alternative wording or "some equivalent modification in the Office for the Ministration of Baptism to Infants."[6] At the same time 22 leading presbyters signed a memorial asking for freedom from use of terminology in the baptismal office that implied baptismal regeneration and for freedom to exchange pulpits with other orthodox Protestant ministers.

Failure of the General Convention to speak definitively on these issues resulted in militancy on both sides. Omission of objectionable phrases from the services of baptism and Holy Communion, which previously had been overlooked, and participation of Protestant Episcopal clergy in services of other denominations came under closer scrutiny. George David Cummins (1822–76), former rector of Chicago's Trinity Church who since 1866 had been suffragan bishop of Kentucky, was accused by Henry J. Whitehouse (1803–74), church bishop of Illinois, of abusing the hospitality of a brother bishop by speaking in Chicago in behalf of the Society for the Propagation of Evangelical Religion.[7] In 1869 Charles Edward Cheney (1836–1916), popular rector of Christ Church, Chicago, was brought to trial and deposed for omitting the (to evangelicals) objectionable phrases from the baptismal office. A civil court reversed the decision, and Cheney and his congregation later went into the Reformed Episcopal Church, taking the property with them. Fearing similar action, William H. Cooper, leader of the clergy who had memorialized the 1869 General Convention, moved from St. John's Church, Lockport, Illinois, to St. Michael's, Mount Pleasant, Iowa. Cooper was a former Church of England presbyter and after two years in Iowa asked Bishop Henry W. Lee, the evangelical diocesan who had welcomed him to the state, for letters dismissory to the Church of England. Instead he was deposed.[8] In the meantime the situation of Bishop Cummins had deteriorated. Differences with his diocesan, Benjamin Bosworth Smith, a former editor of the *Episcopal Recorder* who was then presiding bishop, over the aging bishop's unwillingness to curb Anglo-Catholic practices in Kentucky came to a head after Cummins provoked a massive protest among high churchmen by participating in an ecumenical communion service at an Evangelical Alliance meeting in New York in October 1873.[9] As a result, Cummins wrote Bishop Smith saying he was transfering his "work and office to another sphere of labor." That sphere was the Reformed Episcopal Church, organized in the parlors of the Young Men's Christian Association, New York City, on 2 December 1873, by Bishop Cummins, seven other clergy, and 19 lay persons formerly affiliated with the Protestant Episcopal Church.[10]

Although the *Episcopal Recorder* did not come under the Reformed Episcopal Church for 18 years, its Protestant Episcopal owners and editors gave full coverage to the rise and progress of the new body. The policies pursued by Thomas H. Powers, who purchased the paper in the 1860s, and Charles W. Quick (1822–94), the Protestant Episcopal presbyter serving as editor at the time of the break, were continued without essential change under Reformed Episcopal editors who followed. The Protestant Episcopal tie was maintained by the Reverend G. W. Ridgeley (d. 1883), a former editor, and by the daughter of Francis Wharton (1820–1889), a former editor, who continued to submit articles to the journal after it was taken over by the new group.[11]

On 9 May 1892, Harriet S. Benson (1827–1902), Charles M. Morton (d. 1915), and the Reverend Herman S. Hoffman (1841–1912), proprietors of the then-independent Publication Society, deeded the paper to the Reformed Episcopal Church.[12] This act, not intended to shut out friends in the old church, coupled the paper's interests with those of the denomination. The *Recorder*, which as early as 1875 had provided a "sounding board for all sides" in debate over the founding of a Reformed Episcopal school near Chicago, shifted its focus more and more to church-related issues.[13] By the turn of the century, friends in the Protestant Episcopal Church and leaders inherited from it were fast passing, being replaced by graduates of the Philadelphia-based Reformed Episcopal Theological Seminary. Most, if not all, of the future editors of the *Episcopal Recorder* were to come from this school.

From its beginning, the school welcomed students from other denominations, attracting Presbyterians, Baptists, and Methodists in disproportionate numbers. Few Protestant Episcopalians matriculated. The faculty, though largely Reformed Episcopalian by membership, had for the most part been trained in non-Episcopal schools; several had served churches of other denominations, particularly Presbyterian. The result was that a denomination founded to re-form the Episcopal Church moved steadily toward a Reformed theological orientation. Under the leadership of its alumni, the constituency of the *Recorder* came to include Presbyterians, Baptists, and Methodists in greater numbers than Protestant Episcopalians.

The strong commitment of the Reformed Episcopal Church to fraternity with other Protestant bodies was evinced by early membership in the Federal Council of Churches. Bishop Robert Westly Peach (1863–1936), editor from 1932 to 1936, served on its executive committee.[14] The church withdrew in 1942, however, because of the council's liberalism. The fundamentalist movement of the 1920s and 1930s had a strong impact on the Reformed Episcopal Church.[15] Bishop William Culbertson (1905–71), a president of Moody Bible Institute, served as both assistant and associate editor of the *Episcopal Recorder*. The strongly conservative stance has been continued under Walter G. Truesdell of the Reformed Episcopal Seminary, the present editor. Characteristic are articles opposing the ordination of women and praising private religious schools. In recent years the *Episcopal Recorder* has lost most non-Reformed Episcopalians from its readership. Quality in format and content have also declined markedly.

Notes

1. *Philadelphia Recorder* 1 (5 April 1823).

2. Ibid.

3. Ibid.

4. Frank Luther Mott, *A History of American Magazines* (Cambridge: Harvard University Press, 1938–64), 1:138, mistakenly lists B. B. Smith as the founder.

5. Arthur Carl Piepkorn, *Profiles in Belief: The Religious Bodies of the United States and Canada* (San Francisco: Harper and Row, 1978), 2:247; Raymond W. Albright, *A History of the Protestant Episcopal Church* (New York: Macmillan, 1964), p. 276.

6. Piepkorn, 2:247.

7. Albright, pp. 278–79; Alexandrine Macomb Cummins, *Memoir of George David Cummins, D.D., First Bishop of the Reformed Episcopal Church* (Philadelphia: E. Claxton, 1878), pp. 307–20.

8. Albright, pp. 280–82.

9. Cummins, p. 411.

10. Abraham Gadsden, "Consider the Reformed Episcopal Church," *Episcopal Recorder* 132 (December 1954): 5–6; Piepkorn, 2:248; Albright, p. 286; Cummins, pp. 432–40.

11. Annie Darling Price, *A History of the Formation and Growth of the Reformed Episcopal Church, 1873–1902* (Philadelphia: James M. Armstrong, 1902), p. 292.

12. Ibid., p. 289. Hoffman served as manager of the *Episcopal Recorder* for a time. See Raymond A. Acker, "A History of the Theological Seminary of the Reformed Episcopal Church" (Th.M. thesis, Dallas Theological Seminary, 1964), p. 18.

13. Acker, p. 9; "Offer Made by Mr. Martin," *Episcopal Recorder* 61 (21 April 1883): 4.

14. Acker, p. 79.

15. Illustrative of this trend is the posthumously published article of Bishop Robert K. Rudolph, "The Bible or Chaos," *Episcopal Recorder* 138 (January 1960): 3.

Information Sources

BIBLIOGRAPHY:

Acker, Raymond A. "A History of the Theological Seminary of the Reformed Episcopal Church." Th.M. thesis, Dallas Theological Seminary, 1964.

Albright, Raymond W. *A History of the Protestant Episcopal Church.* New York: Macmillan, 1964.

Cummins, Alexandrine Macomb. *Memoir of George David Cummins, D.D., First Bishop of the Reformed Episcopal Church.* Philadelphia: E. Claxton, 1878.

Mott, Frank Luther. *A History of American Magazines.* 5 vols. Cambridge: Harvard University Press, 1938–64.

Piepkorn, Arthur Carl. *Profiles in Belief: The Religious Bodies of the United States and Canada.* San Francisco: Harper and Row, 1978.

Price, Annie Darling. *A History of the Formation and Growth of the Reformed Episcopal Church, 1873–1902.* Philadelphia: James M. Armstrong, 1902.

INDEX SOURCES: *Guide to Social Science and Religion in Periodical Literature.*

REPRINT EDITIONS: American Periodicals Series, University Microfilms International (vols. 1–28).

LOCATION SOURCES: No known complete collection; partial holdings at American Antiquarian Society, American Congregational Association (Boston), Drew University, Duke University, Episcopal Divinity School, Garrett-Evangelical Theological Seminary, Lehigh University, Library of Congress, New York Public Library, Reformed Episcopal Seminary, Trinity College, and Yale University.

Publication History

MAGAZINE TITLE AND TITLE CHANGES: *Philadelphia Recorder* (5 April 1823–26 March 1831), *Episcopal Recorder* (2 April 1831–   ).

VOLUME AND ISSUE DATA: *Philadelphia Recorder* 1–8 (5 April 1823–26 March 1831); *Episcopal Recorder* 9 (2 April 1831–   ); also listed as *Episcopal Recorder* n.s. 1 (Dec. 1919–   ). Weekly, 5 April 1823–27 November 1919; monthly, December 1919–   .

PUBLISHER AND PLACE OF PUBLICATION: *Philadelphia Recorder*: Sheldon Potter,

Stavely & Bringhurst, William Stavely; *Episcopal Recorder*: Stavely & M'Calla, William Stavely, Stavely & McCalla, Publication Society of the Reformed Episcopal Church. All in Philadelphia.

EDITORS: Edward R. Lippitt (1823–24), Gregory Townsend Bedell (1825–27), Benjamin Bosworth Smith (1829–31), George A. Smith (1831); other nineteenth-century editors include John Alonzo Clark, James May, William W. Spear, William Suddards, H. H. Weld, Francis Wharton, Stephen H. Tyng, Sr., Greenbury William Ridgely, Charles William Quick, and Samuel Ashhurst; twentieth-century editors include Robert Westly Peach, Howard David Higgins, and Walter G. Truesdell.

CIRCULATION: 4000 (1911), 550 (1958), 927 (1983).

Charles E. Jones

EVANGELICAL AND LITERARY MAGAZINE. *See* THE LITERARY AND EVANGELICAL MAGAZINE

EVANGELICAL AND LITERARY MAGAZINE, AND MISSIONARY CHRONICLE. *See* THE LITERARY AND EVANGELICAL MAGAZINE

EVANGELICAL QUARTERLY REVIEW. *See* THE LUTHERAN QUARTERLY

EVANGELICAL REVIEW. *See* THE LUTHERAN QUARTERLY

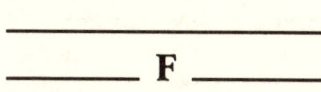

FOUNDATIONS. *See* AMERICAN BAPTIST QUARTERLY

FREE RELIGIOUS STUDY. *See* THE INDEX

THE FUNDAMENTALS

The *Fundamentals* was a series of 12 small, undated, paperbound volumes that appeared at somewhat irregular intervals between 1910 and 1915, comprising mainly essays written from a self-consciously conservative Christian perspective on a wide variety of theological and religious subjects. The periodical became, at least in retrospect, an important symbol and touchstone for the subsequent rise of the fundamentalist movement, which apparently derived its name, though probably not (as it sometimes supposed) its initial impulse, from the title. Whatever its actual relationship to that later movement, however, the *Fundamentals* certainly served, and still stands, as "a monument to conservative evangelicalism"[1] and an important moment in the ongoing controversy that the emergence and spread of liberalism evoked in the United States.

The periodical was the brainchild and personal project of California oil magnate Lyman Stewart, who, with a modest amount of financial assistance from his brother and business partner Milton established the Testimony Publishing House in Chicago for the sole purpose of producing the *Fundamentals*. The title page of every issue included the phrase "Compliments of Two Christian Laymen," for, in order to ensure the widest possible distribution of the periodical, the Stewarts anonymously furnished it free of charge "to every pastor, evangelist, missionary, theological professor, theological student, Sunday school superintendent, Y.M.C.A. and Y.W.C.A. secretary in the English speaking world'' for whom addresses could be obtained.[2]

Their generous subscription policy apparently was successful, for by the third volume, the publication was claiming a circulation of 250,000 and by the fifth, 275,000. All told, some 3 million copies of the 12 volumes were circulated.[3]

The Stewarts' purpose in gratuitously publishing and distributing the *Fundamentals* was unabashedly apologetic. The first issue bore the subtitle ''A Testimony to the Truth,'' and the foreword revealed the perception of the sponsors that ''the truth'' in question was none other than the heart of the Christian faith, which was very much in jeopardy and in need of witnesses: ''Two intelligent, consecrated Christian laymen bear the expense because they believe that the time has come when a new statement of the fundamentals of Christianity should be made.''[4] A later issue elaborated this assertion when it expressed the hopes ''that the Word of God may continue to 'run and be glorified,' that the unbelief, which in the pulpit and pew has been paralyzing the Church of Christ, may be overcome, and that a world-wide revival may be the result.''[5] The following volume further specified three objectives for the publication: ''the strengthening of saints,'' ''the defense of the truth against the insidious attacks of the present day,'' and ''the conversion of sinners.''[6] The ''paralyzing unbelief'' and ''insidious attacks'' referred to modernism (or liberalism) and all of its threatening manifestations, particularly evolutionism and the higher criticism of the Bible; and, as all the volumes of the *Fundamentals* would show, the ''defense of the truth'' would come from conservative, evangelical Christianity, and the essence of the testimony would be the assertion of the verbal inspiration and inerrancy of the Scriptures.

The periodical's founder, editors, and contributors were a curious mix of premillennialists and conservative Calvinists of the Princeton variety[7] and constituted what Sydney Ahlstrom has called ''an uneasy alliance'' of ''two fairly incompatible conservative elements: a denominational, seminary-oriented group, and a Bible institute group with strong premillennial and dispensational interests.''[8] Lyman Stewart himself was a staunch dispensational millenarian, as were the first editor, A. C. Dixon, whom Stewart hand-picked to initiate the project, and all six members of the original editorial committee, two of whom would eventually serve as editor. Moreover, most of the 64 contributing authors had a background in one or another form of millenarianism.[9] Yet there was an interesting degree of diversity among these authors within a narrow range. There was, for example, an international flavor, with over a third of the contributors being non-Americans, but all except one of these were British (English, Canadian, Scottish, or Irish).[10] There was an appearance of interdenominationalism, with authors representing church bodies as diverse as Episcopal, Dutch Reformed, and Plymouth Brethren, yet all of the authors were Protestants, and by far the greater number were Presbyterians and Baptists. Finally, there was an obvious diversity of theological orientation, for numbered among the contributors were representatives as divergent as radical dispensationalist C. I. Scofield, founder and editor of the Scofield Reference Bible, and moderate rationalist James Orr of Scotland, who advocated a reserved acceptance of both higher criticism and biological evolution.[11] Still, all of the writers reflected various shadings of Protestant conservatism, and their views shared far more similarities than differences.

The articles themselves fall neatly into three categories of nearly equal distribution: of the 90, roughly a third were devoted to doctrinal or theological matters; another third to the Bible, its inspiration and authority, and the sticky issue of high criticism; and the rest to a miscellany of mostly practical or polemical concerns. The distribution of these articles suggests the truth of George M. Marsden's contention that the "crucial issue" perceived by the editors and authors was "that of the authority of God in Scripture in relation to the authority of modern science, particularly science in the form of higher criticism of Scripture itself."[12] Indeed, the distinctive stance that the biblical articles assumed in advocacy of verbal inspiration and inerrancy was reflected consistently in all of the articles in the *Fundamentals,* for the viewpoint shared by virtually every author was that the Bible was the Word of God in an unequivocal sense.

The first *Fundamentals* article to deal directly with the question of the inspiration of the Scriptures came in volume 2 with James M. Gray's "The Inspiration of the Bible—Definition, Extent and Proof," which set forth at great length the view of scriptural inspiration and authority that underpinned the periodical.[13] Of the biblical authors, Gray asserted that "however fallible and errant they may have been as men compassed with infirmity like ourselves, such fallibility or errancy was never under any circumstances communicated to their sacred writings." The words of the Bible were God's words, "not in the sense that He uttered them, but that He caused them to be recorded, for our profit. In this sense, the Bible does not merely contain the Word of God, it *is* the Word of God." Gray went on to assert, in Princeton fashion, that he was maintaining this view of inspiration for the original autographs only, which were, by "miraculous control," an "absolute transcript of God's mind," which meant that the Bible had "one Divine author."[14] In a later volume, L. W. Munhall identified this view as a "doctrine of verbal inspiration" and summarized it thus: "The original writings, *ipsissima verba*, came through the penmen direct from God."[15] In an accompanying article, George S. Bishop concurred, speaking of the "dictated inspiration" that made the Bible "a book dropped out of heaven."[16]

This dogmatic position on biblical inspiration turned polemical on the subject of higher criticism. No fewer than a dozen articles echoed and elaborated the longest article contained in volume 1, entitled "The History of Higher Criticism." Its author, Tyson Hague, argued that higher criticism, at least as practiced by its German and Dutch (as opposed to its British and American) advocates, was irreverent, unspiritual, conjectural, hypothetical, rationalistic, arbitrary, and withal un-Christian, as well as unscientific (because of its antisupernaturalistic bias).[17] In the following volume, Franklin Johnson, in an article entitled "Fallacies of the Higher Criticism," intensified Hague's anti-German sentiment and asserted that the best test of higher criticism was the believing reader's "immediate consciousness'' that the Bible was ''the product of the Holy Spirit'' rather than ''a product of human nature working in the field of religious literature.''[18] In the same volume, Robert Anderson tried to distinguish between ''true'' and ''counterfeit'' higher criticism on the basis of the former's being ''open-minded'' and ''without prejudice'' and the latter's being predisposed ''to disprove the genuineness of the ancient writings.''[19] Of constant concern was Wellhausen's four-source hypothesis about the Pentateuch's authorship, which was refuted in 10 *Fundamentals* articles.

In addition to the attention it paid to the Scriptures, the *Fundamentals* also devoted fully a third of its articles to the doctrines of Christianity. In the light of the orientation of so many of those involved with the periodical, it is surprising that premillennialism and dispensationalism did not dominate the *Fundamentals*. The fact is that eschatological matters received very short (and late) shrift, reflecting an apparently conscious editorial decision to elicit a broad consensus on mainline doctrinal issues.[20] Consequently, the first three articles in the first volume were on the Virgin Birth, the deity of Christ, and the Incarnation, respectively, all of which had been key concerns of the recent Bible conferences and would later become cardinal principles for the fundamentalist movement of the 1920s.[21] Beyond the importance implied by the prominent position given to these three tenets, however, at no point did the periodical ever specify these as the most important Christian doctrines; indeed, this volume and the 11 that followed covered virtually the whole gamut of traditional Christian teachings (atonement, grace, justification, providence, and sin) without ever specifying any particular ones as ''the fundamentals of Christianity,'' which the first volume had promised to clarify. Perhaps, in the minds of the men in charge, all of the doctrines treated in the publication were fundamentals. Whatever their intention with that term, however, it is clear, in the light of the disproportionate attention given to them, that the inspiration, authority, and inerrancy of the Bible were the real fundamentals propounded by the entire series.[22]

Virtually all of the doctrinal articles were apologetic in tone, defending each particular teaching either deductively from Scripture or another doctrine, or inductively from Christian experience or Christianity's impact on the world, two methodologies established in the first volume of the series. James Orr's article on the Virgin Birth typified the deductive method by arguing that if Christ was sinless, the Word of God incarnate, the Son of God, the second Adam, and so on, then an advent miracle was required and should be expected in the Scriptures: ''Why then cavil at the narratives which declare the fact of such a miracle?''[23] In the following article, B. B. Warfield explained a twofold basis for belief in Christ's divinity that combined deduction and induction: ''Our conviction of the deity of Christ rests not alone on the scriptural passages which assert it, but also on His entire impression on the world. . . . Both lines of evidence are valid; and when twisted together form an unbreakable cord.'' In other words, he said, an important proof of Christ's divinity was Christianity itself, ''the revolution which

Christ has wrought in the world.'' Warfield's final appeal, however, was to the sensibility of the individual Christian: ''The supreme proof to every Christian of the deity of his Lord is then his own inner experience of the transforming power of his Lord upon the heart and life.''[24] In yet another essay in the same volume, Arthur T. Pierson argued for both the existence and the faithfulness of God on the basis of the believer's experience of answered prayer and offered as an illustration a man who reportedly had devoted 65 years to a ministry to orphans.[25]

The articles that dealt specifically neither with Scripture nor with doctrine covered a wide variety of practical and polemical concerns and became more prevalent in the later volumes. Several of the most substantial of these examined evolution, philosophy, science, and socialism, with attitudes ranging from outright opposition to qualified acceptance.[26] Other articles discussed practical matters like prayer, conversion, money, Sabbath keeping, and evangelism and missions.[27] Four of the first five volumes concluded with a personal testimony, the fifth substituting ''Tributes to Christ and the Bible by Brainy Men Not Known to be Christians,'' a compilation of quotations drawn from Jefferson, Emerson, Napoleon, Goethe, Rousseau, and Disraeli.[28] Beginning with volume 7, the testimonies were replaced with pointed attacks on particular religious groups: Charles Taze Russell's Millennial Dawn movement was called ''a counterfeit of Christianity'';[29] Mary Baker Eddy's Christian Science was vilified as a ''farrago of irreligion and nonsense'';[30] and Mormonism was denounced as ''anti-American,'' ''a depraved and cunning bribe to every kind of social immorality,'' ''something positively Satanic,'' and ''a system of downright heathenism.''[31] Roman Catholicism merited two denunciations, one of which pronounced it the antithesis and enemy of true Christianity and the other of which declared it ''a corrupt and corrupting system of falsehood and idolatry that pollutes our land'' and ''a political system of foreign despotism.''[32]

The vitriol of these attacks, however, was not characteristic of the *Fundamentals* as a whole, which, with a few other notable exceptions, was moderate, even dignified in tone, remarkably so considering the militant conservatism that it espoused.[33] It was also, as William R. Hutchison points out, largely beside the point relative to the key issues that liberalism was raising, preferring to give ''testimonies'' instead of detailed responses. This ''lack of dialogue with Liberalism,'' plus its comparatively tame spirit, may well explain why the *Fundamentals* had little impact in scholarly theological circles, liberal or conservative.[34] Nor, finally, does the *Fundamentals* appear to have been a manifesto that triggered the rise of fundamentalism a few years later.[35] Its importance is rather as a transitional event between the millennialism and Bible conferences of the later nineteenth and early twentieth centuries and the later movement whose name recalled its title. Still, as James Barr rightly points out, the impulse, the concerns, and the issues that underlay the publication did survive, and still do survive, in fundamentalism, albeit in a less temperate form.[36]

Notes

1. Ernest R. Sandeen, *The Roots of Fundamentalism: British and American Millenarianism, 1800–1930* (Chicago: University of Chicago Press, 1970), p. 189. The chapter that this book devotes to the *Fundamentals* (pp. 188–207) appeared earlier in large part as "The Fundamentals: The Last Flowering of the Millenarian-Conservative Alliance," *Journal of Presbyterian History* 47 (1969): 55–73, and remains the most thorough study of the publication. I am greatly indebted to Sandeen's insightful interpretation, as well as to George M. Marsden's more concise chapter on the periodical in his *Fundamentalism and American Culture: The Shaping of Twentieth Century Evangelicalism, 1870–1925* (New York: Oxford University Press, 1980), pp. 118–123.

2. *Fundamentals: A Testimony to the Truth* (Chicago, 1910–1915), 1:4. (Further references to the periodical will be by volume and page numbers only.) By volume 3 (p. 4), the list had grown to include college professors and religious editors, and subscriptions were being offered to laypersons for a nominal fee. Once only, in volume 5 (p. 4), did the list include Roman Catholic priests, but by the following volume (6:4) that category had been replaced by "lay-workers," and the adjective *Protestant* inserted at the head of the list.

3. 3:4; 5:4; and 12:4.

4. 1:4.

5. 5:4.

6. 6:2.

7. Sandeen, "The Fundamentals: The Last Flowering of the Millenarian-Conservative Alliance," pp. 66–68.

8. Sydney E. Ahlstrom, *A Religious History of the American People* (New Haven: Yale University Press, 1972), p. 816.

9. For detailed information about the Stewarts, Dixon, the committee members, and the authors, see Sandeen, pp. 189–203. The two committee members who later served as editor were Louis Meyer, a Jewish Presbyterian Christian, and Reuben A. Torrey, an evangelist with ties to Moody Bible Institute and, later, to the Bible Institute of Los Angeles.

10. The only article by a non-English-speaking author was "The Bible and Modern Criticism," 4:73–80, by Rev. Frederic Bettex of Stuttgart, trans. David Haegle.

11. The article by Scofield was entitled "The Grace of God," and appeared in 11:43–54. Sandeen, in his "Toward a Historical Interpretation of the Origins of Fundamentalism," *Church History* 36 (1967): 66–83, identifies 19 authors responsible for a total of 31 articles in *The Fundamentals* as strict dispensationalists (p. 79). Orr had stated his case on higher criticism in his *Revelation and Inspiration* (1904) and took his positive stance on evolution in his *Fundamentals* article "Science and Christian Faith," 4:91–104, which did, however, dismiss the principle of natural selection as too accidental to comport with divine providence.

12. Marsden, p. 120.

13. 3:7–41.

14. 3:9–10, 14–15, 33.

15. "Inspiration," 7:21.

16. "The Testimony of the Scriptures to Themselves," 7:42–43.

17. 1:87–122.

18. 2:48–68.

19. "Christ and Criticism," 2:69–84.

20. The end-time events are treated directly no earlier than volume 6 with an article by Robert Anderson, "Sin and Judgment to Come," pp. 37–49, and another by John McNicol, "The Hope of the Church," pp. 114–27. Nothing even approaching hard-line premillennialism, however, appears until volume 11 with C. I. Scofield's "The Grace of God," pp. 43–54, and Charles R. Erdman's "The Coming of Christ" pp. 87–99; but the well-attested dispensationalism of the authors is tempered and even conciliatory toward differing views.

21. James Orr, "The Virgin Birth of Christ," 1:7–20; Benjamin B. Warfield, "The Deity of Christ," 1:21–28; and G. Campbell Morgan, "The Purposes of the Incarnation," 1:29–54.

22. Sandeen, *Roots*, p. 204, employs the helpful image of a wheel to represent the interrelationship of the various kinds of *Fundamentals* articles: the hub comprises the biblical essays, the spokes consist of the doctrinal articles, and the rim is formed from the more practical pieces.

23. Orr, "Virgin Birth of Christ," 1:10.

24. Warfield, "Deity of Christ," 1:21, 26–27.

25. Pierson, "The Proof of the Living God, as Found in the Prayer Life of George Müller of Bristol," 1:70–86.

26. See especially George Frederick Wright, "The Passing of Evolution," 7:5–20; James Orr, "Science and Christian Faith," 4:91–104; and Charles R. Erdman, "The Church and Socialism," 12:108–19.

27. See especially Arthur T. Pierson, "Divine Efficacy of Prayer," 9:66–83; H. M. Sydenstricker, "The Science of Conversion," 10:64–73; Arthur T. Pierson, "Our Lord's Teaching about Money," 10:39–47; and Daniel Hoffman Martin, "Why Save the Lord's Day?," 10:5–17. Volume 12 was practically devoted to evangelism and mission, with six articles on the subject, including one by the current editor, Reuben A. Torrey.

28. 2:120–27.

29. William G. Moorhead, "Millennial Dawn: A Counterfeit of Christianity," 7:106–27.

30. Maurice E. Wilson, "Eddyism: Commonly Called Christian Science," 9:111–27.

31. R. G. McNiece, "Mormonism: Its Origin, Characteristics and Doctrines," 8:110–27.

32. T. W. Medhurst, "Is Romanism Christianity?" 11:110–12; and J. M. Foster, "Rome, the Antagonist of the Nation," 11:113–27.

33. Two notable exceptions are Philip Mauro's "Modern Philosophy," 2:85–105, a blanket attack on philosophy (based on Colossians 2:9–10) as too human, rationalistic, speculative, and worldly to be of any use in religious matters; and an anonymous article attributed simply to "An Occupant of the Pew" and entitled "Evolutionism in the Pulpit," 8:27–48, which denounced evolutionism as Satanic in principle. Such anti-intellectual and emotional tirades, however, were extremely rare in the *Fundamentals*.

34. William R. Hutchison, *The Modernist Impulse in American Protestantism* (Cambridge: Harvard University Press, 1976), pp. 196–98; cf. Sandeen, *Roots*, p. 199, and Marsden, p. 119.

35. Marsden, p. 263, n. 3, points out that most of the prominent contributors to the *Fundamentals* who managed to survive into the 1920s were too old by then to take an active part in the fundamentalist movement or related controversies.

36. James Barr, *Fundamentalism* (Philadelphia: Westminster Press, 1977–78), p. 2.

Information Sources

BIBLIOGRAPHY:

Marsden, George M. *Fundamentalism and American Culture: The Shaping of Twentieth Century Evangelicalism, 1870–1925*. New York: Oxford University Press, 1980.

Sandeen, Ernest R. *The Roots of Fundamentalism: British and American Millenarianism, 1800–1930*. Chicago: University of Chicago Press, 1970.

INDEX SOURCES: *Fundamentals: A Testimony to the Truth* 12 (1915): 124–27, provides an index of articles for all 12 volumes.

LOCATION SOURCES: Princeton Theological Seminary, Hamilton College, Cornell University, Vassar College, University of Illinois, General Theological Seminary, Andover-Harvard Theological Library, and others.

Publication History

MAGAZINE TITLE AND TITLE CHANGES: *The Fundamentals: A Testimony to the Truth* (1910); *The Fundamentals: A Testimony* (1910–15).

VOLUME AND ISSUE DATA: Although the volumes themselves were undated, Sandeen, *Roots*, p. 197, dates them as follows: 1 (February 1910); 2 and 3 (1910); 4–6 (1911); 7–9 (1912); and 12 (Spring 1915), with 10 and 11 presumably appearing sometime in 1913 or 1914.

PUBLISHER AND PLACE OF PUBLICATION: Testimony Publishing Company, Chicago.

EDITORS: Amzi Clarence Dixon (1909–11), Louis Meyer (1911–13), Reuben A. Torrey (1913–15).

CIRCULATION: Approximately 275,000 at its peak (1910–11); 250,000 average.

Paul A. Laughlin

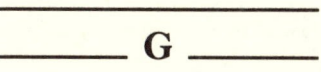

G

THE GORDON REVIEW. *See* CHRISTIAN SCHOLAR'S
REVIEW

THE GOSPEL ADVOCATE

On the back cover of the 24 December 1891 issue, its publisher described the
Gospel Advocate as "The Oldest, The Purest and The Best Religious Paper
Published by the Disciples." Currently in its 126th volume, the *Advocate* has
appeared continuously since July 1855, except for "four dreary years" (1862–
65) of war. It is the only survivor among antebellum periodicals published among
the Churches of Christ or Disciples of Christ.

Tolbert Fanning (1810–74),[1] David Lipscomb (1831–1917),[2] and Benton Cordell Goodpasture (1895–1977), with editorships totaling 98 years, made this
publication the most influential force in the Churches of Christ for over a century.
Goodpasture became a staff writer in 1920, three years after Lipscomb's death,
and was editor from March 1939 to February 1977. By adding his staff years,
the direct influence of these three men spans all but 10 years of the periodical's
life.

No editor has significantly changed policy since the *Advocate*'s beginning.
When Foy E. Wallace, Jr., became editor in 1930, he declared that the *Gospel
Advocate* would be "the same old paper" under new management. His successor,
John T. Hinds, in 1934 "whole-heartedly" accepted and pledged to continue
the policy of strict fidelity to the Word of God. Goodpasture, as editor, claimed
that "the future policy of this great paper will be that of its original founders

and editors and their worthy successors all down the years,'' while repeating
the three earliest policy statements of the paper.[3]

Original editors Tolbert Fanning and William Lipscomb declared in the first
issue:

> We claim not the right to advocate any measures of our own, neither the
> claims of any party; but we regard our position as entirely catholic. Our
> position is to defend the sayings and the doings of Jesus Christ against the
> assaults of the enemy, whether covert or avowed; and we can meet all
> who do in fact acknowledge the authority of the New Testament on common
> ground. With us the gospel is everything or nothing.[4]

Following the four years of war, the editors reissued the *Advocate* with the
following statement:

> We have no local or peculiar institutions to defend and nothing new to set
> forth. We will cheerfully labor with our fellow servants in the kingdom
> of Christ in promoting every interest suggested in the Word of Life, and
> it shall be our constant study to oppose every cause antipodal to the reign
> of the Messiah.[5]

After becoming sole editor in 1867, David Lipscomb, brother of William
whom he replaced as coeditor in 1866, described his intended course for the
Advocate:

> It will constantly strive to separate the church of God from its entangling
> alliances with the institutions of men—to exalt it alone, of the institutions
> of earth, worthy of the undivided fealty and unfaltering service of human
> beings . . . to induce subjects to separate themselves from conformity to
> this world . . . to perfect their character . . . in conformity to the example
> and precepts of Christ and his inspired apostles.[6]

Tolbert Fanning also published and edited two other religious journals in
Nashville, *Christian Review* (1844–47) and *Religious Historian* (1872–74), and
he founded Franklin College in 1844. One writer considered Fanning's contribution ''a great and lasting work in Tennessee and the whole South as educator
and preacher. He was by long odds the most towering form in the Restoration
Movement in the South, and through his work in Franklin College gave direction
to the lives and shaped the destinies of hundreds of young men.''[7]

During its early years, the *Advocate* was consciously southern, but because
of its conscience respecting civil government, its stance was nonpolitical. Although directed to the South at a time when ''Southern independence was threatened both mentally and morally,'' Lipscomb claimed that the paper was not
sectional, although he believed that every community, church, and region should

develop and nurture its own talents and energies.[8] Tension over slavery is an example of sectional attitudes receiving attention. The Lipscomb family regarded slavery as evil. Young David strongly imbibed this view, but he had strong sympathy for southern people. He called slavery an "incubus and hindrance" to the South yet did not hesitate to criticize some of his northern abolitionist brethren. Northern Disciples, through the *Christian Standard* edited in Cincinnati by Isaac Errett, charged that slavery "fostered vice and diabolism" in southern people "that had to be cut out with the terrible swift sword of a wrathful God." Lipscomb considered such an attitude among Christians a "slander born of a very narrow sectional hate."[9]

Lipscomb's views of civil government and moral societies perpetuated those of Fanning and Barton W. Stone, both advocates of nonconformity to the world. For them, the sufficiency of God's pure and primitive church to accomplish all of God's purpose for humanity rendered civil governments (as human creations) and human societies totally unnecessary. Lipscomb championed these views, preaching pacifism even in the face of imprisonment and threat of hanging. "Human government originated in the rebellion of man against his Maker," wrote Lipscomb, "and was the organized effort of man to govern himself and to promote his own good and to conduct the affairs of the world independently of the government of God. It was the organized rebellion of man against God and his government."[10]

Lipscomb also published Justus M. Barnes's temperance message to the Alabama legislature but explained that he had "no faith in human laws." Rather, the world needed the "earnest protest of the word and example of the church of Christ against" such evils as intemperance. The *Advocate* editor sought to educate and arouse the church and the world by bringing the church and every member up to the true standard of Christian holiness on every moral issue. Failing here, the church did much to corrupt society. He concluded that "the church is intended to have a different influence upon the world."[11]

The *Gospel Advocate* has always reflected a strong antimissionary society emphasis such as that found in Alexander Campbell's *Christian Baptist* (1823–30). Fanning and Lipscomb were strong opponents of the American Christian Missionary Society established in 1849. Nothing has been more controversial and divisive among Disciples and Churches of Christ. Such polarization erupted again following World War II when interest in missions intensified and cooperative arrangements among churches met with strong opposition. The *Advocate* was at the center of this controversy.

Churches of Christ, as a restoration or primitivistic group, have always appealed to biblical authority and the oneness of the first century church against sectarianism and denominationalism. The millennial expectancy of the 1820s and 1830s called for a return to the primitive unity believed characteristic of the church before the apostasy. All sectarianism constituted the Babylon of the Apocalypse and would meet with destruction in the wake of restoration. The millennial vision was lost by midcentury, but sectarian opposition continued unabated, and *Advocate* editors led in warning against adopting a sectarian posture. No one was more articulate than Fletcher D. Srygley, front page editor of the *Advocate* from 1889 to 1900, in voicing this emphasis:

> I do not belong to anything larger than a local congregation in the way of church organization. . . . a man can believe on the Lord Jesus Christ, obey the commandments of God, and be a Christian without joining any *party*, *sect*, or *denomination*, in religion, . . . the people of God—Christians—in any locality can form themselves into a church of Christ, keep all the commandments and ordinances of the Lord, and attend to their own business, as a *church of Christ*, without being a part of any general denominational organization or sectarian party in religion.[12]

Further, Srygley pointed out that "each local church of the New Testament was independent of all other local churches. There was no such thing as a denominational federation of churches in a partisan brotherhood, excluding from its sectarian fellowship a large proportion of recognized Christians." Grover Cleveland Brewer (1884–1956), who served on the *Advocate* staff for 45 years, continued to voice this teaching in the twentieth century. These foci of the *Advocate* did create controversy, especially when some abandoned restorationism, but their success is seen in the many members gained in the South and the Southwest where the paper was extensively circulated.

The *Advocate* has treated many other subjects:

Poverty. In the early years wealth and Christianity were viewed as incompatible, although poverty was considered sinful if caused by shiftlessness. For some church members to be wealthy while others were very poor seemed wrong to Lipscomb. To him the unity of the church implied greater equality.

Blacks. The *Advocate* never attacked the legal status of blacks but sought to improve their position by education, by teaching trades, and by church fellowship. Lipscomb felt that it was wrong for black and white congregations to exist separately in the same location.

Education. Traditionally the *Advocate* has promoted church-related schools that are supported as private institutions with no organic ties to churches.

Women's Status. The *Advocate* has encouraged women's activities and has frequently appealed for contributions by women writers.

Bible Revisions. Fanning encouraged the American Bible Union project of the 1850s and 1860s, but this movement lost support by failure to meet expectations. The Revised Version of 1881–85 received strong endorsement. The Revised Standard Version was favorably reviewed when the New Testament appeared in 1946, but publication of the Old Testament and the proliferation of other modern versions brought increasingly frequent criticism.

Clergy. The *Advocate* has published much regarding the role of clergy, along with articles of special doctrinal interest to preachers.

Premillennialism. This topic received special attention when front page writer Robert H. Boll was dismissed in 1915 because of speculative writings on prophecy.

Benevolence. Interest in orphan homes such as the Tennessee Orphan Home, established in 1910, and Fanning Orphan School, founded in 1884, is characteristic of the *Advocate*'s support of church benevolent work. Following World War II, *Advocate* writers stongly rebutted criticism of such work. Guy N. Woods, the present editor, has championed such institutions as a means of charitable work by congregations.

The *Gospel Advocate* remains a vital force among Churches of Christ today. Although it does not adddress many issues of current interest as openly as in its early years—David Lipscomb even invited those with opposing views to the staff—it is still the strongest journalistic force among the Churches of Christ.

Notes

1. James R. Wilburn, *The Hazard of the Die: Tolbert Fanning and the Restoration Movement* (Austin: Sweet Publishing Co., 1969).

2. F. D. Srygley, *Biographies and Sermons* (Nashville: n.p., 1898), p. 163, said of Lipscomb: "His strong points are hard work, close adherence to the right, and cheerful indifference as to consequences in everything he undertakes."

3. "The Future Policy of the Gospel Advocate," *Gospel Advocate* 81 (1939): 196.

4. "The Name of Our Paper," *Gospel Advocate* 1 (1855): 4.

5. T. F., "Salutatory," *Gospel Advocate* 8 (1866): 1.

6. "Prospectus of the Gospel Advocate," *Gospel Advocate* 9 (1867): 900.

7. George Gowen, "Tolbert Fanning," in John T. Brown, *Churches of Christ* (Louisville: J. P. Morton & Co., 1904), pp. 451–52.

8. Lipscomb and Sewell, "Gospel Advocate for 1872," *Gospel Advocate* 13 (1871): 884. Elisha G. Sewell joined Lipscomb as coeditor in 1870. The two conducted *Advocate* for more than 50 years.

9. D.L., "Correction," *Gospel Advocate* 34 (1892): 453.

10. David Lipscomb, *Civil Government: Its Origin, Mission, and Destiny and the Christian's Relation to It* (Nashville: McQuiddy Printing Co., 1913), p. 11. In 1890 Lipscomb expressed the belief that "nothing we ever wrote so nearly affects the vital interests of the church of Christ and the salvation of the world as this little book."

11. Justus Mac Barnes, "To the Senate and House of Representatives of the State of Alabama," *Gospel Advocate* 13 (1871): 1009–13; response by Lipscomb, ibid., p. 1027.

12. F. D. Srygley, *The New Testament Church* (Nashville: McQuiddy Printing Co., 1910), p. 21. This book consists of Srygley's 1889–1900 editorials.

Information Sources

BIBLIOGRAPHY:

Chalk, John Allen. "A History of the Gospel Advocate, 1855–1868: Its Social and Political Conscience." Master's thesis, Tennessee Technological University, 1967.

Choate, Julian E. *The Anchor That Holds: A Biography of Benton Cordell Goodpasture*. Nashville: Gospel Advocate Co., 1971.

Goodpasture, Benton C. *The Gospel Advocate Centennial Volume*. Nashville: Gospel Advocate Co., 1956.

Hooper, Robert E. *Crying in the Wilderness: A Biography of David Lipscomb*. Nashville: David Lipscomb College, 1979.

Rideout, Holbert L. "The Gospel Advocate on Preaching, 1855–1955." Master's thesis, Abilene Christian University, 1956.

West, Earl Irvin. *The Life and Times of David Lipscomb*. Henderson, Tenn.: Religious Book Service, 1954.

Wilburn, James R. *The Hazard of the Die: Tolbert Fanning and the Restoration Movement*. Austin: Sweet Publishing Co., 1969.

INDEX SOURCES: Self-indexed annually, 1855–95, 1945–   ; also in *Christian College Librarians' Index*, 1975–   .

LOCATION SOURCES: David Lipscomb College, Freed-Hardeman College, Harding Graduate School of Religion, Abilene Christian University, Oklahoma Christian College, Pepperdine University.

Publication History

MAGAZINE TITLE AND TITLE CHANGES: *The Gospel Advocate* (1855–   ).

VOLUME AND ISSUE DATA: 1–7 (July 1855-December 1861), monthly; not published, January 1862-December 1865; 8–121 (January 1866–28 June 1979), weekly; 121:6 (12 July 1979–   ), semimonthly.

PUBLISHER AND PLACE OF PUBLICATION: Tolbert Fanning, Nashville, Tenn. (1855–67); Gospel Advocate Publishing Co., Nashville, Tenn. (1868–   ).

EDITORS: Tolbert Fanning and William Lipscomb (1855–61), Tolbert Fanning and David Lipscomb (1866–67), David Lipscomb (1868–69), D. Lipscomb and Elisha G. Sewell (1870–1912), Alexander Bagby Lipscomb (1912–20), H. Leo Boles (1920–23), James A. Allen (1923—30), Foy E. Wallace, Jr. (1930–34), John T. Hinds (1934–38), Benton Cordell Goodpasture (1939–77), J. Roy Vaughan (1977), Ira North (1978–81), Guy N. Woods (1982–   ).

CIRCULATION: 50,000 (1984).

R. L. Roberts

GREEK ORTHODOX THEOLOGICAL REVIEW

The appearance of the first issue of the *Greek Orthodox Theological Review* in August 1954 marked an important stage in the development of the Greek Orthodox Archdiocese of North and South America. Published by the Greek Orthodox Theological Institute, now Holy Cross Greek Orthodox School of Theology, Brookline, Massachusetts, the English-language journal provided a major forum for scholarly articles and the publication of ecclesiastically related materials. Ties with Greece and the Greek language, always strong in the Diocese of North and South America, were reflected in the number of articles by Greek professors and priests translated into English in early issues and in the number of Greek books reviewed for the benefit of American readers over the years. The diocese has always been concerned with one of the main problems of an immigrant church: how to keep a strong bond with the mother church and ancestral language and culture while participating in the nation in which the people now find themselves living. For a time after the great wave of Greek immigration in the later nineteenth and early twentieth centuries the diocese depended on priests from Greece. Of course, this dependence kept a connection with Greek language and theology, but eventually the need for native-born American priests made itself felt. Then the problem of theological education loomed large, for sending men to Greece for training might suffice theologically, but it scarcely prepared them for ministering in American parishes. The founding of a theological school in the United States was an obvious solution, and the Greek Orthodox Theological School was the result. The founders faced severe difficulties, but their perseverance in establishing the school has been rewarded. The *Review* is a continuing witness to the vitality of the Greek Orthodox tradition in the United States.

From the beginning, the *Review* has been concerned with the ecumenical movement. The editorial in the first issue pointed to the "happy coincidence" that the publication of the *Review* coincided with the meeting of the World Council of Churches in Evanston, Illinois.[1] When Iakovos became archbishop in 1959, the commitments of the *Review* to scholarship and of Orthodoxy to ecumenism were strengthened. Both editorials and articles reflect these commitments. The *Review* has published valuable documents from Orthodox Church commissions and delegates, as well as important articles on ecumenical topics.

In recent years single issues of the journal have been dedicated to special ecumenical and interreligious consultations. These consultations have included Greek Orthodox representatives and representatives of Oriental Orthodox Churches (10:2, 13:2, 16:1, and 16:2); Judaism (22:1 and 22:4); Roman Catholicism (24:4); and Southern Baptists (22:4 and 27:1). The published proceedings of these consultations include valuable presentations on common topics (such as authority, Scripture, Torah, and tradition) from the viewpoint of each tradition as well as bibliographies and joint statements. Special issues—"The Authority of Tradition" (15:1), "On Councils and Conciliarism" (24:2, 3), and "Byzantium and Islam" (27:2, 3)—have further significance for understanding within and between faiths. A special issue, "The Future of the Ecumenical Movement," 26:4 honored Archbishop Iakovos by taking note of his special connection with the ecumenical movement before and after his elevation to the archbishopric. Orthodox leaders' deep concern with the ecumenical movement emphasizes the need for theological honesty and difference, along with unity, in a deep appreciation of the possibility that believers may differ in theological expression while being united in mutual concern.

In the first issue, the *Review* was described as "devoted to Greek Orthodox theological thought, scholarship, and discussion."[2] Orthodox theology, presented historically or systematically, has remained central to the journal's purpose, but with volume 5 the emphasis broadened in line with Archbishop Iakovos' vision of scholarship and the role of the church. The purpose was now described as being "the exchange of scholarly articles and reviews in the fields of Biblical, Patristic and Contemporary Orthodox Theology, Church History, Byzantine History, and related Classical Studies."[3] The next year saw a reformulation of the fields: "Orthodox Theology, Church History, Byzantine History, and related Classical, Archaeological and Philosophical Studies."[4] The area of biblical studies was introduced in volume 10. The final formulation, in volume 21, removed the qualification "orthodox" from theology and showed a conformity with the division of fields generally current in seminaries and graduate schools: "Theology, Biblical Studies, Church History, Byzantine History and related Classical, Archaeological, and Philosophical Studies."[5] The changing definition of fields covered reflects directly the movement of Holy Cross and the *Review* into the general climate of theological study and publication.

The fields of historical theology and church history are represented by the largest number of articles. Greek fathers such as Gregory of Nyssa, Pseudo-Dionysius the Areopagite, Gregory Palamas, and Basil the Great have had substantial articles devoted to their thought. In volume 11, George H. Williams presented a lengthy tribute to Georges Florovsky with an important review of the American career of this distinguished Orthodox theologian and historian.[6] In the area of church history, articles cover a wide range of topics, including Orthodox-Islamic relations, the Church of St. Thomas in India, relations with Roman Catholicism, the British Bible Society in Greece, acts of the neomartyrs, Constantinople and the coronation of Charlemagne, late Byzantine dialogues with Jews, and John Henry Newman as a starting point for ecumenism. These and other specialized studies shed light on many aspects of the development of Orthodoxy with emphasis on the premodern period. There are also a number of liturgical studies, several articles on religion and literature (including articles on Fyodor Dostoyevsky and Boris Pasternak), papers on icons, and a few on ecclesiology, canon law, and philosophy.

As would be expected in an Orthodox journal, ascetic-mystic traditions receive attention, with articles on Gregory Palamas, Gregory of Nyssa, Simeon the New Theologian, Pseudo-Dionysius the Areopagite, Thecla, and several general topics in mystical prayer. Biblical studies receive little attention apart from consideration of biblical texts and arguments in the context of theological discussions. Most theological considerations are in the realm of historical theology, although one should note the interesting perspective offered by responses to the "new theology" (the death of God theology) and the "new morality."[7] Supplements to volumes 12, 18, 19, and 20 contain special studies and texts published by N. M. Vaporis in "The Archbishop Iakovos Library of Ecclesiastical and Historical Sources."

Two aspects of contemporary church life and thought are strongly represented. First, various subjects bearing on current ecclesiastical practices have been considered in the pages of the *Review*. Topics include reception of non-Orthodox into the Orthodox Church, the sacrament of marriage, the church hierarchy, Anglican orders, the ecumenical patriarch and the World Council of Churches, the ecclesiology and ecumenism of Vatican II, Orthodox opposition to proselytization by others, Orthodoxy in American culture (a special bicentennial issue,

21:4), Orthodox priestly consciousness in the 1970s and 1980s, Roman Catholicism and Orthodoxy, social concerns in Greek Orthodoxy, and women in the Orthodox Church. The second contemporary emphasis stresses the tension between Orthodoxy and Western culture in general. Part of this is rooted in the gradual separation and final schism of Greek and Latin churches in the medieval period. Part, however, is also grounded in an opposition to certain aspects of Western thought and the gradual secularization of culture, with Orthodoxy seen as presenting a more complete understanding of God, human nature, and the world than contemporary Western thought and culture.

The first four volumes of the *Review* published the "Chronicle" of the Holy Cross Greek Orthodox Theological School. This included notices of events, particularly commencement, and the text of the commencement address in ancient Greek. Later issues contain occasional notices of international and local scholarly conferences of interest.

In closing, mention should be made of the substantial book review section. From its first issue, the journal has provided reviews of publications related to its general purpose. Theology, art history, liturgy, ethics, general history, and other fields are covered as they relate to Orthodoxy. But the book reviews actually embrace a far greater spectrum of theological-historical thought than do the articles in the *Review*. Major books in Protestant and Catholic ethics, theology, historical theology, and similar works are regularly reviewed. A number of publications in Greek are also reviewed.

Notes

1. Nicon D. Patrinacos, "Editorial," *Greek Orthodox Theological Review* 1 (1954): 3–6.

2. Ibid., p. 4.

3. *Greek Orthodox Theological Review* 5 (1959–60): 4.

4. *Greek Orthodox Theological Review* 6 (1960–61): 4.

5. Ibid. 10 (1964–65): 4, 21; 21 (1976): 4.

6. Ibid. 11 (1965–66): 7—107. An editorial in this issue also emphasizes the role of the *Review* in interpreting Orthodoxy to those of other traditions. Also see Thomas E. Bird, "In Memoriam: Father Georges Florovsky," *Greek Orthodox Theological Review* 24 (1979): 342–50.

7. S. S. Harakas, "A Greek Orthodox Evaluation of the 'New Theology,' " *Greek Orthodox Theological Review* 12 (1966–67): 340–68, and "An Orthodox Christian Approach to the 'New Morality,' " *Greek Orthodox Theological Review* 15 (1969–70): 107–39.

Information Sources

BIBLIOGRAPHY:

Kokkinakis, Bishop Athenagoras, "Holy Cross Greek Orthodox Theological School: Twenty Years of Progress, 1937–1957." *Greek Orthodox Theological Review* 3 (1957): 15–22.

Patrinacos, Nicon D. "Editorial." *Greek Orthodox Theological Review* 1 (1954): 3–6.

Romanides, John S. "Editorial: Statement of Purpose." *Greek Orthodox Theological Review* 5 (1959): 7–80

INDEX SOURCES: Contains a five-year cumulative index every five years; also in *Historical Abstracts, Religious and Theological Abstracts, Religion Index One, Old Testament Abstracts, Bulletin analytique bibliographie hellenique.*

REPRINT EDITIONS: University Microfilms International.

LOCATION SOURCES: Duke University, Princeton Theological Seminary, Union Theological Seminary (New York), Yale University, Southern Methodist University, and others.

Publication History

MAGAZINE TITLE AND TITLE CHANGES: *Greek Orthodox Theological Review* (1954–   ).

VOLUME AND ISSUE DATA: 1:1 (August 1954) announced quarterly publication, but 1:2 appeared in March 1955; 2:1 (Easter 1956) announced semiannual publication at Christmas and Easter; 3:1 (Summer 1957) changed date designation to Summer and Winter; 7:1–2 and 8:1–2 each a combined issue; 12:3, a special issue published as "Anniversary Issue 1937–1967: Dedicated to the 30th Anniversary of the Holy Cross Greek Orthodox Theological School," announced redating to Spring and Fall issues; 18:1–2 and 20:1–2 each a combined issue; 21 began quarterly publication in March, June, September, December; 23:3–4, 24:2–3, 26:1–2, 27:2–3 each a combined issue.

PUBLISHER AND PLACE OF PUBLICATION: Greek Orthodox Theological Institute Press, Brookline, Mass. (1954–55); Holy Cross Greek Orthodox Theological School Press, Brookline, Mass. (1956–67); Holy Cross School of Theology, Hellenic College, Brookline, Mass. (1968–75); Holy Cross Orthodox Press, Brookline, Mass. (1976–   ).

EDITORS: Rev. Dr. Nicon D. Patrinacos (1954–55), Rt. Rev. Bishop Athenagoras Kokkinakis (1956–59), Rev. John S. Romanides (1959–65), Rev. Leonidas Contos (1965–67), Rev. Demetrios J. Constantelos (1966–71), Rev. Nomikos Michael Vaporis (1971–   ).

CIRCULATION: 1075 (1983).

Grover A. Zinn

_____ **H** _____

HARVARD THEOLOGICAL REVIEW

Since 1908 the *Harvard Theological Review* has been a leading American religion journal with a scope far broader than the word *theological* in its title might suggest. It has carried articles on topics that span the study of religions, East and West. This broad view is suggested in "The Call to Theology" by Francis Greenwood Peabody, the first issue's lead article. Theology, Peabody argued, should be understood as the "rational interpretation of religion" with the incorporation of "the scientific temper" (objective analysis) and historical study. Theology was thus contrasted to the then dominant aspects of feeling and action in religion.[1] In relation to the purpose of the *Review*, theology therefore had both interpretive and historical-critical dimensions, as well as the more traditional systematic and reflective aspects.

One distinctive mark of the *Review* has been this breadth of purpose, although at times content has been more narrowly focused. A statement of purpose first printed in volume 4 noted, "The Review aims to include discussion in the various Fields of theological study and also in the history of religions, ethics, education, economics, and sociology, in their theological and religious aspects. It is designed to serve the needs not only of clergymen and scholars, but of all who are interested in religious thought and in the place and function of religion in modern life." In 1921 a new statement appeared: "The scope of the Review embraces theology, ethics, the history and philosophy of religion, and cognate subjects. It aims to publish investigations, discussions and reviews, which contribute to the enlargement of knowledge or the advance of thought. From time to time it will present surveys of recent literature in the various fields of learning that fall within its cognizance." Since 1937 this statement has appeared without the last sentence.

The *Review* was founded on the occasion of a bequest that came to the Divinity School. It came from Mildred Everett, daughter of Charles Carroll Everett, a

Harvard Divinity School professor from 1869 and dean from 1878 until his death in 1900. Her purpose, suggested by her father, was to provide funds "for the establishment and maintenance of an undenominational theological review, to be edited under the direction of the Faculty of the Divinity School of Harvard University."[2] The gift came at a propitious moment in the Divinity School's history. Long identified with liberal and Unitarian theology, the school in 1880 appointed to the faculty a Southern Baptist, Crawford Howell Toy, who had studied in Berlin and had been threatened with investigation for teaching theories of Julius Wellhausen at Southern Baptist Theological Seminary. Subsequent appointments of European-trained non-Unitarians made the school "undenominational," as President Charles Eliot had earlier claimed it to be, and what Eliot described as a "broad school of scientific theology and independent research."[3] Thus Harvard quickly moved to the forefront of American institutions influenced by the new historical and critical methods being pursued in Germany. As well, religious-theological scholarship could now be pursued, as in Germany, apart from doctrinal or ecclesiastical loyalties and commitments. Consequently, liberal American scholarship, particularly in theology and history, was becoming dependent on models and ideas imported from Germany, a situation that has not fully vanished in some fields to this day.[4] In the first issue, for example, A. C. McGiffert's "Modern Ideas of God" critically reviewed German theology, philosophy, and scholarship bearing on the idea of God. He referred to a few American and English theologians but only in terms of their relationship to German ideas (1, 1908:10–27).

The breadth of the *Review* over the years can be discerned from a sampling of other articles in the first volume. Topics addressed included synoptic criticism, archaeology in Palestine, New England theology, Hellenism and Christianity, a review of recent work in systematic theology, ethical monism and evil, the minister and his people (by Phillips Brooks), Christianity in the Far East, Catholic modernism (by George Tyrrell), Calvin and the Genevan state, Butler and Newman on religious certitude, surveys of recent literature in Old and New Testament, the Vedic fire god, the psychology of religion (by J. B. Pratt), and the present task of religious thought. The articles, though diverse, are united by a concern to think about religion from a critical perspective. Although contributions on Eastern religions were not numerous in the *Review*'s early decades, interest in the East was present from the beginning.

It is also significant to note that the editors were also committed to freedom of inquiry and an unsectarian attitude. Benjamin B. Warfield, for example, offered an unsparing conservative attack on liberal German scholarship on the life of Jesus in "Christless Christianity" in volume 5. It hardly represented the views of the editor or the Harvard faculty. The conservative-liberal split in American religious thought can also be seen in Warfield's "The Essence of Christianity and the Cross of Christ," a conservative response to D. C. Macintosh's "What is the Christian Religion?" (7, 1914:538–95; ibid., pp. 16–46).

One major new perspective in the *Review* in the early decades was G. F.

Moore's revisionist approach to the study of early Judaism (14, 1921). He called for rejection of Christian misinterpretation of rabbinic thought and application of historical scholarship to recover the thought of early Judaism more accurately.

In the *Review*'s second decade, a shift in emphasis appeared as articles on early Christianity, Greco-Roman religions, and early Judaism came to dominate. This shift reflected the monumental work of Harvard faculty, especially G. F. Moore (Judaism), Hirsopp Lake (early Greek texts of the New Testament), and Arthur Darby Nock (Christianity in the Greco-Roman world). Increasingly the *Review* narrowed its focus as textual, archaeological, literary, and paleographical studies shed new light on the complex religious worlds of Greeks, Romans, Jews, and Christians in the Roman Empire. Depth and clarity compensated for these sacrifices in breadth. As third editor of the journal Nock brought distinguished, distinctive leadership to it.

Similar trends marked the fourth decade of publication, with articles by Robert M. Grant, H. J. Rose, J. Quasten, and others. But the *Review* also published studies in other fields. Among them are Roland Bainton's essays on the early church and war (39, 1936:189–212), Clyde Kluckhohn's classic and often reprinted "Myths and Rituals: A General Theory" (35, 1942:45–79), and Perry Miller's seminal study of Solomon Stoddard (34, 1941:277–320). With volume 40, an expansion of subject matter can be observed. During the decade 1946–56, scholars such as Henry Chadwick, Robert M. Grant, M. S. Enslin, A. H. M. Jones, and Bruce Metzger continued the commitment to scholarship on religion in the Near East and the Greco-Roman world. The larger view is evidenced in articles by N. H. Baynes on icons (44, 1951:93–106), Kenneth K. S. Ch'en on Chinese Buddhism (49, 1956:307–27), D. Geanakoplos on Greek and Latin churches in the thirteenth century (46, 1953:79–89), Perry Miller on Jonathan Edwards (41, 1948:123–45), and Conrad Wright on Ralph Waldo Emerson (49, 1956:19–43). This partial listing indicates both the broadening of emphasis and the high quality of scholarship in the *Review*.

Editor Arthur Darby Nock died in 1963, and Krister Stendahl began his tenure as editor. Old names remained, but work of new scholars increasingly appeared. The range and quality of contributions in the journal's sixth decade may be indicated by a few examples: Werner Jaeger on Greek ideas of immortality (52, 1959:35–47), Helmut Koester on diversification in early Christianity (58, 1965:279–318), George Lindbeck on nominalism (52, 1959:43–60), David Little on Weber and the Protestant ethic (59, 1966:415–28), Jacob Neusner on Judaism's Second Temple period (53, 1960:125–42), Jonathan E. Smith on natural religion (54, 1961:1–19), Harry A. Wolfson on patristic philosophy (57, 1964:360–80), G. Ernest Wright on Shechem (55, 1962:252:66), and Stendahl himself on Paul (56, 1963:199–215). Two new features were also introduced: an annual summary of Harvard doctoral dissertations first appeared in 1961, and "Notes and Observations" debuted in 1964.

The seventh decade saw a continued concentration on Western religious history. However, theological questions were once more raised in articles by Julian

Hartt and Mark C. Taylor on Kierkegaard (60, 1967:133–44; 66, 1973:311–29), Frederick Sontag on Augustinian metaphysics (60, 1967:297–306), and Gordon D. Kaufman on theology and nature (65, 1972:337–66). Black theology and the black church highlighted a special issue in 1971, which featured articles by R. I. McKinney and William Jones. Archaeology, always strong at Harvard, re-emerged in the *Review* in a memorial issue for Paul Lapp that same year. Elaine Pagels published a significant series of articles presenting Gnostic texts in a new light (65, 1972:153–69; 69, 1976:301–24). Ethics received new attention from Clyde A. Holbrook (60, 1967:163–75), Robin Lovin (65, 1972:495–508), and Charles H. Reynolds (65, 1972:509–30).

In recent issues the *Review* has continued to publish the kinds of critical studies of Western religious life and thought that have distinguished it in the past. Among the many significant contributions are those of Paul Ricoeur on a hermeneutic of the idea of revelation (70, 1972:1–37), James H. Charlesworth on Jewish astrology (70, 1977:183–200), Wayne Proudfoot on religious experience and belief (70, 1977:343:67), Ross S. Kraemer on the cult of Dionysius (72, 1979:55–80), Helmut Koester on apocryphal and canonical gospels (73, 1980:105–30), Robert M. Grant on dietary laws (73, 1980:299–310), David W. Lotz on Ritschl (73, 1980:337–72), Jack S. Hawley on yoga in Hinduism (74, 1981:1–20), Phyllis A. Bird on Genesis 1:27b (74, 1981:129–59), Richard R. Niebuhr on symbols (75, 1982:25–33), Stephen J. Stein on Mary Baker Eddy (75, 1982:97–116), Morton Smith on the secret gospel of Mark (75, 1982:449–61), and Michael McGiffert on Elizabethan Puritanism (75, 1982:463–502).

In more than 75 years of publication, the *Harvard Theological Review* has presented scholarship of the highest order, devoted to elucidating critically the history of religion, primarily in the West and primarily in the Jewish and Christian traditions. Its pages testify to the development of a strong American tradition of historical-critical scholarship in religion. When the *Review* began publication, American scholarship was heavily dependent on European, especially German, resources and models. Drawing on their formation in German universities, the Harvard Divinity School faculty created one of the major centers for historical-critical study in the United States. Passed from one generation to the next, this tradition has informed the *Harvard Theological Review* and the study of religion in general.

Notes

1. *Harvard Theological Review* 1 (1980): 1–9. All subsequent references to the *Review* will be in the text in parentheses.

2. Statement in first issue of the *Review*.

3. George Hunston Williams, ed., *The Harvard Divinity School: Its Place in Harvard University and in American Culture* (Boston: n.p., 1954), pp. 166–78.

4. See the reviews of American scholarship in religion in Arnold S. Nash, ed., *Protestant Thought in the Twentieth Century: Whence and Whither?* (New York: Macmillan,

1951), and Paul Ramsey, ed., *Religion* (Englewood Cliffs: Prentice-Hall, 1965). The essay by James Hastings Nichols on the history of Christianity in Ramsey seems overly obsessed with the dominance of English and Continental scholarship in this field.

Information Sources

BIBLIOGRAPHY:

Holbrook, Clyde A. *Religion: A Humanistic Field*. Englewood Cliffs: Prentice-Hall, 1963.

Morison, Samuel Eliot, ed. *The Development of Harvard University since the Inauguration of President Eliot: 1869–1929*. Cambridge: Harvard University Press, 1930.

Nash, Arnold S., ed. *Protestant Thought in the Twentieth Century: Whence and Whither?* New York: Macmillan, 1951.

Ramsey, Paul, ed. *Religion*. Englewood Cliffs, N.J.: Prentice-Hall, 1965.

Williams, George Hunston, ed. *The Harvard Divinity School: Its Place in Harvard University and in American Culture*. Boston: n.p., 1954.

INDEX SOURCES: In supplements of the *Harvard Theological Review* to 30 (1–30), 40 (31–40), and 50 (41–50), in 61 (1968): 659–68 (51–60), and in 71 (1978): 335–46 (61–70); also in *Current Contents, Humanities Index, Old Testament Abstracts, Religion Index One, Religious and Theological Abstracts*.

REPRINT EDITIONS: Microfiche available from *Harvard Theological Review*, Harvard Divinity School.

LOCATION SOURCES: University of Chicago, University of California-Berkeley, University of Texas-Austin, Princeton Theological Seminary, Library of Congress, Duke University, Oberlin College, Harvard University, and many others.

Publication History

MAGAZINE TITLE AND TITLE CHANGES: *Harvard Theological Review* (1908–).

VOLUME AND ISSUE DATA: 1:1 (1908)–68:2 (1975), appeared quarterly, with 64:2–3 (1971) combined; 68:3–4 (1975)–73:3–4 (1980), appeared semiannually with 1–2 and 3–4 combined; 74:1 (1981–), appears quarterly in four numbers annually.

PUBLISHER AND PLACE OF PUBLICATION: Harvard University Press, Cambridge, Mass. 02138.

EDITORS: George F. Moore (1908–30), James H. Ropes (1931–32), Arthur D. Nock (1933–62), Krister Stendahl (1963–74), Helmut Koester (1975–).

CIRCULATION: 1800 (1983).

Grover A. Zinn

HEBRAICA. *See* JOURNAL OF NEAR EASTERN STUDIES

THE HEBREW STUDENT. *See* THE BIBLICAL WORLD

HISTORICAL MAGAZINE OF THE PROTESTANT EPISCOPAL CHURCH

The *Historical Magazine of the Protestant Episcopal Church*, is, with the *Catholic Historical Review*,* one of the two best denominational historical journals published at present in the United States. Both publish articles that meet high scholarly standards; both draw contributors from among professional historians and from outside their denominational ranks; and neither limits itself exclusively to American topics.

The *Historical Magazine* began in 1931 when the Reverend E. Clowes Chorley, historiographer of the Episcopal Church, and a number of other clergy and laymen interested in history persuaded the church's General Convention to authorize such a journal. Three years later, the General Convention provided a modest annual subsidy. The journal was published under the supervision of the Joint Commission of General Convention from 1932 until 1961, when it was transferred to the Church Historical Society, now the Historical Society of the Episcopal Church.[1]

Its first editor, E. Clowes Chorley, was a Methodist minister who emigrated from England, converted to Anglicanism, and was ordained to the priesthood. After studying at the Philadelphia Divinity School, he was employed as a parish priest in the diocese of New York until his retirement in 1940. He was historiographer of the diocese and served as the fifth historiographer of the Episcopal Church from 1919 until his death in 1949. He is best remembered for *Men and Movements in the American Episcopal Church* (1946), a study of the evolution and clashes of evangelical, Anglo-Catholic, and modernist thought in that denomination during the nineteenth and early twentieth centuries.[2]

Under Chorley's editorship, the *Magazine*'s primary objective was to promote "a greater knowledge and an enhanced appreciation of the American church's history on the part of bishops, clergy and laity."[3] It is not strange, therefore, that 94 percent of the articles published between 1932 and 1941 dealt with Anglicanism in what is now the United States. Of the American articles that can be assigned to a particular chronological period, 30 percent dealt with the colonial church; 18 percent with the critical period of the American Revolution and its aftermath (to about 1800), when Anglicanism was disestablished and struggled to adjust itself to republican circumstances; 30 percent with the early nineteenth century; and 21 percent with the period from 1860 to about 1900. The *Magazine* published no articles bearing primarily on the twentieth century.

Among those who contributed articles during this period were John W. Lydekker, archivist for the Society for the Propagation of the Gospel; W. W. Manross and Nelson Burr, distinguished historians of the Episcopal Church; the Venerable George F. Bragg, Jr., pioneer historian of black Anglicanism; the priests G. MacLaren Brydon and Edgar Legare Pennington, who wrote extensively on the local history, sacred and secular, of Georgia, North Carolina, and

Virginia; university professors John Hope Franklin, Frank J. Klingberg, and Samuel C. McCulloch; and the playwright Dubose Murphy.

The Reverend Walter Herbert Stowe succeeded as editor in 1950, serving until his retirement in 1961. Like Chorley, Stowe was a parish priest (in the dioceses of Colorado and New Jersey) whose avocation was history, and he too was historiographer of the Episcopal Church. Stowe's editorial policy did not deviate from that of his predecessor. Although the *Historical Magazine*'s "primary purpose" was "to publish the history of the Protestant Episcopal Church in the United States of America in all its varied aspects," Stowe intended to avoid "a smug provincialism" by publishing some articles on the history of Anglicanism elsewhere in the world. Moreover, Stowe wanted the *Magazine* to help rectify the "distorted picture" of U.S. history to be found in textbooks, which say almost nothing about religion after the Pilgrims and the Puritans. Finally, he wanted to publish articles of interest to the ordinary reader who was not a specialist historian.[4]

Under Stowe's editorship, most of the articles published between 1954 and 1961 (86 percent) continued to be on Anglicanism in the United States, but 11 articles on the Church of England appeared. Of the American articles that can be assigned to a particular chronological period, 17 percent dealt with the colonial period, 50 percent with the Revolutionary era, 29 percent with the early nineteenth century, 34 percent with the later nineteenth century, and 16 percent with the twentieth century. Among the notable contributors were Geoffrey Bill, librarian of the Lambeth Palace library; professors Norman S. Binstead, Frank J. Klingberg, Jr., William A. Clebsch, and Thomas B. Lundeen; and the priests George E. DeMille and Thomas E. Jessett (the latter a noted authority on the history of Washington and Oregon).

The *Historical Magazine* underwent two major changes in 1961. General Convention transferred supervision of the journal to the Church Historical Society although continuing its subsidy.[5] And Lawrence L. Brown became the new editor, serving from 1962 through 1977. Brown, who studied at the University of Texas and the Virginia Theological Seminary, served in the parochial ministry in the diocese of Texas from 1929 to 1951. In 1951 he became associate professor of church history at the newly established Episcopal Theological Seminary of the Southwest, Austin, Texas. He taught there until his retirement in 1973.

Brown planned no "radical departures" in the *Magazine*, although he did want to encourage more studies of the Church of England and other constituent churches in the Anglican Communion.[6] He believed that the function of historical periodicals is to provide an outlet for the close study of particulars: "One can generalize about 'American Christianity,' but there is no such thing apart from the denominations, communions, sects, and persuasions in which it was and is practiced." Hence he thought it important to examine particular leaders, parishes, dioceses, or organizations. A second function that he thought important was to provide an outlet for new interpretations.[7] Under Brown's editorship, the strictly American articles dropped to 69 percent of the total; 21 percent were on English church history. There was little change from past years, however, with respect to the chronological periods covered. Twenty-six percent of the American articles focused on the colonial period, 10 percent on the Revolutionary era, 22 percent on the early nineteenth century, 32 percent on the later nineteenth century, and 11 percent on the twentieth century. With respect to the English articles, 42 percent concentrated on the nineteenth century, 26 percent on the Stuarts, 16 percent on the Tudors, 13 percent on the eighteenth century, and a single article on the twentieth century.

The number of academics who contributed essays grew. One notes such well-known historians as Paul A. Carter, William Gribbin, William P. Haugaard, Derek Holmes, John Lankford, Stanford E. Lehmberg, Ralph E. Luker, Charles F. Mullett, and John Pinnington. Among the clerical contributors were Thomas E. Jessett and John E. Booty (now dean of the School of Theology, University of the South).

John F. Woolverton has been editor of the journal since 1978. Woolverton received the Ph.D. from Columbia University and was professor of church history at the Virginia Theological Seminary from 1958 until 1982, when he left academia for the parish ministry. Woolverton introduced changes in editorial policy that have shifted the *Magazine*'s direction. In a critique of the articles published in the journal from 1932 to 1977, he made several complaints: he found an insufficient number of articles on the twentieth century, the history of theology, minority groups, and liturgy and ministry; he found that the published articles failed to fix their subjects in context or pay attention to changes over time.[8] Perhaps the main goal that he set for himself was to bring the *Magazine* into the twentieth century: "it is my hope that in the last quarter of the twentieth century the magazine will increasingly find it possible to publish articles which deal with the church's history from World War I to the present."[9]

Woolverton has largely succeeded in reaching his goal. The number of articles limited to the United States continues to drop (59 percent of those published between 1978 and 1983), while that of articles on English history continues to rise (to 28 percent). And 24 percent of the English articles deal with the twentieth century. A similar shift may be seen in the chronological distribution of the American articles. The colonial period receives 22 percent of the articles; the Revolutionary era, 5 percent; the early nineteenth century, 22 percent; the later nineteenth century, 20 percent; and the twentieth century, 32 percent.

More difficult to count are the articles' subject matter and methodologies. Over the course of the *Historical Magazine*'s life, the number of articles devoted to biographies of bishops and priests, the histories of dioceses, and the publication of documents has declined; the number of articles dealing with women and blacks, the interaction of church and secular society, and the way that institutions operate has increased. Less attention is paid to the enactments of legislative bodies or the pronouncements of bishops, and more attention is paid to the daily functioning of institutions. As examples, one may cite several recent studies: the first generation of clergy wives in Tudor England; black Anglican hymnody in early nineteenth-century America; the changing attitudes of English evangelicals to the problems of industrialization in early nineteenth-century England; church-state conflicts during the U.S. Civil War; what happened to one urban diocese during the turbulent 1960s; and the role of a certain American priest in the formation of Alcoholics Anonymous. The changing historiographical currents of the 1960s and 1970s therefore are reflected in the journal's pages.

The contributors also mirror the changing nature of the historical profession. Academic historians such as W. Harrison Daniel, Vine Deloria, Jr., Joan R. Gunderson, Francis G. James, Robert W. Kingdon, John Lankford, Wayne N. Metz, and Paul L. Ward continue to contribute, as do historians from the ecclesiastical world—Sister Rachel Hosmer, O.S.H., Charles V. LaFontaine, S.A., and Frederica Thomsett, for instance. An increasing number of contributors who are trained historians, however, do not have academic appointments.

In sum, the *Historical Magazine of the Protestant Episcopal Church* is a major outlet for scholarly work on history, broadly conceived, of Anglicanism in the United States and England. Because of Anglicanism's churchly tradition and because of the historical connections between church and state in the former British Empire, most of the articles published are by no means narrowly denominational in interest.

Notes

1. "Editorial Notes," *Historical Magazine of the Protestant Episcopal Church* 5 (1936): 265; Walter H. Stowe, "Our Twentieth Year! Twentieth Volume!" ibid. 20 (1951): 6; Walter H. Stowe, " 'We Wish You Good Luck in the Name of the Lord,' " ibid. 30 (1961): 227–28.

2. *Historical Magazine* 18 (1949): 347–48.

3. Ibid. 5 (1936): 266.

4. Walter H. Stowe, "The Policy of Historical Magazine," *Historical Magazine* 19 (1950): 4–7.

5. Massey H. Shepherd, Jr., "The *Historical Magazine* Reorganizes," *Historical Magazine* 31 (1962): 2.

6. Lawrence L. Brown, "Editorial," *Historical Magazine* 31 (1962): 4.

7. Ibid. 46 (1977): 379.

8. John F. Woolverton, "The State of the *Historical Magazine*," *Historical Magazine* 48 (1979): 262.

9. John W. Woolverton, "Editorial," *Historical Magazine* 47 (1978): 4.

Information Sources

INDEX SOURCES: *Historical Abstracts, Religion Index One.*
REPRINT EDITIONS: University Microfilms International.
LOCATION SOURCES: Yale University, Library of Congress, University of Chicago, Harvard University, Duke University, and others.

Publication History

MAGAZINE TITLE AND TITLE CHANGES: *Historical Magazine of the Protestant Episcopal Church* (1932–   ).
VOLUME AND ISSUE DATA: 1:1 (1932–   ). Appears quarterly.

PUBLISHER AND PLACE OF PUBLICATION: General Convention of the Episcopal
    Church, Garrison, N.Y. (1932–35), New Brunswick, N.J. (1936–61); Historical
    Society of the Episcopal Church, Austin, Texas (1961–   ).
EDITORS: E. Clowes Chorley (1932–49), Walter H. Stowe (1950–61), Lawrence L.
    Brown (1962–77), John F. Woolverton (1978–   ).
CIRCULATION: 1500 (1982).

Denis G. Paz

HISTORICAL RECORDS AND STUDIES

Historical Records and Studies (*HRS*) was the major periodical of the U.S.
Catholic Historical Society of New York, consisting of 50 annual volumes that
appeared irregularly between 1899 and 1964.

Fascinated by U.S. history and its emergence as a science in the nineteenth
century, John Gilmary Shea (1824–92) abandoned his career as a lawyer for the
life of an unappreciated historian. Posthumously recognized as the Father of
American Catholic History for collecting primary sources and writing extensively, Shea met repeated disappointments in his attempts to encourage American
Catholics to preserve and study records of their past. He and Richard H. Clarke,
a lawyer, had long desired the formation of a Catholic historical society. When
Pope Leo XIII opened the Vatican archives in 1883, they solicited support for
the society from the American hierarchy and set an organizational meeting for
9 December 1884, two days after the close of the Third Plenary Council of
Baltimore. The American bishops endorsed their endeavor, and most became
members of the society.

Recognizing that Protestants were shaping American historiography, Shea and
Clarke argued that Catholics must also contribute to it. They hoped that the U.S.
Catholic Historical Society would "remove the stigma of indifference which
seems to rest on us [Catholics] as a body" by stimulating "an interest in the
glorious labors and struggles of our forebears in faith."[1] Despite ambitious goals
of gathering and housing a national Catholic reference library and archives, the
society was moribund until Shea devoted himself to the publication of a quarterly
and served as its editor.

The *U.S. Catholic Historical Magazine* (*USCHM*) carried book reviews, notes
and queries, the society's proceedings, and primary sources such as the *decreta*
of the First Provincial Council of Oregon, letters of John England (first bishop
of Charleston), and a translation of Thormund Torfason's eighteenth-century
History of Ancient Vinland. Most articles were institutional, episcopal, or mission
history, but some protested contemporary anti-Catholicism and examined its
origins in the colonial period. Between 440 and 500 pages appeared annually
until Shea's death in 1892, when the society again became quiescent.

Charles G. Herbermann (1840–1916) and Archbishop Michael A. Corrigan,
among the original founders in 1884, collaborated to reactivate publication in

1898. Corrigan himself contributed a series of articles on the history of the New York clergy to *Historical Records and Studies*, which Herbermann edited. Professor of Latin at the City College of New York and later editor in chief of the *Catholic Encyclopedia*, Herbermann was the most prolific contributor during the journal's early years, reviewing some 20 books and writing as many articles on topics as diverse as French colonies in North America, the Douai Bible, the Sulpicians, and Catholic universities and parishes. Herbermann also initiated the society's monograph series with a translation of Columbus's journals from his voyages to the New World. Among other contributors were James McGean, Henry Brann, and John Cardinal Farley, who wrote a memoir of Cardinal McCloskey. Adolf Bandelier wrote on native Americans. Articles on Catholicism in the East appeared with greatest frequency, but other geographic areas were not ignored.

A close associate of Herbermann, Thomas F. Meehan (1854–1942), edited *HRS* between 1917 and 1942. Meehan was the son of a newspaper publisher and worked for a number of secular papers. He knew many of the leading figures in the Catholic press and literary movements at the turn of the century.[2] He continued the emphasis on the history of missions, parishes, religious orders, and clerical biography, in addition to articles like "Lincoln's Opinion of Catholics" and "Catholic Contributions to Liberty in America," which demonstrated that Catholics had always been good citizens.

Interest in American Catholic history increased during the twentieth century. Professional organizations appeared, and the publication of primary sources in *HRS* declined. Succeeding editors made no other substantial changes in policy. Among the contributors were prominent Catholic historians such as Peter Guilday, Joseph N. Moody, Henry J. Browne, W. Eugene Shields, S.J., John Tracy Ellis, Anabelle Melville, Thomas T. McAvoy, C.S.C., and James J. Hennesey, S.J. No single individual dominated the publication the way the first two editors had. Volumes ranged from 100 to 500 pages, with most since 1930 having between 130 and 200.

Publication of *HRS* ceased with volume 50 in 1964. An index to *USCHM*, *HRS*, and the monograph series appeared in 1967. By 1979 36 volumes of the monograph series had been published. In 1980 the society launched *U.S. Catholic Historian* (*USCHi*), a quarterly that aims to present sound historical scholarship in a way that appeals to the needs of interested nonprofessionals, especially people engaged in local or community history. The *Historian* publishes some 20 to 30 articles annually in an illustrated quarterly of about 300 pages.

Notes

1. "Report of the Committee on Publications," *Proceedings of the Third Public and First Annual Meeting of the U.S. Catholic Historical Society* (New York: Press of the Society, 1886), pp. 6–7.

2. E. P. Willging and H. Hatzfield, *Catholic Serials of the 19th Century in the U.S.* (Washington: Catholic University of America Press, 1967), 2d ser., pt. XIV, p. 165.

Information Sources

BIBLIOGRAPHY:

Cadden, John P. *Historiography of the American Catholic Church, 1785–1943*. Washington, D.C.: Catholic University of America Press, 1944. Reprint in the American Catholic Tradition, New York: Arno Press, 1978.

Condon, Peter. "Charles George Herbermann." *Historical Records and Studies* 10 (1917): 8–37.

Herbermann, Charles G. "The U.S. Catholic Historical Society." *Catholic Historical Review* 2 (1916): 302–7.

Reardon, T. J. "The Society's Golden Jubilee." *Historical Records and Studies* 25 (1935): 7–20.

INDEX SOURCES: *Index for the Complete Works of the U.S. Catholic Historical Society, 1884–1946*. *Historical Records and Studies* 1–10 (1889–1917) in vol. 11; 11–12 (1917–18) in vol. 13; 13–15 (1919–21) in vol. 15; 16–24 (1924–34) in vol. 24; 25–29 (1935–38) in vol. 30. Also in *Catholic Periodical Index*.

REPRINT EDITIONS: University Microfilms International.

LOCATION SOURCES: *U.S. Catholic Historical Magazine*: Catholic University of America (except vol. 13), St. Joseph Seminary (Dunwoodie), Wisconsin State Historical Society, University of Notre Dame (except vol. 3); *Historical Records and Studies*: Catholic University of America (except vols. 39–40), Wisconsin State Historical Society, University of Notre Dame; *U.S. Catholic Historian*: Library of Congress, Emory University, University of Notre Dame.

Publication History

MAGAZINE TITLE AND TITLE CHANGES: *U.S. Catholic Historical Magazine* (1887–92), *Historical Records and Studies* (1899–1964), *U.S. Catholic Historian* (1980–).

VOLUME AND ISSUE DATA: *U.S. Catholic Historical Magazine* 1–4 (1887–91); *Historical Records and Studies* 1–2 (1899), 3 (1904), 4 (1906), 5 (1908), 6 (1912), 7–9 (1914–16), 10–11 (1917), 12–15 (1918–21), 16 (1924), 17 (1926), 18–19 (1928–29), 20 (1931), 21–22 (1932), 23–24 (1933–34), 25–26 (1935–36), 27–28 (1937), 29–32 (1938–41), 33–37 (1944—48), 38 (1950), 39–40 (1952), 41–42 (1953–54), 43–45 (1955–57), 46 (1958), 47–48 (1959–60), 49 (1962), 50 (1964); *U.S. Catholic Historian* 1- (1980–).

PUBLISHER AND PLACE OF PUBLICATION: U.S. Catholic Historical Society, New York, N.Y.

EDITORS: *U.S. Catholic Historical Magazine*: John Gilmary Shea; *Historical Records and Studies*: Charles G. Herbermann (1899–1916), Thomas F. Meehan (1917–42), Thomas J. McMahon (1942–48), John J. Meng (1950–52), James A. Reynolds (1953–64). *U.S. Catholic Historian*: James J. Mahoney (1980-June 1983), Christopher J. Kauffman (July 1983–).

CIRCULATION: Under 1000 (est., 1982).

Thomas J. Jonas

HISTORY OF RELIGIONS

Under the charismatic and editorial supervision of Mircea Eliade, the University of Chicago's Divinity School published the first issue of *History of Religions* (*HR*) in the summer of 1961. The birth of the international journal fulfilled a dream of the Rumanian-born comparativist to create a special forum for the discussion of world religions.[1] The inaugural issue gave this reason for the journal's founding:

> Despite the manuals, periodicals, and bibliographies today available to scholars, it is progressively more difficult to keep up with the advances being made in all departments of the History of Religions. . . . A scholar regretfully finds himself becoming a specialist in *one* religion or even in a particular period or a single aspect of that religion. This situation has induced us to bring out a new periodical. Our purpose is not simply to make one more review available . . . but more especially to provide an aid to orientation in a field that is constantly widening and to stimulate exhanges of views among specialists who, as a rule, do not follow the progress made in other disciplines.[2]

Eliade and his coeditors, Joseph M. Kitagawa and Charles H. Long, intended for the journal to raise key problems, generate methodological discussions, and give meaning to the varieties of religious data. By 1972 the semiannual had grown, and the editors (including Jonathan Z. Smith) had forged the following statement of purpose: "*History of Religions* is a quarterly journal devoted to the study of historical religious phenomena, either within particular traditions or across cultural boundaries, and seeking to integrate the results of the several disciplines of the science of religion."[3] The priority of religious phenomena, the attention to a historical context, and the relation of particular religious data to general comparative understanding—these elements mark the "science of religion," or *Religionswissenschaft*.

Eliade's presence at Chicago may have been a necessary condition for the journal's beginnings and its success, but he reaped much of what had already been sown. American interest in the study of world religions goes back to a Chicago fair at the turn of the century. At the Columbian Exposition of 1893, which commemorated the 400th anniversary of Columbus's discovery of America, a major international assembly—the World's Parliament of Religions—advanced American interest in exotic, non-Western religions. Presuppositions behind the sessions were those of liberal-Protestant ecumenism.[4] But interest in the history of religions declined with world wars, economic chaos, and the rise of neo-orthodoxy. It was only in the postwar period, with the proliferation of religious studies departments in colleges and universities, the new fascination with Eastern cults, and a concern among social scientists for myth, ritual, and cultural pattern, that the history of religions as a discipline was revived. At this time Joachim Wach (1898–1955), "one of the most universal minds in the field," systematized the comparative study of religions and methodically prepared the ground for Eliade's journal.[5]

Wach viewed the history of religions as an autonomous discipline with roots in nineteenth-century Germany. Following Wilhelm Dilthey's hermeneutics of a "human science," Wach positioned the history of religions squarely between descriptive studies like anthropology, sociology, and psychology on the one hand and normative studies like theology and philosophy of religion on the other.[6] These two kinds of study gave birth to a new discipline, *Religionswissenschaft*, defined by the interaction between a history of specific religious content and an ordered set of generalizations about religious data. From this standpoint, inquiry was interdisciplinary, and it was aimed at meaning. Eliade put it this way: "Like it or not, the scholar has not finished his work when he has reconstructed the history of a religious form or brought out its sociological, economic, or political contexts. In addition, he must understand its meaning—that is, identify and elucidate the situations and positions that have induced or made possible its appearance or its triumph at a particular historical moment."[7] The integration of religious meaning within a particular context promised much for scholarship and for world understanding. For Eliade, the real contribution lay in the ability of the new discipline to pave the way for East-West dialogue, not in the spirit of nineteenth-century liberal Protestantism but in the meeting of others "*on their own plane of reference.*"[8] This was the end of interdisciplinary study and its sensitivity to the many valences of meaning in world religions.

Eliade made his journal-dream a reality with the help of Dean Jerald C. Brauer, and for 10 years the Divinity School at Chicago underwrote the cost of publication, subsidizing the journal in full. In 1970, Brauer's successor, Joseph M. Kitagawa (himself an *HR* editor), arranged for publication to be taken over by the University of Chicago Press. The first decade had been a success, and the press gladly adopted the thriving journal. In 1962, its first full year, *History of Religions* went to an average of 900 subscribers. By 1972, the number of mailings had almost doubled, reaching a high mark of 1731. The twentieth anniversary issue was in the hands of 1947 recipients.[9] The speedy success can be explained in part by the need for interdisciplinary mediums in the academy, through which ever-widening bodies of information could be coherently presented and discussed. Filling such a need was Eliade's design; it certainly helps to account for the fact that within 10 years, *HR* had become the most prestigious journal of its kind. In his assessment of the journal, Jacob Neusner of Brown University ranked *HR* above every other journal in the field. The German and French journals can sustain comparison. But "*HR* is simply at a higher level . . . its articles far broader in scope and interest."[10]

From buddhologists to scholars of native America, from philosophers of religion to anthropologists, contributors have included Kees Bolle, Marcel Detienne, Jan de Vries, Alf Hiltebeitel, Winston L. King, Wayne A. Meeks, Fazlur Rahman, Victor Turner, and Alex Wayman. Eliade is a prolific writer for the journal and other editors, including Wendy D. O'Flaherty, Frank E. Reynolds, and Jonathan Z. Smith have appeared in its pages. Special issues (two bound issues on one theme) are of high quality. The issue "Current Perspectives in the Study of Chinese Religions" was a landmark, updating an area of relative neglect.[11]

An ongoing tension between the historical and the systematic defines *HR*, intellectually and editorially. India receives more attention than any other culture, but this imbalance reflects the large number of scholars working in the area more than it does editorial policy. Christian and Jewish studies appear least frequently, and articles on the West must be of an exceptional quality and speak comparatively. Editors try to balance the regions explored, give equal time to specific and general studies, and (where possible) choose manuscripts that present both data and interpretation. *HR*'s greatest vulnerability lies in the book review department. Begun in May 1969, "critical book reviews" would focus on "important and recent works of the international academic community."[12] Unfortunately, offerings have been more descriptive than critical, European reviewers have not been recruited, and the policy for selecting books to be reviewed lacks criteria.

The strength of *HR* lies in its consistent publication of articles that define the field. *HR* deserves high praise because it not only "serves a field, but it defines the field which it serves, and it does so with genuine scholarly distinction." The journal has been constructed so that "people know how to write for it—and therefore for the field."[13] Authors spice up *HR* with offerings like "Flying Mountains and Walkers of Emptiness," "Two Female Gnostic Revealers," "The Indo-European Cattle-raiding Myth," "The Physiology of Redemption," "Quetzalcoatl's Revenge," "Open Entrance to the Closed Palace: The Greek Labyrinth," and "Iron Working as Spiritual Inquiry."

The common language with which specialists in one area speak to specialists in other areas has been a vital concern. A recent trend has introduced the terms of social-scientific and cultural studies. In the 1960s, much of the dialogue in *HR* was between historians of religions and theologians or philosophers of religion (such as the exchange between Eliade and Paul Tillich). But in the 1970s, as Kitagawa points out, disciplines such as cultural anthropology, cultural area studies, and comparative ethics have become "influential 'conversation partners' of *Religionswissenschaft*." The field "urgently needs to articulate its own identity and to define its own mode of relationship to other fields of inquiry, instead of allowing the other disciplines to define the relationship from their perspective."[14] In this regard, Hans Penner's "The Poverty of Functionalism" steered readers away from the pitfalls of an uncritical use of social-scientific language.[15] In another exciting development, Joanne Punzo Waghorne's "A Body for God: An Interpretation of the Nature of Myth beyond Structuralism" views the quest for "cognitive maps" as a "hidden theology" in the history of religions, bringing the conversation full circle.[16] Debates over a common language for specialists never produce consensus, but they make *History of Religions* a lively journal for interdisciplinary reflection in religious studies.

Notes

1. Mircea Eliade, *Autobiography* (San Francisco: Harper and Row, 1981), vol. 1.

2. Mircea Eliade, "History of Religions and a New Humanism," *History of Religions* 1 (1961): 1 (hereafter cited as *HR*).

3. *HR* 12 (1972): i.

4. George S. Goodspeed, ed., *The World's First Parliament of Religions: Its Christian Spirit, Historic Greatness and Manifold Results* (Chicago: Hill and Shuman, 1895).

5. Jacques Waardenburg, *Classical Approaches to the Study of Religion* (Paris: Mouton, 1973), pp. 63–64.

6. Joseph M. Kitagawa's "Humanistic and Theological History of Religions with Special Reference to the North American Scene," *Numen* 27 (1980): 198–221, is an excellent account that has provided much of the background here. On Wach, see pp. 215–15.

7. Eliade, "A New Humanism," p. 2.

8. Ibid., pp. 2–4.

9. *HR* 20 (August, November 1980); Mary Nell Hoover of the University of Chicago Press kindly supplied the circulation figures and a critical evaluation.

10. Jacob Neusner's assessment of the journal for the University of Chicago Press is titled "Critical Evaluation," dated 1 March 1979, and is used with the permission of the press and the author.

11. *HR* 17 (February, May 1978).

12. Ibid. 8 (May 1969).

13. Neusner, p. 1.

14. Joseph M. Kitagawa, "A Reflection on the History of Religions (*Religionswissenschaft*) Then and Now" (address presented to the faculty of the University of Chicago Divinity School, 21 October 1982), p. 21.

15. *HR* 11 (1971): 91–97.

16. Ibid. 21 (1981): 20–47.

Information Sources

BIBLIOGRAPHY:

Allen, Douglas. *Structure and Creativity in Religion: Hermeneutics in Mircea Eliade's Phenomenology and New Directions*. The Hague: Mouton, 1978.

Culianu, Ioan P. *Mircea Eliade*. Assisi: Cittadella, 1978.

Eliade, Mircea. *No Souvenirs*. New York: Harper & Row, 1977.

Eliade, Mircea, and Joseph M. Kitagawa, eds. *The History of Religions: Essays in Methodology*. Chicago: University of Chicago Press, 1959.

Long, Charles H. "The History of the History of Religions." Appendix to Charles J. Adams, ed., *A Reader's Guide to the Great Religions*. New York: Free Press, 1977.

Reynolds, Frank E. "History of Religions: Conditions and Prospects." Council on the Study of Religion *Bulletin* 13 (December 1982): 129–33.

Sullivan, Lawrence E. "History of Religions: The Shape of an Art." In Mircea Eliade and David Tracy, eds. *What Is Religion?* New York: Seabury Press, 1980.

INDEX SOURCES: Self-indexed at the end of each volume beginning with vol. 11, with an index to vols. 1–10 in vol. 10 (1972); also in *Internationale Zeitschriftenschau für Bibelwissenschaft und Grenzgebiete, Arts and Humanities Citation Index, America: History and Life, Current Contents, Religion Index One, Guide to Social Science and Religion in Periodical Literature, Humanities Index, Religious and Theological Abstracts*.

REPRINT EDITIONS: University Microfilms International, Microforms International Marketing Co., Institute for Scientific Information.

LOCATION SOURCES: Union Theological Seminary (New York), Duke University, Harvard University, Library of Congress, University of California Berkeley, University of Texas-Austin, Princeton University, and others.

Publication History

MAGAZINE TITLE AND TITLE CHANGES: *History of Religions: An International Journal for Comparative Historical Studies* (1961–   ).

VOLUME AND ISSUE DATA: 1–5 (August 1961-May 1966), semiannual; 6 (August 1966–   ), quarterly.

PUBLISHER AND PLACE OF PUBLICATION: Divinity School, University of Chicago, Chicago (1961–69); University of Chicago Press, Chicago (1970–   ).

EDITORS: Mircea Eliade (1961–   ), Joseph M. Kitagawa (1961–   ), Charles H. Long (1961–76), Jonathan Z. Smith (1970–76), Frank E. Reynolds (1977–   ), Wendy D. O'Flaherty (1980–   ).

CIRCULATION: 1796 (1983).

John Kloos

THE HOMILETIC AND PASTORAL REVIEW

Joseph F. Wagner, the German-born head of a Catholic publishing house in New York City, established the *Homiletic Monthly and Catechist* in October 1900.[1] Designed especially for Catholic priests in the parochial ministry, it was published with the approval of the archdiocese of New York. The prosepectus stated that the magazine "undertakes, in fact, to provide in monthly installments a complete set of practical sermons for the ecclesiastical year and, for the catechist, a Sunday School lesson for every Sunday of the Scholastic year."[2] Each number of the first volume contained unsigned sermons for the Sundays and feast days of the coming month, plus a small section on catechetical instruction. Each issue of this volume also included one or more sermons of John Vianney, the saintly curé of Ars, published for the first time in English in the United States.

Wagner obtained the services of a professor at the archdiocesan seminary, Father John F. Brady, as the first editor of the monthly. Brady, trained as a physician, had been ordained in 1898 and, after a year of graduate study at the Catholic University of America, was assigned to St. Joseph's Seminary, Dunwoodie. He taught philosophy, science, and dogmatic theology and served as vice-president of the seminary. From 1905 to 1908 Brady also acted as business manager for the *New York Review*,* a short-lived liberal Catholic theological journal published under the seminary's auspices. In 1916 he was named pastor of a New York City parish and later won renown for his work with the hospital apostolate in the New York archdiocese.[3]

During the years of Brady's editorship (1900–17), the homiletic and catechetical contents of the periodical were supplemented by a pastoral section, which included summaries of new decrees and instructions from the Holy See and a regular question and answer section relating to moral and liturgical questions called "Casus Conscientiae." In 1918 this latter feature became "Questions Answered," a title it retains to the present time.

In 1917 two priests, Charles Callen, O.P. and John A. McHugh, O.P., assumed the editorship of the magazine. During the first three years of their leadership, the periodical underwent three title changes that reflected its expanding scope. It became the *Homiletic Monthly* in 1917 (volume 18), the *Homiletic Monthly and Pastoral Review* in 1918 (volume 19), and finally in 1920 (volume 21) the *Homiletic and Pastoral Review* (*HPR*). The periodical continued to offer sermons for Sundays and feast days, many of them signed by their respective authors, and the monthly "Questions Answered" feature. More significantly, the new editors began publishing articles on topics of interest to priests in their pastoral work. For example, the November 1923 number contained essays on "Congregational Singing," "The Misuse of Scripture by Preachers," "Practical Ascetical Notes for the Priest," and "The Holy Name Jubilee." Book reviews also began to appear in each issue.

Callan and McHugh edited the *HPR* jointly until the latter's death in 1952. Callan continued as sole editor until 1961. Callan, a native of New York State, joined the Dominican Fathers in Kentucky in the same year as McHugh, a native Kentuckian, and the two became immediate friends. Rather early in their respective careers, Callan and McHugh had to be relieved of regular duties because of ill health. As a consequence, their superiors assigned the two young priests to care for a small parish in Hawthorne, New York, in 1915. During their years at the parish, they not only performed their parochial duties but managed to publish jointly over 30 scholarly books, teach theology at the neighboring Maryknoll seminary, and edit the monthly issues of the *HPR*. In 1940 Callan was named the first native-born American member of the Pontifical Biblical Commission.[4]

During the long editorship of Callan and McHugh, most of the articles reflected the predominantly inner-church interests of priests of those years. Little or nothing relating to social issues or to serious theological debates was published. Among the most frequent contributors during these years were Charles Bruehl, Paul E. Campbell, Stanislaus Woywod, O.F.M., John B. Sheering, CSP, and Ernest Graef, O. S. B. Bruehl, a German-born and European-educated priest, professor at St. Charles Seminary, Overbrook, Pennsylvania, and frequent contributor to Catholic periodicals, wrote over 200 essays on a variety of topics for *HPR* between 1920 and 1939. His contributions from 1939 to 1952 were sporadic. Campbell, educator, pastor, and former superintendent of schools for the diocese of Pittsburgh, regularly contributed articles on issues related to education from 1931 to 1962. Woywod, a German-born canon law specialist and editor of the *St. Anthony's Almanac*, joined the regular contributors of *HPR* in 1918. He was responsible for the monthly "Questions Answered" feature from 1918 to his death in 1941.[5] The feature was then conducted by another canon lawyer, Joseph Donovan, C.M., from 1941 to 1952. He was succeeded in this task by John J.

Danaher, C.M. (1952–57), Cecil Parres, C.M. (1957–61), Aidan Carr, O.F.M. Conventual (1962–78), and Joseph Faraher, S.J. (1978 to the present).

John B. Sheerin, C.S.P., the editor of the Paulist Fathers' journal the *Catholic World** from 1948 to 1971, contributed a monthly lead-off essay during the later years of the Callan and McHugh editorship. Ernest Graef, O.S.B., a monk of Buckfast Abbey in England, was a frequent contributor on Scripture questions in the 1930s and 1940s. During the 1920s and 1930s liturgical notes were provided regularly by "the Benedictine Monks of Buckfast Abbey."

In 1957 Aidan Carr, O.F.M. Conventual, a scholarly canon lawyer, was appointed associate editor and in 1961 assumed full editorial responsibility when Callan was named editor emeritus. Carr guided the journal during the era of Vatican II. The debates of the council and the shifts in thinking and praxis it occasioned were reflected in *HPR*. Essays by theologians of the caliber of Bernard Haring, Charles Curran, William Wallace, Richard McCormick, Gregory Baum, Bernard Marthaler, and Gerard Sloyan appeared. Occasionally part of an issue was devoted to a specific question, such as the October 1964 symposium "The Renewed Liturgy." The complacent and sometimes triumphalist attitudes prevalent in the *HPR* essays of pre-Vatican II days were gone. Theological issues were alive and debatable in the pages of Carr's journal.

Only two writers were regular contributors during the 1960s: James Shaughnessy, a pastor from Creve Coeur, Illinois, who provided articles on liturgical renewal, and Aidan Carr, with his monthly feature, "Questions Answered," his editorials, and his occasional essays. Under Carr the *HPR* became a rather traditionally oriented Catholic periodical exploring newer and more liberal theological views.

Carr resigned from the editorship of the journal with the April 1970 number. The resignation coincided with his decision to transfer from the Conventual Franciscan Order to the stricter Cistercian Order (Trappists). Father Carr, later abbot of Mepkin Abbey in South Carolina, continued his monthly contributions to the "Questions Answered" feature until October 1978.

Following Carr's resignation, the monthly was published without an editor for three months. In August 1970 Monsignor Vincent A. Yzermans, former editor of the *St. Cloud Visitor* and former national director of the Bishop's Bureau of Information in Washington, D.C., was named editor of *HPR*. His tenure as editor was brief. In the spring of 1971, the publisher, the Joseph Wagner Company, sold *HPR* to Catholic Polls, Inc. Kenneth Baker, S.J., a theologian from Gonzaga University, became editor and set a new direction for the periodical.

Baker's program entailed the presentation of a conservative yet scholarly treatment of theological issues. His approach was reflected in his choice of articles and contributors, as well as in his own monthly editorials. In his first issue, Baker pledged to continue publishing first-class homily material while seeking to present articles respectful of the magisterium of the church. The theme of the authority of the pope and of the hierarchical church was to become commonplace in the pages of the journal. Essays of scholars of conservative bent, such as

George A. Kelly, James Hitchcock, Hans Urs von Balthasar, Francis Lawlor, Manuel Miguens and Paul Marx, appeared in each issue.

In his editorials in the 1970s, Baker frequently attacked theologians who were dissenting from the teachings of the magisterium of the church. He encouraged the bishops to take the church back from the theologians and even urged excommunication for dissenting theologians.[6] In 1983 the American bishops themselves came under attack from Father Baker because of their pastoral on nuclear warfare, "The Challenge of Peace." Baker wrote that the pastoral "does no credit to the theological, moral, philosophical and political thinking of the American bishops and their advisors." In the September 1983 number the authority of the USSC, the national conference of Catholic bishops, was questioned by the editor. By 1984 the *HPR* had clearly become a haven for conservative Catholic theologians.

Since its founding, the *HPR* has been faithful to its purpose of serving the interests of Catholic parish priests. Each issue has contained homiletic materials such as complete sermons or sermon outlines appropriate to the time of the year and reflecting contemporary theology. In addition most issues have carried advertisements for candles, cassocks, church fund raisers, and architects appropriate to the readership. When the magazine changed hands in 1971, the former publisher maintained that 25,000 priests read *HPR* each month. The priestly nature of the periodical seems to have determined the predominance of priest contributors over the years. *HPR* has published no theological essays of lasting significance. It has basically been a vehicle for the dissemination of contemporary theological ideas to the parochial clergy.

Church historians will find *HPR* valuable in three respects. First, the sermons printed in *HPR* have been influential in the development of Catholic preaching in the United States since 1900. Second, the articles that appeared from 1918 to 1961 were representative of the kind of theological thinking prevalent among the Catholic clergy during that period. Third, the issues of *HPR* from April 1971 to the present reflect the popularization of what might be termed the conservative position among American Catholic theologians.

Notes

1. Cf. "The Homiletic and Pastoral Review, 1900–1960," *Homiletic and Pastoral Review* 60 (1960): 1089–94.

2. "Prospectus," *Homiletic Monthly and Catechist* 1 (1900).

3. Michael De Vito, *The New York Review (1905–1908)* (New York: United States Catholic Historical Society, 1977), pp. 31–33, and Florence D. Cohalan, *A Popular History of the Archdiocese of New York* (New York: U.S. Catholic Historical Society, 1983), p. 309.

4. Cf. "The Homiletic and Pastoral Review, 1900–1960," and "Charles Jerome Callan, 1877–1962," *Homiletic and Pastoral Review* 62 (1962): 587.

5. Cf. Joseph Donovan, C.M., "The Code and the Homiletic: These Thirty-One Years," *Homiletic and Pastoral Review* 50 (1949): 38–44.

6. Cf. Kenneth Baker, S.J., "Editorial," *The Homiletic and Pastoral Review* 71 (April 1971): 80.

Information Sources

BIBLIOGRAPHY:
The Homiletic Index: The Homiletic and Pastoral Reivew, 1900–1953. 2 pts. New York: Joseph Wagner, n.d.
INDEX SOURCES: *Catholic Periodical Index, Religious and Theological Abstracts.*
REPRINT EDITIONS: University Microfilms International.
LOCATION SOURCES: Catholic University of America, St. John's University (New York), Boston College, St. John's University (Collegeville), Loyola University (Chicago), and others.

Publication History

MAGAZINE TITLE AND TITLE CHANGES: *The Homiletic Monthly and Catechist* (1900–17), *The Homiletic Monthly* (1917–18), *The Homiletic Monthly and Pastoral Review* (1918–20), *The Homiletic and Pastoral Review* (1920–   ).
VOLUME AND ISSUE DATA: *Homiletic Monthly and Catechist* 1–17 (October 1900-September 1917), *Homiletic Monthly* 18 (October 1917-September 1918), *Homiletic Monthly and Pastoral Review* 19–20 (October 1918-September 1920), *Homiletic and Pastoral Review* 21 (Oct. 1920–   ). Appears monthly.
PUBLISHERS AND PLACE OF PUBLICATION: Joseph F. Wagner, New York, (October 1900-March 1971); Catholic Polls, New York (April 1971–   ).
EDITORS: Rev. Dr. John F. Brady (1900–17), Charles J. Callan, O.P. (1917–61), John A. McHugh, O.P. (1917–52), Aidan Carr, O.F.M. Conv. (1961–70), Msgr. Vincent Yzermans (1970–71), Kenneth Baker, S.J. (1971–   ).
CIRCULATION: 15,500 (1982).

Bernard Noone

THE HOMILETIC MONTHLY. *See* HOMILETIC AND
PASTORAL REVIEW

THE HOMILETIC MONTHLY AND CATECHIST. *See*
HOMILETIC AND PASTORAL REVIEW

**THE HOMILETIC MONTHLY AND PASTORAL
REVIEW.** *See* HOMILETIC AND PASTORAL REVIEW

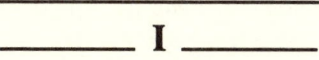

I

ILLINOIS CATHOLIC HISTORICAL REVIEW. *See*
MID-AMERICA

ILLUSTRATED CHRISTIAN WEEKLY. *See* THE
OUTLOOK

THE INDEPENDENT. *See* THE OUTLOOK

THE INDEX

The *Index, a Weekly Paper Devoted to Free Religion*, was first published on
1 January 1870, at Toledo, Ohio, under the editorship of Francis E. Abbot.
According to its prospectus, the *Index* would "aim above all things to increase
pure and genuine religion . . . and freedom in the world." It would be "the organ
of no party in politics and no sect in religion," and, "standing squarely outside
Christianity," it would be based "solely on the authority of right reason and
good conscience."[1] Although Abbot repeatedly denied it, friends as well as
critics noted the affinity between the concerns of the weekly and those of the
Free Religious Association. Indeed, that association had its own "department"
within the *Index* for the first year, and officers and directors of the association
were primary contributors to the paper.[2] In the second year that department was
abolished, and four officers became editorial contributors.[3]

During its first two years, the *Index* maintained a witty, even charming, attitude
toward its competitors, friendly or otherwise. With regard to the *Radical*,* the
monthly edited in Boston by Sidney H. Morse, Abbot held that they would be

"co-workers in the same general movement" and recommended the *Radical* "to every thoughtful person." Later, when the *Radical* suffered a seven-month hiatus because of financial weakness, Abbot confessed that "we should be guilty of a meanness . . . if we secretly exulted in a brother's embarrassment through hopes of profiting by it."[4] Abbot apparently convinced Morse of his authentic goodwill, for not long after the *Radical* finally failed in 1872, Morse became a regular contributor to, and then guest editor of, the *Index*.

As for less familial publications, the Boston *Watchman and Reflector* was "Baptist of the bluest orthodoxy," and the *Christian Register* (Unitarian) was "staid and conservative," with ideas aged "so long that it is positively mellow." And in reply to a *Christian Register* comment that to read the *Index* "always confirms us in our Christian faith," Abbot remarked that the *Register* might "suggest to its Unitarian readers the propriety in taking stock in the Index Association, as the best way to propagate Christianity." The *Index* also was candid enough to apologize for a piece against the Dover, New Hampshire (Abbot's former home), *Morning Star* (Freewill Baptist), praising its editor for his "brain" and "manliness."[5] And through it all, the Index Association, while not propagating Christianity, managed to gain a base of financial support in the amount of $50,000 to secure the future of the *Index* (and the demise of the *Radical*).[6]

By its third year, the *Index* had changed in tone and stance. In an editorial Abbot proclaimed the "Impeachment of Christianity" in the "name of human intelligence," "virtue," "freedom," the "human heart," and "humanitarian religion." He then challenged a proposed "Christian amendment of the Constitution" with a "counter-petition" to the Congress and in 1873 called for "Liberals of America" to organize a family of "Liberal Leagues." Also in September of that year the *Index* moved to Boston, changed its size and format, and declared itself to be "an agitator."[7] Clearly more political than before, the *Index* termed the newly formed World Evangelical Alliance a "league of self-defence" and began to seek distance from the Free Religious Association.[8]

In February 1875, the *Index* argued on behalf of a civil rights bill then before the Congress, claiming that it was "impossible to furnish *separate* schools [*but*] of *equal* excellence for whites and blacks." In August, it challenged the results of the adultery trial of Henry Ward Beecher. In September, it announced a call for a national convention of Liberal Leagues to meet at Philadelphia in July 1876.[9] At that "Congress of Liberals," Abbot was chosen as president of a new national political organization, the National Liberal League, and the *Index* was made its official organ.[10]

Following this broader recognition and involvement, Abbot became more caustic in his criticism; for example, he attacked the Moody-Sankey "revival campaign" in Boston in 1877; he became less effective as well. And when faced with two genuinely radical causes, the woman suffrage issue and the labor issue, the effectiveness and integrity of the "liberal" *Index* collapsed altogether: women and workers must be patient; all good would come to them "when it comes."[11]

One might conclude that the national success of the *Index* contributed directly to its failure to foster "freedom in the world." Abbot's last edition was June 1880.

The *Index* remained in print for six more years, but the forces leading to its demise had been set in motion much earlier. A few years after its founding, the *Index* became formally associated with the Free Religious Association. Conflict between its leaders and Abbot led to Abbot's temporary retirement as editor in 1873, and A. W. Stevens, who had been Abbot's assistant, took over briefly. When Abbot did step down in 1880, the *Index* became the property of the Free Religious Association. The following year (1881), the closer ties to the Free Religious Association brought a name change to the *Free Religious Index*, although the original name was restored after eleven months. When the name change occurred, W. J. Potter became the official editor, but from then until the last issue in December 1886, the bulk of the editorial work fell to Potter's assistant, Benjamin F. Underwood. Even under the ownership of the Free Religious Association, the *Index* retained its independent reputation. Desiring a publication more directly reflecting its own aims, the Free Religious Association announced that the 30 December 1886 issue would be the final edition of the *Index*. The *Open Court* became the official publication of the Free Religious Association in 1887.

Notes

1. *Index* 1 (January 1870):1.

2. O. B. Frothingham, president; T. W. Higginson, vice-president; W. J. Potter, secretary; and Richard P. Hallowell, treasurer; Ednah D. Cheney, Francis Tiffany, John Weiss, C. K. Whipple, Isaac M. Wise, and Abbot, directors.

3. Frothingham, Higginson, Potter, and Hallowell.

4. *Index* 1 (January 1870): 6; (June 1870): 4.

5. Ibid. 2 (May 1871): 164; (December 1871): 391; (October 1871): 325.

6. Ibid. (November 1871): 348–49.

7. Ibid. 3 (January 1872): 4–5; 4 (January 1873): ii; (September 1873): 340.

8. Ibid. 4 (September 1873): 362.

9. Ibid. 6 (February 1875): 6 (August 1875): 366–67, 390.

10. Ibid. 7 (August 1876): 361.

11. Ibid. 8 (February 1877): 78–79. For women, the collapse was the position that they "must wait" for "state [male] secularization," which would, "even if slowly, establish woman suffrage on a permanent basis." Ibid. For labor, "the railroad strikes must be deeply regretted by everyone. [But] pity for the strikers and their families ... cannot become sympathy with riot and lawlessness ... [and] wanton destruction of property." (July 1877):349.

Information Sources

BIBLIOGRAPHY:
Gohdes, Clarence L. F. *The Periodicals of American Transcendentalism*. Durham: Duke University Press, 1931.

Mott, Frank Luther. *A History of American Magazines, 1865–1885*. Cambridge: Harvard University Press, 1957.
INDEX SOURCES: None.
LOCATION SOURCES: Yale University, American Antiquarian Society, Boston Public Library, Cornell University, New York Public Library, Brown University, Swarthmore College.

Publication History

MAGAZINE TITLE AND TITLE CHANGES: *The Index: A Weekly Paper Devoted to Free Religion* (1870–86); known as *Free Religious Index*, January through November, 1881; superseded by *Open Court*.
VOLUME AND ISSUE DATA: 1 (January 1870)–11 (June 1880); n.s. 1 (1881)–6 (1886). Appeared weekly.
PUBLISHER AND PLACE OF PUBLICATION: Francis E. Abbot, Toledo, Ohio (1870); Index Association, Toledo, Ohio (1871–73), Boston (1873–80); Free Religious Association, Boston (1880–86).
EDITORS: Francis E. Abbot (1870–80), A. W. Stevens (1873, 1880), Sidney Morse (summer 1877), W. J. Potter assisted by Benjamin F. Underwood (1881–86).
CIRCULATION: 800 (est.).

Stephen H. Snyder

THE INSTITUTE TIE. *See* THE MOODY MONTHLY

INTERNATIONAL BULLETIN OF MISSIONARY RESEARCH

John Raleigh Mott (1865–1955), a Methodist layman from Postville, Iowa, became the most famous international statesman of the Christian missionary movement in the first half of the twentieth century. On his initiative, the Foreign Missions Conference of North America agreed in 1914 to open a Missionary Research Library in New York City. In 1948 Robert Pierce Beaver became the director of the library, and in 1950 he began publication of the *Occasional Bulletin from the Missionary Research Library*. Although it was mimeographed, it soon developed a widespread influence and respect among missiologists in many parts of the world.[1]

The *Occasional Bulletin* continued to be published by Dr. Beaver's successors, Frank W. Price and Herbert C. Jackson. In July 1967 the Missionary Research Library ceased its independent existence and was incorporated into the library of the Union Theological Seminary, New York City. The *Occasional Bulletin* continued to be issued by the National Council of Churches' Division of Overseas Ministries (NCC/DOM) and was edited for several years by its successive associate general secretaries: David M. Stowe, Randolph Nugent, and Eugene L. Stockwell, with R. Pierce Beaver serving again in 1972–73.

The story of the *Bulletin* is linked as well to the former Houses of Fellowship at Ventnor, New Jersey, established by a donation from Marguerite T. and Ida F. Doane in memory of their father, William H. Doane, composer of many gospel songs and hymns. The Houses of Fellowship (incorporated as the Society for Foreign Mission Welfare) were used for the benefit of Protestant missionaries on furlough. In 1967 the trustees changed the name of the organization to the Overseas Ministries Study Center to promote continuing education in world mission.[2] The program was strengthened in 1973 with the coming of R. Pierce Beaver as director. Gerald H. Anderson, Methodist missionary, scholar, and educator, became associate director in 1974 and director in 1976. The study center became internationally known because of its varied programs of lectures, conferences, study, and research.[3] In 1977 the Overseas Ministries Study Center became the publisher of the *Occasional Bulletin of Missionary Research*, replacing the NCC/DOM in this role. With Anderson as editor, it became a regular quarterly publication. In 1980 *Gospel in Context* was incorporated into the quarterly, and in 1981 it was renamed the *International Bulletin of Missionary Research*.

Any religious publication exhibits a basic theological perspective. Such is eminently the case with a journal dealing with Christian missions. Although the *International Bulletin* does not contain a published theological statement, its editorial policy becomes clear from its contents. It is a theologically open policy in that articles and studies represent a wide spectrum of Christian thought. But the *International Bulletin* is admittedly a Christian missionary journal devoted to the issues related to the proclamation of the gospel to people of different religious persuasions. However, neither the *International Bulletin* nor its editor represents a closed mind or an extreme viewpoint. The theological stance may be called a *via media* between one extreme that is ready to regard anything related to other faiths as evil or false (and therefore to be condemned) and the other that maintains that there should be no missionary or evangelistic efforts whatever on the part of Christians. The *International Bulletin* is therefore ecumenical and in the mainstream of Christian theology. This stance is reflected particularly in items with an explicit theological content and purpose, as, for example, two articles by Lesslie Newbigin[4] and Carl E. Braaten.[5]

The missionary movement has long been the most ecumenically minded arm of Protestantism, helping spur the formation of the World Council of Churches in 1948. Among mission bodies and missiologists, there has been a sustained effort to bridge the gaps that exist within the Christian communities. The Missionary Research Library was an ecumenical venture; so, too, was its *Occasional Bulletin*. In this tradition, the *International Bulletin* and its publisher, the Overseas Ministries Study Center, are thoroughly ecumenical in that the whole spectrum of Christians concerned with mission studies is embraced, going far beyond the traditional mainline Protestant churches. The editorial policy covers Eastern Orthodox and Roman Catholic interests, as well as appealing to representatives of Protestant societies that have no formal ties with such ecumenical bodies as the National Council of Churches or the World Council of Churches.

Missiology and missionary research are broad concepts that include history of missions and history of the churches that came into being because of missionary efforts around the world, theology of missions, phenomenology and sociology, and linguistics, methods of translation, and methods of communicating the gospel across linguistic and cultural boundaries. The *International Bulletin* achieves ecumenical breadth by publishing articles in these fields by scholars from numerous Christian groups, as well as by the broadly based composition of its editorial board. The international scope is wide, including such non-American contributors as Olav G. Myklebust, Hans-Werner Gensichen, J. van den Berg, Kenneth Cragg, Desmond Tutu, Walbert Buhlmann, Andrew Walls, David Bosch, Stanley J. Samartha, John Mbiti, and Mortimer Arias. Countries as varied as Argentina, India, the Philippines, Hong Kong, South Africa, and the Netherlands, to mention a few, are represented. The subject matter as well is international.

In a recent series of articles, the *International Bulletin* elicited the cooperation of a number of ecumenical and international scholars. This series dealt with the legacy of persons who have contributed to the missionary movement. In so doing the journal affirmed a deep consciousness of continuity with the past. The *International Bulletin* contrasts with many recent studies that deplore the fact that missionaries of bygone years were not in possession of the supposedly superior insight of late twentieth-century armchair critics. The Associated Church Press in 1984 gave an award of merit to the quarterly for the "Legacy Series."

The *International Bulletin* is much more than a historical journal. It is also highly contemporary. It has recently published a series of articles on China, discussing the religious situation under Mao Tse-tung and the period of change following his death. The concern with contemporary issues is also demonstrated by articles on Islam and the Near East, the contemporary African religious situation, and the explosive situation in Latin America.

A publication dealing with Christian missionary research will also include studies of other religions. While politics, sociological trends, and economic developments have always been important in the missionary enterprise, its dominant concern has been with religion. Because religion deals with forces that motivate nations and individuals and with ultimate questions, there have always been missionaries who have been informed and productive scholars of the religions of the people with whom they worked. Some secular scholars mistakenly assume that missionary concern with world religions is only polemical and therefore not reliable. On the contrary, the aim of missionary research in these fields has been factual in an effort to understand other traditions and communicate findings and insight to others. Missionary scholarship aims not at falsification of other views but at obtaining reliable knowledge of and insight into other religions. The *International Bulletin* disseminates such understanding.

This journal's perspective and interests are also evident in the books reviewed and in the international background and academic standing of the reviewers. Most of the books reviewed are written in English. But books in Danish, French, German, Norwegian, Spanish, and Swedish have also been reviewed, making it possible to follow what is being published in other countries. In the first issue each year, the editors publish their selection of "Fifteen Outstanding Books for Mission Studies" from the previous year.

A significant contribution in the field of bibliography has recently been added. For several years, the journal offered limited lists of doctoral dissertations in mission studies submitted to universities in the United States and Canada. But in 1983 a complete list of such dissertations at North American universities, covering 1945–81, was published.[6] The list contained 934 dissertations from 145 degree-granting institutions with indexes listing the institutions, authors, and subjects. In addition there have been lists of doctoral dissertations from institutions in Scotland, England, the Netherlands, and South Africa. The *International Bulletin* has published articles giving extensive information about research material available at such institutions as the Billy Graham Center (Wheaton, Illinois) and the Sacred Congregation for the Evangelization of Peoples (Rome, Italy).[7] Such information aids research in almost any area related to Christian missions. Since awareness of this North American research has been limited in Europe, many European scholars have underestimated the quality of American doctoral dissertations. This service of the *International Bulletin* may remedy such misunderstanding.

The *International Bulletin of Missionary Research* fills a vacuum felt for years among North American missiologists. Several countries in Europe, Africa, and Asia have scholarly journals for missionary study and research that carry scholarly work in other languages. The *International Bulletin* offers a welcome opportunity for Americans and others in the international community of scholarship in this discipline. It thereby enriches ecumenical dialogue in North America and worldwide in the field of religious studies. Its standing as having the largest circulation of any scholarly journal in its field testifies to its success.

Notes

1. R. Pierce Beaver, "The Missionary Research Library and the Occasional Bulletin," *Occasional Bulletin of Missionary Research* 1:1 (January 1977): 4.

2. Overseas Ministries Study Center, Ventnor, N.J., *Announcements 1984–85*, p. 5.

3. Robert T. Coote, "Ministry to Missionaries on Furlough: The Overseas Ministries Study Center, 1922–1983," *International Bulletin of Missionary Research* 7:2 (April 1983): 56.

4. Lesslie Newbigin, "Cross-currents in Ecumenical and Evangelical Understandings of Mission," *International Bulletin of Missionary Research* 6:4 (October 1982): 146–51.

5. Carl E. Braaten, "Who Do We Say That He Is? On the Uniqueness and Universality of Jesus Christ," *Occasional Bulletin of Missionary Research* 4:1 (January 1980): 2–8.

6. E. Theodore Bachmann, "North American Doctoral Dissertations on Mission: 1945–1981," *International Bulletin of Missionary Research* 7:3 (July 1983): 97–134.

7. Robert Shuster, "Library and Archival Resources of the Billy Graham Center," *International Bulletin of Missionary Research* 5:3 (July 1981): 124–26; Josef Metzler, "The Sacred Congregation for the Evangelization of Peoples or the Propagation of the Faith: The Mission Center of the Catholic Church in Rome," ibid., pp. 127–28.

Information Sources

BIBLIOGRAPHY:
Beaver, R. Pierce. "The Missionary Research Library and the Occasional Bulletin of Missionary Research." *Occasional Bulletin of Missionary Research* 1:1 (January 1977): 2–4.
Coote, Robert T. "Ministry to Missionaries on Furlough: The Overseas Ministries Study Center, 1922–1983." *International Bulletin of Missionary Research* 7:2 (April 1983): 53–58.
Jackson, Herbert C. "Missionary Research Library." *The Encyclopedia of Modern Christian Missions.* Edited by Burton L. Goddard. Camden, N.J.: Thomas Nelson and Sons, 1967.
INDEX SOURCES: *Bibliografia Missionaria, Christian Periodical Index, Guide to Social Science and Religion in Periodical Literature, Missionalia, Religion Index One, Religious and Theological Abstracts.*
LOCATION SOURCES: Library of Congress, Yale University, Duke University, Union Theological Seminary (New York), Indiana University, Pacific School of Religion, Andover-Harvard Theological Library, and others.

Publication History

MAGAZINE TITLE AND TITLE CHANGES: *Occasional Bulletin from the Missionary Research Library* (1950–76), *Occasional Bulletin of Missionary Research* (1977–80), *International Bulletin of Missionary Research* (1981–   ).
VOLUME AND ISSUE DATA: *Occasional Bulletin from the Missionary Research Library* (March 1950-June 1955), appeared 10 to 16 times per year; *Occasional Bulletin from the Missionary Research Library* (June 1955-December 1976), appeared at irregular intervals; *Occasional Bulletin of Missionary Research* (January 1977-December 1980), appeared quarterly; *International Bulletin of Missionary Research* (January 1981–   ), appears quarterly.
PUBLISHER AND PLACE OF PUBLICATION: Missionary Research Library, New York (1950–76); Overseas Ministries Study Center, Ventnor, N.J. (1977–   ).
EDITORS: R. Pierce Beaver (1950–55), Charles W. Iglehart (1955), Frank W. Price (1956–61), Herbert C. Jackson (1961–67), David M. Stowe, Eugene L. Stockwell, Randolph Nugent, and R. Pierce Beaver (1968–76), Gerald H. Anderson (1977-   ).
CIRCULATION: 7000 U.S., 2000 international (1984).

Per Hassing

INTERPRETATION

"The aim of this new religion quarterly is to bring together the best fruits of biblical study, to stimulate further studies, and to make them available to ministers, teachers, and laymen. The purpose of *Interpretation* may be stated even more concisely: to promote a positive, constructive expression of biblical and theological studies."[1] So wrote the editors in 1947 in the inaugural issue of a journal published under the auspices of the Union Theological Seminary, Virginia. Theoretically the successor to the seminary's *Review*, the venture was in fact a totally different one. Whereas the former *Review* had been primarily a conduit for the Presbyterian school's alumni and had included articles that ranged broadly in all areas of religious studies, the new periodical had a more definite focus and from the start was committed to high standards of scholarship, for material printed was solicited from leading scholars in both the United States and Europe.

Interpretation: A Journal of Bible and Theology is a product of the movement in American theological circles known as neo-orthodoxy. While neo-orthodoxy's European roots stretch back at least to the appearance of Karl Barth's *Commentary on Romans* during World War I and the fresh interest in the dialectical theology in the works of the nineteenth-century Danish philosopher, Søren Kierkegaard, in the United States it began to move to the forefront of theological circles in the 1930s when growing dissatisfaction with the facile optimism of liberal theology moved thinkers such as Reinhold Niebuhr to call for a reappropriation of biblical categories of Christian doctrine without, however, jettisoning the insights provided by the critical interpretive tools that had undergirded the earlier liberalism. The opening issue and many subsequent ones, for example, contained material by Edwin Lewis, a faculty member at Drew University's Theological School, who, like Niebuhr, was a leading advocate of the return to a biblically based theology.

The policy of inviting leading scholars to write for its pages meant that from the start *Interpretation* would offer readers only material of the highest quality. Over the years, the list of contributors reads like a who's who in biblical studies and theology. In its first decade alone, *Interpretation* carried essays by luminaries in the field such as H. H. Rowley, G. Ernest Wright, John Bright, Bruce Metzger, R. B. Y. Scott, Edgar Goodspeed, J. Philip Hyatt, Elmer A. Leslie, Eduard Schweizer, B. Davie Napier, Bernhard W. Anderson, and Walther Eichrodt. And clearly the journal met a need on the part primarily of clergy and scholars, for that same first decade saw circulation rise from 1500 to just over 4000.

Interpretation has also been committed to a practical focus. From its inception, the journal has included not only material reflecting the latest scholarly advances in biblical studies but analyses of the basic tools of biblical interpretation (commentaries and the like) and hints on how to use new views and interpretive materials in sermon preparation ("From Text to Exposition"). In this way, *Interpretation* has been a major vehicle in disseminating rigorous scholarship from the academy to the churches. And while the journal has the sponsorship of a Presbyterian institution, it has not limited its authors to Presbyterians, though for the first decade those from the Reformed wing of Protestantism dominated. Writers represent not only all the major Protestant traditions but for the last 20 years or so the Roman Catholic tradition as well. Indeed, such ecumenicity has cemented *Interpretation*'s self-conscious identification with the larger Christian ecumenical movement.

In 1971, the twenty-fifth anniversary issue contained a reflective editorial and a restrospective essay by Balmer H. Kelly, the first editor. The editorial noted that *Interpretation* continued its subtitle "unchanged as our charter for the past and our vocation in the future," despite the waning of neo-orthodoxy as the reigning thrust of Protestant theology.[2] Kelly's essay did point out that the early years emphasized interpretive principles and consequently witnessed the publication of only a few articles in the area of systematic theology.[3] In the more than a decade that has elapsed since then, however, *Interpretation* has sought to correct that perceived deficiency but without abandoning its primary commitment to biblical studies. One issue in 1974 (28:4), for example, was devoted to "liberation theology," but contributors were quick to highlight the biblical basis for that theological current. Since then, one issue per year generally has concentrated on biblical exegesis, one on doctrinal theology and its biblical grounding, one on a cognate area of religious studies (ethics, sociology, and the like), and one on principles of interpretation.

With circulation in 1983 approaching 12,000, *Interpretation* clearly remains a potent voice in promoting sound practices of biblical interpretation, promulgating current trends in biblical scholarship and theology, and advancing the application of both within the ongoing life of the Christian community. If it no longer manifests the neo-orthodoxy that nurtured its early years, it continues to exhibit a sensitivity to the most recent developments in biblical and theological work, for its greater openness to cross-disciplinary methods and approaches also marks the enterprise of biblical theology in the 1980s.

Notes

1. "The House of the Interpreter: An Editorial," *Interpretation* 1 (1947): 50.
2. "Editorial: The Twenty-fifth Anniversary," *Interpretation* 25 (1971): 10.
3. Balmer H. Kelly, "In Retrospect," *Interpretation* 25 (1971): 15.

Information Sources

BIBLIOGRAPHY:
"Directions: An Editorial." *Interpretation* 5 (1951): 60–61.
"Editorial: The Twenty-fifth Anniversary." *Interpretation* 25 (1971): 3–10.
"The House of the Interpreter: An Editorial." *Interpretation* 1 (1947): 49–51.
Kelly, Balmer H. "In Retrospect." *Interpretation* 25 (1971): 11–23.
McCormick, Scott. "Biblical Theology in the Years 1947–1956." Th.D. dissertation, Union Theological Seminary, 1958.
"The Need Abides: An Editorial." *Interpretation* 8 (1954): 444–45.
INDEX SOURCES: Scott McCormick, Jr., comp., *Interpretation: A Journal of Bible and Theology—Index, Vols. 1–10, 1947–1956* (Richmond: Union Theological Seminary, 1957); *Interpretation: Index, 1957–1971* (Richmond: Union Theological Seminary, n.d.); *Interpretation: Index, 1972–1976* (Richmond: Union Theological Seminary, n.d.); also in *Social Science Index, Old Testament Abstracts, Internationale Zeitschriftenschau fur Bibelwissenschaft und Grenzgebiete, New Testament Abstracts, Book Review Index, Religion Index One, Guide to Social Science and Religion in Periodical Literature, Christian Periodical Index, Humanities Index, Religious and Theological Abstracts.*

REPRINT EDITIONS: University Microfilms International.
LOCATION SOURCES: Yale University, Library of Congress, Duke University, Union
    Theological Seminary (New York), Union Theological Seminary (Virginia), Uni-
    versity of Chicago, San Francisco Theological Seminary, Southern Methodist
    University, and others.

Publication History

MAGAZINE TITLE AND TITLE CHANGES: *Interpretation: A Journal of Bible and
    Theology* (1947–   ); successor to the *Union Seminary Magazine* (1889–1912) and
    Union Seminary Review (1913–46).
VOLUME AND ISSUE DATA: 1:1 (1947–   ). Appears quarterly in January, April,
    July, and October.
PUBLISHER AND PLACE OF PUBLICATION: Interpretation, Richmond, Va. (1947–
    63); Union Theological Seminary, Richmond, Va. (1963–   ).
EDITORS: Balmer H. Kelly (1947–65), Donald G. Miller (1947–63), James L. Mays
    (1963–83), Paul J. Achtemeier (1984–   ); with the assistance of an international
    editorial board chaired since 1963 by the president of Union Theological Seminary,
    Virginia.
CIRCULATION: 1500 (1947), 3000 (1951), 4000 (1957), 5000 (1966), 6000 (1971),
    11,712 (1983).

Charles H. Lippy

J

JOURNAL FOR THE SCIENTIFIC STUDY OF RELIGION

Founded in 1949, the Society for the Scientific Study of Religion provides several forums for those interested in the study of religious phenomena through scientific methodology. In addition to publishing monographs and sponsoring annual conferences, the society since 1961 has published the *Journal for the Scientific Study of Religion*. An editorial foreword in the first issue reviewed the purposes of the society and its members:

> (1) To encourage the study of religion through the media of their respective sciences, (2) To facilitate cooperation between groups and individuals engaging in such studies, (3) To make known, as widely as possible, the nature, progress and findings of their diverse inquiries, (4) To stimulate free and friendly intercommunication between students in the field, and, to this end, to collaborate with other professional organizations such as the American Psychological Society, the Bureau of Research and Survey of the National Council of Churches, etc., (5) To publish a Journal which, by serving these ends, will further free inquiry, knowledge and understanding among religions.[1]

The president of the society and the editor of the *Journal* (Horace M. Kallen and Prentiss L. Pemberton, respectively) proceeded to acknowledge a grant from the J. A. Kaplan Fund that made the *Journal* possible.

The *Journal*'s founders opined that, in view of the Cold War, "the basis of all cooperative study needs to be agreement between those committed to one or another of the world's diversity of religions and those refusing commitment to any particular religion, on the need and promise of the use of scientific disciplines in the study of religion everywhere.''[2] The founders interpreted the widening concern over academic freedom to indicate an ''ethical and intellectual maturity'' on the part of students of religion.[3] They detected, moreover, a growing interest in approaching the study of religion from anthropological, psychological, and economic perspectives and hoped that their fledgling *Journal* might serve as a forum for this interplay of disciplines.

Prentiss Pemberton's retirement as editor several years later prompted more thoughts on the *Journal*'s function. Moving now from infancy into ''robust childhood,'' Pemberton's rather lofty aspirations for the *Journal* had diminished not at all. ''It is my firm conviction,'' he wrote, ''that the *Journal* has a strategic role to play in helping man to discover *The Meaning of the Twentieth Century*.''[4] The key to this discovery, Pemberton believed, lay in the union of religious and scientific resources, which would help to determine the ethical way into the twenty-first century.

James E. Dittes, assuming the editorial reins in April 1967, found a *Journal* that had grown prodigiously in its six years, so much that he faced certain difficult decisions in paring down the number of submissions. On this matter he expressed his preference for relatively pure—as opposed to applied—research problems, convinced that ''progress in our field has been impeded not by a dearth of facts, but by a dearth of theoretical formulations by which facts are comprehended and by which the collection of important new facts is guided and provoked.''[5]

Dittes's preferences have, by and large, set the standard for articles in the *Journal for the Scientific Study of Religion*, and to the extent that that standard has been met, the *Journal* has occupied a place of growing importance as students of religion have reached beyond traditional methodological boundaries. A sampling of recent articles illustrates the interdisciplinary cast of the periodical: ''The Demographic Environment and Church Membership Change'' (C. Kirk Hadaway), ''Subjectivization and the New Evangelical Theodicy'' (James Davison Hunter), ''Two Traditions in the Study of Religion'' (Robert Wuthnow), and ''The Psychodynamics of Demon Possession'' (Colleen A. Ward and Michael H. Beaubrun).

Notes

1. Horace M. Kallen and Prentiss L. Pemberton, ''An Introductory Word,'' *Journal for the Scientific Study of Religion* 1 (1961): 3. On the society's purposes and general information, see also *Encyclopedia of Associations*, 1981 ed., s.v. ''Society for the Scientific Study of Religion.''

2. Kallen and Pemberton, p. 3.

3. Ibid.

4. ''Retrospect and Prospect,'' *Journal for the Scientific Study of Religion* 5 (1965): 3.

5. ''Editorial Foreword,'' *Journal for the Scientific Study of Religion* 6 (1967): 1–2.

Information Sources

INDEX SOURCES: *Journal for the Scientific Study of Religion: 20 Year Index, 1961–1981* (published April 1982). Also in *Arts and Humanities Citation Index, Guide to Social Science and Religion in Periodical Literature, Historical Abstracts, Humanities Index, Old Testament Abstracts, Psychological Abstracts, Religion Index One (Index to Religious Periodicals), Revue d' histoire ecclesiastique, Social Sciences Citation Index* (through 1977), *Sociological Abstracts, Religious and Theological Abstracts.*

REPRINT EDITIONS: University Microfilms International.

LOCATION SOURCES: Yale University, Union Theological Seminary (New York), Princeton University, Library of Congress, University of Texas-Austin, and others.

Publication History

MAGAZINE TITLE AND TITLE CHANGES: *Journal for the Scientific Study of Religion* (1961–   ).

VOLUME AND ISSUE DATA: 1 (October 1961–   ). Published semiannually, October 1961-Fall 1969; quarterly thereafter.

PUBLISHER AND PLACE OF PUBLICATION: Cultura Press, Wetteren, Belgium (1961–69); University of California Press, Berkeley; (1970-Spring 1971); Printing Department, University of Montana (Summer 1971–1975); A & A Printing Co., Akron, Ohio (1976–   ).

EDITORS: Prentiss L. Pemberton (1961–65), Samuel Z. Klausner (interim, 1965–66), James E. Dittes (1967–71), Benton Johnson (1972–74), Richard L. Gorsuch (1975–78), Philip E. Hammond (1979–82), Donald Capps (1983–   ).

CIRCULATION: 2500–2900 (1983).

Randall H. Balmer

JOURNAL OF BIBLE AND RELIGION

The idea for both the *Journal of Bible and Religion* (*JBR*) and its sponsoring organization, the National Association of Biblical Instructors (NABI), came from Ismar J. Peritz, professor of Bible at Syracuse University. Peritz's observations of a professional association and journal for mathematics teachers convinced him that teachers of Bible could benefit from a similar organization and publication. While NABI became a reality in 1909 and met annually with the Society of Biblical Literature and Exegesis (SBLE), the journal materialized only after a long gestation period.

Beginning in 1915, NABI's news and selected papers given at the convention were periodically published in *Christian Education*, whose editor was a NABI member. In 1928 NABI began paying for a regular monthly section in *Christian Education* called the Department of Biblical Instruction and appointed Peritz as editorial secretary to fill it.

When the Great Depression thinned NABI's ranks, the organization, hoping to increase its membership, yielded to Peritz's incessant pleas by giving him permission to edit during 1933 one or two issues of a periodical called the *Journal of the National Association of Biblical Instructors*. The gamble paid off; within a year, membership, which included a free subscription to the journal, jumped 60 percent and secured the journal's continuance.

One of Peritz's early tasks was to allay the fears of SBLE members that the new publication might overlap with its prestigious quarterly, the *Journal of Biblical Literature (JBL)**. Peritz's approach was to concede to SBLE and the *JBL* the specialized role of "creative research" while assigning to NABI and its journal the "humbler task" of finding ways to teach the results of this research to students in an academic setting. For Peritz the ultimate goal of this teaching was an ethical one: the betterment of individual and corporate life by shaping both to be Christ-like. While this meant the defense of Christianity as "the only solution of the problems of universal citizenship," it did not mean rejection of modern knowledge or methods of scholarship. "We make no apology," he declared, "for standing on a modernistic basis of interpretation of Bible and religion, evolution with God back of it and Biblical criticism."[1]

Articles came mainly from papers presented at NABI meetings, including the annual presidential address, and symposia such as "The Bible in Modern Education," and "Teaching the New Testament." Early contributors included Georgia Harkness, Amos N. Wilder, Floyd V. Filson, J. Philip Hyatt, and G. Ernest Wright. East Coast schools dominated both NABI and *JBR*, with only an occasional contribution from the small midwest and fledgling southern sections of NABI. A popular book review section developed over the years, and space was allotted for NABI's business.

When finances permitted the journal to expand to a quarterly in 1937, managing editor Carl E. Purinton suggested a new name to describe more accurately the expanding scope of subject matter being taught by NABI's members. Peritz reluctantly agreed as long as the word *Bible* was retained. The new name, the *Journal of Bible and Religion*, was a compromise between Peritz and Purinton and underscored the tension within NABI that continued into the 1960s. For the Peritz wing, the Bible was always the primary focus and religion a separate and secondary concern. For Purinton and a growing number of other NABI members, the Bible was always a part, albeit a crucial part, of the more inclusive subject of religion.

When Purinton succeeded the retiring Peritz in 1938, apprehension again surfaced within SBLE. Purinton disavowed any interest in competing with *JBL*, although he raised eyebrows by his intention to move *JBR* beyond concern with the pedagogical needs of Bible teachers to the content of biblical research. SBLE had nothing to fear from this approach since, as the editor explained, *JBR* was interested only in the Bible and religion "in so far as it relates to the religion of the Bible."[2] This policy meant moving into such related areas as philosophy of religion, comparative religion, ethics, and theology.

With the coming of World War II, however, there was a renewed interest within NABI in the country's biblical and Christian heritage. As Purinton acknowledged, the "crisis of modern life" was "driving" him and others back to the thoughts and words of Jesus.[3] And after the war, *JBR's* emphasis on theology reflected both the impact of neo-orthodoxy and the emerging field of biblical theology.

Yet *JBR* continued to explore its expanded subject matter even as it benefited from NABI's growth and more even geographical representation. Beginning in 1947, a regular feature, "Research Abstract," kept readers abreast of the latest research in such diverse fields as archaeology, church history, history of religions, psychology of religion, religion and literature, and Old and New Testaments. By 1960 associate editor Dwight M. Beck could say, "Nothing religious is alien to us. The vitality and the variety of our studies is astonishing."[4]

Upon Purinton's retirement in 1961, A. Roy Eckardt, the new editor, launched a crusade through editorials to change NABI's public image to correspond to the development of broadly defined academic departments of religion. The result was a change of name for NABI in 1964 to the American Academy of Religion, but the name of the journal remained unchanged. However, organizational changes accompanying the new AAR shifted responsibility for all nonjournal publishing away from *JBR* to a publications board and added a new *Bulletin* to carry AAR news, thus allowing *JBR* to devote itself to articles and reviews.

An editorial in 1965 on the irony of the journal's name led to quick action by AAR, and in 1967 *JBR* became the *Journal of the American Academy of Religion,** continuing with the same series, editors, and policy. But the change came at a difficult and uncertain time for religion specialists. The prevailing secularity of the times caused Eckardt to wonder if religious study might not come to a state where it was not dominantly or even evidently religious. "What could be more ludicrous," he mused, "than prosperity in the study of a reality that is no longer there."[5]

Notes

1. Ismar J. Peritz, "Editorial," *Journal of the National Association of Biblical Instructors* 1 (1933): 22; Peritz, "Report of the Retiring Editor," *Journal of Bible and Religion* 6 (Winter 1938): 48 (hereafter cited as *JBR*).
2. "The Expansion of the Journal," *JBR* 5 (pt. I, 1937): 32.
3. Carl E. Purinton, "Religious Dynamics," *JBR* 12 (May 1944): 110.
4. Dwight Marion Beck, "Reminiscences," *JBR* 28 (April 1960): 208.
5. A. Roy Eckhardt, "Editorial Preface," *JBR* 34 (October 1966): 303.

Information Sources

BIBLIOGRAPHY:

Eby, Louise S. "Eleven Years of the *Journal*." *Journal of Bible and Religion* 12 (August 1944): 193–97.

Mouls, Elmer W. K. "The National Association of Biblical Instructors: An Historical Account." *Journal of Bible and Religion* 18 (January 1950): 11–28.

Purinton, Carl E. "The Journal of Bible and Religion: The Formative Years." *Journal of Bible and Religion* 28 (April 1960): 209–14.

INDEX SOURCES: *Journal of Bible and Religion* 28 (January 1960), entire issue indexing
   vols. 1–25 (1933–57); *Index to Religious Periodical Literature*.
REPRINT EDITIONS: Johnson Reprint Corporation, American Theological Library Association, University Microfilms International.
LOCATION SOURCES: Yale University, Library of Congress, Union Theological Seminary (New York), Princeton Theological Seminary, Brown University, and others.

Publication History

MAGAZINE TITLE AND TITLE CHANGES: *Journal of the National Association of
   Biblical Instructors* (1933–36), *Journal of Bible and Religion* (1937–66); superseded
   by *Journal of the American Academy of Religion*.
VOLUME AND ISSUE DATA: *Journal of the National Association of Biblical Instructors*
   1–4 (pt. I, 1933–pt. II, 1936), *Journal of Bible and Religion* 5–34 (February 1937-
   October 1966).
PUBLISHER AND PLACE OF PUBLICATION: National Association of Biblical In-
   structors, location varies (1933–64); American Academy of Religion, Chambers-
   burg, Pa. (1964–66).
EDITORS: Ismar J. Peritz (1933–36), Carl E. Purinton (1937–60), A. Roy Eckhardt
   (1961–66).
CIRCULATION: 200 (1933), 3220 (1966).

L. David Lewis

JOURNAL OF BIBLICAL LITERATURE

In 1981, volume 100 of the *Journal of Biblical Literature* (*JBL*) appeared.
One of the oldest scholarly journals still being published in the United States,
JBL provides a rich documentary history of the major advances and controversies
that have marked biblical studies over the past century.

In January 1880 a small group of scholars met in New York City to found
"a Society for the promotion of study in Biblical Literature and Exegesis," a
title formally shortened to the Society of Biblical Literature (SBL) in 1962.[1] By
1881 the society was publishing its proceedings and summaries of papers presented, at this point in booklet form. The *Journal* itself was launched a year
later in response to the society's mandate "to print the papers read at the June
meeting (1881) in full and those of the December meeting as far as the funds
would allow."[2] Since that time, the *JBL* has been the major publication of the
SBL. Volume 1 of *JBL* appeared as an annual, with a circulation of 500 copies,
in 1882. The initial cost for a subscription to *JBL* was $3 annually, a figure not
raised until 1939.[3]

Scholarly papers read at national meetings of the society were regularly published, in full or in abstract form, as were brief notes. Until 1960 accounts of
the proceedings of the annual meetings were printed in *JBL*, along with a number
of official reports. For many years the *Journal* included, in addition, such material

as a membership roster and memorial minutes. Book reviews, which now occupy a prominent place in each issue, did not appear until 1936.[4]

JBL has always featured a wide range of articles, reflecting the variety of approaches being taken by scholars toward the Bible and the discovery of new material, epigraphic and archaeological, that pertains to the Bible. The scope of articles has expanded to include ever-broader categories in terms of geographical, chronological, and methodological coverage.

One of the most convenient places to chart such growth, and its attendant difficulties, is through the annual addresses of the society's presidents, which have traditionally been printed as the first article in the initial issue of each volume. Francis Brown, whose presidential address was an early attempt at an analytical survey of the discipline, issued this modern-sounding cautionary note in 1896: "It is not always possible to decide whether a particular case of criticism should be classed as transmissional or redactional—whether we have to do, in certain cases, with copyists' weaknesses, or with the purposes of a literary workman."[5] Almost 30 years later President Max L. Margolis, judging that "criticism has been overdone, the higher and the lower. Investigations as to date and composition may lie fallow for awhile," challenged his audience: "Away with the multitude of our little publications in which we frequently repeat ourselves! Let us address ourselves to monumental works which will require the cooperation of a large number of us and provide useful occupation beyond the present generation." In so doing, Margolis warned, biblical scholars must avoid reliance on critical positions "hardened into a tradition and woefully lacking in self-criticism."[6]

What has been termed "one of the most remarkable addresses" was delivered by President Julian Morgenstern in 1941. He found fault with "a literary criticism that perpetuated outmoded conclusions and failed to understand the cultural, intellectual, and institutional ambience of documents." According to Morgenstern, the major task of assimilating new evidence from the ancient Near East had fallen to American and Canadian scholars.[7] Bernhard Anderson, in his presidential address of 1980, spoke of the existence of two approaches to biblical study: "the traditio-historical process behind the text and the exegesis of the canonical recension itself."[8] As Anderson saw it: "The relation between tradition and scripture in the community of faith deserves further theological clarification. . . . It is tradition *and* scripture: tradition which still makes its theological witness in scripture, and scripture which theologically incorporates and crystallizes biblical tradition."[9]

Twenty-three individuals have headed *JBL*; since 1938 the title *editor* has been used for this individual. Some of these men, especially those with long years of service, made major efforts to guide the *JBL* in accordance with a particular editorial policy.[10] In recent years the editor of *JBL* has been assisted by two associate editors—one in charge of Old Testament book reviews, the other handling New Testament book reviews—and an editorial board. The editorial board consists of 21 members, seven of whom are selected each year for a three-year term.[11] Under the leadership of this group, four issues, averaging between 160 and 175 pages each, appear annually.

A typical issue from the 1970s contains six or seven articles, ranging in length from eight to 30 pages. The articles are usually heavily footnoted and include such topics as "The Meaning and Usage of RKB in Biblical Hebrew," "Paul's Conversion/Call: A Comparative Analysis of the Three Reports in Acts," and "Coherence and Inconsistency in the Apocalypses: The Case of 'the End' in 4 Ezra." Most issues also contain several critical notes of two to four pages each.

Reviews of scholarly literature occupy between 30 and 50 pages in an average issue. Critical book reviews occupy most of this space, as many as 40 appearing in an average issue. Reviewers are advised that

> there is no room in reviews for personal polemics or rejoinders, nor should a review be employed to show how the reviewer would have treated the subject. Ideally a review should provide the reader with a balanced impression of the book and its value and limitations. . . . Reviewers normally should provide an accurate and balanced description of the relevant *contents* of the book and its *method* of treatment, along with *critical evaluation*, both positive and negative.[12]

Such reviews, which are organized in roughly chronological order according to the subject covered in the book, are usually between 500 and 1000 words in length, although occasionally much longer reviews, almost review articles, are found. A section entitled "Collected Essays," not found in every issue, is basically a listing, with a minimum of critical evaluation, of the contents of festschriften and other collected works. Volumes submitted for review are listed in the quarterly "Books Received," if they "are at all related to the interests of this *Journal*." Inclusion in this section "does not preclude the subsequent review of a book."[13]

An index to books reviewed, arranged in alphabetical order by the author's last name, appears at the close of the March, June, and September issues. The December issue presents an annual index, arranged alphabetically by author, of articles, critical notes, and book reviews (including notices of collected essays). In addition to these annual indexes, four larger ones, each covering at least 20 volumes, have appeared.

In 1928 George Dahl, corresponding secretary of the society (the title given to the individual who edited *JBL* until 1938), gave the following assessment of the publication he headed: "The Journal stands as a bulwark of American Biblical scholarship and, to a great degree, as its index. It provides a channel through which creative thought may find expression."[14]

Anyone who takes the time to go through even a few volumes of *JBL*, noting the topics covered and the scholars who write articles and reviews, will agree that Dahl's statement, valid in 1928, remains an accurate and fair assessment of this major publication in the field of biblical studies.

Notes

1. Ernest W. Saunders, *Searching the Scriptures: A History of the Society of Biblical Literature, 1880–1980* (Chico, Calif.: Scholars Press, 1982), p. 3. Saunders's book, to which frequent reference is made, contains a wealth of information on all facets of SBL's activities.

2. Ibid., p. 4.

3. Ibid., pp. 34, 88. It was difficult to continue publication of the *JBL* during World War I, especially because it was being printed by a firm in Leipzig. On this see ibid., pp. 23, 89, and the personal correspondence of Max L. Margolis, *JBL* editor during this period. (This portion of the Margolis papers is housed in the archives of Dropsie University, Philadelphia.)

4. Ibid., pp. 88–89.

5. Quoted in ibid., pp. 27–28. Brown's address appeared in *JBL* 15 (1896): 63–74.

6. Max L. Margolis, "Our Own Future and a Programme," *JBL* 43 (1924): 6–8. See also Saunders, p. 37.

7. Saunders, pp. 50–51, 58.

8. Ibid., p. 69.

9. Bernhard W. Anderson, "Tradition and Scripture in the Community of Faith," *JBL* 100 (1981): 21.

10. Saunders, esp. pp. 89–90.

11. For the names of those currently occupying these positions, see the inside front cover of a recent issue of *JBL*.

12. "Instructions for Book Reviewers, *Journal of Biblical Literature*," prepared by W. Sibley Towner, associate editor, Old Testament book reviews.

13. As indicated in the statement at the head of the "Books Received" section found in every issue of *JBL*.

14. Quoted in Saunders, p. 88. Future research on topics related to the SBL is being facilitated by the establishment of a national archival center for the American Academy of Religion and Society of Biblical Literature on the campus of the Iliff School of Theology, Denver.

Information Sources

BIBLIOGRAPHY:

Anderson, Bernhard W. "Tradition and Scripture in the Community of Faith." *Journal of Biblical Literature* 100 (1981): 5–21.

Margolis, Max L. "Our Own Future and a Programme." *Journal of Biblical Literature* 43 (1924): 1–8.

————. Personal correspondence. Archives, Dropsie University, Philadelphia.

Saunders, Ernest W. *Searching the Scriptures: A History of the Society of Biblical Literature, 1880–1980*. Chico, Calif.: Scholars Press, 1982.

INDEX SOURCES: *Book Review Index, Poole's Index, Current Contents, Humanities Index, Guide to Social Science and Religion in Periodical Literature, Index to Jewish Periodicals, New Testament Abstracts, Old Testament Abstracts, Religion Index One, Religious and Theological Abstracts*; in addition, the *Journal of Biblical Literature* has published its own indexes, ed. O. H. Gates (vols. 1–40), Ralph Marcus (vols. 41–60), T. H. Gaster (vols. 60–79), and John C. Hurd (vols. 80–99).

REPRINT EDITIONS: University Microfilms International.
LOCATION SOURCES: University of California-Berkeley, Clemson University, University of Michigan, University of Missouri, Vanderbilt University, Yale University, and others.

Publication History

MAGAZINE TITLE AND TITLE CHANGES: *Journal of Biblical Literature* (1882–   ).
VOLUME AND ISSUE DATA: 1 (1882–   ); appeared annually, with a few exceptions, 1882–1905; semiannually, 1906–11; quarterly, 1912–14; quarterly or semiannually, 1915- .
PUBLISHER AND PLACE OF PUBLICATION (1983): Society of Biblical Literature, Scholars Press, Chico, Calif.
EDITORS: Prior to 1938 the secretary or corresponding secretary of the Society of Biblical Literature headed an editorial staff: Frederic Gardiner (1880–83), Hinckley G. Mitchell (1883–89), George Foot Moore (1889–94), David G. Lyon (1894–1900), Lewis B. Paton (1901–4), James Hardy Ropes (1905–6), Benjamin W. Bacon (1907), Julius A. Bewer (1908–9), James A. Montgomery (1910–13), Max L. Margolis (1914–21), George Dahl (1922–29, 1934), Carl H. Kraeling (1930–33), Erwin R. Goodenough (1935–42), Robert H. Pfeiffer (1943–47), J. Philip Hyatt (1948–50), Robert C. Denton (1951–54), David Noel Freedman (1955–59), Morton S. Enslin (1960–69), John Reumann (1970), Joseph A. Fitzmyer (1971–76), John H. Hayes (1977–82), Victor H. Furnish (1983–   ).
CIRCULATION: 6000 (1982).

Leonard J. Greenspoon

JOURNAL OF CHRISTIAN SCIENCE. *See* THE CHRISTIAN SCIENCE MONITOR

JOURNAL OF CHURCH AND STATE

Because of their belief in the voluntariness of religious association and their free congregational ecclesiology, Baptists have made numerous contributions to the concepts of religious liberty and the separation of church and state.[1] It was not strange or inappropriate, then, that the *Journal of Church and State* experienced its birth in a Baptist context. Though currently ecumenical in scope, it has always reflected Baptist leadership and viewpoints, however liberal and academic.

In the colonial period, Roger Williams stated in his *Bloody Tenet*, "It is the will and command of God that . . . a permission of the most Paganish, Jewish, Turkish, or Antichristian consciences and worships, be granted to all men in all nations and countries."[2] This early reference to a private and public (social and civil) liberty of religious expression summarizes well the American Baptist search. That search included a commitment to separation of church and state, for as a minority group, Baptists had dramatically experienced the restrictions and penalties that could be placed by a state church on an individual or a church body. Thus, they have always insisted that the state not interfere in any way with religious beliefs and practices and that in turn churches be completely voluntaristic and not depend on the state in any way for its support. Baptists from the start were committed to the principle of voluntarism, which marked the founding documents of the United States.[3]

In order to implement their political concerns on a national level, a number of Baptist denominations combined efforts in 1938 to found the Joint Conference Committee on Public Relations with headquarters in Washington, D.C. In 1950 the name was changed to the Baptist Joint Committee on Public Affairs. This agency has had an evolving history of defending and preserving the principles of religious liberty and the separation of church and state. Between 1946 and 1953, J. M. Dawson, a Texas Baptist, served as secretary of this agency. Among his many writings, perhaps one of the finest was *America's Way in Church, State, and Society*.[4]

The *Journal of Church and State* saw its first issue in November 1959 and was published by the J. M. Dawson Studies in Church and State, a specially endowed program at Baylor University, a Southern Baptist institution. It was and is the only strictly scholarly periodical expressly concerned with the separation of church and state. The first editorial by the first editor, James E. Wood, quoted the Swiss theologian, Emil Brunner, approvingly: "The relation between Church and State is the greatest subject in the history of the West."[5] Wood then referred to the subject as being perennial and relevant over the entire world. With the launching of this journal, opportunities would be given for the publication of articles, case studies, monographs, and book reviews on matters related to religious liberty and church and state relations. The editor promised that the journal would not be narrow or restrictive and that diverse points of view would be presented with no efforts at glib or easy answers to complex problems. It was hoped that "this journal may find a real place in the growing interest, discussion, and literature concerning church-state relations."[6] In that first issue, however ecumenical were the efforts, all of the writers were Baptists and all of the reviewers were from Baylor University.

The journal has evolved into a truly ecumenical one with writers from other segments of the Christian community than Baptist. For protection against the criticisms of ultraconservative Baptists, however, the second volume carried an editorial notation often repeated: "The opinions freely expressed in this journal are those of the contributors and not necessarily endorsed by the editors or the J. M. Dawson Studies in Church and State."[7] Further, however, the editor welcomed diverse opinions and differing points of view. The journal has continuously expanded its offerings to include a wider variety of services. For example, it began to publish full texts of world organizations on the subjects of its interest such as the United Nations Declaration on Religious Liberty. Full texts of U.S. Supreme Court decisions in relation to church and state matters were published.[8] Lists of doctoral dissertations on church and state also began to appear. Appropriately, Protestant-Catholic interfaith dialogues began to be published, as well as favorable reports on the Second Vatican Council and especially its Declaration on Religious Liberty. More liberal views also began to be aired editorially. For example, in 1981, in relation to Senator Jesse Helms's (North Carolina) suggested prayer legislation, the editorial commented, "Such legislation is unnecessary, ill-advised, and unconstitutional. It does not serve the legitimate interest of the state or true religion."[9]

The autumn 1973 issue was a red-letter publication for a number of reasons.[10] J. M. Dawson had died earlier in the year, and special tributes to him, as well as a survey of his vast contributions, were given. Also, the editorial presented a retrospective statement on the first 15 years of the journal, claiming that although through the years attacks had come from both the extreme Right and Left, efforts were perennially made to "defend and protect the ecumenical character and academic integrity of the journal." Finally, this issue announced that James E. Wood was resigning as editor to become the executive director of the Baptist Joint Committee on Public Affairs and that the new editor would be James Leo Garrett, Jr., one of the more liberal professors on the faculty of Southwestern Baptist Theological Seminary.

During the years of Garrett's editorship (1974–79), there were vastly more guest editorials, and those done by Garrett himself were scholarly articles rather than true editorials. The 1980 volume was directed by James A. Curry, the associate editor, and in 1981 James E. Wood returned as editor. In the 1980s, the journal has been much more ecumenical in its list of contributors and in a recent editorial called for genuine world community: "In the present age of religious encounter, interfaith dialogue is not only a moral imperative but also a practical necessity for the creation of a world community."[11]

The *Journal of Church and State* has made major contributions to a more complete understanding of church and state matters through the years. It has participated actively in the spirit called for in a cogent paragraph by Baptist historian Winthrop Hudson:

> The constitutional provision for the separation of church and state has the great merit of making this responsibility of the churches explicit and of fostering those qualities of initiative, responsibility, relevance, resourcefulness, liberality, missionary zeal, and lay participation, which Philip Schaff, against the background of his knowledge of religious conditions in his native land described as the characteristic consequences of the acceptance of the voluntary principle in religion. The separation of church and state has the additional virtue of guaranteeing the freedom of a church to be a church, to determine its own life, and to appeal to a "higher law" than the statutory enactments of the state. For this reason alone, if for no other reason, the separation of church and state ought resolutely to be guarded—the more so when the prevailing culture is so largely secular.[12]

The *Journal of Church and State* continues to search for the whole meaning of freedom, not away from but in the midst of global responsibility and commitment.

Notes

1. See Robert G. Torbet, *A History of the Baptists*, rev. ed. (Valley Forge, Pa: Judson Press, 1963).

2. H. S. Smith, R. T. Handy, and L. A. Loetscher, eds., *American Christianity* (New York: Charles Scribner's Sons, 1960), 1:153.

3. See Brooks Hays and John E. Steely, *The Baptist Way of Life* (Macon: Mercer University Press, 1981), passim.

4. See Torbet, pp. 454ff.

5. *Journal of Church and State* 1:1 (November 1959): 2.

6. Ibid., p. 3.

7. Ibid. 2:2 (November 1960): 99.

8. For example, see ibid. 23:1 (Winter 1981): 4ff.

9. Ibid. 23:2 (Spring 1981): 213.

10. Ibid. 15:3 (Autumn 1973).

11. Ibid. 25:1 (Winter 1983): 11.

12. Winthrop S. Hudson, *The Great Tradition of the American Churches* (New York: Harper and Bros., 1953), p. 262.

Information Sources

BIBLIOGRAPHY:

Cook, Henry. *What Baptists Stand For*. London: Kingsgate Press, 1947.

Hays, Brooks, and John E. Steely. *The Baptist Way of Life*. Macon: Mercer University Press, 1981.

Hudson, Winthrop S. *The Great Tradition of the American Churches*. New York: Harper and Bros., 1953.

Miller, Perry. *Roger Williams: His Contribution to the American Tradition*. Indianapolis: Bobbs-Merrill, 1953.

Schaff, Philip. *Church and State in the United States*. New York: Scribner, 1888.

Torbet, Robert G. *A History of the Baptists*. Rev. ed. Valley Forge, Pa.: Judson Press, 1963.

Wilson, John F., ed. *Church and State in American History*. Boston: D. C. Heath, 1965.

INDEX SOURCES: *Journal of Church and State* 5 (1963) for vols. 1–5, 15 (1973) for vols. 6–15. Also in *Religion Index One, Christian Periodicals Index, Religious and Theological Abstracts, Legal Resource Index, Educational Administration Index, Public Affairs Information Service, America: History and Life, Historical Abstracts, Current Law Index*.

LOCATION SOURCES: Yale University, Catholic University of America, Union Theological Seminary (New York), University of Texas-Austin, Duke University, University of California-Los Angeles, Princeton Theological Seminary, and others.

Publication History

MAGAZINE TITLE AND TITLE CHANGES: *Journal of Church and State* (1959–   ).

VOLUME AND ISSUE DATA: *Journal of Church and State* 1:1 (November 1959–   ). Published three times a year; about 600 pages per issue.

PUBLISHER AND PLACE OF PUBLICATION: Baylor University, Waco, Texas.
EDITORS: James E. Wood (1959–73), James Leo Garrett (1974–79), James A. Curry
(Winter-Spring 1980), James E. Wood (Autumn 1980–   ).
CIRCULATION: 1365–2000.

George H. Shriver

JOURNAL OF ECUMENICAL STUDIES

The early 1960s launched an era of increased ecumenical activity in American religion, inspired in part by the Catholic overtures to Protestant and Orthodox churches associated with the Second Vatican Council (1962–65). One sign of this new ecumenism was the launching of the *Journal of Ecumenical Studies* in 1964 with its early subtitle, *Catholic-Protestant-Orthodox*. Edited by Leonard Swidler and Elwyn Smith, the journal drew upon an impressive array of associate editors representing the major Christian families in both the United States and abroad. From the beginning, the journal had an international as well as an ecumenical flavor.

The inaugural issue featured a lead editorial explaining the purpose of the new periodical. It would be devoted to an "examination of the issues which concern Catholic, Protestant, and Orthodox Christians." Renouncing polemic, the journal saw itself as a medium for candid analysis, for broaching subjects new to ecumenical discussion, and for presenting scholarly articles, reports of ecumenical conferences and related events, abstracts of articles in other journals from around the world bearing on ecumenicity, and book reviews.[1] Some of these features have distinguished the *Journal of Ecumenical Studies* from other periodicals with a cognate bent, for only this one has tapped a network of international correspondents to abstract articles in foreign languages and comment on international ecumenical activity for an American, English-speaking audience. For many years, numerous associate editors wrote editorials on a regular basis. A shift to devoting some issues to particular themes in 1976 also witnessed a decrease in the number and frequency of editorials. Initially appearing three times each year, the journal became a quarterly in 1966 when the editors joined the faculty of Temple University in Philadelphia and the university became a sponsoring agency for the publication.

During the *Journal of Ecumenical Studies*'s first decade, well-known scholars from a variety of disciplines in religious studies contributed articles. The initial issue featured pieces by biblical scholars Oscar Cullmann and Markus Barth, as well as by Methodist theologian Albert Outler. Other numbers in the first decade featured important essays by noted European Catholic theologians Karl Rahner and Hans Kung, historian Brian Tierney, and New Testament scholar Paul S. Minear.[2] Rather quickly, the purview of the journal expanded beyond intramural Christian concerns. Lowell Streiker's "The Modern Jewish-Christian Dialogue" and Markus Barth's "Can a Jew Believe about Jesus and Still Remain a Jew?"

in the second volume and Jacob Neusner's "Judaism in a Secular Age" in the third marked the beginning of what remains a continuing concern in the journal, Jewish-Christian ecumenical interchange. Arthur Gilbert became the first non-Christian associate editor of the periodical in 1966. Indeed, Jewish-Christian dialogue and Protestant-Catholic dialogue, particularly as the Catholic doctrine of papal infallibility relates to the latter, have been the two most frequent thematic foci over the years.

By 1970, the range of topics perceived as germane to ecumenical discussion broadened. That year, Raymond Panikkar's "Advaita and Bhakti: Love and Identity in Hindu-Christian Dialogue" added an East-West dimension, and Charles E. Curran's "Theology and Genetics: A Multi-Faceted Dialogue" demonstrated that the ramifications of contemporary ethical issues have an ecumenical aspect. As well, practical concerns joined theoretical ones as subjects of inquiry, beginning with James L. Hickey's essay, "Christian Ecumenical Marriages: A Major Pastoral Concern," which appeared in 1970.

In the 1970s, the *Journal of Ecumenical Studies* began to reprint papers from conferences held at the Graymoor Ecumenical Institute, Garrison, New York, in one issue each year. Among the topics addressed under this rubric are "Women and Religion: Scripture-Tradition-Institution" (1983), "Can Religious Education Be Ecumenical?" (1981), "Ecumenical Tensions and Implications" (1980), and "Ecumenical Marriage: A Problem and Possibility" (1979). Some numbers devoted to special topics have been put together by guest editors. The fall 1976 issue, for example, addressed Orthodox-Christian-Jewish dialogue and was co-edited by Nomikos Michael Vaporis and Marc H. Tannenbaum. Other important topics featured in special theme issues include "Religious Liberty in the Crossfire of Creeds," edited by Franklin H. Littell (1977); "Varieties of Christian-Marxist Dialogue," edited by Paul Mojzes (1978); "Can You Still Say 'Christus Victor'? Reflections by Delegates to Amsterdam 1939, in Commemoration of the First World Conference of Christian Youth," edited by R. H. Edwin Espy (1979); "From Holocaust to Dialogue: A Jewish-Christian Dialogue between Americans and Germans," prepared by regular editor Leonard Swidler (1981); "A Critique of Authority in Contemporary Catholicism," edited by Piet F. Fransen (1982); and " 'Baptism, Eucharist, and Ministry' and Its Reception in U.S. Churches," a discussion of a statement from the Commission on Faith and Order of the World Council of Churches edited by Jeffrey Gros (1984).

Two numbers of the *Journal of Ecumenical Studies* were also published as separate anthologies. The first of these, devoted to "Baptists and Ecumenism," edited by William Jerry Boney and Glenn A. Iglehart (1980), appeared in book form under the auspices of Judson Press. Pilgrim Press printed the essays that comprised the summer issue of 1982, "Human Rights in Religious Traditions," edited by Arlene Swidler.

Perhaps the most significant single topic issue to appear to date is the winter number of volume 17 (1980). In that issue Catholic theologians Hans Kung and Edward Schillebeeckx, both of whom have reaped criticism in some Catholic circles for perceived challenges to traditional Catholic doctrine in their writing, offered seminal essays. There then followed a series of responses written by individuals representing not only Christian families—Protestant, Catholic, and Orthodox—but also the Jewish, Muslim, and Hindu traditions. It remains the most vital achievement of the *Journal of Ecumenical Studies* in nurturing genuine interfaith conversation and response.

Although the *Journal of Ecumenical Studies* has increasingly devoted its pages to special thematic issues rather than to individual essays by scholars known and unknown, it remains an important voice in current ecumenical discussion. If ecumenical fervor has become somewhat more restrained in the two decades since Vatican II as continuing dialogue has revealed the complexity of the issues that both divide and unite humanity, the *Journal of Ecumenical Studies* keeps ecumenical discussion alive for an international audience of scholars and lay-persons in a responsible and often penetrating fashion.

Notes

1. "The Purpose of the Journal of Ecumenical Studies," *Journal of Ecumenical Studies* 1 (1964): iii–v (herafter cited as *JES*).

2. Karl Rahner, "Christian Humanism," *JES* 4 (1967): 369–84; Hans Kung, "Participation of the Laity in Church Leadership and in Church Elections," *JES* 6 (1969): 511–33; Brian Tierney, "Origins of Papal Infallibility," *JES* 8 (1971): 841–64; Paul S. Minear, "The Influence of Ecumenical Development on New Testament Teaching," *JES* 8 (1971): 286–99.

Information Sources

BIBLIOGRAPHY:
"The Purpose of the Journal of Ecumenical Studies." *Journal of Ecumenical Studies* 1 (1964): iii–v.

INDEX SOURCES: *Historical Abstracts, America: History and Life, Religion Index One, Religious and Theological Abstracts, Elenchus Bibliographicus Biblicus, Catholic Periodical and Literature Index, Guide to Social Science and Religion in Periodical Literature, Humanities Index, Theologische Literaturzeitung, Internationale Zeitschriftenschau fur Bibelwissenschaft und Grenzgebiete, Infodex, Repertoire bibliographique des institutions chretiennes, Book Reviews of the Month, International Review of Missions, Missionalia.*

REPRINT EDITIONS: Microfilm edition available from the journal.

LOCATION SOURCES: Library of Congress, Princeton Theological Seminary, Emory University, Harvard University, Yale University, University of Chicago, University of California-Los Angeles, Rice University, and others.

Publication History

MAGAZINE TITLE AND TITLE CHANGES: *Journal of Ecumenical Studies: Catholic-Protestant-Orthodox* (1964–65), *Journal of Ecumenical Studies* (1965–   ).

VOLUME AND ISSUE DATA: 1:1–3:3 (1964–66), three numbers per volume in winter, spring, and fall; 4:1 (1967–   ), quarterly numbers in winter, spring, summer, and fall.

PUBLISHER AND PLACE OF PUBLICATION: Duquesne University Press, Pittsburgh (1964–66); Journal of Ecumenical Studies, Temple University, Philadelphia (1967–78, 1980–   ); Ecumenical Press, Temple University, Philadelphia (1979).
EDITORS: Elwyn Smith (1964–71), Leonard Swidler (1964–   ).
CIRCULATION: 2200 (1983).

Charles H. Lippy

JOURNAL OF NEAR EASTERN STUDIES

The *Journal of Near Eastern Studies*, the quarterly publication of the Department of Oriental Languages and Literatures of the University of Chicago, has been published under its present name since 1942. Known as the *American Journal of Semitic Languages and Literatures* from 1895 to 1941 and as *Hebraica* from its inception in 1884 until the first name change in 1895, the *Journal of Near Eastern Studies* publishes original articles and book reviews dealing with a wide array of topics on the ancient and premodern Middle East. In carrying on the traditions of the earlier *Hebraica* and *American Journal of Semitic Languages and Literatures*, the *Journal of Near Eastern Studies* has served as a focus for scientific inquiry into ancient and medieval Middle Eastern civilizations in the United States for over 100 years. As editor George G. Cameron, a Chicago scholar of Persepolis and of Elamite linguistics, noted in the "Editor's Announcement" (1:1, January 1942), the editors of the preceding *American Journal of Semitic Languages and Literatures* "have always welcomed contributions on near eastern languages and literatures outside of the Semitic family (on Egyptian, Sumerian, Hurrian, Persian, Turkish, etc.) as well as on archeology and history—in short, on any scholarly subject dealing with the ancient, medieval, or modern Near East." The earlier *Hebraica*, although closely allied in spirit and functions, represented "the narrower, purely biblical emphasis on Old Testament studies which characterized the beginnings of interest in this field in America."[1]

Thus, the present *Journal* emerges as an evolutionary descendant of the early American understanding of the Middle East, an understanding that was in part rooted in the study of the Bible. Today the *Journal of Near Eastern Studies* describes itself as "the only periodical [in the United States] devoted exclusively to an examination of the ancient and medieval civilizations of the Near East." The *Journal* "also publishes studies of Near Eastern archeology, law, science, and economics."[2] The *Journal* has become, over the last generation, resolutely "premodern"; few studies of a distinctly contemporary interest in what is better known today as the Middle East appear in its pages. In this regard, *Journal* book reviews tend to be broader and more often encompass the present than do the articles. The *Journal*'s emphasis, however, is always on the past. The *Journal* retains the now somewhat curious phrase *Near Eastern* in its title as an indication of its own longevity, predating the use of the term *Middle East* and as a kind of definition of what "Near Eastern" tends to mean today: studies of the Middle

East in premodern periods. In turn, the premodernism of the *Journal* is revealed by its articles that cover the civilizations of the ancient Middle East and of Islam through what is often called medieval Islam.

As the publication of the Department of Oriental Languages and Literatures of the University of Chicago, the *Journal of Near Eastern Studies* can be identified with Orientalism and Oriental studies in the United States over the course of its existence as *Hebraica* and the *American Journal of Semitic Languages and Literatures*. According to Edward Said, author of *Orientalism*, "Orientalism is a style of thought based upon an ontological and epistemological distinction made between 'the Orient' and (most of the time) 'the Occident.' "[3] Orientalism, offers Said, tends to obscure the complexity of Middle Eastern realities by reducing the Middle East, its peoples and civilizations, to stereotypical distinctions between East and West in which the East is always less. But the scholarship displayed in the *Journal of Near Eastern Studies* is premised in bringing Middle Eastern subjects to light—and to a light relatively free from the impurities of Orientalism. The spirit of the *Journal* would seem to be one of evidence found, analyzed, and presented for examination. Conclusions are not always sought, nor are synthetic overviews. The *Journal*'s articles often maintain a narrow perspective, one rooted in the examination of fragments of evidence of antique civilization. In all, the common thread to the articles of the *Journal* is the reasoned analysis of historical evidence from classic Middle Eastern sources.

The traditional and typical subject matter of the *Journal of Near Eastern Studies* focuses on three areas: Middle East archaeology, biblical studies, and studies in the civilization of Islam in the premodern era. The *Journal* typically publishes three to five articles and some six to 10 book reviews; a number of special issues, devoted to a single theme or subject, have appeared. These include the "Erich F. Schmidt Memorial Issue" (24:3–4); the "XVIe Rencontre Assyriologique Internationale" (27:3); "Near Eastern Studies in Memory of Keith C. Seele" (37:2); and "Arab and Islamic Studies in Honor of Nadia Abbott" (40:3–4).

In many ways, the *Journal of Near Eastern Studies* is like a visit to the Oriental Institute at the University of Chicago. Scholars appear and reappear in its pages. Debate, more like conversation, emerges in articles and reviews through the years. Archaeological digs are announced and results presented. A Chicago tone emerges in the *Journal*, which says, "Speak to the evidence, present the case well, and the past shall be understood."

The scholar of religion will find that the *Journal* is a central focus for scholarship concerning ancient Middle Eastern religions, as well as biblical studies. Babylonian and Egyptian religions have been frequent subjects in the *Journal*. Studies in Jewish life also appear in the *Journal*, as in Moshe Gil's "The Jewish Quarters of Jerusalem (A.D. 638–1099) according to Cairo Geniza Documents" (41:261–78), an investigation that cuts across the fabric of traditional Middle Eastern urban society from several important directions. Old Testament studies are recently represented, for example, by Alberto R. Green's "Regnal Formulas in the Hebrew and Greek Texts of the Books of Kings" (42:167–180), or Hayim

Tawil's "The Historicity of 2 Kings 19:24 (=Isaiah 37:25): The Problem of Ye' Ōre Māṣôr" (41:195–206).

The *Journal of Near Eastern Studies* is a scholarly point of encounter for the classicists of Middle Eastern studies. The Middle East—in its many dimensions in the premodern age—is the *Journal*'s purview.

Notes

1. *Journal of Near Eastern Studies* 1:1 (January 1942).
2. Current format of caption page (inside cover), *Journal of Near Eastern Studies*.
3. Edward W. Said, *Orientalism* (New York: Pantheon Books, 1978), p. 2.

Information Sources

BIBLIOGRAPHY:
Said, Edward W. *Orientalism*. New York: Pantheon Books, 1978.
Speiser, E. A. "Near Eastern Studies in America, 1939–45." *Archiv Orientalni* 16 (1948):76–88.
INDEX SOURCES: *Modern Lanugage Abstracts, Current Contents, Social Sciences Citation Index, Language and Language Behavior Abstracts, Religious and Theological Abstracts, Humanities Index, Internationale Zeitschriftenschau für Bibelwissenschaft und Grenzgebiete.*
REPRINT EDITIONS: Walter Johnson Reprints (1942–64), University Microfilms International, Microforms International Marketing Co., Institute for Scientific Information.
LOCATION SOURCES: Union Theological Seminary (New York), Princeton University, Library of Congress, Catholic University of America, University of California-Berkeley, University of Chicago, and others.

Publication History

MAGAZINE TITLE AND TITLE CHANGES: *Hebraica* (1884–95), *American Journal of Semitic Languages and Literatures* (1895–1941), *Journal of Near Eastern Studies* (1942–).
VOLUME AND ISSUE DATA: *Journal of Near Eastern Studies* 1:1 (January 1942–). Appears quarterly in January, April, July, and October.
PUBLISHER AND PLACE OF PUBLICATION: University of Chicago, University of Chicago Press, Chicago.
EDITORS: George G. Cameron (1942–47), George G. Cameron and Keith C. Seele (1948), Keith C. Seele (1949–71), Robert D. Biggs (1972–).
CIRCULATION: 2275 (1982).

James A. Miller

JOURNAL OF PRESBYTERIAN HISTORY

In 1901 the Presbyterian Historical Society initiated publication of the *Journal of the Presbyterian Historical Society*. The starting of the *Journal* was meant to coincide with the fiftieth anniversary observance of the society in 1902. The *Journal* is the oldest denominational historical publication in the United States.[1]

The Presbyterian Historical Society had been organized in 1852 by the Old School Presbyterians. At the second annual meeting of the society, the constitution was amended to make possible the involvement of the New School Presbyterians, as well as other branches of American Presbyterianism. This inclusive spirit would characterize the journal launched by the society in the new century. "The Presbyterian Historical Society belongs to no single branch of the Presbyterian family." The new *Journal* wished to espouse what it called a "catholic Presbyterianism."[2]

The first editor was Louis A. Benson. Benson had served as minister of the Church of the Redeemer, Germantown, Pennsylvania. He was also a scholar, whose articles on hymnody would appear frequently in the ensuing years. Henry C. McCook, minister of the Tabernacle Presbyterian Church, Philadelphia, became editor in 1910 and served until his death in 1911. These two early editors set a high standard of scholarship but at the same time intended to produce a journal that would be read by pastors and laity.

"Catholic Presbyterianism" meant also that from the first the *Journal* was concerned not just with American Presbyterianism but with the larger Reformed tradition and family. Thus there were published in the early years articles on John Calvin, John Knox, and Isaac Watts, as well as on lesser-known European and British figures. At the same time the first issues contained sketches of what were then the nine branches of Presbyterianism in the United States.

Frederick W. Loetscher became editor in 1911. He would serve until 1941, garnering the longest tenure in the life of the publication. Professor of church history at Princeton Theological Seminary, Loetscher brought to the *Journal* a more systematic approach to the history of Presbyterians. Various eras and regions were to be studied, in addition to the regular materials on individuals, congregations, and presbyteries. In 1932, for example, on the occasion of the 225th anniversary of the Presbyterian Church in the United States of America, articles on three eras of American Presbyterian history since 1706 were contributed by William P. Finney, Clarence Edward Macartney, and Loetscher.[3] During Loetscher's tenure, in September 1930, the name of the publication was changed to the *Journal of the Department of History (The Presbyterian Historical Society) of the Presbyterian Church in the U.S.A.*, but in 1944 the title was changed back to the *Journal of the Presbyterian Historical Society*.

For more than three decades the *Journal* included considerable official news and notes about the parent society. In 1934 the format changed to almost exclusively articles and book reviews. Through the first six decades, more and more articles focused on American Presbyterians. There were occasional articles on Presbyterians in India or South Africa, but these essays were few. Within American religion the *Journal* has done better than some others in moving beyond the traditional occupation with the North and East. Sheldon Jackson's travels and church plantings, for example, have been treated by several authors. A bibliography of Clifford Merrill Drury, the foremost Presbyterian writing on the West, appeared in 1970.[4]

Significant changes occurred in the focus and scope of the publication in the 1960s. The present title, the *Journal of Presbyterian History*, was first used in the March 1963 issue. James Hastings Nichols became editor in the same year. Nichols, having just moved from the University of Chicago to Princeton Theological Seminary, brought to the *Journal* his own specialization in modern European church history, plus a variety of specialized interests. The primary focus continued to be American Presbyterians, but his interest in issues of church and state is seen in articles on John Calvin, John Witherspoon, and Woodrow Wilson.[5]

Nichols's ecumenical interests are also apparent during his tenure as editor. Presbyterians in the 1960s were leaders in the larger ecumenical movement while divided for more than a century within their own family. Ernest Trice Thompson put this North and South division in historical perspective with his article in 1965 on the history of efforts toward reunion. A larger perspective was offered by John T. McNeill in a 1966 contribution, "Foundations of Presbyterian Ecumenicity." In these same years, articles appeared giving overviews of the Presbyterian Church in Canada and Ireland.[6] Ecumenical rapprochement entered into the structure of the *Journal* itself. Under the initiative of Nichols, in 1966 the Historical Foundation of the Presbyterian Church in the United States was invited to join with the United Presbyterian Church in the U.S.A. in sponsoring the journal, so that before reunion occurred 17 years later, the *Journal* became a joint publication of the two denominations.[7]

The usefulness of the *Journal* to scholars was enhanced with the preparation in 1967 by Gerald W. Gillette of a "Checklist of Doctoral Dissertations on American Presbyterian and Reformed Subjects, 1912–1965."[8]

The present editor, James H. Smylie, began his service in 1969. Professor of American church history at Union Theological Seminary, Richmond, Virginia, in 1970 he wrote that for the decade of the 1970s, the *Journal* wanted "to cooperate more with the various agencies of the churches in order to give historical perspective to problems in evangelism, education, ethics, ecumenics, mission and other facets of the church's tradition."[9] This initiative has resulted in a number of special issues, including "Evangelism and Christian Experience" (51, 1973); "Black Presbyterians in Ministry" (51, 1973); "Missions and the American Ethos" (53, 1975); and "Changing Attitudes Toward Religion and the State" (54, 1976). "The United Presbyterian Church in Mission: An Historical Overview," was produced in 1979 (55) in cooperation with the Mission Council. In 1981 an issue on "Biblical Authority" (59) highlighted the work of a General Assembly Task Force on the nature of biblical authority.

In conjunction with the American bicentennial, two special issues were produced. "Presbyterians and the American Revolution: A Documentary Account" was published in 1974 (52). It was followed by "Presbyterians and the American Revolution: An Interpretive Account" in 1976 (54). These bicentennial publications were distributed widely and are significant not only because of the quality of the articles but because of the inclusion of chronologies, maps, lists of Presbyterians who served in various phases of the Revolution, prayers, and entries from diaries.

Smylie's creative editorship has brought to the *Journal* the ability to go beyond the usual verbal vehicle in telling the story. Popular culture had its day in a contribution by the editor on the career of William Jennings Bryan that included the lampoons of cartoons from *Punch, Judge*, and *Life*. In a more serious vein, Smylie contributed an article, "Presbyterian History in Stained Glass," with color photographs from churches throughout the country that depict aspects of the Presbyterian story.[10]

By way of format an annual section was added in 1970 that catalogs articles appearing in other journals "relating to Presbyterian and Reformed subjects of historical interest." An updating of doctoral dissertations on "American and Reformed Subjects" also appears from time to time.[11]

Smylie's editorial stance has been to strengthen ties with members of the American Reformed and Presbyterian family. In 1983 the Cumberland Historical Foundation was invited to be represented on the editorial board.

Notes

1. James H. Smylie, "The Presbyterian Historical Society: One Hundred and Twenty-five Years," *Journal of Presbyterian History* 55 (1977): 5 (hereafter cited as *JPH*).

2. *Journal of the Presbyterian Historical Society* 1 (1901–02): 4.

3. *Journal of the Department of History (The Presbyterian Historical Society) of the Presbyterian Church in the U.S.A.* 15 (1932–33).

4. Helen Bliss, "Bibliography of the Works of Clifford Merrill Drury, 1934–1959," *JPH* 48 (1970): 143–57.

5. John T. McNeill, "John Calvin on Civil Government," *JPH* 42 (1965): 166–74; and Arthur S. Link, "The Higher Realism of Woodrow Wilson," *JPH* 41 (1963): 1–13.

6. Ernest Trice Thompson, "Presbyterians North and South—Efforts toward Reunion," *JPH* 43 (1965): 1–15; John T. McNeill, "Foundations of Presbyterian Ecumenicity," *JPH* 44 (1966): 1–23; Allan L. Farris, "Presbyterianism in Canada, 1600–1957," *JPH* 44 (1966): 156–77; John M. Barkley, "The Presbyterian Church in Ireland," pt. I, *JPH* 44 (1966): 244–65, pt. II, 45 (1967): 33–48.

7. Smylie, "The Presbyterian Historical Society," pp. 1–12.

8. Gerald W. Gillette, comp., "Checklist of Doctoral Dissertations on American Presbyterian and Reformed Subjects, 1912–1965," *JPH* 46 (1967): 203–21.

9. James H. Smylie, "Format for the 1970s," *JPH* 48 (1970): 1.

10. James H. Smylie, "William Jennings Bryan and the Cartoonists: A Pictorial Lampoon, 1865–1925," *JPH* 53 (1975): 83–91, and "Presbyterian History in Stained Glass," *JPH* 57 (1979): 93–116.

11. Martha B. Aycock and Gerald W. Gillette, comps., "A Checklist of Doctoral Dissertations on American Presbyterian and Reformed Subjects, 1912–1982," *JPH* 61 (1983): 257–98.

Information Sources

BIBLIOGRAPHY:
Loetscher, Lefferts A. *The Broadening Church*. Philadelphia: Westminster Press, 1954.
INDEX SOURCES: *Poole's Index, Religion Index One, Revue d'Histoire Ecclesiastique,*

"Bibliographie," Writings on American History, Current Theological Discussion, America: History and Life, Religious and Theological Abstracts.

LOCATION SOURCES: Yale University, Princeton Theological Seminary, Presbyterian Historical Society (Philadelphia), Denver Public Library, Southern Methodist University, San Francisco Theological Seminary, and others.

Publication History

MAGAZINE TITLE AND TITLE CHANGES: *Journal of the Presbyterian Historical Society* (1901–30), *Journal of the Department of History (The Presbyterian Historical Society) of the Presbyterian Church in the U.S.A.* (1930–44), *Journal of the Presbyterian Historical Society* (1944–62), *Journal of Presbyterian History* (1962–   ).

VOLUME AND ISSUE DATA: *Journal of the Presbyterian Historical Society* 1:1–14:2 (1901–30), *Journal of the Department of History (The Presbyterian Historical Society) of the Presbyterian Church in the U.S.A.* 14:3–22 (1930–44), *Journal of the Presbyterian Historical Society* 22–40 (1944–62), *Journal of Presbyterian History* 40 (1962–   ).

PUBLISHER AND PLACE OF PUBLICATION: Presbyterian Church (U.S.A.), Philadelphia.

EDITORS: Louis F. Benson (1901–10), Henry C. McCook (1901–11), Frederick W. Loetscher (1911–41), Thomas C. Pears, Jr. (1942–43), Charles A. Anderson (1944–59), Guy S. Klett (1960–63), James Hastings Nichols (1963–68), James H. Smylie (1969–   ).

CIRCULATION: 1400 (1984).

Ronald C. White, Jr.

JOURNAL OF RELIGION

From the time George Burman Foster published *The Finality of the Christian Religion* in 1906, the University of Chicago began to be regarded as a center for radical activity in religion. Three years later, Foster published *The Function of Religion in Man's Struggle for Existence*. This work, and the controversy that arose because of it, sealed the radical reputation of the Chicago faculty, for Foster argued that supernaturalism had no place in religion; rather, religion should concern itself with the naturalism of a scientific approach. Religion, according to Foster, is to be concerned with human ideals, not divine purposes.[1]

Foster's work ushered in the beginning of a development in theology that later came to be known as the Chicago school. Shirley Jackson Case, Gerald Birney Smith, and Shailer Mathews gave this development its more fulfilled expression. The sociohistorical methodology, associated primarily with the work of Case, provided the Chicago school with its trademark.[2] Interested in measuring the religious worth of ideas by their "functional significance in the life of the people by whom they had been espoused," the sociohistorical method applied the presuppositions of pragmatic empiricism to the study of Christian thought and experience.[3] Concern for this scientific understanding of religion gave birth to the *Journal of Religion*, the union of two periodicals published by the Divinity School: *Biblical World** and the *American Journal of Theology**.

Biblical World, subtitled *A Journal of the Awakening Church*, was organized in 1893 in order to promote popular interest in the study of the Bible. At the time of its merger with the *American Journal of Theology*, *Biblical World* was edited by Shailer Mathews and reflected his interest in Social Gospel topics. The *American Journal of Theology*, on the other hand, was much less concerned with the social issues of its day. Its managing editors, Shirley Jackson Case and Gerald Birney Smith, emphasized the scholarly religious thinking of their time. The *American Journal of Theology*, established in 1897, represented a cool, detached, and academic approach to the religious sphere. The merger of these two periodicals, urged by Mathews, was necessitated by a financial crunch at the University of Chicago.

The faculty decided that the new journal should act as a *via media* between the concerns of the readerships of the *Biblical World* and the *American Journal of Theology*. Smith, the designated editor of the *Journal of Religion*, was convinced that the journal should avoid both the popular nature of *Biblical World* and the technical expertise of the *American Journal of Theology*. "This means," he wrote, "that we must exercise particular care to have a sufficient amount of material in each issue which shall not be too 'high brow.' "[4] "While the new journal will be as strictly scientific as the old [*American Journal of Theology*], it will restrict its field to the realm of vital religion."[5]

From faculty response to his inquiry, Smith accumulated a list of prospective contributors for the new journal.[6] In mid-October 1920, he sent a letter to them describing the nature and purpose of the journal:

> We intend to devote the pages of this new journal to the scholarly and persuasive discussion of religion in terms of actual human living. We believe that if the nature of religion is adequately understood, its indispensable place in modern culture will be recognized more widely, and the efforts of religious leaders will be reinforced. Religion in its historical, psychological, social, and theological aspects will constitute the field of the journal.[7]

Articles dealing with "documentary historical presuppositions to a study of religion itself" were to be rejected.[8] The journal was concerned with "vital rather than . . . literary sources of religion."[9]

Shortly after the appearance of the first number of the new journal, several letters were sent to Smith lamenting the loss of the technical aspects of the old *American Journal of Theology*. One disappointed reader went so far as to state that the first number "reads like a copy of the *Outlook.**"[10] Smith defended the new journal on two grounds. First, he claimed that the objectives of the *Journal* included "the task of educating a wider constituency into an appreciation of the scholarly attitude toward the problems of religion."[11] Second, Smith emphasized the pragmatic need "to keep in touch with our constituency." He repeatedly stated his perception that "however much we may lament it, . . . the religious leaders in this country are not as a rule prepared to welcome and appreciate very much technical discussion, unless such discussions are written in distinctly readable form."[12]

Shirley Jackson Case became editor of the *Journal* in 1927. As Bernard E. Meland has observed, "Seldom has an organ represented its sponsors more faithfully in matters of conviction and opinion than did the *Journal of Religion* during the years of Professor Case's editorship."[13] Case emphasized the historical and practical interpretation of religion; purely doctrinal discussions were avoided. But under the combined leadership of Bernard E. Meland and James Hastings Nichols in the late 1940s, the *Journal* underwent a stronger change of emphasis. Meland describes the shift as follows:

> What Professor Case sought to shunt off as doctrinal or philosophical has assumed something of a dominant emphasis. The historical concern has persisted; likewise the attention to practical problems; yet these have assumed a different character under the pressure of new demands. The difference in emphasis here is not one of editorship merely but of climate of thought.[14]

The role of the religious scholar had changed. "He is not only trying to understand Christianity as an objective historical movement; he is concerned to grasp the truth element as a guiding perspective upon problems of man's destiny which have become immediate and urgent."[15] If the Divinity School faculty of the 1940s had moved away from the purely sociohistorical method of the earlier Chicago school, it was still committed to an empirical approach to religious truth. "Abandonment of the empirical method as a source of religious understanding," commented Meland, "would have meant a relinquishment of the traditions of liberalism amounting to a neo-orthodoxy." Hence the *Journal* moved toward awakening all religious fields "to a common concern about the theological import of what they interpret."[16]

Today the *Journal* stands well within the tradition established over the last six decades. The most distinguishing characteristic of the *Journal* has always been its empirical approach to religion. This remains as true now as it ever was.[17] Yet the empirical method exhibited by articles within the present *Journal of Religion* reflects a much broader understanding of empiricism than that of the past. Many more cultural resources are being brought to bear on the study of religious experience. Current contributors to the *Journal* usually regard religious experience as inherently public. Therefore all disciplines interested in the study of human phenomena are used in the attempt to understand more fully and to interpret the nature of religious experience. Even highly specialized areas of religious inquiry are no longer considered off-limits.

Notes

1. For further discussion of Foster's role in the Chicago school, see Larry Axel, "The Root and Form of Meland's Elementalism," *Journal of Religion* 60 (October 1980): 479–82.

2. For a brief description of the sociohistorical method, see Bernard E. Meland, "The Chicago School of 'Theology," in *Twentieth Century Encyclopedia of Religious Knowledge*, ed. Lefferts A. Loetscher (Grand Rapids: Baker Book House, 1955), pp. 232–33. For a more complete treatment, see William J. Hynes, *Shirley Jackson Case and the Chicago School: The Socio-Historical Method* (Chico: Scholars Press, 1981). A brief essay dealing with the topic and written by Case himself appeared in the first number of the *Journal*. See Shirley Jackson Case, "The Historical Study of Religion," *Journal of Religion* 1 (January 1921): 1–17.

3. The phrase in quotation marks is from Shirley Jackson Case, "Education in Liberalism," in *Contemporary American Theology*, ed. Virgilius Ferm (New York: Roundtable Press, 1932), p. 113.

4. Gerald B. Smith to Robert E. Hume, 3 January 1921, *Journal of Religion* Archives, University of Chicago, 1921 box. Also see Gerald B. Smith to James B. Pratt, 21 February 1921, *Journal of Religion* Archives, 1921 box: "We are attempting in the initial numbers the somewhat difficult task of holding the subscribers to the *Biblical World* with the purpose of leading them gently and tactfully into the habit of reading more technical articles than appeared in the *Biblical World*."

5. Gerald B. Smith to Rev. John Donavan, 16 October 1920, *Journal of Religion* Archives, 1921 box. Also see his letter to Robert G. McLeod written on the same date.

6. The prospective contributors included Arthur C. McGiffert, William Adams Brown, Eugene W. Lyman, George A. Coe, Harry E. Fosdick, Henry S. Coffin, Harry F. Ward, Henry Churchill King, William E. Hocking, Charles W. Gilkey, George A. Barton, F. C. Porter, Rufus Jones, Albert Parker Fitch, and C. J. Cadoux.

7. Gerald B. Smith to prospective contributors, 16 October 1920, *Journal of Religion* Archives, 1921 box.

8. Gerald B. Smith to George A. Barton, 8 January 1921, *Journal of Religion* Archives, 1921 box.

9. Gerald B. Smith to C. A. Beckworth, 15 October 1920, *Journal of Religion* Archives, 1921 box.

10. James B. Pratt to Gerald B. Smith, 15 February 1921, *Journal of Religion* Archives, 1921 box.

11. Gerald B. Smith to Harry E. Fosdick, 9 February 1921, *Journal of Religion* Archives, 1921 box.

12. Gerald B. Smith to Edwin D. Starbuck, 5 February 1921, *Journal of Religion* Archives, 1921 box.

13. Bernard E. Meland, "A Time of Reckoning," *Journal of Religion* 29 (January 1949): 2.

14. Ibid.

15. Ibid., p. 3.

16. Ibid. The most celebrated attacks on the Chicago school came from the ranks of neo-orthodoxy. For a critical evaluation of the empirical school according to its own criteria, see H. Richard Niebuhr, "Value-Theory and Theology," in *The Nature of Religious Experience*, ed. J. S. Bixler, R. L. Calhoun, and H. R. Niebuhr (New York:

Harper and Brothers, 1937), pp. 93–116. Niebuhr here asserts that the empirical school belies its claim to disinterested scientific objectivity in the study of value by its arbitrary assumption that human-centered values provide adequate criteria for understanding God as the source of universal value. Also see Thomas Byrnes, "H. Richard Niebuhr's Christian Moral Philosophy" (Ph.D. dissertation, University of Chicago, 1982).

17. For a further analysis of the empirical tradition at the University of Chicago, see Bernard E. Meland, "Introduction: The Empirical Tradition in Theology at Chicago," in *The Future of Empirical Theology*, ed. Bernard E. Meland (Chicago: University of Chicago Press, 1969), pp. 1–62.

Information Sources

BIBLIOGRAPHY:

American Journal of Theology Archives. Regenstein Library Special Collections, University of Chicago.

Arnold, Charles H. *Near the Edge of Truth: A Short History of the Divinity School and the Chicago School of Theology.* Chicago: Divinity School Association, 1966.

Axel, Larry. "God or Man at Chicago: The 'Chicago School' of Theology, with Special Reference to the Roles of G. B. Foster, E. S. Ames, and H. N. Wieman." Ph.D. dissertation, Temple University, 1975.

Biblical World Archives. Regenstein Library Special Collections, University of Chicago.

Hynes, William J. *Shirley Jackson Case and the Chicago School: The Socio-Historical Method.* Chico: Scholars Press, 1981.

Journal of Religion Archives. Regenstein Library Special Collections, University of Chicago.

Meland, Bernard E. "The Chicago School of Theology." *Twentieth Century Encyclopedia of Religious Knowledge.* Lefferts A. Loetscher, ed. Grand Rapids: Baker Book House, 1955.

———, ed. *The Future of Empirical Theology.* Chicago: University of Chicago Press, 1969.

INDEX SOURCES: Indexed annually in no. 4 (October) of each volume. Also in *Religion Index One, Religious and Theological Abstracts, Humanities Index, Guide to Social Science and Religion in Periodical Literature, Internationale Zeitschriftenschau für Bibelwissenschaft und Grenzgebiete, Book Review Digest, Current Contents, Social Sciences Citation Index.*

REPRINT EDITIONS: University Microfilms International, Johnson Associates (microfiche), Microforms International Marketing Co., Institute for Scientific Information. Back issues, vols. 1–41, available from Walter J. Johnson; vols. 42- , from the University of Chicago Press.

LOCATION SOURCES: Atlanta Public Library, Library of Congress, University of Chicago, University of Pennsylvania, University of Southern California, University of Texas-Austin, and others.

Publication History

MAGAZINE TITLE AND TITLE CHANGES: *Journal of Religion* (1921–).

VOLUME AND ISSUE DATA: 1:1 (January 1921–). Published bimonthly, 1921–27; quarterly, 1928- .

PUBLISHER AND PLACE OF PUBLICATION: University of Chicago Press, Chicago.

EDITORS: Gerald Birney Smith (1921–26), Shirley Jackson Case (1927–39), John Knox
(1939–43), John T. McNeill (1943–44), Amos N. Wilder (1944–46), James H.
Nichols and Bernard E. Meland (coeditors, 1946–50), James H. Nichols, Bernard
E. Meland, and J. Coert Rylaarsdam (coeditors, 1950), James Luther Adams,
Bernard E. Meland, and J. Coert Rylaarsdam (coeditors, 1951–58), Bernard E.
Meland and J. Coert Rylaarsdam (coeditors, 1958–63), Bernard E. Meland, J.
Coert Rylaarsdam, and Nathan A. Scott, Jr. (coeditors, 1963–65), J. Coert Ry-
laarsdam and Nathan A. Scott, Jr. (coeditors, 1965–71), Schubert M. Ogden, J.
Coert Rylaarsdam, and Nathan A. Scott, Jr. (coeditors, 1971–72), B. A. Gerrish,
Nathan A. Scott, Jr., and David Tracy (coeditors, 1972–77), B. A. Gerrish, David
Tracy, and James M. Gustafson (coeditors, 1978–79), B. A. Gerrish and David
Tracy (coeditors, 1979–80), B. A. Gerrish, David Tracy, and Anthony C. Yu
(coeditors, 1980–   ).
CIRCULATION: 2300 (1982).

Mark G. Toulouse

JOURNAL OF RELIGIOUS ETHICS

The *Journal of Religious Ethics* was founded in 1973 to provide the emerging
discipline of religious ethics with a scholarly journal to help shape methodological
discussions and to publish new research in the field. It has also sought to encourage communication among religious ethicists, historians of religion, philosophers, and others concerned with religious belief systems, ethical commitment,
and actions claiming a moral basis.[1]

The *Journal of Religious Ethics*, preeminently an academic journal, owes its
origin to what founding editor Charles Reynolds describes as a dream in his
graduate student days. Reynolds, initially joined by Arthur Dyck, Frederick
Carney, and Roland Delattre, soon realized that they were filling an "academic
void."[2] Over 50 scholars served on the journal's editorial board in its first decade,
including many of the most respected ethicists in the United States. By 1981,
the Society of Christian Ethics and the American Academy of Religion were
formally represented on the editorial board, and support had been received from
several universities, foundations, and patrons.[3]

Like other academic disciplines, religious ethics—and the *Journal*—suffer
from and at times even glory in what might be termed an acute identity crisis.
As Glen Stassen has observed:

> For three years the Religious Social Ethics group [of the American Acad-
> emy of Religion] has been debating questions of method in the discipline.
> One question is whether anything holds the discipline together and gives
> it direction and definition, or whether like Don Quixote, it simply jumps
> on its horse and rides off in all directions at once. A second question is
> which candidates for the role of unifying paradigm have more promise and
> less pernicious bias than others.[4]

The *Journal of Religious Ethics* deliberately focuses attention on vexing questions concerning appropriate disciplinary boundaries. The consensus is that the religious ethicist must look in various directions: toward historians of religions, philosophical ethicists, "normative political theorists, cultural anthropologists, developmental and humanistic psychologists, sociological theorists, and interpreters of the aesthetic."[5] One might describe the assumption that unifies this variety of academic interests and approaches as a scholarly pluralism seeking responsible dialogue. In this context, state-of-the-discipline essays are explicitly invited.[6] The *Journal* also participates in the organization of thematic symposia where persons with different areas of expertise in religious ethics are brought together to address problems of mutual concern. Such colloquia are intended to generate material worthy of publication.

In order to serve a constituency with diverse interests, the journal devotes a substantial portion of each issue to a "focus" section that provides extended treatment of a single topic or thinker. One feature generally found in comparable journals, a book review section, inexplicably has not been included. An indication of the scope of the journal may be gathered from a listing of the "focus" sections of its first 10 years: "Virtue and Obligation in Religious Ethics" (Fall 1973), "Selected Issues in Medical Ethics" (Spring 1974), "Max Weber" (Fall 1974), "Religion and Morality: Frankena and the Scope of Religious Ethics" (Spring 1975), "Aesthetics and Ethics (Fall 1975), "Ethics and Mysticism" (Spring 1976), "Love and Society: The Ethics of Paul Ramsey" (Fall 1976), "Analysis and/or Advocacy—Critical Engagement with Ralph Potter on the Scope of Christian Social Ethics" (Spring 1977), "Historical Perspectives on Religious Ethics and Race" (Fall 1978), "Theravada Buddhist Ethics" (Spring 1979), "Liturgy and Ethics" (Fall 1979), "Hermeneutics and Ethics" (Spring 1980), "Jewish Law and Ethics" (Fall 1981), "Practical Moral Reasoning" (Spring 1982), and "The Ethics of Kierkegaard" (Fall 1982).

A commitment to methodological and substantive pluralism in religious ethics, as well as a distaste for "Western parochialism," are most clearly reflected in the singular attention that the fledgling discipline of comparative religious ethics has received in the *Journal of Religious Ethics*. Comparative religious ethics seeks to take seriously the religious and ethical claims of all cultures. In "Paradigms and Parameters for the Comparative Study of Ethics," Frederick Bird acknowledged the extreme difficulty of accomplishing this task:

> Making relevant comparisons of the moral ideas of different religious, ideological and cultural traditions is indeed difficult, especially if due appreciation is made for the particular meanings these ideas have for those who are influenced by them. Typically comparative studies have tended to produce facile superficial comparisons, ripping moral codes out of their social and philosophical contexts or reconceptualizing these norms in a neutral language that distorts their historical significance. Sometimes these errors have arisen out of an apologetic concern to point to the similarities between religious and ideological traditions.[7]

Comparative religious ethics provides a particularly appropriate arena in which to face the methodological dilemmas for religious ethics in general. Among the many questions that arise are: Is comparative ethics primarily descriptive? If so, is it properly subsumable under philosophy of religion? Or is it more properly carried on as part of the disciplines of history of religions or sociology of religions? Should comparative religious ethics address itself primarily to moral discourse and self-consciously philosophical reflection in religiously informed normative traditions, or should the stress fall more heavily on what the practitioners of the traditions have actually done? Should the appropriate conceptual tools be derived from the religious traditions under consideration rather than imported from the outside? In any event, can an outside analysis ever avoid the contamination of imported concerns? How does one construct, evaluate, and test "categories for comparison"? Finally, as the journal's editors pose the problem, "What are the respective contributions of the comparativist and the specialist who has mastered the languages and texts of a particular tradition?"[8] For those who write in the *Journal of Religious Ethics*, the plurality of values is a fact whose necessity may be regretted but never ignored. But, as described by Frederick Bird, what is to be avoided above all are "superficial or distorting comparisons." Rather, the intention is that "as it develops a repertoire of usable concepts and hypotheses, comparative ethics can promote a public, ecumenical discussion of moralities."[9]

Religious ethics, following such disciplines as history (with the rise of social history) and philosophy (such as in the form of ordinary language philosophy), continues to wrestle with the need to broaden its horizons beyond Western European elite culture to include a serious, respectful analysis of other human life-ways in order to see, among other matters, what there may be of enduring normative value in those traditions. Engagement with fundamental problems of this scope is characteristic of the aim and achievement of the *Journal of Religious Ethics*. The prominence of comparative religious ethics in this journal makes it clear that a moral bias in favor of pluralist, public, ecumenical discussion orients the *Journal of Religious Ethics* and the discipline it serves. In its treatment of the comparative study of religious ethics, the *Journal of Religious Ethics* reflects the problems as well as the possibilities of the discipline of religious ethics as practiced in North American academic circles beginning with the 1970s.

Notes

1. *Journal of Religious Ethics* 1 (1973): 3.
2. Ibid. 2 (1974): 1.
3. Ibid. 9 (1981): 153–54.
4. Ibid. 5 (1977): 1.
5. Ibid. 1 (1973): 4.
6. Ibid., pp. 3–4.
7. Ibid. 9 (1981): 161.

8. "Methodological Issues in Comparative Religious Ethics," *Journal of Religious Ethics* 7 (1979): 1–10.

9. Ibid. 9 (1981): 164.

Information Sources

BIBLIOGRAPHY:

Bird, Frederick. "Paradigms and Parameters for the Comparative Study of Ethics." *Journal of Religious Ethics* 9 (1981): 157–85.

"Methodological Issues in Comparative Religious Ethics." Editorial essay. *Journal of Religious Ethics* 7 (1979): 1–10.

INDEX SOURCES: *Religion Index One, Religious and Theological Abstracts, Philosopher's Index; Journal of Religious Ethics* 10:2 (1982) contains an index to vols. 1–10.

LOCATION SOURCES: University of Southern California, University of California-Riverside, University of Chicago, Andover-Harvard Theological Library, Princeton Theological Seminary, Union Theological Seminary (New York), University of Texas-Austin, and others.

Publication History

MAGAZINE TITLE AND TITLE CHANGES: *Journal of Religious Ethics* (1973–   ).

VOLUME AND ISSUE DATA: 1:1 (1973–   ). Published biannually in the spring and fall.

PUBLISHER AND PLACE OF PUBLICATION: American Academy of Religion, Scholar's Press, Missoula, Mont. (1973–77); University of Tennessee, Knoxville, Tenn., in association with other sponsoring agencies (1978–81); University of Notre Dame Press, Notre Dame, Ind. (1981–   ).

EDITORS: Charles Reynolds (1973–77), Charles Reynolds and James Childress (1977–81), James T. Johnson (1981–   ).

CIRCULATION: 1200 (1983).

Richard Milsom

JOURNAL OF RELIGIOUS STUDIES

In the winter of 1973, the Cleveland State University, under the aegis of its Department of Religious Studies, published the first issue of the *Ohio Journal of Religious Studies*. It has continued to appear twice each year, with the exception of 1978, when a delayed fall number was combined with that of spring 1979; that issue bore for the first time the title, *Journal of Religious Studies*.[1] Coinciding with a change of editors, this combined issue and its new title constituted a milestone in the short history of the publication, signaling a distinct and deliberate shift in the intent and character of the entire enterprise.

The comments of editor Frederick H. Holck in the first issue of the journal indicate that the publication's original aim was to function as an organ of the recently formed Ohio Academy of Religion (OAR), founded in 1968 as a successor to the Religion Section of the Ohio College Association (established 1925), and thus to serve as a medium of scholarly communication and dialogue among some 50 colleges and universities within Ohio. Consequently the editor, a faculty member at the sponsoring university, anticipated that contributions would come mainly from Ohio scholars and hoped that the provisional underwriting of expenses and assumption of editorial responsibility by his own university might be supplemented by direct financial and editorial support from other member institutions of the OAR.[2] Unvoiced, but probably implicit, was the expectation that the journal would provide especially the younger scholars in the state an opportunity to break into print in a modest, yet respectable scholarly forum.

From the outset, the *Ohio Journal of Religious Studies* maintained a generalist approach comparable to the broad spectrum of interests reflected in such contemporary national publications as the *Journal of the American Academy of Religion*.* Always well represented have been the areas of non-Christian religions, phenomenology of religion, historical and systematic theology, philosophy of religion, ethics, and American religion. Somewhat surprising, however, has been the paucity of articles in two of the growing areas of interest in the 1970s: women's studies and liberation theology.[3] Whether this fact represents a conservatism toward new trends on the part of either the editorial board or the contributors (or both) or merely a quirk in the availability of papers is not clear. In any case, the articles, though not generally authored by widely known scholars, have been consistently well conceived and well written, reflecting respectable if not rigid editorial standards.

Also explicit at the beginning was the intention of the journal to feature Ohio scholarship. The first five numbers, for example, offered only a single article each by non-Ohio scholars, as compared with four or more by Ohio scholars. In most subsequent numbers, however, out-of-state scholarship has outnumbered in-state scholarship by as much as four to one, though to date Ohio scholarship has managed to maintain a slight edge overall. Owing in part to this trend perhaps and coinciding with the arrival in the summer of 1978 of Derwood C. Smith as the new editor, the publication shortened its name to *Journal of Religious Studies* because, according to the first issue so titled, "its appeal and its circulation both reach beyond the state of Ohio."[4] Indeed recent issues have contained a preponderance of articles by non-Ohio scholars, and circulation statistics show that the distribution of the journal now extends well beyond the small membership of the OAR to libraries, educational institutions, and individuals all over the country.[5]

According to its second and current editor, this divergence from the journal's original intent to remain a parochial and provincial organ reflects its failure to attract a sufficient number of articles by Ohio scholars and the anticipated financial support from member institutions of the Ohio Academy of Religion other than the Cleveland State University, which continues to provide almost total subsidization for the publication. The editorial board, once dominated by faculty of that school, now has members from at least two other institutions of higher learning in Ohio and one from another state. The original ties with the OAR have been relaxed, and the editorial board continues to strive toward its present goal of making the publication an established and credible journal of scholarship representative of religious studies in general.[6]

Notes

1. Vol. 6:2 (Fall 1978) and Vol. 7:1, (Spring 1979). No explanation for the combination accompanied the double issue, but the change in editors was noted briefly, though anonymously and without explanation, on the title page overleaf.

2. "Editor's Note" and "Postscriptum Concludens," *Ohio Journal of Religious Studies* 1 (April 1973): 2, 58.

3. Vol. 4:1 (March 1976) was devoted entirely to women's issues and contained four research pieces and two essays on the subject. With the exception of one article in each of two recent issues, however, this special thematic number constitutes the only attention ever paid to feminist issues by the publication. More surprising still is the fact that on the broader but related theme of liberation, perhaps the most timely and intensely debated issue of the 1970s, not one article has appeared.

4. *Journal of Religious Studies* 6:2–7:1 (Fall 1978-Spring 1979): ii.

5. The circulation information included here was obtained from Susanna Hribsek, a student assistant of the Department of Religious Studies, the Cleveland State University.

6. Most of the observations in this paragraph are based on the reflections and observations of Derwood C. Smith, current editor of the *Journal of Religious Studies*, in a telephone conversation with the author of this article on 6 October 1982.

Information Sources

INDEX SOURCES: *Index to Religious Periodical Literature* (1973–76), *Religion Index One* (1977–   ).

LOCATION SOURCES: Cleveland State University, Library of Congress, Emory University, University of Florida, Pittsburgh Theological Seminary, Andover-Harvard Theological Library, Brigham Young University, and Union Theological Seminary (Richmond).

Publication History

MAGAZINE TITLE AND TITLE CHANGES: *Ohio Journal of Religious Studies* (1973–1978); *Journal of Religious Studies* (1978–   ).

VOLUME AND ISSUE DATA: *Ohio Journal of Religious Studies*, 1–6 (April 1973-April 1978); *Journal of Religious Studies*, 6- (Fall 1978-Spring 1979–   ).

PUBLISHER AND PLACE OF PUBLICATION: Cleveland State University, Cleveland, Ohio.

EDITORS: Frederick H. Holck (1973–78); Derwood C. Smith (1978–   ).

CIRCULATION: Approximately 225 (1982).

Paul A. Laughlin

THE JOURNAL OF RELIGIOUS THOUGHT

The *Journal of Religious Thought (JRT)* is published by the Howard University Press as a vehicle for the publication of papers, scholarly articles, book reviews, and writings of black scholars and others primarily interested in the black religious experience. The *JRT* was founded in 1944 to provide a forum through which scholars might publish articles and addresses presented at Howard University's Institute of Religion. William Stuart Nelson, dean and professor of theology at Howard's School of Religion, was the founding editor and the principal shaper of the journal's editorial policy. Educated at Howard and in Europe at Paris's Sorbonne, at Marburg, and at Berlin, Nelson brought a cosmopolitan and universal tone to the journal.[1] His concerns for civil rights and Gandhian nonviolence also shaped the journal's direction. During the 1940s and early 1950s, Nelson invited not only those papers in which black intellectuals were focusing on the black religious experience in the United States but also those in which they brought their judgments to bear on global problems. A paper by A. Campbell Garnett, "Group Tensions in the Modern World," is representative of this focus.[2] The journal also published articles by such eminent white scholars as Paul Lehmann, Paul Tillich, John C. Bennett, and Reinhold Niebuhr. Still, the central orientation was on the black scholar and his or her thoughts about the black religious experience.

In the 1960s, the journal reflected the activist concerns of that era by publishing articles that treated social ethics and Christian social action. The journal continued to provide articles on non-Christian religious traditions as well. Henry C. Clark's "Communicating the Gospel through Christian Social Action," and articles entitled "Amos of the 1960s," "Reflections on America's Social Ethics," and "God, Evil and Revolution," are representative of this era in the journal's publication focus.[3] The journal's concern for non-Christian religious traditions is evident in J. Deotis Roberts's article, "Madhva Logic According to the Pramanacandrika," and Afglabi Qlabimtan's, "Spiritual Hierarchy in Yoruba Traditional Religion."[4]

According to Cain H. Felder, the current editor, the journal went through a period of reappraisal of the black religious experience in the 1970s and 1980s.[5] This retrospective tone is evidenced in the journal's endeavors to come to grips with the significance of Martin Luther King, Jr., and the "Second Reconstruction Era (1915–1973)."[6]

In the late 1970s and early 1980s, the journal "sought again to diversify the types of articles."[7] This diversification sought to provide not only articles for the academic community, but also articles of special interest to clergy and churches. Acting editor Henry Justin Ferry wrote, "We reiterate our special interest in the particularity of Black religious experience; we affirm our concern to continue a recognized tradition of scholarship in this field."[8] The *JRT* continued these policies into the early 1980s. Retrospectives, articles with an international focus and those with appeal to clergy are evidenced by Herbert Aptheker's reassessment of W. E. B. DuBois's religious views, Patricia Jones-Jackson's article, "Oral Tradition of Prayer in Gullah," and Lawrence N. Jones's article, "Urban Black Churches: Conservators of Value and Sustainers of Community."[9] The journal is published semiannually and currently enjoys a circulation of around 400, describing itself as providing "an interdisciplinary approach to all religion."[10]

Notes

1. *Who's Who in America*, 37th ed. (1972–73), 2:2315.
2. *Journal of Religious Thought* 2 (1945): 123–32 (hereafter cited as *JRT*).
3. Ibid. 20 (1963–64): 3–18; Cain H. Felder, "*The Journal of Religious Thought*: Scholarly Dialogue at Howard about Religion over the Years" (unpublished typescript, 1983), p. 1.
4. *JRT* 20 (1963–64): 61–71, 31 (1974): 44–58.
5. Felder, p. 1.
6. Rayford W. Logan, "The Second Reconstruction Era—Has It Come to an End?" *JRT* 31 (1974): 5–11; George D. Kelsey, "Christian Faith and the Second Post-Reconstruction Era," *JRT*, pp. 12–24; James D. Tyms, "Moral and Religious Education for the Second Reconstruction Era," *JRT*, pp. 25–40; James P. Hanigan, Jr., "Martin Luther King, Jr.: The Images of a Man," *JRT*, pp. 68–95.
7. Felder, p. 1.
8. *JRT* 34 (1977–78): 5.
9. Ibid. 39 (1982): 5–11, 21–33; ibid. 39 (1982–83): 41–50.
10. *Directory of Publishing Opportunities in Journals and Periodicals* (Chicago: Marquis Academic Media, 1981), p. 195.

Information Sources

BIBLIOGRAPHY:
Felder, Cain H. "*The Journal of Religious Thought*: Scholarly Dialogue at Howard about Religion over the Years." Unpublished typescript, 1983.
INDEX SOURCES: *Religion Index One, Religious and Theological Abstracts, Index to Periodical Articles by and about Blacks*.
REPRINT EDITIONS: University Microfilms International.
LOCATION SOURCES: Howard University, Library of Congress, Emory University, Union Theological Seminary (New York), University of Chicago, and others.

Publication History

MAGAZINE TITLE AND TITLE CHANGES: *The Journal of Religious Thought* (1944–).
VOLUME AND ISSUE DATA: 1:1 (Spring-Summer 1944–). Appears twice yearly in Spring-Summer and Fall-Winter issues.
PUBLISHER AND PLACE OF PUBLICATION: Howard University, Washington, D.C.
EDITORS: William Stuart Nelson (1944–67), Samuel L. Gandy (1967–74), J. Deotis Roberts (1975–77, 1978–80), Henry J. Ferry (1977–78, 1981–82), Cain H. Felder (1983–).
CIRCULATION: 400 (1983).

James B. Hunt

JOURNAL OF SEMITIC LANGUAGES AND LITERATURES. *See* JOURNAL OF NEAR EASTERN STUDIES

JOURNAL OF THE AMERICAN ACADEMY OF RELIGION

A quarterly publication of the learned society for religious studies in the United States and Canada, the *Journal of the American Academy of Religion* (*JAAR*) reflects the emergence of the scholarly discipline of religious studies as it meets the professional needs of the academy's membership. The purpose of the journal was defined in the early 1960s: "The scholarly world demands an association and a publication that will effectively report and represent the synoptic realm of religion in and for its varied scholarly dimension."[1] Any sketch of the *JAAR* must begin with the National Association of Bible Instructors (NABI). NABI was founded in December 1909 by Ismar Peritz of Syracuse University, Irving Wood of Smith College, Chaplain Raymond Knox of Columbia, and Olive Dutcher of Mount Holyoke College. They brought instructors of biblical studies into association. Peritz, a Semitist and convert to Christianity, was the man of vision. He delighted in the fact that NABI spelled "prophet" in Hebrew, and he treated the Bible as a "tool," giving priority to students over subject matter. Charles Foster Kent of Yale University, the first president, was the man of organizational skill who did much to popularize the modern study of the Bible.

From the beginning, the *Journal of Bible and Religion**, NABI's periodical, had a pragmatic goal: it sought to educate Americans in the sacred literature of the Judeo-Christian traditions.[2] In the late 1950s, a conscious effort was made to transform NABI into a more scholarly society and the *JBR* into a more academic publication. Since the 1920s, calls for reform had been heard. In 1929, Irwin Beiler proposed a "National Association of Teachers of Religion in Colleges and Preparatory Schools"; from 1939 to 1942, Mary Andrews argued for an "Association for Study and Teaching Religion"; and in 1956, A. Roy Eckardt suggested an "Association of Religion Teachers." The organization of Bible instructors had experienced considerable growth. By the twenty-fifth anniversary in 1934, there were 345 members; by the fortieth in 1949, 760. Ten years later, in 1959, 1180 belonged to NABI.[3] By the early 1960s, agreement was reached for a more inclusive identity and organizational structure. The American Academy of Religion (AAR) officially emerged in January 1964. The AAR's publication took the name *Journal of the American Academy of Religion* with the July 1965 issue. Reports on the transition are found in the "Editorial Prefaces" of the *JBR* and the *JAAR*, where defining "religion" was a major theme. In the old *JBR*, "much is to be said for religion-in-general, as a scholarly principle." Further, "unless the NABI can more tellingly represent and foster religion-in-general . . . it will gradually fail in its essential function and may ultimately cease to exist."[4] A "rechristened" society and journal "can become a strong ally to the scholar seeking to maintain independence of scholarship, commitments of faith, and obligations to a profession." The new journal should be "an international forum cutting across traditional lines in creative conversation."[5] Two areas the *JAAR* would soon "cross-cut" were the philosophy of religion and theology, areas in which scholars had long sought participation in an organization like the American Philosophical Society.[6] In transition, A. Roy Eckardt of Lehigh University and Harry M. Buck of Wilson College served as editor and managing editor, respectively. In the 1960s, a time of change, the journal lost its sharp pedagogical focus. In 1970, the scope was widened and the professional purpose extended by the new editor and chief architect of the new *JAAR*, Ray L. Hart of the University of Montana.[7] At this time, articles like Raymond B. Williams's "Historical Criticism of a Buddhist Scripture: *The Mahāparinibbāna Sutta*," Hiroshi Obayashi's "Pannenberg and Troeltsch: History and Religion," Frederick Ferré's "The Definition of Religion," William A. Beardslee's "Hope in Biblical Eschatology and in Process Theology," Giles Gunn's "F. Scott Fitzgerald's *Gatsby* and the Imagination of Wonder," and David O'Brien's "American Catholicism and American Religion" appeared.

Ten years earlier AAR president Clyde A. Holbrook and the Self-Study Committee had found that most of the American scholarship in religion was done by scholars outside the traditional fields of Bible, theology, church history, and ethics.[8] By 1970, the *JAAR* was publishing articles by scholars in a variety of fields and, throughout the 1970s, the journal distinguished itself from periodicals like the *Journal of Biblical Literature**, the *Harvard Theological Review**, *Church History**, and the *Journal of Religion**. Editor Ray Hart saw the *JAAR* as "the journal of record" for religious studies.[9]

The rise of religious studies as an academic discipline redefined the purpose and the scope of the *JAAR* in the 1970s. Like other fields within the humanities, religious studies had experienced rapid growth in the 1960s, followed by retrenchment in the 1970s.[10] New membership introduced the interests of outside fields, including the cultural reflections on the context of the 1960s: LeRoy Moore's "From Profane to Sacred America: Religion and the Cultural Revolution in the United States," William H. Becker's "The Black Church: Manhood and Mission," James T. Johnson's "The Meaning of Non-Combatant Immunity in the Just War/Limited War Tradition," and John L. Cheek's "Paul's Mysticism in the Light of Psychedelic Experience." Larger trends in *JAAR* content pointed in two directions: studies in Asian religions–history of religions and theology-philosophy of religion. These two areas, represented by Robert S. Elwood, Jr.'s "Shinto and the Discovery of the History of Japan" and James W. Jones's "Reflections on the Problem of Religious Experience," held position in the *JAAR* alongside studies specifically within Judeo-Christian traditions. From 1970 to 1976, these two new interests outdistanced every other area in the number of manuscripts submitted and accepted by a measure of almost two to one. Descriptive studies, East and West, remained strong, as did entries in philosophy-theology. In the late 1970s, interest in religion and the arts, especially literature, came to rank in number with historical and constructive studies.[11]

The format of the new journal was also extended in the 1970s. A book review supplement was published in June 1975 in order to treat the many new publications. Sections for discussion from regional and annual gatherings informed readers of the profession's activities. Theme issues, "New Testament from a

Process Perspective" and a bicentennial piece, "The Restitution of True Religion and the Institutions of Sidney E. Mead," helped organize the new data of religious studies.[12] In 1977, Hart took the journal a step further, introducing the "journal of the future," which contained "three or four articles of general, field-spanning interest" and, in addition to reviews and booknotes, a set of abstracts "of a substantial number (normally, sixteen) in specialized areas." An order form accompanied each new issue so that abstracted articles could be purchased by mail. The innovation promised a professional journal that would "be limited in the number of MSS it can accept only by considerations of *quality*." The new format had the additional advantage of being inexpensive.[13] The new format did not last. Religious studies had grown many times in size, but its members had been specializing in diverse areas. A loss of vitality in the humanities along with area specialization conspired against Hart's innovative journal format. In spite of the fact the the *JAAR* had increased its number of pages over 500 percent (in 1950, 280 pages were published annually; in 1977, the number was 1600), few abstracts were ordered.[14]

Ray Hart's efforts in the 1970s, however, went a long way toward securing membership of the AAR in the American Council of Learned Societies (to which Hart became the AAR's first delegate). In 1980, Robert P. Scharlemann of the University of Virginia became editor. As the seventy-fifth anniversary of the founding of the National Association of Bible Instructors is celebrated, Scharlemann continues to define the new discipline of religious studies by seeing that the *JAAR* "serves the double purpose of being a vehicle for academic publication in all fields of religious studies, and of representing the Academy that sponsors it."[15]

Notes

1. "Editorial Preface," *Journal of Bible and Religion* 30 (July 1962): 185–86 (hereafter cited as *JBR*).

2. Olive Dutcher Doggett, "Golden Memories of a Charter Member," *JBR* 28 (April 1960): 159–60.

3. Dwight Marion Beck, "Reminiscences of the Association," *JBR* 28 (April 1960): 207.

4. "Editorial Preface," *JBR* 30 (July 1962): 185.

5. [Harry M. Buck, Jr.], "Editorial Preface," *JBR* 30 (October 1962): 267–68.

6. John H. Hick, "Theological Table-Talk," *Theology Today* 19 (October 1962): 408–09.

7. Claude Welch, "Editorial Preface," *Journal of the American Academy of Religion* 37 (December 1969): 319–20 (herafter cited as *JAAR*).

8. Clyde A. Holbrook, "Why an Academy of Religion?" *JAAR* 32 (April 1964): 97–98.

9. Ray L. Hart, "The Journal of Changes," *JAAR* 47 (September 1979): 369.

10. Claude Welch, "Identity Crisis in the Study of Religion? A First Report from the ACLS Study," *JAAR* 39 (March 1971): 3–18.

11. Ray L. Hart, "*JAAR* in the Seventies: Unconcluding Unscientific Postface," *JAAR* 47 (December 1979): 513–14.

12. William A. Beardslee and David J. Lull, eds., "New Testament from a Process Perspective," *JAAR* 47 (March 1979); "In Lieu of a Bicentennial Issue: The Restitution of True Religion and the Institutions of Sidney E. Mead," *JAAR* 44 (March 1976).

13. Ray L. Hart, "*Editorial*: The Presence of the Journal of the Future," *JAAR* 45 (March 1977): 4–5.

14. Ibid., p. 5.

15. Robert P. Scharlemann, "'Publishing in Scholarly Journals: Advising Junior Colleagues," *Bulletin of the Council on the Study of Religion* 15 (June 1984): 73.

Information Sources

BIBLIOGRAPHY:

Doggett, Olive Dutcher. "Golden Memories of a Charter Member." *Journal of Bible and Religion* 28 (April 1960): 159–60.

Funk, Robert W. "The Learned Society as Publisher and the University Press." *Bulletin of the Council on the Study of Religion* 4 (June 1973): 3–13.

Hart, Ray L. "*JAAR* in the Seventies: Unconcluding Unscientific Postface." *Journal of the American Academy of Religion* 47 (December 1979): 509–16.

Holbrook, Clyde A. "Why an Academy of Religion?" *Journal of the American Academy of Religion* 32 (April 1964): 97–105.

Welch, Claude. "Identity Crisis in the Study of Religion? A First Report from the ACLA Study." *Journal of the American Academy of Religion* 39 (March 1971): 3–18.

INDEX SOURCES: Self-indexed at the end of each volume, except index for vols. 1–25 in 28 (1960); also in *Old Testament Abstracts, New Testament Abstracts, Social Science Citation Index, Current Contents, Religion Index One, Guide to Social Science and Religion in Periodical Literature, Religious and Theological Abstracts, Humanities Index.*

REPRINT EDITIONS: University Microfilms International.

LOCATION SOURCES: Brown University, Library of Congress, Princeton Theological Seminary, Union Theological Seminary (New York), University of Chicago, Yale University, and others.

Publication History

MAGAZINE TITLE AND TITLE CHANGES: *Journal of Bible and Religion* (1933–64), *Journal of the American Academy of Religion* (1965–).

VOLUME AND ISSUE DATA: *Journal of Bible and Religion* 1:1–32:4 (January 1933-October 1964), *Journal of the American Academy of Religion* 33:1 (January 1965–).

PUBLISHER AND PLACE OF PUBLICATION: National Association of Biblical Instructors, Garden City, N.Y. (1933–38), Somerville, N.J. (1939–46), Baltimore, Md. (1947–52), Brattleboro, Vt. (1953–63), Philadelphia, Pa. (1963–64); American Academy of Religion, Philadelphia, Pa. (1965–70), Missoula, Mont. (1971–79), Chico, Calif. (1980–).

EDITORS: Ismar J. Peritz (1933–36), Carl E. Purinton (1937–60), A. Roy Eckardt (1961–67), Harry M. Buck (Acting, 1963–64, 1968–69), Ray L. Hart (1970–79), Robert P. Scharlemann (1980–).

CIRCULATION: 5120 (1983).

John Kloos

JOURNAL OF THE AMERICAN ORIENTAL SOCIETY

At an informal meeting in the Boston law office of John Pickering in August 1842, a few men discussed the formation of an American Oriental Society. Subsequent meetings on 7 September and 13 October led to the creation of the society, the election of additional members, and preliminary adoption of a constitution and bylaws. An act of incorporation was applied for, and the first meeting of the incorporated society was held on 7 April 1843.[1] The act of incorporation specified the purpose of the society to be "the cultivation of learning in the Asiatic, African, and Polynesian languages." This purpose was further defined in the first constitution and bylaws of the society adopted 7 April 1843, which specified the additional objectives of the society to be "the publication of Memoirs, Translations, Vocabularies, and other works relating to the Asiatic, African, and Polynesian languages" and "the Collection of a Library."[2] Pickering was named president of the society, and William Jenks, Moses Stuart (the distinguished conservative theologian from Andover Seminary), and Edward Robinson were named vice-presidents.

The first volume of the *Journal of the American Oriental Society* consisted of four parts, which were published separately from 1843 to 1849. Pickering was asked to address the society at its first annual meeting in May 1843, and that address was published in full in volume 1. In his address he elaborated the aims of the society and gave eloquent expression to the high expectations for the study of the Orient, which had provided the impetus for the society. He stressed the existing peace with the nations with which it was essential to cooperate in "the investigation of the history, literature and science of the East," the improved communications, and the numbers of missionaries and scholars "who are now spread over the most interesting regions of the civilized East."[3] The recent successes of Edward Robinson, whose research in Palestine in 1838 with his missionary friend and student Eli Smith had been published simultaneously in Halle, Boston, and London in 1841, and Champollion's successful decipherment of Egyptian hieroglyphics some two decades earlier had generated excitement about the potential for great advances in knowledge.

Pickering's recognition of the importance of the missionaries for this advance in knowledge of the Orient is echoed in the report on the relationship of the society to the missionaries in the Orient. In his report to the committee of publication, Dr. Rufus Anderson affirmed the benefits of this mutual relationship in general but emphatic terms: "American missionaries are likely to be our most productive source of information, and that it is among the most important duties of the Society to render their labors, as far as may be, of direct avail to science."[4] The early volumes of the *Journal* reflect this symbiotic relationship in the numbers of articles submitted by missionaries of the American Board of Commissioners for Foreign Missions and other missionary societies.[5]

From their inception, the society and its journal have been characterized by a dominant interest in language, which derives in part from Pickering's own scholarly concerns, as well as from the centrality of language and linguistics to the missionary enterprise.[6] Although language was central, it was by no means the only concern of the society and the *Journal*. Pickering himself identified the subject area as

> of almost boundless extent—the history, languages, literature, and general characteristics of the various people, both civilized and barbarous, who are usually classed under the somewhat indefinite name of *Oriental* nations; including not only those nations who at this day are inhabitants of Asia, but those who in ages past had their origin from Asiatic ancestors, and have been driven by wars, or other causes, from their original home into Africa or Europe, but have still kept up their original character, and are properly to be considered as Orientals.[7]

The aims of the society and its objectives have remained constant. A recent pamphlet describing the society and its publications identifies the aims of the society as humanistic and stresses the centrality of the languages and literatures of Asia in its tradition, while noting the inclusion of "such subjects as philology, literary criticism, textual criticism, paleography, epigraphy, linguistics, biography, and the history of the intellectual and imaginative aspects of Oriental civilizations, especially of philosophy, religion, folklore and art."[8] This variety of interest is reflected in the articles of the first volume, which included, in addition to Pickering's "Address," "A Treatise on Arab Music," "Memoir on the History of Buddhism," "The History of Paper Money in China," "China: Its Population and Trade; and the Prospect of a Treaty," and an "Extract from the *Journal Asiatique*, on the Progress made in reading the Cuneiform Inscriptions."

Some early volumes were given over to the presentation of a critical edition of an important text. Volume 9 (1871) contained only one major article, "The Tâittirîya-Prâtiçâkhya, with Its Commentary, The Tribhâshyaratna: Text, Translation, and Notes," by the distinguished philologist, William D. Whitney, professor of Sanskrit in Yale College. Early volumes had contained articles by missionaries and occasionally by diplomatic personnel; by the fifteenth volume, which coincided with the fiftieth anniversary of the society, articles were by major scholars at the most distinguished educational institutions: George A. Barton of Harvard University, Richard Jewett of Brown University, Maurice Bloomfield of the Johns Hopkins University, Morton W. Easton of the University of Pennsylvania, A. V. Williams Jackson of Columbia University, and Hanns Oertel of Yale University, among others.

The breadth of interest and a high quality of scholarship evident from the beginning have characterized the society and the *Journal* throughout their existence. There has been a remarkable consistency of purpose, subject matter, and scholarship in the *Journal* during its long history. The editors and contributors have been the best scholars in the various fields embraced by the aims of the society. All periods of history are regarded as appropriate subject matter, and although initially membership in the society was by election, membership is now open to all persons who have an interest in the Orient.[9]

Notes

1. "Extract from the Report of a Committee of the American Oriental Society," *Journal of the American Oriental Society* 1 (1943–49): ii (hereafter cited as *JAOS*).
2. Constitution of the American Oriental Society; Adopted April 7, 1843; Article II, printed in *JAOS* 1 (1843–49): vi.
3. John Pickering, "Address at the First Annual Meeting," *JAOS* 1 (1843–49): 1–2.
4. "Proceedings of the Society: Meeting of January 5, 1848," *JAOS* 1 (1843–49): xli.
5. For example, in volume 4 (1853–54), eight of the 12 major articles were by missionaries of the American Board and the American Baptist Missionary Union.
6. A jurist by profession, Pickering served as city solicitor for Boston. His scholarly achievements included the mastery of the principal European and Semitic languages, some acquaintance with Chinese, and an authoritative command of the languages of the North American Indians. His major work was *Comprehensive Lexicon of the Greek Language* (Boston: B. Wilkins, Carter & Co., 1846). Other works were "Remarks on the Indian Languages of North America" (1836) and "Vocabulary of Americanism." Cf. Joseph Thomas, *Universal Pronouncing Dictionary of Biography and Mythology*, new 3d ed. (Philadelphia: J. B. Lippincott Co., 1908), 2:1951.
7. Pickering, "Address," p. 5.
8. *American Oriental Society: Founded 1842* (n.d.).
9. I thank Judy Crocker, American Oriental Society administrator, for technical information and Rosanne Rocher for references to her unpublished typescript on the society's history.

Information Sources

BIBLIOGRAPHY:
American Oriental Society: Founded 1842. n.d.
"Extract from the Report of a Committee of the American Oriental Society." *Journal of the American Oriental Society* 1 (1843–49): ii.
Pickering, John. "Address at the First Annual Meeting." *Journal of the American Oriental Society* 1 (1843–49): 1–60.
"Preface." *Journal of the American Oriental Society* 21 (1900). Details publication of the society's proceedings to 1900.
Rocher, Rosanne. "History of the American Oriental Society." Mimeographed. Philadelphia: South Asia Regional Studies, University of Pennsylvania, 1971.
INDEX SOURCES: "Index to the Journal of the American Oriental Society," *Journal of the American Oriental Society* 21 (1900); *Index to the Journal of the American Oriental Society, Volumes 21 to 60*, comp. Edward H. Schaffer, Isisdore Dyen, Helen E. Fernald, and Harold W. Glidden. American Oriental Series, 40. New Haven: American Oriental Society, 1955, prepared for the society's centennial; *Current Contents, Humanities Index, Religion Index One*.
REPRINT EDITIONS: University Microfilms International.

LOCATION SOURCES: Library of Congress, University of California-Berkeley, Yale University, University of Illinois, Harvard University, Princeton Theological Seminary, Duke University, and others.

Publication History

MAGAZINE TITLE AND TITLE CHANGES: *Journal of the American Oriental Society* (1843–49–   ).

VOLUME AND ISSUE DATA: Published irregularly until 1896; 1 (1843–49), 2 (1851), 3 (1852–53), 4 (1853–54), 5 (1855–56), 6 (1860), 7 (1862), 8 (1866), 9 (1871); 10 (1872–80), 11 (1882–85), 12 (1887), 13 (1889), 14 (1890), 15 (1893), 16 (1894–96), 17 (1896), 18 (1897–   ).

PUBLISHER AND PLACE OF PUBLICATION: George P. Putnam and Co., New York (1849–54); American Oriental Society, New Haven, Conn. (1855–   ).

EDITORS: Committee of Publication (1849–96); committees of editors (1896–1936), with the exception of George F. Moore (1898–1900) and Charles C. Torrey (1915); W. Norman Brown (1937–40), Zellig S. Harris (1941–47), Murray B. Emeneau (1948–51), James B. Pritchard (1952–53), Henry M. Hoenigswald (1954–56), Edward H. Schafer (1958–63), Ernest Bender (1964–   ).

CIRCULATION: 2200 (1984).

Harold O. Forshey

JOURNAL OF THE DEPARTMENT OF HISTORY (THE PRESBYTERIAN HISTORICAL SOCIETY) OF THE PRESBYTERIAN CHURCH IN THE U.S.A.
See JOURNAL OF PRESBYTERIAN HISTORY

JOURNAL OF THE EVANGELICAL THEOLOGICAL SOCIETY

The Evangelical Theological Society was organized in 1949 in Cincinnati, Ohio "to foster conservative Biblical scholarship by providing a medium for the oral exchange and written expression of thought and research in the general field of the theological disciplines as centered in the Scriptures."[1] The single-article doctrinal statement to which members subscribe affirms that "the Bible alone, and the Bible in its entirety, is the Word of God written, and therefore inerrant in the autographs."[2] The confluence of data, location, purpose, and doctrinal statement place the society's roots squarely within the postwar revival of revivalism. The Evangelical Theological Society, however, is rarely recognized for its important contribution to that revival, the attempt to replace fundamentalism's reputation for anti-intellectualism with serious scholarship and an awareness of outside currents of thought.

The society began as a fellowship of like-minded evangelical scholars and students, with a smattering of pastors, writers, missionaries, and others included.

At first ideas were shared informally by word of mouth and mimeographed material. Insofar as they surfaced into the public realm, they did so through the published work of society members. The *Bulletin of the Evangelical Theological Society* appeared in 1958 when the growth of the society required a more formal means of communicating business. In turn, the *Bulletin* became the *Journal of the Evangelical Theological Society* in 1969 to increase the society's influence within and without the evangelical community.

The contribution of the society to the renaissance of scholarship among a broad range of evangelicals is substantial. The single article of doctrine provided a point of unity for scholars who, however much they might disagree on other issues, shared a view of Scripture's authority, which made them feel more at home with one another than with other Protestant biblical scholars. Membership has been drawn from such confessional schools as Concordia, St. Louis (Lutheran Church, Missouri Synod), Calvin College (Dutch Reformed), Westminster Theological Seminary (the seceder Orthodox Presbyterian Church); evangelical strongholds such as Wheaton College; non-Calvinist evangelical schools such as Asbury and Nazarene Theological seminaries; denominational schools such as Trinity, Northern Baptist (Chicago), and Conservative Baptist (Denver) seminaries; Bible schools and related nondenominational seminaries such as Moody Bible Institute, Bible Institute of Los Angeles, Talbot, Fuller, and Dallas seminaries; and such fundamentalist schools as Bob Jones University and William Jennings Bryan University (Dayton, Tennessee). A list of individual members includes Oswald T. Allis, Cleason Archer, Charles L. Feinberg, John Carnell, Merrill Tenny, Harold Lindsell, Kenneth Kantzer, John Warwick Montgomery, Martin J. Wyngarden, R. B. Kuiper, Cornelius Van Til, Frank E. Gaebelein, Merrill Unger, Julian C. McPheeters, William Culbertson, Clark Pinnock, and Carl F. H. Henry.

The society's greatest strength derives from the evangelical rather than the confessional or fundamentalist wings of the Protestant Right. While coincidental, it is significant that Carl F. H. Henry was the first of several editors of *Christianity Today** to be a member. Regionally, the center of membership consists of a band extending from the Middle Atlantic states through the upper Midwest and tapering to California, with the focal point in the Chicago metropolitan area, as witnessed by the number of members drawn from schools close to Chicago and the association of each editor of the *Journal* with Wheaton College.

Lacking commitment to the particulars of a tradition, as well as the ethnicity of many older denominations, the society is but half a home to confessional bodies. The inerrancy banner draws some with a concern for the issue (Missouri Synod Lutheran) or a tradition to contribute (the Princeton theology of some Presbyterian bodies) but is counterbalanced by a spirit of evangelical alliancing— profound disregard for barriers endemic to American ecumenism—so troubling to confessional particularity. Relations with the fundamentalist wing have not been without tension. Militant fundamentalists committed to inerrancy find the brevity of the doctrinal statement, the benign attitude toward doctrinal divergence among members, and the sympathetic observation of nonevangelical Christians problematic. A different issue of style—North versus South, white versus black and ethnic—limits participation by southern Protestants, especially Southern Baptists, as well as members of minority evangelical denominations.

The influence of the evangelicals of the center may be seen in the progress of the *Journal*. As befits the statements of purpose and doctrine, articles lean heavily toward biblical studies. Disciplines traditionally coupled with biblical studies, such as hermeneutics and, for evangelicals, apologetics, are joined by philosophy, linguistics, and church history where they touch or are seen to touch on the meaning and purpose of Scripture. For example, a topic to enter the journal in this manner is the relationship between science and faith, Genesis and evolution, although the society has remained aloof from the creationist controversy. The centrality of biblical studies from a conservative perspective has also been affected over the years by another evangelical concern, the devotion to education and scholarship. This item helps explain the periodic disturbances in the society and the *Journal* over inerrancy itself. From the first issue of the *Bulletin* through the early 1960s, devotion to scholarship could be detected not only in the consistently high quality of the articles presented (usually by younger members close to dissertations and research commitments) but also in the serious attempt to interact with developments among nonevangelical scholars. Neo-orthodoxy in general, and Karl Barth in particular, came in for sympathetic treatment as a hopeful development in Protestantism. From neutral-to-approving critiques to citations from the *Dogmatics* in support of a position, Barth's influence grew. Although few evangelicals would have claimed to have become Barthians, Barth's devotion to scholarship earned him considerable admiration.

In 1965 reaction set in. Concern was mounting over defections from the inerrancy position, among both individual members of the society and formerly secure educational institutions. For the society, concern led president Gordon H. Clark to draw the lines in his 1966 address to the annual meeting, reaffirming the inerrancy position and inviting any who did not accept the position to resign.[3] For the *Journal*, concern led to a counterattack. Old Testament scholar Samuel J. Schultz, its editor, invited a young historian, John Warwick Montgomery, to lead the charge not only as a contributor but also in the fall of 1965 as guest editor. If Montgomery became the knight inerrantist in this contest, Barth became the villain, and positive interaction all but ceased.[4] In its place, the *Journal* was devoted to a detailed working out of the implications of inerrancy. Inerrancy was considered not only for its impact on evangelical doctrine but even for its implications with regard to issues of canonicity, Bible translation, and the nature of God.[5]

In the early 1970s, the agenda interrupted in 1965 began to reassert itself. Interest turned toward developments in the field of biblical studies, and the tools of nonevangelical Biblical scholars came under scrutiny. As the 1970s progressed, observation in some instances became questions of when, how, and how far such tools could be used.[6] Schultz retired as editor and was replaced by Ronald Youngblood. Articles were again written by younger scholars close to their sources. Occasional echoes were heard. Clark Pinnock, who took the inerrantist position against Daniel B. Fuller, Jr., in the early 1970s, was himself called to account by a society "young Turk" in the early 1970s.[7] Ironically, however, the society's credentials on inerrancy were not upheld. When inerrancy became a news item in the late 1970s, the call for a definitive formulation on the question was answered by a new body, the International Council on Biblical Inerrancy. Society members contributed to the deliberations, the position worked out in the *Journal* of the mid–1960s was foundational, and the resulting document (the Chicago Statement on Biblical Inerrancy) was published in its pages, but the society itself played no direct part.[8]

Notes

1. This statement is published on the inside cover of each issue of the *Journal*.
2. Ibid.
3. Gordon H. Clark, "The Evangelical Theological Society Tomorrow," *Bulletin of the Evangelical Theological Society* 9 (1966): 9–12.
4. Demonstrations of this revised view of neo-orthodoxy may be found in ibid., p. 11, and in John Warwick Montgomery, "Guest Editorial," *Bulletin of the Evangelical Theological Society* 8 (1965): 125–26.
5. See, for instance, Burton L. Goddard, "Concerns in Bible Translation," *Bulletin of the Evangelical Theological Society* 10 (1967): 85ff.
6. See, for instance, David O'Brien, "David the Hebrew," *Journal of the Evangelical Theological Society* 23 (1980): 193–206.
7. Rex A. Koivisto, "Clark Pinnock and Inerrancy: A Change of Truth Theory?" *Journal of the Evangelical Theological Society* 24 (1981): 139–51.
8. "The Chicago Statement on Biblical Inerrancy," *Journal of the Evangelical Theological Society* 21 (1978): 289–96.

Information Sources

INDEX SOURCES: *New Testament Abstracts, Christian Periodicals Index, Religious and Theological Abstracts, Religion Index One (Index to Religious Periodical Literature), Old Testament Abstracts.*
REPRINT EDITIONS: University Microfilms International.
LOCATION SOURCES: Back issues available from the Evangelical Theological Society; also at the Billy Graham Archives, Wheaton College, and others.

Publication History

MAGAZINE TITLE AND TITLE CHANGES: *Bulletin of the Evangelical Theological Society* (1958–68), *Journal of the Evangelical Theological Society* (1969–　).
VOLUME AND ISSUE DATA: *Bulletin of the Evangelical Theological Society* 1:1–11:4 (1968–1958); *Journal of the Evangelical Theological Society* 12:1 (1969–　).
PUBLISHER AND PLACE OF PUBLICATION: Evangelical Theological Society, Minneapolis.

EDITORS: Neil J. Winegarden (1958–63), Samuel J. Schultz (1963–75), Ronald Young-
    blood (1975–   ).
CIRCULATION: 1900–2000 (1982).

Daniel L. Swinson

JOURNAL OF THE NATIONAL ASSOCIATION OF BIBLICAL INSTRUCTORS. *See* JOURNAL OF BIBLE AND RELIGION

JOURNAL OF THE PRESBYTERIAN HISTORICAL SOCIETY. *See* JOURNAL OF PRESBYTERIAN HISTORY

JOURNAL OF THE UNIVERSALIST HISTORICAL SOCIETY. *See* PROCEEDINGS OF THE UNITARIAN-UNIVERSALIST HISTORICAL SOCIETY

JUDAISM

From the appearance of its first issue in January 1952, *Judaism: A Quarterly Journal of Jewish Life and Thought* has striven to provide a nondenominational forum for discussion of Jewish religion, philosophy, and ethics.[1] Under the sponsorship of the American Jewish Congress, whose "unwavering support" the journal enjoys, *Judaism* "continues to occupy a special niche among Jewish periodicals the world over."[2]

During the years preceding 1952, a number of Jewish leaders, including Robert Gordis and Milton Steinberg, came to realize the need for a journal "on Jewish theology transcending organizational barriers." After considering several possible directions in which such a publication could go, these individuals secured the support of the American Jewish Congress, which was at that time "casting about for a concrete project which it might undertake to enhance the quality of Jewish life in America." Will Herberg, whose earlier *Commentary** article "From Marxism to Judaism" had attracted wide notice, was the somewhat controversial choice of Gordis and others to serve as *Judaism*'s first editor.[3] Four other men, including Gordis, have also headed this journal.[4]

Judaism appears four times a year, with the first number of each volume being a winter issue (for example, 30:1 is the Winter 1981 issue, followed by issues in the spring, summer, and fall of 1982). The total number of pages in each volume usually runs to just over 500. An index to each volume, arranged alphabetically according to authors and divided into two or three sections (articles, reviews, poems), is found at the close of the last issue of each volume. A cumulative index for the first 20 years (1952–71) appeared in 1972.

In recent years each issue has been introduced by the "First Reader" column, in which the editor briefly summarizes the contents and importance of the articles that follow. These articles cover topics from the Hebrew Bible to contemporary life. A typical issue also includes some fiction and poetry, as well as review essays and shorter book reviews. Some issues of *Judaism* also contain a few letters to the editor.

The symposia or panels that frequently appear are a highlight of *Judaism*. This format allows for a dozen or so experts, representing a wide variety of viewpoints and fields of expertise, to comment on a particular topic. Some of these topics are "Being a Jew and an American—Do They Mesh," "Homosexuals and Homosexuality," "Women as Rabbis," "The Trial of Jesus in the Light of History," "Mordecai M. Kaplan, on His Hundredth Birthday," "The Sabbath Is Forever," "My Jewish Affirmation," and "Toward Jewish Religious Unity."

In selecting authors and material, the editors of *Judaism* have been guided by three principles: (1) to afford "complete freedom of expression for every significant point of view in contemporary Jewish life," (2) to make the publication of interest "to the general intelligent reader and not merely to specialists," and (3) to encourage "younger writers, scholars and thinkers . . . to concern themselves with Jewish life."[5] It is Gordis's judgment that "*Judaism*, it is safe to say, has made a significant contribution to Judaism."

Notes

1. Robert Gordis, "The Genesis of *Judaism*: A Chapter in Jewish Cultural History," *Judaism* 30 (1981): 391. See also the "Statement of Sponsorship" and the "Statement of Purpose" published at the front of each issue. The former is a statement by the American Jewish Congress; the latter is taken from Robert Gordis's introductory article, "Toward a Renascence of Judaism," which appeared in the first issue of *Judaism*. Gordis makes many of the same points in his "Introduction" to the *Twenty Years Cumulative Index of Judaism 1952–1971* (New York: American Jewish Congress, 1972).

2. Gordis, "Genesis," p. 391. See also American Jewish Congress, "Statement of Sponsorship."

3. Gordis, "Genesis," pp. 391ff.

4. In addition to the editor, and in recent years a managing editor, "distinguished scholars and thinkers drawn from every segment of Jewish life" are designated contributing editors. Together they make up the board of editors, which "is vested with full authority and responsibility for the contents of this Journal." See the "Statement of Sponsorship" and the listing of editors found at the front of each issue.

5. Gordis, "Genesis," p. 395. Some of Gordis's comments in his Introduction to the cumulative index also deal with these three principles. Thus, on point 1 he writes: *Judaism* "has served as a non-partisan, non-denominational arena in which religionists and secularists, believers and non-believers, adherents of Orthodoxy, Conservatism, Reform and Reconstructionism, Zionists and non-Zionists, radical, liberal, and conservative Jews and

non-Jews have been able to speak with one another.'' It is to point 2, Gordis writes, that *Judaism* owes much of its uniqueness: "The unique position of this journal, dedicated to Jewish philosophy, religion and ethics, is universally recognized. On the one hand, its pages contain many important contributions to Jewish scholarship in all areas. On the other, it is distinguished from other, more technical journals by its basic concern for making the conclusions of research relevant to contemporary life and the problems which confront our generation. It has sought to keep in creative tension two ideals that superficially may seem to be contradictory, but actually were always complementary in Jewish life . . . 'learning for its own sake' and 'learning for the sake of life.' ''

Information Sources

BIBLIOGRAPHY:
Gordis, Robert. ''The Genesis of *Judaism*: A Chapter in Jewish Cultural History.'' *Judaism* 30 (1981): 390–95.
―――. Introduction. *Twenty Years Cumulative Index of Judaism 1952–1971*. New York: American Jewish Congress, 1972.
―――. ''Toward a Renascence of Judaism.'' *Judaism* 1 (1952): 3–10.
INDEX SOURCES: *Current Contents, Religion Index One, Social Science Citation Index*.
REPRINT EDITIONS: University Microfilms International.
LOCATION SOURCES: University of Alabama, University of Georgia, Hebrew Union College, New York Public Library, Yale University, and others.

Publication History

MAGAZINE TITLE AND TITLE CHANGES: *Judaism: A Quarterly Journal of Jewish Life and Thought* (1952–).
VOLUME AND ISSUE DATA: 1:1 (Winter 1952–). Appears quarterly in winter, spring, summer, and fall.
PUBLISHER AND PLACE OF PUBLICATION: American Jewish Congress, New York.
EDITORS: Will Herberg (1952–54), Theodore Friedman (managing editor, 1954–61); Felix A. Levy (1961–64), Steven Schwarzchild (1964–69), Robert Gordis (1969–).
CIRCULATION: 4000 (1982).

Leonard J. Greenspoon

L

LEHRE UND WEHRE

A scant six years after the formation in 1847 of the German Evangelical Lutheran Synod of Missouri, Ohio and Other States, the seventh general convention of the young church body meeting at Cleveland called for the publication of a technical theological journal to be issued monthly.[1] The biweekly *Der Lutheraner*, founded in 1844 by Ferdinand Walther and published by the congregation of Trinity Church in St. Louis until transferred to synodical auspices in 1847, was meeting the needs of the average reader and would continue to do so. What was needed was a learned journal for the clergy and for educated laity who could profit from scholarly articles with a sound confessional basis. Two pastors, serving congregations in New York and Philadelphia, respectively (and thus close to the major publishing centers), were designated as founding editors. When it was reported at the St. Louis convention of 1854 that no specific steps had been taken to carry out the Cleveland convention's mandate, the synod turned reluctantly to Walther, already overburdened with his duties as rector and professor of the nascent seminary at St. Louis, as pastor of Trinity Church and *Oberpfarrer* of the other St. Louis congregations, and as editor of *Der Lutheraner*.[2]

Walther accepted the task with the understanding that the editorship of *Der Lutheraner* would pass to his successor as seminary rector. He set to work immediately and was able to announce the first number of the new journal in a prospectus published in the second January issue of *Der Lutheraner* for 1855, making clear the aim and scope of the periodical and its relationship to the Missouri Synod:

> The journal is not to be a friend of the church, but a servant of the church.
> It is to take a position not above or alongside, but in and under the church.
> It will not serve as a sort of arena for those whose aim is to attack the

church of the true doctrine and its sacred institutions and who—while they cannot destroy these foundations, for even the gates of hell cannot do this, let alone the bellowing of would-be-wise-men—will at least try to damage and to shake them.[3]

Thus it was that *Lehre und Wehre* ("Doctrine and Defense") came to be published at St. Louis and to be associated—by default rather than design—with the "college" (*Gymnasium*) there, Concordia Seminary, making it the first Lutheran theological journal published west of the Mississippi.[4] The early volumes of *Lehre und Wehre* are a useful guide to the predominant theological concerns and controversies of nineteenth-century American Lutheranism. Articles and editorials on confessional subscription, catechesis, liturgics, church polity, biblical authority and the new science (*Darwinismus und Vulcanismus*), and the doctrine of predestination, together with excerpts in German translation from the Latin works of Luther and the classical dogmaticians of Lutheran orthodoxy, were regularly featured during the period of Walther's editorship, which extended by diminishing degrees until his death in 1887. Although these offerings expressed a consistently Missourian point of view, *Lehre und Wehre* was not limited in its appeal to the Missouri Synod alone, as is shown by the wide reading it received not only in American Lutheran circles but among Lutherans as far distant as Germany and Australia.[5] The regular column on current developments in theology and church ("*Kirchlich-zeitgeschichtliches*"), which was subdivided into foreign (*Ausland*) and domestic (*Amerika*) news, was a useful if cursory source of information, a link between the immigrant separatists of the Stephanite exodus and the lands and churches they left behind.[6]

The specific focus of *Lehre und Wehre* on a theologically literate readership, as distinct from the intentionally popular appeal of *Der Lutheraner*, was very much in evidence during the virulent and protracted predestination controversy that raged in American Lutheranism from 1871 to about 1884.[7] *Lehre und Wehre* contained articles on this subject of such great length that the size of the numbers during this period had to be increased significantly.[8] By contrast, *Der Lutheraner*, under managing editor Martin Guenther, contained few articles on the controversy although the doctrine of predestination and eternal election was the major political and theological issue facing the Missouri Synod at that time.[9]

The death of the great founder and architect of the Missouri Synod in 1887 ushered in a new epoch in the history of both church and seminary and in the history of *Lehre und Wehre* as well. This period of conservation, as the denomination's chief historian termed it, extended from Walther's death to the official adoption of Franz Pieper's "A Brief Statement of the Doctrinal Position of the Missouri Synod" in 1932.[10] Characterized by a concern to consolidate and transmit the theological heritage of the synod's first four decades and by a growing spirit of suspicion and antipathy toward the American religious scene in general and toward Lutherans of other synods in particular, this stance was partly attributable to the threatened and isolated position in which the Missourians found themselves as a result of the predestination controversy.[11] Whereas Walther had used *Lehre und Wehre* initially to plead for "the final establishment of one single Evangelical Lutheran Church of America" by inviting all Lutherans who subscribed constitutionally and personally to the Unaltered Augsburg Confession to a series of "free conferences" to explore the possibilities for church union,[12] any real hope of arriving at doctrinal consensus on a truly national scale seems to have been practically abandoned by the time Friedrich Bente assumed the task of managing editor sometime after his appointment to the Concordia faculty in 1893.[13] In his foreword to the golden anniversary volume, Bente contrasted *Lehre und Wehre*, which "takes a firm position," with the "characterless" content and editorial policy of other church periodicals, a trait not absent from some *Lutheran* periodicals. *Lehre und Wehre*, with its singleminded program of teaching and defense of pure doctrine based on the unity of theological truth flowing from the single source of Holy Scripture, can boast in the face of twentieth-century pluralism and scientific theology that in each issue one and the same spirit speaks.[14]

Bente's claim is as true for the letter as for the spirit of *Lehre und Wehre*. Aside from a slight proportionate increase in the number of articles on biblical inerrancy and on the language question, the topics covered during the journal's last two decades do not differ significantly from the contents of *Lehre und Wehre* under its founder. The same questions continued to be discussed by the same circle of Concordia faculty, disturbed only by infrequent departures and arrivals. The intellectual stagnation that could be inferred from this reluctance to cover new ground should be viewed in the context not only of the ethnic, linguistic, and—as a result of the predestination controversy—theological isolation of the Missouri Synod but also in terms of the increasing cultural isolation and bewilderment of conservative American Protestantism as a whole from the Gilded Age to the Great Depression.[15]

The Missouri Synod had laid the groundwork for a publishing concern as early as 1849 in the form of a stock company, a "publishing society" supported by private and congregational investments. In 1850 the shareholders voted to dissolve what was proving to be an unprofitable enterprise and to lend the shares to the synod for the establishment of a "publishing fund." It was out of this fund that *Lehre und Wehre* was launched, together with a magazine for parochial schoolteachers, the *Ev.-Luth. Schulblatt*. A building was erected on the Concordia Seminary campus, and in 1869 the Synodical Printery was dedicated. A second, larger, and more efficient facility was built off campus in 1874, and in 1878 the corporate name Concordia Publishing House was officially adopted. Martin C. Barthel, son of the first treasurer of the Missouri Synod, was named general agent, with responsibility for manufacture and sales after having served as synodical bookseller for several years previous.[16]

With its publishing concern on a secure footing, the Missouri Synod was in a position to authorize a companion to *Lehre und Wehre* that would supplement its dogmatic, controversial, and church historical offerings with homiletical material. Under general editor Martin Guenther, the first number of the *Magazin für Ev.-Luth. Homiletik* appeared in 1877. It was adopted as an official publication of the synod the following year.

Conceived with the geographically isolated, overworked, and underpaid pastor in mind, the *Magazin* was designed as a miniature library for pastors who could not attend pastoral conferences regularly and who could barely afford the annual two dollar subscription. Although the stated editorial policy of the *Magazin* was identical with *Lehre und Wehre*—the dissemination of pure doctrine—Guenther tried to cover a wide range of Lutheran homiletical literature, including reviews of recently published works together with essays and sermons from the reformers and the classical dogmaticians. The first number of the *Magazin*, for example, contained not only a German translation of the homiletical rules from Quenstedt's *Ethica pastoralis* but a review of a collection of discourses by Søren Kierkegaard as well. A comparison of printing statistics with the total number of pastors in the Missouri Synod at the time shows that by Guenther's death in 1893, the *Magazin* (or "Mag" as it was called) had achieved a wide reading outside the Missouri Synod.[17] By 1897 the format had changed to accommodate more offerings in the field of pastoral care, and the title was correspondingly changed to *Magazin für Ev.-Luth. Homiletik und Pastoraltheologie*, edited collectively by the faculty of Concordia Seminary.

The question of the use of English in worship, preaching, and publication was a thorny problem for all American Lutheran synods, an inevitable transition complicated by successive waves of immigration. Suspicious of English because of the American spirit of materialism, moralism, and doctrinal indifference that went with it and also because of the scarcity of Lutheran literature in English, the midwestern synods especially were reluctant to enter into "English work" on a large scale.[18] In 1860 Pastor Bühl wrote a letter asking the Missouri Synod to consider publishing an English periodical. The response was lukewarm. The difficulties in finding the money and a competent English-speaking editor aside, the 1860 convention pointed out that such a publication would meet with opposition "inasmuch as the American Lutherans do not like to let themselves be taught by Germans." Pastor Bühl, apparently not a Missourian, was directed to discuss his plan with some pastors of the Norwegian Synod who had expressed similar interests and perhaps to launch such a journal as a private undertaking.[19]

At the founding meeting of the Evangelical Lutheran Synodical Conference of North America in 1872, to which the Missouri Synod was party, another voice from outside Missouri was raised on behalf of English publications. Matthias Loy of the Joint Ohio Synod delivered an essay, "Our Duty to the English-Speaking Population of this Country." Loy declared:

It would be disloyal to our Church not to do all in our power to acquaint the English-speaking population, by the spreading of periodicals and books, with the treasures of our Church, and therefore the achievement of this aim must always be considered as our main duty.[20]

The Missouri Synod proceeded with caution. The first attempt at an English theological journal did not come until 1881 and was short-lived. The *St. Louis Theological Monthly* was launched as a trial balloon by the English faculty of Concordia Seminary under editor Rudolf Lange in May 1881 but did not receive synodical endorsement.[21] Its last number was issued in December 1882. The germ of an idea had taken firm root nonetheless. In 1897 another English professional theological journal was founded under A. L. Graebner, also a member of the English faculty. The *Theological Quarterly* achieved approximately half the circulation of *Lehre und Wehre* by the third year of publication and was printed in quantities nearly equal to that of the *Magazin*.[22] In 1903 the *Magazin* adopted a bilingual format. With synodical backing, the *Theological Quarterly* was able to attract a loyal readership as the English counterpart to *Lehre und Wehre*, so much so that in 1920 it achieved synchronous publication with the parent journal and was renamed the *Theological Monthly* under the editorship of W. H. T. Dau, taking its place among five other new English periodicals published under district auspices in the Missouri Synod.[23]

The next logical step was consolidation. At the thirty-fourth regular convention of the Missouri Synod in 1929, it was resolved to merge *Lehre und Wehre*, the *Theological Monthly*, and the *Homiletisches Magazin* into a single monthly periodical.[24] The new *Concordia Theological Monthly*,* published in bilingual format until 1943, combined the scope of *Lehre und Wehre* and the *Magazin*, offering dogmatic, controversial, and historical articles, exegetical essays, studies in pastoral care, and preaching helps. The name *Theological Monthly* had been proposed by the committee on publications. The convention voted instead to include "Concordia," not only evocative of the synod's commitment to the Christian Book of Concord and to the confessional concord so important to Missourians but also gratefully expressive of the firm bond that had been forged between that confessional commitment and the school that had made its articulation possible.[25]

Notes

1. E. Clifford Nelson, ed., *The Lutherans in North America* (Philadelphia: Fortress, 1975), pp. 178–81.

2. William F. Arndt, "The Story of *Lehre und Wehre*," *Concordia Theological Monthly* 26 (December 1955): 885, 886.

3. Ibid., pp. 886–88.

4. Frederick Gebhart Gotwald, *Pioneer American Lutheran Journalism, 1812–1850* ["Reprinted from *The Lutheran Quarterly*, for April 1912, With Additional Illustrations"] (Gettysburg?: Lutheran Theological Seminary?, n.d.), p. 48.

5. Walter A. Baepler, *A Century of Grace. A History of the Missouri Synod, 1847–1947* (St. Louis: Concordia, 1947), pp. 186–89.

6. See Walter O. Forster, *Zion on the Mississippi: The Settlement of the Saxon Lutherans in Missouri, 1839–1841* (St. Louis: Concordia, 1953).

7. See Hans Robert Haug, "The Predestination Controversy in the Lutheran Church in North America" (Ph.D. dissertation, Temple University, 1968).

8. Arndt, pp. 890, 891.

9. James William Albers, "Martin Guenther: Life and Work," (M.S.T. thesis, Concordia Seminary, 1964), pp. 103, 104.

10. See Carl S. Meyer, "The Historical Background of 'A Brief Statement,' " *Concordia Theological Monthly* 32 (July-September 1961): 403–28, 466–82, 526–42.

11. *Lutheran Cyclopedia*, rev. ed., s.v. "Lutheran Church-Missouri Synod, The," by C[arl] S[tamm] M[eyer], VI, 1: "The controversy seems to have made the Mo. Synod even more concerned about correct doctrine and wary of entangling alliances. After Walther's death 1887 this concern and wariness became dominant."

12. "Vorwort zu Jahrgang 1856," *Lehre und Wehre* 2 (January 1856): 4. On these conferences, which were held between 1856 and 1859, see Nelson, pp. 229, 230, and Erwin L. Lueker, "Walther and the Free Lutheran Conferences," *Concordia Theological Monthly* 15 (August 1944): 529–63.

13. The Missouri Synod's *Statistisches Jahrbuch* began listing managing editors of the periodicals of synod in 1921 for the year 1920. Bente's name appears in this issue. Although it is virtually impossible to tell who was managing editor of *Lehre und Wehre* merely from the initials appearing after editorials and editorial forewords (even Walther did not write every editorial or editorial foreword during his tenure as managing editor), it must be assumed that Bente served as managing editor long before 1920 if William Arndt's comment is accurate: "The managing editorship for several decades was in the hands of G. Fr. Bente, favorably known for his live, incisive style."

14. "Vorwort," *Lehre und Wehre* 50 (January 1904): 1–20.

15. See Carl S. Meyer, "The Historical Background of 'A Brief Statement'," *Lehre und Wehre*, pp. 415–28, on Missourian doctrinal concerns in the context of major theological movements in America, 1887–1932.

16. Baepler, pp. 149–51, 209; *Lutheran Cyclopedia*, rev. ed., s.v. "Barthel, Friedrich Wilhelm."

17. Albers, pp. 107–12.

18. On the language problem, see Nelson, pp. 349–51.

19. *Zehnter Synodal Bericht der Allgemeinen Deutschen Evang.-Luth. Synode von Missouri, Ohio u. a. Staaten vom Jahre 1860* (St. Louis, Synodaldruckerei, 1861), p. 75. Bühl is not listed on the clergy roster for 1860.

20. Baepler, pp. 160, 161.

21. Ibid., p. 207.

22. *Lehre und Wehre*: 2350; *Magazin*: 1900; *Theological Quarterly:* 1300; printing statistics as listed in the *Statistisches Jahrbuch der deutschen evangelisch-lutherischen Synode von Missouri, Ohio und andrere Staaten für das Jahr 1899* (St. Louis: Concordia, 1900).

23. *Statistisches Jahrbuch . . .für das Jahr 1920*.

24. *Proceedings of the Thirty-fourth Regular Convention of the Ev. Luth. Synod of Missouri, Ohio and Other States, Assembled at River Forest, Ill., June 19–28, 1929* (St. Louis: Concordia, 1929).

25. Ibid.

Information Sources

BIBLIOGRAPHY:

Albers, James William. "Martin Guenther: Life and Work." S.T.M. thesis, Concordia Seminary, 1964.

Arndt, William Frederick. "The Story of *Lehre und Wehre.*" *Corcordia Theological Monthly* 26 (December 1955): 855–92.

Forster, Walter Otto. *Zion on the Mississippi: The Settlement of the Saxon Lutherans in Missouri.* St. Louis: Concordia, 1953.

Gotwald, Frederick Gebhart. "Pioneer American Lutheran Journalism, 1812–1850." *Lutheran Quarterly* 42 (April 1912): 161–98.

Maug, Hans Robert. "The Predestination Controversy in the Lutheran Church in North America." Ph.D. dissertation, Temple University, 1967.

Lueker, Erwin L., ed. *Lutheran Cyclopedia.* Rev. ed. St. Louis: Concordia, 1975.

Nelson, E. Clifford, ed. *The Lutherans in North America.* Philadelphia: Fortress Press, 1975.

Scharlemann, Martin H. "Born of Anguish and Travail." *Concordia Journal* 1 (January 1975): 4–7.

INDEX SOURCES: None.

LOCATION SOURCES: *Lehre und Wehre*: Library of Congress, Andover-Harvard Theological Library, Catholic Central Verein of St. Louis; *Magazin für Ev.-Luth. Homiletik*: no known complete collection but most complete is that of the Catholic Central Verein of St. Louis.

Publication History

MAGAZINE TITLE AND TITLE CHANGES: *Lehre und Wehre* (1855–1929); *Magazin für Ev.-Luth. Homiletik* (1877–96), *Magazin für Ev.-Luth. Homiletik und Pastoraltheologie* (1897–1902), *Magazin für Ev.-Luth. Homiletik und Pastoraltheologie: Homiletic Magazine* (1903–29); *St. Louis Theological Monthly* (1881–82); *Theological Quarterly* (1897–1920); *Theological Monthly* (1921–29). For successors, see *Concordia Theological Monthly.**

VOLUME AND ISSUE DATA: *Lehre und Wehre* 1–75 (January 1855- December 1929); *Magazin für Ev.-Luth. Homiletik/Magazin für Ev.-Luth. Homiletik und Pastoraltheologie/Magazine für Ev.-Luth. Homiletik und Pastoraltheologie: Homiletic Magazine* 1–53 (January 1877-December 1929); *St. Louis Theological Monthly* 1 (May 1881-December 1882); *Theological Quarterly* 1–24 (January 1897-December 1920); *Theological Monthly* 1–9 (January 1921-December 1929).

PUBLISHER AND PLACE OF PUBLICATION: Synodaldruckerei, St. Louis, Mo. (*Lehre und Wehre*, 1855–1877; *Magazin für Ev.-Luth. Homiletik*, 1877); Concordia-Verlag/Concordia Publishing House, St. Louis (*Lehre und Wehre*, 1878–1929; *Magazin für Ev.-Luth. Homiletik*, 1878–1929; *St. Louis Theological Monthly*, 1881–1882; *Theological Quarterly*, 1897–1920; *Theological Monthly*, 1921–1929).

EDITORS: *Lehre und Wehre*: C. F. W. Walther (1855–87?), Concordia faculty (1887–93?), Friedrich Bente (1893?–1923), Franz Pieper (1924–29?); *Magazin für Ev.-Luth. Homiletik* and immediate successors: Martin Guenther (1877–93?) Concordia faculty (1893–1919?), Georg Mezger (1920?–21), Georg Mezger and Martin Sommer (1921–23), William Arndt and Martin Sommer (1924), William Arndt and O. C. A. Boecler (1925–29?); *St. Louis Theological Monthly*: Rudolf Lange (1881–82); *Theological Quarterly*: Concordia English faculty? (1897–1920); *Theological Monthly*: W. H. T. Dau (1921–29?).

CIRCULATION: (maximum recorded): *Lehre und Wehre*: 2600; *Magazin für Ev.-Luth. Homiletik*: 2300; *St. Louis Theological Monthly*: no surviving record; *Theological Quarterly*: 1500; *Theological Monthly*: no surviving record.

Guy C. Carter

THE LITERARY AND EVANGELICAL MAGAZINE

In 1818, Presbyterian clergyman John Holt Rice launched the publication of the *Virginia Evangelical and Literary Magazine*. In an opening statement, he indicated what he saw as the magazine's purpose: "Our Magazine, as respects religion, is to be Evangelical.—In present usage, (for all living languages are subject to change,) this term designates a peculiar class of sentiments, and system of doctrines from the holy scriptures, in opposition to other systems which are professedly supported by the same authority." But he went on to indicate that those evangelical doctrines were to be identified with the tenets of Calvinism: "1. The total depravity of man. 2. The necessity of regeneration by the Holy Spirit. 3. Justification by faith alone. 4. The necessity of holiness as a qualification for happiness."[1]

The monthly is representative of a genre that emerged in the early nineteenth century and has counterparts in periodicals published elsewhere, often incorporating the same evangelical and literary designation or some similar description in their titles. The impetus for these journals came from the efforts at organized social reform through voluntary societies, many of which were being organized, as well as from the emergence of a secular press that offered the sophisticated reading public a fare of poetry, literature, and "intelligence" (news briefs of general interest). Rice was involved in many of these societies, organizing the Virginia Bible Society in 1813 and the Young Men's Missionary Society in 1819, as well as helping found the American Bible Society in 1816. Earlier, Rice had been the force behind the short-lived (1815–17) *Christian Monitor*, which had been somewhat more explicitly religious in tone. The new magazine would provide coverage of religious matters and include poetry, essays, and articles on topics ranging from navigation to agriculture. Or so Rice hoped.

During its 11 years of publication, the *Magazine* contained many poems and short literary pieces, all designed to edify readers, reports on meetings of the Presbyterian General Assembly, and numerous heady articles on theology, sometimes labeled "Essays on Divinity." Many of these specifically religious essays were written by Rice's friend and associate, Moses Hoge. But a large portion of each issue was devoted to news of various voluntary societies, particularly missionary groups both domestic and foreign. Rice heartily endorsed these efforts as agencies that would help create a Christian culture first in the United States and then elsewhere. In time, however, these societies were to become controversial, for many of them were at first cooperative ventures among the denominations, and individuals in some circles, including the Presbyterian, became convinced that only agencies under denominational control deserved support since only those could be carefully monitored and controlled.

But one area of social reform supported by some of these voluntary societies aroused suspicion in the South: abolition of slavery. An essay in the second volume of the *Magazine* addressed the issue, noting that while slavery was an evil, it was lawful so long as necessity required its continuance. The *Magazine* did not endorse immediate emancipation but rather the efforts of the American Colonization Society, one of the voluntary benevolent groups, to resettle freed blacks in Liberia. It also called for the education and religious instruction of the slaves.[2]

The *Magazine* lent support to religious revivals, another matter that would become a major bone of contention in American religion, one that ultimately caused Rice's Presbyterian denomination to divide. Revivals were seen as another means to convert individuals and thereby aid in the establishment of a Christian society. Another effort to nurture a Christian culture centered around missions to the Indians. The *Magazine* frequently carried reports of work among the southern tribes, especially the Choctaw, Cherokee, and Arkansa.

Circulation, though exact figures are unknown, was always a problem. Rice's endorsement of the voluntary societies was not popular among much of the constituency he hoped to reach. In addition, Rice's work as founder and president of the Presbyterian seminary in Richmond, the Union Theological Seminary, consumed more and more of his energy. And in time, competition from both religious newspapers and the secular press proved too much to meet. In 1828, the journal, then called simply the *Literary and Evangelical Magazine*, published its final issue.

Rice's periodical and the others of its genre are important in providing a perspective on the endeavors to offer wholesome literary material, serious pieces of high quality on religious doctrine, and news of missionary and social reform activity to an educated public as part of what one historian has called the "Protestant quest for a Christian America."[3]

Notes

1. "Introduction," *Virginia Evangelical and Literary Magazine* 1 (1818): 2.

2. "Thoughts on Slavery," *Virginia Evangelical and Literary Magazine* 2 (1819): 293–303.

3. Robert T. Handy, "The Protestant Quest for a Christian America, 1830–1930," *Church History* 22 (1952): 8–20; reprinted, Philadelphia: Fortress Press, 1967.

Information Sources

BIBLIOGRAPHY:

Kuykendall, John. "*Southern Enterprize*": *The Work of the National Evangelical Societies in the Antebellum South.* Westport, Conn.: Greenwood Press, 1982.

Morrison, Alfred J. "The Virginia Literary and Evangelical Magazine, Richmond, 1818–1828." *William and Mary Quarterly*, 1st ser. 19 (April 1911): 266–72.

INDEX SOURCES: None.

REPRINT EDITIONS: University Microfilms International (American Periodicals Series).

LOCATION SOURCES: Library of Congress, University of Virginia, Iowa State Travelling Library, Princeton Theological Seminary, Union Theological Seminary (Virginia), Wisconsin State Historical Society, and others.

Publication History

MAGAZINE TITLE AND TITLE CHANGES: *The Virginia Evangelical and Literary Magazine* (1818–20), *The Evangelical and Literary Magazine, and Missionary Chronicle* (1821), *The Evangelical and Literary Magazine* (1822–23), *The Literary and Evangelical Magazine* (1824–28).

VOLUME AND ISSUE DATA: 1:1–11:12 (January 1818–December 1828). Appeared monthly.

PUBLISHER AND PLACE OF PUBLICATION: William T. Gray (1818); Franklin Press, W. W. Gray, Printer (1819); N. Pollard, at the Franklin Press (1820); N. Pollard, Sign of Franklin's Head (1821–23); Pollard and Goddard, at the Franklin Printing Office (1824–28); all in Richmond, Va.

EDITOR: John Holt Rice (1818–28).

CIRCULATION: Unknown.

Charles H. Lippy

THE LUTHERAN CHURCH QUARTERLY. *See* THE LUTHERAN QUARTERLY

THE LUTHERAN QUARTERLY

The *Lutheran Quarterly* is the most recent name for a journal that earlier sometimes bore that same name. It encompasses five journals and eight titles in a circuitous stream of mergers. It is best understood if each journal is considered separately but in the context of the others.

The Evangelical Review, The Evangelical Quarterly Review, The Quarterly Review of the Evangelical Lutheran Church, and *The Lutheran Quarterly*

Throughout the eighteenth century, Lutherans largely from the Palatinate in Germany migrated to Pennsylvania and neighboring states. By the nineteenth century, they had organized and become independent of their European ecclesiastical ties, but, with few exceptions, they continued to use the German language. By 1830, however, English had become much more prominent and gradually began to predominate.

Simultaneously with the rise of English in the Lutheran churches, Charles Grandison Finney (1792–1875) was plying his "New Measures" brand of revivalism for any church or denomination that would give him a hearing. Many Lutherans listened. Benjamin Kurtz (1795–1865) championed revivalism in the weekly *Lutheran Observer*, which he edited. S. S. Schmucker (1799–1873) was not so strident or obvious an advocate of revivalism, but from his chair of systematic theology at Gettysburg Seminary, he pressed for what he called "American Lutheranism" and broadened confessional Lutheran boundaries until some wondered if any characteristically Lutheran terrain remained. The Lutheran Church on American soil began to look like Methodism and other traditionally English-speaking nonliturgical denominations.

By midcentury some of the Pennsylvania Lutherans were concerned about this state of affairs and started to examine their Lutheran heritage. William R. Reynolds (1812–76), professor at what is now Gettysburg College and later president of Capital University, Columbus, Ohio, was among this group.[1] In 1849 he initiated a quarterly, the *Evangelical Review*, put Luther's statement from Worms in German on the title page, and in the lead editorial explained his intent.[2] "The Lutheran church in the United States," he wrote, "has long felt the necessity of a Journal for the cultivation and criticism of its own theology and literature, and for those questions which, from time to time, excite a peculiar interest in its own bosom."[3] Reynolds detailed some attempts earlier in the century at both German and English journals, indicated that the church was strong enough now to support such an enterprise, and noted that the transition to English rendered a journal even more necessary.[4] He made it clear that the *Review* would be "Lutheran, in the broadest and in the strictest sense of the term,"[5] that it stood between rationalism and Romanism, but that it was not hostile to any other "part of Christendom."[6] In other words, it would be Lutheran with an ecumenical cast.

The following year volume 2 of the *Evangelical Review* was edited by Charles Philip Krauth (1797–1867), soon to retire as president of Gettysburg College so he could devote his energies fully to seminary teaching. Krauth had gradually moved to a more confessional Lutheran posture, and he challenged the church "to examine its position, and to determine its future course."[7] He called attention to Lutheran views of worship, doctrine, sacraments, festivals, and other matters, but he noted division over some points like the nature of Christ's presence in the Lord's Supper.[8] He argued that, while avoiding bitter controversy, the church should use the Augsburg Confession as a creed and move in a more confessional Lutheran direction.[9]

Krauth and Reynolds together edited the *Evangelical Review* until volume 9 in 1857 when they were joined by Martin Luther Stoever (1820–70), who taught at Gettysburg College and compiled numerous memoirs of deceased Lutheran clergymen for publication in the *Review*. In 1861 for volume 13, Krauth dropped out because of his health,[10] and in the following year Reynolds also left the *Review*.[11] In 1862 for volume 14, Stoever changed the title to the *Evangelical Quarterly Review* and continued as the sole editor until he died in 1870.

During the Reynolds-Krauth-Stoever years, the *Evangelical Review* (and from 1862 the *Evangelical Quarterly Review*) largely fulfilled Reynolds's and Krauth's initial intentions. Biblical, church historical, contemporary, educational, theological, liturgical, and other matters were discussed. The editorial posture was moderately confessional for its time and place, but other opinions were admitted. S. S. Schmucker was given space to propound his virtually Zwinglian understanding of the real presence[12] (that is, Christ was not really present in any traditional Lutheran sense), but in the next number H. I. Schmidt argued the more confessional case against Schmucker;[13] and volume 8 contained several articles against Schmucker's "American Lutheranism."

In 1857 when Stoever joined them, Krauth and Reynolds gave a "prospectus." They affirmed that the *Review* had "contributed more to the cultivation of Lutheran literature, history, and theology in the English language, than any publication we have hitherto had." They hoped to enlarge the size of the *Review*, aiming for every Lutheran minister in the country to subscribe. They affirmed the same principles as at the beginning: a cultivated Lutheran theology and literature in the English language, knowing no sect or party, with a liberal and impartial attitude.[14]

These principles sounded much like those from the early years of the *Review*, but the weight seemed to fall now on a broad editorial policy rather than on confessional concerns. When Stoever died, this breadth became even more central. The new editors reaffirmed Reynolds's and Krauth's original vision, but they also made it clear that they stood "unequivocally on the basis of the General Synod."[15]

The General Synod has been aptly described by John Tietjen as an "inclusive federation."[16] It was officially formed in 1820 at the urging of the Pennsylvania ministerium. It tried to unite all Lutheran bodies in the United States with as little regard as possible to faith and practice and with a fear of anything that seemed authoritarian or had a centralized government. Those who found the General Synod not sufficiently Lutheran in 1867 organized the General Council with "subscription" to Lutheran confessions the basis of their organization.[17] In 1871 the new editors of the *Review* articulated the obvious: that the *Review* represented the "inclusive federation" of the General Synod in its editorial policy, not the "confessional subscription" of the General Council.

The new editors, a team of six, were headed by James Allen Brown (1821–82), former president of Newberry College, South Carolina, who at this time was professor of systematic theology at Gettysburg Seminary, and Milton Valentine (1825–1906), then president at Gettysburg College. They changed the title again, this time to *Quarterly Review of the Evangelical Lutheran Church*, without regard to future generations who have to unscramble this maze of similar titles, and began a new series of volume numbers. The title confusion was further compounded when the *Lutheran Quarterly* and the *Quarterly Review of the Evangelical Lutheran Church* were used simultaneously on different pages of the same issue. By the turn of the century, the *Lutheran Quarterly* triumphed.

A careful count might reveal that Brown and Valentine included more articles on topics of current interest, especially ones related to Darwinism, but essentially the past editorial policy was pursued: the journal discussed biblical, church historical, contemporary, educational, theological, and liturgical matters. And it continued to represent a broadly confessional position within the context of the General Synod's all-inclusive stance.

The magazine traveled this same track until 1927. There were editorial shifts during this period, but the editors always remained clustered around Gettysburg Seminary and College as before. They included, among others, James W. Richard (1843–1909) and John Alden Singmaster (1852–1926). Richard is important because he argued an "American Lutheran" liturgical posture in S. S. Schmucker's mold after the church was retrieving a more confessional Lutheran balance.[18] Singmaster served as president of General Synod and on various committees of the church, but his chief claim to fame may be that he fathered the writer Elsie Singmaster Lewars (1879–1958).

The Lutheran Church Review

In 1864 the Pennsylvania Ministerium protested the overly inclusive character of the General Synod by walking out of the Synod and founding what is now the Lutheran Theological Seminary at Philadelphia as a confessional bulwark. (The school is sometimes called Mt. Airy, for the Philadelphia neighborhood where it moved in 1889). Three years later, in 1867, the ministerium initiated the more confessional General Council.

The *Quarterly Review* did not adequately represent the more rigorous Lutheranism the General Council found to its liking, so in 1882, the Alumni Association of the seminary at Philadelphia began to publish its own journal, the *Lutheran Church Review*. No word or article was included about why the journal was being published, but the articles and their authors told the story. The articles were about Lutheran catechetics, preaching, and historical, musical, and liturgical matters. The authors included two of the strongest confessional Lutheran leaders and advocates, Charles Porterfield Krauth (1823–83) and Beale M. Schmucker (1827–88).

Charles Porterfield Krauth imbibed the confessional awakening of his father, Charles Philip Krauth. He served as the first professor of systematic theology at the Philadelphia Seminary, pursued historical studies, and had considerable power in the General Council. The title of his detailed and verbose book of 1871 reveals his stance: *The Conservative Reformation and Its Theology*.[19] B. M. Schmucker shared Krauth's confessional instincts and reacted against the American Lutheranism of his father, S. S. Schmucker. He diligently provided the liturgical scholarship that ultimately led to *The Common Service* of 1887. He served as a parish pastor who knew how to wield power in the General Council, and he wielded it in exactly the opposite direction his father had pursued earlier in the century.

The first issue of the *Lutheran Church Review* was edited by a committee, none of whom was as important as the contributors. In 1883, however, Henry Eyster Jacobs (1844–1932) headed the editorial board until for volume 6 in 1887 he was listed as editor with associates. Jacobs held this position until 1895.

Jacobs took Krauth's place as professor of systematic theology at the Philadelphia Seminary when Krauth died in 1883. He was an exacting Lutheran scholar who exerted a steady influence through study and teaching. With the editorial aid and contributions of men like William Julius Mann (1819–1892) and Adolph

Spaeth (1839–1910), Jacobs continued to pursue the course the first volume of
the journal had plotted: careful, scholarly articles treated Lutheran theological,
historical, and liturgical matters.

In 1895 Jacobs gave up the editorship of the *Lutheran Church Review* to
devote more energies to teaching.[20] In June Theodore E. Schmauk (1860–1920)
was elected editor, and in October he took over, guiding the journal until his
death in 1920. By the turn of the century, Schmauk had become a leader in the
General Council, which elected him president from 1903 until the formation of
the United Lutheran Church in 1918. In 1911 he added the professorship of
apologetics and ethics at Philadelphia Seminary to his editing, writing, and
General Council responsibilities. When he assumed the editorship of the *Lutheran
Church Review* in 1895, he turned his usual articulate verve to the project. In
the journal's first editorial, he indicated what he intended:

> It is the duty of a theological review to introduce, discuss, pass judgment
> on and dispose of such doctrines, principles and tendencies, as may be or
> become timely to its readers, in somewhat ample manner, from its own
> fixed standpoint, and to defend and advance the power of the latter in the
> world of learning. . . . To sum up all in a word, it should furnish the
> scholarly and thinking minds of the church with a point of view.[21]

Schmauk went on to indicate that the point of view need not be authoritative
and that suggestive is probably better. He did not plan to discuss every topic
"that looms up in the horizon," but topics chosen were to be treated in a masterly
and exhaustive fashion. He pointed out, somewhat unfairly to the *Quarterly
Review*, that

> the Lutheran Church in America has no periodical of any kind, which
> presents to our thinking minds a survey of what is going on in all the
> various departments of theological and churchly activities, such as will
> keep the clergy informed and in touch with what is uppermost in the centres
> of learning.[22]

This issue, said Schmauk, would begin to attempt to meet the need. The article
then did what he promised by discussing Protestantism's strengths and weaknesses, Tolstoi's inconsistency, the tasks of country and city, the pope and the
American people, and similar other contemporary concerns.

Schmauk did not mean to neglect the kinds of articles the journal had been
printing for the previous decade. He increased their length and number so that
with his "Editorial Points of View," one volume of the journal soon became
as long as two earlier ones. Articles were sometimes bunched by topics. In 1896,
for instance, education served as the focus. In 1897 articles celebrated the four
hundredth anniversary of Melanchthon's birth (and the four hundredth anniversary of Luther's going away to school) along with a series of monographs on

medieval figures and thinkers from Constantine to Hildebrand. The 1898 issue vigorously discussed liturgy and music.

Like the *Evangelical Review* and its successors, the *Lutheran Church Review* was a quarterly published in January, April, July, and October. Between 1915 and 1917, however, Schmauk had so much material that he increased the journal to six or seven issues each year. Those issues included some curious topics, like "Shakespeare's Attitude toward the Doctrine of the Church." They also provided the opportunity for guest editors to devote more attention to special topics like catechetics, country church, 35 years of Luther research, and liturgy.

In 1918 the journal resumed its former status as a quarterly, and two years later Schmauk died. The faculty of Philadelphia Seminary then assumed the editorial responsibilities, promising to continue the journal's traditional posture. They would, they said, (1) continue to stand for fundamental confessional Lutheran principles, expressed now in the doctrinal basis of the recently formed United Lutheran Church; (2) continue to encourage scholarship based on those principles; (3) encourage discussion and differences of opinion but not print articles that attack or reject the Gospel; (4) deal with practical issues; and (5) acquaint readers with the latest developments in Christian life and thought.[23]

Luther D. Reed (1873–1972) is probably the most important of this last set of editors. A student of Jacobs, he served the Philadelphia Seminary from 1906 until 1950 as librarian (from 1906), professor (from 1911), and president (from 1938 to 1945). His interest lay in liturgy, architecture, and music; he contributed articles on these topics even before the turn of the century.[24]

In 1927 the Philadelphia Seminary faculty edited the last issue of the *Lutheran Church Review* and bade their readers "Farewell."[25] They also announced that a new journal would now be published as a merger of the *Lutheran Church Review* and the *Quarterly Review* of the Gettysburg General Synod circle. The new journal would be called the *Lutheran Church Quarterly* (adding yet more confusion to the series of similar titles).

The Lutheran Church Quarterly

The *Lutheran Church Review* always represented a more confessional Lutheran stance and perhaps a somewhat more scholarly approach than the *Quarterly Review*. But by 1928 the division that had caused the two journals to exist separately had been healed. Ten years earlier the General Council and the General Synod had joined with the General Synod South to form the United Lutheran Church in America (ULCA). In 1926, at the Fifth Biennial Convention of the new church, the following resolution was introduced:

> that, with reference to "a scientific theological quarterly for the cultivation and development of Christian thought," be it resolved that the United Lutheran Church in America approve the idea and recommend that the

Lutheran Quarterly and *Lutheran Church Review* be urged . . . to consider
whether the needs of the Church may not best be served by their
consolidation.[26]

The resolution was carefully worded. Since the journals were not official
church publications and could not be forced to merge, they were "urged . . . to
consider . . . consolidation." The editors reacted positively and swiftly, however.
In 1928 a new journal, the *Lutheran Church Quarterly*, was published. That it
continued the earlier two publications was duly noted on the title page of the
first and every succeeding issue. The editors also made clear that, though it was
not official, it was from and for the ULCA. It aimed "to give intellectual
expression to the faith" of the ULCA, to "promote cordial understandings"
between Lutheran bodies in the United States and Europe, as well as "between
Lutherans and other Christian groups," and to discuss the relation of the Lutheran
faith to contemporary issues. To attain these aims, it would welcome "frank
and fair" contributions of "scholarly and practical value," along with differences
of opinion as long as they were free from "controversial animus"; would seek
contributions in all fields of theology—biblical, historical, practical, systematic,
and those concerning the theory and practice of Christian worship—and would
supplement all this with survey articles and book reviews.[27]

The *Lutheran Church Quarterly* lasted 21 years, from 1928 to 1948. It was
published at Gettysburg rather than Philadelphia, but it always had four editors,
two from the seminary at Gettysburg and two from the one at Philadelphia.[28]
For the first 10 years, through 1937, Raymond T. Stamm (1894–1962) of Gettysburg headed the editors. In 1938, Theodore G. Tappert (1904–73) of Philadelphia took charge and reaffirmed the journal's initial aims. Stamm was graduated
from both Gettysburg College and Seminary and in 1926 received the Ph.D.
from the University of Chicago. He taught New Testament language, literature,
and theology at Gettysburg Seminary, served on the editorial board of the *Lutheran Church Quarterly* for its entire existence, and wrote an overview and
index as a final issue in January 1949.[29] Tappert came from Connecticut, was
graduated from Wagner College, Staten Island, New York, the Lutheran Seminary at Philadelphia, and Columbia University in New York. In 1931, he returned to the Philadelphia Seminary to teach church history and remained there
the rest of his life. Although he edited the Book of Concord and taught in the
former bastion of Lutheran confessionalism at Philadelphia, his sacramental
theology was nevertheless tinged with a Zwinglian bias.[30]

The person and place of the chief editor was not so important as the overriding
historical context. A confessional Lutheran stability had been achieved and was
embodied in the ULCA. Lutheran union even beyond the ULCA was more
important now, and any controversial animus was consciously avoided. Differences of opinion remained, but they were channeled in more carefully conceived,
if sometimes less exciting, formulations. Even the appearance of the journal

bore the look of twentieth-century care and precision, not the more germinal cast of the nineteenth.

The formulations often responded to the issues of the time. The Social Gospel did not compel these Lutherans to renounce their realistic view of human nature, but it did force them to rethink the relation of the individual and society. Ethical issues about race, anti-Semitism, housing, labor, war, wages, and similar concerns were discussed. Nazism demanded a response. Practical twentieth-century matters of church life and union were addressed. Barth's dialectical theology received some positive Lutheran response, but his sacramental stance was not so highly regarded. Biblical studies faced form criticism and twentieth-century pressures, generally trying to walk a line between retaining the notion that the Bible is the Word of God while rejecting the idea that it is to be interpreted literally.

Historical articles also continued. They touched most of the church's history, many of them concerned with the Lutheran part of that history, especially in its American form. Preaching was not forgotten; the importance of the proclaimed Word was characteristically highlighted. Worship too was still discussed as writers developed themes with a tacit acceptance that a common Lutheran heritage within the Western liturgical stream simultaneously allowed a good deal of room for Lutheran freedom.

Articles came not only from the editors and their respective seminaries but from ministers and teachers in various quarters of the church (with the place of residence indicated below the author's name). Past contributors like Luther Reed still wrote articles and reviews from time to time. Abdel Ross Wentz (1883–1976), who made the motion in 1926 to form the *Lutheran Church Quarterly* and who served Gettysburg Seminary as professor of church history from 1909 and eventually as president from 1940 to 1951, contributed many articles and reviews. Joseph Sittler (b. 1904), whose influence and reputation as an incisive thinker, theologian, and churchman would eventually extend beyond the bounds of his Lutheran home, can also be found in these pages when he was still writing as a pastor in Cleveland Heights, Ohio.

The *Lutheran Church Quarterly* for 20 years responsibly did what it said it would with a cross-section of thoughtful ecumenical Lutheran opinion. But in 1949 it went out of business to make yet another merger possible. Before we get to that last chapter of this rather serpentine history, we must pick up a penultimate chapter.

The Augustana Quarterly

Around 1820 and continuing throughout the remainder of the nineteenth century, a million or more Swedes immigrated to North America and settled largely in what is now Illinois, Iowa, Minnesota, and surrounding areas. They organized churches that were welcomed into the General Synod, but soon S. S. Schmucker's American Lutheranism offended their confessional Lutheran loyalties. In 1860, therefore, they formed a synod, college, and seminary, choosing Augustana—the Latin title of the chief Lutheran confessional document—as the name of all three. Until 1863 the schools were housed at Chicago, then Paxton, Illinois. In 1875 they were moved to Rock Island, Illinois, the capital of Swedish immigration.

By 1920 the Swedish immigrants had organized their churches, Synod, schools, and a publishing house. They had watched the tide of immigration cease around World War I. Two journals had also ceased publication: the Swedish *Tidskrift* and the English *Augustana Quarterly*. The Swedes had begun to adapt to the American environment with plans for a lengthy stay. They now needed some English-speaking vehicle to discuss and reflect on their problems and challenges.

After "surveying the field" in 1920,[31] the ministers of the Iowa Conference petitioned the ministerium,[32] who in turn petitioned the Synod,[33] and the Synod authorized the Augustana Book Concern "to publish a theological quarterly."[34] Editors were then elected by the Augustana Book Concern,[35] and in March 1922 the first issue of the *Augustana Quarterly* was published at Rock Island. It was similar to the journals related to the General Synod and General Council, but in two respects it differed: it was initiated by official action and then entrusted to the publishing company of the church, and it began as a bilingual publication.[36]

On the front and back covers of the first issue, the reasons for and positions of the *Augustana Quarterly* were stated. The journal was for pastors and churches of the Augustana Synod; its central concern would be to discuss "problems and questions which are strictly 'inter nos.' "[37] It would not stop there, however, but would "endeavor to serve the cause of Christ in a wider sphere by giving whatever influence and power it may possess to help solve problems of vital importance to the church at large" and to pastors and individual Christians everywhere.[38] The editors made it clear that the quarterly would be "genuinely and thoroughly American in spirit" and "staunchly Lutheran in doctrine," treating church problems and world events "from a positive Christian standpoint."[39] It would "meet all Christians in a spirit of fairness and toleration," though it would also express "its own convictions without fear or favor."[40]

The first editor in chief was Axel F. Almer (1865–1960). Born in Sweden, he was graduated from Gustavus Adolphus College in 1894 and attended Augustana Seminary between 1895 and 1897, when he was ordained.[41] In addition to serving local parishes and deaconess homes, he edited the *China Missionary* from 1903 to 1925 and the *Augustana Quarterly* from 1922 to 1934. Almer imparted to the journal his missionary and practical interests, along with a Swedish brand of pietistic life and faith that colored the confessional Lutheran underlay. Articles in the first years concerned missionary matters, how to secure church attendance, prayer life, infidelity, the Luther League, how to organize the Sunday School, and how to teach a Sunday School lesson. Biblical articles were also included, some with scholarly substance, but they tended to be brief and to aim at the reader's personal life.

The *Augustana Quarterly* was not, however, to be a bland exercise in piety or a Swedish exercise in ethnicity. In it one can see the Augustana Church coming to terms with the American environment and the twentieth century. In 1926 Virgilius Ferm (1896–1974)—an Augustana College and Seminary graduate who a year earlier had finished his Ph.D. at Yale and who would eventually write and edit numerous books on theological and philosophical issues in the United States as a virtual Presbyterian—introduced some dissonance.[42] He took the church to task for failing to face scientific, political, economic, and social changes,[43] and he accused the denominational schools of restricting liberty and the Lutheran Church of surrendering its birthright of honest investigation and study.[44] A lively dialogue ensued. The journal began to print affirmative and negative positions on topics like the Galesburg Rule or limiting enrollments in the colleges or requirements of contemporary theological education.[45] Symposia were featured, and various viewpoints were heard.

Simultaneously with this, the pen and power of Conrad Bergendoff (b. 1895) joined the journal. As early as 1926, Bergendoff contributed an article on evangelism, which at the time might have seemed fairly typical.[46] But already Bergendoff's scholarly depth and his attempt to reach back into the tradition for ballast and direction were evident. In 1928 Bergendoff joined the editorial staff and remained one of its members through the last issue in 1948. He contributed perennial articles largely on confessional Lutheran matters, which he passed through a Scandinavian filter, and he gently guided the journal toward a more scholarly position. Bergendoff was born in Nebraska, completed degrees at Augustana College, the University of Pennsylvania, Augustana Seminary, and the University of Chicago (the last a Ph.D. in 1928), and he devoted his life to teaching and administration as dean at Augustana Seminary and president of both the seminary and the college. A prolific writer, he exerted enormous influence.

In 1935 Oscar N. Olson (1876–1961) replaced Axel Almer as editor in chief. Bergendoff continued on the editorial staff as a guiding force. Olson, like Almer, was born in Sweden. He graduated from Augustana College and Seminary while attending Yale University and the Lutheran Seminary at Philadelphia along the way and served as a pastor, teacher, and researcher.

Olson's appointment as editor did not materially change the *Augustana Quarterly*. Olson was better able to deal with new currents and the present world of reality than Almer, who felt his perspective being pressured out of the "open forum."[47] But for both men the die had been cast. In 1930, C. M. Olander had argued for "an aggressive program of Americanization" in the church, by which he meant using English.[48] Although S. G. Hägglund had argued the opposite case, he lost.[49] The following year and thereafter, the journal used only English. Bergendoff had begun to exert his influence. The practical and evangelistic zeal of Almer was never lost, but it was tempered by a more scholarly and confessional approach that sought to be both devotional and contemporary. The journal continued to do what it set out to do: treat matters of interest to the church by addressing contemporary, creedal, historical, biblical, theological, liturgical, and musical concerns. Writers included mainly Augustana churchmen, but others appeared as well. Abdel Ross Wentz from Gettysburg, Luther Reed from Philadelphia, Arthur Carl Piepkorn of the Missouri Synod, Herbert Willett from Chicago Theological Seminary and contributing editor to the *Christian Century*,* Episcopalian historian Cyril Richardson, and the Swedish theologian with worldwide stature Gustaf Aulen were among those who made contributions to the journal.

In the *Augustana Quarterly* the Swedish Lutherans put their history together, reflected on their relation to other Lutherans and other Christians and the contemporary world, and carved out a sense of who they were. In the process, implicitly and explicitly, they raised the issue of Lutheran union. That leads to the final chapter of this brief journalistic history.

The Lutheran Quarterly

In 1960 four Lutheran groups—three with Norwegian and Danish roots and one with a Germanic heritage—formed the American Lutheran Church (ALC). Two years later four other Lutheran groups—the ULCA, the Augustana Church, the Suomi Synod (or Finnish Evangelical Lutheran Church in America), and the American Evangelical Lutheran Church (earlier called the Danish Evangelical Lutheran Church in America)—formed the Lutheran Church in America (LCA). Soon the seminaries of these formerly separated bodies began to merge even across ALC and LCA lines.

The *Lutheran Quarterly* anticipated these mergers by more than a decade. In 1947 the Association of Lutheran Theological Professors proposed a joint theological journal. This proposal did not work out, but the following year the seminaries at Philadelphia and Gettysburg invited Augustana Seminary along with Capital Seminary in Columbus, Ohio, and Wartburg Seminary in Dubuque, Iowa, to a meeting in Pittsburgh. Philadelphia and Gettysburg at the time were supporting the *Lutheran Church Quarterly*, Augustana Seminary was supporting the *Augustana Quarterly*, and Capital and Wartburg were planning to begin yet another quarterly. The result of the Pittsburgh meeting was that these seminaries, plus Luther Seminary in St. Paul, Minnesota, agreed to merge the existent and planned journals into one "theological magazine." This was intended "as a step toward a theological magazine that will represent all sections" of Lutherans in the United States.[50] Officially it represented seminaries of the ULCA and Augustana, which would become part of the LCA, and the American Lutheran Church and Evangelical Lutheran Church, which would feed into the ALC. It did not include the more conservative Missouri Synod. It was published in Gettysburg.

Four aims were concisely stated. The journal was

to provide a forum (1) for the discussion of Christian faith and life on the basis of the Lutheran confession, (2) for the application of the principles of the Lutheran Church to the changing problems of religion and society, (3) for the fostering of world Lutheranism, and (4) for the promotion of understanding between Lutherans and other Christians.[51]

Except for fostering world Lutheranism, those aims were similar to the ones spelled out in 1928 in the first issue of the *Lutheran Church Quarterly*. The policy even quoted the language from 1928: contributions were to be "frank and fair," "free from controversial animus," and of "real scholarly and practical value."[52] As in 1928, differences of opinion between contributors and editors would not exclude articles; one even sensed that differences were regarded as more normal and expected in 1949 than in 1928.

The "Aims and Policy" were printed on the title page of each issue, as was a statement detailing the *Lutheran Quarterly*'s relation as successor to the quarterlies that had preceded it. Conrad Bergendoff, the powerful Augustana figure, took charge as the first editor. In a foreword, he further detailed the history, embraced the journal's aims and policy, and defined his understanding of a theological journal.[53] Theology as related to a theological journal, said Bergendoff, is not strictly "academic or scholastic"; it is the "thought by which the Church contemplates and directs its life."[54]

For the next five years Bergendoff edited the *Lutheran Quarterly* and saw to it that the thought of the church coursed through its pages. Reports and discussions of the ecumenical movement and Lutheran union, theological challenges and studies, historical articles, liturgical and musical matters, relations of church and state, and ethical studies found their way into the journal along with the book reviews, which had been included from the earliest days of the *Evangelical Review*. In 1951, 11 more Lutheran seminaries joined in supporting the enterprise, which lacked neither vigor, nor direction, nor support.

In 1954 Theodore G. Tappert, who had edited the *Lutheran Church Quarterly* for the last 10 years of its existence and had been book review editor of the *Lutheran Quarterly* itself, took Bergendoff's place. The magazine continued its course, sometimes still with vibrant volumes such as in 1957. But there were also subtle changes. The size of the journal decreased. A volume for one year formerly had included 400 to 500 pages. Now there were between 300 and 400. In 1955, the second year Tappert was editor, the statement of "Aims and Policy" disappeared. A fascination with Rudolf Bultmann and the Word, along with a corresponding un-Lutheran nervousness about the word *Mass* and sacraments, quietly impressed themselves on the journal. These perspectives tended to typify Tappert and the seminary at Philadelphia now, and they were therefore understandable, but they also tended to give the journal an air of arid scholasticism.

None of this immediately hurt circulation, which peaked around 1960. When the next editorial change took place, however, the Tappert years explain why Frederick K. Wentz repeatedly referred to the "staid, old" *Lutheran Quarterly*.[55] Frederick Wentz (b. 1921), the son of Abdel Ross Wentz and a Gettysburg College and Seminary graduate with a Ph.D. from Yale, became president and professor of church history at Hamma School of Theology, Springfield, Ohio, in 1966. In the same year he assumed the editorship of the *Lutheran Quarterly*. With him came a completely new editorial staff, and Wentz seized the opportunity to indicate a new direction: the magazine would make "a renewed effort to provide lively discussion of issues that currently confront the churches."[56] Sponsored now by the 13 seminaries of the ALC and LCA, the journal would be neither neutral nor partisan but would "seek to bring a broadly Lutheran perspective to focus upon any topic and to provide a platform for responsible expression of a variety of viewpoints."[57] To do this, each issue would focus around a theme. As if to illustrate immediately how lively the magazine would be, Wentz's first issue focused on the book that had everyone buzzing at the time, Harvey Cox's *The Secular City*. The cover, which had been dark blue with the Luther rose, was now dressed in brighter colors, new insignia, and the current topic in a band across the bottom.

Wentz served as editor until 1970. His duties at Hamma forced him to delegate responsibilities for the *Lutheran Quarterly*. Philip J. Hefner (b. 1932), a theologian with a Ph.D. from the University of Chicago who taught at Hamma, Gettysburg, and eventually at the Lutheran School of Theology at Chicago, served as acting editor for the first two issues. Robert E. Karsten (b. 1930), pastor to Wittenberg University in Springfield, Ohio, and the managing editor, wrote some of the editorial comments. Guest editors were employed.

A light piece by Robert E. Karsten on the marriage service and Sunday afternoon football evidenced zeal for change and some confusion about what the journal should be, but at the same time associate editor Robert H. Fischer (b. 1918) from the Lutheran School of Theology at Chicago helped the editorial staff develop a new set of aims.[58] These appeared from 1968 through 1970. In them the earlier Lutheran confessional emphasis was absent, and the weight fell on contemporary issues. The journal would provide clergy, seminarians, laypersons, and scholars "with relevant, provocative articles on Christian faith and life, in the context of modern society and of Christian ecumenical concern"; it would "publish scholarly studies, particularly in areas of special Lutheran responsibilities and interests"; and it would "provide a forum" to "encourage creative discussion" of "issues confronting the church."[59]

The ground was obviously shifting, but the journal still seemed vigorous. In 1969 it reached 500 pages and during the Wentz years addressed all sorts of topics: ministry, seminaries, liturgical renewal, social change, black America, preaching, Jewish-Christian and Jewish-Lutheran relations, politics, history, theology, leisure, poverty, biblical studies, and more.

The uncertainty behind the seeming vigor surfaced in 1971 when Daniel F. Martensen (b. 1936) became editor. A Minnesota Lutheran with a Ph.D. from Claremont University, Martensen taught with Wentz at Hamma. He looked ahead to the 1970s as a period of crisis, noted that a "commonality of theological assumptions has eroded within Lutheranism," and then in the ambiguity stipulated that writers must explain why their work is important.[60] He felt the journal could be justified only if it liberated itself "from the ideological trends induced by secular society, the academic establishment, and the ecclesiastical institution."[61] He also wanted to make the journal helpful to ministers in their professional needs.[62]

Martensen stayed until 1975 when he joined the staff of the Lutheran World Federation in Geneva, Switzerland. He continued Wentz's topical focus for each issue until August 1973. Then he returned to a spread of topics. In that same issue his editorial became more ominous. The journal, said Martensen, faced a crossroad. The need for theological faculties to converse with clergy in the parish and the archival function of the *Lutheran Quarterly* argued for its continuation. But low circulation, withdrawal of financial support by the LCA, potential withdrawal by the ALC and some seminaries, and the lack of materials submitted by seminary faculty argued against its continuation. Several possibilities were outlined, and a decision was anticipated by the fall of 1973.[63]

The magazine did not yet fold. In 1975 Keith R. Bridston (b. 1924), a Yale graduate with a Ph.D. from the University of Scotland in Edinburgh who had worked in international Christian circles and taught at Pacific Lutheran Seminary, Berkeley, California, became the editor. He followed what he inherited, continuing the new direction Martensen began in November 1973 when he initiated studies on the new lectionary as a way to help clergy in their ministry. Bridston tried to breathe vitality into the magazine in his first editorial, but three years later he announced the journal might have to cease publication. Citing rising costs, inflation, postage increases, limited income, and small subscriptions with a low price, he indicated there might be no hope. Even the economy rates from the Times and News Publishing Company in Gettysburg, which had always published the magazine, did not save enough and caused delays in getting the journal mailed. Bridston pointed to the high standards the magazine had maintained, its value as a scholarly theological forum, and the fine book review section. Then he noted Martin Luther's warning about churches that neglected scholarship.[64] That was in May 1977. It was the last editorial and the last issue.

These journals were all initiated and controlled by seminary faculties. They provided clergy with scholarly discussions on issues of current concern along with responsible reviews of books. Until the last years, they were clearly in some sense confessional Lutheran organs, and even near the end Lutheran concerns were prominent.

Alert and active pastors read and contributed to these journals. The leaders were precisely those who could be found in these pages, shaping the churches' thought and being shaped by it, engaged in the struggle to think through and act on the insights of their faith. In this sense the circulation statistics are deceiving, for these journals were immensely important despite modest circulation. They provided the turf for thinking through the faith and its implications in each generation. As primary historical sources for Lutherans in the United States, they are invaluable.

Why did the *Lutheran Quarterly* fold in 1977? Rising costs, inflation, and hard economic times are probably part of the answer but not the most convincing part. The earlier journals had survived the Civil War, World Wars I and II, the Great Depression, and perpetually minimal budgets. Low circulation was also a factor but again not too convincing. Circulation had always been low. Failure of supporting faculty to submit suitable materials is also not very convincing. Editors always had that problem, especially when no single controversial issue elicited passionate articles.[65]

One gets closer to a convincing reason for the journal's demise by noting that the *Lutheran Quarterly* had competition from other magazines like the *Lutheran World*, the *Concordia Theological Monthly**, *Dialog**, *Una Sancta*, and *Lutheran Forum*.[66] But that is not a totally satisfactory solution either, for none of those magazines could do precisely what the *Lutheran Quarterly* could do for its constituency.

The *Lutheran Quarterly* went out of business for two reasons. First, the support of so many seminaries, at first a positive influence, proved finally to be negative. Unlike the earlier journals where a faculty or persons from a faculty were committed to the necessity of a magazine and the ideas it would express, the *Lutheran Quarterly* had no single faculty or set of persons with such a commitment to sustain it. Second, and this is probably the more important factor, the journal got caught in the turbulent currents of the 1960s and 1970s. In its closing years, many of the articles sounded as much like sociology as theology. As it searched for an identity and floundered for new directions, it faced the question of whether the theological enterprise itself had any validity. Writers, seminaries, and the church itself answered the question negatively by allowing the journal to go out of business.

Bergendoff and others have lamented the absence of a common theological journal for the whole Lutheran Church.[67] It may be that such a magazine will evolve out of the merger of the LCA, ALC, and the Association of Evangelical Lutheran Churches (AELC). If so the strand begun by the *Evangelical Review* in 1849 will simply have a brief hiatus after 1977. If not, what the *Evangelical Review* and its successors did for a century and a quarter will have to be picked up by other journals.

Notes

1. Cf. Henry E. Horn, ed., *Memoirs of Henry Eyster Jacobs* (N.p.: Huntington Church Management Service, 1974), 2:257.
2. "Es sei denn, dass ich mit Zeugnissen der heiligen Schrift, oder mit 'offentlichen, klaren, und hellen Gründen und Ursachen überwunden und überwieset werde, so kann und will ich nichts widerrufen.' "
3. R. [William M. Reynolds], "Introductory—The Objects and Position of the Evangelical Review," *Evangelical Review* 1:1 (July 1849): 1.
4. For a survey of these early attempts, see Frederick Gebhart Gotwald, "Pioneer American Lutheran Journalism, 1812–1850," *Lutheran Quarterly* 42 (April 1912): 161–98. Also published separately.
5. [Reynolds], p. 17.
6. Ibid., p. 18.
7. C[harles] P[hilip] Krauth, "The Lutheran Church in the United States," *Evangelical Review* 2:4 (July 1850): 1.

8. Ibid., pp. 2–6.

9. Ibid., pp. 11–16. Cf. Gotwald where the private comments of Krauth and Reynolds point even more strongly to the reaction against "new measures" and the need for Lutheran ballast.

10. See "The Review," *Quarterly Review of the Evangelical Lutheran Church*, n.s. 1 (January 1871): 3.

11. Reynolds left the Lutheran Church and entered the Episcopal priesthood in 1864.

12. S. S. Schmucker, "The Nature of the Savior's Presence in the Eucharist," *Evangelical Review* 3:9 (July 1851): 34–64.

13. H. I. Schmidt, "Scriptural Character of the Lutheran Doctrine of the Lord's Supper," *Evangelical Review* 3:10 (October 1851): 198–255.

14. C[harles] P[hilip] Krauth and W[illiam] M. Reynolds, "Prospectus of the Ninth Volume of the Evangelical Review," *Evangelical Review* 9:33 (July 1857): 148–49.

15. "The Review," *Quarterly Review of the Evangelical Lutheran Church*, n.s. 1 (July 1871): 8.

16. See John Tietjen, *Which Way to Lutheran Unity?* (St. Louis: Concordia Publishing House, 1966).

17. Ibid.

18. See, for instance, J. W. Richard, "The Liturgical Question," *Lutheran Quarterly*, n.s. 20 (January 1890): 103–5.

19. Charles P[orterfield] Krauth, *The Conservative Reformation and Its Theology* (Philadelphia: General Council Publication Board, 1871).

20. See Horn, ed., 3:162, n. 103.

21. Theodore E. Schmauk, *Lutheran Church Review* 14 (October 1895): 271.

22. Ibid., pp. 271–72.

23. "Editorial Announcement," *Lutheran Church Review* 39 (October 1920): 385–86.

24. Reed's later books on these topics provide a compendium of his somewhat Anglicized Lutheran posture: *The Lutheran Liturgy* (Philadelphia: Muhlenberg Press, 1947) and *Worship: A Study of Corporate Devotion* (Philadelphia: Muhlenberg Press, 1959).

25. See "Valedictory," *Lutheran Church Review* 46 (October 1927): 409–10.

26. *Minutes of the Fifth Biennial Convention of the United Lutheran Church in America* [1926] (Philadelphia: United Lutheran Publication House, n.d.), p. 119.

27. Raymond F. Stamm, "Editorial Announcement," *Lutheran Church Quarterly* 1 (January 1928): 1–3.

28. From 1939 on, this was even noted on the title page.

29. Raymond F. Stamm, "The Lutheran Church Quarterly, 1928–1948, An Account of Its Stewardship," and "Analytical Index to Volumes I-XXI," *Lutheran Church Quarterly* 22 (January 1949).

30. Theodore G. Tappert et al., eds. *The Book of Concord* (Philadelphia: Fortress Press, 1959).

31. *Augustana Quarterly* 1:1 (March 1922): inside front cover.

32. Ibid.

33. *Minutes of the Sixty-second Annual Convention of the Ev. Luth. Augustana Synod in North America Held in Saron Lutheran Church, Chicago, Ill., June 8–13, 1921* (Rock Island: Augustana Book Concern, n.d.), p. 181.

34. Ibid., p. 120.

35. *Augustana Quarterly* 1:1 (March 1922): inside back cover.

36. Usually proofread quite ably; one slip is interesting. The Swedish article crept into the first sentence of one submission so that it read, "Under de general term 'Missions' we include . . ." See *Augustana Quarterly* 1:1 (March 1922): 73.

37. *Augustana Quarterly* 1:1 (March 1922): inside front cover.

38. Ibid.

39. Ibid., inside back cover.

40. Ibid.

41. Gustavus Adolphus College was founded by the Minnesota Conference of the Augustana Church in 1862.

42. Ferm remained in the Lutheran clergy but was admitted as an affiliate to the Presbytery at Wooster, Ohio, where he taught for most of his life. His sons became Presbyterian ministers and teachers.

43. Vergilius Ferm, "Contemporary Chaos," *Augustana Quarterly* 5:2 (June 1926): 111–19.

44. Ibid., pp. 118–19.

45. The Galesburg Rule is that "Lutheran pulpits are for Lutheran pastors only, and Lutheran altars are for Lutheran communicants only." Formulated in Akron in 1872 and amended at Galesburg in 1875, it grew out of the disputes that formed the General Council.

46. Conrad Bergendoff, "The Individual Christian's Call to Personal Evangelism," *Augustana Quarterly* 5:1 (March 1926): 25–33.

47. Cf. Oscar N. Olson, "Editorial Comments," *Augustana Quarterly* 14:1 (January 1935): 94–96, and A. F. Almer, "A Word of Thanks," *Augustana Quarterly* 13:1 (January 1934): 383–84.

48. C. M. Olander, "What Does the Present Situation Demand of our Synod with Regard to the Language to Be Used in the Upbuilding of God's Kingdom? The English Demand," *Augustana Quarterly* 9:1 (January 1930): 7.

49. S. G. Hägglund, "The Swedish Demand," *Augustana Quarterly* 9:1 (January 1930): 8–16.

50. "The Sponsorship of The Lutheran Quarterly," *Lutheran Quarterly* 1:1 (February 1949): 70.

51. Ibid., pp. 70–71.

52. Ibid., p. 71.

53. Ibid., pp. 3–5.

54. Ibid., p. 5.

55. See F[rederick] K. W[entz], "Editorial Comment," *Lutheran Quarterly* 20:1 (February 1968): 4, or W[entz], "Editorial Comment," *Lutheran Quarterly* 22:1 (February 1970): 2.

56. F[rederick] K. W[entz], "Editorial Comment," *Lutheran Quarterly* 18:1 (February 1966): 2.

57. Ibid.

58. Robert E. Karsten, "This Won't Hurt," *Lutheran Quarterly* 20:1 (February 1968): 5–6.

59. "The Aims of LQ," *Lutheran Quarterly* 20:1 (February 1968): 3.

60. Daniel F. Martensen, "The Lutheran Quarterly and the 1970's: A Statement of Editorial Posture," *Lutheran Quarterly* 23:1 (February 1971): 7.

61. Ibid., p. 8.

62. Ibid.

63. Daniel F. Martensen, "A Note to Lutheran Quarterly Readers," *Lutheran Quarterly* 21:3 (August 1973): 227–30.

64. K[eith] R. B[ridston], "Editorial," *Lutheran Quarterly* 29:2 (May 1977): 107.

65. Almer complained about it. See Almer, pp. 383–84.

66. Martensen, "Statement of Editorial Posture," p. 5, where this is implied.

67. See Glen C. Stone, "An LCA Partners Interview: Conrad J. Bergendoff," *Partners* (February 1980): 29.

Information Sources

BIBLIOGRAPHY:

Archival materials for *Lutheran Quarterly*, Archive of the Lutheran Church in America, Jesuit-Krauss Memorial Library, Lutheran School of Theology, Chicago.

Gotwald, Frederick G. "Pioneer American Lutheran Journalism, 1812–1850." *Lutheran Quarterly* 42 (April 1912): 161–98. Also published separately.

Olson, O. N. "Theological Periodicals of the Augustana Church." *Lutheran Quarterly* 1:3 (August 1949): 331–35.

Stamm, Raymond T. "The Lutheran Church Quarterly, 1928–1948: An Account of Its Stewardship." *Lutheran Church Quarterly* 22 (January 1949): 1–17.

Tietjen, John. *Which Way to Lutheran Unity?* St. Louis: Concordia Publishing House, 1966.

INDEX SOURCES: *Index to the Lutheran Quarterly for Fifty Years, 1871–1920* (N.P.: n.p., 1920); H. Max Lentz, *An Index to the Lutheran Quarterly for Ten Years, January 1871-October 1880* (Gettysburg: J. E. Wible, 1881); Raymond T. Stamm, "Analytical Index to Volumes I-XXI," *Lutheran Church Quarterly* 22 (January 1949): 18–226.

REPRINT EDITIONS: Microfilm in Archives of the Lutheran Church in America, Lutheran School of Theology, Chicago.

LOCATION SOURCES: Lutheran School of Theology, Chicago, and most Lutheran seminary libraries.

Publication History

MAGAZINE TITLE AND TITLE CHANGES: (1) *Evangelical Review* (1849–62), *Evangelical Quarterly Review* (1862–70), *Quarterly Review of the Evangelical Lutheran Church*, and *Lutheran Quarterly* [both titles used simultaneously] (1871–98), *Lutheran Quarterly* (1899–1927); (2) *Lutheran Church Review* (1882–1927); (3) *Lutheran Church Quarterly* (1928–49); (4) *Augustana Quarterly* (1922–48); (5) *Lutheran Quarterly* (1949–77).

VOLUME AND ISSUE DATA: (1) *Evangelical Review* 1–13 (July 1849-April 1862), *Evangelical Quarterly Review* 14–21 (October 1862-October 1870), *Quarterly Review of the Evangelical Lutheran Church* and *Lutheran Quarterly* n.s. 1–57 (January 1871-October 1927); (2) *Lutheran Church Review* 1–46 (January 1882-October 1927); (3) *Lutheran Church Quarterly* 1–22 (January 1928-January 1949); (4) *Augustana Quarterly* 1–27 (March 1922-October 1948); (5) *Lutheran Quarterly* 1–29 (February 1949-May 1977).

PUBLISHER AND PLACE OF PUBLICATION: (1) *Evangelical Review* and successors to 1927: H. C. Neinstadt (1849–64), Aughinbaugh and Wible (1865), J. E. Wible (1866–1901), Barbehenn & Little Ltd. (1902–04), William P. Hammond (1905–

07), Compiler Print (1908–27), all in Gettysburg, Pa.; (2) *Lutheran Church Review*: Alumni Association of the Evangelical Lutheran Theological Seminary (1882–97), Evangelical Lutheran Theological Seminary (1898–1904), General Council Publication House (1905–18), United Lutheran Publication House (1919), probably the Seminary (1920–27), all in Philadelphia; (3) *Lutheran Church Quarterly*: Compiler Print (1928), Gettysburg Times Print (1929–30), Gettysburg Times Press (1931–37), Times & News Publishing Co. (1938–48), all in Gettysburg, Pa.; (4) *Augustana Quarterly*: Augustana Book Concern, Rock Island, Ill.; (5) *Lutheran Quarterly*: Gettysburg Times and News Publishing Co., Gettysburg, Pa. (1949–77).

EDITORS: (1) *Evangelical Review* and its successors to 1927: William M. Reynolds (1849, 1851–62), Charles Philip Krauth (1850–62), Martin Luther Stoever (1857–70), James Allen Brown (1871–79), Milton Valentine et al. (1871–89, 1898–1908), Philip M. Bikle et al. (1890–1909), James W. Richard (1898–1908), John Alden Singmaster et al. (1910–25), Gettysburg Faculty (1926–27); (2) *Lutheran Church Review*: Revere F. Weidner et al. (1882), Henry Eyster Jacobs et al. (1883–85, 1887–85), Ashmead Schaeffer et al. (1886), Theodore E. Schmauk et al. (1896–1919), Philadelphia Seminary Faculty (1920–27); (3) *Lutheran Church Quarterly*: Raymond T. Stamm and Charles M. Jacobs et al. (1928–37), Theodore G. Tappert et al. (1938–48), M. Hadwin Fischer (1938), Harvey D. Hoover (1939–48); (4) *Augustana Quarterly*: Axel F. Almer et al. (1922–34), Oscar N. Olson et al. (1935–48); (5) *Lutheran Quarterly*: Conrad Bergendoff et al. (1949–53), Theodore G. Tappert et al. (1954–65), Frederick Wentz et al. (1966–70), Daniel F. Martensen (1971–74), Keith R. Bridston (1975–77).

CIRCULATION: (1) *Evangelical Review* and its successors to 1927: 500 (approx.); (2) *Lutheran Church Review*: less than 500 (est.); (3) *Lutheran Church Quarterly*: more than 500 (est.); (4) *Augustana Quarterly*: 500–760; (5) *Lutheran Quarterly*: 700–1775.

Paul Westermeyer

THE LUTHERAN CHURCH REVIEW. *See* THE LUTHERAN QUARTERLY

THE LUTHERAN SCHOLAR. *See* ACADEMY

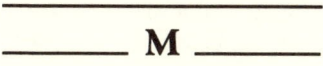

M

MAGAZIN FÜR EV.-LUTH. HOMILETIK. *See* LEHRE
UND WEHRE

**MAGAZIN FÜR EV.-LUTH. HOMILETIK UND
PASTORALTHEOLOGIE.** *See* LEHRE UND WEHRE

**MAGAZIN FÜR EV.-LUTH. HOMILETIK UND
PASTORALTHEOLOGIE: HOMILETIC MAGAZINE.**
See LEHRE UND WEHRE

THE MASSACHUSETTS MISSIONARY MAGAZINE

The *Massachusetts Missionary Magazine* was one of a host of religious magazines founded under the impulse of the benevolent society movement in the late eighteenth and early nineteenth centuries. The rise of the missionary movement in the 1790s included the founding of the Massachusetts Missionary Society on 28 May 1799. Initially the society existed to provide missionaries among the Indians and for growing numbers of settlers in Vermont and Maine.[1] The members of the society recognized that their work was similar to that of other missionary societies across New England. This awareness led directly to the creation of the *Massachusetts Missionary Magazine* after the model of similar ventures by other societies.

In 1803, Nathaniel Emmons, a leading light of Congregational orthodoxy in Massachusetts and president of the society, praised the many religious periodicals in New England as "greatly instrumental of reviving religion at home, and of spreading the gospel far and wide among the poor, ignorant, perishing Pagans.'' He was particularly pleased that the magazines, instead of competing, promoted one another. ''Deeply impressed with these sentiments,'' he reported, ''the Massachusetts Missionary Society unanimously agreed to encourage and support a new Periodical Publication, for the benevolent purpose of promoting the spread of the Gospel and the general cause of Christianity.''[2]

Initially the society conceived of its magazine as a money-making venture rather than a mission in itself. The title page of each edition announced that the ''Profits of this work are to be applied to the support of Missionaries in the New Settlements and among the Indians of North America.''[3] By the time of the first edition of the *Massachusetts Missionary Magazine* in May, 1803, the society was supporting four missionaries: David Avery, Jacob Cram, John Sawyer, and Adoniram Judson.[4] Members of the society hoped to ease financial pressures by realizing a profit from their magazine and providing a forum for promotion of their work.

Perhaps because of this over-arching purpose, the early editions of the magazine did not display great originality in format or content. The editors solicited ''compositions addressed to the conscience and heart,'' preferring those ''calculated for the level of children and persons of but common information'' to articles that were ''learned and highly seasoned with metaphysics.''[5] They particularly requested ''Dissertations on the doctrines and duties of Christianity, Expositions of difficult passages of scripture, lives of eminent persons, Experiences of private Christians, Instances of remarkable conversions, Narratives of special revivals of religion, and every kind of information respecting the spread and success of the gospel in any part of the world.''[6] Each 40-page issue contained a variety of departments, including ''Biography,'' ''Letters,'' ''Religious News,'' and ''Missionary Intelligence.''[7] In addition to these departments, most issues contained an assortment of essays, poems, hymns, and biblical expositions. Many of the features came directly from other religious publications.

Within a very short time the *Massachusetts Missionary Magazine* assumed a prominent role as an organ of Congregational orthodoxy. It began to include articles opposing the Deists, Unitarians, and Universalists.[8] As these controversies began to occupy the pages of the magazine, it came to resemble the *Panoplist*, another Congregational publication with which it shared several officers. In June 1808, this duplication of effort ended when the *Panoplist* absorbed the *Massachusetts Missionary Magazine*.

Notes

1. Benjamin M. Lewis, ''A History and Bibliography of American Magazines, 1800–1810'' (Ph.D. dissertation, University of Michigan, 1955), p. 191.

2. *Massachusetts Missionary Magazine* 1 (May 1803): 2.

3. Ibid., p. 1.

4. Lewis, pp. 191–92.

5. *Massachusetts Missionary Magazine* 1 (May 1803): 159.

6. Ibid., pp. 2–3.

7. "Biography" usually included an exerpt from a larger biographical work. See, for example, "The Character of Bishop Leighton," *Massachusetts Missionary Magazine* 2 (1804).

8. See, for example, "Letter to a Friend," *Massachusetts Missionary Magazine* 2 (April 1805): 443. This trend was especially evident in the last three volumes of the periodical.

Information Sources

BIBLIOGRAPHY:
Lewis, Benjamin M. "A History and Bibliography of American Magazines, 1800–1810."
    Ph.D. dissertation, University of Michigan, 1955.
INDEX SOURCES: None.
REPRINT EDITIONS: American Periodicals Series, University Microfilms International.
LOCATION SOURCES: Library of Congress, Amherst College, Harvard University,
    University of Chicago, Oberlin College, and others.

Publication History

MAGAZINE TITLE AND TITLE CHANGES: *The Massachusetts Missionary Magazine*
    (1803–8); absorbed into the *Panoplist* (June 1808).
VOLUME AND ISSUE DATA: 1–5 (May 1803-May 1808). Monthly issues in annual
    volumes.
PUBLISHER AND PLACE OF PUBLICATION: Massachusetts Missionary Society (J.
    Cushing), Salem, Mass. (1803–4); Massachusetts Missionary Society (E. Lin-
    coln), Boston (1804–8).
EDITOR: Nathaniel Emmons (1803–8), assisted by varying groups of twelve others
    appointed by the Massachusetts Missionary Society.
CIRCULATION: Exact figures unknown; probably not more than a few hundred.

Michael R. McCoy

MENNONITE QUARTERLY REVIEW

The history of the *Mennonite Quarterly Review* centers on one man, Harold S. Bender, the driving force in its creation and its editor for 36 years until his death in 1962. The publication owes its conception and long, steady growth to Bender's vision of the Mennonite place in history and the importance of history in the renewal of the church.

Bender was born in 1897 in Elkhart, Indiana, to devout Mennonite parents. He received his college degree in 1918 from Goshen College, a Mennonite school in Goshen, Indiana. After brief study at Garrett Biblical Institute, Evanston, Illinois, Bender enrolled at Princeton Theological Seminary, where in 1923 he received the Master of Theology degree with a major in New Testament and the Master of Arts degree with a major in Semitic philology. He also studied at the University of Tübingen, Germany, and later would return to Germany to the University of Heidelberg for doctoral studies, which he completed in 1935.

But 1924 found him in Goshen, Indiana, teaching at Goshen College. A colleague and lifetime acquaintance, Guy F. Hershberger, described the times in a 1964 memorial issue of the *Review* dedicated to Bender. About the beginning of the 1900s the Mennonite Church was awakening from a long period of dormancy and lethargy. Goshen College sprang from this awakening. But while the mission activities of the church, in which Bender's father had played an important role, and the church's higher education program were located in Indiana, the church leadership shifted its center to the church publication headquarters in Scottdale, Pennsylvania. As Hershberger recalls, "This geographical dichotomy was symbolic, and in some measure a cause, of an unfortunate intellectual and spiritual dichotomy within the church, productive of much tension . . . the climax of which was reached precisely during Bender's" student days. What might have been a healthy tension between academic and nonacademic communities became instead an "unhealthy conflict of abnormal proportions."[1] So deep were the feelings that in 1923 Goshen College closed for one year to reorganize. When it reopened in 1924, Bender was a leading member of a faculty that set about shaping the direction of school and church.

Upon joining the faculty, Bender and fellow teacher Ernst Correll founded the Mennonite Historical Society. (Correll was still an honorary member of the board of directors of this organization at his death in 1982.) The society directed primary attention to the establishment of a historical library and then, in 1927, to the *Mennonite Quarterly Review*. The society, the library, and the *Review* were each seen as important instruments in the renewal of the church and a "*sine qua non* for a rediscovery of the essence of sixteenth century anabaptism." Bender's perspective extended far beyond the internecine squabbles that rent his church to a reaffirmation of historic Mennonite beliefs and to a vindication before non-Mennonites of the Mennonite vision. Anabaptist historiography, written by non-Mennonites, had been largely pejorative and polemical. The scholarly task, Bender believed, was apologetic: to center the history of Anabaptism in the historiography of the Reformation and to "delineate the ethos and salient features of the movement against innumerable misconceptions."[2]

An editorial in the first issue of the *Review* in 1927 describes its several purposes. It was to be "a quarterly journal devoted to discussion and review of Mennonite history, thought, doctrine, life, literature, and affairs." In the words of editor Bender, although "its chief interests will be those of the Mennonite Church, its content will no doubt be of interest and value to other Mennonite groups, and to non-Mennonites in general." Bender continued: "It is hoped that its contribution to historical scholarship will be worthy of note to historians in general who are interested in the history of the Reformation period and the radical evangelical group which arose at that time and has continued to the present time in Europe and America, once known as Anabaptists, now generally known as Mennonites." Bender emphasized that the *Review* was neither a journal of propaganda serving some radical faction within the Mennonite Church nor a crucible for reheating old Reformation controversies. Nor was it to be "merely a journal of opinion or comment" rounding the distinctive edges of historical Anabaptism or softening the Mennonite position before the growing modernism of the times.

Instead it would be the endeavor of the editors, said Bender, "to present only such material as is scholarly, of literary merit, and of permanent value." Historical articles would be original, authoritative contributions of scholars. Doctrinal or theological articles would be "conservative, vital, biblical and evangelical." Current problems would be discussed by writers of "experience and leadership" who were "sane, sympathetic, constructive and forward-looking." Even the youth of the church, Bender reassured, would find "inspiration and vision and stimulation" in the *Review*.[3]

Since its founding in 1927, the *Review* has appeared continuously and has changed little in size, purpose, or content. Bender remained editor until his death in 1962. He was followed by Guy F. Hershberger (1963–65), John S. Oyer (1966–74; 1977-present), and Walter Klaassen (1975–76). All were colleagues in one way or another with Bender in his lifetime, and all were and are devoted to extending a common legacy. By intention, historical materials have always commanded a large proportion of *Review* space. Included are articles, primary documents, and bibliographical and research notes. Book reviews have remained a regular feature since the beginning. The *Review* is refereed. It receives submissions from Mennonite and non-Mennonite scholars, and its subscribers number many non-Mennonite readers.

Notes

1. Guy F. Hershberger, "Harold S. Bender and His Time," *Mennonite Quarterly Review* 38 (1964): 84. Also see Hershberger, *The Recovery of the Anabaptist Vision: A Sixtieth Anniversary Tribute to Harold S. Bender* (Scottdale, Pa.: Herald Press, 1957).

2. Cornelius J. Dyck, "Harold S. Bender: The Church Historian," *Mennonite Quarterly Review* 38 (1964): 130, 135, 136.

3. "Editorial," *Mennonite Quarterly Review* 1 (1927): 1–3. The purposes were restated and reaffirmed in subsequent issues.

Information Sources

BIBLIOGRAPHY:
Hershberger, Guy F. *The Recovery of the Anabaptist Vision: A Sixtieth Anniversary Tribute to Harold S. Bender*. Scottdale, Pa.: Herald Press, 1957.
INDEX SOURCES: *America: History and Life, Religion Index One, Historical Abstracts*; 1–25 in 26 (1952), 26–30 in 30 (1956), 31–40 in 40 (1966), 41–50 in 50 (1976).
REPRINT EDITIONS: AMS Press.
LOCATION SOURCES: Union Theological Seminary (New York), Library of Congress, Yale University, University of Chicago, Princeton Theological Seminary, Duke University, and others.

Publication History

MAGAZINE TITLE AND TITLE CHANGES: *Mennonite Quarterly Review* (1927–   ).
VOLUME AND ISSUE DATA: 1:1 (January 1927–   ). Appears quarterly.
PUBLISHER AND PLACE OF PUBLICATION: Mennonite Historical Society, Goshen
    College, Goshen, Ind.
EDITORS: Harold S. Bender (1927–62), Guy F. Hershberger (1963–65), John S. Oyer
    (1966–74, 1977–   ), Walter Klaassen (1975–76).
CIRCULATION: 1000 (1983, approx.)

Kent Druyvesteyn

THE MERCERSBURG REVIEW

The Pennsylvania village of Mercersburg lies in the foothills of the Appala-
chian mountain range. Currently the major academic institution there is the
Mercersburg Academy. However, in the mid-nineteenth century, it was the site
of the college and seminary of the German Reformed Church in the United
States.[1] Here was born the famous Mercersburg theology, as well as the major
journalistic outlet of the movement, the *Mercersburg Review*.[2]

The two major figures of Mercersburg as well as the earliest, most important,
and most prolific contributors to the *Mercersburg Review* were John W. Nevin[3]
and Philip Schaff.[4] John W. Nevin experienced a genuine pilgrimage in his
religious outlook, for he grew up in Puritanism and at Mercersburg reacted
against Puritanism or what might be more correctly called low evangelicalism.
After earning his degree from Union College, Schenectady, New York, Nevin
received theological education at Princeton Seminary and studied under Charles
Hodge, who later referred to Nevin as his most brilliant student ever.[5] On
completing his degree, Nevin taught at Princeton while Hodge studied in Europe.
From Princeton Nevin went to Western Seminary (Presbyterian) in Pittsburgh
and remained there for 10 years. There he witnessed the "new measures revivalism" against which he reacted so strongly later. At Pittsburgh he also began
reading European theologians and historians, who would begin to influence his
thinking. In 1840 he came to the small German Reformed Seminary at Mercersburg and joined F. A. Rauch as the entire faculty. When Rauch died un-
expectedly the next year, Nevin was left as the only theological professor there
for several years.

Continuing his wide reading and pilgrimage, Nevin moved on to the positions
that would become hallmarks of Mercersburg theology. Reacting to "anxious
bench" revivalism in Mercersburg, in 1843 Nevin published *The Anxious Bench*,
which attacked this kind of revivalism as sheer quackery.[6] He preferred the
"system of the catechism" as the legitimate approach to Christian nurture. A
few years later, his work turned to liturgics and the Eucharist, both characteristic
concerns of the Mercersburg theology. His *The Mystical Presence* (1846) gave
a more legitimately Calvinistic and Reformed view of the Eucharist than the

Princeton theologians had given.[7] It launched a heated controversy within the German Reformed Church.

After Rauch's death, the search for his successor took the committee to Germany. In Berlin they found Philip Schaff, a young scholar educated at the universities of Halle, Tübingen, and Berlin.[8] His credentials included excellent recommendations from some of the finest scholars in Europe. He began teaching in the fall of 1844 as Nevin's only colleague, delighted to find a scholar in the United States so well read in German theology. Schaff's major contributions to Mercersburg would be multifold but mainly a historical awareness and an ecumenical spirit.

Within two years of his arrival, Schaff had undergone the baptism of fire in the form of two heresy trials.[9] The first trial resulted from his claim that the Reformation evolved naturally out of medieval Catholicism. Expressed first in his inaugural address, this idea formed the thesis of *The Principle of Protestantism* (1845).[10] The second stemmed from his theological questions about a "middle state" of the soul after death, raised in writings done in Germany prior to his coming to the United States.[11] He was exonerated on both counts, and the air was cleared for academic freedom in the German Reformed tradition, for there was never another heresy trial in the denomination. After the stress and turmoil of these early years, Schaff settled in for two decades of diligent work, publishing such works as *What Is Church History?* (1846),[12] *America* (1854),[13] and the first volume of his seven-volume *History of the Christian Church* (1856).[14]

The *Mercersburg Review* began in 1849 when a committee of Marshall College alumni launched it with Nevin as its first editor and chief contributor. In 1851 Nevin resigned from Mercersburg Seminary and the next year from his editorship. Schaff early became an equal contributor and even served as coeditor with E. V. Gerhart from 1857 to 1861. Schaff left the seminary in 1862 on a leave and in 1864 resigned his professorship.[15] Together, Nevin and Schaff dominated the journal during its early history, though Schaff remained an occasional contributor and as late as the year of his death, 1893, an article is found under his name in the *Review*.

Literally dozens of scholarly and semischolarly articles in the early volumes of the *Review* illustrated the major themes of the Mercersburg theology. Nevin attacked "low evangelicalism" in his "True and False Protestantism,"[16] "Early Christianity,"[17] and "Cyprian."[18] Although he presented in these articles Schaff's theory of historical development, Nevin was at times attacked for "Romanism" on the basis of them. He and Schaff called their own church tradition, as well as the American religious scene, to historical consciousness through these and other articles. Both paid attention to liturgics and creeds in such essays as "The Athanasian Creed,"[19] "The New Liturgy,"[20] "The Holy Eucharist,"[21] and "The Anti-Creed Heresy."[22] Ecumenism was found in some way in virtually every article. On all the "contemporary themes of ecumenical study, Nevin and Schaff speak with startling actuality."[23] One additional contribution was made to theological science in the United States by these men through the *Mercersburg*

Review. Their articles, especially Schaff's, served as bridgebuilders between the United States and Europe, acquainting American scholars with the major figures (such as Neander), as well as the most recent scholarship, in Europe.

The influence of the *Mercersburg Review* and its two early and major contributors was more expansive and extensive than would be implied by its small and humble beginnings in the quiet village of Mercersburg. It was one of the most important theological journals published in the United States in the nineteenth century, though in time it became more parochial in focus.

Notes

1. See James I. Good, *History of the Reformed Church in the United States in the Nineteenth Century* (New York: Board of Publication of the Reformed Church in America, 1911), and George W. Richards, *History of the Theological Seminary of the Reformed Church in the United States, 1825–1934, Evangelical and Reformed Church, 1934–1952, at Lancaster, Pennsylvania* (Lancaster: n.p., 1952).

2. James H. Nichols, *Romanticism in American Theology: Nevin and Schaff at Mercersburg* (Chicago: University of Chicago Press, 1961).

3. See Theodore Appel, *The Life and Work of John Williamson Nevin* (Philadelphia: Reformed Church Publication House, 1889).

4. See David Schaff, *The Life of Philip Schaff* (New York: Charles Scribner's Sons, 1897).

5. See George H. Shriver, "Passages in Friendship: John W. Nevin to Charles Hodge," *Journal of Presbyterian History* 58 (1980): 116–22.

6. John Nevin, *The Anxious Bench* (Chambersburg: Printed at the Office of the "Weekly Messenger," 1843).

7. John W. Nevin, *The Mystical Presence*, Lancaster Series on the Mercersburg Theology, vol. 4 (Philadelphia: United Church Press, 1966).

8. See Klaus Penzel, "Church History and the Ecumenical Quest: A Study of the German Background and Thought of Philip Schaff" (Th.D. dissertation, Union Theological Seminary, 1962).

9. See George H. Shriver, *American Religious Heretics* (Nashville: Abingdon Press, 1966), pp. 18ff.

10. Philip Schaff, *The Principle of Protestantism*, Lancaster Series on the Mercersburg Theology, vol. 1 (Philadelphia: United Church Press, 1964).

11. Philip Schaff, *Die Sünde wider den Heiligen Geist* (Halle: J. F. Lippert, 1841).

12. Philip Schaff, *What Is Church History?* (Philadelphia: J. B. Lippincott, 1846).

13. Philip Schaff, *America* (Reprinted, Cambridge: Belknap Press of Harvard University, 1961).

14. Philip Schaff, *History of the Christian Church* (Reprinted, seven volumes in eight, Grand Rapids: Eerdmans, 1950).

15. In 1864, he moved to New York City and in 1870 was appointed to the faculty of Union Theological Seminary. See D. Schaff, *Life*, passim.

16. *Mercersburg Review* 1 (1848): 83ff.

17. Ibid. 3 (1851): 461ff., 513ff.; 4 (1852): 1ff.

18. Ibid. 4 (1852): 259ff., 335ff., 417ff., 513ff.

19. Ibid. 11 (1859): 232ff.

20. Ibid. 10 (1858): 199ff.

21. Ibid. 3 (1851): 446ff.
22. Ibid. 4 (1852): 606ff.
23. Nichols, p. 310.

Information Sources

BIBLIOGRAPHY:

Appel, Theodore. *The Life and Work of John Williamson Nevin*. Philadelphia: Reformed Church Publication House, 1889.

Good, James I. *History of the Reformed Church in the United States in the Nineteenth Century*. New York: Board of Publication of the Reformed Church in America, 1911.

Nevin, John W. *The Anxious Bench*. Chambersburg: Printed at the Office of the "Weekly Messenger," 1843.

————. *The Mystical Presence* (1846). Reprinted. Philadelphia: United Church Press, 1966.

Nichols, James H. *Romanticism in American Theology*. Chicago: University of Chicago Press, 1961.

Schaff, David. *The Life of Philip Schaff*. New York: Charles Scribner's Sons, 1897.

Schaff, Philip. *America* (1855). Reprinted. Cambridge: Belknap Press of Harvard University, 1961.

————. *History of the Christian Church*. 8 vols. Reprinted. Grand Rapids: Eerdmans, 1950.

————. *The Principle of Protestantism*. Reprinted. Philadelphia: United Church Press, 1964.

Shriver, George H. *American Religious Heretics*. Nashville: Abingdon Press, 1966.

INDEX SOURCES: Indexed in *Mercersburg Review* 18 (vols. 1–18), 58 (vols. 1–58), 73 (vols. 59–73); also in *Poole's Index*.

REPRINT EDITIONS: University Microfilms International, ATLA Microtext Project.

LOCATION SOURCES: Library of Congress, University of Chicago, Princeton Theological Seminary, Duke University, Franklin and Marshall College, and others.

Publication History

MAGAZINE TITLE AND TITLE CHANGES: *The Mercersburg Review* (1849–52, 1857–78), *The Mercersburg Quarterly Review* (1853–56), publication suspended (1862–66), *The Reformed Quarterly Review* (1879–96), *The Reformed Church Review* (1897–1926).

VOLUME AND ISSUE DATA: *Mercersburg Review* 1:1–4:4 (1849–52), *Mercersburg Quarterly Review* 5:1–8:4 (1853–56), *Mercersburg Review* 9:1–13:4 (1857–61), publication suspended (1862–66), *Mercersburg Review* 14:1–25:4 (1867–78), *Reformed Quarterly Review* 26:1–43:4 (1879–96), *Reformed Church Review* 44:1–73:4 (1897–1926).

PUBLISHER AND PLACE OF PUBLICATION: Publication Board of the Reformed Church, Lancaster, Pa.

EDITORS: J. W. Nevin (1849–52), Publishing Committee (1853–56), E. V. Gerhart and Philip Schaff (1857–61), publication suspended (1862–66), H. Harbaugh (1867), T. G. Appel (1868–96), W. Rupp (1897–1903), G. W. Richards (1904–11), T. F. Herman (1912–26).

CIRCULATION: In the low hundreds (est.).

George H. Shriver

METHODIST HISTORY

Beginning in 1948, the World Methodist Council and the Association of Methodist Historical Societies joined forces to produce a periodical titled *World Parish*. It was natural for the two agencies to work together since both had headquarters at Lake Junaluska, North Carolina, where American Methodist archival materials were deposited. But *World Parish* was neither scholarly in format, though it did carry occasional pieces by scholars, nor oriented to historical issues. Rather, it was more akin to a sophisticated newsletter, noting important events and meetings of interest to Methodists throughout the world. Hence early on there was a desire among officials of the American Association of Methodist Historical Societies to oversee publication of a journal that would be more academic in tone and treat matters germane to the history of Methodism in the United States. That desire came to fruition in October 1962 when the first issue of the quarterly *Methodist History* appeared. In an editorial statement in the inaugural issue, Methodist historian Elmer T. Clark noted that the journal fulfilled a dream under consideration for more than two decades. At the very least, it was the unstated hope that *Methodist History* would provide one of the United States's largest Protestant denominations with a scholarly vehicle on par with cognate journals published by other denominations, such as the highly regarded *Historical Magazine of the Protestant Episcopal Church** and the *Journal of Presbyterian History.**

Over the years, however, the hopes of creating a historical journal of the first rank met with difficulty. On the one hand, the journal came into existence at a time when the Methodist Church was in the beginning stages of merger with the Evangelical United Brethren Church. The merger, which was effected in 1968 in the creation of the United Methodist Church, considerably broadened the scope of what constituted Methodist history in the United States. And as denominational leaders and agencies became more historically conscious and the archival materials available for scholarly use at the Lake Junaluska site expanded, it became increasingly clear that the facilities were inadequate to provide for serious, sustained research. This latter problem has since been relieved; in 1982 the Commission on Archives and History of the United Methodist Church, in some ways the successor to the old Association of Historical Societies, opened a new archives facility on the campus of Drew University, Madison, New Jersey, which provided proper conditions not only for storage of manuscripts and other materials but also for scholarly research. With materials from the United Methodist Church's predecessor denominations gathered under one roof, a fresh opportunity for production of a solid journal exists.

The first two decades of *Methodist History* were thus times of transition, a situation reflected in the lack of clear focus and uneven quality of articles. For many years the bulk of articles were derived from papers read at meetings of various Methodist historical societies, and although authors had a sincere interest in Methodist history, only a handful were rigorously academic. Many were written by local pastors and bishops with little time for prolonged research. In addition, many of the essays were biographical in focus but occasionally more hagiographic than academic in tone. Until relatively recently, few dealt with historical materials relating to contemporary issues, such as black Methodism or women in the Methodist tradition, which occupied much of the denomination's attention.

But the journal did make valuable contributions in some areas. Durward Hofler's essay, "The Methodist Doctrine of the Church" (6:1, 1967), opened up an important arena in historical theology, as did Paul M. Bassett's article on the theology of the holiness movement (13:3, 1975), a piece complemented by E. Dale Dunlap's historical study of the holiness movement in the same issue. Revivals and camp meetings, which were responsible for much of the growth of American Methodism, received fresh treatment from a literary angle in two important contributions by Elmer F. Suderman: "A Study of the Revival in Late Nineteenth Century American Fiction" (5:2, 1967) and "Washington Irving's Comment on an Early New York Camp Meeting" (6:2, 1968). Perhaps one of the most significant scholarly pieces to appear in the early years was W. Harrison Daniel's article on the role played by the Methodist Episcopal Church, South, during the Confederacy (6:2, 1968). In addition, renowned Methodist theologian Albert Outler provided a judicious assessment of Methodism's founder in "John Wesley as Theologian—Then and Now" (12:4, 1974). Another important role *Methodist History* played in its early years was in printing some hitherto unpublished letters written by figures such as Wesley and Francis Asbury, who are vital to the denomination's story.

Midway through *Methodist History*'s second decade, however, the journal began to assume a much more scholarly and professional quality. With volume 15 (1977), it added two features of interest to researchers in Methodist history: a section entitled "Discoveries," which reported on new materials acquired by the archives or discovered elsewhere and gave a brief description of their contents, and an annual checklist of doctoral dissertations written on topics relating to Methodist history. Reviews of two or three books examining Methodist matters are also now included, though they are brief. The late 1970s also witnessed treatment of topics previously neglected. Black Methodist history was analyzed in such articles as one by William B. Gravely on the Christian (formerly Colored) Methodist Episcopal Church (18:1, 1979), Kirk Mariner's "The Negro's Place: Virginia Methodists Debate Unification, 1924–25" (18:3, 1980), Julius E. Del's "Blacks in the United Methodist Church from Its Beginning to 1968" (19:1, 1980), Reginald Hildebrand's "Ordination of Black Ministers to 1764" (20:3, 1982), and Lewis V. Baldwin's "Black Women and African Union Methodism, 1813–1983" (21:4, 1983). Women's history came under scrutiny in Earl K. Brown's "Women in Church History" (18:2, 1980), Arnold Shankman's "Dorothy Tilley, Civil Rights, and the Methodist Church" (18:2, 1980), Rosemary Skinner Keller's "Creating a Sphere for Women in the Church" (18:2, 1980), and Mary Agnes Daugherty's provocative "The Methodist Deaconess: A Case of Religious Feminism" (21:2, 1983). "The Beginnings of Indian Methodism in Oklahoma" by Walter Vernon (17:3, 1979) opened up another previously neglected dimension of Methodism's story. A few more articles have appeared dealing with Methodist history outside the United States—for example Karl Zehrer's "The Relationship between Pietism in Halle and Early Methodism" (17:4, 1979)—while pieces such as Philip D. Jordan's insightful "Immigrants, Methodists, and a 'Conservative' Social Gospel, 1865–1908" (17:1, 1978) continue to reflect the desire for high standards of scholarship.

Methodist History is now in its third decade, and although it has yet to attain the stature of historical periodicals published by other denominations, it has clearly embarked on a path that may bring it into the front ranks of journals of its genre by its fourth decade. Its greatest contribution to date would seem to have been its role in sparking scholarly interest in American Methodist history primarily among Methodists and, in so doing, bringing a heightened historical consciousness to the United States's second largest Protestant denomination. That contribution alone makes *Methodist History* significant and a journal to watch as it moves toward maturity.

Information Sources

INDEX SOURCES: *Religion Index One, Religious and Theological Abstracts, United Methodist Periodical Index, America: History and Life, Historical Abstracts.*
REPRINT EDITIONS: University Microfilms International.
LOCATION SOURCES: Yale University, Duke University, University of Chicago, Pacific School of Religion, Library of Congress, and others.

Publication History

MAGAZINE TITLE AND TITLE CHANGES: *Methodist History* (1962–   ).
VOLUME AND ISSUE DATA: 1:1 (October 1962–   ). Appears quarterly in October, January, April, and July.
PUBLISHER AND PLACE OF PUBLICATION: American Association of Methodist Historical Societies, Lake Junaluska, N.C. (1962–66); Parthenon Press, Nashville, Tenn., for the American Association of Methodist Historical Societies (1966–68); Parthenon Press, Nashville, Tenn., for the Commission on Archives and History, United Methodist Church (1968–75, 1977–79); Mountaineer, Waynesville, N.C., for the Commission on Archives and History, United Methodist Church (1975–77, 1979–80); Commission on Archives and History, United Methodist Church, Lake Junaluska, N.C. (1980–82); General Commission on Archives and History, United Methodist Church, Madison, N.J. (1982–   ).
EDITORS: Elmer T. Clark (1962–63), Albea Godbold (1963–68), John H. Ness, Jr. (1968–82), Charles Yrigoyen, Jr. (1982–   ).
CIRCULATION: 700 (1982).

Charles H. Lippy

METHODIST MAGAZINE. *See* METHODIST REVIEW

METHODIST MAGAZINE AND QUARTERLY REVIEW.
See METHODIST REVIEW

METHODIST QUARTERLY REVIEW. *See* METHODIST REVIEW

THE METHODIST REVIEW

From its beginning, *Methodist Review*, originally known as *Methodist Magazine*, was a child of its British heritage. John Wesley, responding to attacks from the Calvinist religious press in England, launched the *Arminian Magazine* at the beginning of 1778. This magazine, edited by Wesley and filled with "Extracts and Original Treatises on Universal Redemption," became the inspiration and early model for its American cousin.[1]

Inspired by the British example, the American General Conference of 1796 "authorized the publication of a monthly, to be called the Methodist Magazine, on the ground that the 'propagation of religious knowledge by means of the press is next in importance to the preaching of the gospel.' "[2] John Dickins, founding steward of the Methodist Book Concern, issued the initial numbers of the *Methodist Magazine*, but his death in 1798 interrupted publication. Despite initiatives by the General Conferences of 1812 and 1816, the periodical was not revived until 1818. In that year the *Methodist Magazine*, later known as the *Methodist Quarterly Review* and the *Methodist Review*, began a tenure that lasted until 1931. Its 11 editors guided the publication through 112 years, during which it outlived all of its initial competitors.

Joshua Soule and Thomas Mason published the first volumes of the *Methodist Magazine* beginning in January 1818. The initial article of the magazine explained their guiding principles:

> The great design of this publication is to circulate religious knowledge,— a design which embraces the highest interests of rational existence, as the sum of individual and social happiness increases on a scale of proportion with the increase of spiritual light and information.[3]

They expressed their determination to guard against "the innovations of superstition on the one hand, and of false philosophy on the other."[4] This care to present a moderate path between the opposing hazards of superstition and rationalism led to a format that avoided originality. Most of the articles came, directly or in excerpt, from other publications. From the first edition, the magazine divided its pages among standard departments, which included "Divinity (mostly sermons), Biography, Miscellaneous, Religious and Missionary Intelligence, Obituary, Poetry.'' There was a heavy concentration on church history and biography.[5]

Beginning with the third volume, Nathan Bangs took over as editor of the *Methodist Magazine*. He used much the same format as his predecessors until 1830. In that year Bangs, with the consent of leaders within the church, abandoned the monthly publishing schedule and established a quarterly theological review. Bangs described the need for such a change by pointing to the rise of other Methodist periodicals, including the *Child's Magazine* and the *Christian Advocate and Journal*. Although precise circulation data are difficult to obtain, it is clear that Bangs and his colleagues were confronted with a decline in readership. Their response, the refurbished *Methodist Magazine and Quarterly Review*, was intended to serve a different purpose and reach a different audience from the other Methodist periodicals. The new format permitted longer articles and encouraged original contributions, especially in ''vindication not only of the doctrines, but of the institutions, discipline, and polity, of the Methodist Episcopal Church.''[6] The new format also included book reviews and steel plate engravings of leading ministers in the denomination.

The General Conference of 1840 mandated another important change in the periodical. George Peck, the new editor, changed the title to the *Methodist Quarterly Review* and adopted the style of the English theological review in which ''several (about eight) main articles were placed first, followed by book notices, and everything was anonymous.''[7] At the same time, the magazine adopted a more scholarly demeanor, discussing such topics as Cousin's psychology, Kant's philosophy, and Fourierism.

The strong intellectual cast of the *Methodist Quarterly Review* provoked enough opposition that Peck was not reelected to the editorship by the General Conference of 1848. He was succeeded by John McClintock, who was advised by the General Conference that if the *Quarterly Review* were ''made more practical it would be more popular and useful.''[8]

Under McClintock's leadership, however, the *Methodist Quarterly Review* took on a more, rather than less, scholarly appearance. Puzzled by the advice of the General Conference, McClintock could not accept that he was directed to make the magazine more practical ''by lowering its tone in point of literature and scholarship.'' Indeed, the Book Committee of the denomination advised him that the resolution of the conference should be interpreted as a mandate to elevate the literary character of the quarterly.[9] McClintock was well prepared to do this. He had a long-standing acquaintance with J. L. Jacobi, a pupil of Joachim Neander, who kept the magazine supplied with the latest in critical scholarship from Germany. In 1851 Jacobi supplied McClintock with the first definitive article in English about an important discovery of a text by Hippolytus of Rome. Another series of articles during the McClintock era, presented anonymously by George F. Holmes of the University of Virginia, summarized positive philosophy. These articles came to the attention of Auguste Comte, founder of that movement, who engaged in a long correspondence with McClintock.[10]

Troubled by the continuing scholarly tone and declining circulation of the *Quarterly Review*, the General Conference of 1856 did not reappoint McClintock but replaced him with Daniel Whedon. The new editor was far less interested in profound critical scholarship than in the debates and disputes of his age. Although he made relatively few changes in the structure of the magazine, he turned its attention to controversies about "Calvinism, Universalism, Catholicism, slavery and the things that went with it, all kinds of religious and theological fads, exaggerations, perversions" and other disputes.[11] Whedon continued to direct the magazine for 28 years until his death in 1885.

Whedon was succeeded briefly by his associate editor, Daniel Curry, who had been appointed the year before at the age of 75. Curry filled the post until his death in September 1887.

James W. Mendenhall, a presiding elder from the Ohio Conference, assumed the editorship in 1888. He began his tenure by insisting that the *Review* "must assert itself as a potent instrument in the current strifes of the church with the doctrinal errors of modern thinkers and teachers."[12] Under his leadership the periodical reversed its support of modern biblical scholarship and attacked all forms of higher criticism. This new tenor alienated many scholarly readers and led to a further decline in circulation. Mendenhall died in 1892 and was succeeded by William Valentine Kelley.

Kelley, a leading minister from Connecticut, adopted a more irenic tone, which avoided controversy. The result was a long and peaceful tenure during which the *Methodist Review*, as it now came to be known, combined modest scholarship with a generally uplifting tone. At Kelley's retirement in 1920, George Elliott became the editor. He emphasized scholarly values. His death in 1930 found the publication struggling to maintain its circulation in an era when most denominational theological reviews had long since ceased publication. Noting that the times had changed, "and with them the opinions and tastes of the public, and of the periodicals which serve it," the *Methodist Review* ceased publication in May 1931.[13]

Through more than a century, the *Methodist Quarterly Review* alternated its service between strictly denominational ends and the pursuit of theological scholarship. James R. Joy, the assistant editor who presided over the end of the magazine, offered an assessment of its career:

Methodist periodical literature was Wesley's weapon for fighting the foes of the Arminian doctrine which he taught. In America the Methodist press at first had the same battle on its hands, together with the task of winning recognition as a church worthy of intellectual respect. The Review fought both these fights and won. After 113 years it is the last to leave the field and it marches off with banners flying. It has been demonstrated in its own experience and in that of its whilom denominational contemporaries that the work has been accomplished.[14]

Notes

1. John Wesley, ed., *Arminian Magazine* (London) 1 (1778): title page.
2. John Alfred Faulkner, "The Methodist Review: The First Century," *Methodist Review* 99 (November 1917): 851.
3. Joshua Soule and Thomas Mason, "Address of the Editors of the Methodist Magazine, to Its Patrons and Friends in the United States, and Especially to the Members of the Methodist Episcopal Church," *Methodist Magazine* 1 (January 1818): 3.
4. Ibid., p. 3.
5. Faulkner, p. 852.
6. Nathan Bangs, "Prospectus," *Methodist Magazine and Quarterly Review* 12 (January 1830): 2.
7. Faulkner, p. 853.
8. Ibid., p. 854.
9. John McClintock, "The Editor to the Readers of the Review," *Methodist Quarterly Review* 30 (October 1848): 627.
10. Faulkner, pp. 856–57.
11. Ibid., p. 858.
12. Ibid., pp. 860–61.
13. James R. Joy, "The Methodist Review—1818–1930," *Methodist Review* 114 (May 1931): 425.
14. Ibid., p. 425.

Information Sources

BIBLIOGRAPHY:
Norwood, Frederick A. *The Story of American Methodism.* Nashville: Abingdon Press, 1974.
INDEX SOURCES: Most volumes self-indexed; index for 1818–81 published by Elijah H. Pilcher in 1884; also in *International Index of Periodicals, Poole's Index.*
REPRINT EDITIONS: University Microfilms International.
LOCATION SOURCES: Union Theological Seminary (New York), Wesleyan University, Library of Congress, Emory University, Northwestern University, Boston University, Ohio Wesleyan College, and others.

Publication History

MAGAZINE TITLE AND TITLE CHANGES: *The Methodist Magazine* (1818–28), *The Methodist Magazine and Quarterly Review* (1830–40), *The Methodist Quarterly Review* (1841–84), *The Methodist Review* (1885–1931).
VOLUME AND ISSUE DATA: *Methodist Magazine* 1–11 (1818–28); *Methodist Magazine and Quarterly Review* 12–22 [n.s. 1–11] (1830–40); *Methodist Quarterly Review* 23–66 [3d ser. 1–8, 4th ser. 1–36] (1841–84); *Methodist Review* 67–114 [5th ser. 1–47] (1885–1931); publication suspended November 1827 until December 1827 and through all of 1829.
PUBLISHER AND PLACE OF PUBLICATION: Joshua Soule and Thomas Mason, New York (1818–20); Methodist Book Concern, New York (1820–1931).
EDITORS: Joshua Soule (1818–20), Thomas Mason (1818–24), Nathan Bangs (1820–28, 1832–36), John Emory (1824–31), Beverly Waugh (1830–31), Samuel Luckey (1836–40), George Peck (1840–48), John McClintock (1848–56), Daniel Whedon

(1856–84), Daniel Curry (1884–87), John Mendenhall (1888–92), William Kelley (1893–1920), George Elliott (1920–31).
CIRCULATION: Unknown.

Michael R. McCoy

MID-AMERICA

Established in 1918 by the Illinois Catholic Historical Society, the *Illinois Catholic Historical Review* gradually expanded its scope. In 1929 the name was changed to *Mid-America*, and the quarterly concentrated on Catholicism between the Alleghenies and the Rockies. Since 1936, when Loyola University of Chicago became the publisher, the journal has reflected the varied scholarly interests of its editors, with Jesuit history of the region being particularly strong between 1936 and the mid–1950s.[1]

Frederick J. Siedenburg, a Jesuit and founder of the first American Catholic school of social work, was the society's first president. Appointed to the Illinois Centennial Commission charged with the preparation of the state's official history, Siedenburg argued that the proposed text made derogatory references to Catholicism and neglected its importance in Illinois history. Unable to persuade the commission, Siedenburg concluded that Catholics would be recognized only when they made their history available to all and thereby demonstrated its significance.

In June 1917, Siedenburg raised these concerns in a casual conversation with Joseph T. Thompson, a lawyer assisting the commission. Thompson replied that he had almost completed a history of Illinois Catholics for which he sought a publisher. After reading the manuscript, Siedenburg proposed to publish it serially in order to win wide attention and criticism.[2] Thompson and Siedenburg collaborated with Archbishop Mundelein of Chicago and his suffragans to found the historical society.

Thompson edited the *Review* from 1918 to 1927. Besides his history, the *Review* published studies of missionaries and religious congregations of men and women which had settled in Illinois. Among them were the Jesuits, Franciscans, Vincentians, Sulpicians, Society of Mary, Christian Brothers, Sisters of St. Francis, Sisters of Charity of St. Augustine, Ursuline Sisters, Sisters of Mercy, and the Visitadine Nuns. In addition to biographical sketches and book reviews, primary sources (letters, parish records, and diaries) regularly appeared in the *Review*. Although there was a strong clerical and institutional emphasis in the journal, there were also articles on Catholic immigrants, notably the Germans, Irish, and Slovaks.

Jesuit history figured prominently because of the order's importance to the region. Coverage increased markedly after 1936 when the Illinois Catholic Historical Society asked Loyola University to take responsibility for *Mid-America*. In the same year, the university established the Institute of Jesuit History. It promoted the collection, preservation, and publication of primary sources. It also encouraged their use for articles, monographs, seminars, and theses of graduate students.

The institute flourished until the end of World War II, when its financial problems became severe. Jerome V. Jacobsen, S.J., directed the institute and edited the journal between 1936 and his death in 1970. Jacobsen's editorial interests reflected those of his doctoral mentor, Herbert Eugene Bolton, who created the study of the Spanish borderlands. Articles by Peter M. Dunne, S.J., W. Eugene Shields, S.J., Jean Delanglez, S.J., and others called attention to the Jesuit role in the development of the Western Hemisphere. Gilbert J. Garraghan, S.J., of Chicago and John F. McDermott of St. Louis were among those who saw that the U.S. Midwest was not neglected.

In the 1950s and 1960s, *Mid-America* became a journal of general U.S. history. Articles on progressivism and diplomatic history were the most frequent. John V. Mentag, S.J. (editor 1970–80), continued this broad focus, as did his successor, Louise A. Kerr. The number of articles published yearly has declined as their length increased, but each volume numbers around 300 pages.

Notes

1. I am deeply indebted to John V. Mentag, S.J., who most graciously gave me bibliographic assistance and provided information on Jerome V. Jacobsen, S.J., and the Institute of Jesuit History.

2. Published as *The Archdiocese of Chicago: Antecedents and Development* (Des Plaines, Ill.: St. Mary's Training School Press, 1920).

Information Sources

BIBLIOGRAPHY:

Cadden, John P. *Historiography of the American Catholic Church: 1785–1943*. Washington, D.C.: Catholic University of America Press, 1944. Reprint in the American Catholic Tradition, New York: Arno Press, 1978.

Jacobsen, Jerome V. "The Jesuit Institute of Loyola University: Its Organization." *Mid-America* 18 (July 1936): 147–52.

Thompson, Joseph J. "Editorial." *Illinois Catholic Historical Review* 1 (April 1919): 1.

———. "The Past, Present and Future of the *ICHR*." *Illinois Catholic Historical Review* 3 (January 1921): 329–36.

INDEX SOURCES: Self-indexed in each volume, beginning with vol. 3 (1920–21). Also in *Catholic Periodical and Literature Index* (1930–   ), *Humanities Index* (1974–   ), *Historical Abstracts, America: History and Life*.

REPRINT EDITIONS: University Microfilms International.

LOCATION SOURCES: California State University at Chico, Emory University, Loyola University (Chicago), Yale University, and others.

Publication History

MAGAZINE TITLE AND TITLE CHANGES: *Illinois Catholic Historical Review* (1918–29); *Mid-America* (July 1929–   ).

VOLUME AND ISSUE DATA: *Illinois Catholic Historical Review* 1–11 (July 1918-

April 1929), annual volumes; *Mid-America* 12- (July 1929–), with volumes
also listed as n.s., 1-.

PUBLISHER AND PLACE OF PUBLICATION: Catholic Historical Society, Chicago
(*Illinois Catholic Historical Review*, 1918–29; *Mid-America*, 1929–34); Loyola
University, Chicago (*Mid-America*, 1935-).

EDITORS: *Illinois Catholic Historical Review*: Joseph J. Thompson (1918-April 1927),
F. J. Rooney (July 1927-April 1929); *Mid-America*: Gilbert J. Garraghan (July
1929-April 1934), Jerome V. Jacobsen (January 1935-July 1970), John V. Mentag
(October 1970-January 1980), Louise A. Kerr (April 1980–).

CIRCULATION: 700 (1981).

Thomas J. Jonas

MID-STREAM

Mid-Stream: An Ecumenical Journal has evolved since its founding in 1961
into a major forum for discussion of ecumenical issues. While by content and
circulation it has concentrated primarily on concerns of church union and interdenominational dialogue in the United States, by the late 1970s it was broadening
its scope to consistently include more international authors and issues.

At its modest beginning under the auspices of the Council on Christian Unity,
the ecumenical office of the Christian Church–Disciples of Christ (CCDC), the
journal was described on its title page as "an occasional publication of the
Council on Christian Unity, bringing to the attention of members and friends
significant materials on ecumenical issues." The first issue came forth in November 1961 in the wake of the World Council of Churches (WCC) Third
Assembly in New Delhi. The first issue focused on the ecumenical breakthrough
of that assembly: the reception into full membership of the Orthodox, and particularly the Russian Orthodox, Churches. The second issue appeared in May
1962 with articles by CCDC delegates to the New Delhi meeting, including
denominational figures such as W. B. Blakemore of Disciples House at the
University of Chicago and George Beazley, president of the Council on Christian
Unity (CCU).

Beazley (1914–73) was founding editor of *Mid-Stream* and continued in that
capacity until his untimely death on a trip to the Soviet Union in October 1973.
A CCDC pastor in Missouri and Oklahoma for many years, Beazley became
council president in 1960, soon after starting the journal as an in-house publication originally called "Beazley's Buzz." He held several prominent ecumenical posts, serving as secretary of the WCC Faith and Order Commission from
1968 until his death, as secretary from 1966 to 1968 and vice-chairman from
1968 to 1973 of the Consultation on Church Union (COCU) in the United States,
and as a member of the board of directors of the Ecumenical Institute, Bossey,
Switzerland.

Beazley devoted the first three numbers of volume 2 to internal CCDC discussions of restructure and dialogue with the United Church of Christ. With 2:4,

however, he initiated a long-standing relationship between *Mid-Stream* and COCU with publication of a full collection of documents from the first and second meetings of the consultation in April 1962 and March 1963, respectively. The CCDC then joined COCU at the invitation of its participant denominations, the United Presbyterian Church in the U.S.A., the United Church of Christ, the Protestant Episcopal Church, and the Methodist Church.

By 1970 COCU had expanded to include in its dialogue on church union five additional denominations: the Presbyterian Church U.S., the Council of Community Churches, and the African Methodist Episcopal, the African Methodist Episcopal Zion, and Christian Methodist Episcopal churches. *Mid-Stream* continued to publish a digest of COCU proceedings after every meeting (approximately every 18 months to two years), but after 1974 the digest was published separately, not as a regular number of the journal.

With volume 4 (Fall 1964) *Mid-Stream* settled into a fall, winter, spring, summer quarterly format that continued until Beazley's death. Following a brief interim under a publication committee composed of Robert H. Boyte, Harold E. Fey, and Paul S. Stauffer, the new president of the Council on Christian Unity, Paul A. Crow, Jr., became editor of the journal. Crow (1931–   ) was also a CCDC clergyman and professor of church history at Lexington Theological Seminary. He had served as general secretary of COCU from 1968 until assuming his new CCDC post. Crow's numerous other ecumenical posts included serving on both the WCC Central Committee and Faith and Order Commission, as well as on the Governing Board of the National Council of Churches in the U.S.A., and co-chairing the bilateral dialogue of the CCDC with the Roman Catholic Church.

Under Crow's editorship, *Mid-Stream* expanded in format to include many more articles in each issue on a wider variety of topics, added sections of ecumenical news and book reviews, and settled into a quarterly pattern of publication in January, April, July, and October. It continued its central focus on COCU and the WCC, while printing articles on many other ecumenical dialogues in the United States and worldwide. Its October 1982 issue (21:4) became a major preparatory document for the WCC Sixth Assembly in 1983, with articles by Hugh McCullum of the United Church of Canada, Martin Conway of the Church of England, Jean Tillard, a Canadian Roman Catholic, Wolfhart Pannenberg of the University of Munich, and several U.S. educators and staff of various denominations.

Information Sources

BIBLIOGRAPHY:

Cavert, Samuel McCrea. *Church Cooperation and Unity in America: A Historical Review, 1900–1970.* New York: Association Press, 1970.

Crow, Paul A., Jr., and William Jerry Boney, eds. *Church Union at Midpoint.* New York: Association Press, 1972.

Crow, Paul A., Jr., and George L. Hunt, eds. *Where We Are in Church Union.* A Reflection Book. New York: Association Press, 1965.

Howell, Leon, *Acting in Faith: The World Council of Churches since 1975*. Geneva: World Council of Churches, 1982.

Visser t'Hooft, Willem. *Memoirs*. London: SCM Press, 1973.

INDEX SOURCES: *Religion Index One, Guide to Social Science and Religion in Periodical Literature*.

REPRINT EDITIONS: University Microfilms International.

LOCATION SOURCES: Pacific School of Religion, Pittsburgh Theological Seminary, Union Theological Seminary (New York), Yale University, and others.

Publication History

MAGAZINE TITLE AND TITLE CHANGES: *Mid-Stream, An Ecumenical Journal* (1961–   ).

VOLUME AND ISSUE DATA: Volumes are numbered consecutively beginning with volume 1 in November 1961. Volume 1 had only two numbers; thereafter all volumes had four numbers. Issued quarterly, 1964- .

PUBLISHER AND PLACE OF PUBLICATION: Council on Christian Unity of the Christian Church (Disciples of Christ), Indianapolis.

EDITORS: George G. Beazley, Jr. (1961–73); Publication Committee composed of Robert H. Boyte, Harold E. Fey, and Paul S. Stauffer (1973–74); Paul A. Crow, Jr. (1974–   ).

CIRCULATION: 1000.

Thomas E. Frank

MILLENNIAL HARBINGER

In January 1830 the *Millennial Harbinger* appeared. An organ of the Disciples of Christ, the journal replaced the iconoclastic *Christian Baptist*. Both monthlies were edited and published by Alexander Campbell (1788–1866), a reformer who sought "to restore the ancient gospel and the ancient order of things." Disciples historian Winfred E. Garrison thought the name change was symbolic of Campbell's own shift from a contentious to a more irenic view of church history.[1] The journal's purpose was to unite a divided church: "This work shall be devoted to the destruction of sectarianism, infidelity, and antichristian doctrine and practice. It shall have as its object the development and introduction of that political and religious order of society called THE MILLENNIUM, which will be the consummation of that ultimate amelioration of society proposed in the Christian Scriptures."[2]

The *Millennial Harbinger*, published until 1870 at Bethany, Virginia, now West Virginia, became "the most influential periodical issued by the Disciples" in its day. "There was a generation of Disciples ministers who felt ill equipped without a full set . . . on their library shelves."[3] But it was public demand for copies of Campbell's famous debates with, among others, the communitarian Robert Owen and Archbishop John Purcell, that had encouraged the publishing venture. Consequently, the journal was self-consciously directed toward a lay audience. Campbell wrote most of the articles, and since he thrived on debate, he reprinted much from the antagonistic press. The office of the *Harbinger* was later manned by Robert Richardson, W. K. Pendleton, and C. L. Loos. Contributors included F. W. Emmons, Isaac Errett, John T. Johnson, S. M. M'Corkle, Walter Scott, Elias Smith, Barton Stone, and John Young.

Campbell, born in Ireland and educated at the University of Glasgow, emigrated to the United States in 1809 and joined his father, Thomas Campbell (1763–1854). The impetus for their desire to restore Christianity to New Testament forms stemmed from their break with the Seceder Presbyterian Church of Northern Ireland. Once in the United States, they founded the Christian Association in Washington, Pennsylvania. Thomas's *Declaration and Address* became normative for their followers, especially the phrase: "We speak where the Scriptures speak, where the Scriptures are silent, we are silent." The "Scriptures" meant only the New Testament, and the principle of silence censored instrumental music and the word *Sabbath* since neither was mentioned there. The "Reformers" denounced clergy, sacramental embellishment, and creeds.[4]

One explanation for the zeal with which the *Harbinger* advanced its position lies in what Nathan Hatch calls "a pervasive collapse of certainty within popular culture." After the Revolution, Americans were vexed by a problem of authority as they struggled to practice democracy:

> In exalting the ideas that every man was his own interpreter, [Disciples and "Christians"] brought a measure of certainty to people committed to the principle that all values, rights, and duties originate in the individual. . . . People were expected to discover the self-evident message of the Bible without any mediation. . . . This explicit faith that biblical authority could emerge from below, from the will of the people, was the most enduring legacy of the Christian movement.[5]

In defining areas of religious and social life, the Christian press nurtured the growth of a "theology of the people." As an open forum of democratic exchange, the *Harbinger* helped Christianize the new Republic.[6]

Two issues are illustrative of the *Harbinger*'s message: immersion and voluntary societies. In the first volume, Barton Stone's *Christian Messenger* was attacked for claiming that Christians could commune with the unimmersed. "If the *Christian Messenger* teach the unimmersed to do the things which the Lord commanded none but the immersed to practice, I should like to have his authority."[7] Stone argued from tradition: what was the fate of unimmersed saints? What of the "thief on the cross"? Campbell had his own rigorous interpretation: only Christ could judge the misinformed.

A second issue for the *Millennial Harbinger* was the question of voluntary societies. Missions, temperance orders, and Sunday School societies were not biblically authorized, and the *Christian Baptist* and the early *Harbinger* opposed them. But the tone altered when Stone and Campbell consolidated their followers in 1832.[8] The unity-oriented "Christians" and the strict Disciples found that the experience of common worship, while never free of conflict, outweighed the differences of opinion and strengthened faith in the "millennial church." Reports from new churches, the influence of Walter Scott's evangelical method of preaching, and the naming of an assistant editor marked a new direction. The presence of Robert Richardson, the assistant, at Bethany freed Campbell to visit and report on local churches. Richardson was a student of Walter Scott, and his evangelical stance influenced editorial policy. By the mid–1830s, as Richard T. Hughes notes, "the theme of unity was emerging as the dominant element . . . at the expense of radical restoration."[9] Success of the new program is best measured by the legitimacy granted to key voluntary societies.

The Disciples had always been strong in regions swept by revival, in part because the *Harbinger*'s evangelism was more rational than emotional.[10] When the philanthropic societies spawned by the Second Great Awakening became as schismatic as any sect, the journal advocated "a search for methods of cooperation." In 1845 a new Bible Society was organized by D. S. Burnet in Cincinnati. Both the *Harbinger* and the *Christian Intelligencer* of Charlottesville, Virginia, argued for its union with the American and Foreign Bible Society, formed by the Baptists in 1837.[11] No new society ought to be formed "without a general understanding [and] support of the whole brotherhood."[12] Although such societies were not scriptural, Campbell argued that "*positive* precept for everything" was unnecessary. It was "as unscriptural as to ask for an immutable wardrobe . . . for all persons and ages."[13]

No discussion of the *Harbinger* would be complete without a word about the millennium. Until 1843, Campbell printed regular series of articles on theories about the end of history. Many involved detailed calculations of world ages, not unlike the extrapolations of William Miller.[14] Wisely, the *Harbinger* refused to set a date for the end. In time the journal imagined the millennial age less in terms of catastrophe and more in terms of cooperation designed to combat modern social problems. In 1858, the *Harbinger* declared: "We have too much faith in progress . . . to subscribe to the doctrines of these theological gentlemen who hint the last days are at hand."[15]

In its hopes for the United States, the *Harbinger* approached the vision of what has been called the "Religion of the Republic."[16] A virtuous Republic would advance only as Americans embraced the self-evidence of revelation. The *Harbinger* admired the ability of the state to promote justice in a pluralistic society, but this achievement was believed to depend on America's becoming a Christian nation.[17]

The *Harbinger* lasted four years after the death of Campbell in 1866. The end of publication resulted in part from the Civil War, which divided the denomination. Also, by 1870 numerous weeklies commanded the support of the many local organizations.

Notes

1. Winfred E. Garrison, *Religion Follows the Frontier* (New York: Harper and Bros., 1931), p. 147.
2. *Millennial Harbinger* 1 (1830): 1 (hereafter cited as *MH*).
3. W. E. Garrison and A. T. DeGroot, *The Disciples of Christ: A History* (St. Louis: Christian Board of Publication, 1948), p. 255.
4. Thomas Campbell, *Declaration and Address* (Washington, Pa.: Brown and Sample, 1809).
5. Nathan Hatch, "The Christian Movement and the Demand for a Theology of the People," *Journal of American History* 67 (1980): 564, 566.
6. Ibid., pp. 566–67.
7. *MH* 1 (1830): 474.
8. Lester G. McAllister and William E. Tucker, *Journey of Faith* (St. Louis: Bethany Press, 1975), pp. 146–55.
9. Richard T. Hughes, "From Primitive Church to Civil Religion: The Millennial Odyssey of Alexander Campbell," *Journal of the American Academy of Religion* 44 (1976): 95.
10. Sydney E. Ahlstrom, *A Religious History of the American People* (New York: Image Books, 1975), 1:544.
11. Garrison and DeGroot, p. 243.
12. *MH*, 3d ser. 2 (1845): 372.
13. Ibid. 6 (1849): 269–70.
14. See *MH* 2 (1831): 33; ibid. 3 (1832): 435–38; and ibid. 5 (1834): 548–54.
15. Ibid., 5th ser. 1 (1858): 336.
16. Sidney E. Mead, *The Lively Experiment* (New York: Harper and Row, 1963).
17. Hughes, p. 98.

Information Sources

BIBLIOGRAPHY:
Harrell, David E., Jr. *Quest for a Christian America*. Nashville: Disciples of Christ Historical Society, 1966.
Lunger, Harold. *The Political Ethics of Alexander Campbell*. St. Louis: Bethany Press, 1954.
McAllister, Lester G., and William E. Tucker. *Journey in Faith*. St. Louis: Bethany Press, 1975.
Richardson, Robert. *Memoirs of Alexander Campbell*. 2 vols. Philadelphia: J. P. Lippincott, 1868, 1870.
INDEX SOURCES: David McWhirter, comp. *An Index to the Millennial Harbinger* (Joplin, Mo.: College Press, 1981).
LOCATION SOURCES: Phillips Memorial Archives, Disciples of Christ Historical Society, Nashville, Tenn., and others.

Publication History

MAGAZINE TITLE AND TITLE CHANGES: *Christian Baptist* (1823–30), *Millennial Harbinger* (1830–70).
VOLUME AND ISSUE DATA: *Millennial Harbinger* 1–7 (January 1830-December 1836); n.s. 1–7 (January 1837-December 1843); 3d ser. 1–7 (January 1844-De-

cember 1850); 4th ser. 1–7 (January 1851-December 1857); 5th ser. 1–7 (January 1858-December 1864); last ser. 36–41 (January 1865-December 1870).

PUBLISHER AND PLACE OF PUBLICATION: Alexander Campbell, Bethany, Va. (now W. Va.).

EDITORS: Alexander Campbell (1830–66), Robert Richardson and W. K. Pendleton (1846–66), Charles L. Loos and W. K. Pendleton (1866–70).

CIRCULATION: No estimates available.

John Kloos

MISSIOLOGY

Missiology: An International Review, a quarterly, has its roots in the American Society of Missiology and a predecessor journal, *Practical Anthropology*. The society, founded in 1973, reflected more than three-quarters of a century of consolidation of academic interest in missiology (science of missions) marked by such events as the formation of denominational societies for the study of missions, the establishment of the Missionary Research Library in New York (1914) and the Institute for Social and Religious Research, the creation of the Kennedy School of Missions (Hartford Seminary Foundation), and the organization of the Association of Professors of Missions (1952). The starting of the society culminated a period that witnessed a need to end a totally Euro-American notion of missions, as well as to bridge the gap that had formerly separated evangelicals from other Protestants and Protestants from Catholics in their understanding of the missionary enterprise. Even before the society became official, its leadership commenced publication of *Missiology* in January 1973.[1]

The new periodical absorbed *Practical Anthropology*, a journal started in the 1930s by a group, many of whom had ties to the Translations Department of the American Bible Society, intent on exploring ethnocentrism, cultural relativity, accommodation, and identification as they related to the communication of the gospel, especially in Scripture translation as part of missions.[2] The same forces that led to the American Society of Missiology's establishment by the early 1970s had prompted awareness of the need to broaden the focus of a journal oriented to missions. Fuller Theological Seminary's School of World Mission assumed much responsibility for *Missiology*, with Alan R. Tippett, a professor there and former Australian Methodist missionary, becoming first editor. The subtitle, ''Continuing *Practical Anthropology*,'' testifies to the continuity, although from the start *Missiology* was more scholarly in tone and broader in perspective.[3]

When Tippett resigned in 1976, he noted that *Missiology* had met a scholarly need while pointing out both continuity and changes in approaches to missions. As well, he claimed, *Missiology* sparked awareness of the ethnic diversity within Christianity and of the interdisciplinary nature of missiology.[4] Arthur F. Glassner, then dean of Fuller's School of World Mission, succeeded Tippett and served as editor until 1982. His inaugural editorial emphasized commitment to scholarship, to leadership in debates over the character of missions, to an ecumenical focus, and to refrain from polemics, all within the purview of regarding missiology as an applied science balancing theoretical and practical concerns.[5] His own interests in biblical and theological interpretation of missions, however, did influence the choice and thrust of articles appearing during his tenure.

Glassner was president of the American Society of Missiology when he stepped down as editor. In a farewell essay, he reaffirmed the links between journal and society, calling for participation in both by persons from all branches and movements within Christianity. Both should provide open forums for discussion of all aspects of mission, he noted.[6] His successor, Ralph R. Covell, had been his associate in missionary work in China, and although Covell taught at Denver Conservative Baptist Theological Seminary, he also had ties to Fuller. But his selection highlights the affirmation of ecumenicity characteristic of *Missiology*, for Covell was a Conservative Baptist, whereas Glassner was an evangelical Presbyterian and Tippett an Australian Methodist. As well, two associate editors, one a Roman Catholic priest and the other a minister in the Conciliar Lutheran Church in America, and a Southern Baptist book review editor came on board.

Covell set forth his view of *Missiology*'s role in an editorial that reemphasized the journal's academic orientation and appreciation of a multidisciplinary approach to mission(s). But he also called for greater attention to the practical (while not abandoning the theoretical), pondering whether *Missiology*'s having a lower circulation than had *Practical Anthropology* resulted from its highlighting theoretical concerns. Nonetheless he expressed his commitment to a pluralistic focus in order to retain communication with the broadest possible audience.[7] Under his leadership there has been an increase in articles with a liberation theology bent and a somewhat greater emphasis on missionary spirituality.

In retrospect, *Missiology* retains a sense of continuity with *Practical Anthropology*, though it has made clear that there is more to missiology than anthropological concerns. The continuity is also seen in the emphasis on the practical but one combined with discussion of theory. *Missiology* has consistently recognized religious pluralism in missions, remaining an open forum for discussion of issues from a variety of religious perspectives. The interaction of these forces reveals both the nature of the American Society of Missiology and the character of missiology as a scientific academic discipline.

Notes

1. On the background of the society, see R. Pierce Beaver, "The Purpose and History of the American Society of Missiology" (paper delivered at the annual meeting of the American Society of Missiology, June 1979).

2. On *Practical Anthropology*, see Charles R. Taber, "Change and Continuity," *Missiology* 1 (1973): 7–12.

3. See Gerald H. Anderson, "Introducing *Missiology*," *Missiology* 1 (1973): 4, and Alan R. Tippett, "*Missiology*: 'For Such a Time as This!' " *Missiology* 1 (1973): 15–20

4. Alan R. Tippett, "The Rites of Passage," *Missiology* 4 (1976): 3–4.

5. Arthur F. Glassner, "I Give You My Word," *Missiology* 4 (1976): 7–10.

6. Arthur F. Glassner, "The Mission of *Missiology* and the ASM," *Missiology* 11 (1983): 4–8.

7. Ralph R. Covell, "The Continuing Mandate," *Missiology* 11 (1983): 9–13.

Information Sources

BIBLIOGRAPHY:

Anderson, Gerald H. "Introducing *Missiology*." *Missiology* 1 (1973): 4.

Beaver, R. Pierce. "The Purpose and History of the American Society of Missiology." Paper presented at the annual meeting of the American Society of Missiology, June 1979.

Covell, Ralph R. "The Continuing Mandate." *Missiology* 11 (1983): 9–13.

Glassner, Arthur F. "I Give You My Word." *Missiology* 4 (1976): 7–10.

――――. "The Mission of *Missiology* and the ASM." *Missiology* 11 (1983): 4–8.

Taber, Charles R. "Change and Continuity." *Missiology* 1 (1973): 7–10.

Tippett, Alan R. "*Missiology*: 'For Such a Time as This!' " *Missiology* 1 (1973): 15–20.

――――. "The Rites of Passage." *Missiology* 4 (1976): 3–4.

INDEX SOURCES: *Bibliografia Missionaria, Christian Periodicals Index, Guide to Christian Periodicials, Religion Index One, Religious and Theological Abstracts, Standard Periodical Dictionary*.

REPRINT EDITIONS: University Microfilms International.

LOCATION SOURCES: *Practical Anthropology*: Los Angeles Public Library, Princeton Theological Seminary, Michigan State University, California State University-Northridge, Smithsonian Institute, Southern Illinois University, Brandeis University, American Bible Society, Case-Western Reserve University. *Missiology*: University of California-San Diego, University of California-Los Angeles, University of Illinois, Princeton Theological Seminary, Southern Methodist University, University of Texas-Austin, University of North Carolina-Chapel Hill, and others.

Publication History

MAGAZINE TITLE AND TITLE CHANGES: *Practical Anthropology* (1953–72), *Missiology: An International Review* (1973–).

VOLUME AND ISSUE DATA: *Practical Anthropology* 1:1–19:1 (1953–72), *Missiology* 1:1 (January 1973–). Appears quarterly.

PUBLISHER AND PLACE OF PUBLICATION: Practical Anthropology, Tarrytown, N.Y. (1953–72), American Society of Missiology, South Pasadena, Calif. (1973), Pasadena, Calif. (1974–81), Elkhart, Ind. (1981–82), Scottdale, Pa. (1983–).

EDITORS: Robert Taylor (1955-?), William A. Smalley (1958–68), Charles R. Taber (1968–72), Alan R. Tippett (1973–75), Arthur F. Glassner (1976–82), Ralph R. Covell (1983–).

CIRCULATION: 3000 (1984).

John G. Merritt

THE MOODY BIBLE INSTITUTE MONTHLY. *See* THE MOODY MONTHLY

THE MOODY MONTHLY

In 1891, two years after it had opened, the Moody Bible Institute in Chicago began publication of the *Institute Tie*. Conceived as a means of sustaining the tie between former students and the institute, the biweekly newsletter was discontinued in 1893 for financial reasons. It was resurrected in 1900 by Dwight L. Moody's son-in-law, A. P. Fitt, who served as editor. Published monthly, the *Tie* reported on institute events and on activities of former students. It also included texts of lectures and sermons and suggestions for preaching.

In 1907, under coeditors James M. Gray and R. A. Torrey, the *Tie* was reconceived as an educational publication. Institute news was confined to a specific section of the magazine; articles and devotional pieces appeared in greater number. Regular features such as "Practical and Perplexing Questions" and "Studies in the Life and Teachings of Our Lord" were begun. Both features were of a question-and-answer format. The former answered queries such as, "Is the church a building, or the clergy, or a denomination?"[1] The latter explained church doctrine by presenting lists of Bible references that bore on a particular subject.[2] The objective of the *Tie* became increasingly one of providing church workers—clergy and laypersons—with practical lessons that could be applied to the evangelistic enterprise. This practical emphasis has remained an important part of the magazine, reaching its peak in the 1950s in a column entitled "The Soul-Winner's Notebook." In one such column, "How to Hold to the Point," missionaries are advised that sometimes a "friend will want to discuss 'mistakes' in the Bible or 'contradictions.' Never be led away by this."[3]

Beginning in April 1909, the magazine added the subtitle *The Christian Worker's Magazine* to reflect this change in direction, and the following year, "The Institute Tie" was dropped from the title completely. More educational features were begun. "Studies in Personal Soul-Winning" focused on techniques that might prove helpful in making converts to the church. "The International Sunday School Lesson," a regular department until 1970, and "The Gospel in the World," which survives today in altered form, stated church doctrine in simple, straightforward language and reflected the early and enduring concern of the magazine with missions.[4]

In 1920, the magazine was renamed the *Moody Bible Institute Monthly*. Subscription price was set at two dollars per year, twice that of the *Worker* and quadruple that of the *Tie*. The practical objectives of the magazine came increasingly to the forefront at this time under the editorship of Gray. New columns such as "Sunday School Problems" and "Practical and Doctrinal Application" were added. The *Monthly* consistently linked Bible study with effective preaching and missionizing. To this end, a regular column, "Greek Word Studies" (later renamed "Golden Nuggets for Bible Students"), was begun in 1934.

In 1934, Will H. Houghton became president of Moody Bible Institute, and Gray became president emeritus. When Gray died the following year, Houghton took over as editor of the monthly. The office of editor has since been held concurrently with that of president. In his 13 years as editor, Houghton initiated major changes in the magazine. Houghton himself began a column entitled "Youth Page" in 1935. This was enlarged in 1946 to the "Youth Supplement" section, which was "to provide as much help for Christian youth" as was possible in seven or eight pages.[5] The "Supplement" remains today a part of the magazine as "Teen Focus." Houghton also began publishing articles that placed the interests of the church more clearly within the broader context of American life. When labor disputes erupted after World War II, the *Moody Monthly* (as it was called beginning in 1938) urged Protestant denominations to keep up with Roman Catholics in "cultivating cordial relations with organized labor."[6] The *Monthly* also broadened its vision of missionary work to allow for utilization of the insights of secular learning. Such insights were both practical and theoretical. In the latter case, they served to support and clarify existing church beliefs, as in "A Christian View of Race," in which it was argued that the "science" of anthropology has demonstrated that all persons are equal and that "there is no ground for racial prejudice and hatred, for science confirms the Scriptural record."[7]

When William Culbertson took over as editor in 1947, the *Monthly* became a more distinct voice of theological conservatism and a more determined advocate of education.[8] "In The Study," a regular department that consisted of book reviews and recommendations, as well as essays on history and religion, appeared in 1952. Articles about education, such as "Let's Put More School in Sunday School," appeared with greater frequency.[9] The magazine continued to publish items of an inspirational nature, such as poems and first-person accounts, and collected practical suggestions into a department called "Idea Notebook" in 1953.

In the early 1970s, under the presidency of George Sweeting, the *Moody Monthly* reorganized its regular features under four main headings: "Missions," "Family," "Teen Focus," and "Bible Study." In addition to more frequent articles on Christian family life, and especially on child rearing, the magazine has taken an even more explicitly conservative position. A recent article argues that Moody Bible Institute differs from schools such as Harvard, Yale, and Dartmouth—and other "formerly" Christian schools—by "making known its doctrinal stand so that no one can miss it."[10] As a voice of conservative evangelicalism, the *Moody Monthly* has been very successful. It was chosen as Magazine of the Year by the Evangelical Press Association in 1958 and 1961. Its appeal is not to professionally trained clergy but to laypersons, to those "'ordinary' people who look to us for warmth, encouragement, and Bible teaching."[11]

Notes

1. *Moody Monthly* 46 (September 1945): 32.

2. Both columns, "Practical and Perplexing Questions" and "Studies in the Life and Teachings of Our Lord," responded to questions from readers.

3. Walter L. Wilson, "The Soul Winner's Notebook—How To Hold to the Point," *Moody Monthly* 52 (February 1952): 394.

4. Columns on missions often consisted of accounts of missionaries in foreign countries and the methods they employ in converting the natives.

5. Will Houghton, "Youth's Page," *Moody Bible Institute Monthly* 35 (September 1935): 21.

6. Howard Lehn, "The Gospel and Labor Unions," *Moody Monthly* 46 (July 1946): 659–60.

7. George R. Horner, "A Christian View of Race," *Moody Monthly* 46 (August 1946): 734.

8. "During Dr. Culbertson's more than twenty-five years as president of the Institute and editor in chief of the magazine, his influence was felt at a time when conservatives needed sound theological guidance. In the 1950's and 1960's, when conservative evangelicalism was constantly under fire, Dr. Culbertson's consistent stand built on the MBI tradition and left no doubt as to the steadfastness of the Institute and the magazine." Jerry B. Jenkins, "75 Years at Moody Monthly," *Moody Monthly* 76 (January 1975): 29.

9. The conservatism of the magazine is apparent in the two-part "Why Communism Hates Christianity," by James R. Graham. See part II in *Moody Monthly* 54 (August 1954): 24.

10. George Sweeting,"Why MBI Holds the Line," *Moody Monthly* 76 (June 1976): 59.

11. William Culbertson, quoted in Gene A. Getz, *MBI: The Story of Moody Bible Institute* (Chicago: Moody Press, 1969), p. 264.

Information Sources

BIBLIOGRAPHY:
Getz, Gene A. *MBI: The Story of Moody Bible Institute*. Chicago: Moody Press, 1969.
INDEX SOURCES: *Christian Periodical Literature, Reader's Guide to Periodical Literature, Guide to Social Science and Religion in Periodical Literature*.
REPRINT EDITIONS: University Microfilms International.
LOCATION SOURCES: Yale University, University of Michigan, Ohio State University, Cleveland Public Library, Dropsie College, New York State Library (Albany), University of California-Riverside, Garrett-Evangelical Theological Seminary, University of Illinois, and others.

Publication History

MAGAZINE TITLE AND TITLE CHANGES: *The Institute Tie* (1900–1909), *The Christian Worker's Magazine* (1910–19), *The Moody Bible Institute Monthly* (1920–37), *The Moody Monthly* (1938–   ).
VOLUME AND ISSUE DATA: *Institute Tie* 1–9 (1900–1909), *Christian Worker's Magazine* 10–19 (1910–19), *Moody Bible Institute Monthly* 20–17 (1920–37), *Moody Monthly* 38 (1938–   ). Appears monthly.
PUBLISHER AND PLACE OF PUBLICATION: Moody Bible Institute, Chicago (1900–   ).

John Corrigan

THE MOSLEM WORLD. *See* THE MUSLIM WORLD

THE MUSLIM WORLD

In 1911, Samuel M. Zwemer (1867–1952) began the publication of a proprietary periodical, *Moslem World: A Quarterly Review of Current Events, Literature, and Thought among Mohammedans and the Progress of Christian
Missions in Moslem Lands*. The subtitle reflects some of Zwemer's biases at the
time, for when he launched the periodical, his primary interest was in converting
Muslims to Christianity. Accordingly, he also tended to view Islam negatively,
almost as a form of paganism, since he was convinced of the superiority of
Christianity to all world religions. In the inaugural issue, Zwemer offered a
statement of purpose for the *Moslem World*:

> It is not a magazine of controversy, much less of compromise. In essentials
> it seeks unity, in non-essentials liberty, in all things charity. We hope to
> interpret Islam as a world-wide religion in all its varied aspects and its
> deep needs, ethical and spiritual, to Christians; to point out and press home
> the true solution to the Moslem problem, namely the evangelization of
> Moslems; to be of practical help to all who toil for this end; and to awaken
> sympathy, love, and prayer on behalf of the Moslem world until its bonds
> are burst, its wounds are healed, its sorrows removed, and its desires
> satisfied in Jesus Christ.[1]

Despite its overtly Christian orientation, the *Moslem World* was the first English-language periodical devoted to the religion of Islam. And from the start, it
represented only one focus of the Dutch-American Zwemer's commitment to
missionary activity among Muslims. He also helped found the (British) Fellowship of Faith for the Moslems and the American Christian Literature Society for
Moslems.

For the first two decades or so of publication, the *Moslem World* carried many
pieces by missionaries, as well as news of mission activities among Moslems.
Zwemer himself contributed many articles, averaging nearly one per issue until
he stepped down as editor in 1947. In addition, many articles were translations
of works originally written in languages other than English. Much space was
devoted to reporting on current events in Islamic regions, a matter that received

more obvious treatment when the journal's subtitle was changed in 1930 to *A Christian Quarterly Review of Current Events, Literature, and Thought among Mohammedans*. As well, some leading scholars also contributed to the periodical. Historian of theology Frank Hugh Foster, for example, offered "Fear of God in Islam" (21, 1931), while Coert Rylaarsdam and Frank Laubach authored pieces in volume 25 (1935).

In 1938, Zwemer's proprietary ownership ceased, and the periodical came under the sponsorship of the Hartford Seminary Foundation in Connecticut. Zwemer continued as editor but now shared responsibilities with Edwin E. Calverly. Calverly's association with the *Moslem World* and Zwemer's gradually increasing appreciation of the integrity and complexity of Islam helped lend a more academic focus to the journal. Their joint editorship saw such noted scholars as Harry A. Wolfson (33, 1943), Edward J. Jurji (34, 1944), Harvard's William Ernest Hocking (35, 1945), and renowned missiologist M. Searle Bates (36, 1946) writing for the periodical. Indeed, H. A. R. Gibb, in his *Modern Trends in Islam*, which was published the same year Zwemer turned over full editorial responsibility to Calverly, noted: "To the Western student of the specifically religious aspects of modern Islamic culture, however, most of [the books published] offer little satisfaction. The fullest documentation is to be found in the issues of the *Moslem World* since 1910."[2] With Calverly at the helm, the journal signaled its more rigorous academic commitment with a change in title to the *Muslim World: A Quarterly Review of History, Culture, Religions, and the Christian Mission in Islamdom*.

A quick review of articles and authors in the opening years of the 1950s is instructive in highlighting the heightened scholarly intent of the journal. Columbia University's Arthur Jeffrey, who had contributed several pieces earlier, offered a four-part series, "The Qur'an as Scripture" (40, 1950); J. N. D. Anderson, from the University of London, penned a three-part series on the Islamic view of marriage and an eight-part series on Shari'a Law in volumes 41–42 (1951–52); while respected Islamicist Kenneth Cragg, who became coeditor in 1952, presented a four-part series, "The Christian Church and Islam" (42, 1952). Occasional articles were written by Muslims, whose tone was much different from that which had characterized the early years of the journal. Another change in subtitle in 1953 marks the shift clearly: *A Quarterly Journal of Islamic Study and of Christian Interpretation among Muslims*. Indeed, by the 1950s, few pieces were the work of missionaries. As Christopher Lamb noted in "The Editorials of *The Muslim World*, 1911–1968" (71, 1981: 3-26), "What began as an attempt to supplement Western academic journals on Islam with the experience and convictions of Christian missionaries living amidst Muslims has become itself the standard English language academic journal on Islam, albeit edited from a Christian foundation and by scholars of Christian conviction."[3]

By the time Willem A. Bijelfeld became the periodical's fourth editor in 1967, *Muslim World* was a recognized academic and scholarly journal. Bijelfeld himself, for example, attempted to place the study of Islam in a proper academic focus in his "Islamic Studies within the History of Religions" (62, 1972). As well, the increasingly intricate economic connections between the United States and Muslim nations prompted an interest in Islamic politics and culture in addition to the journal's traditional religious orientation. Philip C. Salzman of McGill University, for example, wrote "Islam and Authority in Tribal Iran," and Mohamed Al-Nowaihi, of the American University, Cairo, "Problems of Modernization in Islam," in 1975 (65), the same year the Iranian hostage crisis would come to dominate American public life. Hence the emphasis on a scholarly approach to all dimensions of Islamic life continued as *Muslim World* moves through its eighth decade of publication. Still the premier American journal on Islam, *Muslim World* is "a gold mine of information, a source book on half a century of mission work among Muslims."[4] Its present stature and focus are also evident in the current full title of the periodical: *The Muslim World: A Journal Devoted to the Study of Islam and of Christian-Muslim Relationship in Past and Present*.

Notes

1. Samuel M. Zwemer, "Editorial," *Moslem World* 1 (1911): 2–3.
2. H. A. R. Gibb, *Modern Trends in Islam* (Chicago: University of Chicago Press, 1947), pp. 232–33.
3. Christopher Lamb, "The Editorials of *The Muslim World, 1911–1968*," *Muslim World* 71 (1981): 5.
4. Lyle L. VanderWerff, *Christian Mission to Muslims, the Record: Anglican and Reformed Approaches in India and the Near East, 1800–1938* (South Pasadena, Calif.: William Carey Library, 1977), p. 226.

Information Sources

BIBLIOGRAPHY:
Bijelfeld, Willem A. "Editorial Introduction." *Muslim World* 57 (1967): 71–75.
Calverly, Edwin E. "Our Plans for the Quarterly." *Moslem World* 37 (1947): 251–54.
Gibb, H. A. R. *Modern Trends in Islam*. Chicago: University of Chicago Press, 1947.
Lamb, Christopher. "The Editorials of *The Muslim World, 1911–1968*." *Muslim World* 71 (1981): 3–26.
VanderWerff, Lyle L. *Christian Mission to Muslims, the Record: Anglican and Reformed Approaches in India and the Near East, 1800–1938*. South Pasadena, Calif.: William Carey Library, 1977.
Wilson, J. Christy. *Apostle to Islam: The Life of Samuel M. Zwemer*. Grand Rapids: Baker Book House, 1952.
———. "The Epic of Samuel Zwemer." *Muslim World* 57 (1967): 79–93.
Zwemer, Samuel M. "Editorial." *Moslem World* 1 (1911): 2–3.
———. "Looking Backward and Forward from the Bridge." *Moslem World* 37 (1947): 73–76.
INDEX SOURCES: Samuel M. Zwemer, *The Moslem World: Index to Volumes I-XXV (1911–1935)* (New York: n.p., 1935); Elmer H. Douglas and Edwin E. Calverly, eds., *The Muslim World: Index, Volumes XXVI-L (1936–60)* (Hartford: Hartford

Seminary Foundation, 1964); *Religion Index One, Religious and Theological Abstracts, Historical Abstracts.*

REPRINT EDITIONS: Kraus Reprint Co.

LOCATION SOURCES: Yale University, University of Chicago, Princeton Theological Seminary, Harvard University, Mount Holyoke College, University of Southern California, Rutgers University, and others.

Publication History

MAGAZINE TITLE AND TITLE CHANGES: *The Moslem World: A Quarterly Review of Current Events, Literature, and Thought Among Mohammedans* (1911–29), *The Moslem World: A Christian Quarterly Review of Current Events, Literature, and Thought among Mohammedans* (1930–47), *The Muslim World: A Quarterly Review of History, Culture, Religions, and the Christian Mission in Islamdom* (1948–52), *The Muslim World: A Quarterly Journal of Islamic Study and of Christian Interpretation among Muslims* (1953–69), *The Muslim World: A Journal Devoted to the Study of Islam and of Christian-Muslim Relationship in Past and Present* (1970–   ).

VOLUME AND ISSUE DATA: *Moslem World* 1:1–37:4 (January 1911-October 1947), *Muslim World* 38:1 (January 1948–   ). Appears quarterly, except 59:3–4 (1969) and 72:3–4 (1982) were combined issues.

PUBLISHER AND PLACE OF PUBLICATION: Christian Literature Society for India, Evangelical Press, Harrisburg, Pa. (1911–16), Missionary Review Publishing Co., Harrisburg, Pa. (1917–32), Moslem World, Harrisburg, Pa. (1933–38), Hartford Seminary Foundation (Duncan Black Macdonald Center), Hartford, Conn. (1938–   ).

EDITORS: Samuel M. Zwemer (1911–47), Edwin E. Calverly (1938–62), Kenneth Cragg (1952–59), Elmer H. Douglas (1960–65), Morris S. Seale (Acting, 1964, 1966–67), Willem A. Bijelfeld (1967–   ), Issa J. Boullata (1970–80), Wadi Z. Haddad (1981–   ), Yvonne Y. Haddad (1981–   ).

CIRCULATION: 1085 (1913), 1377 (1921), 1622 (1931), 1200 (1983).

Charles H. Lippy

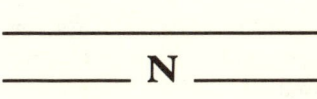

NATIONAL CATHOLIC REPORTER

The Second Vatican Council of the Roman Catholic Church was engaged in its third session on 28 October 1964, the day on which the first issue of a new religious weekly appeared under the title *National Catholic Reporter*. The newspaper, published by an independent corporation in Kansas City, Missouri, was in a real sense a product of Vatican II and for the past two decades has sought to report and interpret events in church life based on a perspective informed by the spirit and direction of *aggiornamento*.

From the beginning, the *Reporter* has seen itself as a unique contribution to the ongoing self-examination of the Catholic Church in America. As John Fallon (president, board of directors), Michael J. Greene (publisher), and Robert G. Hoyt (editor), pointed out in the initial issue, the *Reporter* was an exception to the long-standing rule of clergy-run newspapers and periodicals in that it was owned and controlled solely by laypersons without official accountability to any one diocese, bishop, or religious superior. This independent status allowed the editor and his staff to quote John Courtney Murray to good effect: "the Catholic press is not to serve exclusively any one rank in the Church."[1] This news weekly was to serve the entire Catholic Church:

> Emphatically we do not regard ourselves as spokesmen for the laity or as defenders of lay interests but rather as journalists serving the whole community which is the Church. . . . [We mean to] report the life of the church in the world, pressing for as much information as can be had about events and their meaning and, just as importantly, constantly assessing the overall situation of the Church, the quality of particular aspects of Catholic life.[2]

This was to be a newspaper, a survey of all events and activities relevant to Catholic life in the United States. In this regard, the editors quoted Pope Paul VI that proper journalism ought to "mirror the truth of events, of facts, of daily happenings."[3] The *National Catholic Reporter* would thus cover everything from the implementation in the United States of the reforms of Vatican II (a constant theme in articles on parish life, liturgy, ecumenism, and so forth up to the present day) to the election of the U. S. president ("No one will accuse us of speaking for Rome").[4]

The *Reporter* would not limit itself to any particular audience or constituency but would include articles on every facet of Catholic Christian life. A noted American Protestant historian, Martin E. Marty of the University of Chicago, was brought in to contribute a semiregular column, "The Protestant World." Garry Wills, a conservative Catholic who had worked for William F. Buckley on the *National Review*, played devil's advocate to *Reporter* liberals in his weekly editorial. Michael Novak, a promising young Catholic journalist, sent insightful reports from the closing sessions of Vatican II. It was apparent that the *Reporter* was willing "to enter into dialogue with just about anybody."[5] It seemed that it enjoyed a broad base of support in the religious community: the paper was launched with the help of contributions from over 600 Catholics, Protestants, and Jews and garnered the support of established periodicals such as *Commonweal*.*[6]

It is not surprising, then, that the paper's short history has been colored by controversy and subsequently blessed with an ever-expanding readership. The *Reporter* has been at the vanguard of every major progressive social and religious movement trumpeted by Catholic liberals. Coverage of white parishioners picketing the perceived racism of Detroit's episcopacy headlined a long and thorough analysis of the civil rights movement of the 1960s.[7] Contributors such as Betty Friedan and Rosemary Radford Ruether often have written eloquently of the ongoing struggle for equal rights and opportunities for women.[8] Correspondents from around the nation survey and criticize labor and management, unjust business practices, and union discrimination against blacks.[9]

As the newspaper grew, so did its horizons. Correspondents were stationed not only in Rome and Washington—although reporters like Peter Hebbelwaithe continue to report critically of political subterfuge inside the Vatican—but in Southeast Asia and El Salvador as well. The editions grew in length steadily as funding increased from eight to 12 pages in the 1960s to over 20 pages per issue in the 1980s. Additional space was given to international concerns challenging the life of the Catholic Church in the United States, such as the injustices inherent to governments ruling the Third World and the buildup in nuclear armaments by the world superpowers.[10] As the paper expanded, new departments were added (media, ad random, people in the news), old ones were given more space (forum, reviews), and spinoff products emerged (*Reporter* cassettes).

Amid all the changes, the paper has maintained consistency of method in management and publication. During the tenures of over five different editors and publishers, the format and tone of writing have remained for the most part polished, if at times a bit vitriolic. A glimpse at the layout of one issue might illustrate directly the consistency of theme and concern of the *National Catholic Reporter*.

The issue of 3 September 1982 was a double issue commemorating Labor Day in the United States and included articles on the following topics: Monsignor Charles Owens's five decades of service to the alliance of the Catholic Church and organized labor in Pittsburgh; government prosecution of protestors who attempted a blockade of a Trident submarine; a call by the priests of Portland, Oregon, for the nation's bishops to ordain married people, including women, to overcome a clergy shortage; a strike by destitute migrant workers in Arkansas; and, in the "Forum" section, a penetrating review and analysis of Pope John Paul II's encyclical *Laborem Exercens*.[11]

The *Reporter* appears, then, to interweave sociopolitical and ecclesiastical themes in editing the news. On one front the paper examines critical moral concerns facing individuals and nations—exploitation of religious issues by the New Right, waste and danger involved in the military and nuclear arms buildup, erosion of safeguards for ecology, human rights—but also allots significant space to issues of a more parochial slant—women's spirituality, education for ministry, complete listings of spiritual workshops and institutes, and even a section of classified ads listing job openings in church-related positions.[12] Publisher Jason Petosa defends this integration of international and parochial concerns: "The new church of proud (not chauvinistic) Catholics, young and old, is being born at the grassroots. More Catholics today see the necessary links between church reform, personal renewal and social justice."[13] And Arthur Jones, Washington correspondent, feels that the "religious" is tied inexorably to the "economic" and "political": "When ends and ideals are advocated out of 'economic necessity', the church—Christians—should be at the center of the discussion, proposing workable alternatives."[14]

Thus, by virtue of its independent status, the *Reporter* is free to wander where other Catholic periodicals fear to tread. The editors clearly relish this freedom and the controversy—and readers—that it attracts: "we report what we see, as we see it. No one can tell us what to put in our paper, or what to leave out. That's why for 18 years we've been 'the independent Catholic newsweekly.' "[15]

Notes

1. *National Catholic Reporter* 1 (1964): 1.
2. Ibid.
3. Ibid.
4. Ibid.
5. Ibid.
6. Ibid.
7. These were some of the topics lifted from a survey of the first five years of publication of the *National Catholic Reporter*; similar and even more explosive issues

were covered during these years, such as the War on Poverty, the great numbers who left the Catholic priesthood in the wake of Vatican II, and the advent of the "new morality."

8. *National Catholic Reporter* 1 (1964): 3.

9. Ibid., p. 4.

10. Ibid. 18 (1982): 39.

11. Ibid.

12. Described in an advertisement for the *Reporter* (Box 281, Kansas City, Missouri), January 1983.

13. Ibid.

14. Ibid.

15. Ibid.

Information Sources

BIBLIOGRAPHY:
Hennesey, James, S.J. *American Catholics*. New York: Oxford University Press, 1981.
Marty, Martin E., John G. Deedy, David W. Silverman, and Robert Lechman. *The Religious Press in America*. New York: Holt, Rinehart, and Winston, 1963.
New Catholic Encyclopedia. New York: McGraw-Hill, 1967. Vol. 3.
Reilly, Sister Mary Lonan. *The Catholic Press Association*. Metuchen, N.J.: Scarecrow Press, 1971.
INDEX SOURCES: *Religion Index One, Catholic Periodical and Literature Index*.
REPRINT EDITIONS: University Microfilms International, Bell and Howell Micro Photo Division.
LOCATION SOURCES: University of Notre Dame, Catholic University of America, Loyola University (Chicago), Catholic Theological Union (Chicago), and others.

Publication History

MAGAZINE TITLE AND TITLE CHANGES: *National Catholic Reporter* (1964–   ).
VOLUME AND ISSUE DATA: 1:1 (1964–   ).
PUBLISHER AND PLACE OF PUBLICATION: National Catholic Reporter Publishing Co., Kansas City, Mo.
EDITORS: Robert E. Hoyt (1964–72), Donald J. Thorman (1972–77), Arthur Jones (1977–80), Thomas C. Fox (1980–   ).
CIRCULATION: 50,000 (1982).

R. Scott Appleby

NATIONAL CATHOLIC WAR COUNCIL BULLETIN.
See CATHOLIC ACTION

NATIONAL CATHOLIC WELFARE COUNCIL BULLETIN. *See* CATHOLIC ACTION

NEW CATHOLIC WORLD

In 1865, Father Issac T. Hecker (1819–88), an American and convert to Catholicism, launched "a monthly eclectic magazine of general literature and science." The *Catholic World* quickly won the respect of clergy and laity, Catholics and Protestants, for its handling of issues related to Catholicism and culture. Given a new format and renamed *New Catholic World* in 1972, it is the oldest American Catholic journal still published.[1] With semiannual volumes of between 550 and 770 pages, no other magazine has offered such a comprehensive picture of middle-class American Catholic culture for so long a period.

In 1858 Hecker and four other converts to Catholicism had formed the first American congregation of priests, the Paulist Fathers. Named after the apostle to the Gentiles, Hecker hoped the group would contribute to America's conversion to Catholicism. Like the evangelical Protestants, Hecker understood the United States to be the last, best hope of humanity for the creation of a Christian civilization that would enable Christianity to conquer the modern world. Observing the religious ferment of his day, Hecker concluded that the providential moment was at hand. Willing and energetic souls had only to cooperate with God's grace to hasten its eventual triumph.

Hecker believed God had guided him through a variety of errors (Methodism, reform movements, and transcendentalism) so that he might develop an apologetic sympathetic to Protestants, faithful to the Catholic past, and consistent with the dawning of a providential age.[2] From this perspective, the *World* was one means the Paulists used to protect Catholics from "the poisons of indifferentism and infidelity" in the secular press controlled by Protestants and staunchly to defend Catholicism and propagate it among those the church could reach in no other way.[3]

Although not all the founding Paulists shared Hecker's providential interpretation of history, they did hope for a Catholicism more attentive to the sensibilities of middle-class American culture. This enterprise was bold and controversial in a period when a Protestant United States suspected Catholicism might never be assimilated into American life and when many Catholics feared that accommodation to the American religious situation would lead Catholic immigrants to apostasy. Yet the attempt to integrate Catholicism and American life endured, and the *World* is a barometer of its changing fortunes.

Irreconcilable differences between Catholicism and Protestantism were taken for granted, but American Protestants were generally considered well intentioned if ill informed; "they remain satisfied with their state of spiritual poverty because they are ignorant of the richness of faith."[4] Catholics and Protestants were to speak "not from the two opposite extremes of doctrine where the difference is widest and most palpable, but from the middle terms in which both parties agree ... [then] we may proceed to the extremes, and thus endeavor to settle the points in which we differ by the aid of those in which we agree."[5]

The brilliant and combative Orestes A. Brownson, Hecker's mentor and friend, eventually drew opposite conclusions about the practicality of an irenic apologetic, the compatibility of Catholicism and democracy, and the eventual conversion of the United States. Before he withdrew from the *World* in 1872, he had contributed 70 articles on topics as diverse as theology, apologetics, politics, and science.[6]

Articles from European periodicals on theology, history, philosophy, biography, and science made up most of the first issue. There were also poems and fiction, often with a devotional purpose. Only one article, the book reviews, and a short column on science and art were original. About 100 articles and as many reviews appeared each year in the beginning. By the early 1870s, almost all articles were original, although they appeared anonymously until 1880. High editorial standards were maintained under Hecker (1865–88) and his successor, Augustine F. Hewit (1889–97). An Amherst graduate and Episcopal priest before joining the Paulists, Hewit wrote more articles than anyone else for the *World* during the nineteenth century. Most were on philosophical and theological issues. Other talented contributors around the turn of the century included historian John G. Shea, poet Imogene Guiney, and writers Agnes Repplier, Katharine Tynan, John Talbot Smith, Mrs. Wilfrid Ward, Maurice F. Egan, Katharine Bregy, Richard L. Burtsell, and Anna T. Sadlier.

Important Paulists who wrote for the journal were George M. Searle on science, Alfred Young on music and liturgy, Bertrand Conway on apologetics and history, Joseph McSorley on theology, and Walter Elliott on evangelization and spirituality. Elliott is best remembered for his *Life of Father Hecker*, which first appeared as a serial in the *World* between 1889 and 1891. A French translation of 1897 became the focus of a bitter transatlantic controversy over Catholicism's accommodation to modern culture. In 1899 the pope condemned what he called "Americanism" without mentioning the Paulists by name, but they remained under a cloud of suspicion for years.

Hewit's successor as editor, Alexander P. Doyle (1897–1904), briefly added photographs and more articles of a less scholarly nature in order to appeal to a wider audience. John J. Burke, editor from 1904 to 1922, reversed Doyle's policy but was hindered by the repressive atmosphere and intellectual policies that followed the papal condemnation of modernism in 1907. Prior to that time, the *World* published articles that reflected different theological views. Some explicitly cautioned against an uncritical traditionalism. When such ideas could no longer be tolerated in Catholicism, Burke turned more toward social issues. John A. Ryan, pioneer social philosopher of American Catholicism, and William Kerby, organizer of Catholic social work, wrote frequently on labor policies, socialism, and problems of America's political economy. Articles by and about the militant controversialist Hilaire Belloc and the essayist and historian G. K. Chesterton were frequent during Burke's years.

Although they never lost hope for a better world, Burke and each of his successors became increasingly critical of American culture. In the 1920s Burke denounced "degeneracy in any art, a sign of degeneracy in civilization and morality . . . painting which purveys to lust rather than ideals, music that reflects only vagueness, indefiniteness, and immorality . . . ; drama that exploits the basest things of life."[7]

James M. Gillis (editor, 1922–48), whose incisive and controversial editorials ran from six to 10 pages per issue, was never one to pull punches. He noted that "it is possible to be confident and not arrogant, judicious but not mealy-mouthed. . . . The world, as the world, is not only weak and stupid, it is wicked."[8] In a world "divided in its aims, uncertain in its temper, and spiritually restless" because it was bewildered by "swaggering paganisms," Gillis's recurring theme was that "to save the American Republic and Christian civilization, we must restore or establish the supremacy of the moral element in the conduct of world affairs."[9] Among the contributors during Gillis's years were historian Peter Guilday, sociologist Joseph Fichter, and writers George N. Shuster and Daniel Lord.

The last of the *Catholic World*'s twentieth-century editors, John B. Sheerin (editor, 1948–71), introduced illustrations but made no compromise in editorial quality. More conciliatory than his predecessor, Sheerin engaged non-Catholics in dialogue as Vatican II thawed relations between Catholics and other Christians. Protestants Albert Outler and Paul Ramsey briefly served as contributing editors in the late 1960s. Original articles or excerpts from books by leading scholars such as church historian Francis X. Murphy, moralists Bernard Häring and Richard McCormick, and theologians Gregory Baum, Gustave Wiegel, Hans Küng, Karl Rahner, Jaroslav Pelikan, and George Lindbeck appeared.

Steering a moderately progressive course during the Vatican Council and the turmoil that followed it, Sheerin argued that although "all members of the Church should accept . . . the message of the Holy Spirit for our time, this cannot be done by strong arm methods on the part of progressives who condemn conservatives as old fogies, obscurantist, and reactionaries."[10]

Sheerin's retirement in 1971 marked the end of more than a century of thorough and consistently intelligent treatment of how Catholicism and American culture influenced each other. In 1972 the journal was renamed *New Catholic World*. Each bimonthly issue has a different editor and addresses a single topic. The quality is still high, but the running commentary on current events is absent. Only 280 pages are published annually, down from 1400 for the first 75 years and about 1150 between 1945 and 1972.

Notes

1. Only *Ave Maria*,* a family and devotional magazine, is as old. It also appeared in 1865.

2. Hecker to Brownson [13 April 1851]. Joseph F. Gower and Richard M. Leliaert, eds., *The Brownson-Hecker Correspondence* (Notre Dame: University of Notre Dame Press, 1979), pp. 149–50. The last letters, from 1865 to 1872, offer much information about the *World*. The classical statement on the church in America by Hecker is "An Exposition of the Church . . . " *Catholic World* 21 (April 1875): 117–238 (hereafter cited as *CW*).

3. Articles in the *World* often refuted charges and misstatements from Protestant pulpits or publications like *Harper's Weekly*, the *New Englander*, and the *Church Review*. The *Nation*, the *Roundtable*, and the *Mercersburg Review** were a few of the magazines Hecker followed regularly.

4. "A Few Thoughts about Protestants," *CW* 6 (October 1868): 134.

5. "Dr. Bacon on Conversion to the Catholic Church," *CW* 5 (April 1867): 104–14.

6. John J. Burke, "The *Catholic World*," *CW* 101 (April 1915): 13.

7. "With Our Readers," *CW* 114 (October 1921): 141.

8. "Editorial Comment," *CW* 194 (April 1940): 8.

9. Joseph W. Reilly, "The *Catholic World* in Recent Years," *CW* 192 (April 1940): 17; James M. Gillis, "Valedictory," *CW* 167 (September 1948): 490.

10. "Shall We Wrangle or Reason about Reform?" *CW* 199 (July 1964): 203.

Information Sources

BIBLIOGRAPHY:

Burke, John J. "The Catholic World," *CW* 101 (April 1915): 7–15.

Fichter, Joseph. "Three Quarters of a Century," *CW* 151 (April 1940): 12–17.

Gower, Joseph F. and Richard M. Leliaert, eds. *The Brownson-Hecker Correspondence*. Notre Dame: University of Notre Dame Press, 1979.

Holden, Vincent. *Yankee Paul: Issac Thomas Hecker*. Milwaukee: Bruce Publishing Co., 1958.

McSorley, Joseph. *Father Hecker and His Friends*. St. Louis: B. Herder Book Co., 1952.

Reilly, Joseph W. "The *Catholic World* in Recent Years." *CW* 151 (April 1940): 17–24.

Sheerin, John B. *Never Look Back: The Career and Concerns of John J. Burke*. New York: Paulist Press, 1975.

INDEX SOURCES: *Catholic Periodical and Literature Index* (1930–   ), *Poole's Index to Periodical Literature* (1865–1906), *Reader's Guide to Periodical Literature* (1930–80), *Guide to Social Science and Religion in Periodical Literature*.

REPRINT EDITIONS: *Catholic World*: Library of American Civilization, Library Resources; American Periodicals Series, University Microfilms International. *New Catholic World*: University Microfilms International, Bell and Howell Micro Photo Division.

LOCATION SOURCES: Archives of the Paulist Fathers (New York City), University of California at Los Angeles, Library of Congress, Emory University, University of Chicago, and others.

Publication History

MAGAZINE TITLE AND TITLE CHANGES: *Catholic World* (1865–1971), *New Catholic World* (1972–   ).

VOLUME AND ISSUE DATA: *Catholic World* 1–214 (1965–1971), semi-annual volumes; *New Catholic World* 215–   (1972–   ), annual volumes.

PUBLISHER AND PLACE OF PUBLICATION: Lawrence Kehoe, New York, N. Y. (1865–67); Catholic Publishing House, New York, N.Y. (1867–77), Catholic Publication Society, New York, N.Y. (1877–87), Office of Catholic World, New

York, N.Y. (1887–1901); Paulist Fathers, New York, N.Y. (1972–74); Paulist Press, Paramus, N.J. (1974–   ).
EDITORS: I. T. Hecker (1865–88), Augustine F. Hewit, (1889–97), Alexander P. Doyle (1897–1904), John J. Burke (1904–22), James M. Gillis (1922–48), John B. Sheerin (1948–71), Robert J. Heyer (managing editor, 1972–   ).
CIRCULATION: 16,000 (1982).

Thomas J. Jonas

THE NEW OUTLOOK. *See* THE OUTLOOK

NEW OXFORD REVIEW

The *New Oxford Review*, a monthly journal of ideas and opinion, was founded in early 1977 by Dale Vree, formerly an activist in the Berkeley free speech movement. Vree remains editor, while his wife, Elena, serves as managing editor. The *New Oxford Review* (*NOR*) covers ecclesiastical affairs and "any subject of the day." Its offices are located in Berkeley, California.[1]

Originally Anglo-Catholic in inspiration, addressing itself against modernist currents within the Episcopal Church, the *New Oxford Review* is now officially a lay Roman Catholic periodical following the conversion of its editor.[2] The *NOR*'s changing orientation, however, has not altered its original commitment to both lay evangelism and ecumenism. In the first case, the conviction that the church belongs to laity and clergy alike governs the *NOR*'s position. In the second case, the journal's openness to other Christian denominations stems from the belief "that the things that unite us as believing Christians are more significant than what divides us" and the view that ecumenism is consistent with the position of the Second Vatican Council. The *NOR* has also maintained that an ecumenical heresy—that of secularism—exists that needs to be combatted, as well as an ecumenical orthodoxy that deserves to be fostered.[3]

The *New Oxford Review*'s contributors at the present time include John C. Cort, Robert Coles, James J. Thompson, Jr., and George Rutler, among others. Past contributions have come from such scholars and journalists as Peter Berger, Elaine Pagels, Michael Novak, and William Rusher. The *NOR* seeks both Catholic and non-Catholic readers and writers. It is independent of ecclesiastical control to encourage open and constructive debate among its subscribers.[4]

The *New Oxford Review*'s title and the substance of its articles derive from the nineteenth-century Anglo-Catholic revival in England, the Oxford movement, which combined a reverence of the authority of the church—its sacraments, liturgy, central doctrines, and the apostolic succession of its episcopate—with social activism on behalf of the poor.[5] In fact, the *NOR* is currently published under the patronage of St. Vincent Pallotti, an admirer of the Oxford movement and its principal theologian, John Henry Newman. Pallotti, according to Dale

Vree, "coupled his concern for evangelism with a concern for social justice, never letting one concern overwhelm and obliterate the other."[6]

The Oxford movement as historical model thus explains what one commentator recently described as the *NOR*'s curious mixture of left-liberalism on political and economic issues and conservatism on questions of theology and personal morality.[7] The journal's contributions criticize the nuclear arms race, unrestrained capitalism, abortion, moral relativism, feminist religion, and euthanasia while supporting democratic socialism, workers' rights, and compassion toward the poor.

The standard of measurement for all issues, whether social or political, moral or theological, is the adherence to objective Christian norms and the avoidance of accommodation with secular outlooks that would compromise Christian integrity. Not long after the *NOR*'s founding, Vree argued that "the journal must not be the hostage of any one political 'ism'—for in a secular age it is enough of a handicap to be known as uncompromisingly Christian without also being stigmatized as right wing or New Left or whatever."[8] Later, in a piece specifically critical of feminist theology, Vree attacked judgments that uncritically equated secular social and political projects, be they nazism, communism, or imperialism, with acts of God. "From the viewpoint of orthodoxy, the problem here is that there is a mistaken view whereby Providence is regarded as *manifest* rather than *mysterious*. . . . The result is an idolatrous second source of revelation which rivals or supersedes the teachings of the Bible and the Church."[9] The insistence on Christian norms is not limited to the *NOR*'s editor. A recent article by B. L. Edwards, for example, reproached evangelical television for having submerged the uniqueness of the Christian witness to electronic superficiality, trendiness, consumerism, and materialism.[10]

In sum, the *New Oxford Review* is an emerging journal that, although grounded firmly now in the Roman Catholic tradition, aspires to be a forum for the orthodox and traditionalist in all denominations.

Notes

1. See Fran Schumer, "A Return to Religion," *New York Times Magazine* (15 April 1984): 90ff., and Dale Vree, "Speaking Heart to Heart," *New Oxford Review* 51 (April 1984): 2–4 (hereafter cited as *NOR*).

2. Vree, p.2.

3. Ibid., p. 2, and "On Relations between the American Church Union and the Evangelical and Catholic Mission," *NOR* 45 (December 1978): 2.

4. Vree, "Heart to Heart," p. 4.

5. On the Oxford movement, see Horton M. Davies, *Worship and Theology in England: From Watts and Wesley to Maurice, 1690–1850* (Princeton: Princeton University Press, 1961), pp. 243–82, and Bernard M. G. Reardon, *From Coleridge to Gore: A Century of Religious Thought in Britain* (London: Longman, 1971), pp. 90–157.

6. Vree, "Heart to Heart," p. 4.

7. Schumer, p. 94.

8. *NOR* 45 (February 1978): 28.
9. "Worshipping the Spirit of the Age," *NOR* 45 (June 1978): 14–16.
10. "Evangelical Television," *NOR* 51 (July-August 1984): 10–16.

Information Sources

BIBLIOGRAPHY:
Davies, Horton M. *Worship and Theology in England: From Watts and Wesley to Maurice, 1690–1850*. Princeton: Princeton University Press, 1961.
Reardon, Bernard M. G. *From Coleridge to Gore: A Century of Religious Thought in Britain*. London: Longman, 1971.
Schumer, Fran. "A Return to Religion." *New York Times Magazine*, 15 April 1984.
Vree, Dale, "Speaking Heart to Heart." *New Oxford Review* 51 (April 1984): 2–4.
INDEX SOURCES: None.
REPRINT EDITIONS: University Microfilms International.
LOCATION SOURCES: University of Washington, Emory University, University of Michigan, Brigham Young University, Southern Illinois University, and others.

Publication History

MAGAZINE TITLE AND TITLE CHANGES: *New Oxford Review* (1977–   ). Successor to *American Church News*.
VOLUME AND ISSUE DATA: 44:1 (1977–   ). Monthly except for combined January-February and July-August issues.
PUBLISHER AND PLACE OF PUBLICATION: New Oxford Review, Berkeley, Calif. (1977–   ).
EDITOR: Dale Vree (1977–   ).
CIRCULATION: 10,000 (est. 1984).

Shelley Baranowski

THE NEW PRINCETON REVIEW. *See* THE PRINCETON REVIEW

NEW PULPIT DIGEST. *See* PULPIT DIGEST

THE NEW YORK REVIEW

The *New York Review: A Journal of the Ancient Faith and Modern Thought* was published bimonthly by the faculty of St. Joseph's Seminary at Dunwoodie, New York, from June 1905 to July 1908. The journal has been described by John Tracy Ellis and Robert Trisco as "one of the most learned reviews ever undertaken under American Catholic auspices."[1] James Driscoll, the rector of the seminary, acted as editor, with Francis P. Duffy, professor of philosophy at the seminary and later the celebrated chaplain of the "Fighting '69th" Regiment in World War I, as associate editor and John F. Brady, professor of philosophy and founder of the *Homiletic Monthly* (now the *Homiletic and Pastoral Review**), as managing editor.[2]

The *New York Review* was envisioned by Father Duffy to be "a review in English devoted mainly or altogether to presenting the views of Catholic scholars on religious questions of present interest."[3] From its inception, the project of publishing a first-class critical theological review received the strong endorsement of John M. Farley, the archbishop of New York. Considerable opposition to the periodical came from Edward Dyer, the vicar general of the Sulpician Fathers in the United States. Driscoll and several other professors at the seminary were at the time members of the Sulpician order, and their work was closely supervised by the order. The cautious attitude of the Sulpician superior reflected the intense suspicion of modern critical scholarship among Roman authorities. Sulpician censors had only recently refused an imprimatur to a scriptural commentary authored by Francis Gigot, a Sulpician and the professor of Scripture at the seminary. To assuage the misgivings of the Sulpician superiors, Archbishop Farley personally assumed responsibility for the new review. However, the tensions between the Sulpician members of the Dunwoodie faculty and their superiors led to the secession of most of them from the order early in 1906.

From the first issue the editors of the *New York Review* sought to reconcile their Catholic faith with modern knowledge in a positive, respectful, and constructive manner. The journal was open to modern scientific methods while respecting church tradition. The first article in the premier issue, Wilfrid Ward's "The Spirit of Newman's Apologetics" (1:3–14), exemplified the goals of the editors.

Each number of the review carried scholarly articles of theological significance and substantial book reviews, as well as editorial comments in a feature entitled "Notes." This feature, usually authored by Duffy, contained brief reports of contemporary scholarship, especially of new critical publications, comments on Roman documents, and descriptions of the struggles of European scholars with church authorities.

A significant portion of the articles and reviews appearing in the *New York Review* was concerned with the advances of higher criticism. Francis Gigot, the professor of Sacred Scripture who had already published several important books on both the Old and New Testaments, contributed over one-fifth of these articles. His contributions included a six-part series, "The Higher Criticism of the Bible: Its Relation to Tradition" (1:724–28; 2:66–69, 158–61, 302–5, 442–51, 585–91), in which he attempted to defend Catholic scholarly use of the new methods of biblical criticism against attackers who accused him and others of underrating Catholic tradition. Gigot sought to minimize the threat of higher criticism to the traditional teachings of the Catholic Church. He also published a series on the critical study of the Synoptic Gospels (1:89–102, 217–33, 346–70, 640–61; 2:335–61; 3:181–200) and a series on divorce in the New Testament (2:479–94, 610–20, 749–60; 3:56–58, 545–60, 704–21). His other contributions included essays on the Book of Jonas and a historical study of Abraham.[4]

The second most prolific contributor to the *New York Review* was Gabriel Oussani, the Baghdad-born, Johns Hopkins–educated professor of Scripture and archaeology at the seminary. Oussani, a specialist in Semitic languages and Assyriology, published several essays describing and interpreting recent archaeological discoveries, especially literary artifacts from the Near East. The first volume of the *New York Review* contained four long, detailed, and well-documented articles on the recently discovered and deciphered code of Hammurabi and its comparison with the legislation found in the Pentateuch (1:178–97, 488–510, 616–39, 739–61). He contributed eight additional articles, mostly concerned with archaeology and higher criticism. Other contributors in the area of biblical criticism included James Driscoll, the editor, Marie-Joseph Lagrange, Hugh Pope, and Vincent McNabb.

The review also published articles on topics in apologetics, ecclesiology, and Christology. An important series on the human knowledge of Jesus was written by Edward Hanna, professor of dogmatic theology at St. Bernard's Seminary, Rochester, New York. In three installments entitled, "The Human Knowledge of Christ" (1:303–76, 425–36, 547–615), Hanna discussed the possible limitations of Christ's human knowledge and questioned the then common Catholic teaching that Christ as man enjoyed the beatific vision from birth. Because of ideas expressed in these essays and elsewhere, Hanna's doctrinal soundness came under Roman scrutiny. His appointment as auxiliary bishop of San Francisco was delayed five years because of these suspicions.[5]

During the brief life of the *Review*, the conflict between theologians employing modern critical methods and Roman Catholic doctrinal authority came to a climax. In September 1907, Pope Pius X in his encyclical *Pascendi Dominici gregis* condemned all such theologians under the umbrella term *modernists*. Several theologians who were later explicitly identified by Rome as modernists, as well as others who were to come under suspicion but never explicitly condemned, published articles and reviews in the *New York Review*.

Most prominent among the modernists to appear in the review was George Tyrrell.[6] Two of his articles were published in the first volume. The editors of the journal had a high regard for Tyrrell. In the fall of 1905 they wrote: "Since John Henry Newman laid down his pen, we have had no Catholic writer in English superior to Father Tyrrell in originality of thought, fertility of expression, and an all-pervading sense of religion" (1:375). However, after Tyrrell's dismissal from the Society of Jesus in 1906, Archbishop Farley explicitly prohibited the publication of his works in the review. Two of Tyrrell's protégés, Maude Petre and Henri Bremond, had articles subsequently published in the *New York Review*.

Two other theologians whose writings were eventually condemned also wrote for the *Review*. Joseph Turmel had nine essays on the teachings of the early fathers of the Church published in 1906 and 1907. Ernesto Buonaiuti contributed two essays to the periodical and had his own theological review, *Revista Storico-*

Critica delle Scienze Teologiche, favorably reviewed in the *New York Review* in 1906.[7]

In addition, two contributors to the journal, William L. Sullivan and Thomas J. Mulvey, later publicly abandoned the priesthood and withdrew from the Catholic Church because of the papal condemnation of modernism.[8] Another enthusiastic supporter and early contributor of the *New York Review* was Cornelius C. Clifford who later came under a cloud of suspicion for his writings and was removed from his professorship at Immaculate Conception seminary in New Jersey.[9]

The association of liberal theologians, many of whom were identified as modernists, with the *New York Review* was not accidental. Its editors and other professors at the Dunwoodie seminary had been clearly influenced by such creative thinkers as Alfred Loisy, George Tyrrell, and Baron von Hugel. The rector of the seminary, James Driscoll, carried on correspondence with both Loisy and Tyrrell. Driscoll was intensely interested in intellectual development of future priests. Under his leadership, the intellectual life at the seminary thrived.[10]

The periodical's association with modernists and with those suspected of modernism was responsible for its early demise. The official reason given by the editors for suspending publication in mid–1908 was the financial difficulty arising from the paucity of Catholics interested in supporting the kind of questions addressed in the journal. It is well established, however, that the papal condemnation of modernism and the subsequent suppression of suspected modernists by Roman authorities doomed the *Review*. In early 1908 Archbishop Diomede Falconio, the apostolic delegate to the United States, complained to Farley about the journal, especially the appearance of an advertisement for Tyrrell's book, *Lex Credendi*, in two recent issues of the journal. In response Farley defended the good intentions and doctrinal soundness of his editors; however, the damage had been done. Suspicions arising from Hanna's articles had focused Rome's attention on the *Review*. Its final issue appeared in the summer of 1908.[11]

The *New York Review* has been described as the most learned journal published under American Catholic auspices. Only with the founding of *Theological Studies** in 1940 were American Catholics once again publishing articles of the caliber present in the *New York Review*. It was the first truly scientific Catholic theological journal in the United States.

In recent years the relationship of the *New York Review* to modernism has become a topic of considerable debate. Michael DeVito defended the editors of the *Review* against the accusation of being modernist. He accepted the more traditional understanding of modernism as the heresy defined in the papal encyclical *Pascendi*. He professed the loyalty of the editors of the *Review* to the traditions of the church. No evidence was found by DeVito that would "corroborate the thesis that Driscoll himself was a modernist," despite his close friendships with several modernists.[12]

In recent revisionist approaches to modernism, the papal description of modernism has been criticized as an inadequate description of the project of so many

Catholic scholars who were interested in adapting the Roman Catholic Church to the modern world in the first decade of this century.[13] In their condemnations of error, the Roman authorities assumed a false uniformity of teachings and intentions among the scholars whom they sought to condemn. The qualities of a few (such as Alfred Loisy) were generalized as present in all those theologians who wished to adapt the church to modern times.

Scott Appleby employs the new insights of the revisionists in his study of modernism and the *New York Review*.[14] In this view modernism is seen as a movement among scholars who employed a developmental model of tradition. They did not seek to destroy the faith but to "supervise the application of critical methodologies to the revealed sources of religion."[15] In the light of the revisionist understanding of modernism, the editors and contributors to the *New York Review* were indeed modernists. As modernists loyal to the church, they insisted that religious teaching be informed by the thought world of modern science and that religion might speak to the modern world a relevant word.

During the three years of its publication, the *New York Review* made available the excitement of modern critical scholarship to the young American Catholic theological community. Its suppression was part of a sad anti-intellectual period in Catholic history that persisted until World War II. The review prefigured the rich revival of theological scholarship among American Catholics that has thrived in the aftermath of the Second Vatican Council.

Notes

1. John T. Ellis and Robert Trisco, *A Guide to American Catholic History* (Santa Barbara: ABC-Clio, 1982), p. 200.

2. For more information on the founder of the *Review*, see Michael DeVito, *The New York Review (1905–1908)* (New York: U.S. Catholic Historical Society, 1977), pp. 1–85.

3. Cited by ibid., p. 39.

4. For a complete evaluation Gigot's scholarship, see Bernard Noone, "A Critical Response to the American Catholic Response to Higher Criticism" (Ph.D. dissertation, Drew University, 1976), pp. 322–409.

5. See DeVito, pp. 260–291, and John Tracy Ellis, "The Formation of the American Priest: An Historical Perspective," in J. T. Ellis, ed., *The Catholic Priest in the United States: Historical Investigations* (Collegeville, Minn.: St. John's University Press, 1971), pp. 68–69.

6. Cf. Ellen Leonard, *George Tyrrell and the Catholic Tradition* (New York: Paulist Press, 1982).

7. For additional information on modernism, see *New Catholic Encyclopedia*, s.v. "Modernism" by J. J. Heaney.

8. Michael V. Gannon, "Before and after Modernism: The Intellectual Isolation of the American Priest," in Ellis, *The Catholic Priest*, pp. 338–39.

9. Ellis, "The Formation," pp. 67–68.

10. DeVito, pp. 16–25.

11. Ibid., pp. 291–305.

12. Ibid., pp. 187–246.

13. For example, see Thomas Loome, *Liberal Catholicism, Reform Catholicism, Modernism* (Mainz: Matthias-Grunewald, 1979).

14. Scott Appleby, "American Catholic Modernism: Dunwoodie and *The New York Review*, 1895–1910," in *Working Papers*, ser. 14, no. 3 (Notre Dame: Cushwa Center, 1983).

15. Ibid., p. 29.

Information Sources

BIBLIOGRAPHY:

Appleby, Scott. "American Catholic Modernism: Dunwoodie and *The New York Review*, 1895–1910." *Working Papers,* ser. 14, no. 3. Notre Dame: Cushwa Center, 1983.

DeVito, Michael. *The New York Review (1905–1908)*. New York: United States Catholic Historical Society, 1977.

Ellis, John Tracy, ed. *The Catholic Priest in the United States*. Collegeville, Minn.: St. John's University Press, 1971.

INDEX SOURCES: None.

REPRINT EDITIONS: University Microfilms International (American Periodicals Series).

LOCATION SOURCES: St. Joseph's Seminary (Dunwoodie, N.Y.), University of Chicago, Loyola University (New Orleans), New York Public Library, and others.

Publication History

MAGAZINE TITLE AND TITLE CHANGES: *The New York Review* (1905–8).

VOLUME AND ISSUE DATA: 1:1–6 (June/July 1905-April/May 1906), 2:1–6 (July/Aug. 1906-May/June 1907), 3:1–6 (July/Aug. 1907-May/June 1908). Appeared bimonthly, with 3:4–5 as a single issue.

PUBLISHER AND PLACE OF PUBLICATION: St. Joseph's Seminary, Dunwoodie, N.Y.

EDITOR: James F. Driscoll (Francis P. Duffy, associate editor; John F. Brady, managing editor).

CIRCULATION: Unknown.

Bernard Noone

THE NORTH AMERICAN REVIEW

From its beginnings in 1815 until the 1870s, the *North American Review* was primarily the forum for a Boston-based, Unitarian intellectual and cultural elite. In the late 1870s, it changed its format from lengthy, scholarly, and usually unsigned reviews of books to briefer, more popularly written articles and focused on religious issues along with its traditional literary, political, social, and intellectual concerns. In 1940, however, the *Review*'s career came to an abrupt halt with the arrest of its publisher, Joseph Hilton Smyth, as an unregistered agent of the Japanese government.[1] Revived in 1964 as a literary magazine, the journal has continued since with a limited circulation and with minimal religious content.

The *Review* was founded by the same group of convivial young Boston-area professionals who had earlier produced the *Monthly Anthology* and then had

assisted Unitarian scholar Andrews Norton with his *General Repository*.[2] Frank
Luther Mott describes the tone of these early years under the editorship of,
among others, Jared Sparks, Edward Tyrrel Channing, and Edward Everett as
"Bostonian, Harvardian, Unitarian."[3] As such, it reflected the Unitarian assumption that the proper realm of religious concern was not the metaphysical
but rather the cultural, and treated mainly literary and political matters. Articles
were usually reviews of books; specifically religious content was rare. Entries
on religion over the first two decades included hagiographic accounts of such
Unitarian stalwarts as Joseph Stevens Buckminster and William Ellery Channing;[4] favorable notes on new works of biblical criticism and aids to biblical
study by Gesenius, Moses Stuart, and others;[5] praise for the irenic quality of
Hannah Adams's *Dictionary of All Religions*[6] and for apologetic works in the
"evidences of Christianity" tradition;[7] and occasional mixed notices of works
concerning Catholics and Jews.[8] Emerson's works were reviewed, but he and
his transcendentalist colleagues generally favored their own *Dial** with original
pieces.[9] The publication of Bryant's "Thanatopsis" and "To a Waterfowl" was
the *Review*'s most important direct contribution to romantic religion, albeit in
rather diffuse literary form.[10]

The *Review*'s circulation declined in the years just prior to the Civil War but
revived under the guidance of James Russell Lowell and Charles Eliot Norton
beginning in 1864.[11] Norton's "Immorality in Politics" of that year attacked
biblical defenses of slavery more aggressively than had been characteristic of
earlier years.[12] Although Norton, Lowell, and their successor, Henry Adams,
were all scions of Unitarian families, none was any longer a practicing adherent
of that tradition. The already nascent trend toward secularity thus began to grow.
Muckraking articles later collected in book form as *Chapters of Erie* by Henry
Adams's brother, Charles Francis Adams, Jr., helped set the tone of this era.[13]
Items of particular interest during this period included Chauncey Wright's review
of Henry James's (Sr.) *The Secret of Swedenborg*, written in a gentle but highly
skeptical vein;[14] a critical but friendly notice of Renan's *Life of Jesus* and the
replies it engendered;[15] a favorable notice by William James of Darwin's *The
Variation of Animals and Plants Under Domestication*;[16] Henry James's (Sr.)
characterization of Horace Bushnell's *The Vicarious Sacrifice* as an "attempt to
put old wine in new bottles";[17] and a savage attack on transcendentalism by
editor Henry Adams in his review of Octavius B. Frothingham's history of that
movement.[18]

The *Review*, which had been sold in 1870, moved its offices to New York
City in 1878 and the following year shifted from quarterly to monthly publication.[19] Its format and general approach also changed markedly under the editorship of Allen Thorndike Rice. It became a national forum for the discussion
of contemporary questions, especially religious ones. Articles defending agnosticism appeared, and Felix Adler, founder of the Ethical Culture movement,
contributed a sympathetic two-part treatment of Reform Judaism in 1877.[20]
Symposia were another new feature. In 1878, for example, Frederick Henry

Hedge, John Fiske, and Cardinal Gibbons were among the participants in a discussion of "What Is Inspiration?"[21] The following year saw a similar exchange involving Yale's Noah Porter, Princeton's James McCosh, and Harvard's James Freeman Clarke on "Law and Design in Nature."[22] In 1882, a lively confrontation between Anthony Comstock and Octavius B. Frothingham, among others, on "The Suppression of Vice" added another dimension to the series.[23]

The decade of the 1880s saw some 150 pieces dealing with religious questions, an astonishing increase over previous years and a trend that would continue until around 1930. Contributors included such diverse figures as Elizabeth Stuart Phelps on "The Great Psychical Opportunity"; Cardinal Manning on "The Catholic Church and Modern Society"; David Swing on "The Failure of the Southern Pulpit"; Leonard Bacon on "The Observance of the Sabbath"; James Freeman Clarke on "Rational Sunday Observance"; John Bascom, president of the University of Wisconsin, on "Atheism in the Colleges"; John Fiske on "Theological Charlatanism"; Philip Schaff's comparison of the King James version of the Bible with the new translation recently issued; Nina Morais on "Jewish Ostracism in America"; George Parke Fisher on "The Elements of Puritanism"; Lyman Abbott, Henry Ward Beecher, Newman Smyth, and others in a symposium on "The Revision of Creeds"; Elizabeth Cady Stanton on "The Need for Liberal Divorce Laws"; F. Max Müller on "Buddhist Charity"; Kate Field on "Mormon Blood Atonement"; Richard T. Ely on "Political Economy in America"; and an exchange on Robert Ingersoll's avowed agnosticism. One of the religious highlights of the decade was a long series of articles on the "Why Am I a Methodist?" format, which included not only confessional statements by a Catholic, a Jew, and a wide spectrum of Protestants but also defenses of Swedenborgianism, "Heathenism" (Confucianism), spiritualism, agnosticism, and Islam.

This variety continued in the 1890s, with Madame Blavatsky discoursing on the theosophical scene; Charles A. Briggs on "The Theological Crisis"; Notre Dame's beleaguered Father Zahm on "Christian Faith and Scientific Freedom"; Archbishop Ireland on "The Catholic Church and the Saloon"; Prime Minister Gladstone on "The Future Life and the Condition of Man Therein"; and Josiah Strong on "The Problem of Next Century's City." There were also controversial works on Christian Science and on the ritualist issue in England and several pieces by English Rabbi H. Pereira Mendes and others on the problematic character of contemporary Jewish identity.

In the following decades there appeared similar articles on these and other controversial topics, such as the viability of Christian faith, personal immortality, ecumenism, and the utility of the churches as currently constituted, together with clergymen of a variety of traditions addressing the social questions of the day. The *Review* and its counterparts, such as the *Atlantic* and *Harper's*, were instrumental in providing a widely circulating forum that encouraged the entrance of articulate clergy into the realm of public debate, thus publicizing the thought of liberal Catholics such as Gibbons and Ireland, Social Gospel spokesmen such as Ely and Washington Gladden, and other Protestants such as William Croswell Doane, Chauncey B. Brewster, Borden P. Bowne, Harry Emerson Fosdick, Francis Greenwood Peabody, Charles H. Brent, John Haynes Holmes, Philip S. Moxom, Shailer Mathews, and William Adams Brown. Most of these represented the liberal wing of their denominations, and the number of Episcopal bishops involved indicates the increasing prominence of that denomination in the urban United States. A considerable number of articles by Jewish authors, including Abraham Cahan, continued to deal with Zionism, the situation of the Jew in the contemporary United States, and the increasingly acute issue of Jewish identity in a secular world as well.

Perhaps the best-remembered articles concerning religion from the *Review*, however, were not by clerical writers at all but rather Mark Twain's "To My Missionary Critics" and the series later published as *Christian Science*, both scathing attacks on contemporary participants in the religious scene. Twain's hilarious "Fenimore Cooper's Literary Offences" had earlier appeared in the *Review*, and the serial publication of Henry James's *The Ambassadors* was another major literary highlight of the years around the turn of the century.[24]

Little revolutionary material on religious questions appeared in the early twentieth century; articles on pacifism, prohibition, and fundamentalism simply reflected the controversies of the time. Perhaps the liveliest exchange was when St. Paul's feisty Archbishop Ireland engaged in a lengthy argument with Methodist S. M. Vernon on the tactics of Protestant missionaries in Italy and the rather chilly reception they received from the Vatican.[25] By the 1930s, articles with religious content diminished considerably, and only the increasingly drastic situation of the Jews in Germany received much attention.

With the coming of the war, the *Review* itself came to an ignominious end with the arrest of its editor on charges of covert collaboration with the Japanese. The *Review* has not concerned itself with matters of religious interest since its revival in 1964. Thus ended in 1940 the career of one of the principal vehicles through which the public discussion of religious topics in the United States achieved a degree of ecumenicity, seriousness, and relevance, which it has seldom attained since.

Notes

1. Theodore Peterson, *Magazines in the Twentieth Century* (Urbana: University of Illinois Press, 1964), p. 146.

2. Frank Luther Mott, *A History of American Magazines, 1850–1865* (Cambridge: Harvard University Press, 1938), pp. 219–20.

3. Ibid., p. 223.

4. John Gorham Palfrey, review of Buckminster's *Sermons, North American Review* 10 (1820): 204–17 (hereafter cited as *NAR*); Alexander Hill Everett, "Dr. Channing," *NAR* 41 (1835): 366–406. Authors of usually untitled reviews can be identified through William Cushing's *Index to the North American Review, 1815–1877* (Cambridge, Mass.: John Wilson, 1878.)

5. Moses Stuart, review of Gesenius's "Samaritan and Hebrew Pentateuch," *NAR*

22 (1826): 274–317; Sidney Willard, review of Stuart's *Hebrew Grammar*, *NAR* 13 (1821): 473–77.

6. Sidney Willard, review of Hannah Adams's *Dictionary of All Religions and Religious Denominations*, *NAR* 7 (1818): 86–92.

7. For example, John Brazer, review of Thomas Chalmers's *Evidences of Christianity*, *NAR* 7 (1818): 364–408.

8. For example, letters on Ignatius Loyola and the Jesuits by "Inquisitor," *NAR* 5 (1817): 26–29, 309–12.

9. Mott, pp. 238–39.

10. Ibid., p. 225; Bryant, "Thanatopsis," *NAR* 5 (1817): 338–40; "To a Waterfowl," *NAR* 6 (1818): 383. See also Tremaine McDowell, "Bryant and the *North American Review*," *American Literature* 1 (1929–30): 14–26.

11. Mott, pp. 242–44.

12. Ibid., p. 246; Norton, "Immorality in Politics," *NAR* 98 (1864): 105–27.

13. For example, "A Chapter of Erie," *NAR* 109 (1869): 30–106; later collected with articles by Henry Adams as *Chapters of Erie and Other Essays* (New York: Henry Holt, 1886; reprinted Cornell University Press [Ithaca, 1956].)

14. *NAR* 110 (1870): 463–68.

15. Charles Timothy Brooks, *NAR* 98 (1864): 195–223.

16. *NAR* 107 (1868): 762–68.

17. Ibid. 102 (1866): 556–71.

18. Review of *Transcendentalism in New England*, *NAR* 123 (1876): 468–74.

19. Mott, pp. 249–50.

20. "Reformed Judaism," *NAR* 125 (1877): 133–46; "Reformed Judaism—Part II," *NAR* 125 (1877): 327–50.

21. *NAR* 127 (1878): 304–34.

22. Ibid. 128 (1879): 537–62.

23. Ibid. 135 (1882): 484–501.

24. "To My Missionary Critics," *NAR* 172 (1901): 520–34; "Christian Science" (Part I), *NAR* 175 (1902): 756–68; "Christian Science" (Part II), *NAR* 176 (1903): 1–9; "Christian Science" (Part III), *NAR* 176 (1903): 173–84; "Mrs. Eddy in Error," *NAR* 176 (1903): 505–17; "Fenimore Cooper's Literary Offences," *NAR* 161 (1895): 1–12. *The Ambassadors* appeared in several installments in *NAR* 176 and 177 (1903).

25. The following appear in *NAR* 192 (1910): Ireland, "The Methodist Episcopal Church of America in Italy," 14–33; Rev. S. M. Vernon, "A Reply to Archbishop Ireland," pp. 188–201; Ireland, "The Methodist Episcopal Church in Italy. A Rejoinder," pp. 403–14; Rev. William Burt, "Reply to Archbishop Ireland's Strictures," pp. 543–68.

Information Sources

BIBLIOGRAPHY:

Adams, Herbert B., ed. *The Life and Writings of Jared Sparks*. Boston and New York: Houghton Mifflin, 1893.

Duberman, Martin. *James Russell Lowell*. Boston: Beacon Press, 1966.

Mott, Frank Luther. *A History of American Magazines, 1850–1865*. Cambridge: Harvard University Press, 1938.

Peterson, Theodore. *Magazines in the Twentieth Century*. Urbana: University of Illinois Press, 1964.

Samuels, Ernest. *The Young Henry Adams*. Cambridge: Harvard University Press, 1948.

Simpson, Lewis P., ed. *The Federalist Literary Mind*. Baton Rouge: Louisiana State University Press, 1962.

INDEX SOURCES: *North American Review*, 1815–1940: William Cushing, *Index to the North American Review: Volumes I-CXXV, 1825–1877* (Cambridge, Mass.: Press of John Wilson and Son, 1878; reprinted, Hartford: Transcendental Books, 1967); *Supplementary Index, 1878–80* (Boston: n.p., 1880); William M. Griswold, *General Index to the North-American Review, Vols. 92–134 (1861–1882)* (Bangor: Q.P. Index, 1882); self-indexed, 1964–; *General Index* (Boston: n.p., 1827); also in *Poole's Index, Poole's Abridged, Reader's Guide to Periodical Literature, Annual Library Index, Cumulative Index, Jones' Index, Review of Reviews Index, Engineering Index, Dramatic Index, Current Contents, Humanities Index, Bibliography of English Language and Literature, Index to Little Magazines*.

REPRINT EDITIONS: Bell and Howell Micro Photo Division, University Microfilms International.

LOCATION SOURCES: Yale University, Harvard University, University of Chicago, Los Angeles Public Library, Boston Public Library, University of North Carolina-Chapel Hill, University of Texas-Austin, and others.

Publication History

MAGAZINE TITLE AND TITLE CHANGES: *The North-American Review and Miscellaneous Journal* (1815–21); *The North American Review* (1821–1940, 1964–).

VOLUME AND ISSUE DATA: *North American Review* 1–7 (May 1815-Sept. 1818), semiannual volumes, three numbers each; 8 (December 1818, March 1819); 9 (June, September 1819); 10–183 (1820–1906), regular semiannual volumes (10–30 also called new series, 1–21); 184 (January 4-April 19, 1907); 185 (3 May–16 August 1907); 186 (September-December 1907); 187–221 (January 1908-June 1925), regular semiannual volumes; 222 (September 1925-February 1926); 223 (March 1926-February 1927); 224 (March-December 1927); 225–248 (1928–40), regular semiannual volumes; n.s. 1:1 (o.s. 249) (March 1964–), regular annual volumes. Bimonthly, May 1815-September 1818, January 1877-December 1878; fortnightly, 7 September 1906–16 August 1907; monthly, January 1879-August 1906, September 1907-June 1924, September 1927-March 1935; quarterly, December 1818-October 1876, September 1924-June 1927, June 1935-Winter 1939–40, March 1964– .

PUBLISHER AND PLACE OF PUBLICATION: Wells & Lilly, Boston (1815–16), Cummings & Hilliard, Boston (1817–20, 1824), Oliver Everett, Boston (1821–24), Frederick T. Gray, Boston (1825–28), Gray & Bowen, Boston (1828–31), Charles Bowen, Boston (1832–36), Otis, Broaders & Company, Boston (1837–38, 1843–47), Ferdinand Andrews, Boston (1838–40), James Munroe & Company, Boston (1840–41), David H. Williams, Boston (1842), Charles C. Little & James Brown, Boston (1848–52), Crosby, Nichols & Company, Boston (1853–63), Ticknor & Fields, Boston (1864–67), Fields, Osgood & Company, Boston (1868–69), James R. Osgood & Company, Boston (1870–77), D. Appleton & Company, New York, N.Y. (1878–80), A. T. Rice, New York (1881–89), Lloyd Bryce, New York (1889–94), North American Review Publishing Company, New York (1895–1915), North American Review Corporation, New York (1915–40),

Cornell College, Mt. Vernon, Iowa (1964–69), University of Northern Iowa, Cedar Falls, Iowa (1969–   ).

EDITORS: William Tudor (1815–17), Jared Sparks (1817–18, 1824–30), Edward Tyrrel Channing (1818–19), Edward Everett (1820–23), Alexander Hill Everett (1830–35), John Gorham Palfrey (1836–42), Francis Bowen (1843–53), Andrew Preston Peabody (1853–63), James Russell Lowell (1863–72) with Charles Eliot Norton (1863–68), E. W. Gurney (1868–70), and Henry Adams (1870–72); Henry Adams (1872–76), Allen Thorndike Rice (1877–89), Lloyd Bryce (1889–96), David A. Munro (1896–99), George B. M. Harvey (1899–1926), Walter Butler Mahony (1926–35), John H. G. Pell (1935–40), Robert P. Dana (1964–69), Robley Wilson, Jr. (1969–   ).

CIRCULATION: 500–600 (1820), 3200 (1830), 7500 (1880), 17,000 (1891), 76,000 (1908), 25,000 (1910), 13,000 (1925), 3300 (1982).

Peter W. Williams

THE NORTH-AMERICAN REVIEW AND MISCELLANEOUS JOURNAL. *See* THE NORTH AMERICAN REVIEW

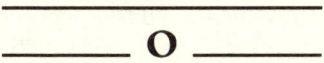

OBERLIN EVANGELIST

On 1 November 1838, the specimen number of a new publication, the *Oberlin Evangelist*, issued from the northern Ohio presses of James Steele. Subtitled *A Semi-Monthly Periodical, Devoted to the Promotion of Religion*, it began to appear on 1 January 1839 in regular biweekly editions and continued virtually without interruption or change in format until 17 December 1862, a victim of Civil War economic conditions. In its 24 years and 624 issues, the *Evangelist* promulgated the religious, theological, and moral concerns of the fledgling Oberlin College, especially revivalism, perfectionism, and abolitionism.

The Oberlin Collegiate Institute, founded in 1833, attracted a faculty and financial supporters who were, for the most part, Presbyterians and Congregationalists with both revivalist and abolitionist sentiments.[1] The *Oberlin Evangelist* was launched to reflect this twofold orientation, as the publication's "Standing Principles" show: (1) "to promote purity, peace and brotherly love, among the saints of every denomination" and thus "the spirit of Christian union" characteristic of the revivals; (2) to clarify the evangelical views of the Oberlin faculty, allegedly suffering from public misrepresentation and misapprehension; (3) to convey "the gospel view of sanctification in this life," a moderate but controversial variety of holiness that concern for Christian nurture had produced, and to set forth a view of the millennium consistent with such sanctification;[2] (4) to deal with a variety of particular issues: "Christian Education, Slavery and Abolition, Moral Reform, Missions, the Christian Sabbath, Revivals of Religion, and any other subject that may seem to be of the highest importance"; and (5) to serve as a vehicle for the sermons of premier revivalist Charles Grandison Finney, himself an Oberlin professor.[3]

The ideas of professor (and later president) Finney maintained a place of prominence throughout the life of the periodical.[4] His theology provided a meas-

ure of coherence to the concerns contained in the "Standing Principles," for it
was as nonsectarian as his revivals and reflected a consensus of the faculty,
particularly on sanctification. Moreover, his mild perfectionist views generated
a moral indignation and reformist zeal that produced activism relative to abolition,
Sabbath keeping, and the like, not to mention articles on such matters.[5]

The principal concern of the *Evangelist*, however, especially in the first five
volumes, was to expound the doctrine of complete sanctification or holiness that
came to be called "Oberlin perfectionism" or simply "Oberlinism." The Oberlin
coterie formulated this doctrine under influences as diverse as John Wesley and
Nathaniel William Taylor, and they took great pains to distinguish it from the
"antinomian perfectionism" of John Humphrey Noyes, with which it had been
confused.[6] This and related matters were treated in Finney's pieces and in regular
contributions by other Oberlin faculty, especially President Asa Mahan, Henry
Cowles, John Morgan, and James A. Thome.[7] The only deliberate change in
policy, announced toward the end of volume 5 (1843), was the shift from the
theoretical to the practical.[8] Accompanying that shift was a detectable change
in tone from apologetic to dogmatic.

In addition to the longer doctrinal articles, each eight-page, quarto-size issue
of the *Evangelist* contained a variety of shorter pieces, including letters from
editors, contributors, and readers; news from denominations, mission fields, and
the secular political arena (the last of these only on such matters as slavery and
abolition); announcements and proceedings of revivals, meetings, conventions,
and other educational and philanthropic events (most notably those connected
with antislavery societies); devotional aphorisms, anecdotes, and poetry; announcements of births, marriages, and deaths of special interest to the readers;
book reviews and ads for books published at Oberlin; news of the college,
including course listings in the early years; nearly endless appeals to subscribers
to pay the one dollar yearly subscription rate; and articles denouncing beverage
alcohol, tobacco, the theater, dancing, and myriad other threats to the sanctified
life.[9] The unifying thread was the perfectionist social ethic.

The Oberlin Evangelistic Association, consisting of the Prudential Committee,
faculty, and selected friends of the college, exercised oversight of the *Evangelist*
enterprise.[10] Though the early issues specified no editor, this duty was apparently
performed until 1843 largely by Horace C. Taylor, removed because of his
embezzlement of *Evangelist* funds, his seduction of a young woman employee,
and his complicity in an abortion.[11] For a short period, President Mahan assumed
editorial responsibility but in July 1845 turned it over to Henry Cowles, who
remained sole editor until the publication's demise, except for nine months in
1847–48, when Mahan again took charge.[12] Throughout these editorial transi-
tions, as well as at least two major changes in publisher and printer,[13] it was
Cowles, rather than Finney or Mahan, who was the stabilizing force behind the
periodical.[14]

Early growth in circulation was rapid, but a gradual decline followed. Initially,
3000 copies of each issue were pressed, but soon the subscription lists had grown

to such an extent that 5000 were printed and back issues reprinted.[15] Distribution was also very wide, covering not only northern Ohio and the old Northwest but New England, New York, and Pennsylvania as well.[16] By early 1858, however, the number of subscribers had dwindled to 2500, forcing the editor to declare that the paper was "without visible means of support" and the publisher to announce a temporary suspension.[17] But the *Evangelist* persisted for four more years, ceasing operations with the final number of 1862, which blamed the demise on the Civil War's demand for secular news, its impoverishment of the *Evangelist*'s low-income readership, and its having driven up costs.[18] In fact, the war may have prolonged the feeble life of the paper by vindicating one of its chief issues, abolition. Indeed, the last volumes of the *Evangelist* recovered some of the rhetorical forcefulness of the earliest volumes, with their argumentative edge and sense of urgency that had all but disappeared.[19]

The *Oberlin Evangelist* had been a successful and significant enterprise in three major ways. First, it had represented the views of Oberlin to a large and influential audience, concomitantly garnering enough support to secure the struggling young college's future. Second, it had promoted a nascent brand of revivalism, fortified with an articulate theology of sanctification. Finally, it had championed the cause of abolition long before it was popular, even in the North.[20]

Notes

1. The character of the school was early shaped by the dramatic 1835 influx of abolitionist students, faculty, and even one dissident trustee from Lane Seminary in Cincinnati, where the famous rebellion over the slavery issue had recently occurred. For good accounts of the relationship between the founding of Oberlin and the exodus from Lane, see Gilbert Hobbs Barnes, *The Anti-Slavery Impulse, 1830–1844* (reprinted, Glouchester, Mass.: Peter Smith, 1957), pp. 74–76; Lawrence Thomas Lesick, *The Lane Rebels: Evangelicalism and Anti-Slavery in Antebellum America* (Metuchen, N.J.: Scarecrow Press, 1980), pp. 169–71; and Louis Filler, *The Crusade against Slavery, 1830–1860* (New York: Harper and Row, 1960), pp. 68–70.

2. The orthodox Oberlin view of the millennium was a variety of postmillennialism, most clearly articulated in a series of *Evangelist* articles by Henry Cowles beginning with 3:4 (17 February 1841) and continuing through most of vol. 4. Cowles was especially interested in undermining what he called the "amillennialism" of adventist William Miller and its "day-year theory."

3. The objectives contained in the "Standing Principles," here condensed from the original 10, were published in 1:1 of the *Evangelist* (1 November 1838), as well as in the next six issues.

4. In some of the volumes, Finney has at least one sermon, lecture, or letter in nearly every issue. In others he has far fewer, as, for example, in vol. 12 (1850), which contains only one of his sermons. This unevenness resulted from the vagaries of Finney's health and revivalist travels.

5. On the link between perfectionism and social reform, see Lawrence Lader, *The Bold Brahmins: New England's War against Slavery: 1831–1863* (New York: E. P. Dutton and Co., 1961), p. 106; and John L. Thomas, "Antislavery and Utopia," in

Martin Duberman, ed., *The Antislavery Vanguard: New Essays on the Abolitionists* (Princeton: Princeton University Press, 1965), p. 247.

6. The definitive work on Oberlin perfectionism and its relation to the perfectionist movement in general is still Benjamin Breckinridge Warfield, *Perfectionism*, 2 vols. (New York: Oxford University Press, 1931), 2:3–215. See also Timothy L. Smith, *Revivalism and Social Reform in Mid-Nineteenth-Century America* (New York and Nashville: Abingdon, 1957), pp. 104–13; H. Shelton Smith et al., *American Christianity: An Historical Interpretation with Representative Documents*, 2 vols. (New York: Charles Scribner's Sons, 1963), 2:42–48; and Whitney R. Cross, *The Burned-Over District: The Social and Intellectual History of Enthusiastic Religion in Western New York, 1800–1850* (New York: Harper and Row, 1950), pp. 238–51.

7. For informative (albeit uncritical) individual profiles of these men, see James H. Fairchild, *Oberlin: The Colony and the College, 1833–1883* (Oberlin, Ohio: E. J. Goodrich, 1883), pp. 277–287, 290–91.

8. *Oberlin Evangelist* (11 October 1843):166.

9. The size changed from medium quarto to the larger royal quarto with vol. 6 (1844).

10. Robert Samuel Fletcher, *A History of Oberlin College from Its Foundation through the Civil War*, 2 vols. (Oberlin, Ohio: Oberlin College, 1943), 1:419.

11. *Oberlin Evangelist* (20 December 1843):206. On Taylor's tenure as editor, see Fletcher, p. 419.

12. Fletcher, p. 419, overlooked the first stint of Mahan as chief editor, which is reported in *Oberlin Evangelist* (16 July 1845):119. Cowles's name begins to appear on the masthead with this same issue.

13. R. E. Gillett, publisher until July 1844, served also as printer after the first two volumes, printed by James Steele.

14. Fairchild, p. 285.

15. *Oberlin Evangelist* (13 March 1839):53.

16. Fletcher, p. 421.

17. *Oberlin Evangelist* (20 January 1858):11, anticipated that the delay would be three or four weeks, but the next issue is dated 17 March. Since the following issues appeared weekly, the missing numbers were made up by the end of April. Ten years earlier, a fire at the publisher's office had prevented the two April 1848 numbers from appearing.

18. *Oberlin Evangelist* (17 December 1862):204.

19. The wartime issues are especially interesting. At the same time that the periodical declared that "Slavery must die!" and that President Lincoln was "the man for the hour" and published timely sermons by Henry Cowles and Richard Hatch on the war and its causes, Finney's sermons focused on personal piety rather than social-political issues. See especially *Oberlin Evangelist* (27 February, 6 March, 22 May, 5, 19 June, 9 October 1861). Previously the *Evangelist* had been consistently pacifist in orientation, as, for example, when it opposed the United States's war with Mexico. See the 10 June 1846 issue, p. 95.

20. *Oberlin Evangelist* (17 December 1862):204; Fletcher, p. 421.

Information Sources

BIBLIOGRAPHY:

Fairchild, James H. *Oberlin: The Colony and the College, 1833–1883*. Oberlin, Ohio: E.J. Goodrich, 1883.

Fletcher, Robert Samuel. *A History of Oberlin College from Its Foundation through the Civil War*. 2 vols. Oberlin, Ohio: Oberlin College, 1943.
INDEX SOURCES: None.
LOCATION SOURCES: The complete set of 24 volumes is accessible both bound and on microfilm in Special Collections at the Oberlin College Library, Oberlin, Ohio.

Publication History

MAGAZINE TITLE AND TITLE CHANGES: *Oberlin Evangelist* (1838–62).
VOLUME AND ISSUE DATA: Vols. 1–5 (1 November 1838–20 December 1843); vols. 6–20 (n.s. 1–15) (3 January 1844–22 December 1858); vols. 21–24 (n.s. vols. 1–4) (5 January 1859–17 December 1862).
PUBLISHER AND PLACE OF PUBLICATION: R. E. Gillett (1838–44), J. M. Fitch (1844–58), Shankland and Harmon (1859–62), all Oberlin, Ohio.
EDITORS: Horace C. Taylor et al. (November 1838-September 1844), Asa Mahan (October 1844-June 1845, December 1847-August 1848), Henry Cowles (July 1845-November 1847, September 1848-December 1862).
CIRCULATION: Approximately 5000 at its peak (1839–40).

Paul A. Laughlin

THE OBERLIN QUARTERLY REVIEW

The *Oberlin Quarterly Review* began its short existence in August 1845 with Asa Mahan, president of the Oberlin Collegiate Institute and professor of mental and moral philosophy, and William Cochran, professor of logic and associate professor of intellectual and moral philosophy, as senior and junior editors, respectively. The *Review* was launched as a platform to promote and defend Oberlin theology, especially perfectionism, and to criticize the Calvinist doctrines of original sin and predestination. Oberlinians already had the biweekly *Oberlin Evangelist** as a vehicle for sermons, lectures, and more popular presentations by Mahan, Charles G. Finney, John Morgan, and others involved in the college, church, and community. The *Review* would venture, as Cochran wrote in an introductory essay, into the realm of religious ideas previously accepted on the basis of creedal formulations and inherited tradition. The grand object of the publication was "the development, elucidation, and scientific arrangement of first principles in Religion, Moral Philosophy, and Taste." The controversial nature of the *Review* was unashamedly announced, with focus on the theological questions of moral depravity, necessity, and free will. The *Review* called for unsparing self-criticism and criticism of others, as well as the acceptance of truth wherever found. Cochran also commented on "Christian Polemic," noting the need to be critical of issues while maintaining a respect for persons, however dangerous their ideas.[1] Cochran remained an editor for only one year. Thereafter Charles G. Finney, then professor of theology and later second president of Oberlin, joined Mahan as editor. Cochran published a series of articles on "The

Simplicity of Moral Action,'' but his untimely death ended the series short of completion.

From the beginning, authors advanced one of Oberlin's distinctive doctrines, perfectionism (Mahan's word), entire sanctification (Finney's), or holiness (Morgan's). Mahan had published his influential *Scripture Doctrine of Christian Perfection* in 1839, but he and Finney found a continuing need to clarify and defend the doctrine. The Oberlinians presented perfection neither as a permanent state achieved nor as a perfection of action but as a perfection of the will and intention insofar as one loves God with all his heart and his neighbor as himself.[2] The first issue of the *Review* contained articles of perfection by Mahan and holiness by Morgan. Later issues contained such articles as Finney's summary of his, Mahan's, and Cowles's presentations on perfection with a reply to criticisms by Dr. Woods and by the Troy Presbytery, the same author's "Reply to the Warning against Error," and Mahan's reply to an attack in *Princeton Theological Essays*.[3]

The questions of moral depravity, God's moral government, and predestination were also frequently discussed as contributors sought to elucidate the errors of Calvinism. On a positive note, biblical and historical arguments for accepting the doctrine of free will were presented, including a translation from C. G. Bretschneider's *Manual of Dogmatic History* showing that the oldest church fathers ascribed to humans freedom of will to choose good and evil. The first volume contained a prepublication extract concerning moral depravity from Finney's *Systematic Theology*. In a later issue, Finney replied at length to a review of his theology published in the *Biblical Repertory*.* In a review of Thomas Chalmers on Romans, Samuel D. Cochran directly opposed Chalmers's presentation of absolute and unconditional predestination and election. Mahan reached into the past to review the doctrine of necessity in Anthony Collins's *A Philosophical Inquiry concerning Human Liberty* (1749). Mahan condemned Collins's position but noted that Collins was at least clear, whereas Edwards was obscure on the issue at hand.[4]

Biblical interpretation found its way into the *Review*. Mahan wrote articles on Ecclesiastes and the Song of Solomon, and his review of Albert Barnes's new translation and commentary on the book of Job amounted to Mahan's exposition of the idea of divine retribution. Mahan also introduced a regular feature, "Select Passages of Scripture Considered." Other articles drew heavily on exegetical arguments. The pages of the *Review* were open to diverse views, but spirited responses could be expected—from editors and also from readers who might forward articles in response. In publishing exegetical articles on immortality, resurrection, and judgment, for example, Mahan recorded his disagreement in notes and wrote a reply.[5]

Ecclesiological and disciplinary matters were addressed in articles by Mahan and Edward H. Fairchild. Both opposed divisiveness from adherence to nonessential aspects of creedal statements and the use of creeds as doctrinal tests to establish orthodoxy rather than having recourse to the Bible. Mahan insisted that brotherly love should unite Christians on essential things even when they differed on doctrinal points, for a difference in doctrine ought not to lead one to impute a lack of virtue in an opponent. At a time when doctrinal differences were causing great strife in denominations and new groups were forming over such differences, such an appeal was important.[6]

Emphasis on Christian experience and perfection aroused an interest among Oberlinians in the mystical life. The life and thought of Madame Guyon were examined, and the works of Thomas Upham were reviewed and analyzed in some detail, with a focus on conversion, progress in sanctification, and a deepening interior spiritual life.[7] In addition, articles on literary subjects and notices of new books on various topics were to be found in almost every issue. Authors such as Carlyle, Lamartins, and Charlotte Elizabeth were considered. T. B. Hudson also contributed an essay on the "National Literature" of England with remarks on the future development of an American national literature reflecting the American character.[8] J. A. Thome, an Oberlin professor until 1848 and later professor at the short-lived Cleveland University under Mahan's presidency of that institution, wrote on "The Education of the Sensibility."[9] In line with his usual method of reconciling opposites in a synthesis, Thome sought to show that an aesthetic sense (often identified with classicism and thus opposed to biblical religion) could be incorporated into a Christian view.

Issues of reform dear to Oberlin were not only presented, they were debated. While all opposed slavery, the issue of come-outerism, or complete separation from all institutions that had any relations with slaveholders, was a moot question.[10] And the matter of the relation of voluntary benevolent societies to the churches was of burning interest. Some supported only benevolent societies subservient to the churches; others advocated separate voluntary societies, arguing that the churches had failed to take up the cause of reform.

Meanwhile, at Oberlin the question of woman's role in society was being discussed and tested. Coeducation was an original principle of the institution. However, the majority of the faculty believed that although women were being educated as equals of men, they were being educated to serve in the household. Two classic presentations of the issue are in the *Review*. James Fairchild, then professor of mathematics and natural philosophy and later president, published an address to students, "Women's Rights and Duties."[11] Fairchild argued that woman's divinely appointed role was in the home. She was not meant to play a public role, to vote, to be a minister, or otherwise to depart from a very traditional concept of female duty. In the same issue, Mahan published (at his initiative) a class paper by Antoinette Brown that presented her exegesis of I Corinthians 14:34–35 and I Timothy 2:11–12, both of which bore directly on the role of women in the church. Brown rejected the idea that the passages were meant to prevent women from speaking in churches. Working from lexical evidence and context, she concluded that nowhere in Scripture is a woman forbidden to act as a public teacher "*provided* that she has a message worth communicating and will deliver it in a manner worthy of her high vocation."[12]

Publication of the *Review* continued for four years. By the end of the second year, financial problems were apparent. The May 1847 issue included a "Publisher's Appeal to All Subscribers," which noted that the number of subscribers was insufficient to meet costs. Authors, the appeal noted, had rarely been paid, but a wider circulation would provide resources to pay them. In the end, financial support was lacking, and the *Review* ceased publication in 1849 with the last issue of the fourth volume.[13] In its brief life, the *Oberlin Quarterly Review* succeeded in giving voice to scholarly presentations of ideas and issues dear to the hearts of Mahan, Finney, and others. The *Oberlin Evangelist* would continue to spread Oberlin views until 1862, but the *Review* had failed to find an audience. Yet the pages reveal a rich tapestry of thought and an amazing breadth of topics of interest to the faculty, students, alumni, and friends of a small, struggling college in what was then "the West."

Notes

1. *Oberlin Quarterly Review* 1 (1845–46): 3–24.
2. On Mahan and perfectionism, see Edward H. Madden and James E. Hamilton, *Freedom and Grace: The Life of Asa Mahan* (Metuchen: Scarecrow Press, 1982), pp. 59–67. Oberlin perfectionism and reform are set in a wider perspective in Timothy L. Smith, *Revivalism and Social Reform in Mid-Nineteenth Century America* (New York: Abingdon Press, 1957).
3. See *Oberlin Quarterly Review* 1 (1845–46): 317–64, 463–80; 2 (1847): 449–72; 3 (1848): 362–70, 373–417.
4. See ibid., 1 (1845–46): 261–79, 446–500; 2 (1847): 1–24, 68–92; 3 (1848): 23–81.
5. See ibid. 2 (1847): 131–57, 263–83; 4 (1849): 59–85, 155–93.
6. See ibid. 2 (1847): 364–76, 473–89; 3 (1848): 121–50; 4 (1849): 4–17.
7. See ibid. 4 (1849): 101–27, 250–74.
8. See ibid. 3 (1848): 219–27.
9. See ibid. 4 (1849): 450–77.
10. See ibid. 2 (1847): 93–110; 3 (1848): 287–310, 419–49.
11. Ibid. 4 (1848): 326–408, with 326–44 misnumbered as 236–54.
12. Ibid. 4 (1849): 358–73.
13. In a brief notice concerning the *Review*, Robert S. Fletcher, *A History of Oberlin College*, 2 vols. (Oberlin: Oberlin College, 1943), 1:418, incorrectly gives August 1848, not October 1849, as the date of the terminal issue.

Information Sources

BIBLIOGRAPHY:
Cazden, Elizabeth. *Antoinette Brown Blackwell*. Old Westbury, N.Y.: Feminist Press, 1983.
Finney, Charles G. *Memoirs of Rev. Charles G. Finney*. New York: A. S. Barnes and Co., 1876.
Fletcher, Robert S. *A History of Oberlin College from Its Foundation through the Civil War*. 2 vols. Oberlin: Oberlin College, 1943.

Klukas, Arnold W., ed. *Building Utopia: Oberlin Architecture, 1833–1933*. Bulletin of the Allen Memorial Art Museum 41 (1983–84).

Madden, Edward H., and James E. Hamilton. *Freedom and Grace: The Life of Asa Mahan*. Metuchen, N.J.: Scarecrow Press, 1982.

Smith, Timothy L. *Revivalism and Social Reform in Mid-Nineteenth Century America*. New York: Abingdon Press, 1957.

INDEX SOURCES: None.

LOCATION SOURCES: Oberlin College, Yale University, University of Chicago, New York Public Library, Congregational Library (Boston), Drew University, Iowa State Travelling Library, Chicago Theological Seminary, Western Reserve Historical Library, State Historical Society of Wisconsin.

Publication History

MAGAZINE TITLE AND TITLE CHANGES: *The Oberlin Quarterly Review* (1845–49).

VOLUME AND ISSUE DATA: 1:1 (August 1845)–4:4 (October 1849).

PUBLISHER AND PLACE OF PUBLICATION: James M. Fitch, Oberlin, Ohio.

EDITORS: Asa Mahan (1845–49), William Cochran (1845–46), Charles G. Finney (1846–49).

CIRCULATION: Unknown.

Grover A. Zinn

OHIO JOURNAL OF RELIGIOUS STUDIES. *See* JOURNAL OF RELIGIOUS STUDIES

THE OLD AND NEW TESTAMENT STUDENT. *See* THE BIBLICAL WORLD

OLD TESTAMENT ABSTRACTS

The first issue of *Old Testament Abstracts*, a publication of the Catholic Biblical Association, appeared in February 1978. As its name implies, this journal, which appears three times a year, publishes abstracts of articles and books relevant to the study of the Old Testament and related fields.

The general editor for the initial issue was Bruce Vawter, who remains in this position, as does managing editor Joseph Jensen. Eight or nine distinguished scholars serve as associate editors.[1] The bulk of the work is performed by a group of approximately 20 abstractors, some of whom have been with the journal since its inception. Over 300 journal articles and close to 50 books are abstracted in a typical issue. The number of journals surveyed has grown to almost 300 from an earlier total of approximately 215.

Old Testament Abstracts maintains the same format every issue. The first, and longer, section is devoted to periodical abstracts and is subdivided into the following headings: "General"; "Archaeology, Epigraphy, Philology"; "History and Geography"; "The Pentateuch: Genesis, Exodus-Deuteronomy"; "Historical Books: Joshua–2 Kings, 1 Chronicles–2 Maccabees"; "The Writings: Psalms, Job to Sirach"; "Major Prophets"; "Minor Prophets"; "Biblical Theology"; and "Intertestamental and Apocrypha." The shorter section of book notices has these headings: "Introduction and General," "Pentateuch," "Historical Books," "The Writings," "The Prophets," "Biblical Theology," "Varia," and "Other Books Received." The last issue for each year contains three cumulative indexes: an author index; an index of Scripture texts (including, in addition to biblical material, pseudepigraphal and early patristic Books; Dead Sea Scrolls; Targumic material; Mishna, Talmud; other rabbinic works); and an index of words in Hebrew and other ancient languages (formerly index of Semitic words).

Each issue also closes with a list of periodicals available for abstraction. In that list an address is given for journals that exchange with *Old Testament Abstracts* or provide free copies. According to Vawter, the reader "will notice by the lack of address some noteworthy hold outs."[2]

Obtaining desired journals and making them available to potential abstractors remain difficult: "We continue to some extent to rely on the availability of various journals to particular abstractors, since some publishers have been and continue to be reluctant to make an exchange with us; on the other hand, certain publishers who held out for two or three years have finally agreed to an exchange."[3] Even greater difficulty has been experienced in obtaining books for inclusion: "We continue to be surprised by the shortsightedness of some book publishers in either ignoring us or deliberately passing us by as an avenue for the advertisement of their wares. Every book that we receive, and they remain far and few, is noted either in our notices or in the category of 'Books Received.' "[4] Cooperative ventures with other abstracting journals have been explored; however, "they have not come to much because of logistical problems beyond our control."[5]

Notwithstanding these problems, Vawter states that the international scholarly community has reacted very favorably to *Old Testament Abstracts*: "I have received numerous commendations on the journal and appreciations on the part of scholars whose names are well known in our field. . . . We have had very generous press given us by the international Old Testament community by and large."[6] These sentiments are shared by Jensen: "We can state without reservation that the goals set in producing this new journal are being abundantly met . . . and from the first issue *Old Testament Abstracts* was greeted as an indispensable tool."[7]

Notes

1. See the "Editorial Foreword" found in *Old Testament Abstracts* 1:1 (February 1978).

2. Bruce Vawter, personal correspondence (May 1982).

3. Ibid.
4. Ibid.
5. Ibid.
6. Ibid.
7. Joseph Jensen, personal correspondence (June 1982).

Information Sources

BIBLIOGRAPHY:
"Editorial Foreword." *Old Testament Abstracts* 1:1 (February 1978).
Personal correspondence.
INDEX SOURCES: Indexed annually in the third issue of each volume.
LOCATION SOURCES: Library of Congress, University of California—Riverside,
    Clemson University, University of Illinois—Urbana, Smith College Library, Yale
    Divinity School Library, and others.

Publication History

MAGAZINE TITLE AND TITLE CHANGES: *Old Testament Abstracts*.
VOLUME AND ISSUE DATA: 1:1 (February 1978–   ).
PUBLISHER AND PLACE OF PUBLICATION: Catholic Biblical Association, Wash-
    ington, D.C.
EDITOR: General editor, Bruce Vawter; managing editor, Joseph Jensen.
CIRCULATION: 1600 (1982).

Leonard J. Greenspoon

THE OLD TESTAMENT STUDENT. *See* THE BIBLICAL
WORLD

ORATE FRATRES. *See* WORSHIP

THE OUTLOOK

When Theodore Roosevelt praised the *Outlook* and its noted editor, Lyman
Abbott, for their "adherence to a high ideal with ready recognition of the need
of practical methods in the achievement of that ideal," he paid them the Progressive era's highest compliment.[1] "Practical idealism" was the ruling slogan
of the day, particularly for publications considered definers of public morality
or, in Henry F. May's phrase, "custodians of culture." The *Outlook* and the
Independent, with which it later merged, along with periodicals such as the
Nation, the *Century*, *Harper's*, and *Scribner's*, formed "a solid front in defense
of American nineteenth century culture."[2]

But no other magazine exemplified this practical idealism within Protestant
circles more than Abbott's *Outlook*. The first issue in 1900 is typical. The weekly

contained first several pages of news summary: items describing action in the Boer War; political reform in Cuba; fighting in the Philippines; bribery and corruption in Montana; municipal reform in Ohio; rising wages in the steel industry ($1.50 a day); the burial of Dwight L. Moody in Northfield, Massachusetts; and advances in sanitation and hygiene in the public schools. Such news was chosen with an editorial advocacy of moderate reform and modest piety. The Department of Indian Affairs was applauded for doing away with Indian exhibition shows in which the natives could get money for their savagery and for requiring future exhibitions to "show the progress of the Indians in education and civilization." William DeWitt Hyde, president of Bowdoin College, was quoted favorably for criticizing indiscriminate scholarship aid to seminarians on the grounds that "natural selection does not get a fair chance to do its wholesome work of toning up the manhood of the ministry" when life was made too comfortable.

Major editorial articles followed. Booker T. Washington, subject of the first, received endorsement for his stress on self-support, education, and industrial training for the Negro and thus implicit contentment with the newly reinforced separate-but-equal system. Typically Protestant Progressivism placed improvement of character before reform of society:

> The character of the negro is more important to him than his place, and the best way to secure for him his right place is to endow him with a right character. It has been a grievous mistake to put agitation for his recognition before strenuous effort to give him a character which deserves to be recognized.[3]

The *Outlook* and its contemporaries placed the building of character through self-control, physical vigor, and moral certainty at the forefront of progress in all areas of society. Numerous biographies were included as if to reinforce the examination of character: profiles of military men; a history of nursing and its founding figures; photographs and stories on college presidents, in this case, two well-known female educators, Caroline Hazard of Wellesley College and Elizabeth Agassiz of Radcliffe.

A Family Paper was for years the subtitle of the *Outlook*'s cover page, and varieties of other materials appeared in its double-columned pages. Poetry, serialized novels, literary criticism, short stories, book reviews, sermons, and a children's section, along with correspondence from readers, rounded out a typical issue of 88 pages.

Abbott's *Outlook*, not related to any denomination, was unalterably opposed to all forms of sectarianism. It promoted the faith that "all human progress is divinely ordered progress, and that all events are to be measured, not by their relation to a political or church organization, but by their relation to human welfare and human development." Christianity was "larger than any church . . . a man can possess the Christian spirit, not only if he is a Friend or a Unitarian, but if he is a Jew or an agnostic.'' Abbott believed that the ''solution of all problems, whether individual or social, is to be found in the principles inculcated and in the spirit possessed by Jesus Christ.''[4] The 65-year history of the *Outlook*, however, marked a general gravitation from the specifically religious to secular political commentary.

The antecedents of the journal lay with another periodical. In 1869 Henry Ward Beecher, some trustees of Brooklyn's Plymouth Church, and Beecher's publisher acquired *Church Union*, a tiny periodical devoted to Protestant denominational reunion which had been established the previous year. Beecher changed its name to *Christian Union*, for he was more interested in ''a unity of feeling and a co-operation of effort of all Christian churches.''[5] In association with the Beecher name, *Christian Union* blossomed from a circulation of perhaps 2000 to over 130,000 in less than two years. It became a Beecher family project, with articles by Henry's brothers, Edward and Thomas, both clergymen; Henry's wife, Eunice; and his novelist sister, Harriet Beecher Stowe.[6]

The *Brooklyn Daily Eagle* considered ''the editorial page of Mr. Beecher's new journal . . . almost wholly secular,'' probably because of Beecher's broad Christian interpretation reflected in the *Christian Union*'s subtitle: *A Family Journal, drawing materials of interest and instruction from every department of human life*.[7] More radical advocates of social change such as Elizabeth Cady Stanton dismissed it as ''a dull paper without a new thought in morals, religion or politics.''[8] Such comments derive from Beecher's stance in the middle ground of Protestant liberalism.

Earlier Beecher had written social commentary for the *Independent*, a Congregationalist journal established in 1848. After a brief stint as the *Independent*'s editor, he became disenchanted with the policies of its managing editor, Theodore Tilton, and severed his connections with the journal in 1867. *Christian Union* provided a new vehicle for Beecher's social commentary and soon became the *Independent*'s chief rival. But the scandal that erupted when Tilton's wife claimed she had engaged in a lengthy affair with Beecher drove *Christian Union* into bankruptcy, although Beecher was acquitted in a church trial (1874) and a civil trial (1875).[9]

Some of Beecher's friends formed the Christian Union Publishing Company in 1875, and with Beecher as nominal editor, the magazine never suspended publication. In 1876, Lyman Abbott became the journal's associate editor. Abbott, born in 1835, prepared for a law career until he felt called to the ministry during Beecher's great revival of 1858. After a five-year pastorate in Terre Haute, Indiana, Abbott returned to New York in 1865 with his wife, Abby, to work for the Freedmen's Commission. In 1866 he began to write for magazines such as *Harper's*, and in 1870 he took on the editorship of the American Tract Society's *Illustrated Christian Weekly*. Abbott was drawn to a broader, more progressive editorial stance than the *Weekly* allowed, and when the job at *Christian Union* was offered, he accepted at once. He gladly worked as Beecher's shadow editor until Beecher resigned in 1881. Abbott then became editor.[10]

The circulation of *Christian Union*, erratic in the 1870s, leveled off at about 20,000 and remained there into the 1890s. The staff began to grow, and when Beecher and his friends were ready to sell their interests in 1885, Abbott's neighbor, Lawson Valentine, a gentleman farmer and entrepreneur, bought controlling interest, forming the New York and Brooklyn Publishing Company. Abbott's life was complicated by Beecher's death in 1887 since the Plymouth Church called Abbott as interim pastor for a year, then as permanent pastor until his resignation because of ill health in 1898. He was primarily a pulpiteer, though, as he continued full time as editor, leaving pastoral duties at Plymouth to others.

In the early 1870s Abbott had contributed a pseudonymous column to the *Christian Union* commenting on moral issues. After his formal association with the magazine, he broadened the column's focus to cover all current affairs and named it "The Outlook." When he became restive with the journal's title because 20 other papers had the word *Christian* in their headings and the word itself sounded too ecclesiastical, Abbott made the name of his column the name of the journal (1 July 1893), and the publisher's name became the Outlook Company.

Only two subscribers were lost in the transition, according to Abbott, and the *Outlook* soon entered its heyday. Circulation multiplied to 80,000 by 1900 and peaked at 105,000 by 1910. The weekly changed from a quarto to a magazine format in 1897.[11] Abbott's moderate progressivism also began to mature as he supported organized labor (but not violent strikes), government control over railroads and telegraph companies (but strong free enterprise), industrial education for blacks (but separate from whites), justice for Indians (but under the reservation system), and international arbitration (but condemnation of barbarism in the Spanish-American War).

Abbott's prominence as an editor, preacher, and lecturer brought contact with eight presidents, but his closest relationship was with Theodore Roosevelt. Abbott induced Roosevelt to write a number of articles for the *Outlook* and to become an associate editor for five years when Roosevelt's presidency ended in 1909. The *Outlook* was hurt by its endorsement of Roosevelt's candidacy in 1912, though, and thereafter stayed out of direct political activity.[12]

The peculiar chemistry of Protestant progressivism that compounded social progress with traditional Christian terminology and reference to the person and teachings of Jesus began to break apart after World War I. The *Outlook* reflected the change in its increasing secularity. Notices of church business were dropped; no weekly sermon was published. Lyman's son, Ernest Hamlin Abbott, after serving as shadow editor in the last years of his father's life, became editor in 1923, but he lacked his father's evangelical heritage and religious interests. In 1928 the magazine passed out of its historic family connections.

The *Outlook* was purchased by Francis Rufus Bellamy, who in an act of historical irony merged it with the *Independent*. The first joint issue appeared 24 October 1928. Neither magazine was competing well in the secular general interest market, nor did they do well together. Circulation fell, and in 1932, the *Outlook and Independent* was sold again. After a brief suspension from May to

September 1932, it was reissued as a monthly under the editorship of Alfred E. Smith, the 1928 Democratic presidential candidate. Smith called his journal the *New Outlook* and used it as a platform to criticize the New Deal. By 1934 Smith had lost interest, and his friend Francis Walton took over and presided over the magazine's demise in June 1935.

An era was over. The nineteenth-century journals celebrating social progress had all merged, died, or unrecognizably changed. Yet in its day, no magazine was more influential in shaping and reinforcing the Protestant Progressive milieu of powerful elements of American society than the *Outlook*.

Notes

1. *Outlook* special edition in honor of the 70th birthday of Lyman Abbott (18 December 1905): 16.

2. Henry F. May, *The End of American Innocence* (Chicago: Quadrangle Books, 1964), pp. 14, 30, 75.

3. *Outlook* 64 (6 January 1900): 9, 12, 14.

4. Lyman Abbott, *Reminiscences* (Boston: Houghton Mifflin, 1915), pp. 336, 338, 347.

5. Milton Rugoff, *The Beechers* (New York: Harper and Row, 1981), p. 476; Abbott, p. 328.

6. Rugoff, pp. 476, 516, 529.

7. Clifford E. Clark, Jr., *Henry Ward Beecher: Spokesman for a Middle-Class America* (Urbana: University of Illinois Press, 1978), p. 187.

8. Rugoff, p. 476.

9. Clark, p. 243.

10. Abbott, pp. 328, 338, and passim.

11 Ibid., pp. 347–50; *Outlook* special edition (18 December 1905): 1–3.

12. Abbott, p. 446; *Outlook* 91 (6 March 1909): 509; Ira V. Brown, *Lyman Abbott, Christian Evolutionist* (Cambridge: Harvard University Press, 1953), p. 210.

Information Sources

BIBLIOGRAPHY:

Abbott, Lyman. *The Evolution of Christianity*. Boston: Mifflin and Co., 1896.

———. *Reminiscences*. Boston: Houghton Mifflin Co., 1914.

———. *The Rights of Man: A Study in Twentieth Century Problems*. London: James Clarke and Co., 1901.

Brown, Ira V. *Lyman Abbott, Christian Evolutionist: A Study in Religious Liberalism*. Cambridge: Harvard University Press, 1953.

Clark, Clifford E., Jr. *Henry Ward Beecher: Spokesman for a Middle-Class America*. Urbana: University of Illinois Press, 1978.

May, Henry F. *The End of American Innocence: A Study of the First Years of Our Own Time, 1912–1917*. Chicago: Quadrangle Books, 1959.

Rugoff, Milton. *The Beechers*. New York: Harper and Row, 1981.

INDEX SOURCES: *Nineteenth Century Reader's Guide to Periodical Literature* (1890–99); *Poole's Index to Periodical Literature* (1892–1906); *Reader's Guide to Periodical Literature* (1900–35); and Ernest Cushing Richardson, *Periodical Articles in Religion, 1890–99* (New York: Charles Scribner's Sons, 1907).

REPRINT EDITIONS: American Periodicals Series, University Microfilms International; Andover-Harvard Theological Library (56 microfilm reels).

LOCATION SOURCES: Union Theological Seminary (New York) has the only complete original set of *Christian Union* and *Outlook*.

Publication History

MAGAZINE TITLE AND TITLE CHANGES: *Christian Union* (1870–93), *The Outlook* (1893–1928), *The Outlook and Independent* (1928–32), *The New Outlook* (1932–35).

VOLUME AND ISSUE DATA: Volumes are numbered continuously, 1–165 (1870–1935) regardless of title changes; publication suspended, May-September 1932. Weekly, 1870–1932; monthly, October 1932-June 1935.

PUBLISHER AND PLACE OF PUBLICATION: J. B. Ford Co., New York (*Christian Union*, 1870–75); Christian Union Publishing Co., New York (*Christian Union*, 1875–85); New York and Brooklyn Publishing Co., New York (*Christian Union*, 1885–93); The Outlook Company, New York (*Outlook, Outlook and Independent, New Outlook*, 1893–1935).

EDITORS: Henry Ward Beecher (1870–81), Lyman Abbott (1881–1922), Ernest Hamlin Abbott (1923–28), Francis Rufus Bellamy (1928–32), Alfred E. Smith (1932–34), Francis Walton (1934–35).

CIRCULATION: 14,000–130,000 (1870–72), 20,000 (1880s), 80,000–120,000 (1900–20), 85,000 (1930).

Thomas E. Frank

THE OUTLOOK AND INDEPENDENT. *See* THE OUTLOOK

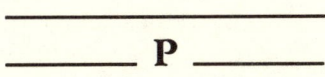

P

THE PANOPLIST. *See* MASSACHUSETTS MISSIONARY
MAGAZINE

**PAPERS OF THE AMERICAN SOCIETY OF CHURCH
HISTORY.** *See* CHURCH HISTORY

THE PASTOR. *See* AMERICAN ECCLESIASTICAL
REVIEW

THE PERKINS SCHOOL OF THEOLOGY JOURNAL

Although published by a denominational seminary, the *Perkins School of
Theology Journal* offers an ecumenical and scholarly perspective on problems
and trends in the life of the church. The *Journal* was inaugurated in the fall of
1947 when Eugene B. Hawk was dean of the Methodist (now United Methodist)
school, a part of Southern Methodist University, Dallas, Texas. The seminary
at that time was undergoing a period of unprecedented vitality and growth made
possible by Dean Hawk's able leadership and by substantial gifts from a number
of benefactors, including Mr. and Mrs. J. J. Perkins of Wichita Falls, Texas,
after whom the school was renamed. In the inaugural issue, Dean Hawk explained
that the *Journal* "is a magazine from Perkins School of Theology to the friends
and ex-students of the institution."

The seminary has never offered the *Journal* by subscription. From its initial
issue through the last issue of volume 29 (Summer 1976), the magazine was
sent to all of the school's alumni, the clergy of the South Central Jurisdiction

of the (United) Methodist Church, and the benefactors of the school. Beginning with the first issue of volume 30 (Fall 1976), the mailing list was pared down to the alumni of Perkins, institutions that had previously received the *Journal*, plus others who asked to be kept on the mailing list.

Through the years, the *Journal* has served several functions. Under its first two editors, Thomas H. Marsh (1947–53) and Howard Grimes (1953–59), its issues carried sections on alumni and faculty news, in addition to the articles, lectures, sermons, books reviews, and the like that have remained the staples of the magazine. Although the news and announcement sections were transferred to a separate publication in 1957, the *Journal* continues to function primarily as an organ of the school. Almost all of its published materials—lectures, symposia, faculty essays, and chapel sermons—originate in the life of the Perkins community and are offered as a means of continuing the theological education of the *Journal*'s readers.

The practice of publishing symposia of related articles in individual issues was begun by Howard Grimes, the second editor. With this development, the *Journal* became a more substantive theological publication. Under Grimes's editorship, symposia themes included such topics as "The Ecumenical Movement" (contributors included the noted ecumenist, Albert C. Outler), "Clinical Pastoral Education," and "The Situation in Contemporary Protestant Theology" (contributions by Schubert M. Ogden, Van A. Harvey, and others). A symposium, "Christianity and Race," was published in the spring 1958 issue under editor pro tempore H. Neill McFarland. Its contributors included John Deschner, Joseph L. Allen, and Douglas Jackson.

The first two editors succeeded in establishing the *Journal* and making it a substantive theological publication. Under the third editor, Roger Ortmayer (1959–66), the magazine took on a distinctively new appearance. Using the art of several contemporary artists—Margaret Rigg, Jim McLean, Robert O. Hodgell, and others—to grace the covers and interior pages, Ortmayer made the *Journal* a visual delight. Commenting on this transformation some years later, Fred D. Gealy observed: "If Augustus found Rome brick and left it marble, so Roger did the same with the *Journal*, if in another medium."[1]

During the Ortmayer years, several issues of the *Journal* presented materials of notable scholarly significance. The second issue of volume 14 (Winter 1961) presented Albert C. Outler's "Towards a Re-Appraisal of John Wesley as a Theologian," representing his distilled reflections from the work that produced his highly acclaimed volume on John Wesley in the Library of Protestant Thought. A later issue (15:2, Winter 1962) celebrated the publication of Schubert M. Ogden's *Christ without Myth* with an essay by Ogden on "The Significance of Rudolf Bultmann" and another by Bernard Meland, "Analogy and Myth in Postliberal Theology." Meland's essay offered a critique of both Ogden's criticism of Bultmann's theological method and Ogden's own alternative proposals for postliberal theology. Another issue (17:1, Fall 1963) presented an English translation of Philipp Vielhauer's seminal essay, "On the 'Paulinism' of Acts," which initiated redaction-critical work on Luke-Acts. Translated by William C. Robinson, Jr., and Victor P. Furnish, this essay was later included in L. E. Keck and J. L. Martyn, eds. *Studies in Luke-Acts* (Abingdon, 1966).

With Ortmayer's departure from the seminary in 1966, the *Journal* had a succession of editors—Klaus Penzel, David Robertson, James F. White, and James M. Ward—who each served for a single year (Robertson's term was two years). Leroy T. Howe became editor in 1971 and has continued to serve in that capacity to the present, having the longest term of any editor of the *Journal*.

Although the period between Ortmayer and Howe was somewhat of an editorial interregnum, the quality of the *Journal* did not suffer. The work of Friedrich Gogarten, visiting professor of systematic theology for 1966–67, was featured in a double issue under Penzel's editorship (20:1–2, Fall-Winter 1966–67); and four studies of Vatican II (by John W. Deschner, Walter J. Burghardt, S.J., Albert C. Outler, and John T. Noonan) were published in a later issue that same year (20:3, Spring 1967). David Robertson published three lectures on "The Church and Social Revolution," given at Perkins by M. Richard Shaull, Carl F. H. Henry, and Van A. Harvey (21:2–3, Winter-Spring 1968). James Ward devoted an issue to Jewish-Christian relations, publishing three Perkins addresses on the subject (24:1, Fall 1970). Authors included Marc H. Tannenbaum and Albert C. Outler.

Leroy Howe, in his second year as editor, began the current practice of publishing the *Journal* four times a year. Three issues a year had been the previous standard, although the third issues of volumes 13, 23, 24, and 25 were never published. Howe also published several monograph-length essays in single issues, plus two bilingual issues (English and Spanish), one on the new evangelism (32:2, Winter 1979). This issue featured four lectures by Mortimer Arias, former bishop of the Methodist Church in Bolivia.

The first monogaph-length essay to be published in the *Journal* was William R. Farmer's, "Jesus and the Gospels: A Form Critical and Theological Essay" (28:2, Winter 1975). This was followed by Marvin T. Judy's "The Professional Ministry: The Call, Performance, Morale, and Authority" (30:2, Winter 1977); Ronald E. Sleeth's, "The Crisis in Preaching" (30:4, Summer 1977); and James A. Carr's, "The Children's Sermon: An Act of Worship for the Community of Faith" (36:1, Spring 1983).

The return of Schubert M. Ogden to Southern Methodist University from the University of Chicago was the occasion for a special colloquy issue on the theme "Schubert Ogden on the Task of Theology" (36:2, Winter 1973). Other occasional issues of a similar nature were prompted by the retirement of Albert Outler (27:3, Spring 1974), Dean Joseph Quillan (34:3, Spring 1981), and Howard Grimes (35:3, Summer 1982). The issue honoring Outler included "the first comprehensive bibliography of Outler's published writings."

The summer 1980 issue (33:4) was devoted to the theme of "Reappraisal and Fresh Approaches in Gospel Research." Here Howe chose to publish several essays that question the adequacy of the two-source theory (priority of Mark and

Q) for understanding the relationships of the synoptic gospels to each other. Explictly or implicitly, the essays (by William R. Farmer, Edward D. Hobbs, Thomas W. R. Longstaff, and others) plead for a return to the Griesbach hypothesis (priority of Matthew, and so forth). Another special issue under Howe's editorship was "Science and Religion" (36:4, Summer 1983), publishing the Isthmus Foundations lectures of 1982–83, which included addresses by four Nobel Laureate scientists (Ilya Prigogine, Roger Sperry, B. D. Josephson, and John C. Eccles).

The *Journal* has not published a cumulative index since 1969. The fall issue of that year (23:1) published an index that encompassed everything in volumes 1–22, superseding two previous indexes (10:3, Spring 1957, and 12:3, Spring 1959).

Notes

1. Fred D. Gealy, "The Perkins Journal: Twenty-five Years," *Perkins School of Theology Journal* 25:2 (Spring 1972): 5.

Information Sources

INDEX SOURCES: *Religion Index One.*
LOCATION SOURCES: Southwestern Baptist Theological Seminary, Rice University, University of Tulsa, Southern Methodist University.

Publication History

MAGAZINE TITLE AND TITLE CHANGES: *The Perkins School of Theology Journal* (1947–   )
VOLUME AND ISSUE DATA: 1:1 (Fall 1947–   ).
PUBLISHER AND PLACE OF PUBLICATION: Perkins School of Theology, Southern Methodist University, Dallas.
EDITORS: Thomas H. Marsh (1947–53), Howard Grimes (1953–59), H. Neill McFarland (1957–58), Roger Ortmayer (1959–64, 1965–66), Klaus Penzel (1964–65, 1966–67), David Robertson (1967–69), James F. White (1969–70), James M. Ward (1970–71), Leroy T. Howe (1971–   ).
CIRCULATION: Under 5000 (est.).

Carl D. Evans

PHILADELPHIA RECORDER. *See* EPISCOPAL RECORDER

THE POST-AMERICAN. *See* SOJOURNERS

PRACTICAL ANTHROPOLOGY. *See* MISSIOLOGY

PREACHING HELPS. *See* CONCORDIA THEOLOGICAL MONTHLY

PRESBYTERIAN AND REFORMED REVIEW. *See* PRINCETON THEOLOGICAL REVIEW

PRESBYTERIAN QUARTERLY AND PRINCETON REVIEW. *See* THE PRINCETON REVIEW

THE PRESBYTERIAN REVIEW. *See* AMERICAN PRESBYTERIAN AND THEOLOGICAL REVIEW

THE PRINCETON REVIEW

In 1825, Charles Hodge of the Princeton Theological Seminary offered to the public the first number of his new journal, *Biblical Repertory: A Collection of Tracts on Biblical Literature*. The quarterly, wrote Hodge, had "arisen, from the conviction of the importance of Biblical studies, and from the desire of exciting greater interest in their cultivation." But there was an underlying concern: approaches to biblical studies then fashionable seemed to Hodge "inimical to religion" because their advocates had "loose Theological opinions."[1] From the start the *Repertory* and most of its later incarnations thus had a vigilante character: orthodoxy would be protected at all costs.

For four years, the *Repertory* presented reprints or translations of classical texts on biblical hermeneutics, concerned itself with textual minutiae and biblical languages, and sought to expose unorthodox methods. But in 1829, Hodge broadened the focus of the journal and changed the subtitle to *A Journal of Biblical Literature and Theological Sciences*. The revamped periodical consisted primarily of review essays, carefully analyzing the latest publications in all areas of the biblical and theological enterprise. These essays were not simply book reviews of the standard sort. Rather, new books provided a springboard for the *Repertory*'s writers to offer their own views on a particular subject. And although the essays were not signed (authors' names did not appear with their material until 1871) and Hodge's name no longer appeared as editor, Hodge and Princeton orthodoxy remained the major force behind the journal.[2] Officially the editors were "An Association of Gentlemen" in the Princeton area, most of them faculty members at the university or seminary there. Besides Hodge, the major figures were Archibald Alexander and his two sons, James W. Alexander and J. Addison Alexander. All were Presbyterians, and the *Repertory* made no bones about its commitment to defend Presbyterian orthodoxy. Years later, Hodge wrote:

The conductors of the *Princeton Review* [the name added as a subtitle in 1838 and the full title after 1878], however, were Presbyterians. They firmly believed that the system of doctrine contained in the Westminster Confession of Faith, the system of the Reformed Church, and of Augustinians in all ages, is the truth of God revealed for his glory and the salvation of men. They believed that the upholding of that system in its integrity, bearing witness to it as the truth of God, and its extension through the world, was the great duty of all who had experienced its power.[3]

Hodge was so convinced that the journal had carried out this mandate that he proudly proclaimed, "Whether it be a ground of reproach or of approbation, it is believed to be true that an original idea in theology is not to be found on the pages of the *Biblical Repertory and Princeton Review* from the beginning until now [1871]."[4]

This apologetic character may be seen in the many review essays over the years that attacked, for example, the New Divinity movement associated with Timothy Dwight, Nathaniel William Taylor, and others; the Arminian approach that undergirded both the revivalism and perfectionism of Charles Grandison Finney and the Oberlin theology; the nascent liberalism of Horace Bushnell; transcendentalism and its ally, the philosophy of Victor Cousin; and the historical romanticism advanced by John Williamson Nevin and Philip Schaff known as the Mercersburg theology. All were major currents in American religious thought in the mid-nineteenth century that left an enduring imprint on the nation's religious landscape. But transformations sweeping Protestantism were not the only foes. Over the years, the *Review* repeatedly attacked Roman Catholicism as a bastardization of the truth of Christianity.

But the *Biblical Repertory and Princeton Review*, the journal's name from 1838 to 1871, was also involved in the issues that shaped its beloved Presbyterian denomination. In addition to reporting on each meeting of the Presbyterian General Assembly, Hodge and his associates offered critical commentary on Presbyterian developments. The *Review*, for example, vigorously supported the Presbyterian position regarding ordination and church polity over the years. As well, it criticized the many interdenominational voluntary societies oriented toward social and religious reform, urging support instead for agencies under the control of the denomination itself. The *Review* also criticized the temperance movement, for it claimed that total abstinence, the movement's real goal, lacked biblical warrant. Nevertheless, Hodge and his allies were saddened by the schism in 1837–38 that divided Presbyterians into Old School and New School groups, though their sympathies were clearly with the Old School. Later in the century, when Old School and New School in the North prepared to reunite, the *Review* deplored the reunion, for it would infect the denomination with unorthodox views.

The pages of the *Review* reveal that some of the social turmoil of the nineteenth century that confronted not only religious groups but American society as a whole also left their mark on defenders of Presbyterian orthodoxy. Three important essays addressed the vital question of slavery (8, 1836:268–306), abolition (16, 1844:545–80), and emancipation (21, 1849:582–607). Consequently, the *Review*'s writers claimed that slaveholding was not in and of itself sinful or criminal and that the abolitionist perspective was subversive to biblical authority. But they were by no means pro-slavery advocates. Rather, they insisted that slaves were rational, moral, immortal creatures who themselves had a right not only to religious instruction and education but also to hold property themselves. Laws that impeded such were evil. Had the position advanced in the *Review* held sway, the end result would have been gradual abolition; however, when war erupted between the North and South, *Review* writers to a man endorsed the northern cause, claiming that southern complaints were unfounded (31, 1861:1–36), condemning the expected English support of the Confederacy (34, 1862:147–77), and urging support for the war to preserve the Union, not to end slavery (35, 1863:140–68).

Hodge stepped down as editor in 1871, turning over the reins to Lyman H. Atwater who the following year renamed the journal the *Presbyterian Quarterly and Princeton Review*. Under Atwater's direction and that of his successors, the journal lost some of its parochial character. Signed articles, now more often reflecting original work than reviews, began to appear on a broader range of topics. Clearly, the defensive character that Hodge had brought to the *Review* was gone. The first decade under fresh leadership saw articles, for example, on "The Buddhist and Christian Ideas of Hell" (n.s. 4, 1875:38–45), "Our Industrial and Financial Situation" (n.s. 4, 1875:517–29), and the Indian policy of the U.S. government (which was soundly criticized for it had as its implicit end the extermination of the tribes). No longer were writers necessarily Presbyterian or even American.

By the early 1880s, a total transformation had been effected. Some volumes carried only three or four articles dealing with religious subjects. More and more, the periodical was a cultural organ, discussing current trends in art, literature, and music. It thus again reflected the changing character of American culture in the Victorian age. But the transformation was also to mean a loss of readers, for the *Review* faced stiff competition from the growing number of secular periodicals that offered much the same fare. Publication was suspended for a year in 1885, and when the *New Princeton Review* made its debut in 1886, it was a journal that Hodge would not have recognized, much less supported, for it was essentially a literary review, mixing short stories and poetry of a secular bent with articles on topics ranging from the Knights of Labor to principles in education. It took only three years for the *New Princeton Review* to fold.

The *Biblical Repertory and Princeton Review*, however, remains one of the more significant religious periodicals of the nineteenth century, for the position it took, defending a Princeton orthodoxy that Hodge once claimed never existed, was as influential a current as any of the other stands it attacked. It provides an important prism through which to view the major religious and social controversies that marked American life during its more than half-century of existence.

Notes

1. "Introduction," *Biblical Repertory* 1 (1825): iii.
2. An attempt to identify authors as much as possible is found in "Index to Authors," *The Biblical Repertory and Princeton Review: Index Volume from 1825 to 1868* (Philadelphia: Peter Walker, 1871), pp. 40–326.
3. Charles Hodge, "Retrospect of the History of the Princeton Review," *Biblical Repertory Index Volume*, p. 3.
4. Ibid., p. 11.

Information Sources

BIBLIOGRAPHY:
Hodge, Charles. "Retrospect of the History of the Princeton Review." *The Biblical Repertory and Princeton Review: Index Volume from 1825 to 1868*. Philadelphia: Peter Walker, 1871.
Hoffecker, W. Andrew. *Piety and the Princeton Theologians: Archibald Alexander, Charles Hodge, and Benjamin Warfield*. Grand Rapids: Baker Book House, 1981.
INDEX SOURCES: *The Biblical Repertory and Princeton Review: Index Volume from 1825 to 1868* (Philadelphia: Peter Walker, 1871); *Poole's Index*.
REPRINT EDITIONS: University Microfilm International (American Periodicals Series).
LOCATION SOURCES: Andover-Harvard Theological Library, Princeton University, Princeton Theological Seminary, Yale University, University of California-Berkeley, Detroit Public Library, McCormick Theological Seminary, St. Louis Public Library, Brown University, and others.

Publication History

MAGAZINE TITLE AND TITLE CHANGES: *Biblical Repertory: A Collection of Tracts on Biblical Literature* (1825–28), *Biblical Repertory: A Journal of Biblical Literature and Theological Sciences* (1829), *Biblical Repertory and Theological Review* (1830–37), *Biblical Repertory and Princeton Review* (1838–71), *Presbyterian Quarterly and Princeton Review* (1872–77), *The Princeton Review* (1878–84), *The New Princeton Review* (1886–88).
VOLUME AND ISSUE DATA: 1:1–4:4 (1825–28), n.s. 1:1–43:4 (1829–71), n.s. 1:1–6:4 (1872–77), 4th ser. 1:1–14:12 (1878–84), 5th ser. 1:1–6:12 (1886–88). Published quarterly, 1825–77, and bimonthly thereafter; publication suspended, 1885.
PUBLISHER AND PLACE OF PUBLICATION: Princeton Press, Princeton, N.J. (1825), G. and C. Carvill, New York (1826–28), Hugh Madden, Princeton, N.J. (1829), Jas. K. Jun & Co. Library, Philadelphia (1830), Russell and Martien, Philadelphia (1831–33), William S. Martien, Philadelphia (1834), Henry Perkins, Philadelphia (1835–37), James A. Peabody, Philadelphia (1838–39), M. B. Hope, Philadelphia (1840–47), William H. Mitchell, Philadelphia (1848–52), Office of the Biblical Repertory, Philadelphia (1853–56), Peter Walker, Philadelphia (1857–68), C. Scribner & Co., New York (1869–71), J. M. Sherwood, New York (1872–77), no publisher listed, New York (1878–84), A. C. Armstrong & Son (1886–88).

EDITORS: Charles Hodge (1825–28, 1856–71), An Association of Gentlemen (1829), An Association of Gentlemen in Princeton, N.J., and Its Vicinity (1830–36), none listed (1837–55), Lyman H. Atwater (1869–77), Henry B. Smith (1872–76), James M. Sherwood (1877), none listed (1878–82), Jonas M. Libbey (1883–84), none listed (1886–88).

CIRCULATION: Unknown.

Charles H. Lippy

PRINCETON THEOLOGICAL REVIEW

In 1902, the *Presbyterian and Reformed Review* suspended publication after 13 years in print. The *Review* had largely become a forum for the faculty of Princeton Theological Seminary and the perpetuation of the rigidly orthodox Princeton theology with which it was identified. Princeton Seminary professor Benjamin B. Warfield at that time was clearly the most well-known vocal proponent of the Princeton theology and had been a leading figure among the *Review*'s authors. The year after the *Review*'s demise, the seminary faculty, with a subsidy from the school's board of trustees, launched the *Princeton Theological Review* to provide a continuing voice for the articulation of its interpretation of Reformed doctrine. Although Warfield was not the official editor, he was expected to play a prominent role, lending his support so long as the new journal was committed to the infallible authority of Scripture and Reformed doctrine.

Indeed until 1918, the title page included a roster of the seminary faculty and occasional individuals (mostly associated with Princeton University) as editors, although an undesignated person served as chairman. John DeWitt assumed that responsibility the first year, sharing chairmanship with W. P. Armstrong through 1907. Armstrong continued in this role through 1917. From 1918 until the journal ceased publication in 1919, seminary professor Oswald T. Allis was formally listed as editor. When Allis resigned, the journal folded.

From its inception, the *Princeton Theological Review* offered a fare of lengthy scholarly articles defending the conservative position central to the Princeton theology. Many were continuing series that would have formed significant monographs if published separately. Many had a polemic tone, vigorously attacking presumed enemies of true Reformed faith: those who espoused use of all the tools of scientific biblical criticism, for example, or those who sought to harmonize evolutionary theory with Christian affirmation. What is evident, however, is that authors (who were by no means restricted to the Princeton faculty although nearly all were identified with the Presbyterian or larger Reformed tradition) were thoroughly familiar with writings they criticized. Their defense of Reformed orthodoxy was not a casual one but based on a careful reading and understanding of the positions they sought to condemn as dangerous to authentic faith. Besides ponderous articles on biblical exegesis, systematic theology, philosophy of religion, and church history, the *Review* from the start devoted considerable space to book reviews, again examining a wide range of literature, which included works antithetical to the principles that the seminary faculty espoused. Book reviews covered the full spectrum of theological inquiry, under such headings as "Apologetical Theology," "Exegetical Theology," "Historical Theology," "Systematic Theology," "Practical Theology," and "General Literature." As well, there were brief notices of articles of interest appearing in other periodicals, many of them published abroad.

The *Princeton Theological Review* was consistently committed to arguing for the ultimate authority of Scripture. Over the years, much of this argument was grounded in belief in miracle and the supernatural. Although writers did espouse many of the tenets of textual criticism—the endeavor to determine the most accurate rendering of the actual biblical text—they rejected most of the other apparatus of biblical criticism because they believed that it undermined the supernatural dimension, challenged the orthodox affirmation of biblical inspiration, and consequently destroyed the foundation of Christian belief. Their position, however, was grounded in careful study of the Hebrew and Greek texts, and they regularly included quotations from them in their articles. As early as volume 3 (1905), for example, J. Gresham Machen argued for a literal, historical interpretation of the gospel birth narratives in "The New Testament Account of the Birth of Jesus." In volume 8 (1910), William Hallock Johnson argued for belief in the miraculous in "Miracles and History." Liberal espousal of critical method came under attack in such pieces as "The Authority of Scripture" by George Johnson (12, 1914), the two-part "Scientific Biblical Criticism" by Robert Dick Wilson (17, 1919), "The Inspiration of the Bible" by William Brenton Greene, Jr. (22, 1924), "The Testimony of the Scriptures to Their Own Trustworthiness" by S. G. Craig (22, 1924), "The Historical Method in the Study of the Old Testament" by Edouard Naville (22, 1924), and "Modern Views about Inspiration—and the Truth of Scripture" by P. E. Kretzmann (27, 1929).

Since the newer methods of biblical scholarship were associated with the liberal movement in theology, particularly as advanced by such German thinkers as Albrecht Ritschl and Adolf von Harnack, the *Review* also relentlessly exposed what its contributors regarded as the pitfalls of liberal thought. The Ritschlian school came under attack, for example, in C. Wistar Hodge's "Modern Positive Theology" (8, 1910) and was sustained in the venerable Warfield's assault in "Albrecht Ritschl and His Doctrine of Christian Perfection" (17, 1919; 18, 1920) and in Jan Karl van Baalen's "The Ritschlians and the Preexistence of Christ" (18, 1920). Harnack came under scrutiny especially in Finley DuBois Jenkins's "Is Harnack's *History of Dogma* a History of Harnack's Dogma?" (21, 1923). The tenor of the *Review* in looking at then-current theological trends is vividly apparent in the titles of two essays: J. Gresham Machen's "Liberalism or Christianity" (20, 1922) and editor Allis's "Was Jesus a Modernist?" (27, 1929). For the *Review*'s writers and sponsors the choice posed by the first was clear-cut: to advocate liberalism was to reject genuine Christianity. The only answer to the question posed by the second was equally clear: a resounding "no."

What made liberalism so pernicious was its sympathetic response to evolutionary theory. A passion to deny the validity of evolutionary theory in any form became more pronounced in the *Review* over the years. In its last decade, which was also the era of the Scopes trial, the *Review* attacked evolutionary thinking in virtually every issue. But the concern was not one born of the moment. The stance of the *Review* was set in volume 1 (1903) with William Hallock Johnson's "Evolution and Theology To-day." But between 1922 and 1929, 10 articles addressed evolution directly, and at least a score of others contained indirect criticism: William Brenton Greene, Jr., "Yet Another Criticism of the Theory of Evolution" (20, 1922); F. D. Jenkins, "The Problem of Mental Evolution," a two-part series (22, 1924); Floyd E. Hamilton, "The Evolutionary Hypothesis in the Light of Modern Science" (22, 1924) and "Modern Aspects of the Theory of Evolution" (24, 1926); David S. Clark, "Theology and Evolution" (23, 1925); Oswald T. Allis's three-part series, "Old Testament Emphases and Modern Thought" (23, 1925; 24, 1926); J. Gresham Machen, "The Relation of Religion to Science and Philosophy" (24, 1926); English scholar Ambrose J. Wilson's "What Charles Darwin Really Found" (26, 1928); and George Johnson, "The Religion of the Scientifically Minded" (27, 1929).

Other current issues of the 1920s also received appraisal in the *Princeton Theological Review*. As was the case in the discussion of evolutionary theory, the approach was both critical and conservative. Several pieces written by W. M. Clow are illustrative. In volume 19 (1921), Clow offered a stinging critique in "Marxian Socialism", as well as a strident defense of laissez-faire capitalism and condemnation of organized labor in "The Elements of the Industrial Strife." His encomium of capitalism was continued in two subsequent articles: "The Justification of Capitalism" (20, 1922) and "The Charge against Capitalism" (21, 1923). But the movement to include discussion of such contemporary issues and the vitriolic tone in these pieces and in the several essays on evolutionary theory may well signal the degree to which controversy and dissension had invaded Princeton Seminary and other circles that sought to advance an orthodox Reformed position, for the ranks of the conservative Reformed were realigning as some, such as J. Gresham Machen, began to espouse fundamentalism while others continued to move within the time-honored orbit of the Princeton theology and its understanding of the Reformed heritage.

The death of Benjamin Breckinridge Warfield in 1921 may signal that these undercurrents were beginning to simmer. Warfield, although staunchly conservative, had become a symbol of Reformed orthodoxy as resistant to an aggressive fundamentalism as he was to liberalism. Although Warfield had never held the title of editor of the *Review*, he had long been one of its more prolific contributors and a force supporting the continued adherence to the *Review*'s commitment to Scripture and the Reformed heritage. In later years, to be sure, he had attacked many movements and currents in theology other than liberalism. His "The

Victorious Life'' (16, 1918) and two-part ''The 'Higher Life' Movement'' (16, 1918; 17, 1919) attempted to show the shortcomings of holiness theology, but his condemnation was still rooted in an orthodox Reformed perspective. Holiness theology erred, in his mind, primarily because it was Pelagian and asserted some positive role for human endeavor in religious experience. Only in ''Oberlin Perfectionism,'' his final four-part series for the *Review* (part of which appeared posthumously), did he occasionally lapse into a tone that was more ranting than reasoned polemic. For example, his linking Oberlin founders and perfectionist advocates with John Humphrey Noyes and the Oneida Perfectionists cannot be supported by evidence. Generally, however, the estimate of Francis L. Patton in a memorial address printed in the *Review* holds: ''Men may agree with Dr. Warfield or they may differ from him, but they must recognize his unswerving fidelity to what he believed to be the truth.''[1] Warfield's death removed not only the *Review*'s most esteemed voice but also part of its conscience.

It is also difficult to assess the degree to which the growing rift in conservative circles over espousal of fundamentalism played into the decision to discontinue publication with the July 1929 issue. The *Review* itself referred only to a ''decision of the Editors.''[2] Allis resigned as editor in the midst of a sweeping reorganization of the Princeton Seminary faculty that witnessed the departure of several members from its ranks. Among those leaving was J. Gresham Machen, who probably had the widest reputation after Warfield's death. Machen readily aligned himself with the fundamentalist posture, helping organize the Westminster Theological Seminary, which some years later would launch its own journal, the *Westminster Theological Journal.** But the disarray for a time meant a lack of theological consensus on the part of the faculty that generated the *Princeton Theological Review*. Consequently there was little hope that it could continue. With its demise, the American religious scene lost an organ that had long represented the most responsible articulation of Reformed orthodoxy.

Notes

1. Francis L. Patton, ''Benjamin Breckinridge Warfield—A Memorial Address,'' *Princeton Theological Review* 19 (1921): 369.
2. *Princeton Theological Review* 27 (1929): 313.

Information Sources

BIBLIOGRAPHY:

Gapp, Kenneth S., comp. ''The Princeton Review Series and the Contribution of Princeton Theological Seminary to Presbyterian Quarterly Magazines.'' Unpublished typescript, n.d.

Loetscher, Lefferts A. *The Broadening Church: A Study of Theological Issues in the Presbyterian Church since 1869*. Philadelphia: Westminster Press, 1954.

Rian, Edwin H. *The Presbyterian Conflict*. Grand Rapids: Eerdman's, 1940.

VanderStelet, John C. *Philosophy and Scripture: A Study in Old Princeton and Westminster Theology*. Marlton, N.J.: Mack Publishing Co., 1978.

INDEX SOURCES: William P. Armstrong, ''Index of the Presbyterian and Reformed

Review XI (1900)-XIII (1902) and the Princeton Theological Review I (1903)-
XXVII (1929)," *Princeton Theological Review* 27 (1929): 487–587.
REPRINT EDITIONS: ATLA Board of Microtext.
LOCATION SOURCES: University of Chicago, Princeton Theological Seminary, Duke
University, and others.

Publication History

MAGAZINE TITLE AND TITLE CHANGES: *Princeton Theological Review* (1903–29);
supersedes *Presbyterian and Reformed Review*.
VOLUME AND ISSUE DATA: *Princeton Theological Review* 1:1 (1903)–27:4 (1929).
Appeared quarterly in January, April, July, and October.
PUBLISHER AND PLACE OF PUBLICATION: MacCalla and Co., Philadelphia (1903–
06); Princeton University Press, Princeton, N.J. (1907–29).
EDITORS: Committee of the Princeton Theological Seminary Faculty (1903–17), Oswald
T. Allis for the Princeton Theological Seminary Faculty (1918–29).
CIRCULATION: 2000 (est.).

Charles H. Lippy

THE PROCEEDINGS OF THE CATHOLIC THEOLOGICAL SOCIETY OF AMERICA

The *Proceedings of the Catholic Theological Society of America* (CTSA), an
annual publication, contain papers and reports delivered at the yearly meetings
of this society of Roman Catholic theologians. The CTSA was founded in 1946
at the initiative of several professors of the School of Theology of the Catholic
University of America. Father Eugene Burke, professor of dogmatic theology
and the prime mover of the project, proposed the formation of the society so
that critical issues in Roman Catholic theology could be openly aired by professional theologians. The society was to be American oriented and would serve
to raise the professional standards of seminary teaching.[1]

Papers in the *Proceedings* have been commissioned and selected by the society's board of directors, which plans the annual meetings. In the early years
of its existence, the CTSA's Committee on Current Problems proposed topics
for papers to the board. Since 1967, each volume has treated a single topic. For
example, the theme for the 1981 meeting (volume 36) was "The Local Church."
In recent years the president of the society has set the theme for the convention
to be held during his or her term. Consequently the duties of the editors have
been restricted primarily to emending texts of papers for publication.

Essays in the *Proceedings* from 1946 to the present record rapid and dramatic
developments in Roman Catholic theology. Notable have been the expansion of
the kind of persons designated Roman Catholic theologians, several significant
shifts in the content and methodologies of theology, and the growing openness
of Roman Catholic theologians to broader contexts for their work.

From its establishment, ordained priests have dominated the CTSA, and until

1958 all articles in the *Proceedings* were contributed by priest-theologians. In 1958 Brother Luke Salm, a Christian Brother, became the first nonpriest published. His summaries of convention discussions had appeared in earlier volumes. Brother Salm also served as the first nonpriest president of the CTSA in 1975. The first essay by a female theologian, Sister Agnes Cunningham, did not appear until 1969. She served as the first female president of the CTSA in 1978.[2] By then, Roman Catholic theology was no longer considered the exclusive preserve of ordained priests.

In the early volumes, topics and approaches of the papers were quite traditional, usually bound to the categories of seminary theology. For example, volume 6 (1951) contains essays on "The Doctrinal Value of the Ordinary Teaching of the Holy Father in View of *Humani Generis*," "The Morality of Gambling," and "The Senses of Sacred Scripture." By the 1960s, papers demonstrated Catholic theology's gradual openness to non-Catholic theological thought, with contributions from Jaroslav Pelikan (1962), John Meyendorff (1964), and Rabbi Marc Tannenbaum (1966).

In the 1970s and 1980s Catholic theology began to broaden its contexts to include serious dialogue with the social sciences and contemporary thought. Themes of annual meetings reflect this movement: "Catholic Theology in Social and Political Context" (1975) and "Power as an Issue in Theology" (1982).

Three important topics recur in the *Proceedings*: (1) the nature of Roman Catholic theology and its methodology and pedagogy, (2) the relationship between theologians and the teaching authority (magisterium) of the church, and (3) the development of a distinctively American theology. Concern for the appropriate method for teaching theology was taken up in volume 4 (1949), which includes Eugene Burke's "The Scientific Teaching of Theology." In 1956 John Courtney Murray debated the adequacy of the thesis form of theological instruction with Eugene Burke. The issue of biblical scholarship and dogmatic theology, long a problem in Catholic theological circles, was aired in several essays in the late 1950s. In the 1960s serious consideration of non-Catholic thought was evidenced in papers by Jaroslav Pelikan (1962), John Meyendorff (1964), and George Lindbeck (1966), all non-Catholics. In the 1970s and 1980s entire volumes have been devoted to the question of the nature of theology: "Is There a Catholic Theology?" (1974), "Christian Orthopraxis and the Emergence of New Meaning in Theology" (1980), and "Theology and the Study of Religion" (1977).

The question of how theology relates to the magisterium of the church has also been a recurring theme. At first theology was portrayed primarily as the interpreter of the magisterial statements, as in John M. Fearns, "The Theological Content of the Utterances of Pope Pius XII" (1953). A more critical examination of theology's place in this relationship appeared in Walter Burghardt, "The Catholic Concept of Tradition in the Light of Modern Theological Thought" (1951), and in the 1957 presidential address of George Shea, "Theology and the Magisterium." In the aftermath of Vatican II, Roman Catholic theologians took a more independent stance regarding the magisterium as reflected in the theme of the 1967 meeting: "The Church's Teaching Authority and Theology as a Science." Some idea of the ferment within the CTSA over this issue can be gleaned from comparing the presidential addresses of Austin Vaughan (1969) and Charles Curran (1970). The issue remained alive in the 1970s and 1980s.[3] It is interesting to note that since 1972 no statement of ecclesiastical approbation has appeared on the copyright page.

Although the development of an American theology was an original goal of the CTSA, it began to receive concentrated attention only in the late 1960s, primarily stimulated by issues relating to the Vietnam War. Following Walter Burghardt's presidential address in 1968, volume 26 (1971) was devoted to "The Impact of American Culture and Experience on Theology" and volume 28 (1973) to "American Theologians in the Service of the American Church." Issues of political and pastoral theology arising from the American experience have received considerable attention in more recent volumes.

Three papers published in the *Proceedings* can be identified as seminal. The earliest of these is "Government Repression of Heresy," in which John Courtney Murray developed his argument that a historical approach to the question of religious liberty was essential to the solution of the problem.[4] The ideas in this paper, at first severely criticized by Murray's colleagues in public and one of the causes of his silencing by the Holy See in the 1950s, eventually won the day when Vatican II adopted its "Decree on Religious Liberty."

A second seminal essay was the 1953 paper of Gustav Weigel, "A Survey of Protestant Theology in Our Day."[5] This commanding exposition of Protestant theology both foreshadowed and encouraged the trend toward ecumenical theology characteristic of much Roman Catholic thought since Vatican II. Weigel deplored the ignorance of Protestant theology among Catholic theologians. In addition to the study of the Reformers' teachings, he urged serious consideration of contemporary Protestant theology by Catholic thinkers.

A third seminal paper was delivered as the 1968 presidential address of Walter Burghardt, "Toward an American Theology."[6] Reflections on the spiritual and political conditions of the United States in the early summer of 1968 led him to bemoan the failure of Americans to produce a theology that addresses the real issues and experience of the United States. As a result, the CTSA began reevaluation of its aims. In the 1970s and 1980s many essays appeared directed to the issues of pastoral and political theology such as women, homosexuality, nuclear war, liberation theology, and the like.[7]

Papers in the *Proceedings* have exhibited a high caliber of theological scholarship and have been carefully edited with scholarly apparatus. In addition, a wide spectrum of serious theological opinion can be found in them. The writers have been characterized by a profound respect for the faith and tradition of the Roman Catholic Church. The *Proceedings* will be an important source when the history of American Catholic theology since World War II is written.

Notes

1. E. Burke, "A Personal Memoir on the Origins of the CTSA," *Proceedings of the Catholic Theological Society of America* 35 (1980): 337–47 (hereafter cited as *Proceedings*).

2. Elizabeth Farlans and Cathleen Going were accepted as the first female members of the CTSA in 1965.

3. See, for example, Avery Dulles, "The Theologian and the Magisterium," *Proceedings* 31 (1976): 235–46.

4. John Courtney Murray, "Government Repression of Heresy," *Proceedings* 3 (1948): 26–97.

5. Gustav Weigel, "A Survey of Protestant Theology in Our Day," *Proceedings* 8 (1953): 43–76.

6. Walter Burghardt, "Towards an American Theology," *Proceedings* 23 (1968): 20–27.

7. See, for example, Joseph Nearon, "The Situation of American Blacks," *Proceedings* 30 (1975): 177–202; Joseph Gremillon, "North American Ecclesial Consciousness in its Global Context," *Proceedings* 31 (1981): 113–29; and Mary Buckley, "Women, Power, and Liberation," *Proceedings* 32 (1982): 109–12.

Information Sources

BIBLIOGRAPHY:
Bourke, M. "Rudolf Bultmann's Demythologizing of the New Testament." *Proceedings* 12 (1957): 103–31.
Burghardt, W. "Towards an American Theology." *Proceedings* 23 (1968): 20–27.
Burke, E. "A Personal Memoir on the Origins of the CTSA." *Proceedings* 35 (1980): 337–47.
Fenton, J. C. "The Foundations and Progress of the Society." *Proceedings* 1 (1946): 5–12.
Hennesey, J. *American Catholics.* New York: Oxford University Press, 1981.
Murray, J. C. "Government Repression of Heresy." *Proceedings* 3 (1948): 26–97.
Salm, L. "Past Perspectives and Future Prospects for the CTSA." *Proceedings* 30 (1975): 239–50.
Weigel, G. "A Survey of Protestant Theology in Our Day." *Proceedings* 8 (1953): 43–76.
INDEX SOURCES: *Catholic Periodical and Literature Index.*
REPRINT EDITIONS: University Microfilms International.
LOCATION SOURCES: Catholic University of America, Loyola University (Chicago), St. John's University (Collegeville), and others.

Publication History

MAGAZINE TITLE AND TITLE CHANGES: *The Proceedings of the Catholic Theological Society of America* (1946–   ).
VOLUME AND ISSUE DATA: 1 (1946–   ). Published annually.
PUBLISHER AND PLACE OF PUBLICATION: Catholic Theological Society of America, St. Joseph's Seminary, Dunwoodie, N.Y. (1946–69); Catholic Theological Society of America, Manhattan College, Bronx, N.Y. (1970–   ).

EDITORS: Aloysius McDonough (1946–50), John H. Harrington (1951–63), James F. Rigney (1964), Daniel V. Flynn (1965–67), Raymond T. Powers (1968–69), Luke Salm (1970–   ).
CIRCULATION: 1500 (1983).

Bernard Noone

THE PROCEEDINGS OF THE UNITARIAN HISTORICAL SOCIETY. *See* THE PROCEEDINGS OF THE UNITARIAN-UNIVERSALIST HISTORICAL SOCIETY

THE PROCEEDINGS OF THE UNITARIAN-UNIVERSALIST HISTORICAL SOCIETY

The Unitarian Historical Society, founded in Boston in 1901, first published its *Proceedings* in 1925. The first issue[1] announced a desire to make available the addresses delivered at the society's annual meetings (usually held at King's Chapel, Boston)[2] in order to "create a fresh interest in the historical background of our churches; to preserve and to make readily accessible information which is liable otherwise to be lost; and to stimulate the interest of the local churches in the preservation of their records."[3] In addition to articles by William Wallace Fenn[4] and Kenneth B. Murdock,[5] records of the annual meetings, and a piece on the "Historical Exhibit, Centenary of the American Unitarian Association," the issue also contained a list of addresses delivered before the society from 1901 to 1925. Most were the work of Boston-area clergy, but a few were presented by European scholars.[6]

The two parts of volume 1 came at three-year intervals; subsequently, issues appeared nearly every year until the mid–1960s, with a six-year hiatus during World War II. The range of articles published indicates the framework within which Unitarians interpreted their identity and development. As annual addresses antedating the *Proceedings* demonstrate, Unitarian scholars did not regard their movement as indigenously American but as rooted in such figures as Servetus, Socinus, and kindred liberals of the Reformation era.[7] Attention was also paid to British Unitarianism, especially in the figure of Joseph Priestley, as well as to colonial Congregationalists, from which American Unitarianism directly arose.[8] Transcendentalism, regarded by Boston liberals as little short of heresy, was by the twentieth century considered a legitimate part of the movement's heritage. Other topics covered included ministerial biographies, articles on prominent laity, histories of individual churches or societies, area studies (such as "Unitarianism in Maine"), thematic essays (such as "Tensions in Unitarianism One Hundred Years Ago"), studies of aspects of worship and education, and historical source materials.[9]

Until the late 1950s, most of the contents of the *Proceedings* was traditional, often celebratory in tone, and not always characterized by great scholarly rigor. In 1957, with the appointment of the Reverend David B. Parke as editor, came a change in editorial policy: "the contents of the *Proceedings* will no longer be limited to papers presented before meetings of the Society. Henceforth it will be more truly a journal of liberal religious history, drawing upon a wide variety of authors, articles, and points of view."[10] A perceptive editorial by Parke in 1958 suggested that, with the recent death of historian Earl Morse Wilbur, a transition was taking place to a new era of Unitarian historiography.[11] According to Parke, the preparatory tasks of gathering and editing source materials had already been accomplished to a significant degree; in the years to come, the emphasis would shift to "interpretation, reconstruction, and synthesis."[12] In the same issue appeared the principal address at the 1957 meeting of the Unitarian Historical Society by Sidney E. Mead, then president of the denomination's seminary, the Meadville Theological School.[13] Mead's address, very much in consonance with many of Parke's themes, was a sophisticated exposition of the philosophical dimensions of the historian's task, with particular reference to the relevance of that task to Unitarian self-understanding.

Since then, the *Proceedings* have appeared somewhat less frequently but have been characterized by the increasing professionalization that at that time was overtaking the enterprise of church history as a whole. The change in scholarly tone resulted in part from the emergent scholarship of George H. Williams and C. Conrad Wright at the Harvard Divinity School, which was then in the process of academic revitalization. Some issues continued to consist of articles on a wide variety of topics, including Unitarianism in India and Hungary, and book reviews have appeared from time to time.[14] Two volumes, each spanning several years of *Proceedings*, were devoted to monographic studies: Harold Field Worthy's massive *An Inventory of the Records of the Particular (Congregational) Churches of Massachusetts, 1620–1805*[15] and George Hunston Williams's almost equally extensive study of the Polish Brethren.[16] Other individual issues consisted entirely of articles on Theodore Parker, once the bête noir of the Boston Unitarian establishment, and the more orthodox New Yorker Henry W. Bellows.[17]

Beginning with volume 19 (1980–81), the name of the journal was changed to *Proceedings of the Unitarian-Universalist Historical Society*, reflecting the union of the two denominations in 1961 and the subsequent merger of their historical societies in 1978. This combined publication also superseded the *Journal of the Universalist Historical Society*, published periodically since 1959. Although occasional articles on Universalism appeared both before and after the merger, Unitarian history has always been the focus of attention.

Other kinds of materials appeared from time to time, including occasional plates (usually portraits), indexes of articles, reports to the board of trustees, proceedings of annual meetings, and lists of officers. A list published in 1954 revealed that the society consisted of 93 members (mostly individuals, a few institutional), 54 of whom were from Massachusetts; 16 others from New England; nine from other northeastern states; and the remaining 14 primarily from the Midwest and Far West.[19] Without question, the society's primary constituency continues to abide in "the neighborhood of Boston": the present geographical distribution of contributors and the quality of the contents, however, indicate that the *Proceedings* have come to transcend the parochial.

Notes

1. The first issue, copyright 1926, was simply designated as volume 1. In 1928, volume 1, part 2 appeared, setting a pattern for subsequent issues in which two consecutively published numbers would constitute parts 1 and 2 of a volume.

2. King's Chapel, although originally Anglican, was the first American church formally to declare its Unitarian predilections when its congregation voted to delete Trinitarian references in the *Book of Common Prayer* in 1785.

3. "Announcement," *Proceedings of the Unitarian Historical Society* 1, pt. 1 (1925): facing list of officers (hereafter cited as *Proceedings*).

4. "How the Schism Came," *Proceedings* 1, pt. 1 (1925): 3–21.

5. "Notes on Cotton and Increase Mather," *Proceedings* 1, pt. 1 (1925): 22–44.

6. T. G. Masaryk, Prague, "The Los von Rom Movement in Austria" (1902); Alfred Alther, Basle, "The Origin and Growth of the Liberal Church in Switzerland" (1903); W. W. Fenn, "Historical Sketch of British Unitarians" (1925).

7. For example, Earl M. Wilbur, "Socinian Propaganda in Germany Three Hundred Years Ago," *Proceedings* 3:1 (1933): 22–41; John C. Godbey, "Faustus Socinus in the Light of Modern Scholarship," *Proceedings* 15:1 (1964): 66–92.

8. Frederick R. Griffin, "Joseph Priestley," *Proceedings* 3:2 (1934): 1–12; Charles Edward Park, "The First Four Churches of Massachusetts Bay," *Proceedings* 2:1 (1931): 1–19.

9. *Proceedings* 8:1 (1947): 5–16 (Frederick May Eliot).

10. Initialed by Parke, "Editor's Note," *Proceedings* 11:2 (1957): vii. The same "Note" announces the beginnings of a book review section edited by George H. Williams and Conrad Wright of the Harvard Divinity School.

11. "Editor's Note," pp. vii–xii. Also see Wilbur's "How the History Came to Be Written," *Proceedings* 12:1 (1958): 5–23. A bibliography of Wilbur's writings is appended to this article.

12. "Editor's Note," p. vii.

13. "The Historian's History: A Pathway to Freedom," *Proceedings* 12:1 (1958): 1–11. Following this is another work by Mead, "An Address to Unitarians" (pp. 12–26).

14. Spencer Lavan, "Unitarians and Acculturation: Jabez T. Sunderland in India (1895–1896)," *Proceedings* 17: 2 (1973–75): 73–91; Joseph Ferencz and John Szasz, "When Hungarian Unitarianism Was Born," *Proceedings* 17:1 (1970–72): 57–62.

15. *Proceedings* 16:1–2 (1966–69), published together in one volume; also issued as *Harvard Theological Studies* 25.

16. Ibid. 18:1 (1976–77) and 18:2 (1978–79), published in two issues and distributed by Scholars Press.

17. Ibid. 13:1 (1960) on Parker; ibid. 15:2 (1965) on Bellows.

18. The Universalist Historical Society was founded in 1834 and published 10 volumes of a *Journal* beginning in 1959. According to a recent flyer (c. 1980), copies of all back issues are available through the Unitarian-Universalist Historical Society.

19. *Proceedings* 10:2 (1954): 32–34. The same issue contains a "List of Officers" from 1901 to 1954 and an index for vols. 1–10 of the *Proceedings*.

Information Sources

BIBLIOGRAPHY:
Unitarian Universalist Association. *1980 Directory*. Boston: Beacon Press, 1980.
Williams, George H., ed. *The Harvard Divinity School*. Boston: Beacon Press, 1954.
Wright, Conrad, ed. *A Stream of Light: A Sesquicentennial History of American Unitarianism*. Boston: Beacon Press, 1975.
INDEX SOURCES: *Proceedings of the Unitarian Historical Society* 10:2 (1954): 35–36, for vols. 1–10; *Proceedings of the Unitarian Historical Society* 13:2 (1961): 107–8, for vols. 8–13.
LOCATION SOURCES: Copies of selected back issues are available from the society, c/o Prof. Conrad Wright, Harvard Divinity School, Cambridge, Mass. 02138.

Publication History

MAGAZINE TITLE AND TITLE CHANGES: *The Proceedings of the Unitarian Historical Society* (1925–79), *The Proceedings of the Unitarian Universalist Historical Society* (1980–   ).
VOLUME AND ISSUE DATA: Two parts to each volume. 1:1 (1925), 1:2 (1928), 2:1–7:2 (1931–41) issued annually; 8:1 (1947), 8:2–10:2 (1950–54) issued annually; 11:1 (1956), 11:2 (1957), 12 (1958) only one part; 13:1 (1960), 13:2 (1961), 14:1–2 (1962–63), 15:1 (1964), 16:1–2 (1965–69), 17:1 (1970–72), 17:2 (1973–75), 18:1 (1976–77), 18:2 (1978–79), 19:1 (1980–81–   ).
PUBLISHER AND PLACE OF PUBLICATION: Beacon Press, Boston (1925–56); the society using various printers (1957–   ). Vol. 16 also published as *Harvard Theological Studies* 25; vol. 18, distributed by Scholars Press, Missoula, Mont.
EDITORS: Vol. 1:1 lists an editorial committee (Henry Wilder Foote, Julius H. Tuttle, and Charles E. Park). Officers of the society are listed in each subsequent issue, but only with 9:1 (1951) is there a list of a Publication Committee and Editors of Proceedings, which identifies Christopher Rhodes Eliot as editor (1931–41) and Frederick Lewis Weis as editor (1941–51). Vol. 11:2 (1957) announced the appointment of David B. Parke as editor, with the officers and directors serving as an editorial board. Harold F. Worthley is listed as editor beginning with 17:1 (1970–72). No editor is listed for 18, and Richard E. Myers is listed in the most recent issue (19:1, 1980–81) as editor.
CIRCULATION: 250 (est., 1980).

Peter W. Williams

THE PULPIT. *See* THE CHRISTIAN MINISTRY

PULPIT DIGEST

Pulpit Digest continues two earlier professional journals for preachers, *Pulpit Preaching* and the old *Pulpit Digest*. Merged in 1972 for economic reasons, the two then had little substantive difference, in marked contrast to their early years.[1]

The separate beginnings, converging courses, and eventual merger illuminate developments not only in pulpit resources but in the twentieth-century pulpit.

Pulpit Digest was founded in 1936 by Lester L. Doniger (1909–71). His experience as a cub reporter covering prominent New York City pulpits inspired several business ventures aimed at pastors. The *Digest* was the first. The second, offering publications to clergy at reduced rates, became the Religious Book Club in 1954. The third, providing resources for pastoral counseling, was *Pastoral Psychology*, founded in 1949.[2] These ventures were not new approaches to servicing the needs of the ministry, but they were conditioned by changes that professionalism wrought in those needs.

Attempts to formulate a theology of proclamation or to instruct in techniques of public speaking were rare in the early *Pulpit Digest*. Such a role was disavowed. The *Digest* "set out to reform nothing, to influence no one, to uphold no thesis, but merely to lend a hand wherever it might be welcome."[3] While this hand might include articles on a variety of subjects, it involved primarily the publication of complete sermons. The printed sermons were intended only coincidentally to ease weekly sermon preparation. The *Digest* met a far greater need by providing an affirmation of preaching itself.

The need for affirmation resulted in part from a deterioration in the self-image of the preacher. W. Wesley Shrader recalled in the twentieth anniversary issue that to many, the preacher of the 1930s "was a sad little man with an umbrella. He was easily frightened. His intellectual level was slightly above that of a moron."[4] Hollywood was blamed for projecting this image.[5] *Pulpit Digest* aimed to counteract the influence of this view on the morale of preachers. Moreover, in affirming preachers and preaching, not only were works of "princes of the pulpit" chosen, but "examples of the best that is being said and done in the Protestant ministry, *and* that which seems to be significant" were accepted regardless of source.[6]

Any uncertainty about the preaching role was largely dissolved in the revitalization experienced by American Protestantism at midcentury. The clearest indication of this change was the rebirth of a strong, well-defined pulpit aristocracy. Such men as Paul Scherer, Joseph Fort Newton, Ralph Sockman, Clarence Macartney, Clovis Chappell, and George Buttrick attained the seniority necessary to become paradigms for a younger generation of preachers. In the process they influenced the founding of *Pulpit Preaching*, governing both its format and policy.

Pulpit Preaching was founded in 1947 by Methodist pastor Charles L. Allen who envisioned a "journal for the minister's study" that would furnish enough substance on two themes "to give an over-abundance of material that can be preached."[7] This substance was to come in essay form from an editorial board consisting of the nation's leading preachers. Other contributions were not solicited. The tone was that of a craft journal for a professional constituency whose place in society was to be assumed rather than affirmed. *Pulpit Preaching* did not address other clergy needs and eschewed such marks of commercial venture as advertising. Preaching was the sole focus of the journal.

Interestingly, *Pulpit Digest* entered the 1950s on a course parallel to that of its younger competitor. In 1953 the *Digest* modified its policy to the extent that, through its "Man on the Cover" series, it became something of an arbiter of pulpit taste.[8] For 12 years each issue featured a photograph of one of the great preachers of the day who was usually a contributing editor of *Pulpit Preaching* as well. Further, the sermons printed in the *Digest* represented a smaller body of contributors. This change generated an identity crisis for the *Digest*'s constituency. The hinterland felt slighted by the attention given leading figures, expressing dissatisfaction in a slow, steady stream of mail. The editors reaffirmed their pledge to print quality from whatever source, but with one addition. Who should be surprised, the editors demurred, if quality were most often found among those who had become a presence in the land?[9] The dissatisfied continued a minor campaign to alter the cover format to a table of contents. The resulting compromise—a table of contents on both the cover and within—has stood as a monument to the struggle since 1965.

This struggle reveals an antipodal tendency in the attitude of American preachers to pulpit resources. Preachers were of two minds: one eagerly seeking the example of the master craftsman, the other jealously guarding a collegiality won in the creation of a professional ministry. A format of printed sermons emerged that served the dual purpose of affirming the craft and instructing the craftsmen. Confirmation of this tendency may be gleaned from changes in *Pulpit Preaching*, which at first ignored the issue of collegiality, during its first year in print. Essays changed to printed sermons, the list of contributing editors that served as the cover for the first volume disappeared, a call was issued for contributions from subscribers, and in 1951 a new editor responsive to this tension came on staff. Charles L. Wallis proved his sensitivity by becoming an influence as enduring as that of either Doniger or Allen. While *Pulpit Digest* moved hesitantly through the 1950s to resolve this tension, Wallis rather quickly established the balance between the preachers' two minds, which allowed *Pulpit Preaching* to experience explosive growth.[10]

Unintentionally, the constituency created its journals out of the crucible of its own experience. For this reason, the two publications provide valuable insight into the vicissitudes of the twentieth-century Protestant pulpit, for they mirrored the struggles and soul searchings, prejudices and ambivalences of their clientele. For example, the *Digest* placed a somewhat greater stress on social issues, engaging Samuel McCrea Cavert as senior editorial adviser in 1958 to guide preachers in the critical questions of the day.[11] *Pulpit Preaching*, on the other hand, stressed stylistic concerns in such series as "Preaching Values in *Reader's Digest*" (which capitalized on that periodical's popularity and quotability) or associate editor E. Paul Hovey's long-running "Worth Quoting."[12] Since both journals included the points stressed by the other, the distinction was essentially intramural. When the two merged in 1972, the differing emphases were drawn under one roof with hardly a ripple.

Pulpit Digest during its last 20 years of independent publication reveals both the nature and limits of social issues for the pulpit. Peace, racial equality, and economic justice were frequently discussed.[13] On the other hand, Roman Catholics were the objects of sermons rather than their contributors, as were the faith healers, politico-religious preachers, and revivalists such as Oral Roberts, Kathryn Kuhlmann, and Billy James Hargis.[14] Although a strong sympathy for the civil rights movement and a commitment to the ecumenical agenda of the Federal (now National) Council of Churches created a new appreciation for ethnic minority and non-Western preaching traditions, few examples of them were published. Those that were seem much like the standard body of published sermons. The tradition that on both counts garnered most sympathy—the black American— is found least often in authentic form. Black preachers who published did so largely outside their own traditional forms.[15]

Such lacunae point to the prejudices of those who occupied the pulpit but even more to the style of preaching (and preacher), the audience, and to some extent the content of message assumed by both journals—all of which fit squarely within the continuum of the received Protestant culture still under the shadow of preaching's Gilded Age. Nothing could entirely dispel the heritage of the literate, polished, exegetical, multipoint-structured sermon bequeathed to this century. But changes of the 1970s have deflected the shadow. The merged journal has a more ambivalent evangelical following, a stronger mainline cast.[16] More women are publishing.[17] Articles on new forms of proclamation have appeared, and the older forms are used more self-consciously.[18] Non-Western, ethnic minority, charismatic, and socially radical forms have been quarried for insights. Yet the sermon derived from the tradition continues to have an honored and important place in the format of the *Digest*, if not the prominent place in the hearts of both preachers and people.

Notes

1. Letter from LaVerne Lowry, *Pulpit Digest* business manager, to the author, 3 February 1983.

2. "In Memoriam," *Pulpit Digest* 51 (June 1971): 5.

3. "Editorial," *Pulpit Digest* 37 (December 1956): 11.

4. W. Wesley Shrader, "1,040 Sundays," *Pulpit Digest* 37 (December 1956): 13.

5. Ibid.

6. "Editorial," *Pulpit Digest* 37 (December 1956): 12. Cf. Charles C. Morrison, "Editorial," *Christian Century Pulpit* 1 (October 1929): 23.

7. Charles L. Allen, "Last Page Comment," *Pulpit Preaching* 1 (October 1947): 19.

8. "The Man on the Cover," *Pulpit Digest* 33 (January 1953): 11.

9. "Letters to the Editor," *Pulpit Digest* 33 (June 1953): 7, 8.

10. *Pulpit Preaching* 4 (May 1951): 1; 4 (July 1951): 1.

11. Samuel McCrea Cavert, "Pentecost—Then and Now," *Pulpit Digest* 38 (May 1958): 7, 8, was the inaugural editorial of this series.

12. "Preaching Values in *Reader's Digest*," *Pulpit Preaching* 5 (August 1952); on the significance of these emphases, see DeWitte Holland, ed., *Preaching in American History* (Nashville: Abingdon Press, 1969), pp. 11–15, and Holland, ed., *Sermons in American History* (Nashville: Abingdon Press, 1971), pp. 13–24.

13. *Pulpit Digest* 34 (June 1954), for example, was given over entirely to the issue of the hydrogen-cobalt bomb. Such, however, was the exception rather than the rule.

14. For examples of Protestant–Roman Catholic concerns, see *Pulpit Preaching* 14 (October 1962), esp. Everett W. Palmer, "What Can We Do for Catholic-Protestant Concord?" (pp. 20–23); *Pulpit Digest* 40 (November 1959) and 45 (July-August 1965), especially Samuel McCrea Cavert's editorial on Pope John XXIII and Vatican II (pp. 7ff.). On faith healers and others, see William Goddard Sherman, "What about Oral Roberts?" *Pulpit Digest* 36 (June 1956): 17ff., and Samuel McCrea Cavert, "The Healing Ministry of the Church," *Pulpit Digest* 39 (September 1958): 11–12.

15. The primary difficulty seems to have been stylistic: the contrast between the auricular quality and congregational dynamics of the black tradition and the formal literary approach of the received culture. See Henry H. Mitchell, *Black Preaching* (Philadelphia: J. B. Lippincott Co., 1970), pp. 95–109, 148–95, 230–48. The first black preacher featured in the Man on the Cover series was James H. Robinson, pastor in the Presbyterian Church, U.S.A. (*Pulpit Digest* 36 [April 1956]). *Pulpit Preaching* featured W. O. Carrington of the AME Zion Church in the original list of contributing editors in 1947.

16. Evangelical participation in both journals has always been ambivalent. Some well-known evangelicals such as Stephen F. Olford have published regularly, while others have never published. In *Pulpit Digest* 33 (January 1953): 41, Moody Bible Institute advertised the speakers for Founder's Week, an annual pulpit event of the evangelical-fundamentalist tradition, but none of the featured preachers published in the *Digest*.

17. In 1954 *Pulpit Digest* featured an extract, Margaret Blair Johnstone, "Would People Accept You—A Woman?" 35 (October 1954): 11–14, taken from her *When God Said "No": Faith's Starting Point* (New York: Simon and Schuster, 1954). Beginning in 1952, Alice Geer Kelsey provided a regular feature on children's sermons. The first and only woman to publish a sermon prior to 1972 was Georgia Harkness, "Have You Seen the Lord," *Pulpit Digest* 38 (March 1958): 37–41. The situation for *Pulpit Preaching* was similar.

18. John Killenger, author of *Experimental Preaching* (Nashville: Abingdon Press, 1973) and critic of traditional sermon form, has recently begun publishing in *Pulpit Digest*.

Information Sources

BIBLIOGRAPHY:
Holland, DeWitte, ed. *Preaching in American History*. Nashville: Abingdon Press, 1969.
———, ed. *Sermons in American History*. Nashville: Abingdon Press, 1971.
Hoyt, Arthur S. *The Pulpit and American Life*. New York: Macmillan, 1921.
Killenger, John. *Experimental Preaching*. Nashville: Abingdon Press, 1973.
Mitchell, Henry H. *Black Preaching*. Philadelphia: J. B. Lippincott Co., 1970.
INDEX SOURCES: None.
LOCATION SOURCES: Colgate-Rochester Divinity School.

Publication History

MAGAZINE TITLE AND TITLE CHANGES: *Pulpit Digest* (1936–72) and *Pulpit Preaching* (1947–72), *New Pulpit Digest* (1972–77), *Pulpit Digest* (1978–   ).

VOLUME AND ISSUE DATA: *Pulpit Digest*: 1:1 (1936)–51:386 (1971); *Pulpit Preaching*: 1:1 (1947)–24:4 (1971); *New Pulpit Digest*: 52:387 (1972)–58:434 (1978); *Pulpit Digest*: 59:435 (1978–   ).

PUBLISHER AND PLACE OF PUBLICATION: *Pulpit Digest*, 1936–65: Pulpit Digest Publishing Co., Great Neck, N.Y.; *Pulpit Digest*, 1965–72: Merideth Publishing Corp., Manhasset, N.Y.; *Pulpit Preaching*, 1947–53: Charles L. Allen, Publisher, Thomson, Ga.; *Pulpit Preaching*, 1953–55: Oxford Press, Jackson, Miss.; *Pulpit Preaching*, 1955–72: Tombigbee Pub. Co., Jackson, Miss.; *New Pulpit Digest*, 1972–77; *Pulpit Digest*, 1978–80: Walter Dell Davis, Jackson, Miss.; *Pulpit Digest*, 1980–   : Pulpit Publishing Co., Great Neck, N.Y.

EDITORS: *Pulpit Digest*: Lester L. Doniger (1936–45), Richard A. Newhouse (1945–46), Ralph C. Raughley (1946–68), Charles Wheeler Scott (1968–72); *Pulpit Preaching*: Charles L. Allen (1947–72), Charles L. Wallis (1951–72), E. Paul Hovey (1958–72); *New Pulpit Digest/Pulpit Digest*: Charles L. Wallis (1972–81), W. T. Edwards (1981–82), James W. Cox and David A. Farmer (1982–   ).

CIRCULATION: 7500 (1983).

Daniel L. Swinson

PULPIT PREACHING. *See* PULPIT DIGEST

PURITAN RECORDER. *See* CONGREGATIONALIST AND HERALD OF GOSPEL LIBERTY

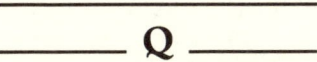

QUAKER HISTORY

In 1904 a group of Quakers in the Philadelphia area interested in promoting historical awareness of their religious tradition organized the Friends' Historical Society of Philadelphia. High on the agenda of the society was the publication of a journal that would treat topics related to Quaker history in a scholarly fashion. Two years later the first issue of the *Bulletin of Friends' Historical Society of Philadelphia* appeared. A notice on the title page indicated the intent of the society in producing the periodical: "We should like to make [our pages] a depository of new material or of new and fresh presentations of old material which is not accessible. We should wish to stimulate in the minds of the readers a knowledge of the importance of historical facts to coming generations." The introductory statement also noted that the *Bulletin* would appear at irregular intervals until such time as it was determined whether interest would make a regular publication schedule feasible. Over the next 15 years, 10 volumes of the *Bulletin* were published, with all but the last containing three issues each printed over a period of one and one-half years. The tenth volume (1920–21) contained only two numbers and marked the transition to a regular publication schedule. Beginning with volume 11 (1922), two issues have appeared annually, one in the spring and one in the fall.

The *Bulletin* from the start adhered to high standards of scholarship and academic quality, a practice aided by the presence of large repositories of Quaker materials in library collections at Haverford and Swarthmore colleges, both Quaker institutions in the greater Philadelphia area, and the association of several of the editors with one of these schools. The commitment to quality and the professional appearance of the *Bulletin* received a boost after the Philadelphia Society merged with the older Friends' Historical Association in 1923. The combined group maintained the journal but changed its name to reflect the stronger backing it had to the *Bulletin of Friends' Historical Association* in 1924. Later, in 1941, the apostrophe after *Friends* was dropped, and in 1962 the present name, *Quaker History: The Bulletin of Friends Historical Association*, was adopted.

Over the years, *Quaker History* has combined a farc of scholarly articles and reviews of books treating Quaker matters with reprints of brief documents and occasional letters detailing early Quaker history in the United States. Until the early 1970s, the main orientation was to the story of the Friends in colonial America, and most of the articles were written by members of the historical association. Recently, the focus of articles has expanded to include a broader time frame, and non-Quaker scholars have begun to contribute a larger proportion of the essays. As well, the journal reports on meetings of the historical association, articles about Quakers appearing in other periodicals, and newly discovered or recently acquired primary materials available for study.

In its first half-century, the *Bulletin* offered appraisals, for example, of the Keithian schism (16:2, 1927), Quaker contributions to music (23:2, 1934), links of early Quaker developments to French quietism (29:2, 1940), and the Quaker influence on the work of John Greenleaf Whittier (27:2, 1937; 28, 1939) and Theodore Dreiser (35:2, 1946). The pace-setting Quaker concern for the abolition of slavery in the United States also came under periodic scrutiny, as did the Friends' commitment to improving the status of free blacks in the antebellum period (32:1, 1943; 30:2, 1941). *Quaker History* has attempted as well to be candid about the diversity within the ranks of the Friends, noting, for example, the plight of Quaker Loyalists in the epoch of the American Revolution (32:2, 1943) and Quaker communitarian experiments (43:1, 1954). But few touched on Quaker theology or religious thought, perhaps because the Quaker conviction that religious experience is intensely individualistic in nature, that the inner light comes to different persons in different ways, has meant that the tradition as a whole has deemphasized matters of doctrine.

Winds of change, however, were apparent as early as 1947 when Quaker scholar Frederick B. Tolles served as acting editor for one issue. Tolles seized the opportunity to write an editorial entitled "Desiderata in Quaker History" (36:1, 1948), in which he outlined several areas neglected by students of the tradition. In particular, he singled out the links of the Quakers to Puritanism, Quaker experiments in government, Quaker social and economic thought, and the Hicksite division of the nineteenth century as areas needing exposition and analysis. Two years later, Tolles began a 19-year tenure as editor of the journal. Under his leadership, *Quaker History* began to pursue more wide-ranging coverage. Quaker contributions to U.S. foreign policy, for example, came under scrutiny (48:1, 1959), as did Quaker concern for educational reform (58:1, 1969). Tolles's insistence that Quaker connections with Puritanism be explored received treatment in an essay arguing that both the Baptists and the Quakers had roots in the left wing of English Puritanism (62:2, 1973). Quaker theology also came under occasional study, as in an article detailing Baptist influence on the Quaker notion of the inner light (56:1, 1967). Revisionist approaches to Quaker history have been evidenced in Joseph E. Illick's "The Flight to Pennsylvania: Affirmation or Denial of Quakerism?" (59:2, 1970), but traditional concerns have not been neglected, as seen in the article by J. William Frost, which reviewed recent literature on abolitionism and antislavery movements (67:1, 1978). The impact of contemporary society on subject matter is apparent in articles such as one that discussed nineteenth-century Quaker women ministers (63:2, 1974).

Quaker History has been a vehicle for careful consideration of the tradition of the Friends for over three-quarters of a century. Although its circulation thas remained small, quality has remained high. It is a journal of specialized interest, which has made a signal contribution in highlighting the impact on American life of a religious group whose significance far exceeds its numbers.

Information Sources

INDEX SOURCES: *Quaker History* and its predecessors have published separate index volumes for 1–15 and each five-year sequence since through vol. 65; also in *Religious Index One*.

REPRINT EDITIONS: University Microfilms International.

LOCATION SOURCES: Henry E. Huntington Library, Duke University, Yale University, Princeton Theological Seminary, University of Chicago, Library of Congress, Haverford College, and others.

Publication History

MAGAZINE TITLE AND TITLE CHANGES: *Bulletin of Friends' Historical Society of Philadelphia* (1906–23), *Bulletin of Friends' Historical Association* (1924–40), *Bulletin of Friends Historical Association* (1941–61), *Quaker History* (1962–   ).

VOLUME AND ISSUE DATA: 1:1–3 (October 1906-November 1907), 2:1–3 (1908), 3:1–3 (February 1909-February 1910), 4:1–3 (March 1911-November 1912), 5:1–3 (April 1913-May 1914), 6:1–3 (November 1914-November 1915), 7:1–3 (May 1916-May 1917), 8:1–3 (November 1917-November 1918), 9:1–3 (1919–20), 10:1–2 (1920–21); 11:1 (1922–   ). Spring and fall issues each year starting with 11:1 (1922).

PUBLISHER AND PLACE OF PUBLICATION: Friends' Historical Society of Philadelphia, Philadelphia (1906–8); Ferris and Lynch, Philadelphia (1909–18); Friends Historical Association, Philadelphia (1919–44); Publication Office, Haverford College Library, Haverford, Pa. (1945–   ).

EDITORS: None designated (1906–7), Allen C. Thomas (1907–21), none designated (1922–24), Rayner W. Kelsey (1925–27, 1930–32), Henry J. Cadbury (acting, 1928–29), Thomas K. Brown, Jr. (1933–44), Thomas E. Drake (1945–48), Frederick Tolles (acting, 1947; 1949–67), Opal Thornburg (acting, 1947), Lyma W. Riley (1967–72), John M. Moore (1974–80), Arthur J. Mekeel (1981–   ).

CIRCULATION: 890 (1982).

Charles H. Lippy

QUARTERLY REVIEW

Throughout the nineteenth and early twentieth centuries, the two major branches of American Methodism, North and South, published scholarly journals under various titles such as *Quarterly Review*, *Methodist Review*,* and *Methodist Quarterly Review*.* Enjoying wide circulation and usage, especially prior to World War I when Methodism was America's largest Protestant denomination, the journals of both groups began to lose readership thereafter and were discontinued by 1931.

The Methodist Episcopal Church (North), under the leadership of its book editor, John W. Langdale, moved to fill the void in 1932 with a different type of publication. While still Methodist in sponsorship, the new journal took a broader name, *Religion in Life*, and was intended to appeal to a wide ecumenical constituency across the Christian world.

Religion in Life was liberal in scope of content and in breadth of authorship. Writers were drawn from many fields, including comparative literature, education, philosophy, geology, sociology, and economics, as well as theological studies. Pastors of major Protestant churches, executives of ecumenical organizations such as the Federal Council of Churches, academicians, and church leaders from England, Canada, Japan, and other nations, were represented in its pages.

While clearly religious in interest, articles ranged over not only traditional fields such as contemporary theology, biblical criticism, church music, prayer, homiletics, and church life in various nations but also over national and international issues such as war and peace, capitalism, and communism. The journal reflected interest in literature, and it published sermons and extensive book reviews.

Over the years the editorial board and advisory council rosters were dotted with names of prominent Methodist scholars, such as Lynn Harold Hough, Harris Franklin Rall, Albert Edward Day, and Walter Muelder, but recognized scholars and church leaders of many denominations were always included as well: Kenneth Scott Latourette, Gerald Cragg, Joseph Haroutunian, Douglas Steere, Elton Trueblood, Leslie Weatherhead, and Stephen Neill.

If *Religion in Life* was liberal in scope and authorship, it was also liberal in viewpoint, reflecting the mainstream Protestantism of its day. The tone was well set by the lead article of the winter 1932 issue. Methodist Bishop Francis T. McConnell of New York, then perhaps the major leader of northern Methodism, wrote an explanation of the journal's title. In keeping with Protestant progressivism of the preceding 50 years, he argued that religion was to be involved in "actual living problems," sharing responsibility for "progressive ideas" that would "cause society to advance." Religion was not mystical but active, a doing of the divine will; for "in the teaching and example of Jesus religion and life are indissolubly bound together."

In genuine liberal fashion, McConnell defended religion against the critiques of modern thought, insisting against Freud that belief was not just an illusion or psychological need and against humanism that theistic belief was essential to a moral world. He restated the mutual accommodation of religion and science as broadly accepted in mainstream Protestantism: that each was properly limited to its own sphere, science to the natural world of immediate causes and facts, religion to the supernatural world of ultimate causes and interpretation, each needing and respecting the domain of the other.

McConnell's viewpoint was reinforced by the next article, in which a Harvard geologist, Kirtley F. Mather, noted an increasing "attitude of friendly and orderly cooperation" between science and religion. He also called for scientists to allow for several ways of approaching reality and for the "intelligent layman to distinguish between theological husks and religious kernel" in determining the effects of scientific evidence on foundations of belief. This approach was concomitant with historical critical method in biblical studies as well, which scholarship also was presupposed and often presented in the pages of *Religion in Life*.[1]

Over its nearly 50 years of publication, the journal reflected contemporary discussion on many religious issues and in retrospect could serve almost literally as a journal or diary of theological trends and social change during those years. Numbers were devoted to the "Honest to God" debate, provoked by Anglican Bishop John Robinson's book of that name, to the emergence of Third World churches, and to post–Vatican II Roman Catholicism. As religious studies fields became more professionalized, articles tended to become more specialized, couched more in scholarly jargon. The range of concerns never diminished, however.

The 1939 Uniting Conference of Methodism ordered official sponsorship of *Religion in Life* by the merged denomination. Shortly thereafter the book editorship and consequent editorship of the journal passed to a scholar of the southern tradition, Nolan B. Harmon, who served from 1941 until his election to the episcopacy in 1956. During his tenure, the publication changed to a larger format with the 1951–52 volume. It added the words *of Opinion and Discussion* to the earlier subtitle, *A Christian Quarterly*, printed slightly fewer articles in each number, replaced the older narrative items called "Bookish Notices" with more formal "Book Notices," and continued a "Book Review" section.

Always partially underwritten by the Publishing House, *Religion in Life* suffered falling circulation in the 1970s and issued its last number in winter 1980. Meanwhile plans were being laid by book editor Ronald P. Patterson for a new journal to be published jointly with the Board of Higher Education and Ministry of the United Methodist Church. Picking up the older traditional name of Methodist journals, it was called *Quarterly Review* and commenced with an advance edition in fall 1980.

Quarterly Review is "unashamedly directed toward Methodists," though its editorial board has included Leander Keck, dean of Yale Divinity School, and Sallie McFague, dean of Vanderbilt Divinity School.[2] Authorship is not limited to Methodists. Taking the subtitle, *A Scholarly Journal for Reflection on Ministry*, the journal is intended as a continuing education tool, with space devoted to articles on the practice of ministry and on biblical exegesis useful for sermon preparation. The half-dozen or so major articles range broadly over literature and social issues, as well as theological studies, often with three or four brief responses printed as well. A thematic issue was printed in spring 1982 on "The Professional Ministry," and another in spring 1984 on the Methodist bicentenary. In-depth book reviews are also included in each issue's approximately 100 pages. Charles E. Cole is editor.

Notes

1. *Religion in Life* 1 (Winter 1932): 4, 13, 14.
2. *Quarterly Review* 1 (Fall 1980): 3.

Information Sources

BIBLIOGRAPHY:
Bucke, Emory Stevens. *History of American Methodism*, Vol. 3. New York: Abingdon Press, 1964.
Harmon, Nolan B., Jr., ed. *Encyclopedia of World Methodism*. Nashville: United Methodist Publishing House, 1974.
INDEX SOURCES: *Religion Index One, Guide to Social Science and Religion in Periodical Literature, Humanities Index, Old Testament Abstracts*.
REPRINT EDITIONS: University Microfilms International, American Theological Library Association Board of Microtext.
LOCATION SOURCES: Yale University, Library of Congress, University of Chicago, Union Theological Seminary (New York), Duke University, Andover-Harvard Theological Library, Princeton University, Southern Methodist University, San Francisco Theological Seminary, and others.

Publication History

MAGAZINE TITLE AND TITLE CHANGES: *Religion in Life* (1932–80), *Quarterly Review* (1981–   ).
VOLUME AND ISSUE DATA: *Religion in Life* 1:1–49:4 (Winter 1932-Winter 1980); appeared quarterly by calendar year (winter, spring, summer, fall), 1932–41, then quarterly with the first number late in the year (winter 1941, spring 1942, etc.), 1941–66; 35 (1965–66) contained five numbers to permit return to calendar year issues, 1966–80; *Quarterly Review* 1:1 (Fall 1980–   ); 1 (1980–81) had five numbers, an advance edition and quarterly numbers by season in 1981; thereafter (1982–   ) issued quarterly by calendar year.
PUBLISHER AND PLACE OF PUBLICATION: *Religion in Life*: Abingdon Press of the Methodist Publishing House, New York, and Nashville, Tenn. *Quarterly Review*: United Methodist Board of Higher Education and Ministry and the United Methodist Publishing House, Nashville, Tenn.

EDITORS: John W. Langdale (1932–41), Nolan B. Harmon, Jr. (1941–56), Emory Stevens
    Bucke (1956–76), Ronald P. Patterson (1976–80), Charles E. Cole (1980–   ).
CIRCULATION: 3000–4000 (1960), 1300–1400 (1975), 3000 (1984).

Thomas E. Frank

QUARTERLY REVIEW OF THE EVANGELICAL LUTHERAN CHURCH. *See* THE LUTHERAN QUARTERLY

THE RADICAL

The *Radical*, edited in Boston by Sidney H. Morse (and Joseph B. Marvin for volumes 3–5), appeared monthly from September 1865 through June 1872 but for a suspension from July 1870 through January 1871. Self-consciously "post-Unitarian," Morse and his journal sought to advance religion as devotion to "the True, Beautiful and Good Providence . . . the One Reality."[1] The journal was to be "a medium for the freest expression of thought on all religious and social topics," with its contributors "responsible each for his or her own production, but for no others."[2] Among such responsible contributors were O. B. Frothingham, W. J. Potter, and John Weiss, organizers of the Free Religious Association; Samuel Johnson, minister of the Free Church at Lynn, Massachusetts; Bronson Alcott; T. W. Higginson; Wendell Phillips; Elizabeth Cady Stanton; C. K. Whipple; and David A. Wasson, president of the Theodore Parker Society.

Parker was patron saint of the *Radical*. His name and memory (d. 1860) were often recalled by the editor and others, including Frothingham in a major piece, and his *Works* were prominent in the journal's "book-list."[3] Another symbol of a carefully chosen tradition was Ralph Waldo Emerson, whose addresses and writings were also published in the journal, including the address of 1838 to the Harvard Divinity senior students in which Emerson identified the "religious sentiment" as that which "makes our highest happiness."[4]

Another source of happiness for Morse and the *Radical* was a good quarrel, whether with another publication, such as the *Atlantic* over a book review (and subscription lists), or the *New York Independent* over sermons or remarks by Henry Ward Beecher; or with such sundry types as "conservative Unitarians," "liberals of calvinistic sects," "bad old-fashioned orthodoxy," the Boston YMCA, and erstwhile colleagues, James Freeman Clarke and F. E. Abbot. In one instance Morse asserted that the journal, even by its title, "must represent the radical change which is taking place in the religious convictions of the American people. . . . Mere Liberalism is a doubtful commodity. The departure from the old is to be marked and unmistakable."[5]

Marked indeed was a quarrel begun in 1866 by Morse with Abbot, then minister at Dover, New Hampshire, over distancing oneself from the body of "conservative Unitarians."[6] Very probably this led to the termination of the journal. Abbot responded in the journal to Morse's criticism, soon resigned his position at Dover and his membership in the American Unitarian Association, and moved to Toledo, Ohio, to found his own publication, the *Index*.* With a touch of paternalism, Morse announced the forthcoming weekly in December 1869, allowing that his action alone "should be sufficient to ensure success."[7] Two months later, in a review article, Morse found the *Index* to be a "fitting companion sheet to the *Radical*, and especially is it so for all who are interested in the many items which a monthly [his], for the most part, has to let slip."[8]

Many items were not all that the monthly let slip, for Morse soon found also that the *Index* had drawn away many of his most important contributors and his subscribers as well. When the *Index* organized an association to pledge a base of support in the amount of $50,000 and was successful in its endeavor, the *Radical* followed with its own association. The names on the pledge list were impressive; the amount of money promised was not. The project and the journal ended. On 1 June 1872 Morse published the last issue of the *Radical*, including a valedictory in which he expressed disappointment for the present, but pride for the past.

He had cause for such pride. The *Radical* had offered a number of significant pieces during its publication, including: Samuel Johnson, "Discourses Concerning the Foundations of Religious Belief"; O. B. Frothingham, "The Radical's Attitude toward the Bible"; Samuel Longfellow, "Some Radical Doctrine"; F. E. Abbot, "A Radical's Theology"; Frothingham, "Two Religions in the New Testament"; E. About, "Progress"; John Weiss, "Woman Suffrage"; Frothingham, "What Is Religion and What Is It For?"; C. D. B. Mills, "Zoroaster and His Religion"; and Frothingham, "The Religion of Humanity." This last piece Morse described as "the outlines of a new rational religion," and it was published in book form in 1872.[9]

Notes

1. Sidney H. Morse, "Religion," *Radical* 1 (September 1865): 4.

2. Morse, "Notes," *Radical* 2 (March 1867): 448.

3. O. B. Frothingham, "On Theodore Parker," *Radical* 6 (August 1869): 89–112; "The Radical Book-list," *Radical* 4 (December 1868): 485–87.

4. Ralph Waldo Emerson, "Address," *Radical* 1 (October 1865): 36.

5. Morse, "Notes," *Radical* 7 (January 1870): 67.

6. Morse asked, "Has the time not arrived when the cause demands of us all, that we come out from the midst of our opponents?" *Radical* 2 (November 1866): 186.

7. Morse, "The *Index*," *Radical* 6 (December 1869): 518. Abbot's reply, not an apology, had appeared in the *Radical* 2 (December 1866): 219–25.

8. Morse, "The *Index*" *Radical* 7 (February 1870): 158.

9. Morse, *Radical* 10 (April 1872): 310. Johnson, *Radical* 1 (November 1865): 73–85, (December 1865): 113–26, (January 1866): 154–68, (March 1866): 233–46, (May 1866): 313–25, (July 1866): 401–13; Frothingham, *Radical* 1 (August 1866): 449–58; Longfellow, *Radical* 2 (May 1867): 513–25; Abbot, *Radical* 2 (June 1867): 585–97; Frothingham, *Radical* 3 (September 1867): 11–17, (October 1867): 89–96, (November 1867): 149–54, (December 1867): 208–14, (January 1868): 284–92; About, *Radical* 3 (September 1867): 40–46, (October 1867): 121–28, (November 1867): 165–74, (December 1867): 243–54, (February 1868): 403–16, (March 1868): 487–95, (May 1868): 637–52; Weiss, *Radical* 5 (June 1869): 445–62; Frothingham, *Radical* 7 (June 1870): 433–49; Mills, *Radical* 9 (October 1871): 161–75, (November 1871): 261–77; Frothingham, *Radical* 10 (April 1872): 240–72, (May 1872): 321–36, (June 1872): 401–17.

Information Sources

BIBLIOGRAPHY:
Gohdes, Clarence L. F. *The Periodicals of American Transcendentalism*. Durham: Duke University Press, 1931.
Mott, Frank Luther. *A History of American Magazines, 1865–1885*.Cambridge: Harvard University Press, 1957.
INDEX SOURCES: *Poole's Index*.
REPRINT EDITIONS: University Microfilms International.
LOCATION SOURCES: Library of Congress, Yale University, Princeton University, University of Texas-Austin, Harvard University, University of Chicago, and others.

Publication History

MAGAZINE TITLE AND TITLE CHANGES: *The Radical: A Journal for Social and Religious Culture* 1 (June-July 1865); *The Radical* 1 (September 1865)–10 (June 1872).
VOLUME AND ISSUE DATA: *Radical: A Journal for Social and Religious Culture* 1 (June-July 1865); *Radical* 1 (September 1865)–7 (June 1870), 8 (February 1871)–10 (June 1872).
PUBLISHER AND PLACE OF PUBLICATION: A William & Co., Boston.
EDITORS: Sidney H. Morse (1865–67), Sidney H. Morse and Joseph B. Marvin (1867–69), Sidney H. Morse (1869–72).
CIRCULATION: 500 (est.).

Stephen H. Snyder

RECORDER. *See* CONGREGATIONALIST AND HERALD OF GOSPEL LIBERTY

RECORDER AND TELEGRAPH. *See* CONGREGATIONALIST AND HERALD OF GOSPEL LIBERTY

REFORMED JOURNAL

The appearance of the *Reformed Journal* in March 1951 was the culmination of the vision of five men: cousins George Stob and Henry Stob, James Daane, Harry Boer, and Henry Zylstra. While devoted to the Christian Reformed Church, these five desired an independent periodical that would consider current issues apart from denominational publications. If a single theme has characterized the journal, it is that of viewing denominational and societal concerns from a prophetic and critical stance within the Reformed tradition.

As a distinctly ethnic denomination, the Christian Reformed Church drew from its rich Reformed tradition in the Netherlands, but in the United States it was confronted with Americanization—the process of adapting to the American way of life. Both of these phenomena shaped the denomination and provided the context out of which the journal was born. Three patterns have shaped the denomination's life. In a 1974 article in the journal, Nicholas Wolterstorff called them pietism, doctrinalism, and "Kuyperianism."[1] Pietism denoted an emphasis on disciplined devotional life and separation from society, but its effect, said Wolterstorff, was to measure spiritual achievement by adherence to such activities as daily devotions, keeping the Sabbath, and other proscriptions relating to individual conduct. As well, the tradition emphasized doctrinalism, acceptance of and adherence to correct doctrine. Hence elucidation and clarification of doctrine has been "an immensely important enterprise."[2] "Kuyperianism" takes its name from Abraham Kuyper, Dutch theologian and national leader of the Netherlands in the later nineteenth century. Kuyperians did not deny the importance of the other two emphases but believed that the proper response to the gospel was to reform society in accordance with God's laws and precepts. Their concern was to penetrate society and make it conform to God's laws. The problem, then, confronting both the denomination and the journal was the proper balance of these three, complicated by Americanization.

When the Kuyperian agenda received a fresh hearing at the Free (Reformed) University of Amsterdam in the 1920s and 1930s, its effects were felt at the Christian Reformed Church's Calvin College and Seminary. In partial response to these currents, the *Calvin Forum* was established by a group of academics at the college and seminary in 1935 to promote the Kuyperian cultural imperative. World War II interrupted their plans. In addition and more important, the denominational hierarchy was less receptive to Kuyperianism than to pietism and doctrinalism. At the war's end, the denomination faced a critical juncture. By the early 1950s, new theological currents, questions of interchurch relations, standards of separation from worldliness, and the role of the church in a secular society threatened Christian Reformed ethnic insularity. The journal's editors represented a minority voice of intellectuals who felt that these concerns and the direction of the church needed further articulation. They were also a homogeneous group. All five were Dutch and were associated in some way (by education and/or teaching experience) with Calvin College and Seminary.

The history of the *Reformed Journal* can be roughly divided into two periods. During its first two decades, the journal reflected an "in-house" mentality (as George Stob put it). It dealt primarily with theological, ecclesiastical, and practical issues of concern to the Christian Reformed Church. By the late 1960s, the editors shifted the content to reach a wider audience. There were several reasons for reorientation. By then the issues of earlier years had been addressed, resolved, or discarded. Also, the *Journal* was attracting evangelical readers outside the denomination. Finally, the addition of Nicholas Wolterstorff and Richard Mouw to the editorial board brought the new blood of a younger generation whose concerns were wider than specific denominational issues.

The subject matter of the *Journal* in its first two decades varied from philosophy, theology, social ethics, ecclesiology, and reviews of literature, but there was a preoccupation with denominational concerns. Always the impact of the Kuyperian tradition is discernible, while the pietistic and doctrinal aspects of the Reformed faith were downplayed, questioned, revised, or clarified.

The question of the denomination's posture toward such worldly amusements as movie attendance, dancing, and card playing was raised several times. To the editors, prohibitions of these kinds of entertainment reflected the unfavorable side of American fundamentalism, resulting in a legalism that defined Reformed faith by personal standards of separation. A more balanced view, argued Henry Stob, would recognize the necessity of personal discernment over legislation for all.[3]

One long-standing issue predating the *Journal* was the labor question: would Christian Reformed members compromise loyalty to the faith by taking an oath of loyalty to a union? In the early 1950s this question revolved around whether the AFL and CIO were anti-Christian or neutral labor organizations. More specifically, the issue revolved around the awarding of building contracts for the Calvin College Commons Building to contractors who hired union labor. Behind this issue lay a larger question: should church members withdraw into their own enclaves and form their own separate organizations, or should they engage the world in dialogue and seek to influence existing social structures? The *Reformed Journal* editors, showing Kuyperian sympathies, supported the latter approach. That this issue was explosive is indicated by the amount of ink spilled and passions expressed on both sides over a 12-year period (to 1964) in the journal's pages.[4]

Another social concern was race relations. During the journal's first year, editors George Stob and Harry Boer favorably reported on the position taken by the Young Calvinists on black-white relations.[5] This denominational youth organization issued a statement urging evangelism to and fellowship with blacks. Not until 1969, however, did a specific racial issue confront the Christian Reformed Church on a large scale: the Lawndale-Cicero problem. From 1965 to 1969 black parents from the Lawndale Christian Reformed Church in Chicago sought admission for their children at the nearest denominational school, located in the all-white, racist community of Cicero. The school board denied their admission. The *Journal*'s editors and contributors urged admission as a matter of Christian conviction and love. The issue was practically resolved when the school in Cicero moved to the western suburb of Elmhurst where a Christian Reformed school already admitted blacks. Yet for the editors, this solution deflected the primary issue of racism.[6]

In dealing with practice and doctrine, though, the journal came into more direct conflict with the denomination. Missions is one example. "The path we have followed," wrote Harry Boer from Nigeria in 1954, "effective though it has been in keeping the CRC a compact Dutch-American community, has only one defect. Our missionary effort remains sterile, relatively fruitless, and on the whole quite frustrating. . . . Is our concern to protect the CR status quo worth being poor in fruits to present to Christ?"[7] Boer's criticisms became more strident, causing the Grand Rapids South classis to suggest disciplinary action. The threat confirmed the denomination's defensive posture. For others, the sociological reasons Boer offered could not fully answer the lack of missionary outreach. Harold Dekker wrote a series of articles that spawned a controversy known as the Dekker case, or the "love of God controversy." Dekker contended that it was biblical to say "God loves all men" and since that love was expressed by Christ on the cross, it was also acceptable to proclaim that "Christ died for you."[8] A study committee of the Synod of 1964 accepted Dekker's first proposition, with qualifications, but rejected the second. More debate ensued, various rulings were made by subsequent synods, and finally the 1967 Synod admonished Dekker for literary and methodological faults. The *Journal*'s editors were dissatisfied because issues were left unresolved.

Biblical infallibility also provoked controversy. Marvin Hoogland wrote an article for a Calvin Seminary student publication in which he questioned the scientific and grammatical accuracy of Scripture. The *Journal* ran nearly 20 articles from 1959 to 1961 addressing this and related issues of inerrancy and inspiration.

In these controversies, the *Reformed Journal* fulfilled its self-appointed role as a forum for openness and debate. But since the late 1960s, denominational issues and prolonged controversies have receded into the background as the *Journal* has sought a broader evangelical clientele. Articles have treated such topics as social engagement, the Moral Majority, women's place in the church, abortion, homosexuality, pornography, liturgical renewal, and sacramental theology. Thus the *Reformed Journal* remains "a periodical of Reformed comment and opinion," as its subcaption suggests, offering to readers a window to the world through the eyes of the Reformed faith.

Notes

1. Nicholas Wolterstorff, "The AACS in the CRC," *Reformed Journal* 24:10 (1974): 10.

2. Ibid.

3. See Henry Stob, "What Did 1928 Say?" *Reformed Journal* 1:3 (1951): 11–13;

"The Majority Report Examined . . . 'Worldly Amusements,' " *Reformed Journal* 1:4 (1951): 5–9; "Synod on Worldly Amusements," *Reformed Journal* 1:5 (1951): 5–7; "Movies, Television and the Christian," *Reformed Journal* 2:2 (1952): 10–12.

4. The following are only George Stob's *Reformed Journal* articles on labor: "The Church and the Labor Problem," 2:6 (1952): 13–15; "The Heart of the Matter," 2:7 (1952): 14–16; "The Christian and the Labor Union," 3:5 (1953): 5–8; "World Calling— Separation or Involvement," 3:9 (1953): 10–12; "The Christian Duty toward Society," 4:2 (1954): 8–10; "Synod 1956 on the Labor Question," 6:8 (1956): 9–12; "Critical Issues in the Labor Problem," 6:10 (1956): 4–8; "The Burden of the Laboring Man," 7:2 (1957): 3–8.

5. George Stob, "Negro Evangelism," *Reformed Journal* 1:6 (1951): 1–2; Harry R. Boer, "The Young Calvinists on the Race Question," *Reformed Journal* 1:7 (1951): 2– 4, 7–10; Boer, "One Fellowship in Christ," *Reformed Journal* 1:9 (1951): 3–5. See also "Young Calvinists on the Race Question," *Reformed Journal* 1:5 (1951): 12; and Clarence Boomsma, "Cursed Be—Whom?" *Reformed Journal* 1:6 (1951): 6–8.

6. See Nicholas P. Wolterstorff, "When Did We See Thee?" *Reformed Journal* 19:9 (1969): 2–3; "An Event That Shames Us All," *Reformed Journal* 20:3 (1970): 2–13; Wolterstorff, "Eternity or Lawndale," *Reformed Journal* 20:4 (1970): 2–3; "One of America's in Crisis," *Reformed Journal* 20:5 (1970): 5–13; Martin LaVlaire, "Acts of a Minor Assembly," *Reformed Journal* 21:1 (1971): 14–17; and George Stob's contributions to *Reformed Journal*: "Cicero, the Gospel, and the Integrity of the Church," 21:7 (1971): 8–13; "Where Is Your Brother?" 21:8 (1971): 9–11; "Who Will Show Any Good?" 22:1 (972): 8–11; and "Busing for Reconciliation,"22:5 (1972): 6–7.

7. Harry R. Boer, "The Christian Reformed Church and the American World," *Reformed Journal* 4:11 (1954): 8.

8. Harold Dekker, "God So Loved—All Men!" *Reformed Journal* 22:11 (1972): 7.

Information Sources

INDEX SOURCES: *Christian Periodical Index, Religious and Theological Abstracts, Religion Index One.*

LOCATION SOURCES: Calvin College and Seminary Library, Union Theological Seminary (New York), Princeton Theological Seminary, Union Theological Seminary (Virginia), Yale University, Concordia Theological Seminary, McCormick Theological Seminary, New Brunswick Theological Seminary.

Publication History

MAGAZINE TITLE AND TITLE CHANGES: *Reformed Journal* (1951–   ).

VOLUME AND ISSUE DATA: 1:1–10 (monthly, March-December 1951), 2–3:1–12 (monthly, 1952–53), 4–12:1–11 (monthly, with combined July-August issue, 1954– 62), 13–26:1–10 (monthly, with combined May-June and July-August issues, 1963–76), 27–30:1–12 (monthly, 1977–80); 31:1–11 (monthly, combined November-December issue, 1981–   ).

PUBLISHER AND PLACE OF PUBLICATION: William B. Eerdmans, Grand Rapids, Mich.

EDITORS: Harry R. Boer (1951–   ), James Daane (1951–65, 1966–   ), George Stob, (1951–79), Henry Stob (1951–79), Henry Zylstra (1951–57), Lester DeKoster

(1957–69), Lewis B. Smedes (1964–   ), Nicholas Wolterstorff (1979–   ), John Timmerman (1981–   ), Richard Mouw (1972–   ), George Marsden (1980–   ), Marlin VanElderen (1982–   ).
CIRCULATION: 3000 (1984).

David Kling

RELIGION IN LIFE. *See* QUARTERLY REVIEW

RELIGIOUS EDUCATION

Religious Education is the official scholarly journal of the Religious Education Association, organized in 1903 by a group of predominantly white, male, urban Progressives. They founded the journal three years later as a "center, a clearing house, a bureau of information," for the promotion of moral and religious education in public education. According to an early statement, "The threefold purpose of the Religious Education Association is: to inspire the educational forces of our country with the religious ideal, to inspire the religious forces of our country with the educational ideal, and to keep before the public mind the ideal of Religious Education and the sense of its need and value."[1] At the outset, the Religious Education Association was influenced by the Progressive dream of establishing a "democracy of God" through moral and religious education, but the journal and the association have shifted along with changing theological and educational currents.

Three persons were central to the founding of both the association and the journal: William Rainey Harper, president of the University of Chicago; George Albert Coe, professor at Teacher's College, Columbia University; and Henry F. Cope, general secretary of the association from 1906 to 1923. Harper died in 1906, passing intellectual leadership of the enterprise to Coe. To a large extent, Coe was the mentor of the entire religious education movement. Theologically to the left of mainline Protestantism in rejecting evil as an irremediable flaw in human nature, he celebrated the social force of education as a sure avenue toward the Kingdom of God.[2] Through the collaborative efforts of Sunday Schools, young people's societies, the YMCAs and YWCAs, catechisms, and lesson plans, society, in his mind, would be culturally transformed. Cope, on the other hand, was the administrative catalyst of the organization and oversaw the publication of the journal. Throughout its first 20 years, under Coe's and Cope's leadership, the journal "raised the question of religious and moral values in relationship to public education."[3]

The principal accomplishment of the journal in its early years was to provide support for Sunday Schools and churches. To this end, it successfully promoted the use of contemporary pedagogical techniques and graded lesson plans in religious instruction, and it stimulated the practice of critical biblical scholarship in adult education programs of the churches. The articles therefore struck an optimistic note that nurture was the key to unlocking innate human religious sensibilities. But scant attention was paid to either Catholic religious educators or the Protestant fundamentalists, to women or blacks (apart from echoing racial stereotypes). Several Jewish authors, however, published in its pages. As well, neither the association nor the journal had much impact in influencing public education to become a forum for character and moral education. In time, the journal became supportive of the new professionals, the directors of religious education being hired by large, mainline Protestant churches. On the whole, then, the journal in its formative years reflected the values and the aspirations of its white, liberal, male founders and constituencies.

Cope's death in 1923 left a leadership void, eventuating in an outside evaluation of the association. According to Stephen Schmidt, who has examined the unpublished portion of the evaluative review, critics claimed that Coe and Cope had excessively dominated the journal's pages, authoring 36 and 27 articles, respectively. Hence the journal exaggerated the importance of the behaviorist psychology and deterministic philosophy to which they were sympathetic.[4] Under the administrative leadership of Joseph M. Artman, named general secretary of the association in 1926, the group hoped to broaden its focus, as well as that of its journal. Expansionism was the word of the day. Increasingly the periodical became a professional journal with more articles by academics, a better book review section, and greater coverage of international educational efforts and controversial issues. For example, articles addressed war and peace issues, papal infallibility, the nature of biblical authority, and the need for the churches to take stands on social issues. Artman's attempt to change the name of the journal to *Character* to mirror his commitment to character education rather than religious education failed, but he did gain support to launch a companion journal that emphasized secular rather than religious approaches to public morality.

In the 1930s, *Religious Education* also sought to incorporate perspectives other than those reflecting Protestant views. Numerous articles explore Jewish-Catholic-Protestant dialogue, race relations, native American Indians, and the concerns of other ethnic minorities, as well as those identified with women. The journal, however, continued to regard race as almost exclusively a southern problem, and its openness to women's issues still limited its orientation to female contributions within the traditional nuclear family. But the depression of the 1930s brought hard times financially to the association and the journal, a loss of membership, and a decline in readership (causing the publication to become a quarterly rather than a monthly in 1934). As well, the founding generation of optimistic liberals was being replaced by those who imbibed the neo-orthodox theological currents associated with Karl Barth, Emil Brunner, and Reinhold Niebuhr. While the liberal old guard had difficulty adjusting to theological shifts, the upshot of the new currents was the reconsideration of religious education as specifically Christian education.

The new focus became clear by the 1950s, when Yale's Randolph Crump

Miller began a 20-year tenure as editor (1958–78), Herman Wornom served as general secretary of the association (1952–70), and Union Theological Seminary's Lewis J. Sherrill exerted considerable influence on both the journal and the association. Miller brought to bear his passion for seeking a mediating position between neo-orthodoxy and liberalism, Sherrill his commitment to the individual psychological dimensions of education, and Wornom his skill in increasing the size of the organization (including the addition of Catholics and Jews to its governing board) and enriching the academic reputation of the journal. As *Religious Education* became more ecumenical, it also treated with more seriousness Catholic and Jewish contributions to religious education. But it also backed away from dealing with the controversial social issues of the 1950s and 1960s: nuclear war, civil rights, women's rights, Vietnam, and the like (though the association confronted all of them at its annual conventions).

But an underlying concern, typified in the analysis offered by John Westerhoff in introducing an anthology of articles from the journal, was one of identity.[5] Did either the association or the journal have a clear sense of identity as they simultaneously affirmed pluralism and cooperation, diversity and unity, apart from engagement in the issues of the times? Regardless of how history resolves that question, in the early 1980s the Religious Education Association and *Religious Education*, with a circulation hovering near 5500, remain important forums for the dissemination of educational ideas to church schools and for sharing ideas in religious education among Protestant, Catholic, and Jewish religious educators.

Notes

1. *Religious Education* 1 (1906–07): 2.
2. George Albert Coe, *A Social Theory of Religious Education* (New York: Scribners, 1923), pp. 53–54.
3. Stephen A. Schmidt, *A History of the Religious Education Association* (Birmingham: Religious Education Press, 1981), p. 43.
4. Ibid., pp. 60–63.
5. John H. Westerhoff, ed., *Who Are We? The Quest for a Religious Education* (Birmingham: Religious Education Press, 1978), p. 13.

Information Sources

BIBLIOGRAPHY:
Schmidt, Stephen A. *A History of the Religious Education Association.* Birmingham: Religious Education Press, 1981.
Westerhoff, John H., ed. *Who Are We? The Quest for a Religious Education.* Birmingham: Religious Education Press, 1978.
INDEX SOURCES: *Education Index, Religion Index One, Religious and Theological Abstracts, Current Contents, Psychological Abstracts, Index to Jewish Periodicals, International Index to Periodicals, Sociological Abstracts.*
REPRINT EDITIONS: University Microfilms International.

LOCATION SOURCES: Claremont College, University of Texas-Austin, Union Theological Seminary (New York), University of Chicago, Duke University, Emory University, Harvard University, and others.

Publication History

MAGAZINE TITLE AND TITLE CHANGES: *Religious Education: The Journal of the Religious Education Association* (1906–   ).

VOLUME AND ISSUE DATA: 1:1 (1906–   ). Monthly until 1934, quarterly thereafter.

PUBLISHER AND PLACE OF PUBLICATION: Religious Education Association, Chicago (1906–48), Oberlin, Ohio (1948–58), New Haven (1958–78), Durham, N.C. (1978–   ).

EDITORS: Henry F. Cope (1906–23), Frank G. Ward (1923–24), George Albert Coe (1924–26, 1935–48), Laird T. Hites (1926–29), Joseph M. Artman (1929–35), Leonard A. Stidley (1948–58), Randolph Crump Miller (acting, 1956–57; 1958–78); acting, 1984–   ). Paul H. Vieth (acting, 1959–60, 1966–67, 1970), John H. Westerhoff III (1978–84).

CIRCULATION: 5500 (1984).

James B. Hunt

RELIGIOUS HUMANISM

Religious Humanism was first published in its present form in 1967 as a successor to the *Religious Humanism Bulletin* of the Fellowship of Religious Humanists. The humanist movement was and is made up of those who regard "reason as the chief means of solving problems and the belief that mankind can survive and humans can enjoy a significant life."[1] Some adherents enlarged on that intellectual point by carefully examining the tenets of world religions and moving beyond them to the concept of interior spiritual guidance based on scientific truth. Persons of this ilk formed the Fellowship of Religious Humanists in 1963. Affiliated with the American Humanist Association and the Unitarian-Universalist Association, the fellowship has spearheaded a movement based on a naturalistic thesis combined with the accumulated discoveries of the human spirit as the basis for meaning in life.

Religious Humanism serves as the fellowship's quarterly forum for education and discussion of humanistic issues and acts as a "bridge organization among ethical, philosophic, and religious non-conformists who have a naturalistic emphasis and orientation."[2] In keeping with these aims, the journal provides for open discussion of any subject pertaining to the general scope of humanistic interests. The first issue was published at the Humanist Center, Yellow Springs, Ohio. Edwin H. Wilson was the first editor, with the editorship subsequently revolving among the officers of the fellowship. Paul H. Beattie and Lucinda Beattie are the current editors. Each issue contains articles, commentaries, book reviews, poetry, letters, and short biographical descriptions of the contributors.

The main educational tasks of *Religious Humanism* are to explain the concept of religious humanism itself to those who believe that humanism and religion are mutually exclusive and then to explore selected topics from that viewpoint. As John Wren Lewis pointed out in an early essay in the quarterly, a religious viewpoint in a scientific world need not be anachronistic if worldly realities are faced instead of denied in the facile assumption that the world is a stage prop for some larger metaphysical drama. The scientific age has done away with many traditional spiritual beliefs, but Lewis argued that religion could be strengthened and expanded if humans took their "inner imaginative life seriously as something worthy of attention in its own right."[3]

Lester Mondale further developed this theme in his definitive article, "What Is a Humanist and What Does He Do about It?"[4] Examining various humanistic movements as they emerged chronologically, he skillfully built the argument for religious humanists today by comparing them favorably with like-minded scholars and activists of the past. He claimed that there was a bond of common ancestry in that all persons are *homo sapiens*, that Marxists, existentialists, and Jesuits are all linked in spite of their differing ideologies. A contemporary humanist's beliefs are thus the natural outcome of all previous humanistic movements. Humanists can celebrate the essential oneness of humanity because they are "looking on Sundays and throughout the week for something more . . . satisfying to live for than either the golden streets of a heaven in the hereafter or the heaven of . . . suburban values in the here and now."[5]

An essay that clearly illustrates the spirit behind *Religious Humanism* is Joseph Fletcher's "An Odyssey: From Theology to Humanism" (Autumn 1979).[6] In this essay, Fletcher explains how he went from being an Anglican theologian to a secular humanist. He points out that formal religion lost all appeal for him in part because religious "enthusiasm" had clouded the real issue of true righteous living. For him, the only way to be at peace with himself and his friends, agnostic and Christian of many dogmas, was to turn to the "free man's worship" (citing Bertrand Russell) and simply accept and live by what one knows. Contained in this short essay is the spirit of tolerance for others, along with the loving concern for all of humanity, that permeate the whole of the quarterly's offerings.

Religious Humanism may be characterized as providing a loose collection of articles dealing with humanistic questions, but it serves a purpose in offering an exchange of ideas among a self-selected, generally highly educated readership, those humanists who feel that a spiritual religious experience is a necessary part of their existence.

Notes

1. Paul Kurtz, ed., *The Humanist Alternative* (Buffalo: Prometheus Books, 1973), p. 7.

2. *Religious Humanism* 1:1 (1967): 2.

3. Ibid., p. 4.

4. Ibid. 7:3 (1973): 100.

5. Ibid., p. 107.

6. Ibid. 13:4 (1979).

Information Sources

INDEX SOURCES: *Guide to Social Science and Religion in Periodical Literature, Philosopher's Index, Arts and Humanities Citation Index, Religious and Theological Abstracts.*

REPRINT EDITIONS: University Microfilms International.

LOCATION SOURCES: Yale University, University of California-Santa Barbara, Union Theological Seminary (New York), Library of Congress, Duke University, University of Texas-Austin, and others.

Publication History

MAGAZINE TITLE AND TITLE CHANGES: *Religious Humanism* (1967–   ).

VOLUME AND ISSUE DATA: 1:1 (Winter 1967–   ). Appears quarterly.

PUBLISHER AND PLACE OF PUBLICATION: Fellowship of Religious Humanists, Yellow Springs, Ohio.

EDITORS: Edwin H. Wilson (1967–70), Robert S. Hoagland (1970–77), Harold Hadley (1977–81), Paul and Lucinda Beattie (1981–   ).

CIRCULATION: 1500 (1983).

Linda K. Varkonda

RELIGIOUS HUMANISM BULLETIN. *See* RELIGIOUS HUMANISM

RELIGIOUS STUDIES REVIEW

After years of planning, in 1974 the Council on the Study of Religion, a federation of the nine most learned and prestigious societies in the field of religious studies in the United States and Canada, announced a forthcoming new publication. It was to be a quarterly journal devoted to the review of books, articles, issues, and research in the field of religion and related areas and would be named *Religious Studies Review*. A carefully worked out network of scholars from the United States and Canada would contribute to this major undertaking, and their work would be skillfully coordinated by five editors, while the directing general of the operation would be the managing editor, Harold Remus of Wilfrid Laurier University and the Council on the Study of Religion. Remus brought years of expertise in publishing to the new journal. Within a few years, it had become the major review journal of publications in the field of religion and related disciplines in the United States and Canada.

The inaugural issue appeared in September 1975. In the years following, issues appeared in January, April, July, and October, with the annual index always appearing in the October number. Remus's editorial comments also appeared in each issue's "Postscript."

The journal appeared in the larger context of learned societies in religion arriving at a "heightened self-consciousness about 'scholarly communication and publication.' "[1] In fact a special task force of the Council on the Study of Religion (CSR) with the assignment of studying the question produced a volume with the title *Scholarly Communication and Publication*. Developing a journal dedicated solely to reviewing was only one of numerous options suggested for attaining the goals of a thorough coverage of publications. But this option was picked up by the CSR as it authorized the publication of *Religious Studies Review* (*RSR*) on the recommendation of its Research and Publications Committee, chaired at the time by Robert Funk. The new journal would not rival but would rather complement existing journals in the field.

Through the years, *RSR* has sought to meet three interrelated needs in the field of studies in religion: "(1) The need for intensive and extensive evaluation of major works in the field of religion by the best qualified persons. (2) The need for brief assessments of the large current body of literature about religion. (3) The need for literary discussion among the subdisciplines of religious studies and between religious studies and related disciplines."[2]

These goals have been achieved in a variety of ways. Each issue publishes a limited number of reviews of major works in religion, allowing the reviewers 4000 words or more per review and sometimes reviewing certain works from more than one point of view. This is an illustration, also, of the interdisciplinary commitment of *RSR*. Retrospective reviews are sometimes done of a most important work or of an important corpus or author. Reviews of the state of the art in a particular discipline or subdiscipline often appear. "Notes on Recent Publications" fill the second stated goal, with hundreds of works being critically assessed by a wide range of scholars from a delicately balanced network of reviewers in every area of religious studies across the United States and Canada. In relation to the third goal, major bibliographical essays appear that contribute to interdisciplinary study and communication. Interdisciplinary topics hold an especially lively interest for those involved in religious studies, and this remains a major contribution of *RSR*. Other services include lists of reprintings and lists of dissertations completed, as well as of those in progress, in religious studies as provided by the Council on Graduate Studies in Religion.

Reception of *RSR* has been positive and appreciative, largely because the editorial board and the managing editor have been committed to the principle of openness and the concept of a journal *in via*. Ongoing evaluations come from an advisory committee, as well as from suggestions from the wide network of reviewing scholars and readers. The editors remain sensitive to changing times and the needs of its readers. This attitude has sustained the most qualitative review journal in the field of religious studies in the United States and Canada, *Religious Studies Review*.

Notes

1. *Religious Studies Review* 1:1 (1973): 63.
2. White paper distributed at the 1974 meetings of the American Academy of Religion and Society of Biblical Literature.

Information Sources

INDEX SOURCES: Self-indexed in the October issue each year; also in *Religion Index One, New Testament Abstracts, Old Testament Abstracts*.

LOCATION SOURCES: Yale University, University of Chicago, Princeton University, University of North Carolina-Charlotte, University of California-Riverside,Texas A&M University, and others.

Publication History

MAGAZINE TITLE AND TITLE CHANGES: *Religious Studies Review* (1975–   ).

VOLUME AND ISSUE DATA: 1:1 (January 1975   ). Appears quarterly in January, April, July, October.

PUBLISHER AND PLACE OF PUBLICATION: Wilfrid Laurier University, Waterloo, Ontario, Canada.

EDITOR: Harold Remus (managing editor, 1975–   ).

CIRCULATION: 2900 (1983).

George H. Shriver

THE RELIGIOUS TELESCOPE. *See* THE TELESCOPE-MESSENGER

REVIEW OF RELIGIOUS RESEARCH

In 1959 the Religious Research Association published the first volume of its journal, *Review of Religious Research*. The journal was established to publish and disseminate the association's lectures in honor of Harlan Paul Douglass, pioneering researcher in the sociology of religion. Another purpose of the journal was to draw academics into an association whose roots went back to attempts by Protestant churches to achieve "interfaith comity" in the 1920s.[1]

A precursor to the association was the Religious Research Fellowship organized 21 June 1951. The fellowship was formed in part to contend with the dissolution of the Committee for Cooperative Field Research, headed by Douglass, when the National Council of Churches was formed. The fellowship consisted at the outset of a group of 56 members known as the Augmented Technical Staff, basically a research staff for Protestant churches. The technical staff chose to reorganize as the fellowship in order to become an independent, interfaith group not specifically tied to Protestant denominations.

The goals of the fellowship and, later, the association were (1) to improve the quality of research among its members, (2) to expand contacts with scholars in the sociology of religion, (3) to achieve and establish professional standards for the development and use of social research on religion, and (4) to move beyond intrafaith Protestant ties to interfaith contacts among Catholics and Jews.[2] Thus, originating out of a predominantly Protestant background, the fellowship and the association have increasingly moved toward professionalization of standards. A large number of members still retain close ties to ecclesiastical organizations. Rank-and-file membership is predominantly academic; as early as 1973, 54 percent were college or university faculty.[3]

With the formation of the Society for the Scientific Study of Religion in 1949 and the publication of its journal, the *Journal for the Scientific Study of Religion*,* the focus of the Religious Research Association began to center on the denominations.[4] By 1964, the Board of the Religious Research Association affirmed the policy that it was not only concerned with fostering professional standards of research and methodology but was also "interested in bringing the theory and methods and empirical approach of social science research to the service of organized religion."[5] This emphasis on service to ecclesiastical organizations was affirmed in an April 1977 policy statement by the board that articles written for the *Review of Religious Research* would have to have "usable implications ... for policy decisions of religious organizations."[6]

As a vehicle for the publication of empirical research for organized religion, the *Review* has provided important contributions to knowledge in the field of the sociology of religion. As one of three journals in the field, it has provided a forum for the theoretical, methodological, and empirical research of such scholars as Gerhard Lenski, Seymour Martin Lipset, Gibson Winter, Horace R. Clayton, Liston Pope, Walter Muelder, Thomas O'Dea, Jay Demerath, Philip Hammond, Samuel Klausner, and those who have given the prestigious Harlan Paul Douglass Lectures. Some of the important or seminal articles that have appeared in its pages include a study of "unchurched Americans" (Summer 1980); Gordon F. DeJong and Joseph E. Faulkner, "Religion and Intellectuals" (Fall 1972); James D. Davidson, "Patterns of Belief at the Denominational and Congregational Levels" (Spring 1972); Samuel A. Mueller, "The New Triple Melting Pot: Herberg Revisited" (Fall 1971); David Elkind, "The Origins of Religion in the Child" (Fall 1970); and Charles Y. Glock and Rodney Stark, "The 'New Denominationalism' " (Fall 1965).

A 1973 survey of its 335 members found that the Religious Research Association continued to be predominantly male (94 percent), Protestant (73.2 percent), clergy (62 percent ordained), and well educated (65 percent with doctorates). By 1983, membership had increased to 434, and there were 593 subscribers to the journal. Most of the members are clustered in the Northeast, Chicago, Atlanta, Los Angeles, and San Francisco. Over 70 percent also belong to the Society for the Scientific Study of Religion. The two associations have held joint meetings in Denver and Boston.

In 1980 the *Review of Religious Research* became a quarterly, reaffirming its goals of publishing broader articles, such as the Douglass Lectures, and denominational research, whereas the shorter, more scientifically and interdisciplinary articles are published by the *Journal for the Scientific Study of Religion*. *Sociological Analysis* publishes the more theoretical pieces in the sociology of religion. Each journal in the field thus has its own market, with the central emphasis of the *Review of Religious Research* being the more applied denominational research along with broader statements in the sociology of religion.

Notes

1. Jeffrey K. Hadden, "A Brief Social History of the Religious Research Association," *Review of Religious Research* 15 (Spring 1974): 128–29. Also see Jeffrey K. Hadden, "H. Paul Douglass: His Perspective and His Work," *Review of Religious Research* 22 (September 1980): 66–88.

2. Hadden, "Social History," p. 130.

3. Ibid., p. 132.

4. William M. Newman, "The Society for the Scientific Study of Religion: The Development of an Academic Society," *Review of Religious Research* 15 (Spring 1974): 142–45.

5. Form letter signed by Hart M. Nelsen, ed., *Review of Religious Research*, ca. 1977.

6. David O. Moberg, "Characteristics and Perspectives of Religious Research Association Constituents," *Review of Religious Research* 15 (Spring 1974): 173–75; telephone interview, 7 November 1983, with Constant Jacquet, Development Committee chair, Religious Research Association.

Information Sources

BIBLIOGRAPHY:

Hadden, Jeffrey K. "A Brief Social History of the Religious Research Association." *Review of Religious Research* 15 (1974): 128–36.

INDEX SOURCES: *Religious and Theological Abstracts, Religion Index One, Sociological Abstracts, Current Contents, Social Sciences Citation Index.*

REPRINT EDITIONS: University Microfilms International.

LOCATION SOURCES: Union Theological Seminary (New York), Yale University, Princeton Theological Seminary, University of North Carolina-Chapel Hill, University of Southern California, Rice University, and others.

Publication History

MAGAZINE TITLE AND TITLE CHANGES: *Review of Religious Research* (1959–).

VOLUME AND ISSUE DATA: 1:1 (Summer 1959–). Quarterly since 1980.

PUBLISHER AND PLACE OF PUBLICATION: Religious Research Association, New York (1959–60), Sandberg Printing Co., Minneapolis (1960–66), Mennonite Press, North Newton, Kansas (1966–).

EDITORS: Frederick A. Shippey (1959–64), Walter Kloetzli (1965), W. Widick Schroeder (1965–69), David O. Moberg (1969–73), Richard Knudten (1973–77), James Davidson (1978–80), Hart M. Nelsen (1980–84), Edward Lehman (1984–).

CIRCULATION: 600 (1983).

James B. Hunt

THE RUSSIAN AMERICAN ORTHODOX MESSENGER

The first issue of the *Russian American Orthodox Messenger* appeared on 1/ 13 September 1896 under the editorship of Father Alexander Hotovitsky, as the official organ of the North American Mission of the Russian Orthodox Church with the blessing of its bishop, Nicholas (Ziorov).[1] The ambitious goals Father Hotovitsky set for the periodical were similar to those set for other ethnic journals. It was established, he wrote at the end of the first year of publication,

> to proclaim in a non-Orthodox milieu the dogmatic and historical truths of Orthodoxy, both as a means of discovering the true teachings of the Church and of explaining and refuting opponents' errors;
>
> To defend the work of Russian Orthodoxy against vicious attacks in several local newspapers hostile toward the successes of the Russian missionaries in this country;
>
> To instill a feeling of love and commitment to their faith and homeland in all Orthodox immigrants from the "Old Country," so that inspired by them, they can not only withstand the influences of the surrounding non-Orthodox society, but influence it in return;
>
> While joining, by means of the printed word, the souls and hearts of these people to their homeland, at the same time, to invite readers in the Old World to participate in the life of their distant countrymen;
>
> To acquaint, gradually, the local non-Orthodox American readers with the true Russian person, with the spirit and customs of the Russian land, implanting in the American environment sympathy to our native people in the place of prejudice.[2]

The American Mission had only recently entered a new phase of its existence. It had been founded by Russian missionaries in Alaska in 1794 and was originally directed toward the conversion and support of the Alaskan natives: Aleuts, Eskimoes, and Tlingit Indians. A handful of immigrant parishes developed during the mid-nineteenth century, mainly in the major cities of the United States. In 1891, however, Father Alexis Toth of Minneapolis entered the Orthodox Church from the Roman Catholic Byzantine Rite (Unia) and brought his parish with him. This move began a wave of such conversions. By Father Toth's death in 1909, for example, nearly 30,000 Uniates had returned to the Orthodox Church, along with more than 15 parishes. This exodus was the cause of the "vicious attacks" mentioned by Father Hotovitsky, and the defense of the Mission against those attacks was a primary impetus for the establishment of the *Messenger*. By 1905, however, the need for such polemics was greatly reduced, and the *Messenger* turned to other matters, such as education and the assimilation of Orthodoxy to the American way of life.

Messenger articles attempted to address the various goals that had been set by Father Hotovitsky. The following articles appeared in the first issue: "Orthodoxy and Its Meaning in the Work of Salvation in Comparison with Hetero-doxy,'' by Bishop Nicholas (in Russian and English); ''Some Data on Orthodoxy in America''; ''Holy Days of the Orthodox Church''; a letter from Chicago describing a Baptist preacher's enthusiastic sermon on the occasion of the cor-onation of Czar Nicholas II; and official notices of ordinations, promotions, and transfers (all in Russian).[3] In the issues that followed, there were articles by Father Toth responding to attacks in the Uniate press, news of the Russian imperial family, reports of the bishop's travels around the country, and articles of theological and historical content.

During the early years, the primary contributor to the *Messenger* was Father Hotovitsky. This situation—the editor as the major contributor—was to last the life of the periodical. Later he was assisted by Fathers Alexander Nemolovsky and Leonid Turkevich, who also shared editorial responsibilities, Nemolovsky substituting for Hotovitsky during his trips to Russia and Turkevich succeeding Hotovitsky in 1914. The ethnic diversity of American Orthodoxy was also dem-onstrated in the pages of the *Messenger* during those early years. Father Sebastian Dabovich, a Serb; Father Raphael Hawaweeny, a Syrian; and Father Michael Andreades, a Greek; all contributed heavily. Two of them later went on to found their own journals. In 1905, Dabovich established the *Glasnik Srpske Crkve u Americi* (*Herald of the Serbian Church in America*, through 1906) and Hawa-weeny estabalished *Al Kalimat* (*The Word*, still the official publication of the Antiochian Orthodox Christian Archdiocese of North America). Also, before his consecration in 1909 as bishop of Alaska, Nemolovsky was editor of the Carpatho-Russian newspaper *Svit* (*The Light*), which, under his direction, merged editorial opinion with the *Messenger*.

The year 1917 brought an element of change to the American Mission and to the *Messenger*. In March Czar Nicholas II abdicated the throne of Russia, and, in October-November, the Bolsheviks took over. As a result, communication with the church in Russia was difficult at best, and the substantial funds that had kept the Mission running were cut off completely. In addition, Bolshevik sympathizers in the United States and Soviet intervention in church affairs made life even more difficult. Court battles for the control of the Mission and its parishes ensued. In the face of all this, publication of the *Messenger* faltered in 1917 and stopped completely in 1918.

The next few years were a time of groping for ways to cope with the new situation in which the North American Mission found itself. Archbishop Evdokim (Meschersky), who had headed the diocese since 1914, traveled to Russia in August 1917 to attend a church council. He never returned to the United States. Bishop Alexander (Nemolovsky), Evdokim's first assistant, was elected in 1919 to replace him but proved unequal to the task of guiding the Mission through such difficult times and left for Europe in 1922. Metropolitan Platon (Rozh-destvensky), who had headed the Mission from 1907 to 1914 and went on to become the metropolitan of Kherson and Odessa in the south of Russia by 1917, found his way to the United States as a refugee by 1921. Following Alexander's departure, Platon was elected to lead the diocese. Toward the end of this confusing period, in January 1922, the *Russian American Orthodox Messenger* reappeared, setting for itself the same goals as before.

After 1922, publication was interrupted twice. The entire year of 1928 was lost because of the closing of the printing plant.[4] In 1930, publication again stopped, most likely because of the economic crisis of the Depression, and was begun again in March 1936. The *Messenger* continued to be published until 1973. Two factors contributed to the final demise of the *Messenger*: rising costs in printing the magazine and declining subscriptions due, in part, to the establishment in 1965 of the *Orthodox Church*, the official English-language newspaper of the Orthodox Church in America.

Throughout most of its history, the *Messenger* was bilingual. In the early years, one or two of the articles in each issue were printed in English, frequently in parallel columns with the Russian. The difficulties of this procedure, however, led to the founding in 1902 of the *Russian Orthodox American Messenger Supplement*, an all-English monthly. While a complete run of the supplement does not exist, making full analysis impossible, it seems to have been directed primarily at Episcopalians, for whom the Russians felt a special affinity. The *Supplement* lasted until 1910, during which time the *Messenger* itself was entirely Russian. Following 1910, English returned to the *Messenger*, although on a much smaller scale than before. One or two articles in each issue continued to be printed in English until publication stopped in 1930. When publication resumed in 1936 under Father Feofan Buketoff, the *Messenger* was again entirely in Russian. During the 1940s, a small amount of English began to be used. Apparently if an article was submitted in English, it was printed in English. With the appearance of the all-English newspaper the *Orthodox Church* in 1965, the *Messenger* once again became entirely Russian.

Throughout its 69-year history, the *Russian American Orthodox Messenger* remained faithful to the task originally set for it, constantly striving to present the Orthodox faith to those within and without the Orthodox Church and to provide news and information about the church, both in the United States and throughout the world, to its readers.

Notes

1. The two dates indicate the difference between the Julian calendar, used in the Russian Empire and church, and the Gregorian calendar, used in the West. In the nineteenth century, the two calendars were 12 days apart, so that 1 September on the Julian calendar was the same day as 13 September on the Gregorian. In the twentieth century, the difference increased to 13 days.

2. *Russian Orthodox American Messenger* 1 (15/27 August 1897): 541.

3. "Novoe Izdanie: Pravoslavnyi Amerikanskii Viestnik" *Pribavleniia k tserkovnym viedomostiam* 9 (5 October 1896): 1468–69.

4. According to Father Turkevich, a special reference book covering 1928 would be published. Since it was to carry the sequential volume 29, there is no break in the numbering of volumes.

Information Sources

INDEX SOURCES: No comprehensive index to the *Russian American Orthodox Messenger* exists. An index to references to Alaska in the *Messenger* is being prepared by Barbara S. Smith of the Alaska Historical Commission.

REPRINT EDITIONS: Microform edition under preparation by the Library of Congress.

LOCATION SOURCES: No known complete collection; partial holdings at Archives of the Orthodox Church in America (Syosset, N.Y.), Library of Congress, St. Vladimir's Seminary, St. Herman's Seminary (Kodiak, Alaska), New York Public Library.

Publication History

MAGAZINE TITLE AND TITLE CHANGES: *Amerikanskii Pravoslavnyi Viestnik* (*The Russian Orthodox American Messenger*) (1896–1918), *Amerikanskii Pravoslavnyi Viestnik* (*The American Orthodox Messenger*) (1922–29), *Russko-Amerikanskii Pravoslavnyi Viestnik* (*The Russian American Orthodox Messenger*) (1930, 1936–73).

VOLUME AND ISSUE DATA: *Russian Orthodox American Messenger*: 1–22 (1/13 September 1896-October/November/December 1918 [single issue]), *American Orthodox Messenger* 23–30 (January 1922-December 1929); *Russian American Orthodox Messenger* 31, 32–69 (January 1930-October/November 1930 [single issue], March 1936-December 1973).

PUBLISHER AND PLACE OF PUBLICATION: The church was always the publisher under the name of the diocese of the Aleutian Islands and Alaska (1896–1900), diocese of the Aleutian Islands and North America (1900–7, archdiocese from 1905), Russian Orthodox Greek Catholic Church in North America (1907–70), Orthodox Church in America (1970–73); always published in New York except for 1928, when published in Cleveland, Ohio.

EDITORS: Alexander Hotovitsky (1896–1914), Leonid Turkevich (1914–30), Feofan Buketoff (1936–61), Boris Borisewitsch (1961), Alexis Yonov (1961–68), editorial committee consisting of Archbishop Sylvester (Haruns), Alexis Yonov, George Benigsen, and Cyril Fotiev (1968–69); Cyril Fotiev (1969–73).

CIRCULATION: Unknown.

Dennis R. Rhodes

THE RUSSIAN ORTHODOX AMERICAN MESSENGER.
See THE RUSSIAN AMERICAN ORTHODOX MESSENGER

RUSSKO-AMERIKANSKII PRAVOSLAVNYI VIESTNIK.
See THE RUSSIAN AMERICAN ORTHODOX MESSENGER

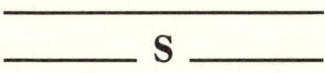

S

ST. LOUIS THEOLOGICAL MONTHLY. *See* LEHRE UND WEHRE

SAINT LUKE'S JOURNAL OF THEOLOGY

Saint Luke's Journal of Theology first appeared in 1957 at a time when the American South and the Episcopal Church were beginning to feel the stirrings of the civil rights movement and other social movements that challenged the status quo. The journal's editorial policy was "to provoke serious, scholarly consideration in the catholic tradition of the innumerable problems that are facing the Church at the present."[1]

During the first 15 years or so of its publication, the *Journal* served chiefly to provide a scholarly outlet for the students of the School of Theology of the University of the South and to serve as a vehicle for postordination continuing education for the school's alumni. During this period, almost every issue included one article written by a student, and students served as the editorial staff. One finds practical articles of interest to parish priests on church music, liturgics, pastoral theology, and the history of theology. The *Journal* also published papers originally delivered as endowed lectures and matriculation and baccalaureate sermons. Finally, short inspirational or devotional pieces appeared with some regularity.

The *Journal* then became caught up in the theological and political ferment of the late 1960s and early 1970s. Its pages reflect interest in and excitement about Harvey Cox's *Secular City*, J. A. T. Robinson's *Honest to God*, death of God theology, radical theology, and other trends of the day. One article uses an eisegesis of the lyrics of "Winchester Cathedral" (a popular song of the day) to convict the institutional church of indifference; another rests its theological reflections on the ideas in Charles Reich's *The Greening of America*. The *Journal* was the first periodical in the United States to publish an English translation of some of Ho Chi Minh's prison poems (11:4, 1967–68).

Beginning in the early 1970s and accelerating under the editorship of John M. Gessell, the *Journal* changed direction. Fewer papers by students and faculty appear, and there are fewer how-to essays for parochial clergy and more scholarly articles by people unconnected with the School of Theology or the Episcopal Church. Among the authors published are the Episcopalians John H. Westerhoff and O. C. Edwards and the Roman Catholics Theodore Hesburgh, Charles V. LaFontaine, and Henri J. M. Nouwen (the last as a reprint). Forty-three major articles appeared in the 10 issues between September 1979 and June 1982, of which only 30 percent (13) were on subjects of primary interest to Anglicans alone. Of the authors, 42 percent can be identified as Episcopalians. Topics include the new religious Right, sacramental confession in the Anglican tradition, the theologies of Schillebeeckx and Barth, alcoholism, homosexuality, and liturgical art.

Six issues have been devoted to special topics: "The Prayer Book Liturgy and the Proposed Revision" (1973); "Liturgics" (1974); "Papers from the Conference of Anglican Theologians on the Ordination of Women to the Priesthood and Episcopate" (1975; a joint issue with the *Nashotah Review*); "Religion in Appalachia" and "The Black Episcopalian: Evaluating the Past and Planning the Future" (both 1979); and "The Professional Model of Ministry—and Beyond" (1982).

In sum, the *Saint Luke's Journal of Theology* has evolved from its in-house origins to become one of the more significant regional organs in the Episcopal Church today. It draws heavily on contemporary Roman Catholic thought but within the context of a peculiarly Anglican interest in the historical approach and historical questions.

Note

1. *Saint Luke's Journal of Theology* 1 (1957–58): 3.

Information Sources

INDEX SOURCES: *Old Testament Abstracts, Religion Index One.*
REPRINT EDITIONS: University Microfilms International.
LOCATION SOURCES: Trinity College (Connecticut), University of the South, Louisiana State University, Boston University, Library of Congress.

Publication History

MAGAZINE TITLE AND TITLE CHANGES: *Saint Luke's Journal of Theology* (1957–   ).
VOLUME AND ISSUE DATA: 1 (December 1957–   ).
PUBLISHERS AND PLACES OF PUBLICATION: School of Theology, University of the South, Sewanee, Tenn.
EDITORS: For the first 21 years of publication, the journal was directed by student editors

who served one-year terms, under the supervision of a faculty committee headed by deans of the seminary, George M. Alexander (1957–1972) and Urban T. Holmes III (1973–76). Craig B. Anderson served as student editor for two years (1974–76), the only student to do so. The first permanent nonstudent editor was appointed in 1976: John M. Gessell (1976–   ).

CIRCULATION: 2500.

Denis G. Paz

ST. VINCENT DE PAUL QUARTERLY. *See* CATHOLIC CHARITIES REVIEW

ST. VLADIMIR'S SEMINARY QUARTERLY. *See* ST. VLADIMIR'S THEOLOGICAL QUARTERLY

ST. VLADIMIR'S THEOLOGICAL QUARTERLY

Since its initial publication in September 1952, the *St. Vladimir's Seminary Quarterly* (title changed in 1969 to *St. Vladimir's Theological Quarterly*) has served as a forum written in English for reflection about the Eastern Orthodox tradition in the United States. In addition, the founders of the journal, led by the Reverend Georges Florovsky (1893–1979), then dean of St. Vladimir's Orthodox Theological Seminary in New York City, expected that the *Quarterly* would also chronicle the life of the seminary. From its beginnings, the *Quarterly* has provided opportunities for St. Vladimir's faculty and others to communicate with academic and ecclesiastical colleagues within and beyond the Eastern Orthodox tradition.

As first editor in chief, Florovsky elaborated an agenda for the *Quarterly* that was also aimed at fortifying a fragile, heterogeneous group of Eastern Orthodox Christians whose numbers had increased dramatically as a result of immigration patterns during the first half of the twentieth century. He wrote in 1952,

> There is no Orthodox literature in English. There are occasional books, often of modest quality, and rarely on the most urgent basic subjects. The real problem, however, is not that of books, but of study. Each generation especially in a new country, has to assess the Christian truth afresh, in continuous contact with the past, as well as in close contact with the changing present.[1]

To a large extent Florovsky's own interests in patristics, ecumenism, and Russian history and culture, undergirded by a profound conviction of the unity of Orthodoxy, stamped the *Quarterly* from its inception. The journal was to exercise a unitive influence in American Eastern Orthodoxy just as the seminary, based in the tradition of Russian Orthodoxy, rapidly began to include representatives of other national and ethnic traditions as well. Florovsky's engagement with Orthodoxy as a focus of unity across time and space provided a rostrum during a period of fervid ecumenical activity from which to assay the broader ecumenical possibilities intimated by such organizations as the Faith and Order Commission of the World Council of Churches.

In the years following Florovsky's departure to Harvard Divinity School in 1956, under the leadership of Alexander Schmemann (1921–1983) and John Meyendorff (1926–   ), the *Quarterly* sustained the interests that motivated its founders while conveying an increasing sense of self-consciousness and stability in the United States. Both Schmemann and Meyendorff, like Florovsky, had come to St. Vladimir's from St. Sergius Orthodox Theological Institute, Paris. Like Florovsky they were influenced by the Russian *émigré* culture, which had flourished in Paris during the period following the 1917 Bolshevik Revolution.

The American context, like that of France, provided an opportunity to overcome historic patterns of symbiosis between the Eastern Orthodox tradition and a number of national and ethnic cultures. As a small population within the American denominational system, Eastern Orthodoxy could develop theologically and liturgically without the necessity of also serving as the bearer of a culture. The *Quarterly* continues to reflect a substantial concern for the cultivation of a denationalized and deethnicized Orthodox Christianity.

While sustaining its role as a focal point for the particular concerns, both pastoral and academic, of Eastern Orthodox Christians in the United States, the *Quarterly* has also provided careful analyses of the ecumenical consultations that have taken place between representatives of Orthodoxy and representatives of Roman Catholicism and Anglicanism since the 1950s. The broadening scope of the *Quarterly* and, in particular, its mission beyond St. Vladimir's Seminary and Eastern Orthodoxy, is well symbolized by the 1969 decision to change the title from a "seminary" to a "theological" quarterly.

Note

1. *St. Vladimir's Seminary Quarterly* 1:1 (1952): 5.

Information Sources

BIBLIOGRAPHY:
Meyendorff, John. *Byzantine Theology: Historical Trends and Doctrinal Themes.* New York: Fordham University Press, 1974.
———. *The Orthodox Church: Its Past and Its Role in the World Today.* New York: Pantheon Books, 1962.
Piepkorn, Arthur C. *Profiles in Belief: The Religious Bodies of the United States and Canada.* Vol. 1: *Roman Catholic, Old Catholic, Eastern Orthodox.* New York: Harper and Row, 1977.
Tarasar, Constance, gen. ed., and John H. Erickson, assoc. ed. *Orthodox America, 1794–*

1976: Development of the Orthodox Church in America. Syosset, N.Y.: Department of History and Archives, Orthodox Church in America, 1975.

INDEX SOURCES: "Index of St. Vladimir's Theological Quarterly," *St. Vladimir's Theological Quarterly* 20:1–2 (1976); *Religion Index One, Old Testament Abstracts, Religious and Theological Abstracts.*

REPRINT EDITIONS: University Microfilms International.

LOCATION SOURCES: University of Chicago, Union Theological Seminary (New York), Princeton Theological Seminary, Garrett-Evangelical Theological Seminary, University of Iowa, Duke University, Andover-Harvard Theological Library, and others.

Publication History

MAGAZINE TITLE AND TITLE CHANGES: *St. Vladimir's Seminary Quarterly* (1952–68), *St. Vladimir's Theological Quarterly* (1969–).

VOLUME AND ISSUE DATA: *St. Vladimir's Seminary Quarterly* 1:1–4:4 (1952–56), n.s. 1:1–12:4 (1957–68); *St. Vladimir's Theological Quarterly*, n.s. 13:1 (1969–).

PUBLISHER AND PLACE OF PUBLICATION: St. Vladimir's Orthodox Theological Seminary, New York (1952–62), Crestwood, N.Y. (1962–).

EDITORS: Georges Florovsky (1952–55), Alexander Schmemann (1957–61), John Meyendorff (1961–).

CIRCULATION: 2000 (1984).

Eugene Y. Lowe

SEMEIA

Semeia is an experimental journal sponsored by the Society of Biblical Literature (SBL) as part of its research and publication program. The journal is "devoted to the exploration of new and emergent areas and methods of biblical criticism" and publishes "studies employing the methods, models, and findings of linguistics, folklore studies, contemporary literary criticism, structuralism, social anthropology, and other such disciplines and approaches."[1]

Semeia had its genesis in the work of the Parables Seminar of the SBL. The seminar, whose first sessions were held at the annual meeting of the SBL in 1973, was organized to sponsor research and facilitate discussions among scholars who recognized the potential of the methods and insights of literary criticism and linguistics in the study of the New Testament parables. Robert W. Funk, who was instrumental in organizing the Parables Seminar, drew up a proposal for an "Experimental Journal for Linguistic and Literary Arts in Biblical Study" to serve as a publishing vehicle for the Parables Seminar and the several other working groups within the SBL with similar interests. The proposal was approved by the Research and Publications Committee of the SBL in January 1974, and the first two issues of the journal appeared later that year.[2]

Each issue of the journal has been edited by a member of the editorial board.

Robert W. Funk was the first editor of *Semeia*, serving in that capacity until 1980 (issues 1–16), when he was succeeded by John Dominic Crossan (with the title general editor).

A central theme or literary genre unifies the essays in each issue, thus allowing for the adoption of experimental formats. The format often provides both major essays and critical discussions of those essays, all within the same issue. Occasionally, issues include responses to the critical comments by the authors of the major essays. This type of format, coupled with the use of typescript (which was changed to regular type beginning with issue 17), was adopted, in the words of Funk, to "permit scholars freedoms they had forgotten, such as rapid, almost instant publication."[3] Any uncertainty about scholars' willingness to accept "serious communication in a cheap format" was soon dispelled; the journal was given an enthusiastic reception both within the SBL and in circles beyond.[4]

The real significance of this journal—the attempt to be experimental in content—lies in its movement beyond the traditional methods of biblical criticism while maintaining, in the words of Amos N. Wilder, that "there is no reason to disparage older methods and contributions of biblical study or to make undue claims for new strategies."[5] Both continuity and discontinuity with the older methods of biblical scholarship are evident in every issue, but the main thrust is always to experiment with the insights and methods of the nonbiblical disciplines: comparative literature, linguistics, structuralism, and social anthropology, among others. To a large extent, *Semeia* has sought to bring biblical scholars into conversation with their colleagues in related disciplines.

The first two issues of the journal, edited by Robert W. Funk and John Dominic Crossan, respectively, featured new approaches to the study of the New Testament parables. These issues explored a structuralist approach to the parables, with special attention to the differences between parables and exemplary stories. A special feature of the inaugural issue was a basic bibliography for parables research.

A later issue (no. 9) took up the subject of the parables again, this time focusing on the parable of the prodigal son. This issue, edited by Crossan, featured several essays under the rubric "Polyvalent Narration," including psychoanalytic and structuralist interpretations of this parable.

Several issues of the journal have featured the work of individual scholars: Erhardt Güttgemann's "generative poetics" (no. 6), Paul Ricoeur's hermeneutics (nos. 4, 19), Jacques Derrida's "deconstructive" approach (no. 23), Vladimir Propp's morphological studies of folktales (no. 10), and reflections on Julius Wellhausen's influential *Prolegomena zur Geschichte Israels* a century after its publication (no. 25).

Two issues (12 and 13) honored the work of Amos Wilder. The first presented essays by prominent New Testament scholars on "Rhetoric, Eschatology, and Ethics in the New Testament"; the second, on "Imagination, Rhetoric and the Disclosure of Faith," honored Wilder's work as a literary critic. Both issues were edited by William A. Beardslee. A special feature of the second issue was a bibliography and vita of Wilder.

Many other issues of the journal have been devoted to genre studies. In most cases, these issues also reflect the work of units with the SBL. Among the genres featured have been classical Hebrew narrative (nos. 3, 15), early Christian miracle stories (no. 11), apocalypse (no. 14), various forms of gnomic wisdom (no. 17), pronouncement stories (no. 20), and ancient letters (no. 22). Several of these genre studies cover a broad spectrum of ancient literature. Thus, for example, issue 17 provides "a comprehensive survey of all the texts which might be or have been classified as apocalypses and can be dated with any plausibility in the period 250 BCE–250 CE, with the purpose of establishing how far they can purposefully be regarded as members of one genre."[6] Similarly, issue 22 provides studies of cuneiform, Aramaic and Greek letters. The essay "Aramaic Epistolography" by Joseph A. Fitzmyer contains comprehensive listings of known Aramaic letters.

Occasionally, issues are devoted to a particular theme, such as "Oral Tradition and Old Testament Studies" (no. 5), structural readings of Genesis 2 and 3 (no. 18), "Anthropological Perspectives on Old Testament Prophecy" (no. 21), "Old Testament Interpretation from a Process Perspective" (no. 24), the study of discourse in structural exegesis (no. 26), and current methods in the study of rabbinic literature (no. 27).

Semeia was published irregularly in issues numbered consecutively from 1974 to 1979. Since 1980 it has been published quarterly (August, November, February, and May), but still in consecutively numbered issues.

As "an experimental journal for biblical criticism," *Semeia* has broadened the horizons of biblical study. At the same time, its issues reflect the ferment that has characterized biblical studies in recent years.

Notes

1. From cover 2 of the journal.
2. For a fuller account, see Amos N. Wilder, "*Semeia,* an Experimental Journal for Biblical Criticism: an Introduction," *Semeia* 1 (1974): 1–16, esp. pp. 1–3.
3. Robert W. Funk, "*Semeia* and the Stuff and Style of Scholarship," *Semeia* 1 (1974): 276.
4. Ibid., p. 275.
5. Wilder, p. 3.
6. John J. Collins, "Preface," *Semeia* 17 (1979): v.

Information Sources

BIBLIOGRAPHY:

Funk, Robert W. "*Semeia* and the Stuff and Style of Scholarship." *Semeia* 1 (1974): 275–78.

Saunders, Ernest W. *Searching the Scriptures: A History of the Society of Biblical Literature, 1880–1980.* Chico, Calif.: Scholars Press, 1982.

Wilder, Amos N. "*Semeia*, an Experimental Journal for Biblical Criticism: An Intro-
duction." *Semeia* 1 (1974): 1–16.
INDEX SOURCES: *Religion Index One, Elenchus Bibliographicus Biblicus, Interna-
tionale Zeitschriftenschau für Bibelwissenschaft und Grenzgebiete, New Testament
Abstracts.*
LOCATION SOURCES: Library of Congress, University of California-Riverside, Emory
University, Yale University, University of Chicago, University of California-Santa
Barbara, and others.

Publication History

MAGAZINE TITLE AND TITLE CHANGES: *Semeia* (1974–   ).
VOLUME AND ISSUE DATA: 1:1 (1974–   ).
PUBLISHER AND PLACE OF PUBLICATION: Scholars Press, Missoula, Mont. (1974–
79), Chico, Calif. (1980–   ).
EDITORS: Robert W. Funk (1974–80), John Dominic Crossan (1980–   ); frequent
guest editors for special issues.
CIRCULATION: 800 (1982).

Carl D. Evans

SOCIAL JUSTICE REVIEW

*Central-Blatt and Social Justice** began as the chief means of social inquiry
of the Central Verein, the oldest foundation of mutual aid societies to be established by German Catholic immigrants in the United States. Begun in 1855,
Central Verein spoke to the common concerns of most immigrants by providing
economic and employment assistance, as well as a whole host of other supportive
services. Although engaged in the significant issues of the time (Cahenslyism,
the Americanist controversy in the church, and others), Central Verein gradually
expanded its interest in various social justice issues. In 1908 Central Verein
established a Central Bureau to serve as headquarters of its various social reform
activities and began publication of a monthly journal, *Central-Blatt*. The next
year the journal became a bilingual monthly and was called *Central-Blatt and
Social Justice*.

Until his death in 1952, Frederick P. Kenkel, director of the Central Bureau,
greatly influenced the journal. Kenkel felt that "a society as ill as that founded
in the principles of Liberalism demands reformation. . . . It is futile to hope that
anything but changes of a fundamental nature can establish what has come to
be known as 'social justice.' "[1] He envisioned a Christian cooperative order
modeled on the organic society of the Middle Ages. Society would be bound
together in a series of voluntary organizations in just relationship with each other.
In 1913 J. Elliot Ross wrote that this system, known as solidarism, was a
"principle of economic organization based upon the essential unity of mankind
flowing from human nature."[2] The journal spelled out this system in future
issues. Because all social problems were structural, according to Kenkel, virtually

all secular social reform failed to address the root problem. Only total reform—only Catholic reform—would remind true reformers that man has an immortal soul, and this would "color and direct both his aims and his methods."[3] Hence, the constant call throughout the early years—and, indeed, until Kenkel's death—was the need for the complete social, economic, and spiritual reform of the country. Against this ideal all problems were to be evaluated and all programs judged.

In 1940 the journal's name was changed to *Social Justice Review*. Use of the German language, growing less prominent every year, was dropped completely in 1946. During the war years, Central Bureau and the journal promoted chaplains' aid societies and aid to displaced persons. It also examined the causes of the war and the proper course for complete social reconstruction after hostilities ceased. In the immediate postwar years, the journal recognized the dawn of a new era and declared that the United States should "magnanimously discontinue the use of the atomic bomb." Despite changing circumstances, the "immutable principles of the encyclicals" were still alive, and the great social problems would be solved only by a "change of heart and mind of men and women of all classes of societies."[4]

Always opposed to socialism, *Social Justice Review* was virulently anti-Communist in the postwar years. Resolutions of the ninety-first Verein convention stated that "Communism, no less than Naziism, is a bitter enemy of the Catholic Church." By 1954 the menace had grown to "such ominous proportions as to dominate all national and international planning in the Free World." Communism, like other social ills, had its roots in the "whole complexity of Liberalistic ideas which have progressively alienated the modern world from the Church, from Christ, from God and His law."[5] Given this apocalyptic view, it was no surprise in 1956 that the Central Verein recommended that the United States break diplomatic relations with the Soviet Union. More than a decade later, it still reflected Cold War concerns when it argued that the U.S. Supreme Court had "voided most of our legal safeguards against Communism."[6]

Strident anticommunism blinded the journal to the moral dilemmas of Vietnam and Watergate. Other articles continued to discuss labor issues, and Central Verein's Declaration of Principles in 1977 spoke of various human hungers: justice among the aged, blacks, and Indians. The journal called for liturgical reform according to the dictates of Vatican II and also lamented reports of those who saw the council as a battle between liberals and conservatives.

A gloomy outlook pervades the contemporary stance of the journal. Articles in the early 1970s entitled "The Perverts Revolution," "Soviet Police Terror Rising," "Sodom-Gomorrah Rock Festivals and Civic Authorities" bear witness, in the journal's view, to the diagnosis made in 1950: "gone into well-nigh total eclipse is the national law and the law of nations. The repudiation of religion and of the existence of an Absolute is now almost complete."[7]

Recent issues continue to take a variety of stances across the social spectrum. Firm opposition to birth control and abortion, occasional support for neutron bombs, and opposition to the equal rights amendment were mixed with awareness of racial injustice and the need for international economic reform, especially with regard to superpowers' treatment of Third World countries. Thus does Kenkel's imprint remain in the message of the journal: radical alienation from a degenerate (and degenerating) society, concern for the physical and spiritual condition of Catholics, and fear of modern ideologies that will bring spurious social change destined to entrap man in the bonds of injustice and spiritual disequilibrium.

Notes

1. Quoted in Joseph Matt, "Centenary of the Catholic Central Verein of America, Its Foundation and History," in *Official Program—125th Convention, The Catholic Central Union (Verein) of America* (St. Louis: Catholic Central Union [Verein] of America, 1980), p. 86.

2. J. Elliot Ross, C.S.P., "Not Individualism, Not Socialism, But Solidarism, II," *Central-Blatt and Social Justice* 6 (May 1913): 37.

3. "Not By Bread Alone," *Central-Blatt and Social Justice* 4 (April 1911): 8.

4. *Social Justice Review* 38 (September 1945): 173.

5. Both quotes from ibid. 48 (February 1955): 354.

6. Ibid. 61 (October 1968): 202.

7. Ibid. 43 (April 1950): 31.

Information Sources

BIBLIOGRAPHY:

Barry, Colman J. *The Catholic Church and German-Americans*. Milwaukee: Bruce Publishing Co., 1953.

Brophy, Mary L. *The Social Thought of the German Roman Catholic Verein*. Washington, D.C.: Catholic University of America Press, 1941.

Central Bureau of the Catholic Central Union. Free Leaflet No. 107. St. Louis: Central Bureau of the Catholic Central Union, 1960.

Gleason, Philip. *The Conservative Reformers: German-American Catholics and the Social Order*. Notre Dame: University of Notre Dame Press, 1968.

Matt, Joseph. "Centenary of the Catholic Central Verein of America, Its Foundation and History." In *Official Program—125th Convention, The Catholic Central Union (Verein) of America*. St. Louis: Catholic Central Union of America, 1980.

Olson, James S. *The Ethnic Dimension in American History*. New York: St. Martin's Press, 1979.

INDEX SOURCES: *Catholic Periodical and Literature Index.*

LOCATION SOURCES: Yale University, University of Illinois, Harvard University, St. John's University (Collegeville), University of Scranton, and others.

Publication History

MAGAZINE TITLE AND TITLE CHANGES: *Central-Blatt* (1908–9), *Central-Blatt and Social Justice* (1909–40), *Social Justice Review* (1940–   ).

VOLUME AND ISSUE DATA: *Central-Blatt* 1 (April 1908-March 1909), *Central-Blatt and Social Justice* 2–32 (April 1909-March 1940), *Social Justice Review* 33-

(April 1940–   ). Monthly from April 1909 (vol. 2) until February 1977 (vol. 69) when publication was suspended; publication resumed bimonthly in January-February 1979 (vol. 70).

PUBLISHER AND PLACE OF PUBLICATION: Central Bureau of the Catholic Central Union (Verein) of America, St. Louis.

EDITORS: Rudolph Krueger (1908), Rev. Dr. August Brieg and Rev. Peter C. Dietz (1909–10), Frederick P. Kenkel (1910–52), Rev. Victor T. Suren (1952–62), Harvey J. Johnson (1962–   ).

CIRCULATION: 1615 (1982).

Edward Tabor Linenthal

SOCIAL THOUGHT. *See* CATHOLIC CHARITIES REVIEW

SOJOURNERS

In 1971, a handful of seminarians pooled $700 to pay for the first issue of the *Post-American*. Printed in tabloid style, 30,000 copies were hand distributed throughout the country by these seminarians and a network of friends at a cost of 25¢ or "whatever you can afford." Within a decade, the *Post-American* had assumed a new name (*Sojourners*), a new format (attractive magazine style), and use of computer services to facilitate distribution to over 50,000 subscribers and readers.

The precipitant of the *Post-American* was the People's Christian Coalition of Deerfield, Illinois, composed primarily of seminary students at Trinity Evangelical Divinity School. Unhappy with the seminary's silence on such social issues as the war in Vietnam and poverty, these young evangelicals espoused a theology of Christian radicalism. Their purpose was to relate the mandates of biblical faith to contemporary social and political issues. On the cover of the first issue of the *Post-American* (Fall 1971), Jesus was pictured with a crown of thorns on his head and wrapped in the American flag. The caption read: "And they crucified him." The message was clear: Jesus was being crucified again by American Christianity. To editor Jim Wallis, in the United States, "the gospel had become almost completely lost in a church that had become captive to its culture and trapped by a narrow vision of economic self-interest and American nationalism. . . . The brutality of the war in Vietnam, the persistence of white racism, and the grinding oppression of the poor all screamed to heaven over the church's silence. A pervasive American civil religion was in fact sanctioning these manifold national sins, and the prophetic character of biblical faith was almost never invoked."[1]

The message of the *Post-American* was not popular with establishment Protestants, liberal or conservative. Agreeing with liberal Christianity's emphasis on social justice and orthodoxy's demand for personal regeneration, the *Post-American* rejected both for lacking a prophetic dimension. Neither alternative was adequate in itself, nor was a combination of the two. Both required a transcendent vision.[2] What was needed was a Christian radicalism that "provided the vehicle for people willing to change their own lives, to challenge the system, to take the problems of change seriously." This radicalism would be found in the "movemental church," a "new order," whose members would live "by the values and ethical priorities of Jesus Christ and His Kingdom in the midst of the indifference and injustice of the American church and state."[3] The *Post-American* "emerged as an evangelical publication radically committed to social justice and peace."[4]

A community that seeks to live out what it boldly espouses in print has always been associated with the journal. The change in name from *Post-American* to *Sojourners* illustrates this connection. In the fall of 1975, the *Post-American* community moved from Chicago to Washington, D.C., and shortly after renamed itself Sojourners Fellowship and the magazine, *Sojourners*. The new name revealed a new identity.

"The *Post-American* years," relates Wallis,

> were characterized by a prophetic stance that was alienated from the government, the system, and the established church. The change to *Sojourners* reflected the deepening of our identity as a Christian community and a new commitment growing among us to the rebuilding of the church at the local level . . . to the forging of a new vision, a new style of life that could be offered for the sake of the church's future in this country.[5]

Since its inception, Jim Wallis has been the editor and guiding light of *Sojourners*. In a recent book, Richard Quebedeaux stated that *Sojourners* "really *is* Jim Wallis," but the point is well taken.[6] Raised in the Plymouth Brethren Church, Wallis was an antiwar activist at Michigan State University before enrolling at Trinity Evangelical Divinity School in 1970. He has since emerged as a leading voice of the young evangelical social conscience.

Two of the earliest contributors to the journal were Clark Pinnock, then professor of theology at Trinity Evangelical School, and U.S. Senator Mark Hatfield. Pinnock was the only teacher at the seminary to give the *Post-American* his unqualified support. He continues to contribute articles on theology and discipleship. Hatfield, who offered early encouragement to the *Post-American*, remains a contributing editor.[7] Other major evangelical contributors include a distinguished list of the evangelical Left: William Stringfellow; Mennonite scholar John Howard Yoder; Art Gish; Dale Brown; Robert Webber of Wheaton College; John F. Alexander, Jr.; N. Gordon Crosby of the Church of the Savior, Washington, D.C.; Samuel Escobar, a Latin American evangelical theologian; William Pannell; John Perkins of the Voice of Calvary; and John R. Stott, British Anglican bishop.

In addition, *Sojourners* propounds other Christian traditions. In his article, "What Nurtures Us," Wes Michaelson contended that the stance of *Sojourners* is reflected in the following traditions: Anabaptist, charismatic, social justice activist, Catholic contemplative, and Catholic Left.[8] The focus of the articles in *Sojourners* bears this out. The Anabaptist commitment to discipleship, nonviolence, and Christian community has filled the journal's pages since its beginning. An emphasis on the gift of the Spirit is discernible in *Sojourners'* contents since 1975.[9] Throughout its brief history, *Sojourners* has given predominant space to social and political issues. It has dealt with such matters as poverty, hunger, housing shortages, labor, racism, and war—in the United States and in the world. This emphasis stems from a conviction that truly biblical people identify with the dispossessed. More recently, the spread of international torture and the proliferation of nuclear arms have received increasing attention. Finally, the Roman Catholic tradition has supplied "two tributaries . . . which uniquely feed those called to a radical gospel."[10] On the one hand there is the Catholic Left, represented by Dorothy Day and the Catholic Worker movement and social activist Philip Berrigan. On the other hand, there is the contribution of Catholic contemplatives. *Sojourners* has featured cover stories on St. Francis of Assisi and Thomas Merton.

The *Sojourners* audience mirrors this diversity of traditions. A 1979 poll taken by publisher Joe Roos revealed the readership to be evangelical (33 percent), liberal (23 percent), Catholic (21 percent), Anabaptist (12 percent), charismatic (9 percent), and fundamentalist (2 percent). Nearly all readers are college educated (86 percent), and two-thirds have had some graduate training.[11] *Sojourners*'s diverse audience provides the journal with a broad base of appeal. More important, its very nature as a publication dedicated to a radical alternative gives *Sojourners* a loyal and committed readership. Another strength is its financial stability. As one of the few reader-sponsored journals, *Sojourners* has never overextended its resources. In addition, the commitment of Sojourners Fellowship to live at near poverty level has kept staff salaries minimal. A final strength is that *Sojourners* results from the efforts of a group bound together by personal and spiritual ties. What would happen to *Sojourners* if the community fell apart? Perhaps it would be accurate to say that as Sojourners Fellowship goes, so goes *Sojourners*.

Notes

1. "Ten Years," *Sojourners* 10 (September 1981): 4.
2. "What Is the People's Christian Coalition?" *Post-American* 1 (Winter 1972): 7.
3. Ibid.
4. "Ten Years," p. 4.
5. Ibid., p. 5.
6. Richard Quebedeaux, *The Worldly Evangelicals* (New York: Harper & Row, 1978), p. 150.
7. See his letter in "Feedback," *Post-American* 1 (Winter 1972): 6.

8. *Sojourners* 7 (May 1978): 16–19.

9. See "Crucible of Community: A Dialogue in the Shaping of Sojourners," *Sojourners* 6 (January 1977): 14–21.

10. "What Nurtures Us," *Sojourners* 7 (May 1978): 18.

11. "Into 1980 Together," *Sojourners* 9 (Jan. 1980): 5.

Information Sources

BIBLIOGRAPHY:

Quebedeaux, Richard. *The Worldly Evangelicals*. New York: Harper & Row, 1978.

———. *The Young Evangelicals*. New York: Harper & Row, 1974.

Wallis, Jim. *Agenda for Biblical People*. New York: Harper & Row, 1976.

———. *The Call to Conversion*. New York: Harper & Row, 1981.

INDEX SOURCES: *Religion Index One, Christian Periodical Index*.

REPRINT EDITIONS: American Theological Library Association (microfiche).

LOCATION SOURCES: George Washington University, Southern Methodist University, Princeton Theological Seminary, and Swarthmore College.

Publication History

MAGAZINE TITLE AND TITLE CHANGES: *Post-American* (1971–75), *Sojourners* (1976–   ).

VOLUME AND ISSUE DATA: *Post-American*: 1–4 (1971–75), number of issues per year varies; *Sojourners*: 5 (1976–   ), number of issues per year varies, but monthly except for combined July-August issue since 1982.

PUBLISHER AND PLACE OF PUBLICATION: Joe Roos, Chicago (*Post-American*, 1971–75); Joe Roos, Washington, D.C. (*Sojourners*, 1976–   ).

EDITOR: Jim Wallis (1971–   ).

CIRCULATION: 50,000 (est., 1982).

David Kling

SOUNDINGS

In 1910, the boards of education of several Protestant denominations decided to combine their efforts in fostering Christian education and founded the Council of Church Boards of Education. It was affirmed that "the Council stands for inter-denominational co-operation in Christian education" and "holds to the ideal that all of the processes of education should be carried on by methods permeated with religion as a fundamental human impulse." By 1924 the council included representatives from 20 denominations, with which were affiliated some 400 colleges and numerous secondary schools. Moreover, the council assumed that "every educational institution, whether directly or indirectly affiliated with the churches or maintained by public taxation, is profoundly interested in the moral and religious welfare of all its members." It therefore established relationships with 60 tax-supported colleges and universities, coordinating the work of student pastors and religious instruction with the needs of respective university communities. The purpose of the council beyond this was to create "a body of literature on Christian education."[1]

Accordingly, in 1917, *Christian Education* was founded for the purpose of disseminating information about religion in higher education in the United States. Each issue of the monthly magazine reported on religious studies programs at public and private institutions and often included a short article by an educator or church leader defining the mission of the council to higher education.[2] A section entitled "The Worker's Bookshelf," which was added to the magazine in the 1920s, reviewed books on higher education and religion.

In 1953, the journal was renamed the *Christian Scholar*. Founded on the premise that "the twentieth century is the greatest age in theology since the thirteenth," the *Christian Scholar* identified itself as "a publication devoted to a full explanation of the meaning of Christian faith and thought, as expressed in the current theological renaissance, in relation to the whole range of intellectual life and the whole task of higher education." Moreover, the journal sought "to overcome some of the current academic fragmentations" that hindered "the integration of faith and scholarship" and described the new Christian scholar, who would prosecute this integration, as follows: "Faith and thought are, for him, not divorced but in constant tension and dialectic."[3] It was nevertheless assumed that this dialectic took place at all times within the context of Christian belief: "The Christian professor finds that his Christian worldview is a perspective from which he can interpret facts and deal with issues in his field more adequately than from a different or opposing worldview."[4]

This shift in purpose from *Christian Education* was immediately apparent in the format of the *Christian Scholar*. Reports on academic programs were replaced by articles of a more thoughtful nature, many of which sought to demonstrate connections between religion and the various academic disciplines.[5] The quality of the book section in particular was dramatically upgraded and featured long review-articles by leading scholars.[6] In the wake of such changes, circulation increased sharply, from 350 to 1800 in the first year. However, as the hope for a Christian theological renaissance faded over the course of the next 10 years, the original optimism and ambition of the *Christian Scholar* diminished. The project of overcoming "academic fragmentation" with a coherent Christian worldview gave way finally to an admittance of the fragmented character of life in the world:

> The world which God created . . . is not simply the world as grasped in one or another "Christian interpretation" but *the* world itself, of which the abstract world of modern arts and sciences is the only viable contemporary model. The Christian must stand before God in this admittedly fragmented world.[7]

In 1968, the Society for Religion in Higher Education (a reorganization of the council) proposed that the *Christian Scholar* be replaced by a journal concerned with "the relation of common human concerns to the life of society and culture as reflected in active scholarship, research and creative thought." The new publication, entitled *Soundings: A Journal of Interdisciplinary Studies*, rejected the notion that there had been "a disintegration of the bonds between faith and knowledge" since the optimistic early years of the *Christian Scholar* but admitted "the arrival of a radically different understanding of how religion can and ought to be related to learning." Such an understanding rested on the premise that "it is in man, in whatever dignifies him, illumines his reality, tells a truth about him, and challenges him to fuller potential, that the various disciplines make contact with religion as understood in our Western tradition today."[8]

The task of a scholar in general therefore was seen as one of relating the methods of inquiry and the body of knowledge associated with a particular discipline to "common human concerns." *Soundings*, as a forum for this enterprise, defines itself as interdisciplinary. Contributions to the journal generally address some broad concern with human values or religious sensibilities through analysis of texts, historical events, and social forces.[9] Because of its rich potential for interdisciplinary studies, structuralist method and its application is of particular interest to the journal.[10] Articles that comment on various aspects of social and political life from a feminist point of view also appear regularly.[11] Articles analyzing the ideas of Christian theologians and church leaders are still published in *Soundings*, just as they were published by its predecessors. For *Soundings*, however, such articles constitute a part of a dialogue with other disciplines rather than a statement of religious or philosophical truth itself.

Notes

1. *Christian Education* 7 (April 1924): 311, 313; (May 1928): 496.

2. James C. Baker, "The Educational Task of the Church at College and University Centers," *Christian Education* 11 (March 1928): 365–73.

3. *Christian Scholar* 36 (March 1953): 3, 4.

4. Ibid. 36 (June 1953): 84.

5. Charles Hartshorne, "Biology and the Spiritual View of the World: A Comment on Dr. Birch's Paper," *Christian Scholar* 37 (September 1954): 408–9; William G. Pollard, "The Relation of the Christian College to the Scientific World," *Christian Scholar* 37 (Autumn 1954): 247–56; Irvin Miller, "The Responsibility of the Christian College to Business, Industry and Labor," *Christian Scholar* 37 (Autumn 1954): 257–63.

6. W. H. Auden, "Fog in the Mediterranean: A Review-Article of *The Rebel* by Albert Camus," and Nathan A. Scott, Jr., "The Realism of Eric Auerbach—A Review-Article of *Mimesis* by Eric Auerbach," *Christian Scholar* 37 (December 1954): 531–34; 538–547.

7. *Christian Scholar* 46 (Winter 1963): 276.

8. *Soundings* 51 (Spring 1968): 2, 3.

9. Wayne Elzey, " 'What Would Jesus Do?' *In His Steps* and the Moral Codes of the Middle Class," *Soundings* 58 (Winter 1975): 463–89; Marilyn French, "Macbeth at My Lai: A Study of the Value Structure of Shakespeare's *Macbeth*," *Soundings* 58 (Spring 1975): 54–68.

10. See the issue guest edited by Susan Wittig, *Structuralism: An Interdisciplinary Study*, *Soundings* 58 (Summer 1975).

11. Florence Howe, "Feminism, Fiction and the Classroom," *Soundings* 55 (Winter 1972): 369–89; Rosemary Ruether, "The First and Final Proletariat: Socialism and Women's Liberation," *Soundings* 58 (Fall 1975): 310–28.

Information Sources

INDEX SOURCES: *Current Contents, Historical Abstracts, Humanities Index, Old Testament Abstracts, Religion Index One, America: History and Life, Arts and Humanities Citation Index, Language and Language Behavior Abstracts, Sociological Abstracts, Religious and Theological Abstracts, Guide to Social Science and Religion in Periodical Literature, Current Index to Journals in Education, Film Literature Index.*

REPRINT EDITIONS: University Microfilms International, Microforms International Marketing Co., KTO Microform Division.

LOCATION SOURCES: Princeton University, University of Michigan, Williams College, North Carolina State University, University of Arizona-Tucson, Oberlin College, Stanford University, New York Public Library, Texas Tech University; partial collections elsewhere.

Publication History

MAGAZINE TITLE AND TITLE CHANGES: *Christian Education* (1917–52), *Christian Scholar* (1953–67), *Soundings: A Journal of Interdisciplinary Studies* (1968–   ).

VOLUME AND ISSUE DATA: *Christian Education*: 1–35 (1917–52), 1932–34 combined as 16–17; *Christian Scholar*: 36–50 (1953–68); *Soundings: A Journal of Interdisciplinary Studies*: 51 (1968–   ).

PUBLISHER AND PLACE OF PUBLICATION: *Christian Education*: Council of Church Boards of Education, Somerville, N.J. (1917–46); National Protestant Council on Higher Education, Somerville, N.J. (1947–50); Commission on Christian Higher Education of the National Council of the Churches of Christ in the U.S.A., Somerville, N.J. (1951–53). *Christian Scholar*: Commission on Christian Higher Education of the National Council of the Churches of Christ in the U.S.A., Somerville, N.J. (1953–64); Department of Higher Education of the National Council of the Churches of Christ in the U.S.A., Somerville, N.J. (1965–67). *Soundings*: Society for Religion in Higher Education, New Haven (1968–71); Society for Religion in Higher Education and Vanderbilt University, Nashville, Tenn. (1971–75); Society for Values in Higher Education and Vanderbilt University, Nashville, Tenn. (1975–   ).

EDITORS: *Christian Education*: Robert L. Kelly (1917–34), Gould Wickey (1934–47), Bernard J. Mulder (1947–53). *Christian Scholar*: J. Edward Dirks (1953–63, 1965–66), William R. Mueller (1963–65, 1967), Merle Allshouse and George Allan (1967). *Soundings*: Sallie TeSelle (1968–75), Thomas W. Ogletree (1975–80), Don Sherburne (1980–   ).

CIRCULATION: 1800 (1983).

John Corrigan

THE SOUTHERN PRESBYTERIAN REVIEW

Begun in the spring of 1847 by a group of Presbyterian ministers, the *Southern Presbyterian Review* offered its readers a broad range of theological literature. Throughout its history, each quarterly issue consisted of five to eight articles whose themes treated dogmatic theology, Presbyterian polity, and social ethics. A "Critical Notices" section, whch consisted mostly of reviews of scholarly books, concluded each issue.

Perhaps no other journal has ever been quite as faithful to its title as was the *Southern Presbyterian Review*. The *Review* was first and foremost a southern production. In the antebellum years, it concerned itself primarily with the ecclesiastical issues relevant to southern Presbyterians. As the war approached, the *Review* increasingly addressed the political and social ills that precipitated America's bloodiest war. In this, the *Review* serves as an interesting window on a troubled period in U.S. history. Articles on southern identity, especially the ethical and political dimensions of the slavery question, make the *Review* useful as a primary source document for historians of antebellum and reconstructionist America.

Donald G. Mathews's *Religion in the Old South* deals at some length with southern evangelical thinking about the slave system. In addition to discussing the economic and social justifications of slavery, Mathews carefully delineates the southerners' religious justification of the institution. In this regard—though the *Review* is not specifically cited in Mathews's work—the *Southern Presbyterian Review* can be seen as a classic apologia for distinctly southern culture and religion.

As early as 1850, the pages of the *Review* addressed the question of the Christianization of black slaves. In the face of warnings "to watch with jealous care all combinations of blacks," the *Review* praised one church that erected a separate building to house a slave congregation. Of course, Christian slaves who met for corporate worship had no civil rights, nor were ecclesiastical rights extended to them. These Christian slaves were not "a church, but a simple congregation" that would "always remain under the ecclesiastical control of the Second Presbyterian Church."[1]

The *Review*'s defenses of slavery never waned, even after the military defeat of the South. Moreover, in its zeal to defend slavery against the abolitionists, the *Review* published several articles that sought to establish the positive good of the system. In 1858, a Presbyterian writer claimed that the system "is not only good for us, but good for them [the slaves]."[2] Indeed, more than a decade after emancipation, the spiritual utility of the slave system was still heralded in the *Review*. Noting the vast cultural differences between the orderly churches of the freedmen (the Colored Baptist Association of Virginia was mentioned specifically) and the barbarism of tribal life in Africa, an anonymous author argued for this "important proposition": "Slavery accomplished this wonderful, beneficent work. . . . The whole truth, however, is not expressed by the proposition that slavery has made for the negro the difference between civilization and barbarism; it needs to be expanded negatively by adding—and nothing else could have effected it.''

The *Review* consistently served as a journalistic mouthpiece for southern regionalism and confederate nationalism. The issue of slavery aside, other titles demonstrate the publication's parochial character: "Southern Views Not Extinguished by the War," "The Battle of Fort Sumter: Its Mystery and Miracle— God's Mastery and Mercy," and an enthusiastic review of Jefferson Davis's *The Rise and Fall of the Confederate Government*, which ended with the charge that the "south was degraded by Northern Christianity."[3]

Second, the *Review* helped to describe mainline southern Presbyterianism in the middle decades of the nineteenth century. Throughout its 36 volumes, the reader found detailed expositions of controverted points in Presbyterian doctrine. The sacraments, polity, evangelism, and the freedom of the will are all treated at length. Perhaps the best description of southern Presbyterianism is revealed in an article entitled "Paul, a Presbyterian." According to the author, the apostle, like his southern Presbyterian descendants, affirmed an educated ministry, "practical calvinism," Presbyterian polity, and Presbyterian preaching—that "middle between the one extreme of dispassionate calmness and the other of excited declamation."[4]

Finally, the *Southern Presbyterian Review* functioned as a fine example of the classic review—a literary genre not to be confused with the regular inclusion of a book review section. Many article-length contributions were closely reasoned essays concerning current theological literature. One example of this scholarly enterprise was R. L. Dabney's treatment of Charles Hodge's three-volume *Systematic Theology*.[5] Dabney, perhaps the greatest of the southern Reformed systematists, was often compared to his northern counterpart, Hodge. Thus it was fitting that the great Princetonian's magnum opus should have been reviewed by Dabney. This particular essay was quite technical; indeed only a reader familiar with Presbyterian history and theology would have found it intelligible.

Despite the *Review*'s parochial concerns, the publication's final years chronicled a growing interest in worlds outside the South. The *Review* began to include articles concerned with missions, both within the United States and in foreign lands. Indeed, in 1884 the *Review* published an article entitled "The Chief Glory of the Nineteenth Century."[6] Given the tenor of the previous issues, a reader might have expected Presbyterianism or southern culture to have earned this attribution. Yet from John B. Adger's perspective, these earthly concerns paled before the chief glory of his day: foreign missions.

Notes

1. Anon., "The Revival of the Slave Trade," *Southern Presbyterian Review* 11:2 (1857): 104.

2. Anon., "Slavery and the Religious Instruction of the Coloured People," *Southern Presbyterian Review* 4:1 (1850): 106.

3. *Southern Presbyterian Review* 14:1 (1860): 61ff, 14:3 (1860): 365ff., 33:2 (1881): 290ff.

4. T. W. Hooper, "Paul, a Presbyterian," *Southern Presbyterian Review* 23:3 (1871): 412.

5. R. L. Dabney, "Hodge's Systematic Theology," *Southern Presbyterian Review* 24:2 (1872): 167ff.

6. John B. Adger, "The Chief Glory of the Nineteenth Century," *Southern Presbyterian Review* 35:3 (1884): 521ff.

Information Sources

BIBLIOGRAPHY:
Mathews, Donald S. *Religion in the Old South*. Chicago: University of Chicago Press, 1977.
INDEX SOURCES: James L. Martin, "Alphabetical Index to the Titles in the Southern Presbyterian Review, Volumes 1–34," *Southern Presbyterian Review* 34:1 (1884): 1–59.
LOCATION SOURCES: Princeton Theological Seminary, New York Public Library, University of South Carolina-Columbia, Union Theological Seminary (Richmond), Duke University, Columbia Theological Seminary, Historical Foundation of the Presbyterian and Reformed Churches.

Publication History

MAGAZINE TITLE AND TITLE CHANGES: *The Southern Presbyterian Review* (1847–85).
VOLUME AND ISSUE DATA: 1:1–2:4 (June 1847-March 1849), published quarterly in June, September, December and March; 3:1–36:4 (July 1849-October 1885), published quarterly in July, October, January, and April; publication interrupted during the Civil War: 16 contained the following numbers: 1 (July 1863), 2 (October 1963), 3 (April 1864), 4 (March 1866); regular publication resumed with 17.
PUBLISHERS AND PLACE OF PUBLICATION: I. C. Morgan (1847–49), A. S. Johnston (1849–56), R. W. Gibbes (1856–59), P. C. Pelham (1859–63), the Presbyterian Publishing House (1863–85); all in Columbia, S.C.
EDITORS: "An Association of Ministers in Columbia, South Carolina" (including, among others, R. L. Dabney, James Woodrow, and John B. Adger).
CIRCULATION: Unknown.

John R. Fitzmier

SUNSTONE

In 1975 *Dialogue**, the original independent Mormon periodical, was almost 10 years old. Its editors and contributors were an impressive list of who's who in Mormon society and letters. But Scott Kenney, a Mormon student at Berkeley's Graduate Theological Union (GTU), felt that there was not much chance for the student or not-yet-established writer to be heard. He enlisted the help of some friends, including Peggy Fletcher, another Mormon student at GTU, and the first issue of *Sunstone* came off the press in 1975. The third number carried this description of the new periodical:

> *Sunstone* is an independent quarterly journal of Mormon experience, scholarship, issues, and art addressed to an LDS [Latter-day Saint] student readership and to those of whatever age or conviction with similar concerns and interests. Submission of articles for the journal is in no way restricted, but priority will be given both to articles by younger writers and to topics which deal with Mormon culture, Mormon history, or Mormon faith, albeit indirectly.[1]

But like many other infant periodicals, *Sunstone* was still struggling for a clear identity. "Why another journal?" was the most frequently asked question. Its continuation could not rest on the support of students, most of whom were too poor to subscribe and too busy with their own studies to contribute or volunteer. In the second year of publication, the format of the publication was changed from the standard scholarly journal format to a larger magazine-size format, the first step toward a new identity for the publication as a magazine rather than a journal—the *Atlantic Monthly* of Mormonism, its ambitious editors would quip.

But there were only two numbers of the magazine in 1976. At the end of the year, *Sunstone* merged with a short-lived publication, the *New Messenger and Advocate*, which had been started by Kevin Barnhurst, a student at Brigham Young University. Barnhurst had conceived his publication as a magazine of contemporary news and views on Mormon life but had published only two issues. But many of his ideas for columns—"Update," "One Fold," "Mormon Associations," "The Law of the Land"—were adopted into *Sunstone*, which also absorbed the *New Messenger and Advocate*'s mailing list, advertisers, and subscribers (and for one issue its editors as well). At this juncture *Sunstone* became a bimonthly rather than a quarterly publication.

In early 1978, artist Randall Smith redesigned the format, which had varied considerably from issue to issue. Each number would now contain news columns, book reviews, and several longer feature articles. That same spring, editor Scott Kenney resigned his duties. New coeditors and publishers were Peggy Fletcher, who had been with the publication from the beginning, and Allen Roberts, an architectural designer in Salt Lake City. Fletcher began working full time on the venture in May 1978, which signaled the beginning of a professional operation instead of an intermittent, volunteer one. Susan Staker Oman, who later became managing editor of the magazine, arrived in January of 1979. The *Sunstone* editors, who had previously operated out of someone's bedroom or office, moved to independent offices in November 1979. When Roberts left *Sunstone* in the summer of 1980, Fletcher became publisher-editor.

The next major change occurred in the summer of 1981. The news and book reviews sections had expanded to the point that it was impossible to print all the desired information. So the *Sunstone Review* came into existence, a new periodical published by the same group. *Sunstone* magazine had about 5000 subscribers, but the circulation of the *Review* was planned at 20,000. Advertising revenue from the *Review*, a monthly newsprint publication, would help to support the more expensive magazine. Since the news and reviews sections of the magazine were now printed in a more expanded version in the *Review*, the editors launched a new series of opinion columns in the magazine. Regular columnists included a non-Mormon humorist, a lawyer, a family counselor, a psychologist, a collector of folklore, and the president of the Temple School of the Reorganized LDS Church.

The editors could now define the goals of the magazine as follows:

> *Sunstone* is a bimonthy magazine which publishes personal essays, history, fiction, art, theology, social issues, and interviews. Edited for Mormons and Mormon-watchers, it strives to be professionally excellent, balanced, and objective yet sympathetic to the Mormon church. It publishes articles by Mormons and non-Mormons alike and is dedicated to the following goals:
>
> —To provide a forum for a variety of perspectives on knotty and complex issues concerning Mormonism and Mormon group life
>
> —To encourage writing which looks at the problems of the world through specifically Mormon eyes and thus celebrates Mormon insights
>
> —To introduce readers, in the spirit of the Thirteenth Article of Faith [a Mormon tenet], to people, events, and ideas which might not otherwise come within their circle of concern
>
> —To establish a standard of graphic excellence in layout and design and provide opportunities for artistic expression
>
> —To establish networks between Mormons and non-Mormons.[2]

The identity crisis had long since passed.

Response to *Sunstone* by members of the Mormon community always has been varied. "Unholy" it was labeled by one angry reader. "The writers of the articles and reviews all try to be sophisticated and to get attention in any way possible. It is a very ridiculous magazine," wrote another. Some readers urged the editors not to be too careful: "Don't be afraid of offending." "*Sunstone* has the potential to develop the radical consciousness of individuals in the Church who are frustrated, thwarted, stifled." Still others have thanked *Sunstone* for strengthening their commitment to Mormonism: "I am a new convert; *Sunstone* assisted me greatly in answering many questions during my period of instruction." Many readers commented that the coverage was "well balanced," which was what the editors wished to achieve.[3]

Sunstone's editors could also boast a string of related projects and accomplishments. In 1979 *Sunstone* sponsored the first Mormon Theological Symposium (later changed to Sunstone Theological Symposium), which has become an annual August event with hundreds of participants. In addition to participating Mormon scholars, *Sunstone* also brought in major non-Mormon scholars of religious studies to comment on both Mormonism and religion in general.

In 1980 *Sunstone* began sponsoring an annual fiction contest. The annual prizes total $1000 ($500 for first prize). *Sunstone* has also been committed to running articles on contemporary society. Topics such as women in the church, the institutional church and the individual, church and state, social welfare issues, and excommunication have been treated in *Sunstone*.

In 1982, a controversy over the writing of history, which had been going on for some time in the church, was intensified by the discovery of a controversial blessing by Joseph Smith to his son and by national publicity in *Newsweek* and the *New York Times*. In response *Sunstone* began running a series of articles on the writing of history.

Other projects sponsored by the editors of *Sunstone* include seven Mormon history calendars (1975–81), two best-selling cartoon books on Mormon life, and a reprint of the Hebrew Grammar used by Joseph Smith.

Like other similar periodicals, *Sunstone* operates precariously close to a survival level. It has always been dependent on donations from patrons, in addition to subscription and advertising revenue. Yet its young editors had reason for pride in its accomplishments. Any future historian of twentieth-century Mormonism will have to consider it an indispensable source. And for the present it has established itself as a positive stimulus in Mormonism's intellectual, artistic, and cultural life.

Notes

1. *Sunstone* 1:3 (1976): inside front cover.
2. "Guideline for Writers," available at the *Sunstone* editorial office.
3. Selected at random from the "Readers Forum" column in various issues of *Sunstone*.

Information Sources

INDEX SOURCES: None.

LOCATION SOURCES: Princeton University, Harvard University, Yale University, University of California-Berkeley, University of California-Los Angeles, University of Utah, Brigham Young University.

Publication History

MAGAZINE TITLE AND TITLE CHANGES: *Sunstone* (1975–   ); *Sunstone Review* (1981–   ).

VOLUME AND ISSUE DATA: *Sunstone*: 1:1 (Winter 1975), 1:2–4 (Spring-Fall 1976), 2:1–2 (Spring-Summer 1977), 3:1 (November-December 1977), 3:2–6 (January-October 1978), 4:1–6 (January-December 1979), 5:1–6 (January-December 1980), 6:1–6 (January-December 1981), 7:1–6 (January-December 1982), 8:1- (January 1983–   ). *Sunstone Review*: 1:1 (July-August 1981), 1:2–3 (September-December 1981), 2:1 (January-February 1982), 2:2 (March 1982), 2:3, 2:4–12 (April-

December 1982), 3:1- (January 1983–   ). *Sunstone* became bimonthly begin-
ning with 3:1 (November-December 1977).
PUBLISHER AND PLACE OF PUBLICATION: *Sunstone*: Berkeley, Calif. (1975),
    Provo, Utah (1976–77); Salt Lake City (1977–   ); *Sunstone Review*: Salt Lake
    City (1981–   ).
EDITORS: Scott Kenney (1975–77), Kevin Barnhurst (1977–78), Scott Kenney (1978),
    Allen Roberts and Peggy Fletcher (1978–80), Peggy Fletcher (1980–   ).
CIRCULATION: 7000 (*Sunstone*, 1982), 15,000 (*Sunstone Review*, 1982).

Davis Bitton

SUNSTONE REVIEW. *See* SUNSTONE

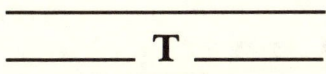

THE TELESCOPE-MESSENGER

In May 1833, the General Conference of the Church of the United Brethren in Christ appointed three trustees for a new denominational periodical and printing office, to be located in Circleville, Ohio. Within a year and a half, these men had purchased printing equipment and a publishing site and had secured as editor William R. Rhinehart, who only recently had begun a newspaper for his own Virginia Conference entitled *Union Messenger* (later, *Mountain Messenger*). On New Year's Eve 1834, Rhinehart issued the first number of the *Religious Telescope*, which would remain the chief official publication of the United Brethren for over a century.

The character of the new periodical was much affected by the strong personality of its editor. Rhinehart was, by all accounts, a progressive thinker, especially on the subjects of temperance and slavery, and not at all averse to joining actively in the controversies of his day. In fact, his unequivocal advocacy of abolition caused a great deal of dissension among the Brethren, probably accounted for the notable decrease in the number of *Telescope* subscribers between 1835 and 1838, and certainly contributed to Rhinehart's abrupt resignation in 1839.[1] Nevertheless, Rhinehart had indicated that he wanted the *Telescope* "to be devoted to the interests of religion, literature, and morality, and every useful information associated with Christianity," including foreign and domestic news of religious interest, and indeed this breadth of interest would be exhibited to a greater or lesser extent throughout the life of the paper.[2]

The *Telescope* underwent a number of changes during its long history. It began as a four-page semimonthly of folio size but became a weekly in 1845, assuming quarto size for a short time before resuming its former folio proportions permanently in 1850. By the turn of the century, each issue was running upwards of 30 pages in length. The press itself was moved from its original location in

Circleville first to the basement of the local United Brethren Church in 1845 and in 1853 to its final local in Dayton, Ohio, which thenceforth became the denominational publishing center and headquarters. The original subscription list of 1197, after an initial decline, reached 5400 in 1851 and 15,000 in 1891, though occasional purges of delinquent subscribers kept the numbers fluctuating markedly.[3]

It is not surprising, therefore, that finances were always a problem with the *Telescope* and the cause of much consternation at virtually every Annual and General Conference throughout its history. The only other significant trouble that the periodical appears to have had was a legal battle in the late 1880s that stemmed from a doctrinal dispute between "radicals" (conservatives) and "liberals," with the latter prevailing and retaining editorial control.[4] Despite its problems, however, the *Telescope* managed to spawn a German-language counterpart in 1846, *Der Deutsche Telescop*, which was renamed *Der Fröliche Botschafter (Joyful Messenger)* in 1851 and survived until 1930.[5]

After the resignation of Rhinehart, the *Telescope* quickly became a fixture of United Brethren denominational life, largely because of the personality of his successor, William Hanby. A man of limited editorial ability who regularly turned over responsibility for the *Telescope* to its printer because of his own immersion in church affairs, Hanby nevertheless not only rescued the struggling young paper from financial disaster but also gave it credibility by virtue of his standing and reputation as a church leader.[6] A measure of the paper's centrality in the denomination is the fact that, of the 10 men who served as editor throughout its history, no fewer than four eventually would be elected to the episcopacy, not to mention one of its original trustees and one of its last publishing agents.[7] Moreover, the *Telescope*'s own self-image, as reflected in retrospectives in two of its centennial editions, revolved around its official standing with respect to the denomination and its having tried to meet the needs and interests of all members of the Brethren, its unwelcome reputation as "a preachers' paper" notwithstanding.[8] Nevertheless, the publication accurately claimed that, far from being a merely servile denominational instrument, it had performed a leadership role by being open to modern scholarship and progressive on many issues, including some that were not strictly denominational, such as temperance and slavery.[9]

The *Religious Telescope* persisted in the face of nearly continual financial problems and vagaries in subscriptions until late in 1946, when the United Brethren in Christ merged with the Evangelical Church to form the Evangelical United Brethren Church. With that event, the *Religious Telescope* joined with its counterpart, the *Evangelical-Messenger*, to create the *Telescope-Messenger*, with a total combined subscription list of 50,000. By 1950, however, that number had dropped to fewer than 42,000 and continued to decline until 1958, when the General Conference voted to discontinue publication of the *Telescope-Messenger* and another floundering publication, and to replace both with a semimonthly entitled *Church and Home*.[10] The last issue of the *Telescope-Messenger* appeared on 7 December 1963, thus closing volume 129 and bringing to an end a long history of service to the Brethren.

Notes

1. John H. Ness, Jr., *One Hundred Fifty Years: A History of Publishing in the Evangelical United Brethren Church* (Dayton, Ohio: Board of Publication of the Evangelical United Brethren Church, 1966), pp. 268–99; J. Bruce Behney and Paul H. Eller, *The History of The Evangelical United Brethren*, ed. Kenneth W. Krueger (Nashville: Abingdon, 1979), pp. 124–27; Delbert R. Krumm, *A History of the Scioto, Southeast and Ohio Conferences of the Evangelical United Brethren Church* (Circleville, Ohio: Advocate Publishing House, 1958), pp. 44–46.

2. *Religious Telescope* 1:1 (31 December 1834): 2.

3. Ness, pp. 269, 304–6, 318–22, 401.

4. Ibid., pp. 394–99.

5. Behney and Eller, p. 180.

6. Krumm, p. 16; cf. Ness, p. 283.

7. A. W. Drury, "Editors of the Religious Telescope," *Religious Telescope* 100:52 (29 December 1934): 11–13; Ness, p. 459; Behney and Eller, pp. 175–78. The editors who became bishops were William Hanby, David Edwards, Milton Wright, and J. W. Hott. Original trustee John Russel served as bishop in the 1860s, and publisher J. Balmer Showers in the 1940s.

8. *Religious Telescope* 100:1 (6 January 1934): 6–7.

9. J. Balmer Showers, "A Century of Progress," *Religious Telescope* 100:52 (29 December 1934): pp. 8–10.

10. Ness, pp. 463–67, 483.

Information Sources

BIBLIOGRAPHY:
Behney, J. Bruce and Eller, Paul H. *The History of The Evangelical United Brethren Church.* Ed. Kenneth W. Krueger. Nashville: Abingdon, 1979.

Ness, John H., Jr. *One Hundred Fifty Years: A History of Publishing in The Evangelical United Brethren Church.* Dayton, Ohio: Board of Publication of the Evangelical United Brethren Church, 1966.

INDEX SOURCES: None.

LOCATION SOURCES: Historical Society of the Evangelical United Brethren Church, United Theological Seminary, Dayton, Ohio.

Publication History

MAGAZINE TITLE AND TITLE CHANGES: *The Religious Telescope* (31 December 1834–28 December 1946), *The Telescope-Messenger* (4 January 1947–7 December 1963).

VOLUME AND ISSUE DATA: 1 (31 December 1834)–129 (7 December 1963). Appeared semimonthly, 1834–44; appeared weekly, 1845–1963.

PUBLISHER AND PLACE OF PUBLICATION: United Brethren in Christ, Circleville, Ohio (1834–1853), Dayton, Ohio (1853–1946); Evangelical United Brethren Church, Dayton, Ohio (1947–1963).

EDITORS: William R. Rhinehart (1834–39); William Hanby (1839–45, 1849–52); David Edwards (1845–49); John Lawrence (1852–64); Daniel Berger (1864–69); Milton Wright (1869–77); J. W. Hott (1877–89); I. L. Kephart (1889–1908); J. M. Phillippi (1909–26); William E. Snyder (1926–46); Joe Willard Krecker (1947–63).
CIRCULATION: Approximately 50,000 at its peak (1947).

Paul A. Laughlin

THEOLOGICAL EDUCATION

Theological Education is the journal of the [American] Association of Theological Schools ([A]ATS).[1] Published since 1964, it has served as the primary means by which the association has communicated with its several member schools.

In order to give a place to the journal, a brief review of the history of the association is in order. The beginnings stem from a gathering called in 1918 by A. Lawrence Lowell, president of Harvard University. Comprised of representatives from a number of Protestant theological schools in Canada and the United States, this group became the Conference of Theological Seminaries and Colleges in the U.S. and Canada in 1920. Membership in the conference was by invitation and member recommendation. Prior to 1936, the goals of the conference were organized around communication among the schools, the solving of common problems, and the advancement of "the highest ideals of training for the Christian ministry."[2]

In 1936, the conference became the American Association of Theological Schools and added the accrediting of theological schools to its list of primary concerns. The [A]ATS published its first list of accredited schools in 1938. From that date forward, the regular accrediting of theological schools became an increasingly central service.

Prior to 1956, the work of the [A]ATS was directed by a series of executive secretaries who served on a voluntary basis. In that year, Charles L. Taylor, former professor and later dean of the Episcopal Theological School, Cambridge, Massachsetts, became the first full-time executive director. It was during the directorship of Charles Taylor that *Theological Education* began publication.[3]

"There is a notable lack of communication within the theological education enterprise when one takes into account its basic unity of purpose."[4] With these words *Theological Education* began. The journal was intended to help ameliorate this problem. Specifically, it was intended "to provide a medium of communication among those who are most intimately involved in the enterprise": the faculties and administrators of the member schools. With the aid of the Lilly Foundation, the [A]ATS was able to provide all full-time faculty members with complimentary subscriptions of *Theological Education* for three years. In this way, communication might be fostered all the more. The initial circulation was approximately 1700.[5]

The journal's first editor was Jesse H. Ziegler, associate director of [A]ATS under Charles Taylor and, following Taylor's retirement in 1966, executive director and editor until his own retirement in 1980. In that year, Leon Pacala, former president of Colgate-Rochester/Bexley Hall/Crozier, became executive director and editor.

The preoccupation of *Theological Education* is theological education, understood primarily as the educating of candidates for ordination by Christian churches. The journal has not been concerned with Christian education (or religious education) in the usual parochial or congregational sense. At the same time, although initially concerned with theological education in a Protestant setting, the journal increasingly has reflected the presence and influence of Roman Catholic schools in [A]ATS.

Unlike journals concerned with the variety of traditional theological disciplines (such as theology, Scripture, church history, and worship), *Theological Education* has focused more on the analysis of the educational enterprise, particularly the purpose of theological education and the nurturing or reform of the process. A brief survey of assorted article topics is instructive: accreditation (Autumn 1977), continuing education for clergy (Summer 1965), theological libraries (Autumn 1969), field education (Summer 1971, Summer 1975), governance (Autumn 1970, Fall 1975), academic freedom and tenure (Winter 1976), evaluation (Winter 1974), and the teaching office of the church (Spring 1983).

There have also been articles on topics with a higher socioeconomic profile. Examples are numbers given over to the role of women in theological education (Summer 1972, Winter 1975) and the black experience and theological education (Spring 1970, the supplement to Spring 1970, and the special issue in Winter 1980). Single articles on these subjects also appear in other issues. To date, consideration of Hispanic theological education has yet to receive a full number, although three articles appeared in the Winter 1977 issue: "Hispanic Ministries Education at Fuller Seminary" by George Gay, "Hispanic Ministry: New York Theological Seminary" by George Webber, and "Towards a Bilingual Seminary: A Catholic Effort" by Urban Voll. "Theological Education and Liberation Theology: A Symposium" was the focus of the Autumn 1979 issue.

As diverse as the topics are in these listings, the subject that receives the most extensive treatment remains to be named. Evidenced in a variety of ways, the concern on the part of the [A]ATS to influence (as well as to report on) the nature, purpose, and direction of theological education in North America finds most frequent expression in the pages of *Theological Education*. For example, "The Purpose of Theological Schools" was the central theme of two numbers, 12 years apart (Winter 1966, Spring 1978). In the fall of 1966, *Theological Education* published a book-length volume, "Education for Ministry," written by Charles R. Fielding and others. The intention of this study was to answer the question the author put at the outset: "How can our present system of theological education (so often based on the model of a graduate school in the humanities, with practical subjects added) be converted into genuinely professional education?"[6] Hence, curriculum reform became a primary concern.

Perhaps the most influential study undertaken by [A]ATS and published by *Theological Education* was "Readiness for Ministry," begun in 1973 and completed three years later. The work was done under the administrative directorship of David S. Schuller, associate director of [A]ATS. The intent of the study was to determine "competencies" ("qualities, abilities and knowledge") appropriately or necessarily possessed by "the fledgling minister which make him or her able to do the work of ministry acceptably and to continue growing toward professional maturity outside the formal institutional setting."[7] The completed project was published in two volumes in 1976 as *Readiness for Ministry Project.*[8] Progress reports and analysis are regularly reported in *Theological Education.*[9]

It was Schuller's expectation that the results of the project might bring about "the most thorough transformation of theological education experienced" in the twentieth century.[10] If perhaps too bold a hope, it is nonetheless true that the findings made available to theological schools carried that potential, and certainly such was the aspiration of the researchers and the editorial intent of *Theological Education.* The extent to which that aspiration bears fruit remains to be seen.

In order for any periodical to have impact, it needs to be read by the intended constituency. As part of a project designed to assess the program of the [A]ATS, data were gathered that present a picture of the extent of *Theological Education*'s potential influence. The evidence indicated that the journal was read often by only 30 percent of those surveyed, though 54 percent read it occasionally; that 35 percent found it "quite valuable" and another 39 percent "of some value"; and that 76 percent felt that the journal should continue publication in its current manner.[11] The public presentation of this information attests to the editor's intention that the journal, like the sponsoring body, be self-critical.

Notes

1. In 1974, the AATS became the Association of Theological Schools, dropping the word *American* from its title. Throughout this profile, unless in a quotation, the association will be designated [A]ATS.

2. Jesse H. Ziegler, "The AATS and Theological Education," *Theological Education* 2:4 (Summer 1966): S–67.

3. Ibid., p. S–68.

4. Jesse H. Ziegler, "Editorial Introduction," *Theological Education* 1:1 (1964): 1.

5. Ibid.

6. "Education for Ministry," *Theological Education* 3:1 (1966): 18.

7. David S. Schuller, "Readiness for Ministry," *Theological Education* 9:3 (Spring 1973): 221; David S. Schuller, Merton P. Strommen, and Milo L. Brekke, "The Assessment of Readiness for the Practice of Professional Ministry: Rationale and Research Method," *Theological Education* 10:1 (Fall 1973): 51.

8. *Readiness for Ministry Project* (Vandalia, Ohio: AATS, 1976).

9. See, for example, *Theological Education* 9:3 (Spring 1973), 10:1 (Fall 1973), 12:3 (Spring 1976), and 13:1 (Autumn 1976).

10. Schuller.

11. Jackson W. Carroll, "Project Transition: An Assessment of ATS Programs and Services," *Theological Education* 18:1 (Autumn 1981): 91–92, 150.

Information Sources

INDEX SOURCES: *Religion Index One, Current Contents.*
REPRINT EDITIONS: University Microfilms International.
LOCATION SOURCES: Union Theological Seminary (New York), Yale University, Library of Congress, Princeton Theological Seminary, University of Chicago, Emory University, and others.

Publication History

MAGAZINE TITLE AND TITLE CHANGES: *Theological Education* (1964–).
VOLUME AND ISSUE DATA: *Theological Education* 1–12 (1964–76), four numbers annually; 13 (1977), three numbers; 14 (1978–), two numbers annually; occasional supplements and special issues.
PUBLISHER AND PLACE OF PUBLICATION: [American] Association of Theological Schools, Vandalia, Ohio.
EDITORS: Jesse H. Ziegler (1964–80), Leon Pacala (1980–).
CIRCULATION: 1700 (1964), 3200 (1983).

William S. Adams

THE THEOLOGICAL MEDIUM. *See* THE CUMBERLAND PRESBYTERIAN REVIEW

THEOLOGICAL MONTHLY. *See* LEHRE UND WEHRE

THEOLOGICAL QUARTERLY. *See* LEHRE UND WEHRE

THEOLOGICAL STUDIES

The successive papal condemnations of Americanism in 1899 and modernism in 1907 had a disastrous effect on American Catholic theological research.[1] Gerald Fogarty maintains that as a result of these two Roman censures, "the American Catholic Church lapsed into an intellectual slumber from which it did not awaken until the 1940s."[2] Nowhere was the blighting of Catholic scholarship more obvious than in the archdiocese of New York. Prior to 1907, the archdiocesan seminary, Saint Joseph's at Dunwoodie, N.Y., had been home both to a gifted and progressive faculty and the *New York Review** (1905–8), an equally progressive theological journal. In the aftermath of the modernist controversy, several suspected modernists on the faculty were dismissed from the seminary, and the *Review* was forced to cease publication.[3] After the demise of the *Review*, until 1940, the only specifically theological journal published in the American church was the *American Ecclesiastical Review (AER)** (1889–1975). Its theological outlook was squarely and sagely integrist. As a result, it enjoyed the blessing of the hierarchy, the Roman Curia, and the American Jesuits who, with their Roman brethren, had fought against both Americanism and modernism.[4]

Ironically in the light of their earlier hostility to creative theological research, the American Jesuit community brought forth a successor to the *New York Review*. In 1937, responding to a felt need to provide the American church with a progressive theological journal, "the Directors of the America Press judged that it would be advisable . . . for the Society in this country to inaugurate the publication of a periodical devoted to theology."[5] In 1939, at the instigation of Francis X. Talbot, S.J., the editor of *America*,* representatives of the American Jesuit schools of theology[6] met at St. Ignatius College, Inisfada, New York,[7] to discuss the project. The representatives endorsed Talbot's suggestion and on receipt of approval from both the American fathers provincial and the Very Reverend Father General, Wlodimir Ledochowski, S.J., William J. McGarry, S.J., the president of Boston College, was named editor of the new quarterly, named *Theological Studies (TS)*. From its inception *TS* has remained a project of all the American Jesuit provinces. As a result, it receives both manpower and financial assistance from the American provinces.

During McGarry's short tenure as editor, the editorial offices were located in New York City, and the new journal's ties to the America Press remained strong. Although he was editor for less than two years (1940–41), McGarry had an extraordinary impact on the young publication. As the parent publication, *America*, noted, under McGarry both the aims and the audience of the new journal were identified:

> it will not be theology for beginners. Theological Studies is a scientific publication. Its aim is to present the fruits of serious theological research in the various fields comprised under such studies: Dogma, Scripture, Liturgy, etc.[8]

> William J. McGarry, S.J. . . . is fulfilling the original aim of this theological venture, namely, that of creating an organ through which theologian might speak to theologian, the latest research might be transmitted to research workers.[9]

In addition, on a more practical level, McGarry hit upon the three-part division of contents that has always characterized *TS*: articles dealing with theological topics, notes of a more pastoral nature synthesizing the latest thought on a range of topics, and book reviews.

Following McGarry's sudden death in 1941, the provincials named John Courtney Murray, S.J., a theology professor at Woodstock College, as editor of the journal. As a result of Murray's appointment, the editorial offices were moved to Woodstock, Maryland, the journal's ties to the America Press were severed, and Theological Studies, Inc. became the publisher of the periodical.[10] During Murray's long tenure (1941–67) as editor, *TS* became the preeminent Catholic theological journal in the United States.[11] This growth in stature under Murray is ironic in the light of the fact that at the time of his appointment, Murray had grave misgivings concerning both his own abilities and the value of *TS*.[12] Murray's self-doubts stemmed from the fact that within a short time of his appointment to the editorship of *TS*, he was also made religion editor of *America*. As a result, he felt himself pulled in two different directions. In his eyes, the *TS* post demanded that he devote himself to scholarly research, while the *America* post dragged him more and more into a concern for what he called "religion and society," a more practical branch of theological reflection. He felt that if he were required to do both jobs, he would do neither very well. In spite of his requests to be relieved of one or both of his positions, his superiors asked him to continue his work for both publications.[13] As it turned out, the pull he felt toward "religion and society" served to focus his own theological reflections and those of *TS*. As Donald Pelotte notes, as a result of Murray's fascination with practical theology, which led him ever more deeply into a study of American church life and its pluralistic context,[14] both he and *TS* were able to have a profound impact on the social thought of Roman Catholicism. In short, in many ways, the history of *TS* under Murray is inextricably bound to the history of Murray's intellectual growth, troubles, and triumphs.[15]

Murray's pioneering work in the areas of religious freedom and church-state relations led to a heated controversy between *TS* and the more integrist *AER*, edited by Joseph C. Fenton of Catholic University. The *AER* championed the traditional Catholic view concerning church-state relations: there should be one religion in the state, and "Catholicism should be professed by the state."[16] To buttress their views, *AER* writers appealed to a strict and uncritical reading and acceptance of papal utterances concerning church and state.[17] In short, Fenton and his colleagues believed in a static Catholic position on the proper relation of church and state. For his part, Murray believed that this position confused the historical conditioning behind papal pronouncements with the unchanging principles that should guide Catholic thought.[18] As a result, Murray proposed to use historical method to distinguish the temporal conditioning of any papal statement from the authoritative teaching of the same,[19] and since modern Catholic social thought was rooted in the writings of Leo XIII, he turned his attention to the Leonine corpus in a series of five articles for *TS*.[20]

Murray's articles on Leo drew fire immediately. Fenton and the *AER* were joined by the apostolic delegate in Washington and the Holy Office in Rome in denouncing Murray's conclusions, all of which seemed to smack of both Americanism and modernism.[21] As a result, Murray was required to "submit all of his writings on Church and State to his superiors in Rome for censorship," and in 1955 he was told to stop writing on the subject.[22]

While Murray and *TS* were embroiled in this controversy, the journal continued to function. Indeed, it thrived at the same time in providing a forum for Jesuit experts in various fields. Gerard Ellard, S.J., contributed articles on liturgy; Gustav Weigel, S.J., addressed Protestant theological developments; the Canadian Bernard Lonergan, S.J., wrote on Thomism; and following Pius XII's promulgation of *Divino Afflante Spiritu* (1943), Laurence J. McGinley, S.J., authored articles on form criticism. In addition, the annual "Notes on Moral Theology" written by such men as John C. Ford, S.J., John J. Lynch, S.J., and Richard McCormick, S.J., of the Kennedy Center for Bioethics of Georgetown University became a regular and important feature of *TS*.

Following the death of Murray in 1967, Walter J. Burghardt, S.J., of Woodstock College assumed the editorship. Under his leadership the journal has moved twice: to New York City in 1970 and to Washington, D.C., in 1975. Burghardt has continued the editorial policies that marked the editorships of McGarry and Murray. As a result, *TS* continues to be a lively and important presence in the field of theological research in the United States. The only discernible changes are reflections of the practical and ideological climate of the age: on the practical level, because of the closing of several of the Jesuits' schools of theology that oversaw publication of the journal, the editorial board has been expanded to include theologians who are not professors at Jesuit theologates, and in the aftermath of Vatican II, articles by non-Catholic authors have appeared with great regularity in *TS*.

Notes

1. See Thomas T. McAvoy, *The Great Crisis in American Catholic History* (Chicago: Henry Regnery, 1957), on this topic.

2. Gerald P. Fogarty, *The Vatican and the American Hierarchy from 1870 to 1965* (Stuttgart: Anton Hiersemann, 1982), p. 193.

3. Ibid.

4. James Hennesey, *American Catholics* (New York: Oxford University Press, 1981), p. 198.

5. "Obituary: Father William McGarry, S.J.," *Woodstock Letters* 71 (1942): 208.

6. The schools represented were Alma College, St. Mary of the Lake, St. Mary's (Kansas), West Baden College, Weston College and Woodstock College.

7. "In Memoriam: William J. McGarry, S.J.," *Theological Studies* 2 (1941): 449 (hereafter cited as *TS*).

8. "Comments," *America* (9 March 1940): 591.

9. "Comments," *America* (4 May 1940): 87.

10. Since 1941, *TS* has remained identified with Woodstock College and its successor institution, the Woodstock Theological Center.

11. Donald E. Pelotte, *John Courtney Murray: Theologian in Conflict* (New York: Paulist Press, 1975), p. 6.

12. Ibid., p. 7.

13. Ibid., p. 8.

14. Ibid., p. 7.

15. During the 1940s and 1950s, Murray's own concerns for intercreedal cooperation, freedom of religion, and church-state relations were reflected in the contents of the journal. Although he did not exclude other topics, in the period between 1949 and 1954, no fewer than 18 articles on these subjects appeared, 12 of which were written by Murray.

16. Hennesey, p. 302.

17. Fogarty, p. 370.

18. Thomas T. Love, *John Courtney Murray: Contemporary Church-State Theory* (Garden City: Doubleday, 1965), p. 62.

19. Ibid., p. 181.

20. Murray's articles on Leo were "Leo XIII on Church and State: The General Structure of the Controversy," *TS* 14 (1953): 1–30; "Leo XIII: Separation of Church and State," *TS* 14 (1953): 145–214; "Leo XIII: Two Concepts of Government," *TS* 14 (1953): 551–67; and "Leo XIII: Government and the Order of Culture," *TS* 15 (1954): 1–33.

21. Love, p. 121.

22. Fogarty, pp. 380–81.

Information Sources

BIBLIOGRAPHY:

Fogarty, Gerald P. *The Vatican and the American Hierarchy from 1870 to 1965*. Stuttgart: Anton Hiersemann, 1982.

Hennesey, James. *American Catholics*. New York: Oxford University Press, 1981.

Love, Thomas T. *John Courtney Murray: Contemporary Church-State Theory*. Garden City: Doubleday, 1965.

McAvoy, Thomas T. *The Great Crisis in American Catholic History*. Chicago: Henry Regnery, 1957.

Pelotte, Donald E. *John Courtney Murray: Theologian in Conflict*. New York: Paulist Press, 1975.

INDEX SOURCES: *Catholic Periodical and Literature Index, Religious and Theological Abstracts, Religion Index One*, the Catholic Magazine index of the *Catholic Bookman, New Testament Abstracts, Old Testament Abstracts, Current Contents*.

REPRINT EDITIONS: University Microfilms International.

LOCATION SOURCES: Yale University, University of Chicago, Andover-Harvard Theological Library, Catholic University of America, Princeton Theological Seminary, and others.

Publication History

MAGAZINE TITLE AND TITLE CHANGES: *Theological Studies* (1940–).

VOLUME AND ISSUE DATA: 1:1 (1940–).

PUBLISHER AND PLACE OF PUBLICATION: America Press, New York (1940–41), Theological Studies, Woodstock, Md. (1942–70), New York (1970–75), Washington, D.C. (1975–).

EDITORS: William J. McGarry, S.J. (1940–41), John Courtney Murray, S.J. (1941–67), Walter J. Burghardt, S.J. (1967–).

CIRCULATION: 6200 (1982).

Joseph R. McShane, S.J.

THEOLOGY DIGEST

In the fall of 1951 two Jesuit priests, Cyril O. Vollert and Gerald Van Ackeren, found themselves together on the faculty of St. Mary's College, St. Mary's, Kansas. St. Mary's was a Jesuit theologate, a school of theological studies for members of the Society of Jesus, a Roman Catholic religious order, who were preparing for ordination. Van Ackeren had just joined the faculty after several years of studying in Europe. He had taken a doctorate in theology at the Gregorian University, Rome, in May 1950 and had then spent a year studying under the Jesuit theologian, Karl Rahner, in Innsbruck, Austria. Vollert was a veteran of many years on the faculty and in 1951 was the dean of the college.

The two priests began to discuss the possibility of starting a theological periodical at St. Mary's, a project that Vollert had had in mind for more than a decade. Vollert suggested that some sort of digest of significant theological literature then appearing in European periodicals would be a significant contribution to the English-speaking world. He even had a title for the journal in mind: *Theology Digest*.

Van Ackeren eagerly took up the suggestion and agreed to serve as editor. Vollert explained the project to the Jesuit seminarians at St. Mary's, many of whom knew one or more foreign languages, and appealed for their help. They would have to find articles in European journals suitable for condensation, translate them, and then digest them. It was decided to try an experimental issue, which appeared in December 1951.[1]

The preface to this experimental issue described the rationale and the scope of the proposed publication. *Theology Digest* was "based on the belief that a considerable number of priests, seminarians, and educated Catholic laity in this country are interested in present-day theological thought." However, the vast quantity of theological publications and the fact that most of the literature was not in English prevented many in this audience from reading widely in contemporary theology. The *Digest* would present "in short, readable form the best of the theological thought that is contained in current periodicals."

The new journal would publish digests only. There would be no original articles and no book reviews. The emphasis would be on the speculative rather than the pastoral aspects of theology. "The reader of *Theology Digest*," the editor promised, "will not obtain a complete coverage of what is being accomplished in theological circles, but he will be kept aware of the more significant contributions." For the first year the journal would be published on an experimental basis until a satisfactory method of selecting and condensing articles had been developed.[2]

After a second experimental issue in May 1952, *Theology Digest* began regular publication in the winter of 1953. Although the first experimental issue had carried five articles on the recent encyclical of Pope Pius XII, *Humani generis*, the issues were not devoted to single themes. This experimental issue had also carried eight articles on a variety of topics. In 1962, lectures as well as published articles began to be digested in the journal's pages. The Winter 1963 issue reprinted the annual Bellarmine Lecture presented by a distinguished theologian at St. Mary's College that year. In subsequent years the Bellarmine Lecture appeared regularly in the winter issue.

From the beginning *Theology Digest* was meant to serve a Catholic readership. The first article by a Protestant to appear was Vissert Hooft's piece on the World Council of Churches meeting in Evanston, Illinois, which was printed in the Spring 1954 issue. Thereafter, the work of Protestant and other non-Catholic writers began to appear in the pages of the journal.

The original prospectus for *Theology Digest* in December 1951 had announced that the journal would not carry book reviews. For the first 10 years of its existence, the journal adhered to this policy. The Winter 1963 issue carried a "Book List" compiled by W. Charles Heiser. This first list was limited to books published in the United States since the summer of 1962 and was intended as an aid especially to theology teachers and librarians in charge of the religious sections of large college libraries. Publication information, the Library of Congress catalog card number, and the price were listed, along with an annotation of a few lines identifying the author and the nature and scope of the book. Beginning with the issue for summer 1964, Heiser's book list became a standard feature of every issue of *Theology Digest*. At first, books by authors who were not Catholics were marked with an asterisk, and the readers were warned that for Catholics the restrictions on reading material that fell under the ban of the Index of Forbidden Books might apply to some of them. The following year, with Vatican II fully embarked on its program of renewal, the warning was no longer printed, although the asterisks continued to appear until 1966. By then the compiler of the survey was content to note simply that the listing of a book did not imply a recommendation.

With the conclusion of Vatican II in December 1965 and the gathering momentum of ecumenism in the Catholic Church, *Theology Digest* began to digest the work of more and more non-Catholic writers. As theological studies in the United States came to maturity in these same years, the journal ceased to limit its scope to European periodicals and authors who wrote in a language other than English. When St. Mary's College was closed in 1967 and the school and students were moved to St. Louis, *Theology Digest* moved there as well. Van Ackeren, still the editor, was now also the dean of the Divinity School. In 1975, Theology Digest, Incorporated, took over the publication of the journal.

The editors continued to experiment with new formats for presenting the work of theologians to a wide readership. In 1968 a supplement consisting of seven lectures of Karl Rahner was published to commemorate the sesquicentennial of the founding of St. Louis University in 1818. In the Winter 1980 issue, an annotated bibliography was published on "Kung, Schillebeeckx, and the Magisterium." The Winter 1981 issue carried an annotated bibliography, "Women and the Ministerial Priesthood." Van Ackeren continued to direct and edit *The-*

ology Digest until his death in January 1978. He was succeeded by Wendell E. Langley. Under Van Ackeren, the journal had reached a circulation of more than 13,000, impressive for a theological perodical.

Notes

1. Cyril O. Vollert, "How *Theology Digest* Began," *Theology Digest* 28 (Winter 1980): 303.
2. "Introducing *Theology Digest*," *Theology Digest* (December 1951): 1.

Information Sources

INDEX SOURCES: *Catholic Periodical and Literature Index, Religious and Theological Abstracts, Theology Digest 20-Year Cumulative Index* (1953–72), *Old Testament Abstracts.*
REPRINT EDITIONS: University Microfilms International.
LOCATION SOURCES: Library of Congress, Catholic University of America, Emory University, Duke University, St. Louis University, and others.

Publication History

MAGAZINE TITLE AND TITLE CHANGES: *Theology Digest* (1953–   ).
VOLUME AND ISSUE DATA: Experimental issues in December 1951 and May 1952. Vol. 1:1 dated Winter 1953; 1–9 (1953–61) had three issues per year; thereafter there have been four issues per year except for 20 (1972), which had five issues.
PUBLISHER AND PLACE OF PUBLICATION: St. Mary's College, St. Mary's, Kans. (Winter 1953-Summer 1967); School of Divinity, St. Louis University, St. Louis, Mo. (Autumn 1967-Spring 1975); Theology Digest, St. Louis, Mo. (Summer 1975–   ).
EDITORS: Gerald F. Van Ackeren (experimental issues and 1–25, 1953–77), Wendell E. Langley (1978–   ).
CIRCULATION: 13,000.

James T. Connelly, C.S.C.

THEOLOGY TODAY

In September 1943, a group of friends—college, university, and seminary professors and clergy all identified with the Reformed tradition in American Protestantism—met in Princeton, New Jersey, to discuss the possibility of establishing a periodical that would present current issues in theology for a sophisticated clergy and lay audience. They felt a need for a journal that would disseminate the fruits of academic scholarship in such areas as systematic and philosophical theology, church history, social ethics, biblical studies, and practical theology but in a tone that avoided the technical jargon of specialists. The group formed itself into an editorial council, designating Princeton Theological Seminary's John Mackay as editor and fixing on "the life of man in the light of God" as a motto for the periodical. Articles were solicited from prominent scholars, and the first issue of *Theology Today* appeared in April 1944.

The inaugural editorial outlined the aims of the journal. The same aims continue to guide the publication of *Theology Today* after more than 40 years and have been reprinted in the journal from time to time when anniversary issues have prompted reflection on goals and achievements. The stated goals were and are:

1. "To contribute to the restoration of theology in the world of today as the supreme science."
2. "To study the central realities of Christian faith and life and to set forth their meaning in clear and appropriate language."
3. "To explore afresh the truth rediscovered by the Protestant Reformation, especially the tradition called the Reformed, and to show their relevancy to the contemporary problems of church and society."
4. "To provide an organ in which Christians whose faith is rooted in the revelation of God in the Bible and in Jesus Christ, and who are in different spheres of intellectual activity, may combine their insights into the life of man in the light of God, with a view to interpreting our human situation and developing a Christian philosophy of life."[1]

Clearly reflecting the impact of neo-orthodox thought in theological circles and the assumption that the events of World War II would demand rethinking of theological perspectives, these aims were to be carried out through editorials by members of the council, scholarly articles, essays of comment on contemporary religious events ("The Church in the World") and on theological trends ("Theological Table-Talk"), and reviews. The approach was to solicit most of the material from leading scholars, though occasionally material has been excerpted or reprinted from other works. In October 1961, a section called "Critic's Corner" was added. Initially the brief essays in this feature represented reactions of scholars to articles appearing in previous issues, though in recent years commentary on articles has been solicited in advance of publication so that an essay and response frequently appear in the same issue. As well, "Critic's Corner" has provided a forum for authors to offer terse appraisal of contemporary issues not treated elsewhere in the journal. Occasionally *Theology Today* has featured religious poetry.

In its more than four decades of publication, *Theology Today* has demonstrated remarkable consistency in purpose and quality. Several factors account for this constancy. One is the association of the periodical with Princeton Theological Seminary. Although the seminary does not officially sponsor the journal, it has provided editorial leadership, and its faculty have been frequent contributors to its pages. Another vital factor is editorial continuity. Only two persons have served as editor: Mackay, the founding editor and Princeton Seminary president, remained at the helm until 1951, when he was succeeded by Hugh T. Kerr, Jr., a member of the seminary's faculty, who continues to oversee publication. Except for minor changes in technical design and the restatement of the motto to "Our

Life in God's Light'' in 1974 (perhaps indicating a sensitivity to feminist concerns), *Theology Today* has maintained the same basic format instituted in its first issue.

The roster of contributors during the first decade of *Theology Today*'s publication history reads like a who's who of scholars in various religion disciplines in the United States and abroad. Historical essays, for example, were offered by such distinguished scholars as Wilhelm Pauck, E. Harris Harbison, and Roland Bainton. England's C. H. Dodd joined with Americans Paul Minear and Bruce Metzger to present essays on current trends in biblical scholarship, while ethicist-theologians of the caliber of Reinhold Niebuhr, H. Richard Niebuhr, Paul Ramsey, Paul Lehmann, John C. Bennett, Joseph Fletcher, and George Kelsey directed attention to social ramifications of Christian belief. Theological giants of the age such as Karl Barth, Paul Tillich, and Emil Brunner are also represented in the first decade's issues.

Within the first decade, *Theology Today* expanded its horizons well beyond the Reformed tradition and has not yet returned to a narrow Reformed focus. In the tenth anniversary year, for example, Pius Parsch presented ''The New Renaissance of Biblical Studies in the Roman Catholic Church'' (10, 1953–54). Two years later, the July issue of volume 12 was devoted to Christianity's relations with other religions and included essays on the theology of Martin Buber and the resurgence of a vital Hindu tradition. Interfaith relations were also the focus of a theme issue in volume 16 (1959–60), and world religions were the subject of a symposium of essays in volume 23 (1966–67). More recent manifestations of this broader perspective include John C. Carey's ''An Overview of Catholic Theology'' and Catholic theologian Rosemary Radford Ruether's ''Anti-Semitism in Christian Theology,'' both in the thirtieth anniversary year (1973–74), and George W. Braswell, Jr.'s ''Iran and Islam,'' which appeared in 1980 in the midst of the United States's confrontation with Iran over the hostage crisis.

Traditions other than the Protestant Reformed have not been the only subjects of special theme issues or symposia of articles within a single issue. There has been a consistent affort to link material in each issue together either explicitly or implicitly in an editorial that discusses the relationships among the various articles. Notable theme issues over the years are those devoted to an analysis of the thought of Danish philosopher-theologian Søren Kierkegaard on the occasion of the centennial of his death (12, 1955–56), an appreciation of the theological contribution of Karl Barth at the time of his seventieth birthday (13, 1956–67), a discussion of the philosophical theology of Paul Tillich (15, 1958–59), a wide-ranging roundtable on ''The Christian in Politics,'' which included essays by scholars as well as by political leaders such as Senator Charles Percy (26, 1969–70), a detailed examination of clinical pastoral education in the training of clergy (36, 1979–80), and a provocative colloquy on the interrelationships of anthropology and theology that attracted articles by scholars such as Jacob Neusner and Mary Douglas (41, 1984–85).

But *Theology Today* has always been conscious of the contemporaneous dimension of its task, which the title of the journal itself indicates. In this regard, the editors and editorial council are to be commended for addressing numerous social issues in the journal's pages just as they were coming in vogue. As early as volume 14 (1957–58), which also contained a symposium on racial segregation, Edward A. Tiryakian called attention to "*Apartheid* and Religion," while Joseph R. Washington, Jr., launched what has remained a continuing interest in black religion and theology in volume 20 (1963–64) with his "Are American Negro Churches Christian?" The role of women in the church represents another example of a current issue that has received careful treatment in *Theology Today*. Volume 28 (1971–72) is a case in point; it contained essays by Howard Moody on "Abortion: Woman's Right and the Legal Problem" (reprinted from *Christianity and Crisis**) and Marilyn Bowen on "Women's Liberation: A Catholic View," as well as a reprinted interview with Catholic feminist theologian Mary Daly on "The Church and Women." The entire January issue of 1978 (volume 34) was given over to consideration of similar topics. Two other areas of current concern addressed in *Theology Today* merit mention. Both Gabriel Fackre and Joseph Fletcher have highlighted issues in the field of biomedical ethics, the former in "Biomedical Reproduction" (27, 1970–71) and the latter in "Medicine, Morals, and Religion" (31, 1974–75), while Patrick Henry turned to the more controversial matter of "Homosexuals: Identity and Dignity" in a provocative essay in volume 33 (1976–77).

At the same time, *Theology Today* has not lost sight of the emphasis demanded by the first word in its title. In addition to articles by or about the thought of seminal figures such as Karl Barth, Reinhold Niebuhr, Paul Tillich, and Emil Brunner, *Theology Today* has kept readers apprised of the latest major developments in Christian religious thought. This ongoing concern is evidenced in essays by Carl E. Braaten on "Toward a Theology of Hope" (24, 1967–68), Daniel Day Williams on "The New Theological Situation" (24, 1967–68), Norman Pittenger on "Process Theology Revisited" (27, 1970–71), Robert McAfee Brown on "New Data for a New Bonhoeffer" (29, 1972–73), Jurgen Moltmann on "The Crucified God" (31, 1974–75), and Jerry Irish on "Moltmann's Theology of Contradiction" (32, 1975–76). Two special symposia also testify to the journal's commitment in the theological arena: one on "The Rhetoric of Theology" based on papers presented at the Gallahue Conference on Theology at Princeton Theological Seminary in April 1968 (25, 1968–69), and one on "Story and Narrative in Theology" (32, 1975–76).

The inaugural editorial drew attention to *Theology Today*'s special interest in matters relating to the Reformed heritage within Protestantism. That interest has not been forgotten over the years; numerous articles have directed attention to topics dealing with worship, history, and theology pertaining to the Reformed tradition. Historian James Hastings Nichols provided a brief overview of "The Liturgical Tradition of the Reformed Churches" in volume 11 (1954–55), and Howard G. Hageman offered a comparison of current worship practice with earlier expressions in "Reformed Worship: Yesterday and Today" (18, 1961–62). Interest in Reformed history may be seen not only in the theme issue entitled "A Reformed Jubilee," which marked the four-hundredth anniversary of the publication of the Geneva Bible (17, 1960–61), but in individual essays such as Lefferts A. Loetscher's thoughtful "C. A. Briggs in the Retrospect of Half a Century" (12, 1955–56), John A. Mackay's "Witherspoon of Paisley and Princeton" (18, 1961–62), Georges A. Barrois's "Calvin and the Genevans" (21, 1964–65), James I. McCord's "The Faith of John Knox" (29, 1972–73), and Wolfhart Pannenberg's "Freedom and the Lutheran Reformation" (34, 1981–82). Of the numerous articles exploring the theological thrust of Reformed Protestantism, four merit mention for their efforts to show the relevance of the heritage to contemporary concerns or to apply new interpretive constructs to understand the tradition: James D. Smart, "Scripture and the Confession of 1967" (23, 1966–67); B. A. Gerrish, "The Lord's Supper in the Reformed Confessions" (23, 1966–67); Paul W. Pruyser's especially provocative "Calvin's View of Man: A Psychological Commentary" (26, 1969–70); and Edward A. Dowey, "Law in Luther and Calvin" (41, 1984–85).

Three other topical areas have also been prominent in *Theology Today*'s efforts to probe "our life in God's light": the ecumenical movement, biblical scholarship, and religious expression in the arts (especially in music and architecture). As early as volume 7 (1950–51), eminent Orthodox theologian Georges Florovsky contributed an important piece, "The Eastern Orthodox Church and the Ecumenical Movement," and in later volumes, H. Richard Niebuhr looked at "The Seminary in an Ecumenical Age" (17, 1960–61), leading ecumenist Henry Pitney VanDusen wrote about "Ecumenical Christianity Tomorrow" (18, 1961–62), John Dillenberger added a theological twist in "Church Union: Theology and Culture" (19, 1962–63), and former executive secretary of the Consultation on Church Union Paul A. Crow, Jr., explored the significance of "The Lord's Supper in Ecumenical Dialogue" (22, 1965–66). Representative of the attention paid to biblical studies are Frederick C. Grant's "Biblical Studies: View and Reviews" (14, 1957–58), James M. Robinson's "The Quest of the Historical Jesus Today" (15, 1958–59), a symposium on servant imagery in Bible and theology (15, 1958–59), and Bruce Metzger's "The New Testament of the Church" (19, 1962–63). Concern for the arts is evidenced in the several articles over the years written by literary critics such as Roland M. Frye, Robert Detweiler, Arthur H. Driver, Wilbur Dwight Dunkel, and Carlos Baker, as well as in symposia on architecture (19, 1962–63) and the arts (34, 1977–78), and such articles as "What Should a Congregation Sing?" by William H. Scheide (20, 1963–64) and "Folk Singing in Worship" (26, 1969–70).

A questionnaire asking for reader information was included in the October 1983 issue. The results, based on 1200 replies, were reported in the July 1984 issue. They reveal that the typical reader is a married male between the ages of thirty-five and sixty, holder of a postbaccalaureate degree, pastor of a church with approximately 500 members, receiving a salary of $25,000, a home owner, and the purchaser of more than 20 books each year. In addition, the typical reader regularly attends continuing education programs, views some 10 movies each year, and watches television 10 hours each week. Moreover, the survey showed that just over one-quarter of the readers hold an earned doctoral degree. Approximately the same proportion had also published a book, monograph, or article within the five years preceding the survey. Hence it is safe to conclude that *Theology Today* reaches an intellectually sophisticated audience committed to the advancement of theological inquiry and knowledge.

Theology Today after more than four decades of publication remains one of a handful of periodicals dedicated to disseminating scholarly work in a popular but sophisticated manner. As such, it provides a valuable service to thousands of clergy and laity intent on keeping abreast of current thinking on a variety of areas dealing with religion in general and the state of Christianity in the world in particular.

Note

1. Editorial by John A. Mackay, *Theology Today* 8 (1951–52): 5, citing his editorial, "Our Aims," in *Theology Today* 1 (1944–45): 3ff.

Information Sources

BIBLIOGRAPHY:
Kerr, Hugh T., Jr. "Forty Years and So?" *Theology Today* 40 (1983–84): 391–93.
Mackay, John A. "Our Aims." *Theology Today* 1 (1944–45): 3ff.
———. "Our Aims." *Theology Today* 10 (1953–54): 447–55.
Wiggins, James B. "Scholarly Quarterly Sounds: Some Reflections." *Quarterly Review* 3 (1983): 95–104.
INDEX SOURCES: Index to 1–20 in *Theology Today* 20 (1963–64): 595–635, to 21–30 in *Theology Today* 30 (1973–74): 445–67; also in *Book Reviews of the Month, New Testament Abstracts, Old Testament Abstracts, Book Review Index, Current Contents, Religious and Theological Abstracts, Religion Index One, Guide to Social Science and Religion in Periodical Literature, Humanities Index.*
REPRINT EDITONS: University Microfilms International, Microforms International Marketing Co.
LOCATION SOURCES: Princeton Theological Seminary, Princeton University, Duke University, Southern Methodist University, University of Chicago, Los Angeles Public Library, Union Theological Seminary (New York), and many others.

Publication History

MAGAZINE TITLE AND TITLE CHANGES: *Theology Today* (1944–   ).
VOLUME AND ISSUE DATA: 1:1 (April 1944–   ). Appears quarterly in April, July, October, and January.
PUBLISHER AND PLACE OF PUBLICATION: Lancaster Press, Lancaster, Pa. (1944–   ).
EDITORS: John A. Mackay (1944–51), Hugh T. Kerr, Jr. (1951–   ).
CIRCULATION: 10,000 (1984).

Charles H. Lippy

THE THOMIST

The *Thomist*, a speculative quarterly review, was established in 1939 by Dominican priests (Order of Preachers) who taught at the Dominican House of Studies, Washington, D.C. In February 1938 Dominican Fathers Arthur McMahon, Walter Farrell, Paul Skehan, and Robert Slavin were requested by their religious superior, Father T. S. McDermott, the provincial of the province of St. Joseph, to "outline a program for the publication of a scientific review."[1] Little over a year later, the first issue of the *Thomist* appeared, dated April 1939. Listed as its editors were "The Dominican Fathers of the Province of St. Joseph." This anonymous group editorship listing persisted through 1967. In January 1968, the name of the chief editor was listed for the first time in the periodical. Walter Farrell (1902–51), a noted interpreter of the *Summa Theologica* of St. Thomas Aquinas and professor of dogmatic theology at the Washington House of Studies, was the key figure in getting the quarterly into print. For all practical purposes he should be called the founder and first editor of the *Thomist*. At his death Father Farrell was eulogized in the pages of the periodical as "the guiding genius in the first critical years of its existence."[2]

The first issue of the *Thomist* contained an editorial note explaining the purpose of the new quarterly.[3] The *Thomist* was to be a serious periodical designed to be read not only by specialists in the fields of theology and philosophy but also by the educated nonprofessional "who has maintained an interest in the worthwhile things of life." The editors intended their journal "to be solidly scientific." Its contents were to be "vital" ("possessed of a personal and fundamental pertinence") and presented in a clear style in English. The quarterly was to specialize in speculative essays in theology and philosophy "of significance for humans living in the age in which we live."

From its inception the *Thomist* has adhered consistently to the criteria set out by the first editors. Each issue has almost invariably carried three or four articles of a highly theoretical nature concerning issues in philosophy or theology. Some have been authored by scholars of renown, others by little-known writers. Most writers have been Roman Catholic. Several reviews of serious theological or philosophical works have been printed in each number. Editorial comment has appeared only occasionally in the *Thomist*. The first two volumes contained a series of essays by Mortimer Adler, then a young philosophy professor at the University of Chicago. The series, a study of a complicated issue in Thomistic philosophy, was entitled "The Problem of Species" and was later published in book form. Walter Farrell, who contributed extensively to the quarterly in its early years, joined with Mortimer Adler in the volumes of 1941 to 1944 to present a long series of articles, jointly authored, on "The Theory of Democracy."

In addition to those of Adler and Farrell, the essays of other prominent philosophers and theologians found their way into the pages of the *Thomist*. They included Jacques Maritain, Yves Simon, Maurice Blondel, Charles E. Curran, James Collins, Paul Ramsey, and Dominican scholars Otto Pesch, William A.

Kane, William A. Wallace, Jerome Hamer, William Hill, Thomas O'Meara, and James Weisheipl.

Over the course of its history, single issues and, in some cases, whole volumes of the *Thomist* have been dedicated to specific topics. In 1943 the January number, which formed volume 5, consisted of articles in honor of Jacques Maritain, the renowned Thomist and prominent Catholic layman, on the occasion of his sixtieth birthday. Included were essays by distinguished scholars such as Mortimer Adler, Anton Pegis, and Robert Hutchinson. The January 1957 number was devoted to a series of articles concerned with the recent papal proclamation of the dogma of the Assumption of the Virgin Mary, *Munificentissimus Deus*. In 1961 the April, July, and October numbers were combined into a festschrift entitled "The Dignity of Science" to honor the sixtieth birthday of William A. Kane, O.P., an American Dominican writer of some distinction.

"Vatican II: The Theological Dimension" was the theme of volume 27 in 1963. It contained essays by prominent Catholic theologians on specific topics being considered at the council. In 1974 the seventh centenary of the death of St. Thomas Aquinas was commemorated in the *Thomist*. Each of the four numbers that year presented essays written by significant Thomistic scholars, including Mortimer Adler, Otto Pesch, and James Weisheipl. Fellow Dominicans of repute, Meister Eckhart of Hochheim and St. Albert the Great, were honored in special issues of April 1978 and October 1980, respectively. The January 1979 number honored Karl Rahner with a number-length essay by Andrew Tallon on Rahner's Christian anthropology. "Foundational Theology" was the theme of the April 1981 issue and included articles by important contemporary American Catholic theologians including Avery Dulles, William Shea, Charles E. Curran, and John Komonshak.

Apart from the nine special numbers or volumes mentioned, the editors of the *Thomist* have made no special effort to thematize the contents of the periodical beyond adhering to the rather broad guidelines established in 1939. The common denominator among the articles appearing in the quarterly continues to be their speculative nature. In content, the essays in any one issue might range from a study of some abstract mathematical principle to one on the teleological suspension of the ethical. In a few cases frequent contributors have concentrated on specific areas of investigation in their articles. Important examples are the numerous articles of William A. Wallace on the relationship between philosophy and science.[4]

In summary, the *Thomist* can be described as a well-edited quarterly containing serious essays of a highly theoretical nature on topics of theology and philosophy. The theology is done primarily by Roman Catholic theologians. The philosophy is generally, though not necessarily, concerned with issues arising from Thomistic philosophy. Only occasionally and almost by coincidence do the essays relate to issues of current importance on the contemporary Roman Catholic scene. As a consequence the quarterly has not become identified with either the conservative or liberal factions among contemporary American Catholic intellectuals. The ahistorical attitude of the *Thomist* is also apparent in the fact that not a single article in recent years has been concerned with social questions such as nuclear war.

The Catholic hierarchy exercises no control over the periodical. The sponsorship of the Dominican Fathers has not prevented its editors from publishing worthwhile essays by Dominicans and non-Dominicans, by Roman Catholics and non-Roman Catholics. The editors have been faithful to their goals, especially in encouraging the exploration of truth in the pages of their journal.

Notes

1. Data concerning the founding of the *Thomist* is found in Reginald M. Coffey, O.P., "The Way of the Eagle," an unpublished biography of Walter Farrell.

2. Robert E. Brennan, O.P., "Walter Farrell: *Apud Posteros Sacer*," *Thomist* 15 (1952): 200.

3. See "Editorial Notes," *Thomist* 1 (1939): 123–26.

4. See William A. Wallace, O.P., "Thomas and Modern Science," *Thomist* 32 (1968): 67–83, and "Aquinas on Creation: Science, Theology and Matters of Fact," *Thomist* 38 (1974): 485–523.

Information Sources

INDEX SOURCES: *Catholic Periodical and Literature Index, Philosopher's Index, Religious and Theological Abstracts, Current Contents.*
REPRINT EDITIONS: Kraus Thompson Organization, Ltd. (reprints and microfilm).
LOCATION SOURCES: Catholic University of America, Loyola University (Chicago), New York Public Library, St. John's University (Collegeville), University of Southern California, and others.

Publication History

MAGAZINE TITLE AND TITLE CHANGES: *The Thomist* (1939–   ).
VOLUME AND ISSUE DATA: 1 (1939–   ); generally appears quarterly (January, April, July, October); 1 (1939) had three numbers (April, July, October), 5 had only one (January 1943), 6 contained the other three numbers for 1943, 26 had one (January 1963), and 27 had the remaining three for 1963.
PUBLISHER AND PLACE OF PUBLICATION: Sheed and Ward, New York. (1939–45); Thomist Press, Washington, D.C. (1945–   ).
EDITORS: Dominican Fathers of the Province of St. Joseph (1939–67), Nicholas Halligan, O.P. (1968–75), William J. Hill, O.P. (1975–83), J. A. DiNoia, O.P. (1983–   ).
CIRCULATION: 1085 (1983).

Bernard Noone

TIDSKRIFT. *See* THE LUTHERAN QUARTERLY

THE TRUE WESLEYAN. *See* THE WESLEYAN
ADVOCATE

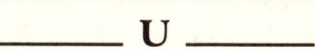

UNION SEMINARY QUARTERLY REVIEW

In December 1939, the students of Union Theological Seminary (UTS), New York City, published the first issue of the *Union Review*, later titled *Union Seminary Quarterly Review*. Its first editors were students, Ernest A. Becker, Jr., and Roger Shinn, who along with their editorial board selected as the *Review*'s motto the somewhat pretentious "To give expression to the best of student Christian thought and to promote further thought and action in the service of Christ." Its original stated intent was to register student thought, to provide a kind of public forum through which Union students (mostly) could explore and appraise the problems of their contemporary world.[1] The first issue included articles on diverse topics, ranging from civil liberties, war and pacifism, democracy and fascism, to religion and science, and anti-Semitism. Throughout its brief existence (1939–45) the *Union Review* published three issues annually; its format was informal; its editorials, wide ranging, sometimes inflammatory; its articles, brief (three to seven pages) and largely popular, not scholarly.[2]

In 1945 a major step was taken to upgrade the *Union Review*; it would now be published jointly by the students, faculty, and alumni of the seminary. In November 1945, the first issue of *Union Seminary Quarterly Review* was published, formed by uniting two previously independent UTS publications: the *Union Review* and the *Alumni Bulletin*. Its aim was "to give students, faculty, and alumni an opportunity for exchange of ideas and free expression of opinion."[3] Other changes were made. The motto was simplified: "To promote thought and action in the service of Christ"; the responsibilities of chief editor were shared by a student and a member of the UTS faculty; and the earliest volumes (1–10) included alumni news and information, alumni necrology, and a column, "Quadrangle Notes," usually by the president of the seminary. Otherwise the *Quarterly* remained faithful to the original purpose of the *Union Review*.

During the years 1954–55, the *Review* took the step that made it the academic, scholarly journal it is today. There was now a single editor, a student. It is perhaps the only scholarly religion journal in the United States completely edited and produced by students. At this time or shortly after, the *Quarterly*'s function as an alumni bulletin ceased; alumni news and necrology were dropped and the "Quadrangle Notes" replaced by brief editorial comments.

Of much greater interest is the way in which this journal carried out its aim of showing how "theological thinking [can] respond both critically and responsibly to the concrete realities of time."[4] Two of the most frequent and significant issues raised in the earliest volumes of the *Union Review* were neo-orthodoxy and war and pacifism.

If any theological raison d'être can be singled out, the *Union Review* was begotten on behalf of what came to be known as neo-orthodoxy. Union Seminary at the time was, perhaps, the fulcrum of this movement in the United States, and the journal provided a forum for a theological school whose students and distinguished faculty, in the 1940s and 1950s, were largely, although not entirely, persuaded of "dialectical" theology. This was, in fact, the *Review*'s self-perception from the start. In a 1942 editorial preface, the student editor, John Dillenberger, reflected that when the journal began, "the struggle between a liberal and more orthodox theology was in the foreground. . . . [Since then] the student body as a whole has definitely swung to a more 'orthodox' theology and in some cases even more so than the faculty. . . . But in no sense is it to be construed as a return to an old orthodoxy. Nor is it devoid of the valid contributions which liberal theology has made."[5] More than 25 years later, in 1970, the *Union Seminary Quarterly Review*'s self-perception was much the same: "The publication of the *Quarterly Review* (begun in 1945) is roughly coextensive with the maturity of neo-orthodoxy." Over the years, the editors pointed out, the essays in this journal had "consistently presupposed the 'over-againstness' of the theological discipline, the need to bring a theological perspective to bear upon the alien condition of culture." Then, in a declaration of renewed commitment to their neo-orthodox heritage, the editors reaffirmed that the procedure of theology cannot assume "the benignity of the world situation" on the one hand or "the cultural success of the church" on the other. Instead, current events seemed to have "rendered theological innocence a permanent impossibility." Accordingly, concluded the editors, "we sense the need for this tradition to 'come of age' in a revolutionary and intensely diverse world, the need for theology to begin again in the midst of cultural experience."[6]

Two early articles illustrating this neo-orthodox bent appear in volume 1, (May 1940) of the *Union Review*: "Permanent Values in Liberal Christian Theology" by Eugene W. Lyman and "Evangelical Christianity and Social Action" by A. H. Behrenberg. In these two articles a critical assessment is made in such a way that a—perhaps precarious—middle course is negotiated between liberalism and evangelicalism. Both authors attempt to expose the insurmountable faults of these two traditions while distilling their enduring values. Essays focusing on existentialism and existentialist philosophers, along with essays by prominent dialectical theologians—including Reinhold Niebuhr, Paul Tillich, Dietrich Bonhoeffer, Martin Buber, and others—reinforce the view that the journal functioned as a forum for neo-orthodox theology.

A second problem attracting many articles and much editorializing was war and the Christian response to it. One issue of the *Union Review*, for example, includes an interview with Canon Charles E. Raven, a vocal English pacifist, who attacks Reinhold Niebuhr's claim that there is "no evidence that tyranny could be overcome except by force" as denying the gospel of grace and salvation. The Christian, rejoins Raven, should work to redeem society in wartime in the same way he works to redeem society in peacetime.[7] Of the two editorial responses included in the same issue, one editor was favorably challenged by Raven's pacifism and the other vehemently assaulted pacifism as an apostasy.

Years later (1968) and another war later, however, the editors of *USQR* disregarded a policy of no editorial comment and with a single voice signed and published a statement unconditionally castigating the war in Vietnam as "an affront to human dignity and respect for human life."[8] This statement was signed and republished in 1970 by a different board of editors, who added, "Our war in Vietnam is an inhuman, cruel, and senseless tragedy."[9] Such editorializing, although uncommon in the scholarly *USQR*, exemplifies the profound conviction of the editors to bring, in the service of Christ, a theological perspective to bear upon the alien condition of culture.[10]

Since the mid–1950s, when it evolved into its present scholarly character, *Union Seminary Quarterly Review* has devoted its pages to a potpourri of material and formats. It has regularly included surveys of recent theological literature, annotated bibliographies, or lengthy book reviews; topical (thematic) issues, such as on black theology, feminist theology, psychology and religion, religion and the arts, to name only a few; mixed issues, with essays on any number of subjects; festschrift issues, such as "In Honor of Daniel Day Williams"; special supplementary issues, customarily containing the inaugural lectures of newly appointed senior professors at UTS; occasional poems, such as "Prison" by D. Bonhoeffer, and photographic essays, such as "Fat City" in volume 25 (Winter 1970).

The *Union Seminary Quarterly Review* was originally cultivated in the fertile soil of neo-orthodox theology. Today vestiges of this tradition survive, but mostly it has been surpassed by a smorgasboard of theologies from which Americans select and indulge their sometimes fastidious theological palates. That *USQR* has survived its theological progenitor is the result of an ongoing editorial conviction that its function in American society is prophetic. Its editors have never been much interested in printing minutiae of biblical and theological scholarship simply for digestion by scholars. Instead, they have had an enduring interest in approximating an ideal of theological thinking that responds critically and responsibly to the concrete needs and evils of the present age.

Notes

1. Roger Shinn, "Making No Promises," *Union Review* 1:1 (December 1939): 1.
2. One exception was the year 1944 when only two issues were published. In "A Word from the Editor" John E. Smith explains: "Conditions resulting from the war have made it impossible for us to follow our former schedule of publication. Despite these conditions we are publishing two editions this year, because it is our conviction that when serious and responsible thinking is no longer carried on, a situation such as the one in which we find ourselves today has often been the result." See *Union Review* 5 (March 1944):2.
3. "Editorial," *Union Seminary Quarterly Review* 1 (November 1945): 1 (hereafter cited as *USQR*).
4. "Editorial," *USQR* 15 (Fall 1961): 1.
5. John Dillenberger, "From Vol. I to Vol. IV," *Union Review* 4 (December 1942): 1.
6. "Editorial," *USQR* 25 (Winter 1970): 1.
7. Charles E. Raven, "From an English Pacifist," *Union Review* 1 (March 1940): 15–16.
8. "Statement," *USQR* 23 (Winter 1968): 1.
9. "Statement," *USQR* 25 (Winter 1970): 1.
10. One other such statement, a "Loyalty Oath," was published in USQR 5 (January 1951). It was a signed statement endorsing the efforts of Protestant theological faculties to achieve academic freedom at the University of California.

Information Sources

BIBLIOGRAPHY:
Bennett, John C. "Change and Continuity in the Theological Climate at Union Seminary." *Union Seminary Quarterly Review* 18 (May 1963): 7–67.
Coffin, Henry Sloane. *A Half Century of Union Theological Seminary, 1896–1945: An Informal History*. New York: Charles Scribner's Sons, 1954.
Vorkink, Peter, ed. *Bonhoeffer in a World Come of Age*. Essays by Paul M. Van Buren and others; foreword by John C. Bennett. Philadelphia: Fortress Press, 1968. Originally published as *Union Seminary Quarterly Review* 23 (Fall 1967).
INDEX SOURCES: *Old Testament Abstracts, New Testament Abstracts, Religion Index One, Religious and Theological Abstracts*.
REPRINT EDITIONS: University Microfilms International.
LOCATION SOURCES: Yale University, Library of Congress, Union Theological Seminary (New York), University of Chicago, University of Michigan, Princeton Theological Seminary, and others.

Publication History

MAGAZINE TITLE AND TITLE CHANGES: *Union Review* (1939–45), *Union Seminary Quarterly Review* (1945–   ).
VOLUME AND ISSUE DATA: *Union Review* 1–6 (1939–45); *Union Seminary Quarterly Review* 1–   (1945–   ). Occasional supplementary issues or combined issues.
PUBLISHER AND PLACE OF PUBLICATION: Union Theological Seminary, New York (*Union Review, Union Seminary Quarterly Review* 1–17); Union Theological Seminary, Worcester, Mass. (*Union Seminary Quarterly Review* 18–19); Heffer-

nan Press, Worcester, Mass. (*Union Seminary Quarterly Review* 20); Capital City Press, Montpelier, Vt. (*Union Seminary Quarterly Review* 21–   ).

EDITORS: *Union Review*: Ernest A. Becker, Jr., and Roger Shinn (1939–40), Roger Shinn (1940–41), John Dillenberger (1941–43), John E. Smith (1943–45); *Union Seminary Quarterly Review*: Theodor Mauch and David E. Roberts (1945–46), Raymond Gibson and David E. Roberts (1946–57), Paul Meyer and John C. Bennett (1947–48), William Hamilton and John C. Bennett (1948–49), Robert Hutchinson and John C. Bennett (1949–50), David W. Jewell and John C. Bennett (1950–51), Doris C. Watson and John C. Bennett (1951–52), Philip J. Ramstad and John C. Bennett (1952–53), Edward Eastman and John C. Bennett (1953–54), Richard Kahlenberg and John C. Bennett (1954–55), James F. White (1955–56), William H. Hudnut III (1956–57), Ronald V. Perrin (1957–58), Carl N. Edwards (1958–59), Thomas B. Cox (1959–60), David P. McPhail (1960–62), Thomas R. Laws (1962–64), Mark K. Juergensmeyer (1964–65), Charles E. Brewster (1965–66), Garrett Green (1966–67), James H. Stentzel (1967–68), John C. Cendo, Jr. (1968–69), Robert A. Harsh (1969–70), Willis H. Logan (1970–71), Nancy R. Krasa (1971–72), Richard Strum (1972–74), Mark Zier (1974–75), Paul A. Bernabea (1975–76), Arthur M. Jester, Jr. (1976–77), Richard P. Hordern (1977–78), Mary Edwardsen (1978–81), James Waller (1981–82), Margaret McGuinness (1982–   ).

CIRCULATION: 1500 (1983).

James E. Gilman

U.S. CATHOLIC MISCELLANY

During the first decades of the nineteenth century, the Roman Catholic Church in the United States was an undistinguished and feared minority numbering roughly 200,000 out of a national population of 8 million. In 1822, the newly founded diocese of Charleston embraced the states of North Carolina and Georgia, as well as South Carolina, and the Catholic parishioners found themselves surrounded by hostile Huguenots fleeing Catholic persecution in France and displaced Anglicans fighting border wars with Catholics in southern Florida. The diocese itself was composed of poor families fleeing religious and economic turmoil in Ireland and on the island of Santo Domingo. Newly arrived as the spiritual leader of these refugees was Bishop John England, hardly a stranger to religious persecution.[1]

England had already distinguished himself as a defender of Catholic liberty in his native Ireland. In 1809, he had written a series of tracts entitled *Religious Repository* that sought to diffuse among his people a spirit of piety and to warn them against perusal of any books or articles of heretical and immoral tendency.[2] In the atmosphere of anti-Catholic suspicions and prejudices articulated in the secular press of the Carolinas, England saw the opportunity to use his editorial skill to good effect. Thus, on 5 June 1822, with the financial support of his sister Johanna, Bishop England established the *U.S. Catholic Miscellany*, the earliest genuine Catholic journal in the United States.[3] As a potential antidote to the poisonous misinformation about Catholics circulated in the secular press, the *Miscellany* sought to relieve Americans (including many Catholics) of their ignorance regarding Catholic doctrine and, in so doing, to win the tolerance, if not the allegiance, of the Protestant landed aristocracy of the diocese.[4] The purpose of the journal, as expressed in its prospectus, was to "give a simple explanation and defense of Catholic doctrine . . . employing a vigorous, persuasive, yet inoffensive style . . . [in order to] 'undeceive' the public press."[5]

England had begun a campaign that was slow to catch on but was eventually to serve the American Catholic Church with distinction. As early as 1837 his literary efforts were hailed in a pastoral letter issued at the close of the Third Provincial Council of Baltimore. The bishops of the council exhorted the clergy and faithful to support these nascent journals, "which though not officially sanctioned by us still are most useful to explain our tenets, to defend our rights, and to vindicate our conduct."[6]

In spite of this ringing endorsement, most American bishops failed to follow England's lead. Perhaps their hesitancy was occasioned by a sober appraisal of the financial and societal obstacles that the bishop of Charleston faced.

In the first place, the Protestant press did not welcome this sudden, lone voice of refutation. After the publication of the first issue of the *Miscellany*, the *Charleston Courier* launched a vitriolic attack on Catholicism and refused to sell advertisement space to Catholic businessmen because of the availability of such in the new periodical.[7] In two early encounters with Protestant publicists, England, writing in his "Curiosity" column in the *Miscellany*, refuted charges made in a sermon at the dedication of a Unitarian church and printed in the *Washington Gazette* regarding papal power of moral law dispensations and battled heresies voiced as Catholic teaching by an apostate Spanish priest employed by the secular press.[8] England felt that his journal of apologetics only began to meet the need of confronting anti-Catholic prejudice:

> How many volumes of religious tracts, how many Gospel and Evangelical and Christian periodical publications teem with misrepresentation and abuse of our creed! Nay, look at the common newspapers of the day whose editors boast of their liberty and confirm their claim to the title by the most copious quotations from every British hireling and malevolent infidel; in the midst of all this, how is it possible for us to expect that we shall be held in just estimation by our fellow citizens? It is a duty which we owe to them and to ourselves to attempt our vindication.[9]

Perhaps England's greatest enemy was the Evangelical Association of America. In one of its organs, the *Southern Religious Telegraph*, the tone for the debate was set: "The *beast* numbers half a million subjects in the United States . . . [all under] Popery, a monster forging chains to bind the people."[10] And, in

1831, when the *Miscellany* ran a series of 12 letters demonstrating Catholic claims to civil freedom, the association called England "an enemy to the State who is even now concocting in our midst a servile insurrection most brutal and bloody of all revolutions. . . . Come, let us root him out."[11]

The most serious attack on American Catholics answered by the *Miscellany* in England's 21-year tenure as editor came from Duff Green of the *Baltimore Pilot and Transcript*. In October 1840, Green charged that England had influenced Catholics to vote against the election of President William Henry Harrison as part of a larger scheme to overthrow all republican institutions in the land. The *Pilot and Transcript* took up the political question of priests seen as emissaries of a despotic foreign government and called for modification or outright repeal of the laws of naturalization.[12] The *Miscellany* wasted no time in defending the patriotism of American Catholics and insisted that Catholic clergy were bound by U.S. law just like other citizens.

In addition to these intense disputes with the Protestant press, England faced a difficult, often insurmountable, financial challenge in operating the *U.S. Catholic Miscellany*. In its initial printing, the journal was a scant eight pages, quarto size; nonetheless it folded only six months after beginning because of a lack of financial support. England had hoped to woo over 300 contributors in those early months but failed miserably. Publication was not resumed until 7 January 1824. Even then, with new publishers Gray and Ellis, a smaller format of 16 pages, and a renewed drive to sell shares in the journal, the bishop had to dig into his personal funds to the tune of $500 to keep it afloat. Indeed, until England's death in 1843, the *Miscellany* was often literally a one-man publication, produced, written, edited, and sold by either the bishop or his assistant, Rev. John McEncroe. Articles were often hastily written and poorly proofread. In addition, the journal suffered from neglect in New York and Philadelphia, which preferred a similar journal entitled *Truth Teller*. The biggest blow to England's fortunes came, however, in 1827 with the death of his sister Johanna, who had donated much of her small personal wealth to the ongoing struggle to finance the *Miscellany*. By the time of his own death, England had built a publication with about 6000 supporters and subscribers which was over $700 in debt.[13]

For the next five years, England's two successors, Bishops Reynolds and Lynch, managed the *Miscellany* in his spirit, the former contributing articles on doctrinal and ethical themes such as mixed marriage and the latter printing excerpts from the letters and personal works of the journal's founder.[14]

The final editor of the relatively short-lived *Miscellany* was Rev. James Andrew Corcoran, who later continued the periodical's polemics in his own *American Catholic Quarterly Review*.* Corcoran's days as editor of the *Miscellany* were colored by his series of essays impugning the work and character of Martin Luther and by the ravages of a devastating fire that left the *Miscellany* office in Charleston a ruin in 1858.[15] The death blow to the *U.S. Catholic Miscellany* did not come until the outbreak of Civil War in 1861, which effected the end of various organs of thought and debate in the South. Among them was this Catholic journal, a 39-year attempt at American Catholic apologetics aimed at a skeptical Protestant public and at a demoralized Catholic one.

Notes

1. C. Reilly, *Catholic Journalism: A Study of Its Development in the United States, 1789–1930* (New York: Columbia University Press, 1931), p. 2.

2. Paul J. Foik, C.S.C., *Pioneer Catholic Journalism* (New York: U.S. Catholic Historical Society, 1930), p. 73.

3. Reilly, p. 3.

4. Foik, p. 74.

5. "Prospectus," *United States Catholic Miscellany* 1 (1822): 1–3.

6. Peter Guilday, ed., *National Catholic Pastorals of the American Hierarchy, 1792–1919* (1923; reprinted, Westminster, Md.: Newman Press, 1954), p. 114.

7. Foik, p. 80.

8. Ibid., p. 85.

9. Quoted in Foik from *The Works of the Right Rev. John England* (Baltimore: John Murphy & Co., 1849), 3: 109.

10. *The United States Catholic Miscellany* 9 (1830).

11. Quoted in Foik, p. 86.

12. Ibid., p. 90.

13. Ibid., pp. 90–93.

14. For a discussion of the patterns in continuance of the original aims of a journal's founder, see Martin E. Marty et al., *The Religious Press in America* (New York: Holt, Rinehart and Winston, 1963).

15. Foik, p. 93.

Information Sources

BIBLIOGRAPHY:

Foik, Paul J. *Pioneer Catholic Journalism.* New York: U.S. Catholic Historical Society, 1931.

Marty, Martin E., et al. *The Religious Press in America.* New York: Holt, Rinehart and Winston, 1963.

New Catholic Encyclopedia. New York: McGraw-Hill, 1967. Vol. 3.

Reilly, Sister Mary Lonan. *The Catholic Press Association.* Metuchen, N.J.: Scarecrow Press, 1971.

INDEX SOURCES: *Catholic Periodical Index.*

REPRINT EDITIONS: American Periodicals Series, University Microfilms International.

LOCATION SOURCES: According to Foik, "It is doubtful (due to age and Civil War) whether a complete set of this periodical can be found in the United States."

Publication History

MAGAZINE TITLE AND TITLE CHANGES: *U.S. Catholic Miscellany* (1822–61).

VOLUME AND ISSUE DATA: 1:1–3 (June-November 1822); 2:4–3:11 (January 1824-November 1825); 4:11–38, no. 148 (January 1827-January 1861).

PUBLISHER AND PLACE OF PUBLICATION: Gray and Ellis, Charleston, S.C.

EDITORS: Bishop John England (1822, 1824–25, 1827–43), Bishop Patrick N. Lynch and Bishop Reynolds (1843–48), Rev. James A. Corcoran (1848–61). CIRCULATION: 300 (1822); 6000 (peak, 1848).

R. Scott Appleby

UNIVERSALIST QUARTERLY AND GENERAL REVIEW

Editor Hosea Ballou II, writing in the inaugural issue of the *Universalist Quarterly and General Review* in 1844, clearly envisioned a journal with ambitious goals and broad purposes. He proposed "to take in a much wider field" than "any publication which has appeared among Universalists in this country." Accordingly, the *Quarterly*'s contents ranged from reviews, denominational news, and expositions of Scripture to poetry, philosophy, and "dissertations in Biblical literature." Seeking to be in the vanguard of denominational thought, the *Quarterly* promised "considerable latitude . . . for the different views which different minds will take of the same subject." The editor's highest aspiration for the *Quarterly* was that it might promote "the cause of sound knowledge and genuine piety."[1]

Throughout its history (1844–91) the *Quarterly* served as both a forum for Universalist views on such issues as slavery, Unitarianism, German rationalism, and Utilitarianism, and a barometer of the denomination's concerns and its approach to a rapidly changing nineteenth-century America. "It is true, that every change is not, necessarily, an improvement," one contributor wrote in 1849, "but it is equally true, that where no modification of original views, no enlargement of mind, or no change in early habits of thought occurs, there can be no advancement in knowledge."[2]

Universalist reactions to Charles Darwin's *Origin of Species* provide a case in point. Unlike many other American religious groups, Universalists took note of Darwin's work in 1860, the year after its publication, and over the ensuing four decades the *Quarterly* contained a long succession of articles on Darwinism. Although greeted at first with hostility, evolutionary theory met with an increasingly favorable response in the pages of the *Quarterly*. Believing that religion had nothing to fear from science, Universalists began cautiously to consider Darwin's theory and in the final decades of the century accepted it fully.[3]

The inauguration of a new series in 1864, under the direction of Thomas B. Thayer, author of *Theology of Universalism* (Boston, 1862) and the denomination's first systematic theologian, brought subtle changes to the *Quarterly*. The new editor eliminated some of the broad-ranging departments of the original series in favor of more strictly theological and philosophical matters and included a regular listing of articles appearing in other theological journals. The *Universalist Quarterly and General Review* retained this character and format until recurring financial losses forced its closing in 1891.

Notes

1. Editor's introduction, *Universalist Quarterly and General Review* 1 (1844): 1–2.
2. "Changes in the Religious Views of Universalists," *Universalist Quarterly and General Review* 6 (1849): 6.
3. For a survey of Darwin's reception in the *Quarterly*, see Ernest Cassara, "The Effect of Darwinism on Universalist Belief," Universalist Historical Society *Journal* 1 (1959): 32–42.

Information Sources

INDEX SOURCES: *Universalist Quarterly and General Review* 48 (n.s. 28) (1891), *Poole's Index to Periodical Literature*.
REPRINT EDITIONS: American Periodicals Series, University Microfilms International.
LOCATION SOURCES: Library of Congress, Los Angeles Public Library, Newberry Library (Chicago), Boston Public Library, Harvard University, and Oberlin College.

Publication History

MAGAZINE TITLE AND TITLE CHANGES: *Universalist Quarterly and General Review* (1844–91).
VOLUME AND ISSUE DATA: 1:1 (January 1844)–48:4 (October 1891). New series begun January 1864. Appeared quarterly.
PUBLISHER AND PLACE OF PUBLICATION: A. Tompkins, Boston (1844–61), Tompkins & Co., Boston (1862–65), N.E. Universalist Publishing House, Boston (1865–91).
EDITORS: Hosea Ballou II (1844–58), George H. Emerson (1858–64), Thomas B. Thayer (1864–86), Richard Eddy (1886–91).
CIRCULATION: Unknown.

Randall H. Balmer

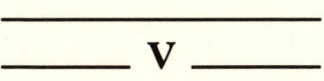

VIRGINIA EVANGELICAL AND LITERARY MAGAZINE. *See* THE LITERARY AND EVANGELICAL MAGAZINE

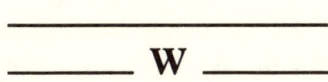

THE WESLEYAN. *See* THE WESLEYAN ADVOCATE

THE WESLEYAN ADVOCATE

On 7 January 1843 the *True Wesleyan* made its debut. This four-page weekly publication was the climax of almost a decade of abolitionist activities by its editor and owner, Orange Scott. A Methodist minister, Scott was sensitive to the discrepancy between the Methodist Episcopal Church's statement of opposition to slavery and its refusal to act against the practice. Repeatedly rebuked in his efforts to have the Methodist Church renounce slavery as a moral sin and work for its eradication, Scott withdrew from the denomination in November 1842.

Slavery challenged American Methodism throughout its first century of existence. In its early years, the church took a strong stand against the institution, but when the denomination faced the loss of southern support, founding Bishop Francis Asbury decided compromise was best. Henceforth the church officially condemned slavery while permitting its existence internally. Increasingly the church avoided discussion of slavery so as not to provoke its supporters, until the abolitionists of the 1830s gained a substantial following within the denomination. In 1843, frustrated by their unsuccessful efforts to end such compromise, numerous abolitionists seceded from the nation's largest Protestant group to form the Wesleyan Methodist Connection, thus foreshadowing Methodism's division into northern and southern branches two years later and the nation's division in 1860.[1]

Scott started his antislavery evangelism in 1834 by attempting to convert his colleagues in Methodism's New England Conference to his position. He purchased subscriptions to the antislavery publication, the *Liberator*, for all its members. In January 1835 he initiated the first extended discussion of slavery in a Methodist periodical in a series of abolitionist articles in *Zion's Herald*, the conference's official paper. Antiabolitionist rejoinders were presented by Dr. Wilbur Fisk, president of Wesleyan University, who described the abolitionist position as "moral quackery." This antiabolitionist position was deeply entrenched among the church's leadership, and most Methodist publications refused to carry material about slavery.

At the General Conference of 1836, the bishops declared that the scriptural way to deal with slavery was "to refrain from this agitating subject" and to support civil laws governing it.[2] The conference emphasized its willingness to "use all prudent means" to stop Methodist abolitionists from interfering with slavery.[3] Scott was so disheartened that he distributed to the members of the conference an anonymous pamphlet, arguing that the real question was not political expediency but the justice or injustice of excluding from 2 million Americans their inalienable rights.[4] The pamphlet caused an outrage, but elevated Scott to the forefront of leadership in Methodist abolitionism.

In the following months, Methodist abolitionists saw the bishops use their authority to prevent conferences from considering antislavery resolutions. Consequently Scott turned to extraecclesiastical structures, joining and becoming an agent for the American Anti-Slavery Society and writing his "Appeal to the Methodist Episcopal Church," which comprised the only edition of the *Wesleyan Antislavery Review*. In it he attacked the church's ethics concerning slavery and proclaimed the church's position to be "a stench in the nostrils of the Almighty!"[5] Returning to the pastorate in 1839, Scott found the church's publications still closed to the abolitionist message, so he started the *American Wesleyan Observer*. This antislavery publication was discontinued following the General Conference of 1840, which defeated every antislavery resolution presented. By 1841 Scott held "little hope that the church will ever be reformed in relation to slavery."[6] He admitted in June 1842 that he had "no expectation" that the church would ever "take action against slavery.... There is, therefore, no alternative but to submit to things pretty much as they are, or secede."[7] On 8 November 1842, Orange Scott withdrew from the Methodist Episcopal Church.

Scott then joined other abolitionists in calling for a convention to organize a new denomination, one free from the evil of slavery, to be called the Wesleyan Methodist Connection. In addition, Scott initiated the *True Wesleyan* as the voice of Methodist abolitionists and the new church, announcing that "on the absorbing question of the day, our paper will be decidedly anti-slavery both in its editorial and general character."[8] In the first issue, Scott also argued that in withdrawing from the Methodist Episcopal Church, he dissolved only his connection with slavery and episcopacy, not with anything essential to "pure Wesleyan Methodism.... We are still Methodist in doctrine ... [and] with the venerable Wesley in his views of slavery."[9] Thus Scott continued to combine his antislavery activities and his churchly enterprise.

The abolition of slavery was the major topic in the *True Wesleyan* for the next two decades. The journal regularly reported on antislavery activities and specifically about such within Methodist circles, local, regional, and national antislavery conventions, and significant slavery events in the South. In addition, the paper provided readers with a history of the American antislavery movement, a review of John Wesley's vigorous antislavery position, and details of the English Wesleyans' action on the issue.[10] At the conclusion of the paper's first year, Scott correctly observed "that our Wesleyan movement has given a tremendous impetus to church anti-slavery."[11] Following the Wesleyan secession, there was a revival of antislavery sentiment within New England Methodism. Fearing further secessions, the church's leadership allowed abolitionists to conduct conventions and voice their views. Methodist officials and publications, to keep abolitionists within the church, became more vocal against slavery. The general theme of pronouncements from northern Methodism was that good Methodists could be good abolitionists, and vice-versa.[12] In 1844 antislavery delegates dominated the Methodist General Conference, and the conference arranged for the church to split into independent northern and southern branches. The *True Wesleyan* covered the conference, concluding:

The Northern men took the ground of expediency. The Southern men that of right, as secured by civil law, the constitution, and laws of the church. The great question is whether slavery is a moral evil. . . . This question was not [answered]. . . . No voice was raised to show that Southern slaves were men and women, entitled to life, liberty, and property, as much as their masters. . . . The Northern men did not take the ground that slaveholding was sinful. This is trifling with the subject![13]

One of the more significant articles in the history of the *True Wesleyan* was the editorial entitled "Division of the M.E. Church: Its Effect on the Union of the States." The editors claimed that the division of the Methodist Episcopal Church would cause other denominations to divide and hasten the abolition of slavery in the United States. In fact they believed the Methodist split would "greatly weaken the cords of union. . . . The glory of God and the happiness of man requires a severance of the 'Union,' both in church and state."[14] The editors, like most other abolitionists, made one miscalculation, insisting that this dissolving of the Union would not entail physical force. For the next 16 years the *True Wesleyan* kept readers abreast of the gradual dissolution of the Union and its results.

Orange Scott did not live to see the liberation of the American slaves, for he died of tuberculosis on 31 July 1847. The spectacular growth (from 6000 to 15,000 members the first year) of his new Wesleyan Methodist Church, however, had ceased before his death. The switch of the denomination on slavery stopped the exodus to the Wesleyan Church and encouraged a number of Scott's followers to return. Among those were former editors of the *True Wesleyan* Jothan Horton, Luther Lee, and Lucius Matlack. So effective were the Methodist Episcopal

Church's efforts to prevent a migration of abolitionists that in 1865 the membership in the Wesleyan Church was no larger than it had been in 1843, and once the slavery issue was resolved, Wesleyan Methodist growth remained slow over the next century.

As the official publication of the Wesleyan Methodists, the *True Wesleyan* treated other subjects the new church felt important. The most prominent, besides slavery, was church polity, particularly denunciation of the episcopacy system of the Methodist Episcopal Church. The Wesleyans were committed to a representative system of government, which included lay participation.[15] The paper frequently dealt with social issues such as capital punishment, temperance, and the Sabbath Day movement. It opposed use of tobacco and membership in secret societies. The doctrine of Christian perfection or entire sanctification was given strong emphasis by the paper and was taught as a normative spiritual experience for all believers, placing the Wesleyan Church within the nineteenth-century holiness movement.

Following the Civil War and the emancipation of the slaves, the significance of the *True Wesleyan* to the general public declined. The paper became less provocative and more provincial as it concerned itself more with the church's own sectarian matters. The *True Wesleyan* has, however, survived to the present although it has undergone several name changes, as has the denomination it represents. Today it is the *Wesleyan Advocate*, the official publication of the Wesleyan Church.

Notes

1. *Zion's Herald* (7 January 1835): 2; ibid. (11 March 1835): 37.

2. *Christian Advocate and Journal* (17 June 1836): 171.

3. *Journals of the General Conference of the Methodist Episcopal Church, 1796–1836* (New York: n.p., 1855), p. 443.

4. Orange Scott, *Address to the General Conference of The Methodist Episcopal Church by the Rev. O. Scott, A Member of that Body* (New York: H. R. Piercy, 1836).

5. Orange Scott, *An Appeal to the Methodist Episcopal Church* (Boston: David H. Ela, 1838), p. 128.

6. *Zion's Watchman* (February 1841): 26.

7. *Zion's Herald* (15 June 1842): 96.

8. *True Wesleyan* (7 January 1843): 3.

9. Ibid., p. 2.

10. *True Wesleyan* (6 April 1844): 56; 20 (April 1844): 64; (4 May 1844): 72.

11. Ibid. (9 December 1843): 195.

12. Donald G. Mathews, "Orange Scott: The Methodist Evangelist as Revolutionary," in *The Antislavery Vanguard: New Essays on the Abolitionists*, ed. Martin Duberman (Princeton: Princeton University Press, 1965), pp. 96–97.

13. *True Wesleyan* (20 July 1844): 113.

14. Ibid. (3 August 1844): 121.

15. Ibid. (7 January 1844): 1.

Information Sources

BIBLIOGRAPHY:
McLeister, Ira F. *History of the Wesleyan Methodist Church of America*. Rev. ed. Marion, Ind.: Wesley Press, 1959.
Mathews, Donald G. "Orange Scott: The Methodist Evangelist as Revolutionary." *The Antislavery Vanguard: New Essays on the Abolitionists*. Ed. Martin Duberman. Princeton: Princeton University Press, 1965.
————. *Slavery and Methodism: A Chapter in American Morality, 1780–1845*. Princeton: Princeton University Press, 1965.
Matlack, Lucius C. *The Antislavery Struggle and Triumph in the Methodist Episcopal Church*. New York: Phillips and Hunt, 1881.
————. *The History of American Slavery and Methodism from 1780 to 1849*. New York: n.p., 1849.
————. *The Life of Rev. Orange Scott*. New York: Wesleyan Methodist Book Room, 1847–48.
Scott, Orange. *Address to the General Conference of the Methodist Episcopal Church by the Rev. O. Scott, a Member of That Body*. New York: H. R. Piercy, 1836.
————. *An Appeal to the Methodist Episcopal Church*. Boston: David H. Ela, 1838.
————. *The Grounds of Secession from the M.E. Church*. New York: O. Scott for the Wesleyan Methodist Connection of America, 1846.
————. *The Methodist E. Church and Slavery*. Boston: Scott, 1844.
INDEX SOURCES: *Guide to Social Science and Religion in Periodical Literature* (*Wesleyan Advocate* only).
REPRINT EDITIONS: Department of Photoduplication, Regenstein Library, University of Chicago; ATLA Board of Microtext Project; Wesleyan Church Archives.
LOCATION SOURCES: Partial holdings at Library of Congress, Clements Library (University of Michigan), Yale University, Boston Athenaeum, American Antiquarian Society, and Drew University.

Publication History

MAGAZINE TITLE AND TITLE CHANGES: *True Wesleyan* (1843–52), *The Wesleyan* (1853–60), *American Wesleyan* (1861–83), *The Wesleyan Methodist* (1884–1968), *The Wesleyan Advocate* (1968–   ).
VOLUME AND ISSUE DATA: *True Wesleyan* (7 January 1843–25 December 1852), *Wesleyan* (6 January 1853–26 December 1860), *American Wesleyan* (2 January 1861–26 December 1863), *Wesleyan Methodist* (2 January 1844–3 July 1968), *Wesleyan Advocate* (15 July 1968–   ). Published weekly.
PUBLISHERS AND PLACES OF PUBLICATION: O. Scott, Lowell, Mass. (1843); O. Scott, Boston (1843–44); O. Scott, New York (1844–47); C. Prindle, New York (1847–53); Wesleyan Methodist Connection, Syracuse, N.Y. (1853–60); Wesleyan Methodist Publishing Association, Syracuse, N.Y. (1861–83); Wesleyan Methodist Church of America, Syracuse, N.Y. (1884–1957); Wesleyan Church of America, Marion, Ind. (1957–68); Wesleyan Publishing House, Marion, Ind. (1968–   ).
EDITORS: Jothan Horton (1843), Orange Scott (1843–44), Luther Lee (1843, 1844–52), Lucius C. Matlack (1852–56), Cyrus Prindle (1856–64), Adam Crooks (1864–74), L. N. Stratton (1875–81), Nathan Wardner (1881–91), Arthur T. Jennings

(1891–1913), F. A. Butterfield (1913–27), Ira F. McLeister (1927–43), Roy S. Nicholson (1943–47), Oliver G. Wilson (1947–59), George E. Failing (1959–68, 1973–   ), Robert McIntire (1968–73).
CIRCULATION: 4700 (1852), 18,300 (1984).

Paul G. Chappell

THE WESLEYAN METHODIST. *See* THE WESLEYAN ADVOCATE

WESLEYAN THEOLOGICAL JOURNAL

Frank Baxter, British Methodist and professor emeritus at Duke Divinity School, observed:

> One sight of the theological ferment of these last twenty years is the presence since 1966 of *The Wesleyan Theological Journal*, which has published more than a hundred studies of various aspects of Wesley's theology, especially as that theology was focused on the work of the Holy Spirit in human life. The articles vary in quality—as do those of most journals—but most are well written and carefully documented; occasionally they are of major importance. The fact that membership in the publishing body, the Wesleyan Theological Society, is restricted by a conservative doctrinal test—one, however, to which Wesley himself would have had little difficulty subscribing—may sound uncompromising to many, but the thousand members are drawn from many different denominations, including both non-Methodist and non-American.[1]

This evaluation reflects the importance, orientation, and scope of the *Wesleyan Theological Journal* and its links to the Wesleyan Theological Society, the theological commission of the Christian Holiness Association, which was founded in 1965 as a learned society comparable to the Evangelical Theological Society but for scholars in the Wesleyan holiness tradition.[2]

Charles W. Carter (editor, 1965–72), assisted by a committee, produced the first number of the journal in the spring of 1966. According to Robert A. Mattke, "The publication of an annual Journal continues to be one of the more significant contributions of the Wesleyan Theological Society to the Holiness movement."[3] Two years after the journal was launched, discussion commenced about expanding from an annual to a quarterly publication in cooperation with seminaries associated with the Christian Holiness Association, but no change ensued. In 1979, however, semiannual publication began. Book reviews were added in 1981. These years also witnessed efforts to publicize the existence of the journal more widely.

The thematic orientation of the journal is apparent from the first issue, with its emphasis on the distinctive theological features of the Wesleyan holiness movement. The lead article by Wilbur T. Dayton, for example, addressed "Entire Sanctification as Taught in the Book of Romans," while Kenneth Geiger focused on "The Biblical Basis for the Doctrine of Holiness," and Milton S. Agnew wrote about "The Works of the Holy Spirit." These articles unwittingly presaged concerns that became critical later in both the society and its journal: the problem of biblical inerrancy-infallibility and the debate over how "baptism with the Holy Spirit" was linked to Wesley's idea of "entire sanctification." Much of the discussion was conducted in the business meetings of the society rather than in the pages of the journal, particularly in debates over doctrinal standards for membership in the society.

Two articles that appeared in 1981, "John Wesley's Approach to Scripture in Historical Perspective" by R. Larry Shelton and "Early Wesleyan Views of Scripture" by Daryl McCarthy, indicate tension over inerrancy, especially with regard to form and content and the subtle distinction between inerrancy and infallibility. Even earlier, the relation between pneumatology (doctrine of the Spirit) and entire sanctification erupted in both meetings of the society and the journal. Articles articulated viewpoints that included affirmation of baptism with the Holy Spirit as indeed related to entire sanctification, whether Wesley himself and the early Methodists made such a connection, whether the connection was related more to the American holiness tradition rather than to Wesley or to Scripture, and possible links to Oberlin's Asa Mahan and Charles G. Finney and their notions of Christian perfection. Others debated whether relating the baptism with the Spirit with the experience of perfect love was consistent with Scripture and early Wesleyan tradition. No consensus has yet been reached nor has a synthesis emerged from the diverse angles of the debate.

The first crisis regarding Scripture was a philosophical one with historical overtones and theological consequences. The debate over the relation of Spirit-baptism to Christian perfection was a hermeneutical one, both biblically and historically, which bore profound theological significance for the Wesleyan holiness tradition in North America. Together they indicate that the *Wesleyan Theological Journal* is at the forefront of ferment within holiness circles.

Notes

1. Frank Baker, "Unfolding John Wesley: A Survey of Twenty Years' Studies in Wesley's Thought," *Quarterly Review* advance edition (Fall 1980): 44–45.

2. The Christian Holiness Association, organized in 1867 at Vineland, N.J., as the National Camp Meeting Association for the Promotion of Holiness, became the National Association for the Promotion of Holiness in the later nineteenth century, following which it was known as the National Holiness Association until 1971. It "is a body of churches, organizations and individuals who accept" the traditional evangelical doctrines, with special concern for the doctrine of sanctification. See Charles W. Carter, *The Person and Work of the Holy Spirit: A Wesleyan Perspective* (Grand Rapids: Baker Book House,

1974), pp. 157–90, and Vinson Synan, *The Holiness-Pentecostal Movement* (Grand Rapids: Eerdmans, 1971).

3. Wesleyan Theological Society president's report to the Christian Holiness Association Board of Administration, April 1972, p. 1.

Information Sources

BIBLIOGRAPHY:

Baker, Frank. "Unfolding John Wesley: A Survey of Twenty Years' Studies in Wesley's Thought." *Quarterly Review* advance edition (Fall 1980): 44–45.

Carter, Charles W. *The Person and Ministry of the Holy Spirit: A Wesleyan Perspective.* Grand Rapids: Baker Book House, 1974.

Synan, Vinson. *The Holiness-Pentecostal Movement.* Grand Rapids: Eerdmans, 1971.

Wesleyan Theological Society Archives. Asbury Theological Seminary, Wilmore, Ky.

INDEX SOURCES: *Christian Periodical Index, Religion Index One.*

REPRINT EDITIONS: University Microfilms International.

LOCATION SOURCES: Yale University, Union Theological Seminary (New York), Duke University, Asbury Theological Seminary, Nazarene Theological Seminary, Western Evangelical Seminary, and others.

Publication History

MAGAZINE TITLE AND TITLE CHANGES: *Wesleyan Theological Journal* (1966–   ).

VOLUME AND ISSUE DATA: 1–13 (1966–78), one number per volume; 14 (1979–   ), two numbers per volume.

PUBLISHER AND PLACE OF PUBLICATION: Wesleyan Theological Society, University Park, Iowa (1966–67), Wilmore, Ky. (1968), Concord, Mich. (1969–71), Kansas City, Mo. (1972), Lakeville, Ind. (1973–75), Marion, Ind. (1976–84), Wilmore, Ky. (1985–   ).

EDITORS: Charles W. Carter (1965–72), Harvey J. S. Blaney (1972–73), W. T. Purkiser (1973–75), Leon O. Hynson (1975–78), Lee M. Haines (1978–81), Alex R. G. Deasley (1981–   ).

CIRCULATION: 1500 (1984).

John G. Merritt

THE WESTMINSTER THEOLOGICAL JOURNAL

In 1929 the tensions of the fundamentalist-modernist controversy within the Presbyterian Church, U.S.A., led to the reorganization of the faculty of the Princeton Theological Seminary and to the subsequent withdrawal of several of its members, notably J. Gresham Machen, generally considered the most prominent intellectually respectable defender of the fundamentalist position. Machen had been to that time influential in the *Princeton Theological Review**, which ceased publication that same year. Machen was central in the organization, also in 1929, of the Westminster Theological Seminary, Philadelphia, later removed to suburban Chestnut Hill. Founded as a bastion of Presbyterian orthodoxy, the seminary became the nucleus of the Presbyterian Church of America, which separated from the Presbyterian Church in 1936 and as the result of court action was renamed the Orthodox Presbyterian Church in 1939. Founded as the organ of Westminster Seminary's faculty in the midst of that turmoil, and a year after Machen's death, the *Westminster Theological Journal* was clearly established with a view to carrying on Machen's work: surveying from orthodoxy's height every doctrinal equivocation or open heresy of modernism and using every intellectual weapon available to challenge the latter and make the former the more impregnable.

The published intention of the founders in the *Journal*'s first volume was "to uphold historic Christianity." They stated further: "The *Journal* is based upon the conviction that the Holy Scriptures are the word of God, the only infallible rule of faith and practice, and that the system of belief commonly designated the Reformed Faith is the purest and most consistent formulation . . . of the system of truth set forth in the Holy Scriptures."[1]

While the *Journal*'s explicit aim was to defend historic Calvinism at large, the striking resemblance it bore in format and typography to the *Princeton Theological Review* suggests a much more particular, implicit purpose: to carry on the Princeton theology from a new outpost when the old citadel had been breached by the enemy.

A striking characteristic of the *Journal*, especially in its first two decades, was that much seems to have been written with an eye over the shoulder toward Princeton. In Spring 1941, the lead review of Princeton Seminary president John A. Mackay's *A Preface to Christian Theology* assumes that "the major interest of a reader of the book who has any religious awareness will be in what it reveals concerning President Mackay's relation to the Princeton tradition." It then asks, "What sound do we hear today from the Princeton trumpet?" and in answer suspects Mackay of being a "fellow traveler" with Barth or Brunner "in holding that the Bible is less than infallible."[2] A Spring 1944 review of Mackay's *Heritage and Destiny* opines regretfully: "Had Dr. Mackay, in the providence of God, relied more completely upon the theology of the Princeton of the Hodges rather than upon that of Karl Barth, *Heritage and Destiny* would have been a volume to rejoice the hearts of Calvinists."[3] If President Mackay's books are reviewed critically, he is himself consistently treated with studied courtesy. Lesser figures on Princeton Seminary's faculty fared less well. Edited by David Hugh Jones, the Presbyterian *Hymnbook* of 1955 is dismissed as a "bland juxtaposition of the gospel of Christ with hymns of the gospel of man."[4]

A good proportion of the *Journal*'s articles are not likely to attract the interest of anyone not committed to its theological stance or to the study of the history of Calvinism. The editors were addressing a faithful remnant. Articles in the first two decades of publication come largely from the pens of the Westminster Seminary faculty. The point of view is consistently conservative, both theologically and politically. In "The Days of Genesis," Edward J. Young argues that the days must be interpreted chronologically.[5] In "Justice in the Social Order," William Matheson argues that Peter's confrontation with Ananias in *Acts* recognizes private property rights as a matter of foundational principle for Christianity.[6] From 1960 on articles become more narrowly confessional in their scope and interest.

In the first issue of the *Journal*, the editors listed as the first of three points of policy, "To maintain the highest standard of scholarship." Earlier they stated, "The position we maintain, therefore, necessarily involves the bringing of every form of thought that may reasonably come within the purview of a theological faculty to the touchstone of Holy Scripture and the defining of its relations to our Christian faith."[7] Under the tutelage of the original faculty-editors, the *Journal* fulfilled this aim admirably in terms of its contributors' erudition, diction, and use of scholarly methods consonant with their interpretation of the Bible. Nowhere was the scholarship better exhibited than in the range of books and authors reviewed. Like its ancestral Princeton journals, the *Westminster Theological Journal* saw a major part of its calling as the surveying of every shifting current of doctrine from its rock of orthodoxy, treating each view fairly and answering it decisively. The answers will strike many as unsatisfactory and perhaps more as uncharitable: "Dr. Hocking gives the cause of true religion a setback of two hundred years. Even that is a serious understatement. . . . The volume under review deals with a future world religion. The Word of God says something on that subject. It tells of the beast which will open its mouth against God in blasphemy. . . . The reviewer cannot help thinking of the words of Jeremiah. . . . 'They have rejected the word of Jehovah; and what wisdom is in them?' "[8] Another example will suffice to show that the reviewers did not mince words: "If Professor Rall's view of Christianity were the only one open to us today, we might well exclaim that its glory has departed."[9]

The range of writers reviewed, especially in the *Journal*'s first two decades or so, is impressive: John Baillie, Karl Barth, Emil Brunner, Ernst Cassirer, C. N. Cochrane, Benedetto Croce, Gregory Dix, Nels Ferré, Harry Emerson Fosdick, Etienne Gilson, E. C. Hoskyns, Karl Jaspers, C. E. M. Joad, C. S. Lewis, D. C. McIntosh, Jacques Maritain, E. L. Mascall, Reinhold Niebuhr, Anders Nygren, Paul Tillich, and A. E. Taylor. The list is partial. Frequently reviewed as well are republications of theologians of the previous century, such as A. A. Hodge ("not the theologian his father was"),[10] B. B. Warfield, and E. B. Pusey.

From the early 1950s, the faculties of other conservative colleges and seminaries (Wheaton [Illinois], Fuller, Gordon-Conwell) began to contribute reviews, especially of Westminster Seminary authors. As the original editors' names began to disappear from the masthead because of retirement or death, the *Journal* developed a narrower, more in-house character, clearly appealing to a conservative readership, less concerned to review a broad spectrum of literature.

In 1967 Edward J. Young (faculty, 1939–67) died, and Paul Woolley (editor, 1938–56, managing editor, 1956–67) retired. Thereafter the scope of reviews narrowed noticeably. Scholars familiar to a general audience occur occasionally: Bernhard W. Anderson, Hans Freiherr von Campenhausen, Ernst Grillmeier,

Gordon Rupp, Roger L. Shinn, and Claude Welch. Notably, many of these scholars are historians. History received more attention from the *Journal* in the 1970s than earlier. Liberal theologians (Langdon Gilkey, Martin Marty, Jürgen Moltmann, Paul Van Buren) are reviewed only rarely. Somewhat more attention is paid to well-known, conservative theologians such as G. C. Berkouwer, Carl F. H. Henry, and Cornelius Van Til (of Westminster). Still, many of the books reviewed and most of the articles are by authors one assumes familiar chiefly within denominational and connectional circles.

In Spring 1982, the *Journal* announced two changes of policy. Henceforth volumes would be numbered according to the calendar rather than the academic year (its previous practice). At the head of the issue appeared a notice "To Our Contributors and Readers" in which a "new editorial team" reaffirmed "the statement of purpose that appeared in the initial volume." It called attention to the intellectual ideals of the *Journal*'s founders and the tension between loyalty to "Christian tradition" and the demand that it "be interpreted 'in the present.' " While differing from those who reject tradition and closing the *Journal* to those of differing theological loyalties, the staff, "representing the faculty as a whole," announced it "regretfully cannot accept articles which, while seeking to promote Christian orthodoxy, show isolation from current scholarship (including foreign literature when applicable), or criticize opposing viewpoints uncharitably, or otherwise fail to advance scholarly discussion in original fashion."[11]

This notice would seem to indicate the editors' or the faculty's opinion that in recent years their journal had drifted from the standards hoisted by those gentlemen of the Old School who founded the *Westminster Theological Journal*. Their aim was to defend their faith with a scholarship able to challenge all comers and to command the respect and attention of foes as well as the faithful. The success of the *Journal*'s attempt to raise that standard anew cannot as yet be assessed.

Notes

1. "To Our Readers," *Westminster Theological Journal* 1 (1938): i, ii (hereafter cited as *WTJ*).

2. Robert Strong, review of *A Preface to Christian Theology* by John A. Mackay, *WTJ* 3 (1941): 133–35.

3. Richard W. Gray, review of *Heritage and Destiny* by John A. Mackay, *WTJ* 6 (1944): 209.

4. Arthur W. Kuschke, Jr., review of *The Hymnbook*, ed. David Hugh Jones, *WTJ* 19 (1956): 68.

5. Edward B. Young, "The Days of Genesis," *WTJ* 25 (1962): 1–34; 26 (1963): 143–71.

6. William Matheson, "Justice in the Social Order," *WTJ* 8 (1946): 127–48.

7. "To Our Readers," *WTJ* 1 (1938): i-ii.

8. R. B. Kuiper, review of *Living Religions and a World Faith* by William Ernest Hocking, *WTJ* 3 (1941): 174–75.

9. N. B. Stonehouse, review of *Christianity: An Inquiry into Its Nature and Truth* by Harris Franklin Rall, *WTJ* 3 (1941): 162.

10. Arthur W. Kuschke, Jr., review of *Outlines of Theology* by A. A. Hodge, *WTJ* 13 (1950): 57.

11. "To Our Readers and Contributors," *WTJ* 44 (1982): i–iii.

Information Sources

BIBLIOGRAPHY:

Loetscher, Lefferts A. *The Broadening Church: A Study of Theological Issues in the Presbyterian Church since 1869.* Philadelphia: Westminster Press, 1954.

Marsden, George M. *Fundamentalism and American Culture: The Shaping of Twentieth Century Evangelicalism.* New York: Oxford University Press, 1980.

————. "J. Gresham Machen: History and Truth." *Westminster Theological Journal* 42 (1971): 157–75.

Rian, Edwin H. *The Presbyterian Conflict.* Grand Rapids: Eerdmans, 1940.

Sandeen, E. R. *The Roots of Fundamentalism.* Chicago: University of Chicago Press, 1970.

Sloat, Leslie W. "American Calvinism Speaks." *Westminster Theological Journal* 7 (1944–45): 122–35.

Stonehouse, N. B. *J. Gresham Machen: A Biographical Memoir.* Grand Rapids: Eerdmans, 1954.

VanderStelet, John C. *Philosophy and Scripture: A Study in Old Princeton and Westminster Theology.* Marlton, N.J.: Mack Publishing Co., 1978.

Woolley, Paul. *The Significance of J. Gresham Machen Today.* Nutley, N.J.: Presbyterian and Reformed Publishing Co., 1977.

INDEX SOURCES: *Religion Index One, Biblica, Elenchus Bibliographica, Christian Periodical Index, Internationale Zeitschriftenschau für Bibelwissenschaft und Grenzgebiete, New Testament Abstracts, Religious and Theological Abstracts.*

REPRINT EDITIONS: University Microfilms International, Johnson Reprint Corporation.

LOCATION SOURCES: Westminster Theological Seminary, Princeton Theological Seminary, University of Denver, Union Theological Seminary (Va.), and others.

Publication History

MAGAZINE TITLE AND TITLE CHANGES: *The Westminster Theological Journal* (1938–   ).

VOLUME AND ISSUE DATA: 1:1 (November 1938–   ). Originally two numbers (November, May) per volume. Vols. 35–38 had three numbers. Vols. 39 and on have two numbers (Fall, Spring). No Fall 1981 issue. Beginning with vol. 44 (Spring 1982), volumes are numbered by the calendar year.

PUBLISHER AND PLACE OF PUBLICATION: Westminster Theological Seminary, Chestnut Hill, Philadelphia.

EDITORS: Paul Woolley and John Murray (1938–53), Paul Woolley and John H. Skilton (1953–54), N. B. Stonehouse (1954–58), Meredith G. Kline (1958–59), Edward

J. Young (1958–68), John H. Skilton (1968–73), D. Clair Davis (1973–75), Robert
D. Knudsen (1975–80), W. Robert Godfrey (1980–81), Moisés Silva (1982–   ).
CIRCULATION: 1200 (1983).

Howard J. Happ

WORLD PARISH. *See* METHODIST HISTORY

WORLD TOMORROW. *See* THE CHRISTIAN CENTURY

WORSHIP

While the genesis of the twentieth-century liturgical revival in the Roman
Catholic Church may generally be traced to Western Europe and to the Benedictine monks, in the United States it was largely the fruit of the work of one
man, Dom Virgil Michel, a Benedictine monk of St. John's Abbey, Collegeville,
Minnesota.[1] Born in St. Paul in 1890, Michel had been educated at St. John's
Preparatory School and University in Collegeville. He entered the monastery in
1909, made solemn vows as a monk of the Order of St. Benedict in 1913, and
was ordained a Roman Catholic priest in 1916. In 1918 he received a Ph.D. in
English and a licentiate in theology from the Catholic University of America.
After teaching at St. John's for several years, Michel went to Rome in February
1924 to begin studies in philosophy.

Disappointed with the teachers in Rome, Michel transferred to the University
of Louvain in Belgium. It was in the Benedictine monasteries of northern Europe,
principally in Belgium and Germany, that he encountered the liturgical revival,
which had been gathering momentum in Europe for several decades. Returning
to his abbey in Minnesota in the fall of 1925, Michel persuaded the abbot, Alcuin
Deutsch, that English-speaking Catholics needed the liturgical movement that
he had found in Europe and that St. John's should promote it and be its center.[2]

By the end of 1925, Michel had founded Liturgical Press, a printing house
for the publication of books and materials concerned with upgrading public
worship. In November 1926, there appeared the first issue of a monthly review,
Orate Fratres, edited by Michel. The foreword of this issue announced that
Orate Fratres was being launched to further a "liturgical awakening" among
American Catholics:

Our general aim is to develop a better understanding of the spiritual import
of the liturgy, an understanding that is truly sympathetic . . . not aiming at
a cold scholastic interest in the liturgy of the Church, but at an interest
that is more thoroughly intimate, that seizes upon the entire person, touching not only intellect but also will, heart as well as mind.

Orate Fratres, Michel wrote, sought to foster participation by Catholics in the public prayer of their church, and he confidently predicted that "ultimately the liturgical movement is bound to come."[3]

Under Virgil Michel's editorship, *Orate Fratres* functioned as the organ of the liturgical movement in the United States, as well as in much of the rest of the English-speaking world. Popular in character and pastoral in approach, the review brought the work of European writers to the notice of American Catholics. Although the liturgical movement in Europe was largely a Benedictine enterprise, Michel sought wide collaboration among English-speaking Catholics, as the list of associate editors from the early years attests. Several monks of St. John's Abbey also worked closely with Dom Virgil, and several of them were sent to Europe for training. The first to go was Godfrey Diekmann, and when Michel died suddenly in 1938, Diekmann took over the editorship of the journal.

Orate Fratres, with Diekmann as editor (1939–64), displayed several emphases. Significant European liturgical theologians, such as Odo Casel, were presented in English translation. A popular understanding of the Bible was promoted. Mother Kathryn Sullivan began to contribute a series of commentaries on the books of the Old Testament in 1955, and from 1957 to 1962 there was a "Scripture" section edited by Kilian McDonnell. This section was discontinued with the appearance of the popular biblical magazine, the *Bible Today*, published by Liturgical Press. Catechetics, another of Michel's interests, had its own section in the review from 1962 until 1964 when a popular catechetical publication, the *Living Light*, was announced. Diekmann's concern for artistic excellence led to his inviting Frank Kacmarcik to design the covers and the typographical format that continue to grace the review. With the number of December 1951, the Latin title was dropped in favor of a one-word English name, *Worship*.[4]

Diekmann resigned as editor at the end of 1964, and another monk of St. John's Abbey, Aelred Tegels, succeeded him. By the conclusion of Vatican Council II in 1965, liturgical reform and renewal had come of age in the Roman Catholic Church. Most Catholic newspapers and magazines were carrying articles and columns on the liturgy, and books on the liturgy could be found in the lists of many publishing houses. Tegels reoriented *Worship* so that it became the more scholarly review foreseen by Michel, providing a "basically theoretic—yet pastorally very concerned—approach to the problems of renewal."[5]

The Second Vatican Council also brought Catholics into the ecumenical movement, and in 1967 *Worship* announced the appointment of its first associate editors who were not Roman Catholics. From that time, the journal opened its pages to an increasing number of articles concerning liturgical renewal in other Christian churches. In January 1976, *Worship* became a bimonthly review, and in that same year it also became the official organ of the North American Academy of Liturgy, with the annual proceedings of the academy being published each year in the July issue. A threatened termination of this arrangement in 1982 was reversed, and *Worship* continues to publish the proceedings.

Notes

1. L. C. Sheppard, "Liturgical Movement, Catholic," in *The New Catholic Encyclopedia* (New York: McGraw-Hill, 1967): 7:900–05.

2. Paul Marx, *Virgil Michel and the Liturgical Movement* (Collegeville, Minn.: Liturgical Press, 1957).

3. Foreword to *Orate Fratres* 1:1 (November 1926): 1–4.

4. Aelred Tegels, "Fifty Years of *Worship*," *Worship* 50:6 (November 1976): 466–71.

5. Ibid.

Information Sources

INDEX SOURCES: The last issue for each year contains an index for that year. Also in *Religion Index One, Catholic Periodical and Literature Index, Religious and Theological Abstracts, Old Testament Abstracts*.

REPRINT EDITIONS: University Microfilms International.

LOCATION SOURCES: Back issues available from the publisher. Also at Catholic University of America, Loyola University (Chicago), Boston College, St. John's University (Collegeville), St. Louis University, and others.

Publication History

MAGAZINE TITLE AND TITLE CHANGES: *Orate Fratres* 1–25 (1926–51), *Worship* 26 (1951–).

VOLUME AND ISSUE DATA: *Orate Fratres* had 13 issues in vol. 1. Thereafter it appeared monthly. *Worship* appeared monthly from December 1951 (26:1) through November 1953 (27:12). From December 1953 (28:12) through December 1975 (49:10), *Worship* appeared 10 times per year. With vol. 40 (1965), the first issue was dated January instead of November as had previously been the custom. With the first issue of vol. 50 (January 1976), *Worship* began to appear six times per year.

PUBLISHER AND PLACE OF PUBLICATION: Liturgical Press, Collegeville, Minn. (vols 1–27); Monks of St. John's Abbey, Collegeville, Minn. (vol. 28–).

EDITORS: Virgil Michel (1926–38), Godfrey Diekmann (1939–64), Aelred Tegels (1965–).

CIRCULATION: 7500 (1982).

James T. Connelly, C.S.C.

Z

ZYGON

In the 1940s Hudson Hoagland and Harlow Shapely, officers of the American Academy for the Advancement of Science (AAAS), suggested that the AAAS consider the role of science in providing knowledge of good and evil. Led by executive officer Ralph W. Burhoe, the AAAS moved in 1950 to found the Committee on Science and Values. That same year, Boston University professor E. P. Booth spoke to a group of theologians meeting on Star Island, New Hampshire, about the necessity for bringing formulations of religious truth more into line with the discoveries of science. The Star Island group and Burhoe's committee eventually recognized their mutual interest and jointly founded the Institute on Religion in an Age of Science (IRAS) in 1954. IRAS found encouragement and support from religious denominations and from theological schools, particularly those with a Unitarian-Universalist affiliation. Between 1961 and 1964, Malcolm R. Sutherland, Jr., president of Meadville Theological School in Chicago and an IRAS admirer, invited scientists associated with IRAS to Chicago to speak to students and faculty. In 1964, the Committee on Theology and the Sciences was formed at Meadville. The next year this committee, together with IRAS, chartered *Zygon: Journal of Religion and Science*.

Zygon was envisioned as "a workshop for those seeking ways to unite, in full integrity, the sciences with what men hold to be their sacred values, their religion."[1] Religion is understood to be "civilization's core institution for acculturating its long-range apex values."[2] The choice of title reflected this concern: *zygote* is a scientific term for the union of two gametes, while *zygos* refers to the union of the individual with ultimate reality. Founding editor Burhoe understood the mission of the journal more specifically to be essentially one of reformulating religion to fit the new conditions of life brought by science and technology. During his tenure as editor, this purpose became more focused on the need to establish "an objective standard that transcends individual values" and to make possible a "sounder conviction" of truth.[3]

The format of *Zygon* has from its beginning been coincident with its ends; articles are often published together with responses from other scholars, and at times theologians will critique the ideas of scientists and vice-versa. Such carefulness to encourage dialogue and to remain reflexive is evident as well in the willingness of the journal to publish articles with conclusions totally at odds with the aspirations of the editors. For example, in "The Dilemma of Science and Morals," Gunther S. Stent concluded that the gulf between science and religion is unbridgeable.[4]

The journal publishes articles from scholars in nearly every discipline, writing on topics that range from claims for the neurobiological basis of myth, to mathematical statements on the problem of evil, to conversations on the physics and chemistry of life processes, to discussion of religious views of history.[5] Occasionally entire issues are reserved for the publication of papers delivered at an IRAS conference on a specific topic. Accordingly, issues of *Zygon* have been organized exclusively around topics such as "Science and Human Purpose," "Symposium on Human Prospect," "Science, Religion and Social Change," and "Sociobiology, Values, and Religion."[6]

The common denominator of the contributions to *Zygon* is a concern for values. In an early issue, *Zygon* republished an essay by Clyde Kluckhohn entitled "The Scientific Study of Values and Contemporary Civilization." This essay has set the tone for much of what has appeared in the journal since by calling for a "cross-cultural study of values" and "a thorough examination of the relation of instrumental and ultimate values in a specific culture."[7] This focus on values is evident as well in the statement of purpose of the Center for Advanced Study in Religion and Science (CASIRAS), an organization founded in 1972 when Meadville could no longer afford to fund the Committee on Theology and the Sciences. The aims of CASIRAS are "to resolve new problems of morals," "to resolve new problems of morale," and "to resolve the problem of creating the cultural universality of values" necessary for global civilization.[8]

Zygon is bold and optimistic about its enterprise. In 1968 Burhoe wrote that "*Zygon* is sailing into an uncharted sea on an incredible mission: . . . to reach religion by using the sciences." Nine years later he declared that a "genuine synthesis of religion and science" lay in the "near future." Karl E. Peters, who took over as editor in 1979, has likened the project of the journal to "Columbian voyages of the mind from spaceship earth outward to the stars."[9]

Notes

1. Ralph W. Burhoe, "Editorial," *Zygon* 1 (March 1966): 2.
2. Ralph W. Burhoe, "Editorial," *Zygon* 9 (June 1974): 96.
3. Ralph W. Burhoe, "Editorial," *Zygon* 1 (March 1966): 1, 7; Ralph W. Burhoe, "Editorial," *Zygon* 4 (June 1969): 110.

4. Gunther S. Stent, "The Dilemma of Science and Morals," *Zygon* 10 (March 1975): 95–112.

5. Eugene D. d'Aquili, "The Neurobiological Bases of Myth and Concepts of Deity," *Zygon* 13 (December 1978): 257–75; William S. Hatcher, "A Logical Solution to the Problem of Evil," *Zygon* 9 (September 1974): 245–55; Gerald Holton, Michael Polanyi, Ernest Nagel, John R. Platt, and Barry Commoner, "Do Life Processes Transcend Physics and Chemistry?" *Zygon* 3 (December 1968): 442–72; Langdon Gilkey, "Robert L. Heilbroner's Vision of History," *Zygon* 10 (September 1975): 215–33.

6. *Zygon* 8 (September-December 1973); *Zygon* 10 (September 1975); *Zygon* 10 (March 1975); *Zygon* 15 (September and December 1980).

7. Clyde Kluckhohn, "The Scientific Study of Values and Contemporary Civilization," *Zygon* 1 (September 1966): 240.

8. "Proposal to Establish a Center for Advanced Study in Religion and Science," *Zygon* 7 (September 1972): 176. The Center for the Advanced Study in Religion and Science is affiliated with the Chicago Cluster of Theological Schools. In 1972, at the time of its separation from Meadville, the original Committee on Theology and the Sciences was called the Center of Advanced Study in Theology and the Sciences.

9. *Zygon* 3 (March 1968): 2; 12 (March 1977): 3; 15 (March 1980): 3.

Information Sources

INDEX SOURCES: *Current Contents, Humanities Index, Historical Abstracts, Psychological Abstracts, Social Sciences Citation Index, Arts and Humanities Citation Index, America: History and Life, Philosopher's Index, Religious and Theological Abstracts, Religion Index One, Guide to Social Science and Religion in Periodical Literature.*

REPRINT EDITONS: University Microfilms International, Microforms International Marketing Co.

LOCATION SOURCES: Harvard University, Princeton University, Duke University, Oberlin College, University of Michigan, University of Chicago, University of Texas-Austin, Stanford University, University of Arizona, and others.

Publication History

MAGAZINE TITLE AND TITLE CHANGES: *Zygon: Journal of Religion and Science* (1966–).

VOLUME AND ISSUE DATA: 1:1 (March 1966–); appears quarterly.

PUBLISHER AND PLACE OF PUBLICATION: University of Chicago Press, Chicago, for the Institute on Religion and Science and the Center of Advanced Study in Theology and the Sciences (1966–72); University of Chicago Press, for IRAS and the Center for Advanced Study in Religion and Science (1972–79); Council on the Study of Religion and Wilfrid Laurier University, Waterloo, Ontario, for IRAS and CASIRAS (1979–).

EDITORS: Ralph W. Burhoe (1966–79), Karl E. Peters (1979–).

CIRCULATION: 1945 (1983).

John Corrigan

Chronological Capsule

The column on the left indicates the founding year of the periodical noted; the column on the right marks selected events and movements in American religious history.

Year	Journal	Event
1784		Christmas Conference led by Francis Asbury organizes American Methodism
1789		First General Convention of the Protestant Episcopal Church
1800		Camp meeting revival in Logan County, Ky.
1803	*Massachusetts Missionary Magazine*	
1808	*The Panoplist*	Andover Theological Seminary founded to promote orthodoxy; John Carroll named archbishop of the Roman Catholic diocese of Baltimore
1815	*The Christian Monitor*	
	North-American Review and Miscellaneous Journal	
1816	*Recorder*	Founding of the African Methodist Episcopal Church
1817	*Boston Recorder*	
1818	*Methodist Magazine*	
	The Virginia Evangelical and Literary Magazine	
1819		William Ellery Channing preaches "What Is Unitarian Christianity?"

Year	Journal	Event
1821	The Evangelical and Literary Magazine and Missionary Chronicle	
	North American Review	
1822	The Evangelical and Literary Magazine	Charles Hodge (1797–1878) joins Princeton Theological Seminary faculty
	U.S. Catholic Miscellany	
1823	Christian Baptist	
	Philadelphia Recorder	
1824	The Literary and Evangelical Magazine	
1825	Biblical Repertory	Charles Grandison Finney inaugurates "new measures" revivalism at Western, N.Y.
	Recorder and Telegraph	
1826	Boston Recorder and Religious Telegraph	
1830	Biblical Repertory and Theological Review	Joseph Smith publishes the Book of Mormon
	Methodist Magazine and Quarterly Review	
	Millennial Harbinger	
1831	The Biblical Repository	
	Episcopal Recorder	
1833		American Antislavery Society founded; Oberlin College established
1834	Religious Telescope	
1835	The Biblical Repository and Quarterly	
1836		Founding of Union Theological Seminary (New York); heyday of transcendentalism
1837	The American Biblical Repository	Presbyterians divide over merits of revivalism
1838	Biblical Repertory and Princeton Review	
	Oberlin Evangelist	
1840	The Dial	John Williamson Nevin joins the Mercersburg Seminary faculty; adventist excitement becomes prominent
	Methodist Quarterly Review	
1843	Bibliotheca Sacra, Tracts and Essays on Topics Connected with Biblical Literature and Theology	
	The True Wesleyan	

Year	Journal	Event
1844	*Bibliotheca Sacra and Theological Review*	Methodists split over slavery
	Universalist Quarterly and General Review	
1845	*The Biblical Repository and Classical Review*	Baptists divide into Northern and Southern denominations
	Oberlin Quarterly Review	
	The Theological Medium	
1847	*The Southern Presbyterian Review*	
1849	*Evangelical Review*	
	Mercersburg Review	
	Puritan Recorder	
1851	*Bibliotheca Sacra and Biblical Repository*	
1853	*Mercersburg Quarterly Review*	
	The Wesleyan	
1855	*Gospel Advocate*	Central Verein founded in St. Louis
	Lehre and Wehre	
1857–1859		Holiness revivals sweep the United States
1859	*American Theological Review*	
	Congregational Quarterly	
1861	*American Wesleyan*	U.S. Civil War begins
1862	*Evangelical Quarterly Review*	
1863	*American Presbyterian and Theological Review*	
1865	*Ave Maria*	U.S. Civil War ends
	Catholic World	
	The Radical	
1867	*Congregationalist and Recorder*	Free Religious Association founded; first Orthodox diocese in United States established; organization of the National Association for the Promotion of Holiness
1870s		Sunday School movement flourishes; evangelical liberalism takes shape in Protestant circles; biblical criticism becomes prominent
1870	*Christian Union*	Colored (now Christian) Methodist Episcopal Church founded
	Congregationalist	
	The Index	
1871	*Bibliotheca Sacra and Theological Eclectic*	

Year	Journal	Event
1872	*Presbyterian Quarterly and Princeton Review*	
1873–1875		Dwight L. Moody's London revivals give him a national reputation in the United States
1874		Founding of the Women's Christian Temperance Union
1875		Mary Baker Eddy publishes *Science and Health, with Key to the Scriptures*; Hebrew Union College founded in Cincinnati
1876	*American Catholic Quarterly Review*	Meeting of first Prophetic Bible Conference, which feeds emergent fundamentalism
	Bibliotheca Sacra	
1877	*Magazin fur Ev.-Luth. Homiletik*	
1878	*Princeton Review*	Salvation Army starts in London; comes to United States two years later
	Quarterly Review of the Evangelical Lutheran Church	
1879	*Reformed Quarterly Review*	
1880s		Impact of immigration, urbanization, and industrialization brings the rise of the Social Gospel movement
1880	*The Cumberland Presbyterian Review*	Founding of the Society of Biblical Literature
1881	*Free Religious Index*	
	St. Louis Theological Monthly	
1882	*The Hebrew Student*	
	Journal of Biblical Literature	
	Lutheran Church Review	
1883	*Journal of Christian Science*	
	The Old Testament Student	
1884	*A.M.E. Church Review*	
	Andover Review	
	Christian Oracle	
	Hebraica	
	The Wesleyan Methodist	
1885	*Christian Science Journal*	Promulgation of Reform Judaism's Pittsburgh Platform
	Methodist Review	
1886	*New Princeton Review*	
1887	*U.S. Catholic Historical Magazine*	
1888	*Papers of the American Society of Church History*, 1st ser.	Founding of the American Society of Church History

Year	Journal	Event
1889	*American Ecclesiastical Review*	
	The Old and New Testament Student	
1890s		Americanization crisis in Roman Catholicism
1892		Founding of the University of Chicago, which becomes a major center for the academic study of religion
1893	*The Biblical World*	World's Parliament of Religions meets in Chicago
	The Outlook	
1895	*American Journal of Semitic Languages and Literatures*	Founding of Anti-Saloon League, which leads move to Prohibition
	St. Vincent de Paul Quarterly	
1896	*Reformed Church Review*	
	Russian Orthodox American Messenger (Amerikanskii Pravoslavnyi Viestnik)	
1897	*American Journal of Theology*	First World Zionist Congress meets in Basel
	Magazin fur Ev.-Luth. Homiletik und Pastoraltheologie	
	Theological Quarterly	
1899	*The Christian Century of the Disciples of Christ*	
	Historical Records and Studies	
	Lutheran Quarterly	
1900	*The Homiletic Monthly and Catechist*	
	The Institute Tie	
1901	*Congregationalist and Christian World*	
	Ecclesiastical Review	
	Journal of the Presbyterian Historical Society	
1902	*The Christian Century*	
1906	*Bulletin of Friends Historical Society of Philadelphia*	Azusa Street revivals give birth to modern pentecostalism
	Religious Education	
1908	*Central-Blatt*	Federal Council of Churches founded
	Christian Science Monitor	
	Papers of the American Society of Church History, 2d ser.	
1909	*America*	National Association of Biblical Instructors (NABI) organized
	Central Blatt and Social Justice	

Year	Journal	Event
1910	*Christian Worker's Magazine*	Edinburgh Conference leads to formation of the International Missionary Council
	The Fundamentals	
1911	*The Moslem World*	
1915	*Catholic Historical Review*	
1917	*Catholic Charities Review*	U.S. enters World War I; founding of the National Catholic War Council (renamed National Catholic Welfare Conference in 1921)
	Christian Education	
	The Homiletic Monthly	
1918	*Anglican Theological Review*	
	Christian Union Quarterly	
	Homiletic Monthly and Pastoral Review	
	Illinois Catholic Historical Review	
1919	*National Catholic War Council Bulletin*	Founding of the Catholic Historical Association
1920s		Age of the fundamentalist-modernist controversy; evangelist Billy Sunday dominates American revivalism
1920	*The Homiletic and Pastoral Review*	
	National Catholic Welfare Council Bulletin	
	The Moody Bible Institute Monthly	
1921	*Congregationalist*	
	Journal of Religion	
	Theological Monthly	
1922	*American Orthodox Messenger (Amerikanskii Pravoslavnyi Viestnik)*	
	Augustana Quarterly	
	National Catholic Welfare Conference Bulletin	
1924	*Bulletin of Friends' Historical Association*	
	Commonweal	
1925	*Proceedings of the Unitarian Historical Society*	
1926	*Orate Fratres*	
1927	*Mennonite Quarterly Review*	
1928	*Lutheran Church Review*	Founding of the National Conference of Christians and Jews
	Outlook and Independent	
1929	*The Christian Century Pulpit*	
	Mid-America	

Year	Journal	Event
1930s		Rise of neo-orthodox theology in American Protestantism
1930	*Concordia Theological Monthly*	Greek archdiocese of North and South America established
	Congregationalist and Herald of Gospel Liberty	
	Journal of the Department of History (The Presbyterian Historical Society) of the Presbyterian Church in the U.S.A.	
	National Catholic Welfare Conference Review	
	Russian American Orthodox Messenger (Russko-Amerikanskii Pravoslavnyi Viestnik)	
1932	*Catholic Action*	Founding of the Catholic League for Social Justice
	Church History	
	Historical Magazine of the Protestant Episcopal Church	
	New Outlook	
	Religion in Life	
1933	*Journal of the National Association of Biblical Instructors*	Dorothy Day launches Catholic Worker movement
1935	*Christendom*	
1936	*The Christian Front*	
	Pulpit Digest	
	Russian American Orthodox Messenger (Russko-Amerikanskii Pravoslavnyi Viestnik)	
1937	*Journal of Bible and Religion*	Catholic Biblical Association founded
1938	*The Biblical Archaeologist*	
	The Chronicle	
	Contemporary Jewish Record *The Moody Monthly*	
	Westminster Theological Journal	
1939	*Catholic Biblical Quarterly*	Merger creates The Methodist Church
	Christian Social Action	
	The Thomist	
	Union Review	
1940	*Social Justice Review*	
	Theological Studies	

Year	Journal	Event
1941	*Bulletin of Friends Historical Association*	U.S. entry into World War II
	Christianity and Crisis	
1942	*Journal of Near Eastern Studies*	
	The Pulpit	
1943	*American Ecclesiastical Review*	
	Contemporary Jewish Record	
	Lutheran Scholar	
1944	*Journal of the Presbyterian Historical Society*	
	Journal of Religious Thought	
1945	*Commentary*	
	Conservative Judaism	
	Union Seminary Quarterly Review	
1946	*Proceedings of the Catholic Theological Society of America*	
1947	*Interpretation*	
	Perkins School of Theology Journal	
	Pulpit Preaching	
	Telescope-Messenger	
1948	*Church and State*	World Council of Churches organized as ecumenical movement flourishes
	The Ecumenical Review	
	The Muslim World	
	World Parish	
1949	*Lutheran Quarterly*	Founding of the Evangelical Theological Society and of the Society for the Scientific Study of Religion
1950s		Popular revival of religion in the United States; emergence of Billy Graham as the nation's premier evangelist
1950	*Cross Currents*	Organization of the National Council of Churches
	Occasional Bulletin from the Missionary Research Library	
1951	*Reformed Journal*	Founding of the Full Gospel Businessmen's Fellowship marks the emergence of the new pentecostalism
	Worship	
1952	*Judaism*	
	St. Vladimir's Seminary Quarterly	

Year	Journal	Event
1953	*Christian Scholar*	
	Theology Digest	
	Greek Orthodox Theological Review	
1955	*Gordon Review*	
1957	*St. Luke's Journal of Theology*	Merger creates the United Church of Christ
1958	*Bulletin of the Evangelical Theological Society*	
	Foundations	
1959	*Journal of Church and State*	
	Review of Religious Research	
1961	*History of Religions*	
	Journal for the Scientific Study of Religion	
	Mid-Stream	
1962	*Chicago Studies*	Consultation on Church Union convenes for the first time; opening session of Vatican II (closes in 1965)
	Dialog	
	Journal of Presbyterian History	
	Methodist History	
	Quaker History	
1964	*National Catholic Reporter*	National Association of Biblical Instructors becomes the American Academy of Religion
	Theological Education	
1965	*Baptist History and Heritage*	Death of God theology and secular Christianity become fashionable
	Journal of the American Academy of Religion	
1966	*Calvin Theological Journal*	
	Diakonia	
	Dialogue	
	Zygon	
1967	*Religious Humanism*	
1968	*St. Vladimir's Theological Quarterly*	Merger creates the United Methodist Church; founding of the Jewish Anti-Defamation League
	Soundings	
	The Wesleyan Advocate	
1969	*The Christian Ministry*	Conservative J. A. O. Preus elected president of Missouri Synod Lutherans
	Journal of the Evangelical Theological Society	
1970s		Rise of the ''new evangelicalism'' and increasing appeal of charismatic religion

Year	Journal	Event
1970	*Christian Scholar's Review*	Elizabeth Bayley Seton's canonization makes her the first native-born American Roman Catholic saint
1971	*Post-American*	
1972	*New Catholic World*	
	New Pulpit Digest	
1973	*CTM*	
	Journal of Religious Ethics	
	Ohio Journal of Religious Studies	
1974	*Academy*	
	Currents in Theology and Mission	
	Preaching Helps	
	Semeia	
1975	*Biblical Archaeology Review*	
	Concordia Journal	
	Religious Studies Review	
	Social Thought	
	Sunstone	
1976	*Association for Jewish Studies Review*	
	Biblical Archeologist	
	Sojourners	
1977	*New Oxford Review*	
	Occasional Bulletin of Missionary Research	
1978	*Journal of Religious Studies*	
	Old Testament Abstracts	
	Pulpit Digest	
1979	*Sunstone Review*	
1980s		Age of the electronic church
1980	*Proceedings of the Unitarian-Universalist Historical Society*	
	Quarterly Review	
	U.S. Catholic Historian	
1981	*International Bulletin of Missionary Research*	
1982	*American Baptist Quarterly*	
1983	*Biblical Archaeologist*	
1984		Mergers among both Presbyterians and Lutherans get underway

Listing by Sponsoring Organization or Religious Orientation

This listing identifies the periodicals profiled by sponsoring agency or religious orientation. Many academic and scholarly publications, for example, appear under the aegis of learned societies, academic institutions, or agencies other than religious bodies. Some have official sponsorship by religious bodies or historically reflect an orientation to concerns identified with a particular religious group. Yet others are independent. Occasionally, too, a journal published by a learned society will also have a particular religious focus. Hence some titles may be listed below in more than one category.

Periodicals Reflecting the Anglican and Episcopal Tradition

Anglican Theological Review
Episcopal Recorder
Historical Magazine of the Protestant Episcopal Church
St. Luke's Journal of Theology

Periodicals Reflecting Sponsorship by Academic Institutions

American Journal of Theology
Andover Review
Biblical World
Catholic University Bulletin
Chicago Studies
Cross Currents
Drew Gateway
Harvard Theological Review
History of Religions
Interpretation
Journal of Church and State
Journal of Ecumenical Studies
Journal of Near Eastern Studies
Journal of Religion
Journal of Religious Ethics

Journal of Religious Studies
Journal of Religious Thought
Moody Monthly
Muslim World
Oberlin Evangelist
Oberlin Quarterly Review
Old Testament Abstracts
Perkins School of Theology Journal
Princeton Theological Review
St. Vladimir's Theological Quarterly
Union Seminary Quarterly Review
Westminster Theological Journal
Worship

Periodicals Reflecting the Baptist Tradition

American Baptist Quarterly
Baptist History and Heritage

Periodicals Reflecting the Christian Science Tradition

Christian Science Monitor

Periodicals Reflecting the Congregationalist–United Church of Christ Tradition

Andover Review
Congregational Quarterly
Congregationalist and Herald of Gospel Liberty
North American Review
Outlook

Periodicals Reflecting the Disciples of Christ and Churches of Christ Tradition

Christian Century
Christian Ministry
Gospel Advocate
Millennial Harbinger

Periodicals Reflecting the Free Religion Tradition

Index
Radical
Religious Humanism

Periodicals Reflecting an Independent Background or Orientation

Biblical Archaeology Review
Brownson's Quarterly Review
Christian Century
Christian Ministry
Christian Social Action

Christianity and Crisis
Christianity Today
Dial
Fundamentals
Journal of Religious Ethics
Missiology
Princeton Review

Periodicals Reflecting Judaism's Tradition

Association for Jewish Studies Review
Commentary
Conservative Judaism
Judaism
Mid-Stream

Periodicals Reflecting Learned Societies' Interests

Association for Jewish Studies Review
Baptist History and Heritage
Biblical Archaeologist
Catholic Biblical Quarterly
Catholic Historical Review
Christian Scholar's Review
Church History
Journal for the Scientific Study of Religion
Journal of Bible and Religion
Journal of Biblical Literature
Journal of Presbyterian History
Journal of the American Academy of Religion
Journal of the American Oriental Society
Journal of the Evangelical Theological Society
Old Testament Abstracts
Proceedings of the Catholic Theological Society of America
Proceedings of the Unitarian-Universalist Historical Society
Quaker History
Religious Education
Religious Studies Review
Semeia
Soundings
Theological Education
Wesleyan Theological Review
Zygon

Periodicals Reflecting the Lutheran Tradition

Academy
Concordia Theological Monthly
Dialog
Lehre and Wehre
Lutheran Quarterly

Periodical Reflecting the Mennonite Tradition

Mennonite Quarterly Review

Periodicals Reflecting the Methodist and Wesleyan Tradition

A.M.E. Church Review
Drew Gateway
Methodist History
Methodist Review
Perkins School of Theology Journal
Quarterly Review
Telescope-Messenger
Wesleyan Advocate
Wesleyan Theological Journal

Periodicals Reflecting the Mormon Tradition

Dialogue
Sunstone

Periodical Reflecting a Non-Denominational Protestant Perspective

Sojourners

Periodicals Reflecting the Orthodox Tradition

Diakonia
Greek Orthodox Theological Review
Russian American Orthodox Messenger
St. Vladimir's Theological Quarterly

Periodicals Reflecting the Presbyterian and Reformed Tradition

American Presbyterian and Theological Review
Biblical Repository and Classical Review
Bibliotheca Sacra
Calvin Theological Journal
Cumberland Presbyterian Review
Interpretation
Journal of Presbyterian History
Literary and Evangelical Review
Mercersburg Review
Princeton Review
Princeton Theological Review
Reformed Journal
Southern Presbyterian Review
Theology Today

Periodicals Reflecting the Roman Catholic Tradition

America
American Catholic Quarterly Review

American Ecclesiastical Review
Ave Maria
Brownson's Quarterly Review
Catholic Action
Catholic Biblical Quarterly
Catholic Charities Review
Catholic Historical Review
Catholic University Bulletin
Central Blatt and Social Justice
Chicago Studies
Commonweal
Cross Currents
Diakonia
Historical Records and Studies
Homiletic and Pastoral Review
Mid-America
National Catholic Reporter
New Catholic World
New Oxford Review
New York Review
Proceedings of the Catholic Theological Society of America
Social Justice Review
Theological Studies
Theology Digest
Thomist
U.S. Catholic Miscellany

Periodical Reflecting the Society of Friends' Tradition (Quakers)

Quaker History

Periodicals Reflecting the Unitarian-Universalist Tradition

Proceedings of the Unitarian-Universalist Historical Society
Universalist Quarterly and General Review

Periodicals Sponsored by Other Agencies and Associations

Church and State
Ecumenical Review
Massachusetts Missionary Magazine
Pulpit Digest
Review of Religious Research

Index

Guttgemann, Erhardt, 474
Guyon, Madame, 403

Hadaway, C. Kirk, 264
Hageman, Howard G., 509
Hagglund, S. G., 331
Hague, Tyson, 213
Hallock, Gerard, 169–70
Hamer, Jerome, 513
Hamilton, Floyd E., 423
Hamma School of Theology, 333
Hammond, Philip, 462
Hammurabi, code of, 397
Hanby, William, 494
Handy, Robert T., 77
Hanna, Edward, 387
Hanna, Septimus J., 124
Harbison, E. Harris, 508
Hardy, Charles A., 18
Hargis, Billy James, 435
Haring, Bernard, 247, 381
Harkness, Georgia, 266, 436
Harmon, Nolan B., 443
Harmony, Christian Science doctrine of, 126
Harms, Oliver, 3
Harnack, Adolf von, 101, 144, 422
Haroutunian, Joseph, 442
Harper's, 392, 407
Harper, William Rainey, 59–60, 454
Harrington, Michael, 154
Harris, George, 31–32
Harrison, Everett F., 65–66
Harrisville, Roy, 189
Hart, Charles A., 84
Hart, Ray L., 299–300
Hartford Seminary Foundation, 372–73; Kennedy School of Missions of, 365
Hartnett, Robert C., 10–11
Hartt, Julian, 231–32
Harvard Divinity School, 229–32, 430
Harvard Theological Review, 299
Harvard University, 32
Harvey, Van A., 414–15
Haselden, Kyle, 112
Hatch, Nathan, 362
Hatfield, Mark, 480
Haugaard, William P., 236

Haverford College, 439
Hawaweeny, Raphael, 465
Hawk, Eugene B., 413
Hawley, Jack S., 232
Hawthorne, Nathaniel, 72
Hayes, Carlton J. H., 154
Haynes, George Edmund, 7
Hazard, Caroline, 408
Hebbelwaithe, Peter, 376
Hebermann, Charles G., 238–39
Hebraica, 60, 279–80
Hebrew, biblical, 270
Hebrew Student, xiv, 59
Hecker, Isaac T., 71, 379–80
Hedge, Frederick Henry, 184, 391–92\
Hefner, Philip J., 334
Hegel, Georg, 188
Heiser, W. Charles, 505
Hellenism, 230
Helms, Jesse, 274
Hennesey, James J., 239
Henry, Carl F. H., 135–37, 306, 415, 537
Henry, Patrick, 509
Herald of the Serbian Church in America. See *Glasnik Srpske Crkve u Americi*
Herberg, Will, 154, 198, 309, 462
Heresy, 143, 347, 427
Hermeneutics, 101, 241, 291, 307; biblical, 417. *See also* Bible, interpretation of
Herron, L. S., 105
Hershberger, Guy S., 344–45
Hesburgh, Theodore, 470
Heschel, Abraham J., 172
Heuser, Herman J., 19, 21–23
Hewit, Augustine F., 380
Hickey, James L., 277
Hicksites, 440
Hierarchicalism, ecclesiastical, 154
Higginson, T. W., 447
Higher Life movement, 424
Hildebrand, Reginald, 351
Hill, William, 513
Hiltbeitel, Alf, 242
Hincks, Edward Y., 31
Hinds, John T., 219

Contributors

WILLIAM S. ADAMS, Ph.D. (Princeton University), is the J. Milton Richardson Professor of Liturgics and Anglican Studies at the Episcopal Theological Seminary of the Southwest, Austin, Texas. He previously taught at the Vancouver School of Theology.

R. SCOTT APPLEBY, a graduate of Notre Dame University, holds the Ph.D. from the University of Chicago. A specialist in American Catholic modernism at the turn of the century, he is currently on the religious studies faculty of St. Xavier College, Chicago.

RANDALL H. BALMER, visiting lecturer at Rutgers University, holds degrees from Trinity College (B.A.), Trinity Divinity School (M.Div.), and Princeton University (M.A., Ph.D.). The former editor of *Voices*, he has published scholarly articles in several theological and historical journals.

SHELLEY BARANOWSKI received the Ph.D. from Princeton University. Her scholarly interests center on American religious history. She currently resides and teaches in Ohio.

DAVIS BITTON, professor of history at the University of Utah, received the doctorate at Princeton University in 1961. Author of *The French Nobility in Crisis, 1560–1640* (1969) and, with Leonard J. Arrington, *The Mormon Experience: A History of the Latter-day Saints* (1979), he is a former president of the Mormon History Association.

GUY C. CARTER, Ph.D. (Marquette University), is a ministerial student at the Lutheran School of Theology in Chicago. A specialist in Lutheran biblical hermeneutics, he has also been a fellow of the Institute for European History, Mainz, West Germany, where he researched the Bethel Confession of 1933.

PAUL G. CHAPPELL is associate dean of academic affairs in the Graduate School of Theology, Oral Roberts University, where he is professor of American church history. He holds degrees from Oral Roberts University (B.A.), Asbury Theological Seminary (M.Div.), Princeton Theological Seminary (Th.M.), and Drew University (M.Phil., Ph.D.).

The Reverend JAMES T. CONNELLY, C.S.C., is archivist for the Indiana Province, Priests of Holy Cross. He received the Ph.D. in church history from the University of Chicago (1977) and has taught at King's College, Wilkes-Barre, Pennsylvania, and at Alokolum National Seminary, Gulu, Uganda.

JOHN CORRIGAN, M.A. (Miami University) and Ph.D. (University of Chicago), is presently assistant professor of American religious history at the University of Virginia, Charlottesville. His academic interests currently focus on the beginnings of the Enlightenment in the United States.

KENT DRUYVESTEYN received the Ph.D. in the history of American religion from the University of Chicago. He is dean of students and director of the M.B.A. program at the University of Chicago's Graduate School of Business.

CARL D. EVANS, associate professor of religious studies at the University of South Carolina-Columbia, received the Ph.D. in 1975 from the University of Chicago. His specialty is biblical studies.

JOHN R. FITZMIER received degrees from the University of Pittsburgh and the Gordon-Conwell Theological Seminary prior to pursuing doctoral studies at Princeton University. His scholarly focus is the history of American Protestantism, and his current research centers on Timothy Dwight and the New Divinity movement.

HAROLD O. FORSHEY, professor of religion at Miami University, Oxford, Ohio, received the Ph.D. from Harvard University. His academic pursuits center on ancient Hebrew religion and sacred texts.

THOMAS E. FRANK holds degrees from Harvard University (B.A.), Candler School of Theology (M.Div.), and Emory University (Ph.D.). A specialist in American religious history with particular interests in the progressive era of liberal Protestantism (1880–1930), he is currently pastor of University United Methodist Church, St. Louis.

JAMES E. GILMAN holds degrees from Seattle Pacific University (B.A.), Denver Theological Seminary (M.Div.), the University of Colorado (M.A.), and Drew University (M.Phil., Ph.D.). Formerly on the philosophy and religion faculty at Palm Beach Atlantic College, he is currently teaching at Mary Baldwin College, Staunton, Virginia.

LEONARD J. GREENSPOON, Ph.D. (Harvard University) is associate professor of religion and history at South Carolina's Clemson University. A specialist in ancient Near Eastern languages and literature, he has written numerous scholarly articles and is author of or contributor to works on the Old Testament Book of Joshua.

HOWARD J. HAPP is professor of religious studies at California State University-Northridge and assistant rector of St. Nicholas' (Episcopal) Church, Encino. A native of Iowa, he is a graduate of Cornell College and Princeton Theological Seminary. He holds the Ph.D. in religion from Princeton University.

PER HASSING, Ph.D., is professor emeritus, Boston University School of Theology. A Methodist minister, he is a former missionary to Zimbabwe who currently resides in Lake Junaluska, North Carolina.

MARVIN S. HILL, a graduate of Brigham Young University (B.A., M.A.) and the University of Chicago (Ph.D.), is coauthor of *Mormonism and American Culture* and *Carthage Conspiracy*. He is currently working on a multivolume biographical study of Mormonism for Greenwood Press.

JAMES B. HUNT, Ph.D., chairs the department of history and political studies at Whitworth College, Spokane. His research and writing interests include colonial and nineteenth-century U.S. history, American biography, American culture and values, and faith development theory.

THOMAS J. JONAS received the Ph.D. and A.M. from the University of Chicago and holds the A.B. degree from Creighton University. He is research associate at Needham, Harper, and Steers in Chicago.

CHARLES E. JONES holds the Ph.D. in American history from the University of Wisconsin. He has held archival and library positions at Brown University, the University of Michigan, and other institutions. Jones is author of *A Guide to the Study of the Holiness Movement, Perfectionist Persuasion: The Holiness Movement and American Methodism, 1867–1936*, and *A Guide to the Study of the Pentecostal Movement*.

CHRISTA R. KLEIN, Ph.D. (University of Pennsylvania), is a historian of American religion, specializing in the immigrant churches of the nineteenth century. She has taught and is currently engaged in research at Lutheran Theological Seminary, Gettysburg, Pennsylvania. She also serves as a consultant with the Lilly Endowment's Division for Religion.

DAVID KLING, Ph.D., holds degrees from Trinity College, Northern Illinois University, and the University of Chicago. He is assistant professor of history at Palm Beach Atlantic College, with special competence in early nineteenth-century American religious history.

JOHN KLOOS earned the M.A. at Miami University and did doctoral work at the University of Chicago. He is assistant professor of religious studies, with special interests in the history of religion in the United States, at Illinois Benedictine College.

PAUL A. LAUGHLIN received the B.A. in classics from the University of Cincinnati and the M.Div and Ph.D. degrees from Emory University. He is assistant professor of religion and philosophy at Otterbein College, Westerville, Ohio.

L. DAVID LEWIS is adjunct professor of history at Anderson College, Anderson, Indiana. He was pastor of several congregations of the Church of God (Anderson) before earning the Ph.D. in the history of Christianity from the University of Chicago.

EDWARD TABOR LINENTHAL, Ph.D. (University of California-Santa Barbara), is assistant professor of religion at the University of Wisconsin-Oshkosh. He is author of *Changing Images of the Warrior Hero in America* (1982).

CHARLES H. LIPPY, Ph.D. (Princeton University), is professor of religion and history at Clemson University in South Carolina. He is author of *Seasonable Revolutionary: The Mind of Charles Chauncy* (1981) and *A Bibliography of Religion in the South* (1985). He is also, with Peter Williams, editor of the *Encylopedia of Religion in America*.

EUGENE Y. LOWE is a graduate of Princeton University. His doctoral studies in American church history were done at the Union Theological Seminary, New York City. He is dean of students at Princeton.

MICHAEL R. MCCOY is a graduate of Emory and Henry College and Princeton Theological Seminary. His Ph.D. is from the University of Chicago. He is currently assistant professor of religion and philosophy at Ferrum College, Virginia.

JOSEPH M. MCSHANE, S.J., entered the Society of Jesus in 1967. Following ordination to the priesthood in 1977, he completed Ph.D. studies in American church history at the University of Chicago (1982). He is assistant professor of religious studies at LeMoyne College, Syracuse, New York.

Major JOHN G. MERRITT pursued graduate studies in the history of Christianity, with a concentration in American religious history, at the University of Chicago Divinity School. He is on the staff of the Salvation Army's School for Officers' Training in Chicago.

JAMES A. MILLER holds the Ph.D. degree from the University of Texas-Austin. He is currently on the faculty of Clemson University, where he teaches courses in geography and Near Eastern studies.

RICHARD MILSOM engaged in doctoral studies in American religious history at the University of Chicago Divinity School. Currently he is involved in social service work in the area of alcohol and drug education in Oregon.

BERNARD NOONE earned the Ph.D. from Drew University. His main academic interests deal with the history of American Catholicism. He is on the faculty of Manhattan College, Riverdale, New York.

DENIS G. PAZ, Ph.D. (University of Michigan), is assistant professor of history at Clemson University. His special interests include the history of the Anglican communion and nineteenth-century British history.

The Reverend DENNIS R. RHODES is the archivist of the Orthodox Church in America. He holds a degree in Russian from the University of California-Davis and one in theology from St. Vladimir's Orthodox Theological Seminary in Crestwood, New York.

R. L. ROBERTS, B.A. (Abilene Christian University) and M.L.S. (North Texas State University), is archivist for the Center for Restoration Studies at Abilene Christian University, Texas, where he has served as religious librarian since 1966. He has written numerous articles on the history of The Churches of Christ.

GEORGE H. SHRIVER is a graduate of Stetson University (B.A.), Southeastern Seminary (B.D.), and Duke University (Ph.D.). The author of four books and numerous articles, he is working on a biography of Philip Schaff while teaching at Georgia Southern College.

STEPHEN H. SNYDER holds degrees from Stanford University (A.B.) and the University of Chicago (A.M., Ph.D.). The author of numerous book reviews in *Church History* and *Choice*, he is associate professor of religious studies at Linfield College, McMinnville, Oregon.

DANIEL L. SWINSON pursued doctoral work at the University of Chicago. A Methodist pastor in western Illinois, he has special interest in the study of the temperance movement and nineteenth-century religiously based social reform.

MARK G. TOULOUSE, Ph.D. (University of Chicago), is assistant professor of church history at the Phillips University Graduate Seminary, Enid, Oklahoma. He previously was a member of the religious studies faculty of Illinois Benedictine College.

LINDA K. VARKONDA received the Ph.D. from Florida State University. She has taught on the faculties of Limestone College, Tri-County Technical College (Pendleton, South Carolina), and Clemson University.

PAUL WESTERMEYER is a graduate of Elmhurst College, the School of Sacred Music at Union Seminary in New York, and the University of Chicago. The degrees represent his interdisciplinary interests in theology, liturgy, music, and church history. Dr. Westermeyer serves as professor of music and chairman of the music department at Elmhurst College and a cantor (organist-choirmaster) at Ascension Lutheran Church, Riverside, Illinois.

RONALD C. WHITE, JR., Ph.D. (Princeton University), is associate director of the Center for Continuing Education at Princeton Theological Seminary. He is the author of numerous books and articles on the Social Gospel movement of the late nineteenth and early twentieth centuries.

PETER W. WILLIAMS, professor of religion and American studies at Miami University, studied at Harvard and Yale Universities. He is author of *Popular Religion in America* and editor, with Charles H. Lippy, of the *Encyclopedia of Religion in America*.

ROBERT J. WILLIAMS, a United Methodist pastor in New Jersey, earned degrees from the University of Pennsylvania (B.A., M.S.), Eastern Baptist Theological Seminary (M.Div.), and Drew University (Ph.D.). An accredited visitor to the Sixth Assembly of the World Council of Churches, he also teaches Methodist-related courses at Princeton and Eastern Baptist seminaries.

JUDITH WIMMER is a graduate of Marquette University (B.A.), the University of Notre Dame (M.A.), and Drew University (Ph.D.). With special interest in the interaction of religion and culture, she is associate professor of religious studies and chairperson of the religious studies department at the College of St. Elizabeth, New Jersey.

GROVER A. ZINN, Ph.D. (Duke University), is professor of religion at Oberlin College in Ohio. His special interests concern medieval religious thought, particularly the tradition of Christian mysticism.